The Complete Atlas of Britain

Published by The Automobile Association

1st Edition	Apr	1979
2nd Edition	Jan	1980
3rd Edition	Jan	1981
4th Edition	Oct	1981
5th Edition	Jan	1983
6th Edition	Mar	1984
7th Edition	Oct	1984
Reprinted	May	1985

Produced by the Cartographic Department, Publications Division of the Automobile Association.

Based on the Ordnance Survey maps, with the permission of the Controller of Her Majesty's Stationery Office, Crown Copyright Reserved.

Printed and bound in Great Britain by
Hazell Watson & Viney Limited.
Member of the B.P.C.C. Group
Aylesbury, Bucks.

The contents of this book are believed correct at the time of printing. Nevertheless, the publisher can accept no responsibility for errors or omissions, or for changes in the details given.

ISBN 0 86145 239 9

Contents

Journey Planning

The Motoring Atlas of Great Britain combines superb maps with accurate and practical routefinding aids. These aids are designed to help the motorist complete a journey as quickly and with as little stress as possible.

ALERTNESS

Whether a journey is undertaken for business or pleasure, it is essential that the driver should set out feeling alert and confident, and that he should remain so until his destination is reached. A tired, frustrated driver is a potential danger to himself, to his passengers, and to other road users. The driver will feel more confident, and will certainly have a less troublesome journey, if he has planned his journey in advance.

MILEAGE

One of the fundamental considerations to be taken into account when planning a journey of any sort is that of the mileage involved. The mileage chart on page x which gives the distances between a selection of towns in Great Britain, can be used to make a rough calculation of the total journey length. From this an indication of the journey time may be gained.

ROUTE PLANNING

Once an indication of the journey length and time has been ascertained it is necessary to decide on a general route, and for this the route planning maps on pages II–VII are an invaluable guide. They depict principal routes throughout the country, and pinpoint the larger conurbations on those routes. Detailed routes can be worked out from the maps in the main atlas section of this book. The driver may find it useful to make a note of road numbers and route directions before setting out, as this can reduce his need to stop and consult the atlas.

MOTORAIL

If the journey involved is very long, the motorist may find it both more convenient and less exhausting to take advantage of the British Rail Motorail service. The cost of transporting a car and a family of four by rail is between 10% and 20% higher than travelling by road, but there may be considerable gains in travelling time, and saving in vehicle wear and tear. Details of the Motorail Service can be obtained from British Rail stations.

RADIO

Frequent radio bulletins are issued by the BBC and Independent Local Radio stations on road conditions, possible hold-ups, etc. and these can be of great assistance to the driver. By tuning to the local stations of areas being passed through it may be possible to avoid delays, and be prepared to make running changes to the route. The maps and accompanying text on pages viii–ix give details of the wavelengths and reception areas of all local radio stations in Great Britain.

ROAD SIGNS

Considerable help in negotiating the nation's highways can be obtained by understanding the various types of road direction signs. They are illustrated, and their functions described, on page xii. The principal benefit of the system is that primary route signs indicate the most straightforward route between one major town and another. It should be remembered that the shortest route is not necessarily the quickest. The driver is advised, where possible, to avoid driving through towns and built-up-areas, even if such routes appear to be more direct from the map. Delays caused by traffic lights, one-way systems, pedestrians, etc, will almost certainly be encountered in such areas.

THE NATIONAL GRID

The National Grid system, which is explained on page xiii, enables the driver to pinpoint any town or village in the atlas after having first found the reference number of that place by consulting the index. There is a separate index for London. A series of plans of principal towns and cities in Great Britain will be found between pages 153 and 206.

MOTORWAYS

When planning routes, many drivers will consider using motorways. They have several advantages over other types of road; not only are they faster, but they are also very easy to follow and allow a more consistent speed to be maintained. Drivers should, however, be fully conversant with the special rules for motorway driving, which are contained in the Highway Code. Perhaps the most ignored of these is that the outside lanes of a motorway should be used for overtaking only; there is no such thing as a 'fast lane'. Beginning on page 114 is a series of maps of the principal motorways in Great Britain.

Route Planning Maps

Legend:
- Motorway
- Motorway under construction
- Primary route
- Other A Roads

Scale: 0 · 10 · 20 · 30 mls
0 · 10 · 20 · 30 · 40 · 50 kms

Orkney Islands

John o'Groats
Thurso
Melvich
Tongue
Scourie
Altnaharra
Wick
Inchnadamph
Helmsdale
Lairg
Ullapool
Golspie
Bonar Bridge
Tain
MORAY FIRTH
Cromarty
Achnasheen
Dingwall
Nairn
Elgin
Cullen
Portsoy
Macduff
Fraserburgh
Forres
Banff
Beauly
Rothes
Keith
Turriff
Peterhead
INVERNESS
Aberlour
Boddam
Huntly
Drumnadrochit
Grantown-on-Spey
Ellon
Invermoriston
Carrbridge
Tomintoul
Inverurie
Oldmeldrum
Fort Augustus
Aviemore
Invergarry
Newtonmore
Kingussie
ABERDEEN
Braemar
Ballater
Banchory
Fort William
Stonehaven
Blair Atholl
Laurencekirk
Inverbervie
Pitlochry
Brechin
Tyndrum
Aberfeldy
Forfar
Montrose
Dalmally
Blairgowrie
Killin
Crianlarich
Coupar Angus
Arbroath
Lochearnhead
Crieff
DUNDEE
TAY BRIDGE
Callander
PERTH
Newport-on-Tay
Auchterarder
Cupar
St Andrews
Dunblane
Auchtermuchty
Crail
STIRLING
Kinross
Kincardine-on-Forth
Buckhaven
Dysart
KIRKCALDY
DUNFERMLINE
Burntisland
FALKIRK
FORTH BRIDGE
Cunoon
Gourock
DUMBARTON
GREENOCK
ERSKINE BRIDGE
EDINBURGH
Dunbar
Wemyss Bay
GLASGOW
Linlithgow

III

Berwick–upon–Tweed

dstream

A697

Alnwick

Morpeth   ASHINGTON

A696

WHITLEY BAY
NEWCASTLE-   TYNEMOUTH
UPON-TYNE   TYNE TUNNEL
   SOUTH SHIELDS
GATESHEAD   JARROW   SUNDERLAND
Chester-   Ryhope
le-Street
CONSETT

Durham

A689

BISHOP AUCKLAND   A1(M)   HARTLEPOOL

STOCKTON-
ON-TEES   MIDDLESBROUGH
DARLINGTON   A171
A66
Scotch   Whitby
Corner
A684
Leyburn   A684   Northallerton

Thirsk   SCARBOROUGH
A61   Helmsley   Pickering   Filey
A170
Ripon   A64

Boroughbridge   Malton

A166   BRIDLINGTON
HARROGATE   A59
Skipton   YORK   Great
Ilkley   Otley   Wetherby   A163   Driffield
EIGHLEY
Y BINGLEY   SHIPLEY   Market Weighton
BRADFORD   LEEDS   A163   Beverley
orden   HALIFAX   Selby   Howden   A63
BRIGHOUSE   DEWSBURY   PONTEFRACT   Goole   HULL
ALE   WAKEFIELD   HUMBER   Barton-upon-
HUDDERSFIELD   M62   M18   BRIDGE   Humber
HAM   BARNSLEY   Thorne   SCUNTHORPE   Immingham
VCHESTER   A1(M)   M180   GRIMSBY
ASHTON-UNDER-LYNE   DONCASTER   Brigg   CLEETHORPES
ORD   Glossop   M1   A159
OCKPORT   ROTHERHAM   M18   Bawtry   Market
A57   Rasen   Louth
CCLESFIELD   SHEFFIELD   A57   Gainsborough
Buxton   M1   WORKSOP   Mablethorpe
Bakewell   CHESTERFIELD   A57   A158
Leek   Matlock   LINCOLN   Horncastle   Skegness
MANSFIELD   A46   A158
A52   ALFRETON   NEWARK-ON-TRENT
N-TRENT   Ashbourne   Sleaford

NORTH

SEA

v

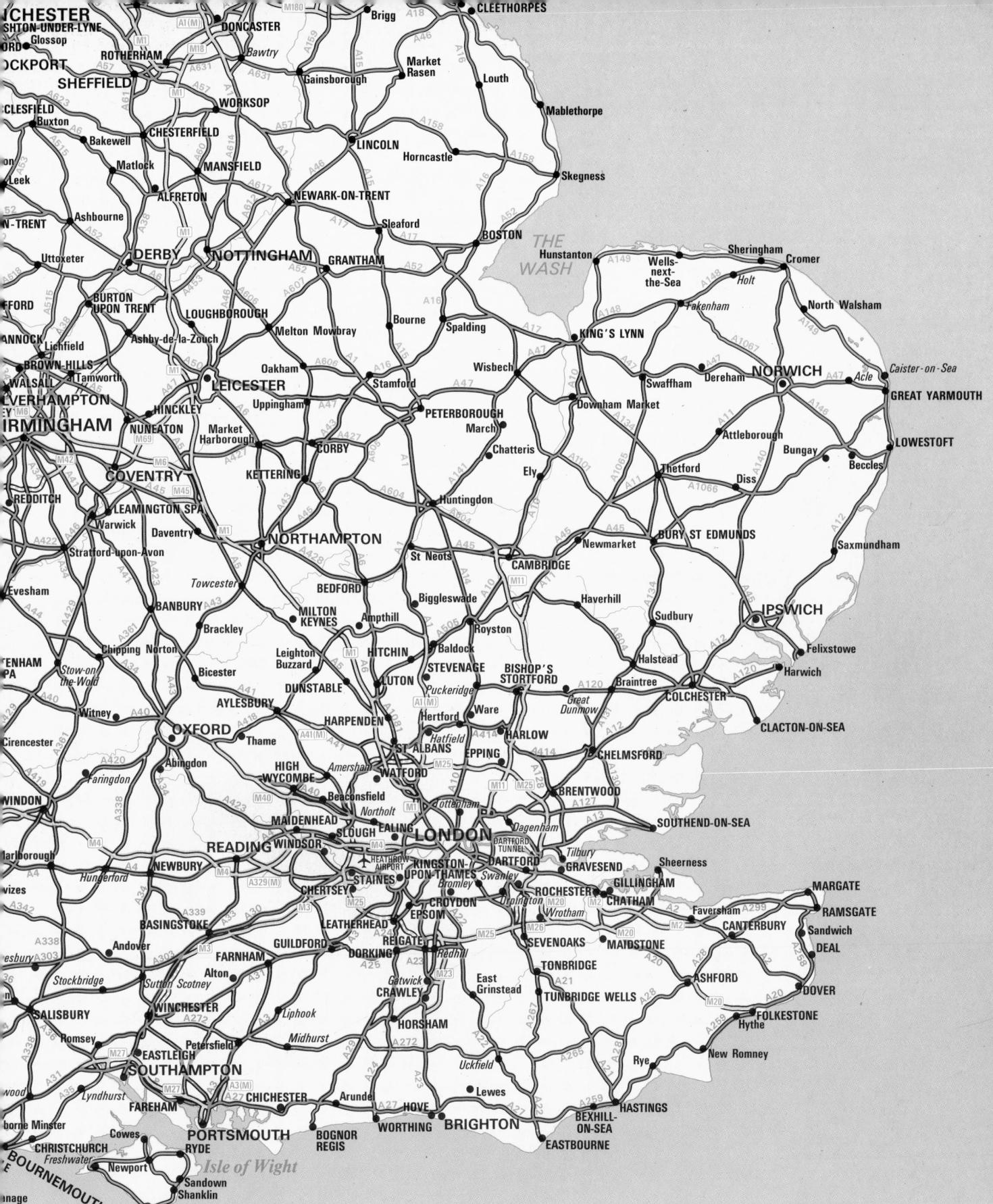

BBC Local Radio

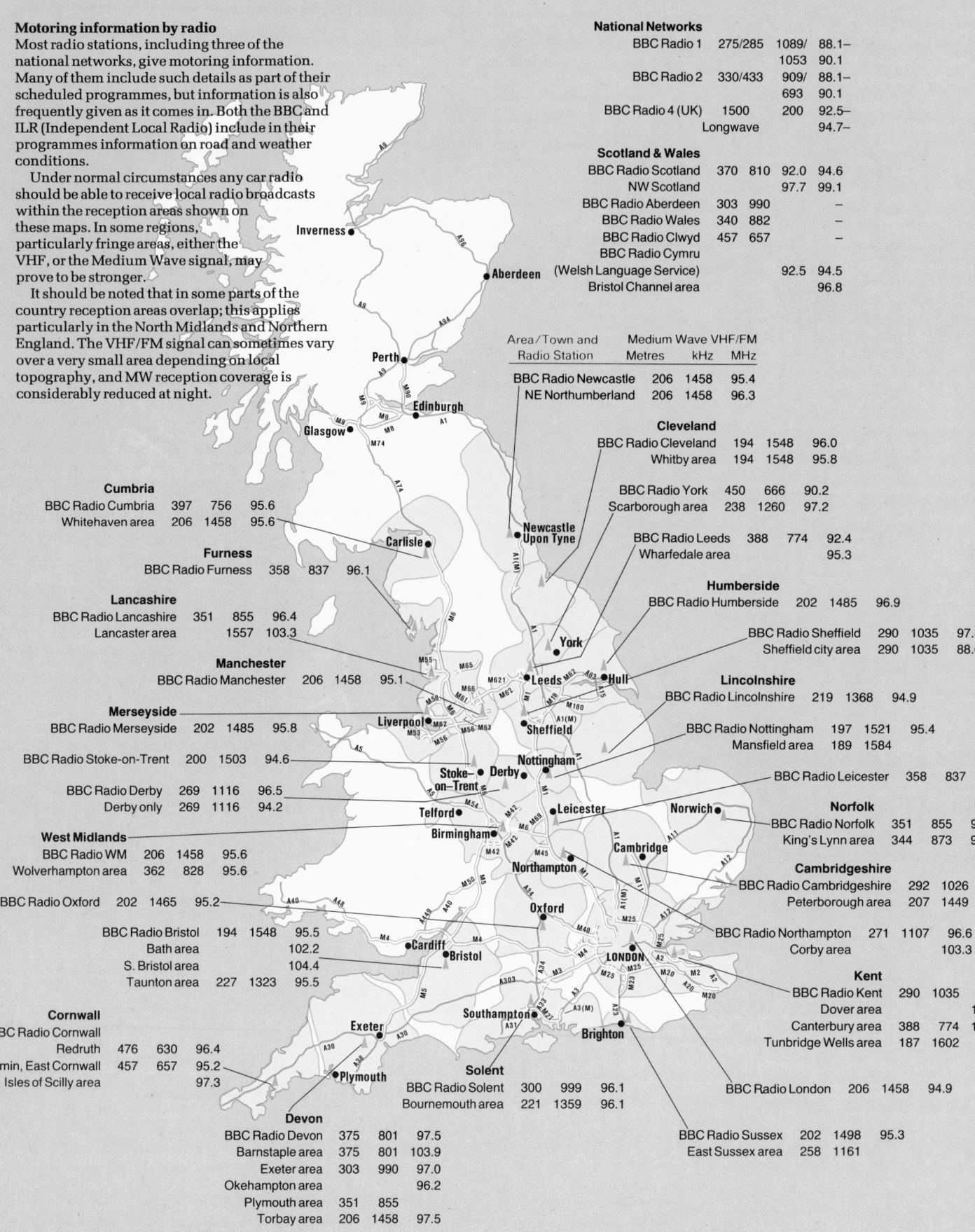

Motoring information by radio

Most radio stations, including three of the national networks, give motoring information. Many of them include such details as part of their scheduled programmes, but information is also frequently given as it comes in. Both the BBC and ILR (Independent Local Radio) include in their programmes information on road and weather conditions.

Under normal circumstances any car radio should be able to receive local radio broadcasts within the reception areas shown on these maps. In some regions, particularly fringe areas, either the VHF, or the Medium Wave signal, may prove to be stronger.

It should be noted that in some parts of the country reception areas overlap; this applies particularly in the North Midlands and Northern England. The VHF/FM signal can sometimes vary over a very small area depending on local topography, and MW reception coverage is considerably reduced at night.

National Networks

	Metres	kHz	MHz
BBC Radio 1	275/285	1089/1053	88.1–90.1
BBC Radio 2	330/433	909/693	88.1–90.1
BBC Radio 4 (UK)	1500	200	92.5–
Longwave			94.7–

Scotland & Wales

	Metres	kHz		
BBC Radio Scotland	370	810	92.0	94.6
NW Scotland			97.7	99.1
BBC Radio Aberdeen	303	990	–	
BBC Radio Wales	340	882	–	
BBC Radio Clwyd	457	657	–	
BBC Radio Cymru				
(Welsh Language Service)			92.5	94.5
Bristol Channel area				96.8

Area/Town and Radio Station	Medium Wave		VHF/FM
	Metres	kHz	MHz
BBC Radio Newcastle	206	1458	95.4
NE Northumberland	206	1458	96.3

Cleveland

BBC Radio Cleveland	194	1548	96.0
Whitby area	194	1548	95.8
BBC Radio York	450	666	90.2
Scarborough area	238	1260	97.2
BBC Radio Leeds	388	774	92.4
Wharfedale area			95.3

Humberside

BBC Radio Humberside	202	1485	96.9
BBC Radio Sheffield	290	1035	97.4
Sheffield city area	290	1035	88.6

Lincolnshire

BBC Radio Lincolnshire	219	1368	94.9
BBC Radio Nottingham	197	1521	95.4
Mansfield area	189	1584	
BBC Radio Leicester	358	837	

Norfolk

BBC Radio Norfolk	351	855	95
King's Lynn area	344	873	96

Cambridgeshire

BBC Radio Cambridgeshire	292	1026	
Peterborough area	207	1449	
BBC Radio Northampton	271	1107	96.6
Corby area			103.3

Kent

BBC Radio Kent	290	1035	9
Dover area			10
Canterbury area	388	774	10
Tunbridge Wells area	187	1602	9
BBC Radio London	206	1458	94.9
BBC Radio Sussex	202	1498	95.3
East Sussex area	258	1161	

Cumbria

BBC Radio Cumbria	397	756	95.6
Whitehaven area	206	1458	95.6

Furness

BBC Radio Furness	358	837	96.1

Lancashire

BBC Radio Lancashire	351	855	96.4
Lancaster area		1557	103.3

Manchester

BBC Radio Manchester	206	1458	95.1

Merseyside

BBC Radio Merseyside	202	1485	95.8
BBC Radio Stoke-on-Trent	200	1503	94.6
BBC Radio Derby	269	1116	96.5
Derby only	269	1116	94.2

West Midlands

BBC Radio WM	206	1458	95.6
Wolverhampton area	362	828	95.6
BBC Radio Oxford	202	1465	95.2
BBC Radio Bristol	194	1548	95.5
Bath area			102.2
S. Bristol area			104.4
Taunton area	227	1323	95.5

Cornwall

BBC Radio Cornwall			
Redruth	476	630	96.4
Bodmin, East Cornwall	457	657	95.2
Isles of Scilly area			97.3

Devon

BBC Radio Devon	375	801	97.5
Barnstaple area	375	801	103.9
Exeter area	303	990	97.0
Okehampton area			96.2
Plymouth area	351	855	
Torbay area	206	1458	97.5

Solent

BBC Radio Solent	300	999	96.1
Bournemouth area	221	1359	96.1

IBA Local Radio

Area/Town and Radio Station	Medium Wave		VHF/FM
	Metres	kHz	MHz
Birmingham			
BRMB Radio	261	1152	94.8
Bristol			
Radio West	238	1260	96.3
Cardiff			
CBC	221	1359	96.0
Edinburgh			
Radio Forth	194	1548	96.8
Glasgow			
Radio Clyde	261	1152	95.1
Liverpool			
Radio City	194	1548	96.7
London			
Capital Radio (General)	194	1548	95.8
LBC (News & Information)	261	1152	97.3
Plymouth			
Plymouth Sound	261	1152	96.0

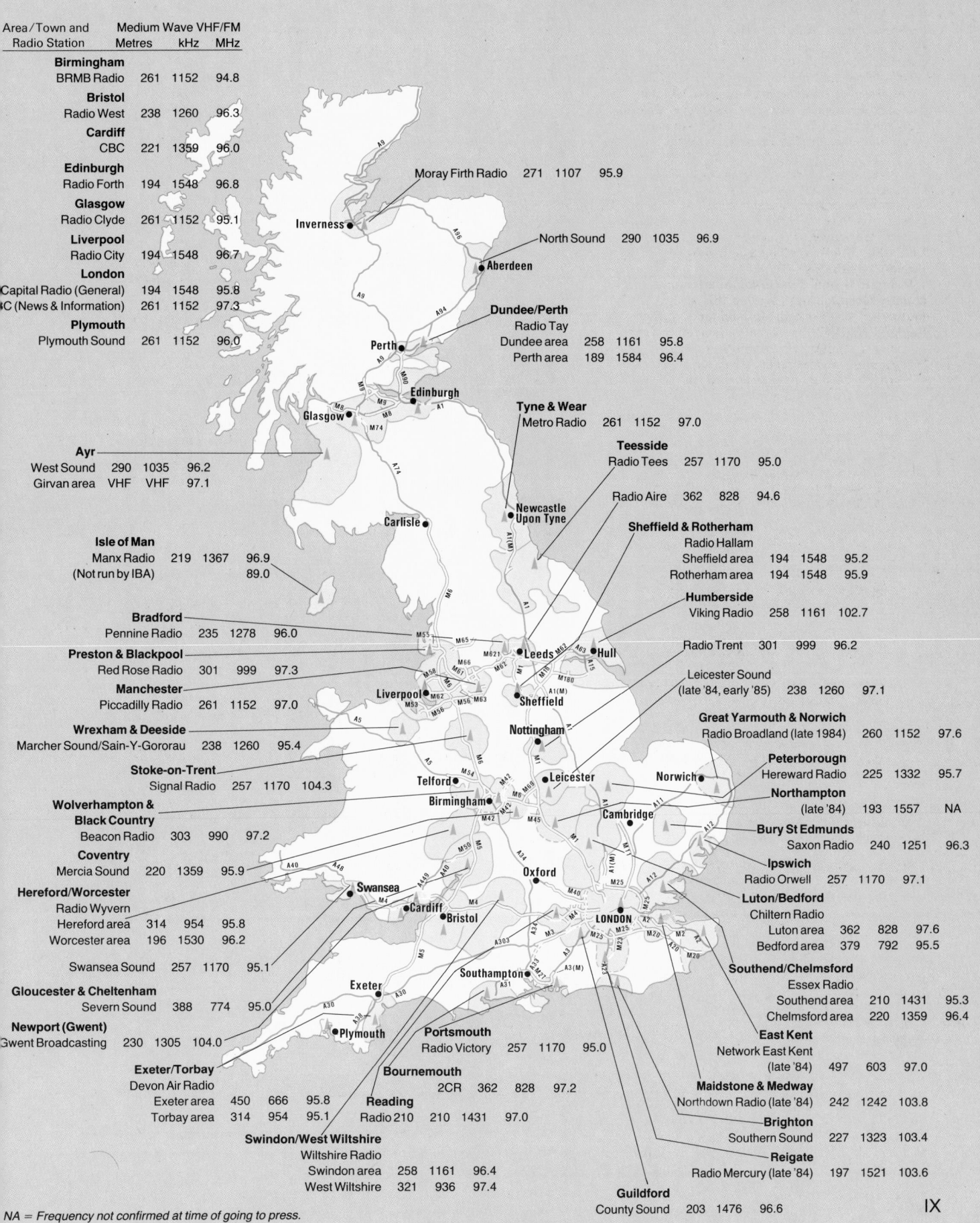

Moray Firth Radio 271 1107 95.9

North Sound 290 1035 96.9

Dundee/Perth
Radio Tay
Dundee area 258 1161 95.8
Perth area 189 1584 96.4

Tyne & Wear
Metro Radio 261 1152 97.0

Teesside
Radio Tees 257 1170 95.0

Radio Aire 362 828 94.6

Sheffield & Rotherham
Radio Hallam
Sheffield area 194 1548 95.2
Rotherham area 194 1548 95.9

Humberside
Viking Radio 258 1161 102.7

Radio Trent 301 999 96.2

Leicester Sound
(late '84, early '85) 238 1260 97.1

Great Yarmouth & Norwich
Radio Broadland (late 1984) 260 1152 97.6

Peterborough
Hereward Radio 225 1332 95.7

Northampton
(late '84) 193 1557 NA

Bury St Edmunds
Saxon Radio 240 1251 96.3

Ipswich
Radio Orwell 257 1170 97.1

Luton/Bedford
Chiltern Radio
Luton area 362 828 97.6
Bedford area 379 792 95.5

Southend/Chelmsford
Essex Radio
Southend area 210 1431 95.3
Chelmsford area 220 1359 96.4

East Kent
Network East Kent
(late '84) 497 603 97.0

Maidstone & Medway
Northdown Radio (late '84) 242 1242 103.8

Brighton
Southern Sound 227 1323 103.4

Reigate
Radio Mercury (late '84) 197 1521 103.6

Guildford
County Sound 203 1476 96.6

Ayr
West Sound 290 1035 96.2
Girvan area VHF VHF 97.1

Isle of Man
Manx Radio 219 1367 96.9
(Not run by IBA) 89.0

Bradford
Pennine Radio 235 1278 96.0

Preston & Blackpool
Red Rose Radio 301 999 97.3

Manchester
Piccadilly Radio 261 1152 97.0

Wrexham & Deeside
Marcher Sound/Sain-Y-Gororau 238 1260 95.4

Stoke-on-Trent
Signal Radio 257 1170 104.3

Wolverhampton & Black Country
Beacon Radio 303 990 97.2

Coventry
Mercia Sound 220 1359 95.9

Hereford/Worcester
Radio Wyvern
Hereford area 314 954 95.8
Worcester area 196 1530 96.2

Swansea Sound 257 1170 95.1

Gloucester & Cheltenham
Severn Sound 388 774 95.0

Newport (Gwent)
Gwent Broadcasting 230 1305 104.0

Exeter/Torbay
Devon Air Radio
Exeter area 450 666 95.8
Torbay area 314 954 95.1

Swindon/West Wiltshire
Wiltshire Radio
Swindon area 258 1161 96.4
West Wiltshire 321 936 97.4

Portsmouth
Radio Victory 257 1170 95.0

Bournemouth
2CR 362 828 97.2

Reading
Radio 210 210 1431 97.0

NA = Frequency not confirmed at time of going to press.

Mileage Chart

The distances between towns on the mileage chart are given to the nearest mile, and are measured along the normal AA recommended routes. It should be noted that AA recommended routes do not necessarily follow the shortest distances between places but are based on the quickest travelling time, making maximum use of motorways or dual-carriageway roads.

Index to Motorways

Index to Town Plans

Road Signs

Considerable help in negotiating the nation's highways can be obtained by understanding the various types of road direction signs illustrated on this page. The principal benefit of the sign system is that the primary route signs (green) indicate the most straightforward route between one town and another. These signs do not necessarily indicate the most direct route, but it should be remembered that direct routes may not be the quickest, or the easiest to follow.

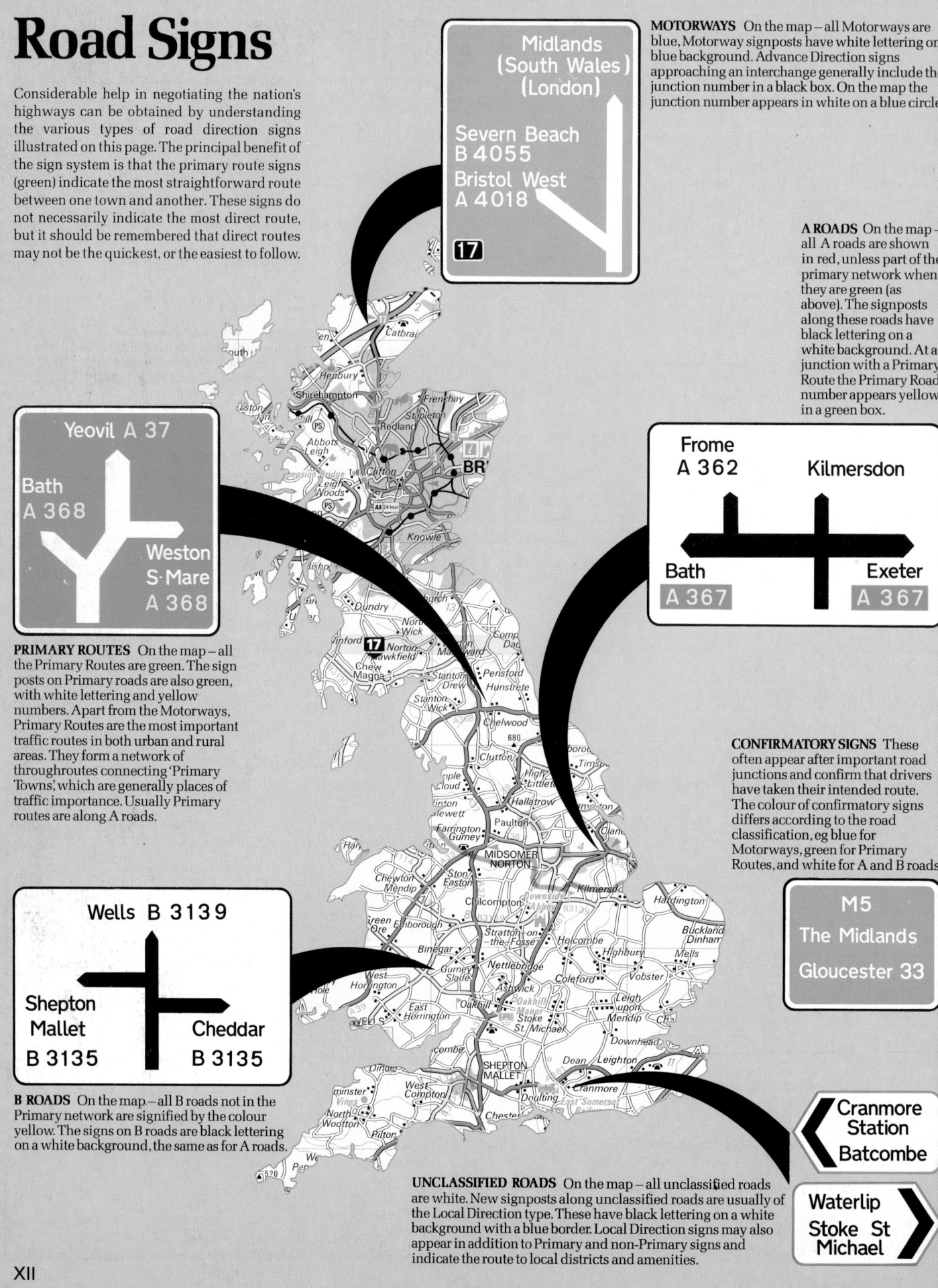

MOTORWAYS On the map – all Motorways are blue, Motorway signposts have white lettering on blue background. Advance Direction signs approaching an interchange generally include the junction number in a black box. On the map the junction number appears in white on a blue circle.

Midlands
(South Wales)
(London)

Severn Beach
B 4055
Bristol West
A 4018

17

A ROADS On the map – all A roads are shown in red, unless part of the primary network when they are green (as above). The signposts along these roads have black lettering on a white background. At a junction with a Primary Route the Primary Road number appears yellow in a green box.

Yeovil A 37

Bath
A 368

Weston
S·Mare
A 368

PRIMARY ROUTES On the map – all the Primary Routes are green. The sign posts on Primary roads are also green, with white lettering and yellow numbers. Apart from the Motorways, Primary Routes are the most important traffic routes in both urban and rural areas. They form a network of throughroutes connecting 'Primary Towns,' which are generally places of traffic importance. Usually Primary routes are along A roads.

Frome
A 362

Kilmersdon

Bath
A 367

Exeter
A 367

CONFIRMATORY SIGNS These often appear after important road junctions and confirm that drivers have taken their intended route. The colour of confirmatory signs differs according to the road classification, eg blue for Motorways, green for Primary Routes, and white for A and B roads.

M5
The Midlands
Gloucester 33

Wells B 3139

Shepton
Mallet
B 3135

Cheddar
B 3135

B ROADS On the map. – all B roads not in the Primary network are signified by the colour yellow. The signs on B roads are black lettering on a white background, the same as for A roads.

UNCLASSIFIED ROADS On the map – all unclassified roads are white. New signposts along unclassified roads are usually of the Local Direction type. These have black lettering on a white background with a blue border. Local Direction signs may also appear in addition to Primary and non-Primary signs and indicate the route to local districts and amenities.

Cranmore
Station
Batcombe

Waterlip
Stoke St
Michael

The National Grid

To locate a place in this atlas, first look up the name of the town or village required in the index, which starts on page 227. Each entry is followed by the page number on which the place can be found, and its National Grid reference.

Eg:
Hyssington	*40*	SO 3194
Hythe (Hants.)	*11*	SU 4207
Hythe (Kent)	*15*	TR 1635

Hythe is on page 15 with National Grid reference TR 1635.

When the required place name and its reference have been found in the index:

a) turn to the page number indicated,
b) find the location using the last four numbers,

Taking Hythe (Kent) as our example:

Take the first figure of the reference 1, this refers to the numbered grid line running along the bottom of the page. Having found this line, the second figure 6, tells you the distance to move in tenths to the right of this line. A vertical line through this point is the first half of the reference.

The third figure 3, refers to the numbered grid lines on the left hand side of the page, finally the fourth figure 5, indicates the distance to move in tenths above this line. A horizontal line drawn through this point to intersect with the first line gives the precise location of the place in question. See example below.

NATIONAL GRID EXPLANATION

The National Grid provides a system of reference common to maps of all scales. The grid covers Britain with an imaginary network of 100 kilometre squares. Each square is identified by two letters eg. TR. Every 100 kilometre square is then sub-divided into 10 kilometre squares which appear as a network of blue lines on the map pages. These blue lines are numbered left to right [0]–[9] and bottom to top [0]–[9]. These 10 kilometre squares can be further divided into tenths to give a place reference to the nearest kilometre.

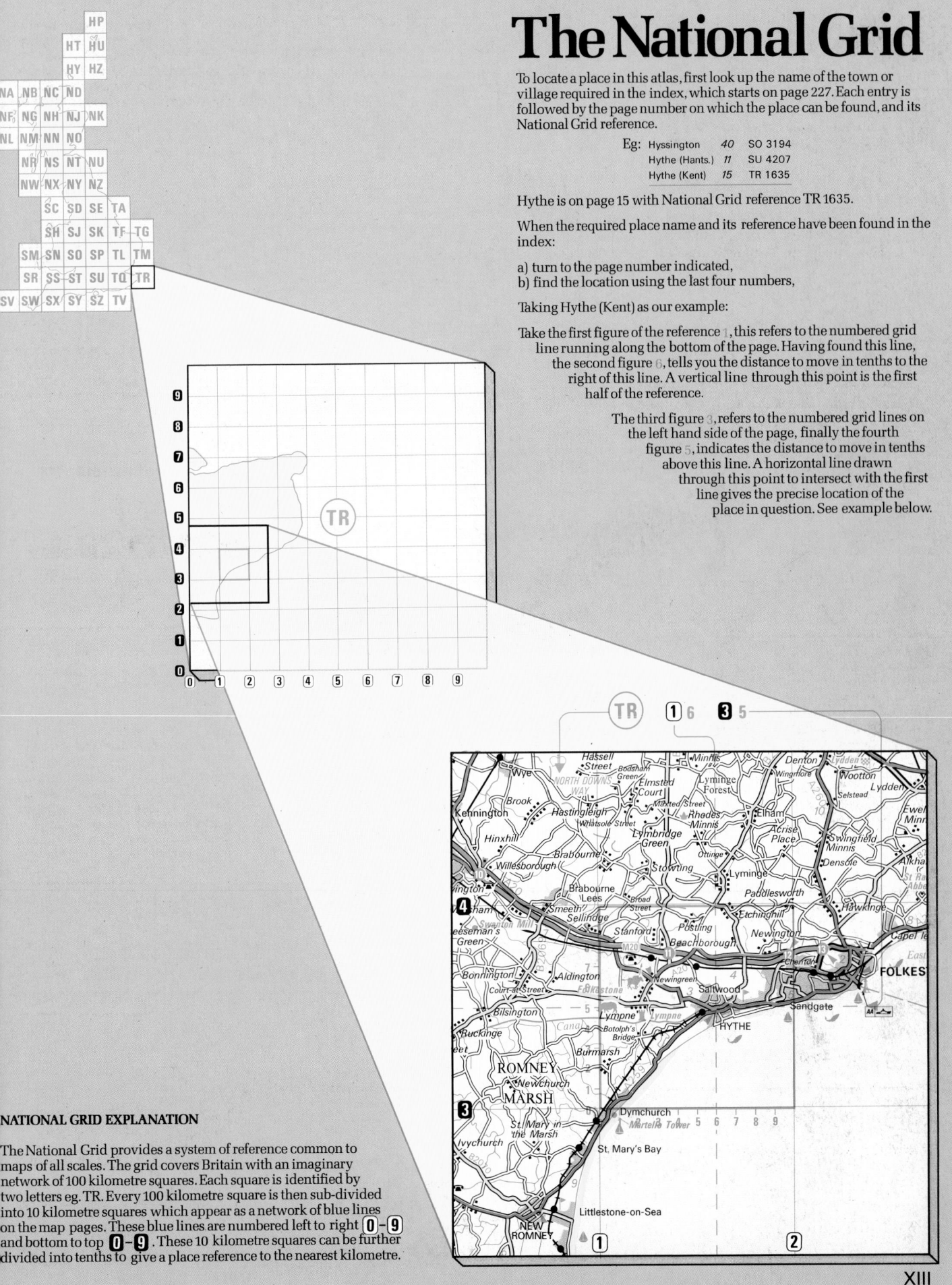

XIII

Legend

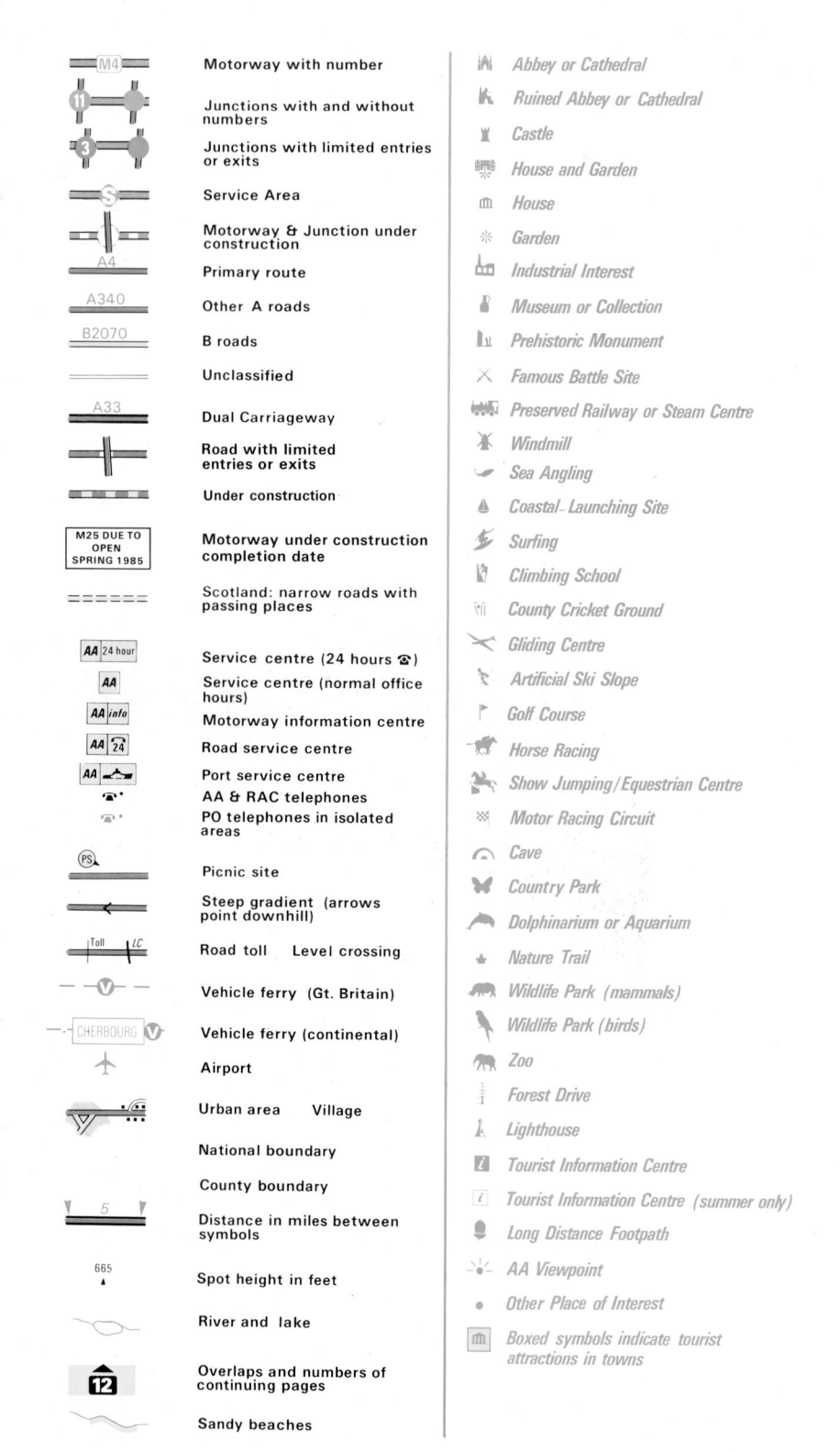

M4	Motorway with number
	Junctions with and without numbers
	Junctions with limited entries or exits
S	Service Area
	Motorway & Junction under construction
A4	Primary route
A340	Other A roads
B2070	B roads
	Unclassified
A33	Dual Carriageway
	Road with limited entries or exits
	Under construction
M25 DUE TO OPEN SPRING 1985	Motorway under construction completion date
	Scotland: narrow roads with passing places
AA 24 hour	Service centre (24 hours ☎)
AA	Service centre (normal office hours)
AA info	Motorway information centre
AA 24	Road service centre
AA	Port service centre
☎	AA & RAC telephones
☎	PO telephones in isolated areas
PS	Picnic site
	Steep gradient (arrows point downhill)
Toll LC	Road toll Level crossing
V	Vehicle ferry (Gt. Britain)
CHERBOURG V	Vehicle ferry (continental)
✈	Airport
	Urban area Village
	National boundary
	County boundary
5	Distance in miles between symbols
665 ▲	Spot height in feet
	River and lake
12	Overlaps and numbers of continuing pages
	Sandy beaches

	Abbey or Cathedral
	Ruined Abbey or Cathedral
	Castle
	House and Garden
	House
	Garden
	Industrial Interest
	Museum or Collection
	Prehistoric Monument
✕	Famous Battle Site
	Preserved Railway or Steam Centre
	Windmill
	Sea Angling
	Coastal Launching Site
	Surfing
	Climbing School
	County Cricket Ground
	Gliding Centre
	Artificial Ski Slope
	Golf Course
	Horse Racing
	Show Jumping/Equestrian Centre
	Motor Racing Circuit
	Cave
	Country Park
	Dolphinarium or Aquarium
	Nature Trail
	Wildlife Park (mammals)
	Wildlife Park (birds)
	Zoo
	Forest Drive
	Lighthouse
	Tourist Information Centre
	Tourist Information Centre (summer only)
	Long Distance Footpath
	AA Viewpoint
•	Other Place of Interest
	Boxed symbols indicate tourist attractions in towns

Key To Map Pages

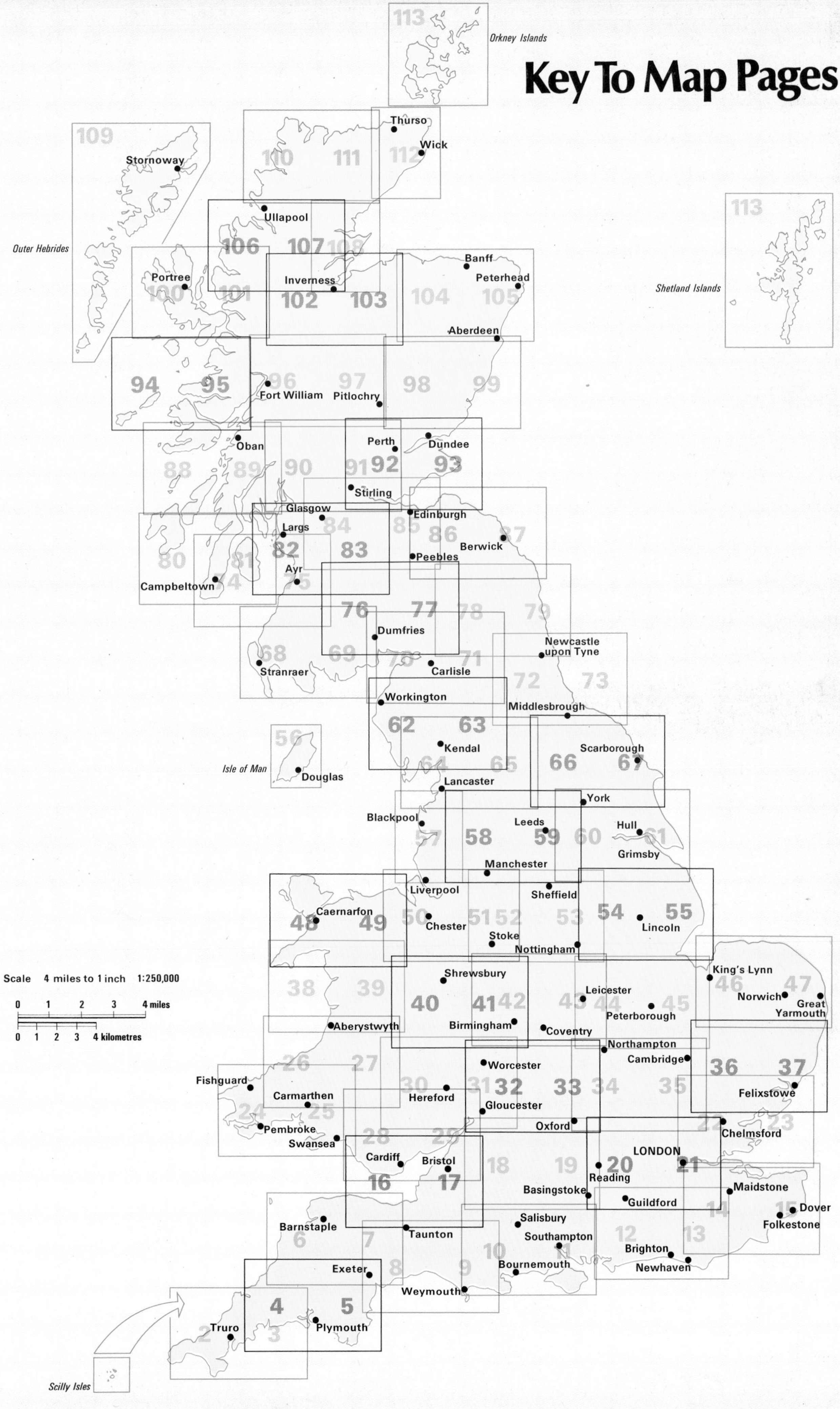

Orkney Islands 113

Shetland Islands 113

Outer Hebrides

109 Stornoway

110 111 112
Thurso
Wick

106 107 108
Ullapool

100 101 102 103 104 105
Portree
Inverness
Banff
Peterhead
Aberdeen

94 95 96 97 98 99
Fort William
Pitlochry

88 89 90 91 92 93
Oban
Perth
Dundee
Stirling

80 81 82 83 84 85 86 87
Glasgow
Largs
Ayr
Edinburgh
Peebles
Berwick

76 77 78 79
Dumfries

68 69 70 71 72 73
Stranraer
Carlisle
Newcastle upon Tyne
Workington
Middlesbrough

62 63 64 65 66 67
Kendal
Scarborough
Lancaster
York

56
Isle of Man
Douglas

Blackpool

57 58 59 60 61
Leeds
Hull
Manchester
Grimsby

Liverpool
Sheffield

48 49 50 51 52 53 54 55
Caernarfon
Chester
Stoke
Nottingham
Lincoln

38 39 40 41 42 43 44 45 46 47
Shrewsbury
Leicester
King's Lynn
Norwich
Great Yarmouth
Aberystwyth
Birmingham
Coventry
Peterborough
Northampton
Felixstowe

26 27 30 31 32 33 34 35 36 37
Fishguard
Worcester
Cambridge
Carmarthen
Hereford
Gloucester
Chelmsford

24 25 28 29 18 19 20 21 22 23
Pembroke
Oxford
LONDON
Maidstone
Swansea
Cardiff
Bristol
16 17
Reading
Basingstoke
Guildford
14 15
Dover
Folkestone

6 7 8 9 10 11 12 13
Barnstaple
Taunton
Salisbury
Southampton
Brighton
Exeter
Bournemouth
Newhaven
Weymouth

4 5
Truro
Plymouth

2 3

Scilly Isles

Scale   4 miles to 1 inch   1:250,000

0 1 2 3   4 miles

0 1 2 3   4 kilometres

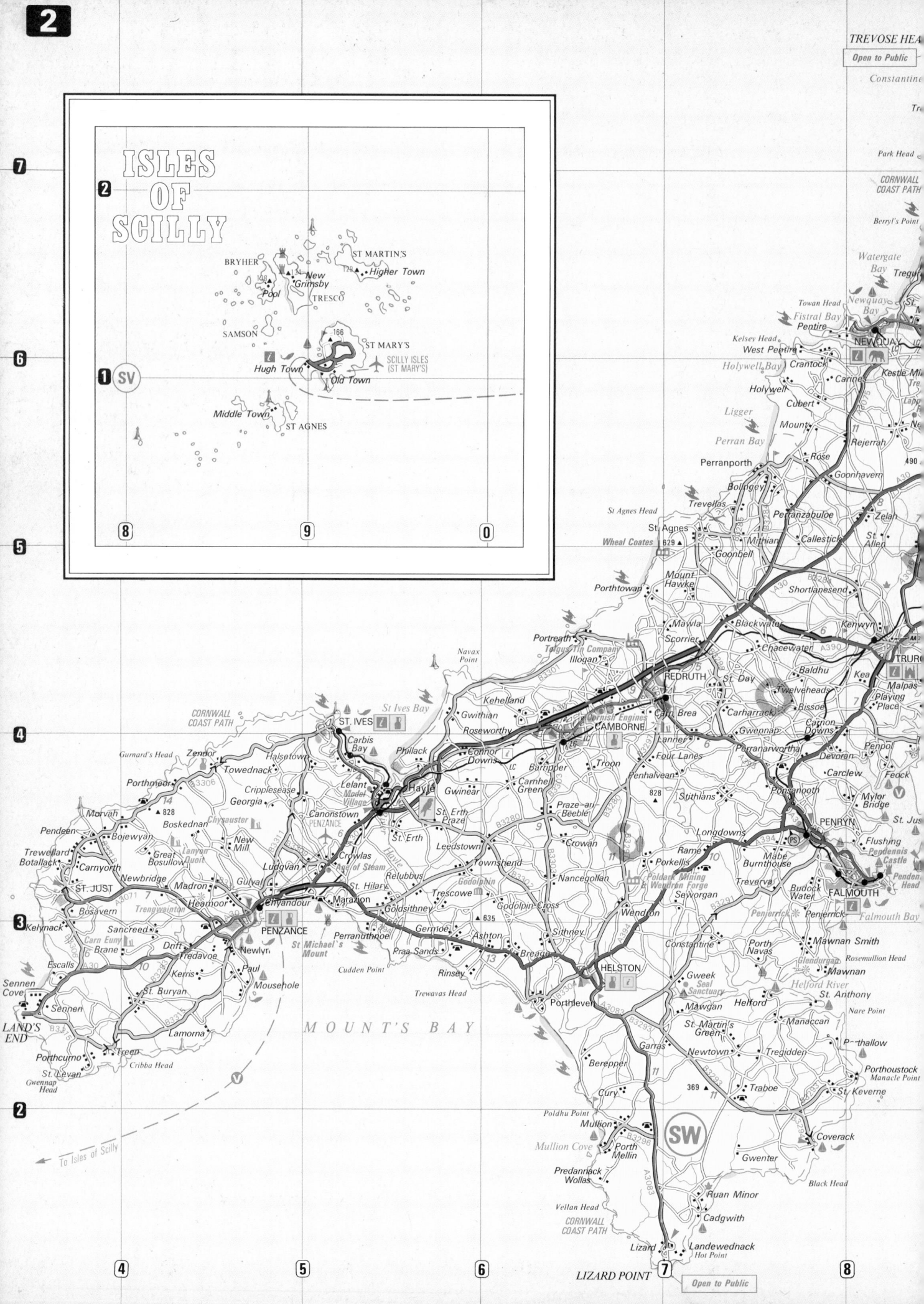

TREVOSE HEA

Open to Public

Constantine

Tre

Park Head

CORNWALL
COAST PATH

Berryl's Point

Watergate
Bay   Tregu

Towan Head   Newquay
Fistral Bay   Bay St.
Pentire   NEWQUAY

Kelsey Head   West Pentire
Holywell Bay   Crantock   Kestle Mi
Holywell   Carnes   Tre
Cubert   Lapp
Ligger   Mount
Perran Bay   Rejerrah
Perranporth   Rose   490
Bolingey   Goonhavern
Trevellas   Pertanzabuloe   Zelah
St Agnes Head   St Agnes   Mithian   St
Wheal Coates   629   Goonbell   Callestick   Allen
Mount   Shortlanesend
Porthtowan   Hawke
Mawla   Blackwater   Kenwyn
Scorrier   6
Portreath   Chacewater   A390
Telgus Tin Company   Illogan   TRUR
Redruth   St Day   Baldhu   Kea
Twelveheads   Malpas
Carn Brea   Carharrack   Playing
Cornish Engines   Bissoe   Place
Navax   Kehelland   Camborne   Gwennap   Cannon
Point   Gwithian   Roseworthy   Lanner   Perranarworthal   Downs
St Ives Bay   Connor   Barripper   Four Lanes   Devoran   Penpol
ST. IVES   Downs   Penhalvean   Ponsanooth   Carclew
Carbis   Phillack   LC   Troon   Feock
Bay   Carnhell   828   Stithians   Mylor
Gurnard's Head   Zennor   Lelant   Hayle   Green   Bridge   St. Ju
Porthmeor   Towednack   Model   Gwinear   Praze-an-   Gwennap   PENRYN
Village   St Erth   Beeble   Flushing
Cripplesease   PENZANCE   Praze   Crowan   Longdowns   Pendennis
Morvah   Georgia   6   Rame   10   Castle
828   Canonstown   Crowan   Porkellis   Burnthouse   Penden
Boskednan   Chysauster   St Erth   Leedstown   Treverva   Head
Pendeen   New   Townshend   Poldark Mining   Budock   FALMOUTH
Bojewyan   Mill   Nancegollan   & Wendron Forge   Water
Lanyon Quoit   Ludgvan   Godolphin   Penjerrick   Penjerrick   Falmouth Bay
Great   Crowlas   Sewgoran
Trewellard   Bosullow   Age of Steam   Trescowe   Sithney   Constantine   Mawnan Smith
Botallack   Madron   Relubbus   Godolphin Cross   Wendron   Porth
Carnyorth   Newbridge   Gulval   St Hilary   Navas
ST. JUST   Hesmoor   Marazion   635   Germoe   HELSTON   Glendurgan   Rosemullion Head
Bosavern   Trengwainton   Goldsithney   Ashton   Gweek   Mawnan
Chyandour   Breage   13   Seal   Helford   St. Anthony
Kelynack   PENZANCE   Perranuthnoe   Sanctuary   Helford River
Carn Euny   Sancreed   Praa Sands   Mawgan   St. Martin's   Nare Point
Brane   Drift   Newlyn   Cudden Point   Porthleven   Green   Manaccan
Escalls   Tredavoe   St Michael's   Rinsey   Garras   Newtown   Tregidden   Porthallow
Paul   Mount   Porthleven   Cury   Porthoustock
Sennen   Kerris   Mousehole   Trewavas Head   Berepper   Traboe   Manacle Point
Cove   St. Buryan   369   St. Keverne
Sennen   M O U N T ' S   B A Y   Poldhu Point   Coverack
LAND'S   Lamorna   Mullion   Gwenter
END   Treen   Porth   Mellin   SW   Black Head
Porthcurno   Cribba Head   Mullion Cove   Predannack
St. Levan   Wollas   A3083
Gwennap   Ruan Minor
Head   To Isles of Scilly   Vellan Head   Cadgwith
CORNWALL
COAST PATH   Lizard   Landewednack
Hot Point
LIZARD POINT   Open to Public

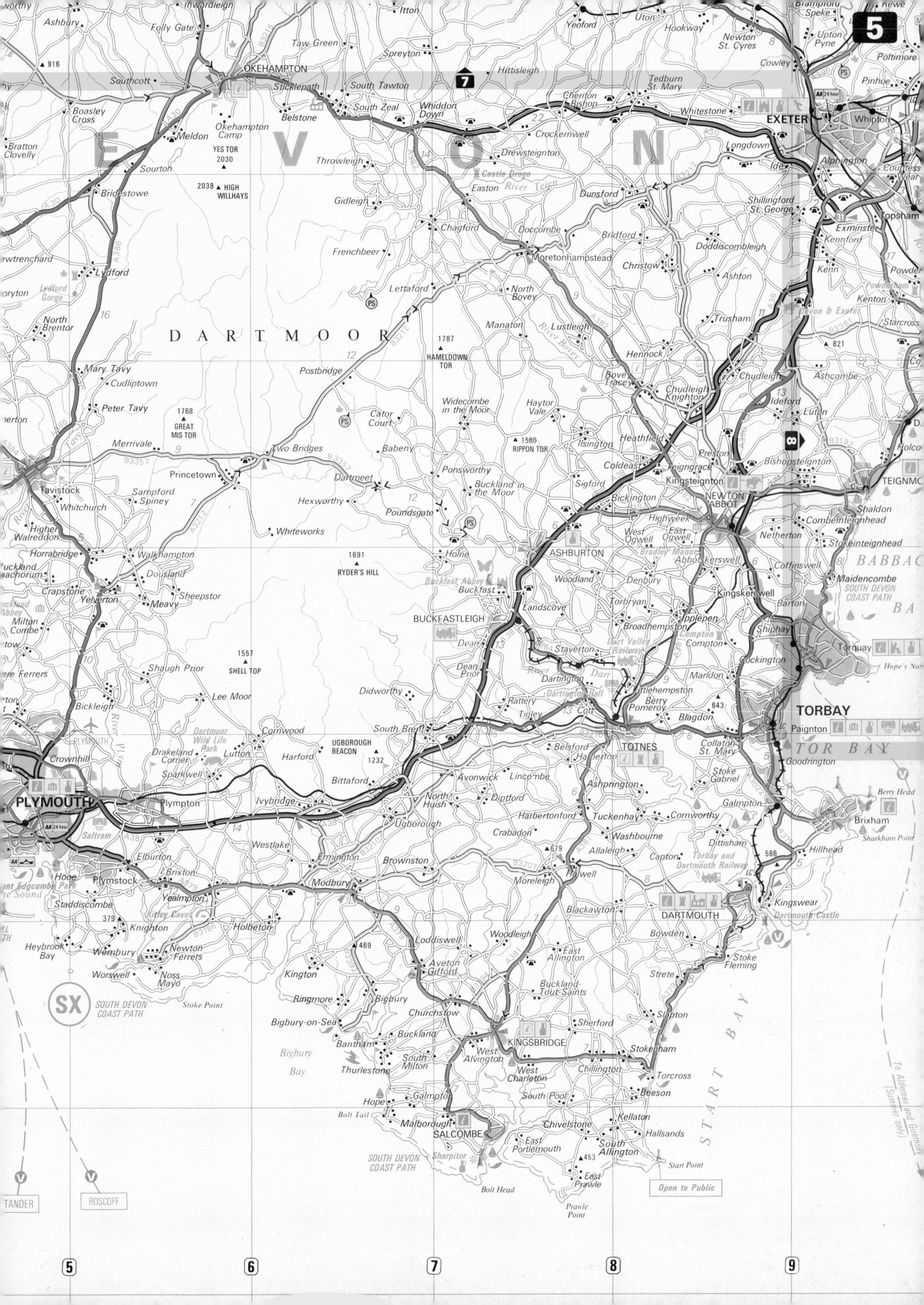

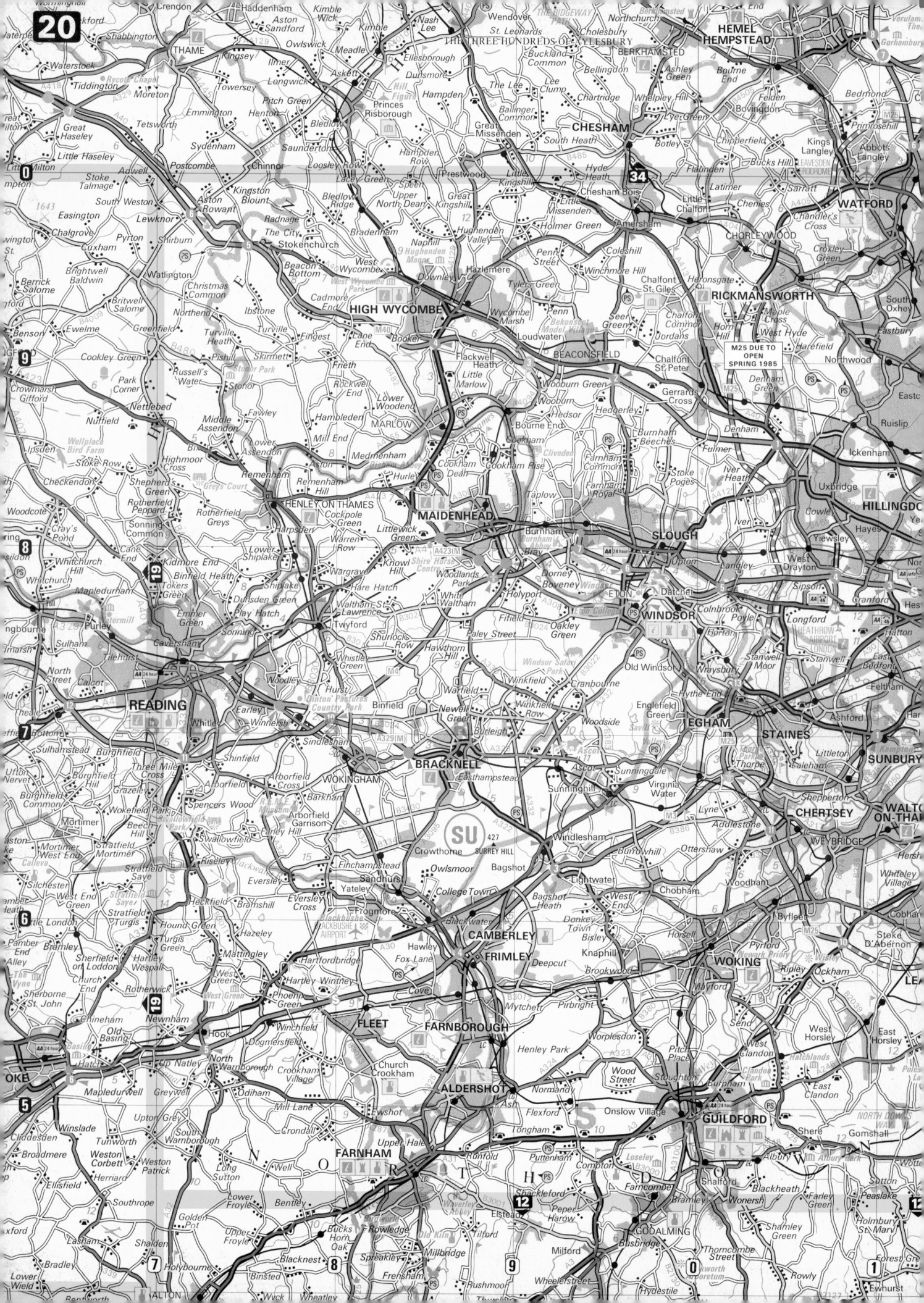

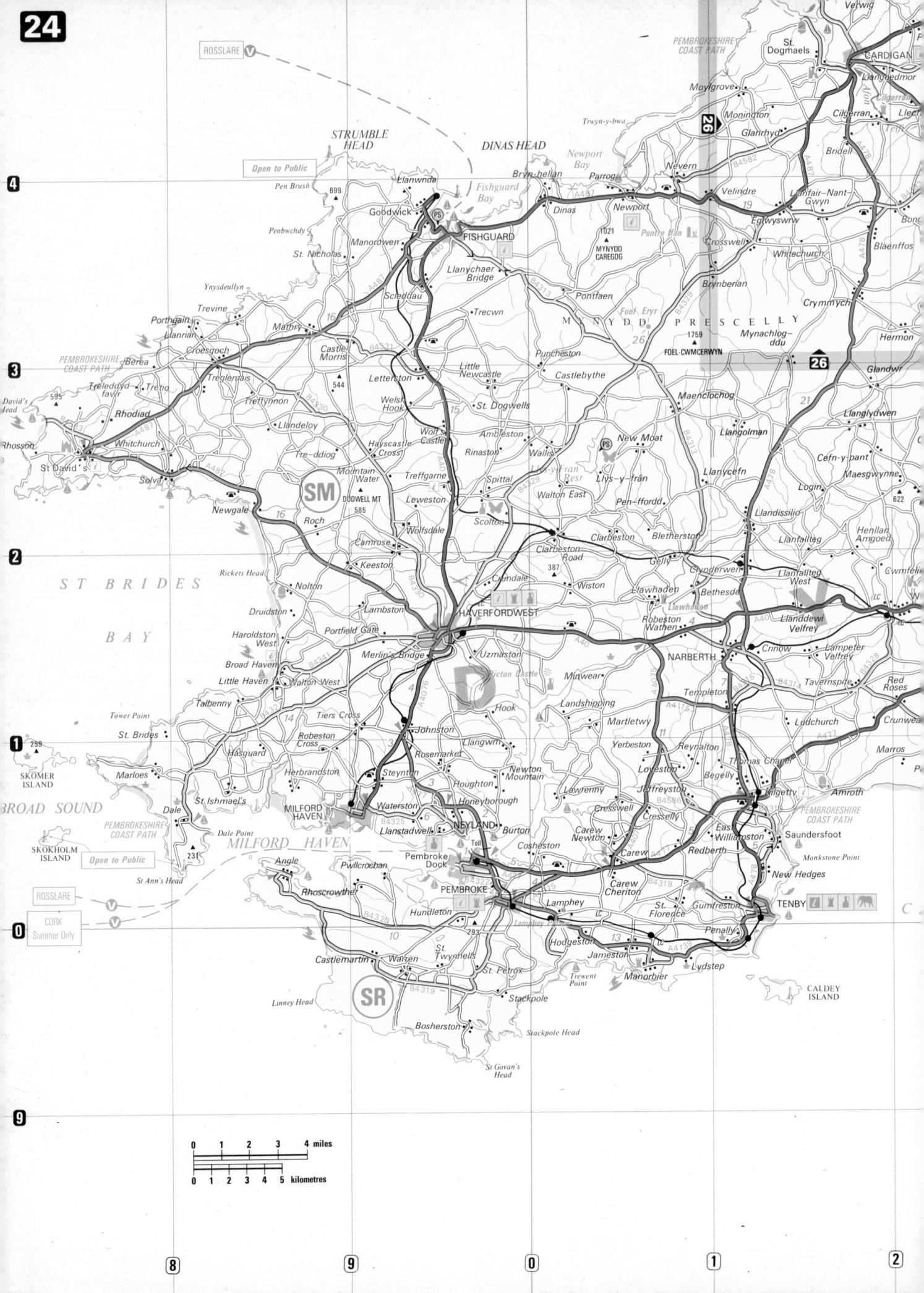

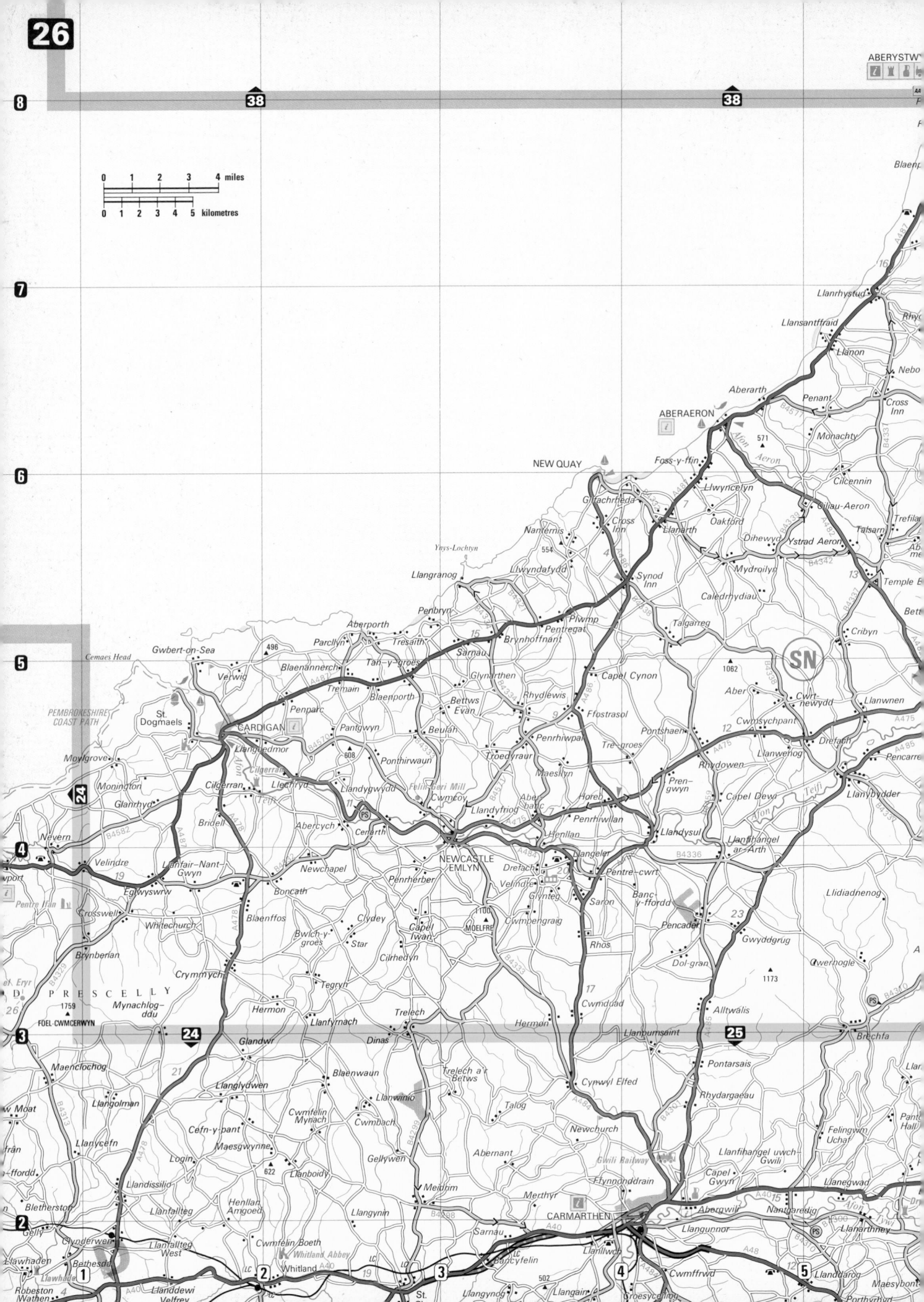

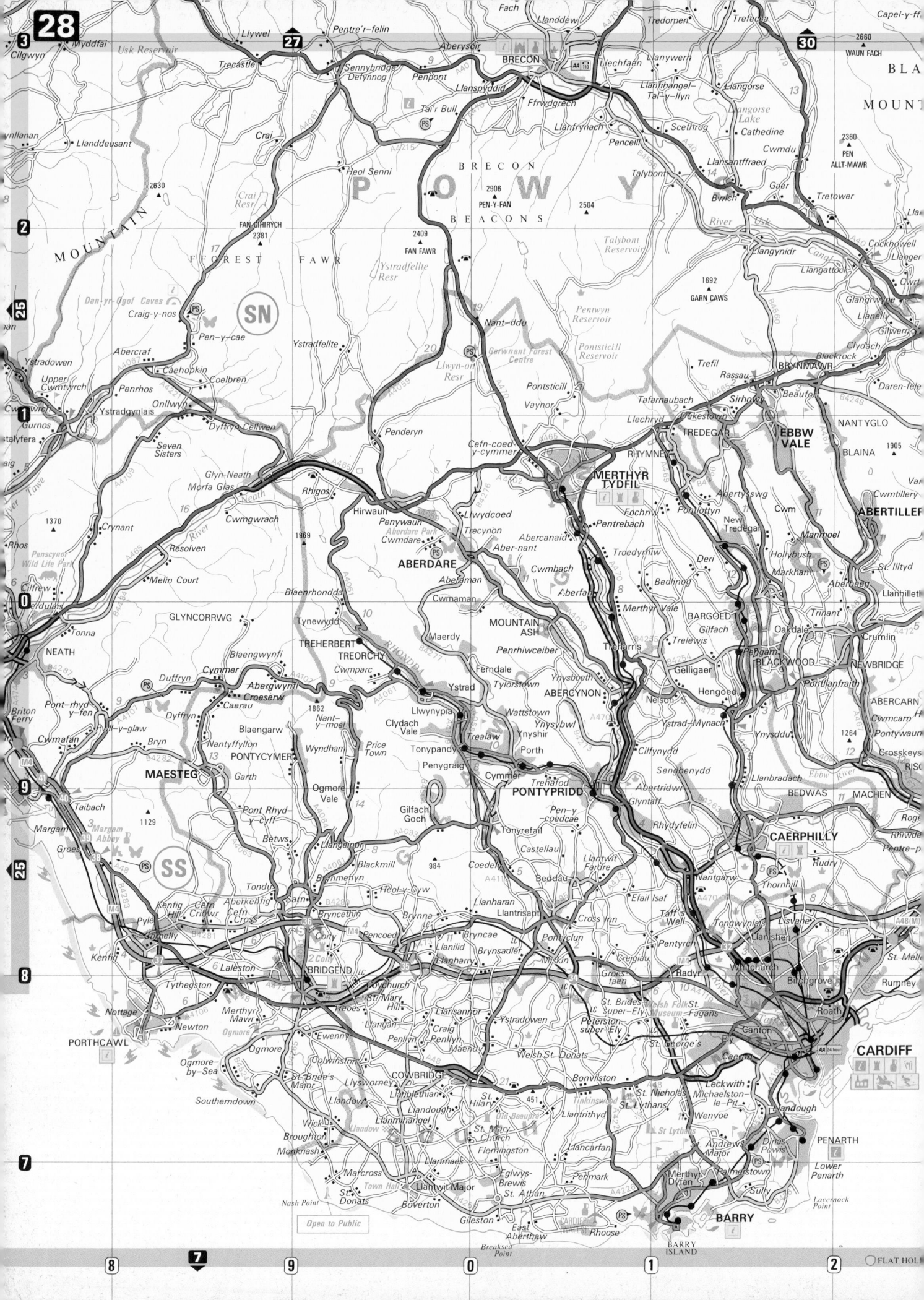

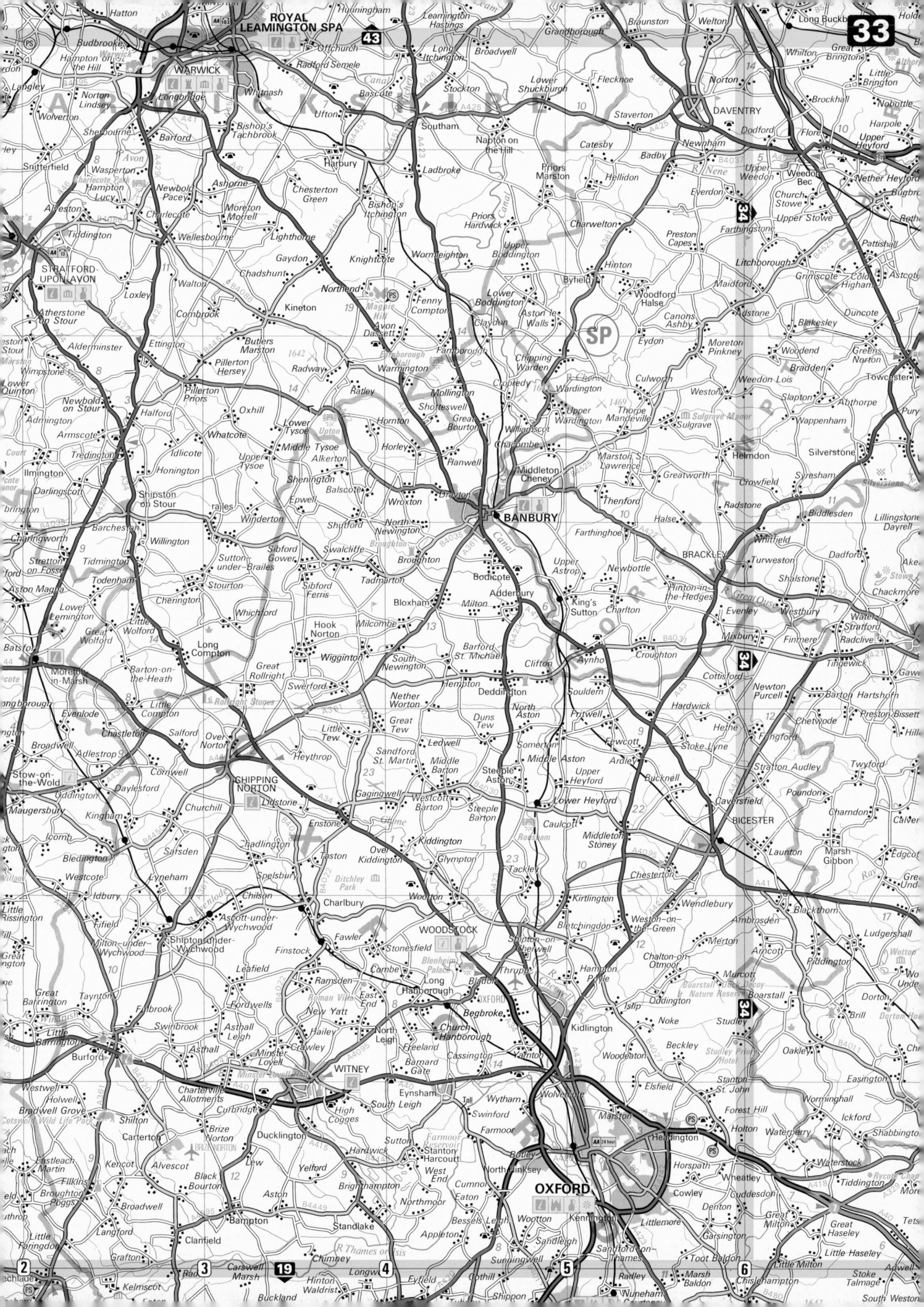

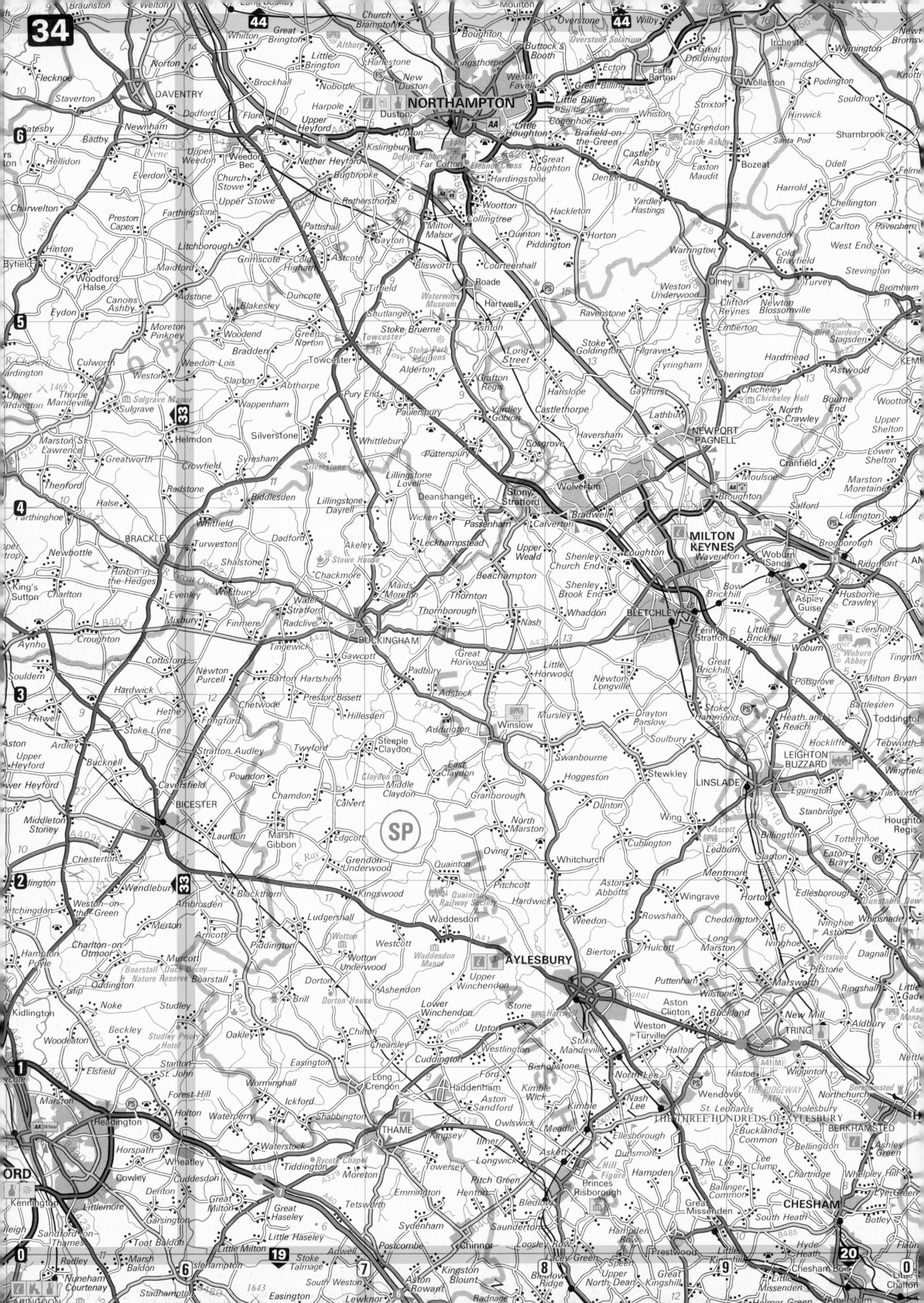

38

4

3

2

1

0

9

8

LLŶN PENINSULA

BARDSEY ISLAND

Open to Public

Bardsey Sound

Braich y Pwll
Uwchmynydd
Pen y Cil

Capel Carmel
Pwlldefaid
Aberdaron

Rhydlios
Ty-hen
Pen-y-graig

Penrhyn Mawr
Llangwnnadl
Tudweiliog
Porth Ysgaden
Rhos-y-llan
Ceidio Fawr
Dinas

Bryncroes
Sarn
Meyllteyrn
Botwnnog
Llaniestyn
Garn
Nanhoron

Y Rhiw
Plas-Yn-Rhiw
Llidiardau
Llangian
Llanengan
Sarn-bâch
Bwlchtocyn
Cilan Uchaf

Porth Neigwl or Hell's Mouth

Trwyn yr Wylfa
Trwyn Cilan

Abersoch
St Tudwal's Road
ST TUDWAL'S ISLANDS

Mynytho
Llanbedrog
Trwyn Llanbedrog
Rhedyn
Penrhos

PWLLHELI
Carreg yr Imbill

Efailnewydd
Rhyd-y-clafdy
Llannor
Abererch

Morfa Nefyn
Edern
Nefyn
Bodfuan
Fron
Y Ffor
Rhos-fawr
Chwilog
Penarth Fawr

Carreg Ddu
Pistyll
Llithfaen
Llwyndyrys
Llanaelhaearn
Pen-Sarn
Cennin

St Cybi's Well
Llangybi
Llanarmon
Llanystumdwy
Rhoslan
Lloyd George
Pen-ychain

CRICCIETH

1850
20
B4417
A499
B4354
A497
B4413
B4415
A499

Bryncir
Garn-Dolbenmaen
Dolbenmaen
Golan
Prenteg
Penmorfa
Pentrefelin
Tremadog
Festiniog Railway
PORTHMADOG
Borth-y-Gest
Morfa Bychan
Minffordd
Portmeirion

1811
MOEL DDU
y-pennant
A487
B4411

Llanfihangel-y-traethau
Harlech
Old Llanfair Quarries
Pen-Sarn
Llanfair
Llandanwg
Llanbed
Llanenddwyn
Dyffryn Ardudwy
Tal-y-
A496
B45

Llanaber

[i] **BARMOUTH**

Tremadog Bay

Barmouth Bay
The bar
Fairbourne Railway

CARDIGAN BAY

Llwyr
Llangelynin
Rhoslefain
Llanfendigaid
Bryncrug
TYW
Cae
Ab
A493

Ynyslas
Borth

ABERYSTWYTH
Penparcau
Rhydyfelin
Blaenplwf
A44

0 1 2 3 4 miles
0 1 2 3 4 5 kilometres

48

48

26

26

2

3

4

5

6

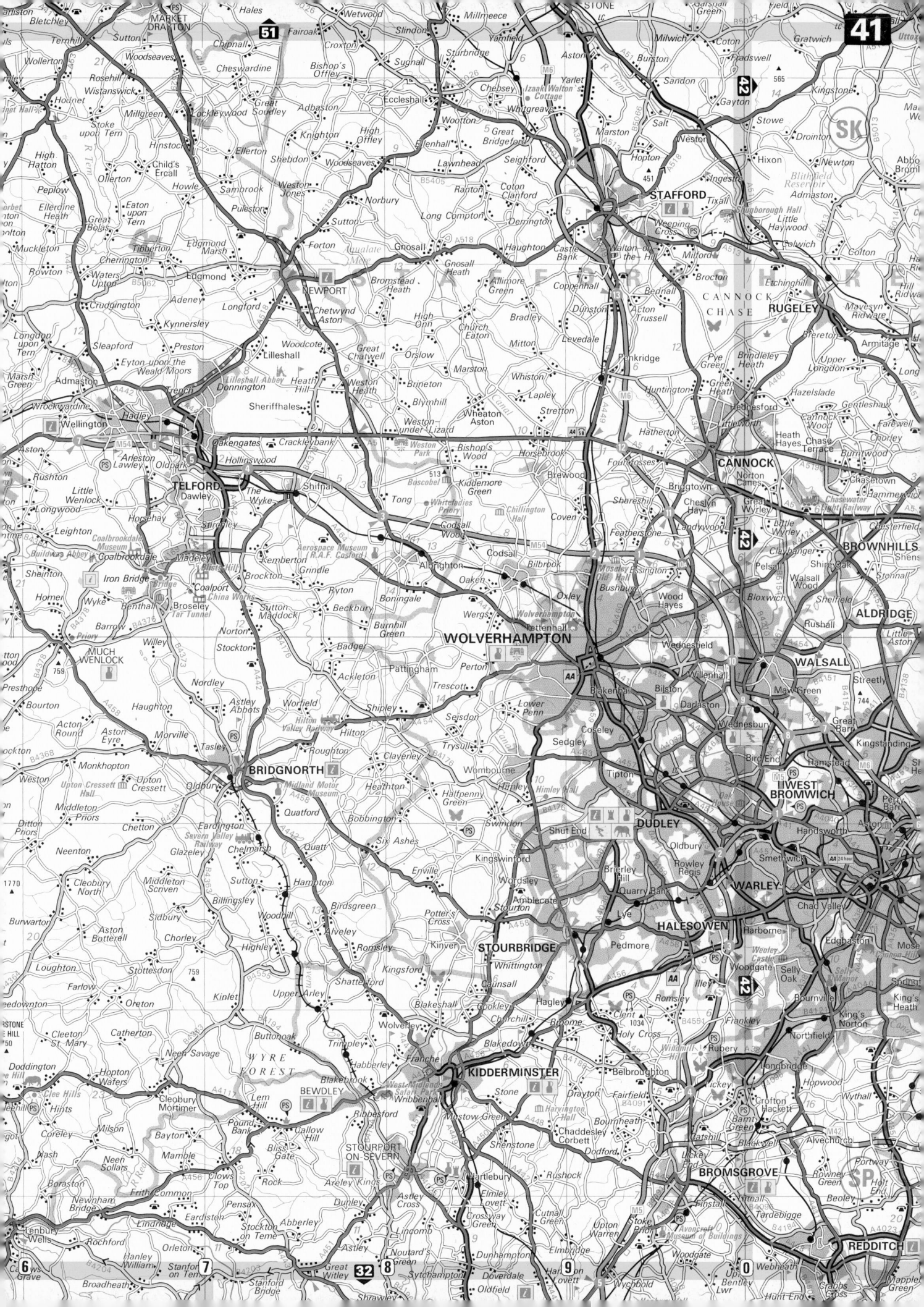

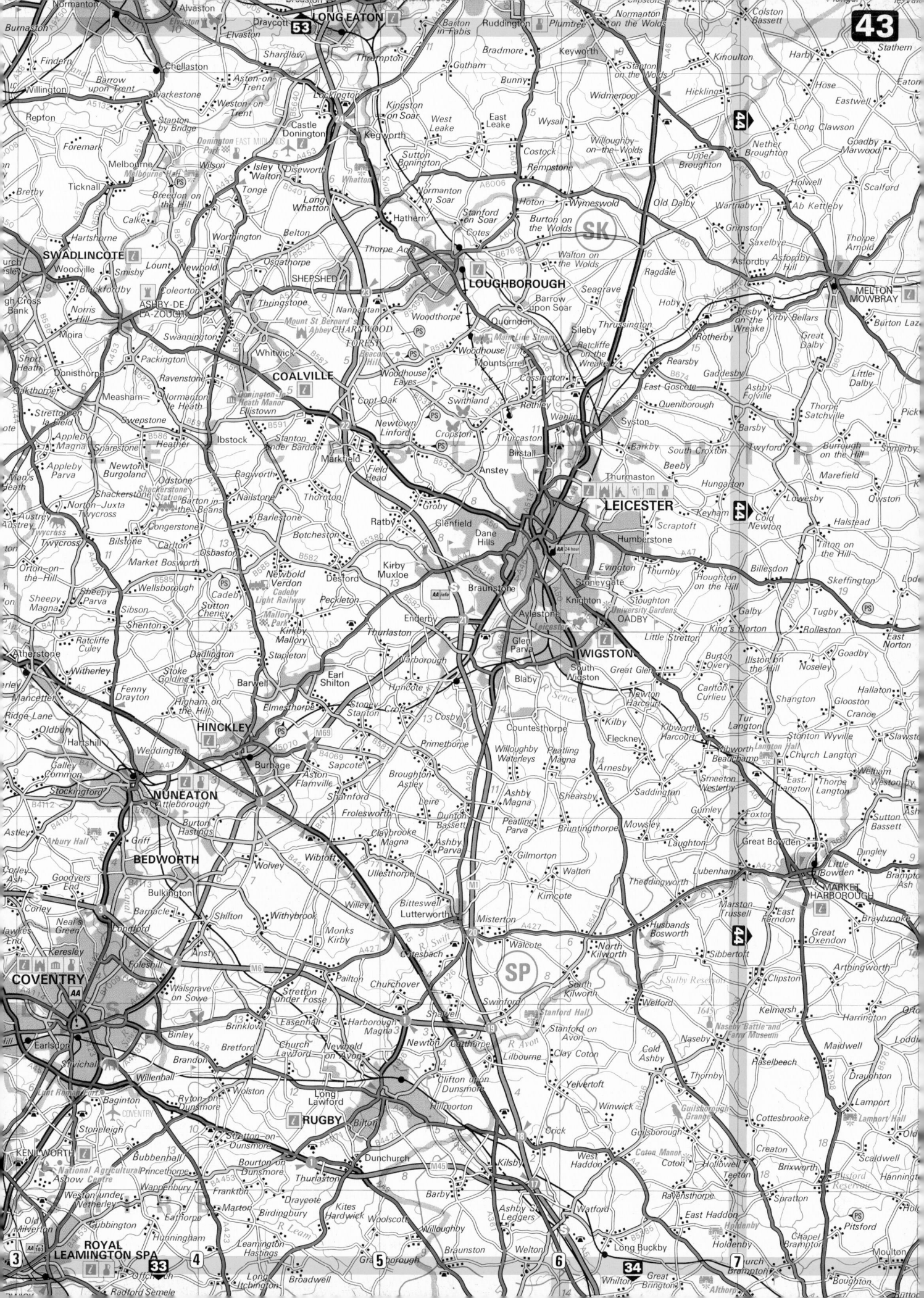

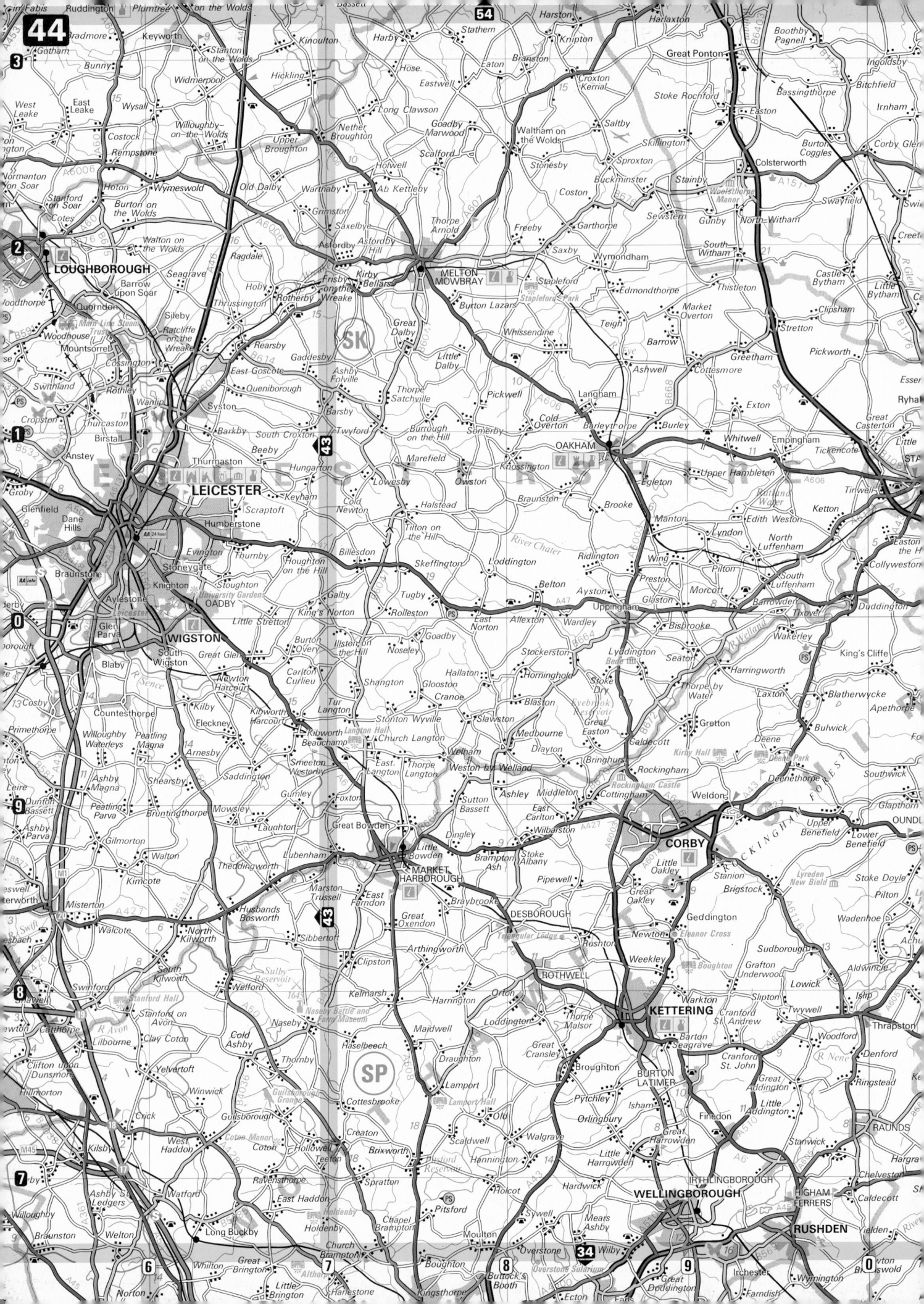

SHERINGHAM · CROMER · Open to Public

0 1 2 3 4 miles
0 1 2 3 4 5 kilometres

Salthouse · Weybourne · West Runton · East Runton · Overstrand · Sidestrand
Kelling · Upper Sheringham · Beeston Regis · Felbrigg · Trimingham
Holt · Bodham Street · Aylmerton · Crossdale Street · Northrepps · Gimingham · Mundesley
West Beckham · East Beckham · Gresham · Roughton · Southrepps · Paston
Baconsthorpe · Bessingham · Sustead · Thorpe Market · Trunch · Bacton · Keswick · Walcott
Hempstead · Plumstead · Hanworth · Thurgarton · Bradfield · Antingham · Edingthorpe · Ridlington · Happisburgh
Edgefield · Little Barningham · Aldborough · Ab Hill · Swafield · Witton · Crostwight · Whimpwell Green
Corpusty · Calthorpe · Colby · Ingworth · Felmingham · NORTH WALSHAM · Honing · Halsburgh Common · Hempstead · Sea Palling
Heydon · Blickling · Aylsham · Tuttington · Westwick · Worstead · Briggate · East Ruston · Lessingham · Ingham · Waxham
Reepham · Cawston · Brampton · Scottow · Sloley · Stalham · Hickling · Horsey
Buxton · Lamas · Fairstead · Tunstead · Sutton · Hickling Green · Hickling Heath
Eastgate · Brandiston · Stratton Strawless · Sco Ruston · Barton Turf · Catfield · Somerton
Alderford · Swannington · Hevingham · Horstead · Coltishall · Neatishead · Irstead · Potter Heigham · Winterton-on-Sea
Lenwade · Felthorpe · Hainford · Belaugh · Hoveton · Horning · Ludham · Martham · Hemsby · Newport
Weston Longville · Horsford · Frettenham · Wroxham · Woodbastwick · Thurne · Repps · Rollesby · Ormesby St Margaret · Scratby · California
Ringland · Drayton · St Helena · Newton St Faith · Crostwick · Upper Street · Ranworth · Clippesby · Burgh St Margaret · Filby · Ormesby St Michael · Caister-on-Sea
Hockering · Honingham · Taverham · Horsham St Faith · Spixworth · Rackheath · Salhouse · Panxworth · Fairhaven · Billockby · Thrigby · Mauby
Costessey · Catton · New Rackheath · Little Plumstead · South Walsham · Upton · Stokesby · West Caister
Hellesdon · Sprowston · Thorpe End Garden Village · North Burlingham · Acle · Runham · West End · Great Yarmouth
NORWICH · Great Plumstead · Blofield · Lingwood · Damgate
Bowthorpe · Thorpe St Andrew · Brundall · Beighton · Tunstall · Halvergate · Stracey Arms Wind Pump
Colney · Postwick · South Burlingham · Freethorpe · Berney Arms Station · Burgh Castle
Eaton · Trowse Newton · Surlingham · Strumpshaw · Southwood · Freethorpe Common · Wickhampton · GREAT YARMOUTH
Lakenham · Kirby Bedon · Buckenham · Limpenhoe · Berney Arms · Burgh · Belton · Gorleston on Sea
Cringleford · Keswick · Bramerton · Hassingham · Cantley · Reedham · Bradwell
Arminghall · Framingham Pigot · Rockland St Mary · Claxton · Langley Street · Hardley Street · Pettitts Rural Industries · Hopton on Sea
WYMONDHAM · East Carleton · Framingham Earl · Hellington · Yelverton · Ashby St Mary · Chedgrave · St Olaves Priory · Fritton · Hobland Hall
Mulbarton · Dunston · Stoke Holy Cross · Howe · Bergh Apton · Norton Subcourse · Lower Thurlton · Lound · Corton
Swardeston · Caistor St Edmund · Swainsthorpe · East Poringland · Thurton · Hales · Thurlton · Somerleyton · Blundeston
Bracon Ash · Toprow · Flordon · Newton Flotman · Brooke · Mundham · Raveningham · Herringfleet · Somerleyton Hall · Lowestoft End
Ashwellthorpe · Saxlingham Nethergate · Kirstead Green · Seething · Thwaite St Mary · Toft Monks · Maypole Green · Oulton · LOWESTOFT
Spooner Row · Tasburgh · Upper Tasburgh · Hemphall · Woodton · Kirby Cane · Haddiscoe · Oulton Broad · Kirkley
Tacolneston · Tharston · Stratton St Mary · Hemphall Green · Hedenham · Stockton · Wheatacre · Pakefield
Bunwell · Forncett St Mary · Topcroft · Ellingham · Kirby Row · Aldeby · Burgh St Peter
Carleton Rode · Forncett End · Forncett St Peter · Long Stratton · Topcroft Street · Ditchingham · Broome · Geldeston · Gillingham · Barnby · North Cove · Carlton Colville
Old Buckenham · Aslacton · Great Moulton · Shelton · Shelton Green · BUNGAY · Shipmeadow · Worlingham · Mutford · Rushmere · Gisleham
New Buckenham · Tibenham · Hardwick · Great Green · Mettingham · Barsham · BECCLES · Gillingham · Kessingland
Banham · North Green · Denton · Earsham · Ringsfield · Ellough · Redisham · Shadingfield · Sotterly · Wrentham
Tivetshall St Margaret · Bush Green · Alburgh · Flixton · Ilketshall St Margaret · Ilketshall St Andrew · Ringsfield Corner · Hulver Street · Benacre
Winfarthing · Gissing · Pulham Market · Wortwell · Homersfield · St Margaret South Elmham · Redisham · Brampton Station · Clay Common · Covehithe
Shelfanger · Tivetshall St Mary · Pulham St Mary · Redenhall · St Michael South Elmham · All Saints South Elmham · Stoven · South Cove
Shimpling · Rushall · Harleston · Starston · St Cross South Elmham · Cox Common · Brampton · Mount Pleasant
Fersfield · Burston · Dickleburgh · Needham · Mendham · Withersdale Street · Rumburgh · Reydon
Shimpling · Scole · Thorpe Abbots · Weybread · Metfield · St James South Elmham · Spexhall · Westhall · Uggeshall
DISS · Billingford · Brockdish · Fressingfield · Wissett · Wangford
Roydon · Palgrave · Stuston · Oakley · Hoxne · Wingfield · Chediston · Bulford · Holton

37

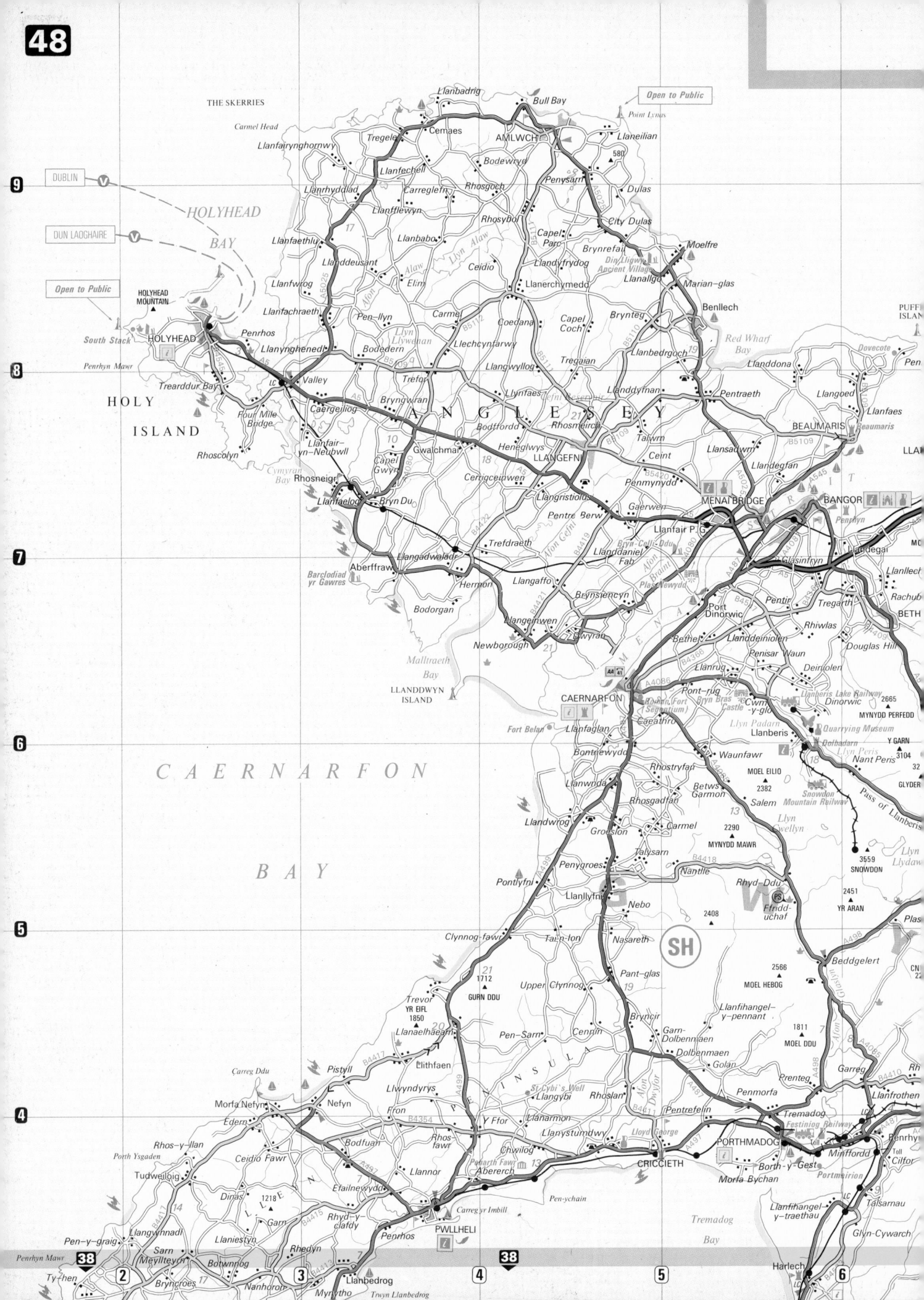

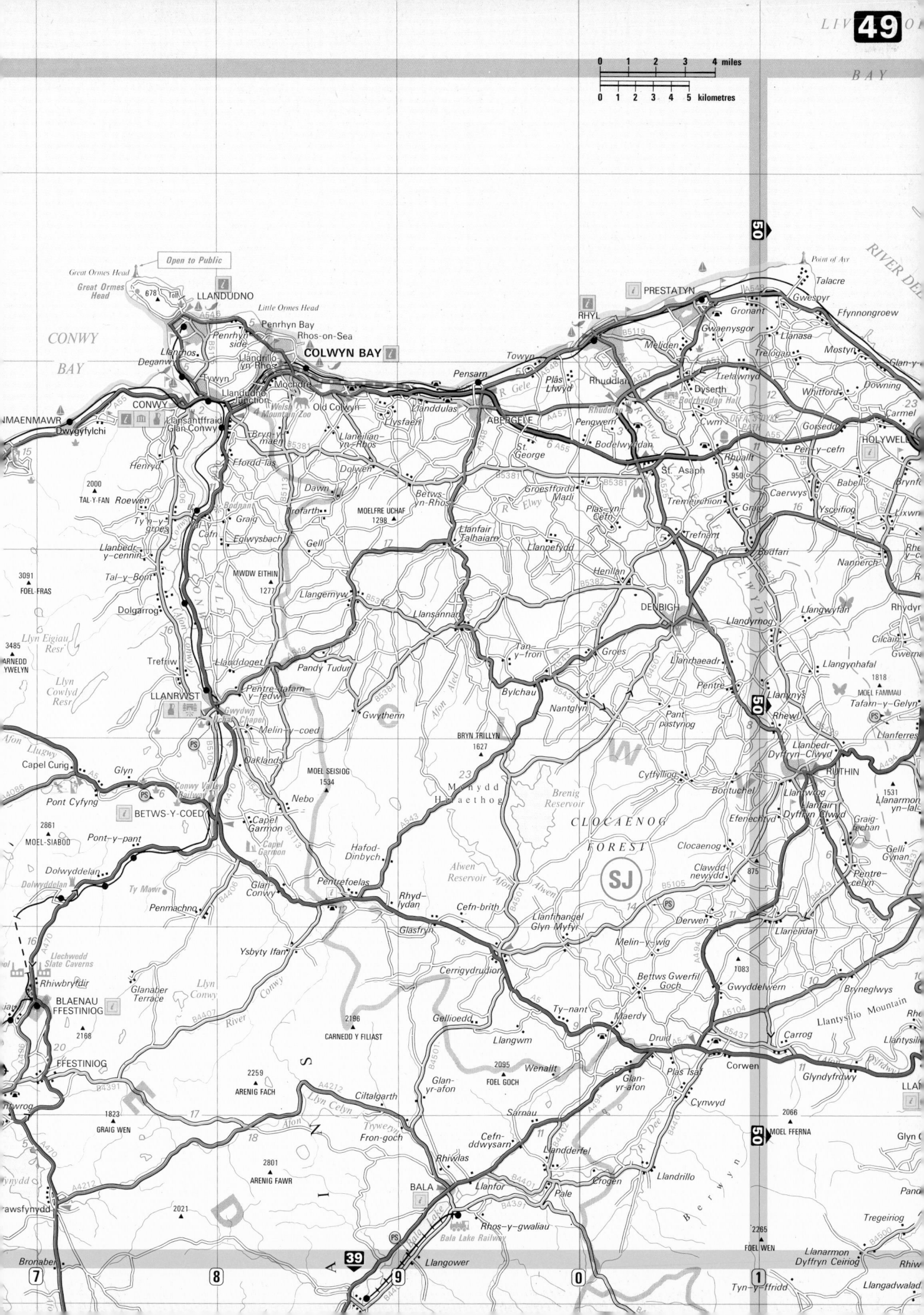

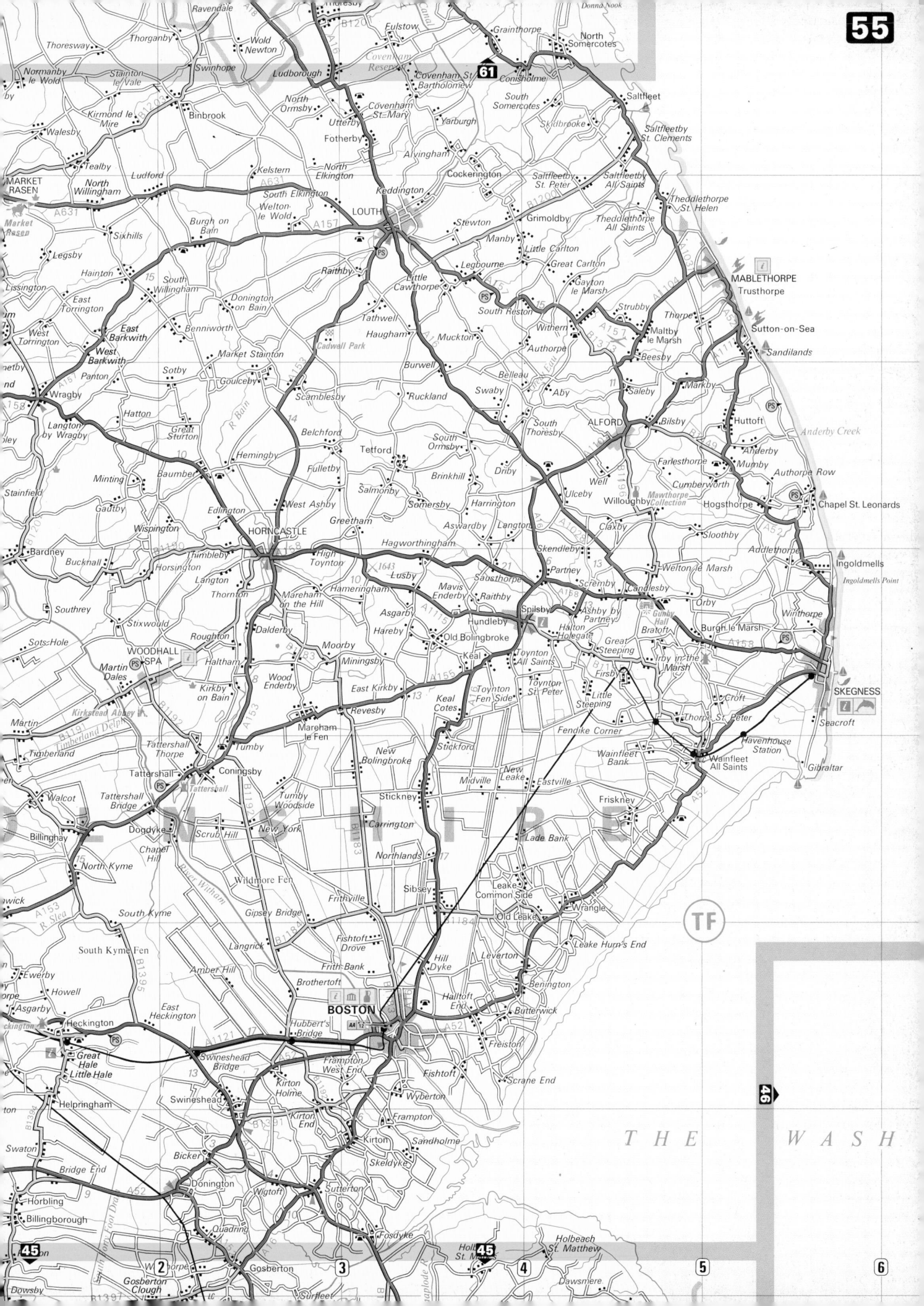

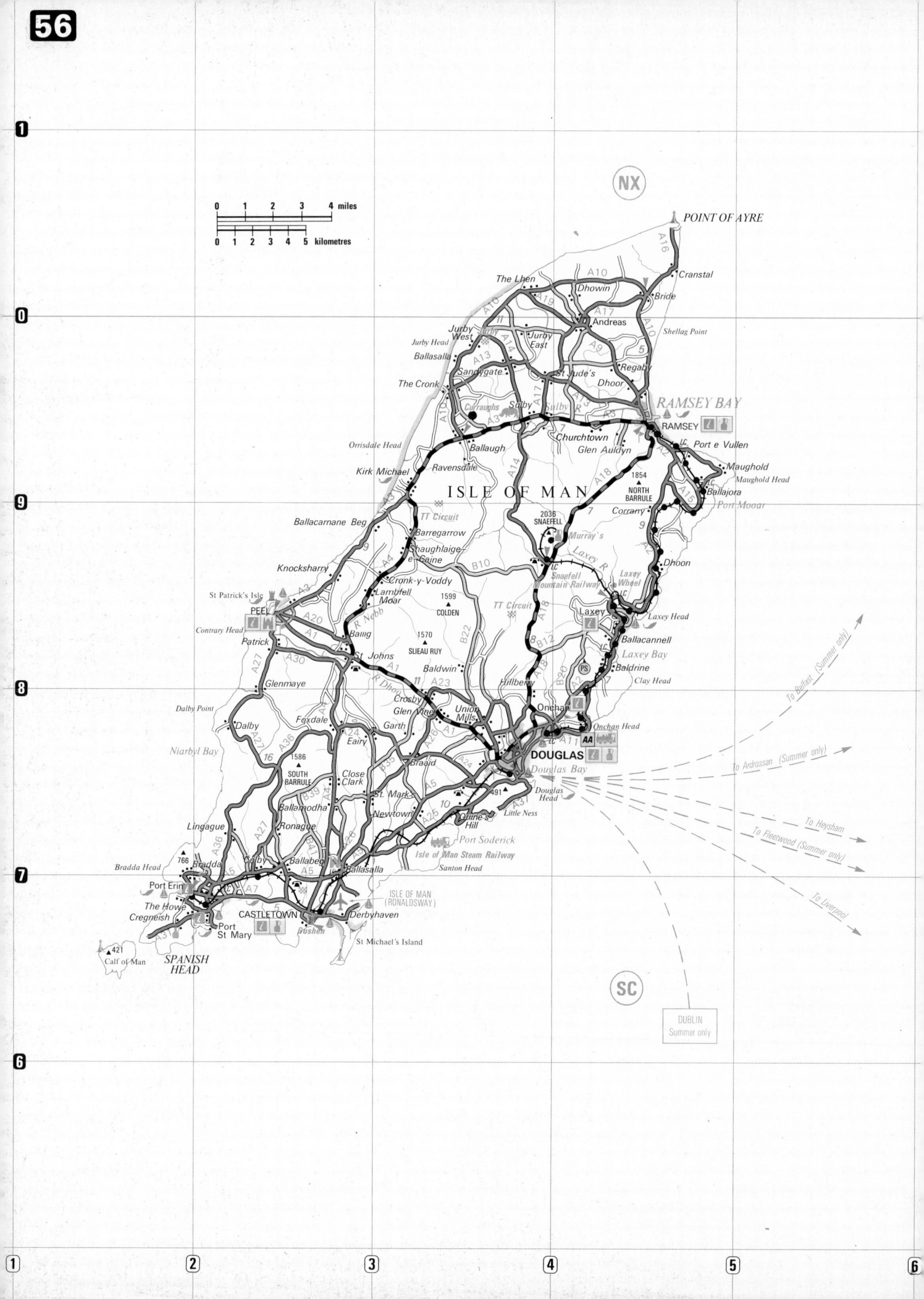

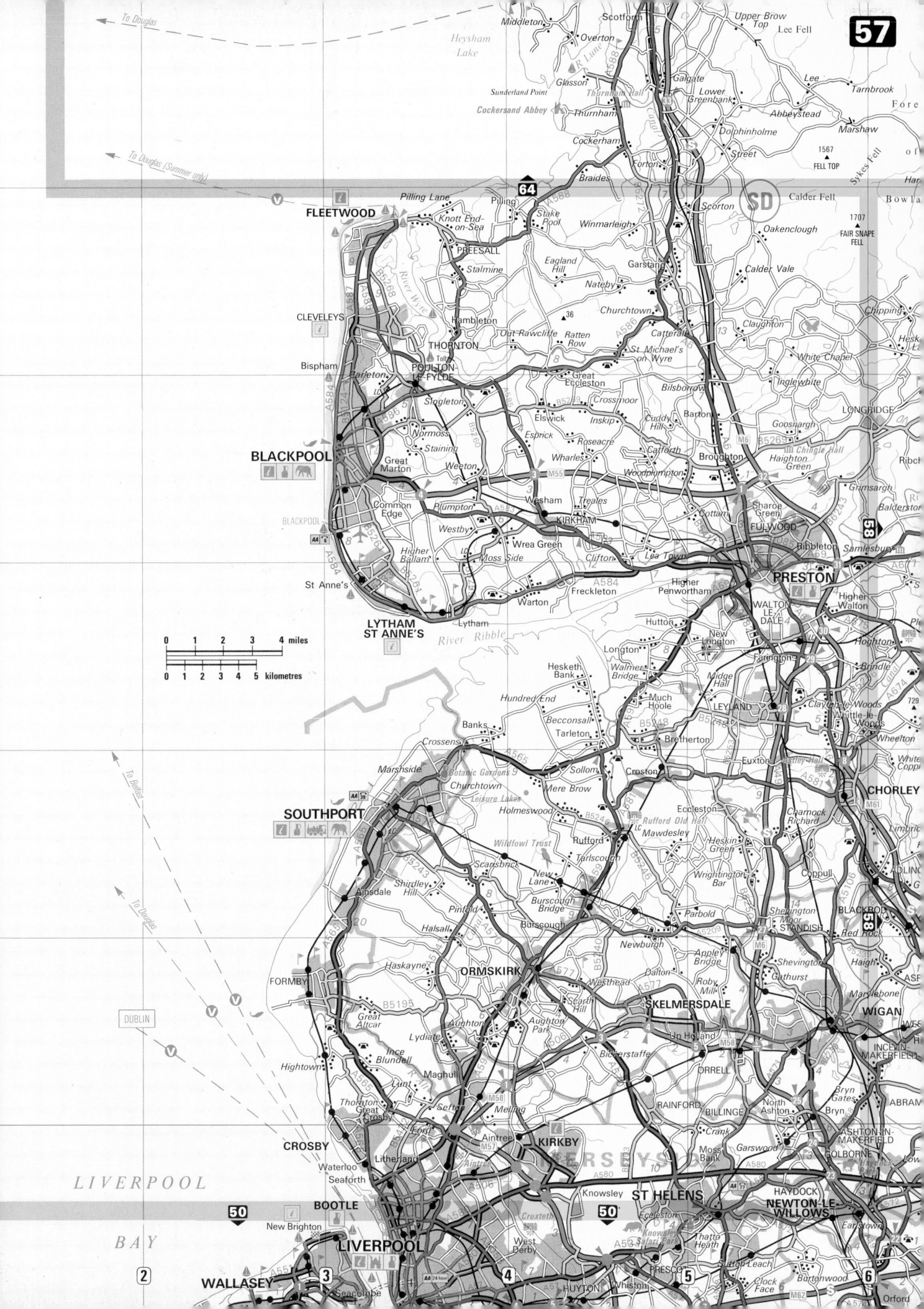

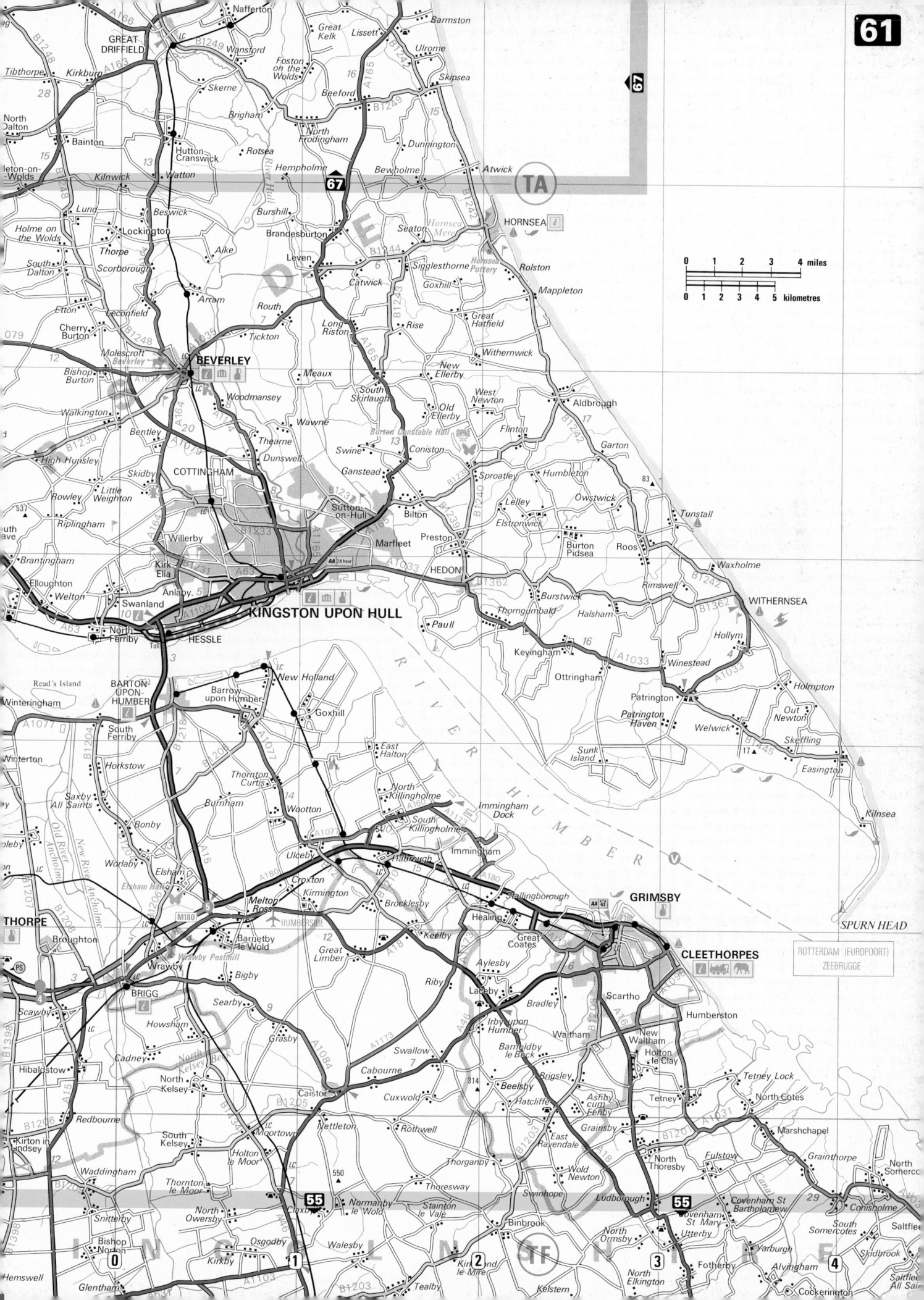

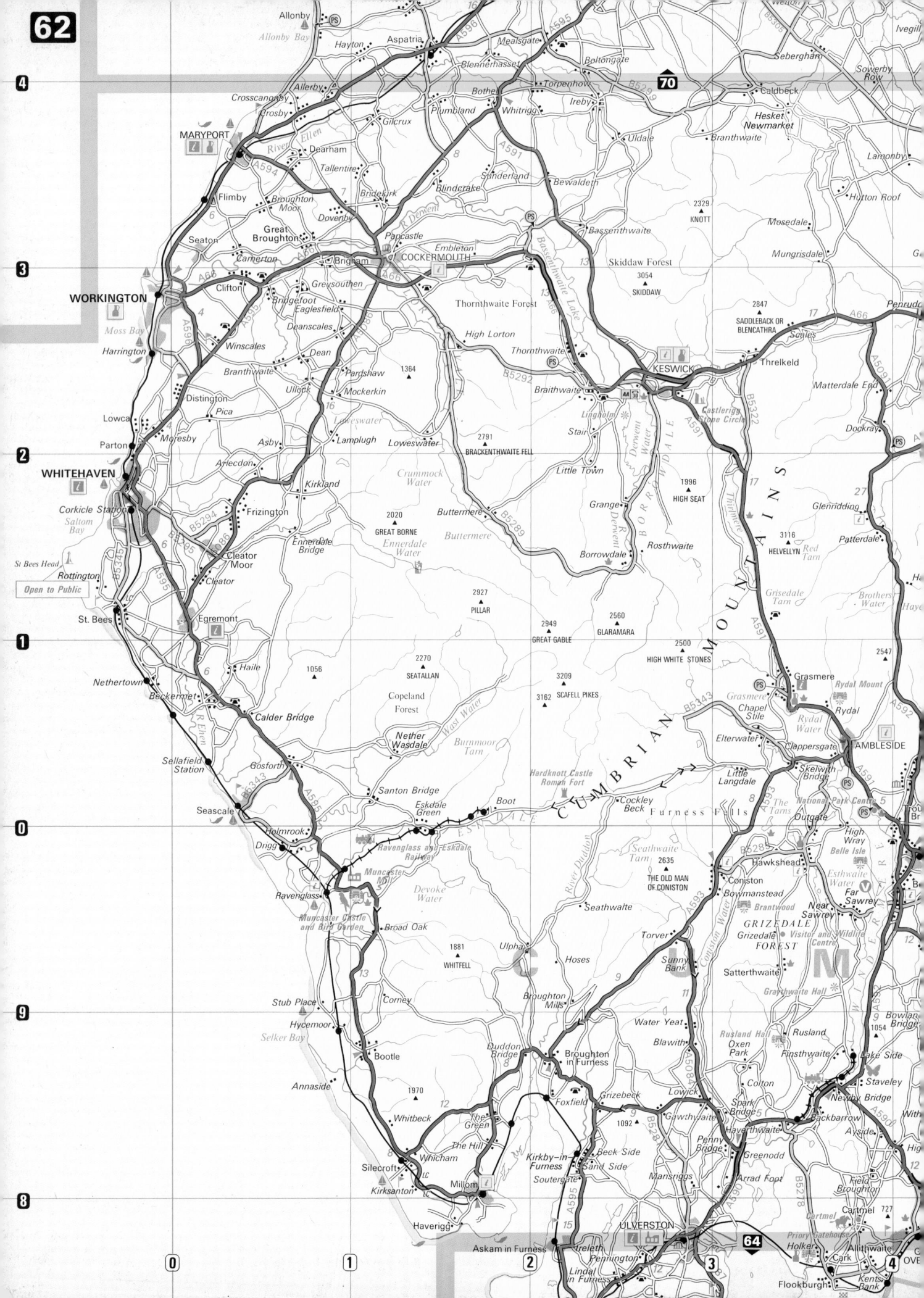

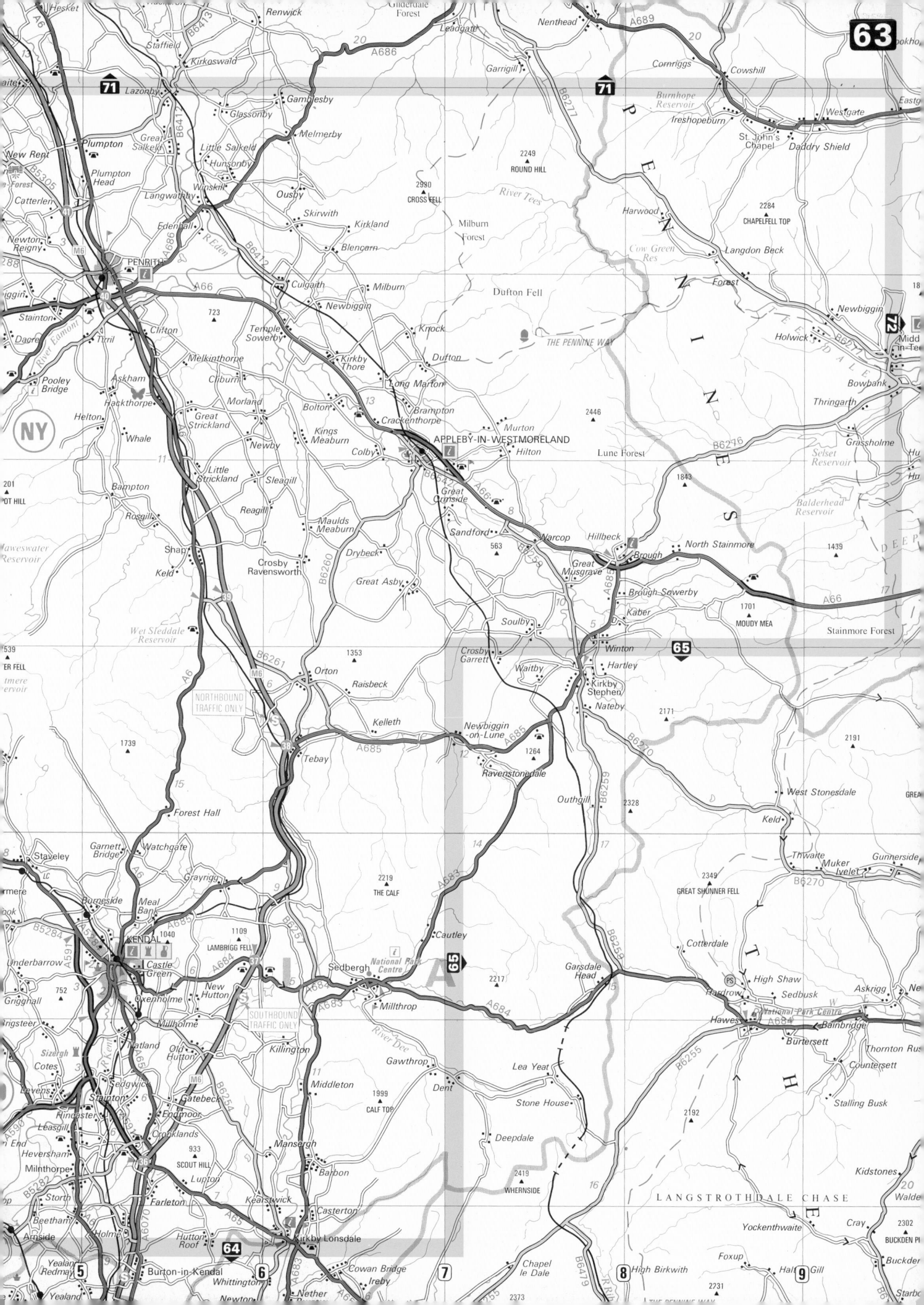

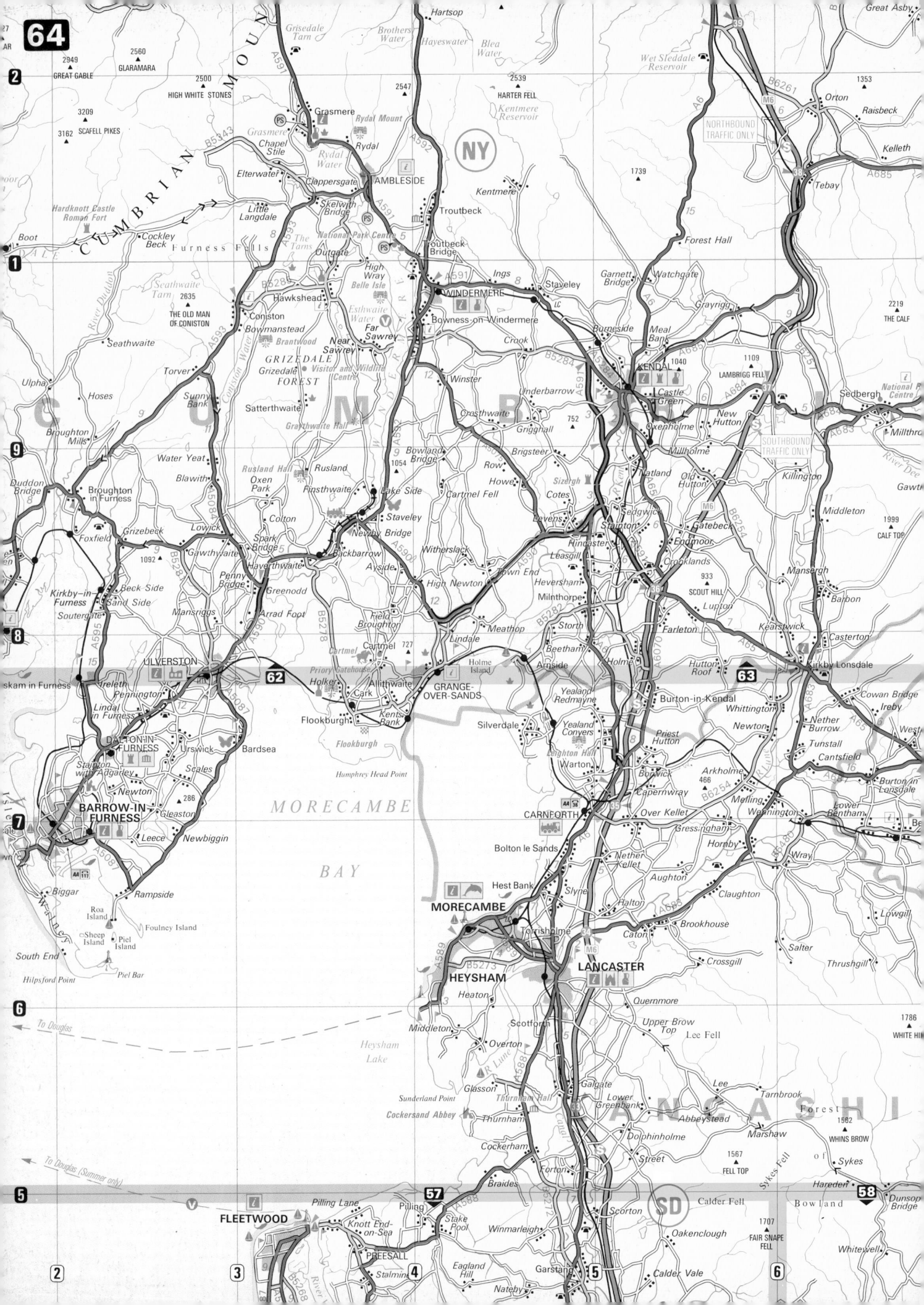

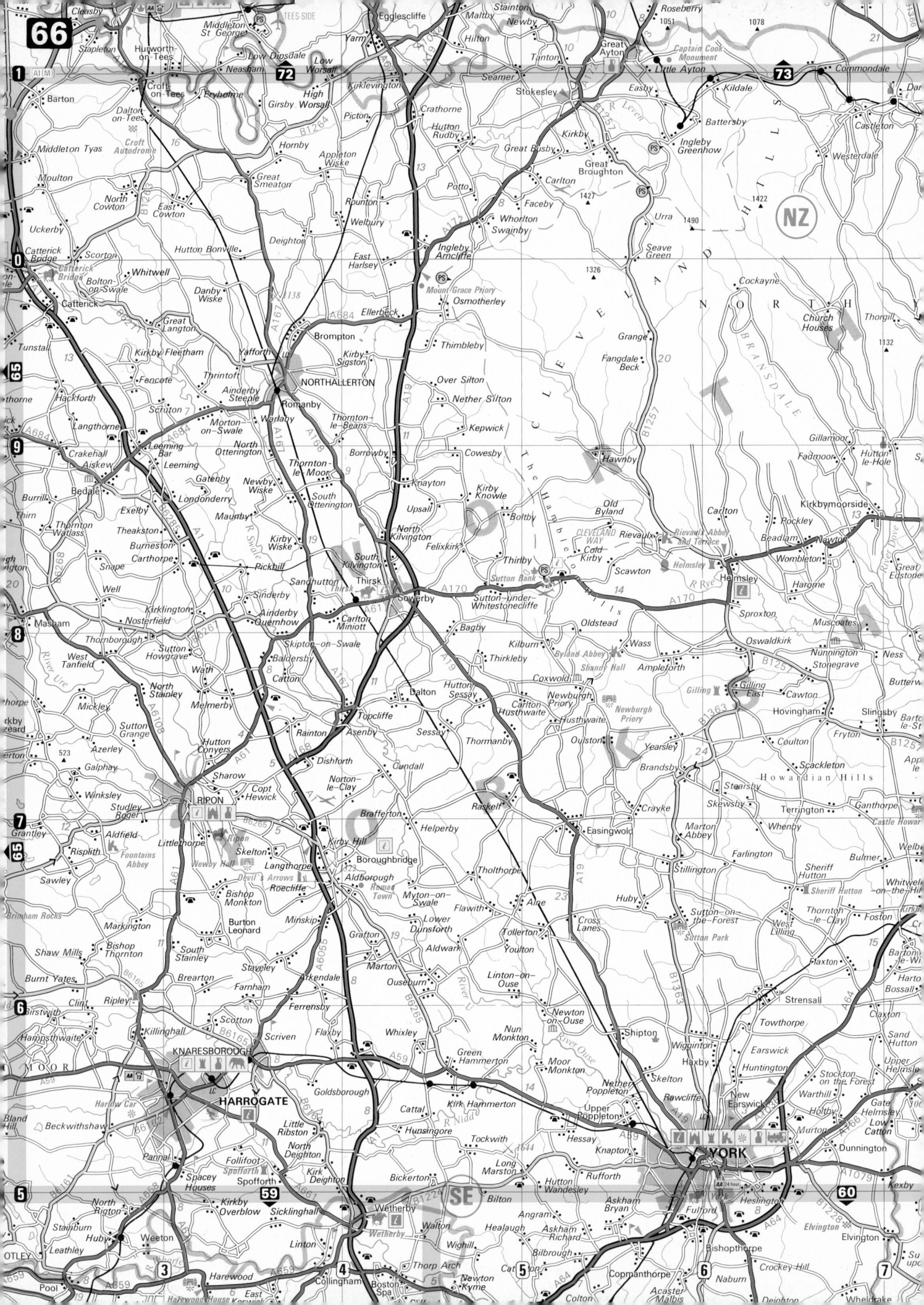

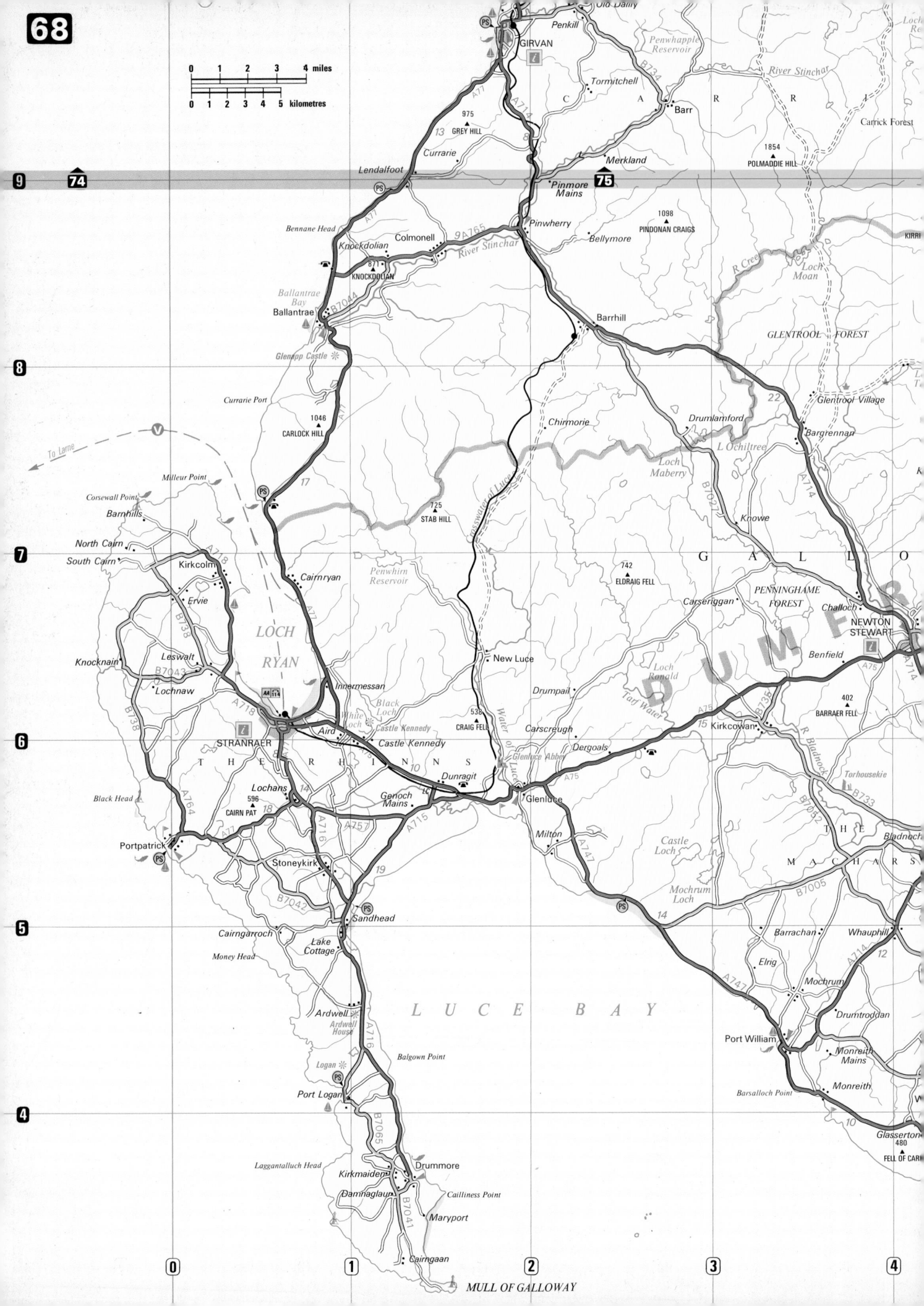

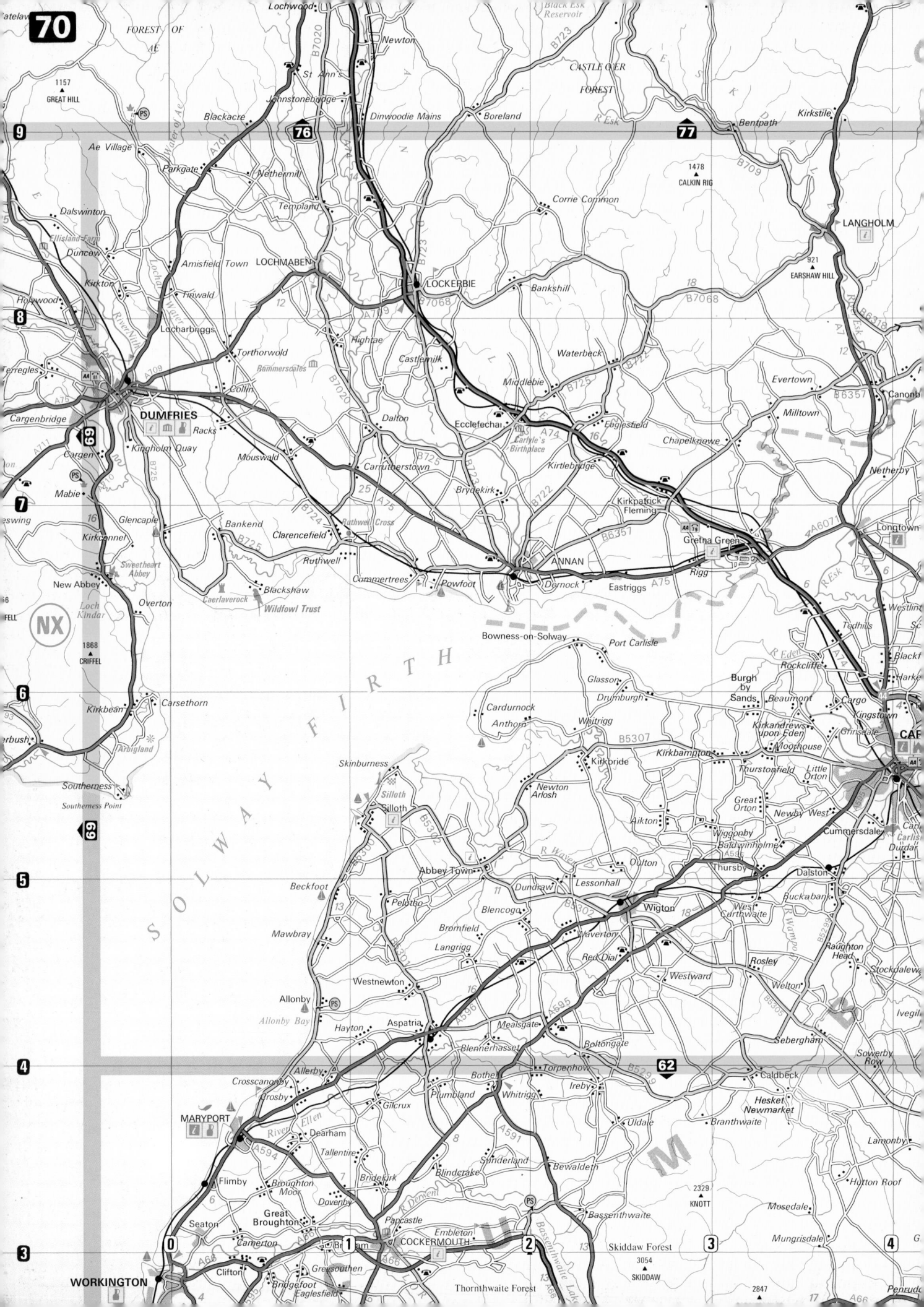

BERGEN
Summer only

GOTEBORG
Summer only

ESBJERG
Summer only

0   1   2   3   4 miles
0 1 2 3 4 5 kilometres

AND

NZ

M

con Point

orden Point

orden

Blackhall
Colliery

den

PS

9

aton

Hart

Elwick

HARTLEPOOL

79

Dalton
Piercy

AA 11

Hartlepool
Bay

Seaton
Carew

9

Greatham

Tees Bay

Newton
Bewley

A178

Coatham

REDCAR

Billingham

Cowpen
Bewley

The Flashes

Redcar

MARSKE-
BY-THE-SEA

Norton

AA 24 hour   Toll

Dormanstown

Kirkleatham

SALTBURN-BY-THE-SEA

Grangetown

New
Marske

Skinningrove

Boulby

South
Bank

Lazenby

Wilton

BROTTON

LOFTUS

Staithes

Port Mulgrave

Tees

MIDDLESBROUGH

Eston

Upleatham

16

Easington

Hinderwell

Acklam

SKELTON

D

Runswick

Marton

Ormesby

Boosbeck

Lingdale

Liverton

Roxby

naby
ees

Nunthorpe

GUISBOROUGH

A171

Stanghow

Ellerby

CLEVELAND WAY

Goldsborough

Gisborough
Priory

Moorsholm

B1266

Maltby
Hilton

Newby

Stainton

Newton under
Roseberry

CLEVELAND WAY

Lythe

1051

1078

Mickleby

Sandsend

Open to Public

Captain Cook
Monument

10

Tanton

Great
Ayton

WHITBY

Saltwick Bay

Seamer

5

Little Ayton

6

66

Commond

7

thorpe

8

Dunsley

Newholm

9

Ruswarp

67

Stokesley

Easby

Kildale

Danby

A171

Stainsacre

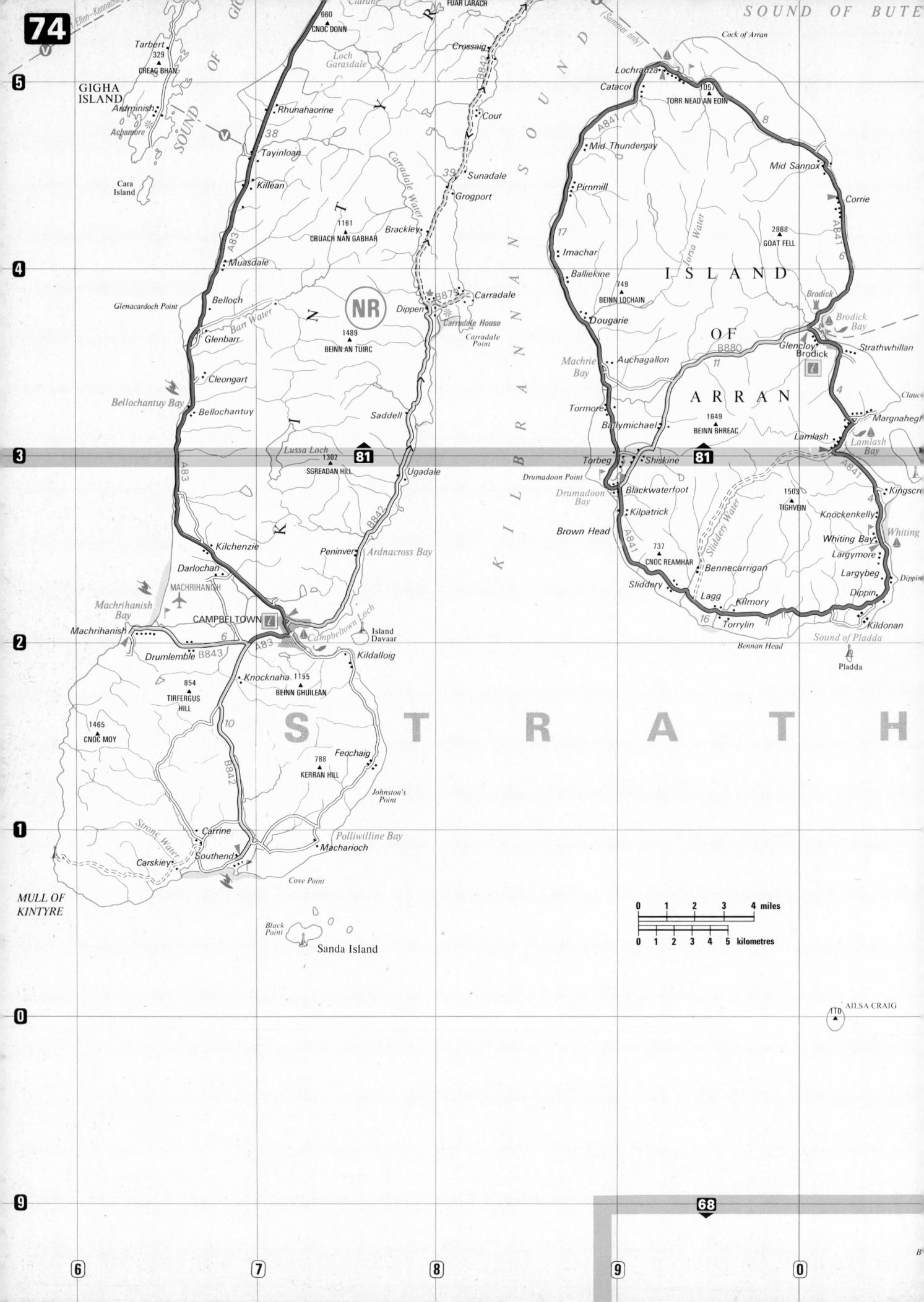

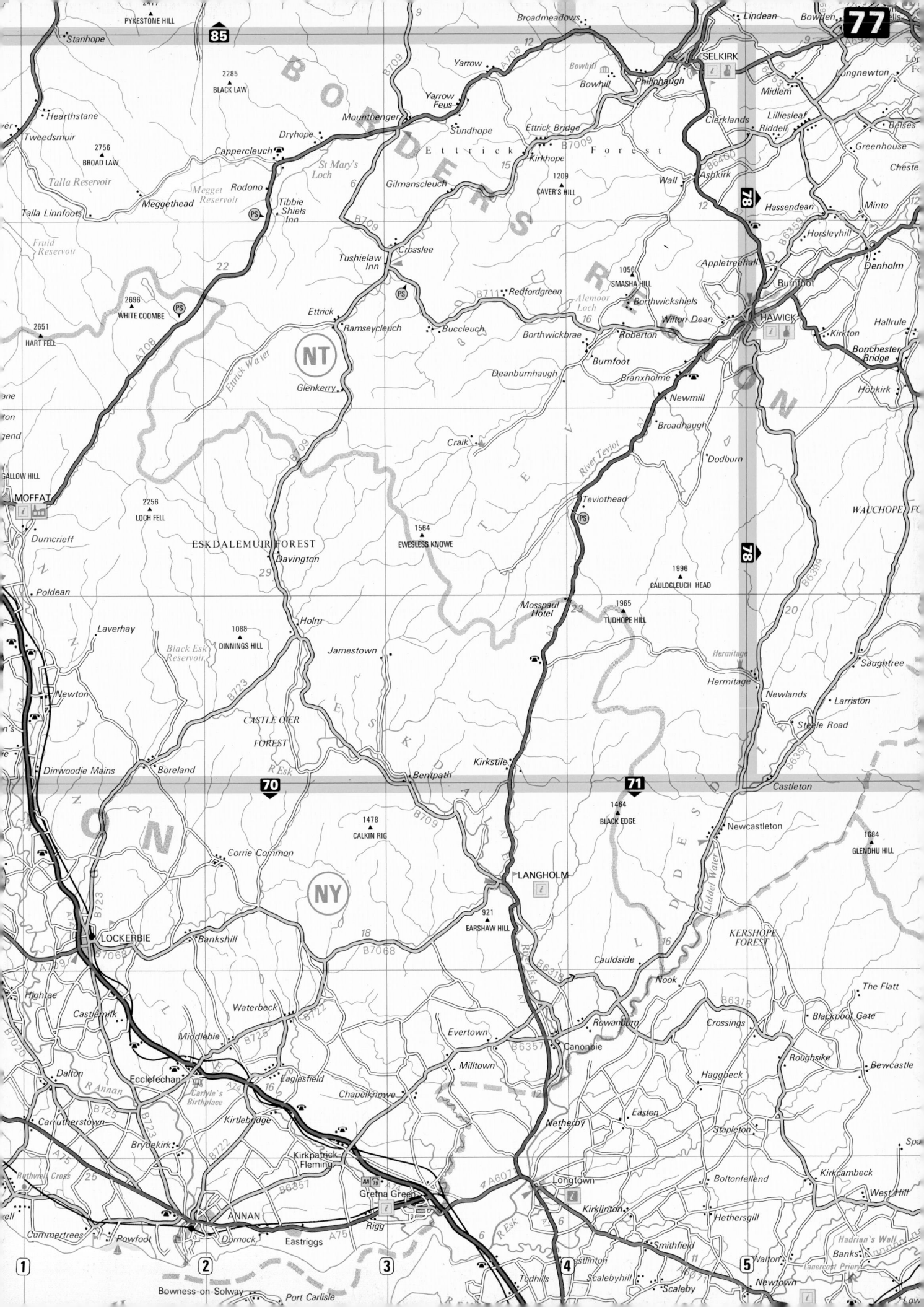

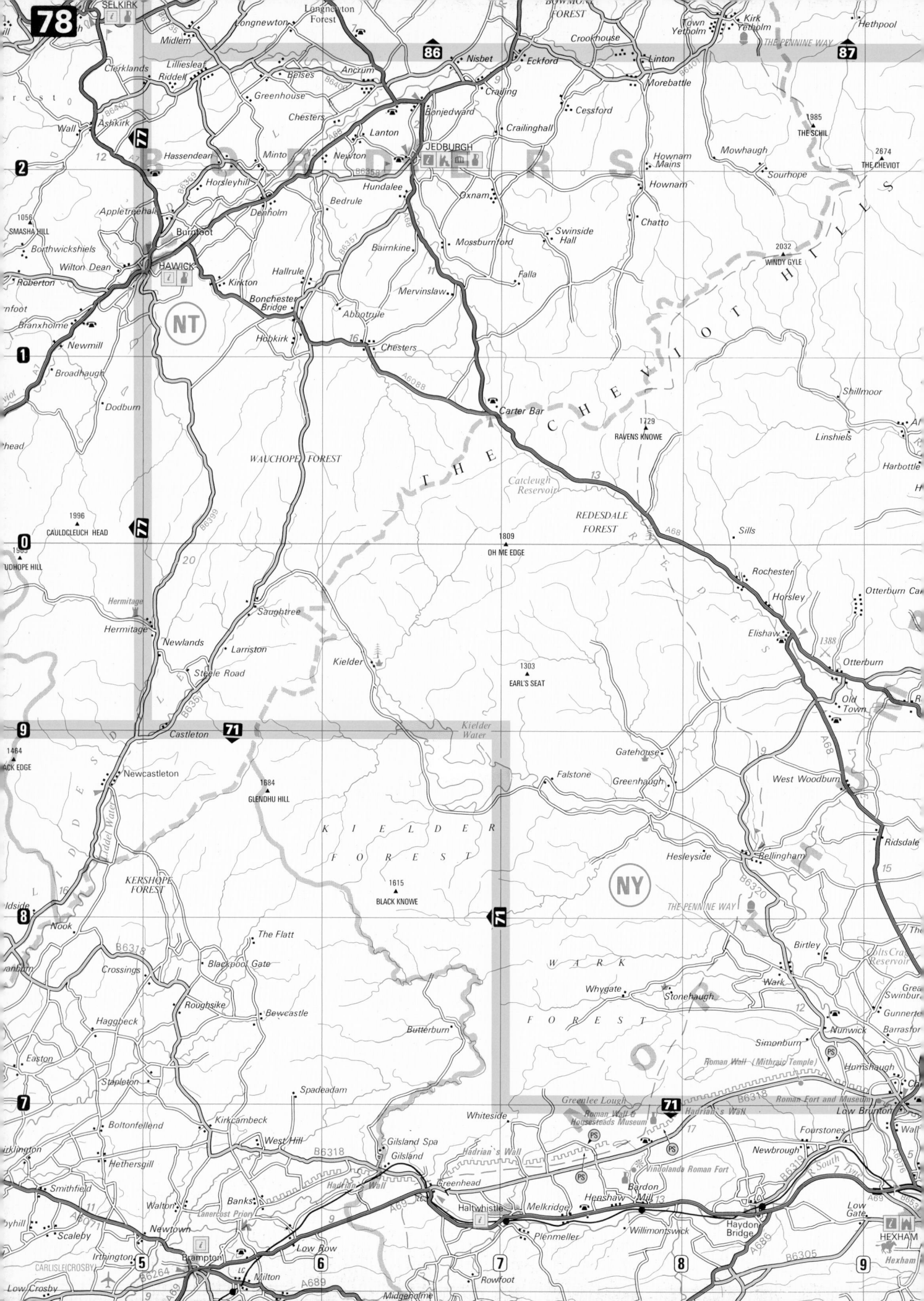

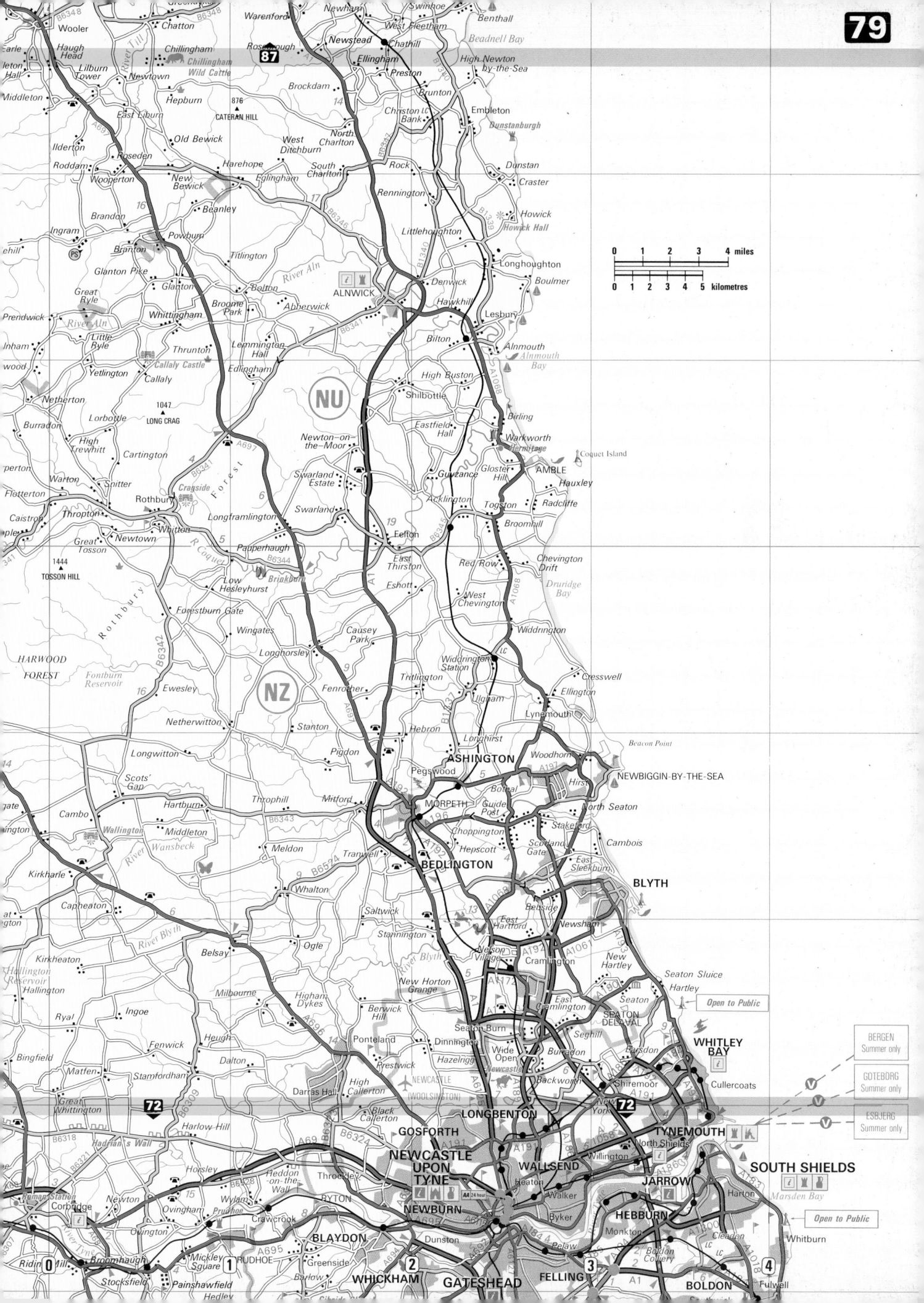

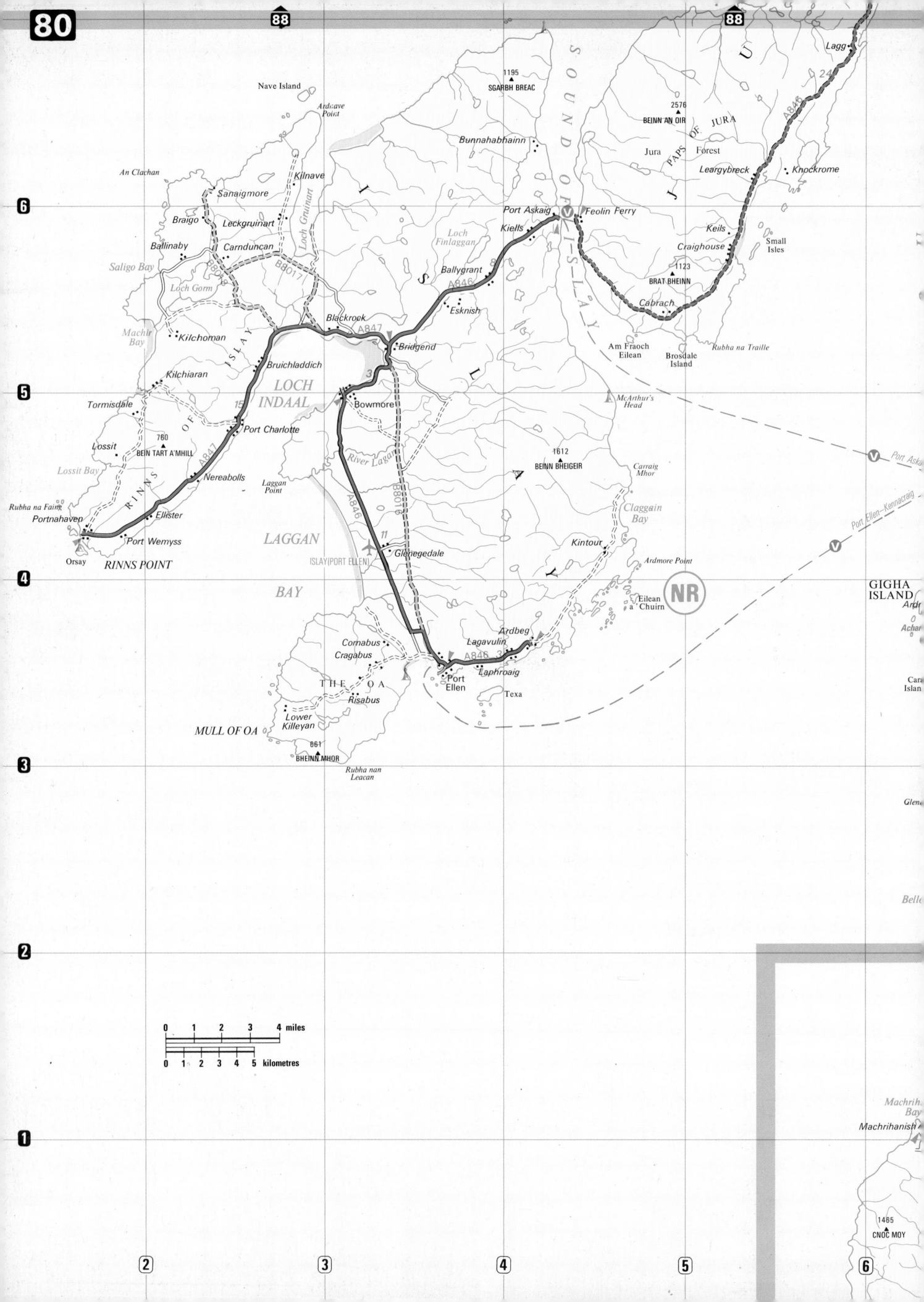

88

88

Lagg

SGARBH BREAC
1195

Nave Island

BEINN AN OIR
2576

Ardnave
Point

Bunnahabhainn

Jura
Forest

PAPS OF JURA

Leargybreck

Knockrome

An Clachan

Sanaigmore

Kilnave

I

Port Askaig

Feolin Ferry

Keils

Braigo

Leckgruinart

Kiells

Craighouse

Small
Isles

Ballinaby

Carnduncan

Loch Gruinart

Ballygrant

B8018

B8017

A846

Brat Bheinn
1123

Saligo Bay

Loch Gorm

S

Esknish

Cabrach

Machir
Bay

Kilchoman

Blackrock

A847

Bridgend

L

Am Fraoch
Eilen

Rubha na Traille

Brosdale
Island

Bruichladdich

LOCH
INDAAL

McArthur's
Head

Tormisdale

15

Port Charlotte

Bowmore

BEINN BHEIGEIR
1612

Carraig
Mhor

Port Ask

Lossit

BEIN TART A'MHILL
760

OF ISLAY

River Laggan

B8016

Claggain
Bay

Port Ellen–Kennacraig

Lossit Bay

RINNS

Nereabolls

Laggan
Point

Rubha na Faing

Ellister

A846

Kintour

Portnahaven

LAGGAN

ISLAY(PORT ELLEN)

11

Glenegedale

Ardmore Point

GIGHA
ISLAND

Orsay

Port Wemyss

RINNS POINT

BAY

Eilean
a' Chuirn

NR

Ardr

Achar

Cornabus

Lagavulin

Ardbeg

Cragabus

A846

Laphroaig

Cara
Islan

THE OA

Port
Ellen

Texa

Lower
Killeyan

Risabus

MULL OF OA

Rubha nan
Leacan

Glen

BHEINN MHOR
B861

Belle

SOUND OF ISLAY

Machrih.
Bay

Machrihanish

CNOC MOY
1465

0 1 2 3 4 miles

0 1 2 3 4 5 kilometres

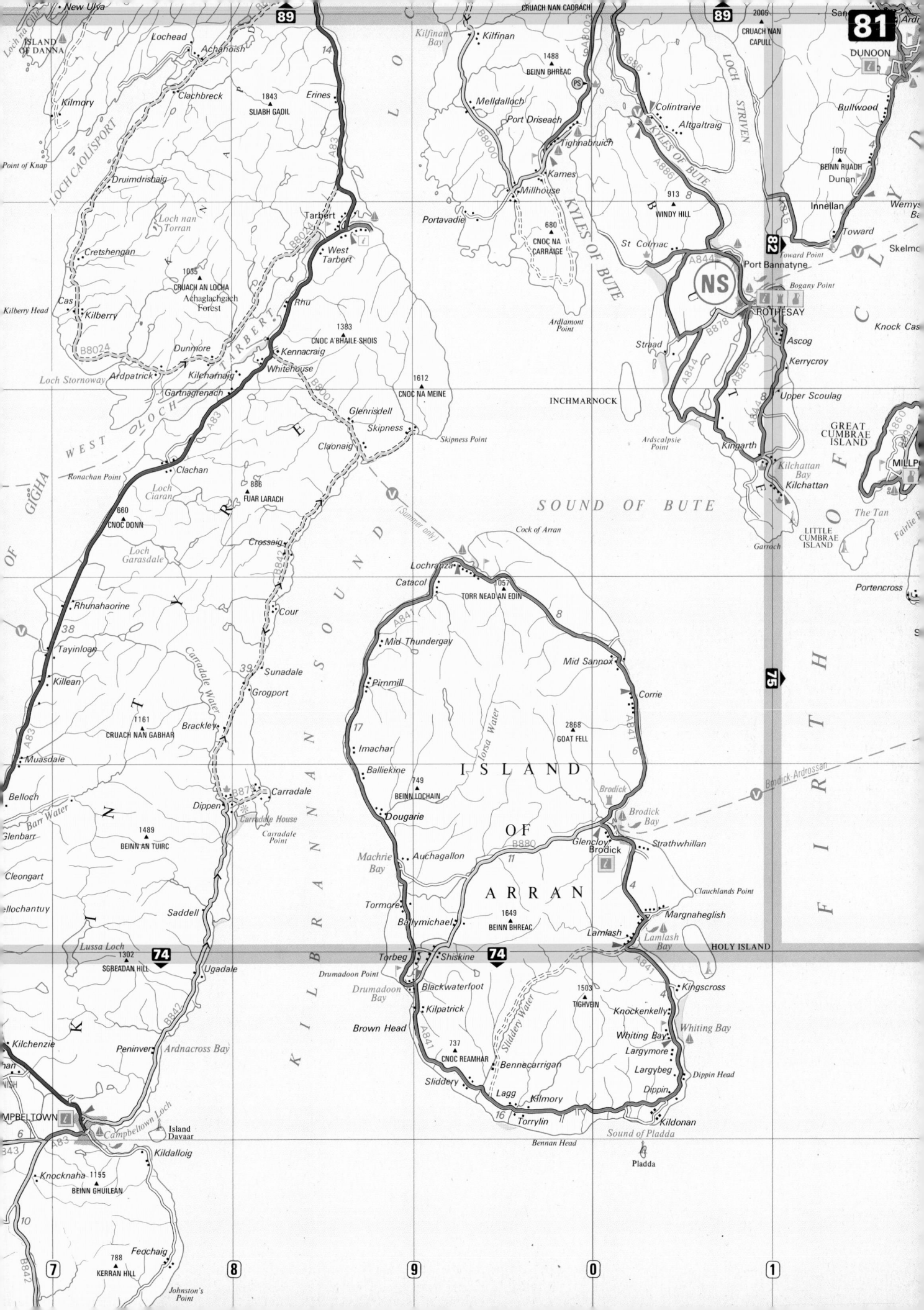

0 1 2 3 4 miles
0 1 2 3 4 5 kilometres

Reed Point
Cockburnspath
ST ABB'S HEAD
Northfield
St Abbs
Grantshouse
Coldingham
Houndwood
Gairncross
EYEMOUTH
21
ey Bathans
Auchencrow
B6438
Reston
Burnmouth
Marygold
Ayton
Lintlaw
Preston
Chirnside
Foulden
Lamberton
Chirnsidebridge
Edrom
Clappers
1333
Allanton
Hutton
Paxton
Blackadder
B6461
Whitsome
Fishwick
Loanend
Tweedmouth
Spittal
BERWICK-UPON-TWEED
Fogo
Horncliffe
Murton
Thorntonpark
Ladykirk
Scremerston
Swinton
Norham
Thornton
Cheswick
Shoreswood
West Allerdean
Swintonmill
Shoresdean
Ancroft
Goswick
Simprim
Grindon
Leitholm
Felkington
Haggerston
CAUSEWAY FLOODED AT HIGH TIDE
HOLY ISLAND
Berrington
Beal
Holy Island
Duddo
15
Lindisfarne Priory
Castle Point
Lennel
Bowsden
Burrows Hole
COLDSTREAM
Castle Heaton
Kyloe
Fenwick
Cornhill on-Tweed
Etal
Lowick
Buckton
Crookham
Heatherslaw Mill
B6353
Wark
The Lady Waterford Hall
Ford
Elwick
Ross
Carham
Learmouth
Branxton
Holburn
Detchant
Staple Sound
FARNE ISLANDS
Hadden
Pressen
Flodden
Kimmerston
Middleton
Inner Sound
Lempitlaw
Downham
Milfield
Nesbit
Belford
Budle Bay
Budle
Bamburgh
Waren Mill
Mindrum
Pawston
Fenton Town
Doddington
Warenton
Bellshill
Spindlestone
Burton
Seahouses
Open to Public
Kilham
Lanton
Newtown
Horton
Bradford
Carr End
North Sunderland
78
Shotton
Coupland
Warenford
Tucker
Newham Hall
Newham
Kirknewton
Akeld
Wooler
Greendykes
Adderstone
Swinhoe
Benthall
79
Humbleton
Haugh Head
Chatton
Rosebrough
Newstead
West Fleetham
Chillingham
Kirk Yetholm
Earle
Middleton Hall
Lilburn Tower
Newtown
Chillingham Wild Cattle
Ellingham
Preston
High Newton by-the-Sea
THE PENNINE WAY
Morebattle
COLD LAW
1485
Middleton
East Lilburn
Hepburn
CATERAN HILL
Brockdam
Brunton
Christon Bank
Embleton
Dunstanburgh
Beadnell Bay
Beadnell
Town Yetholm
NORTHUMBERLAND

8   9   0   1   2

1985

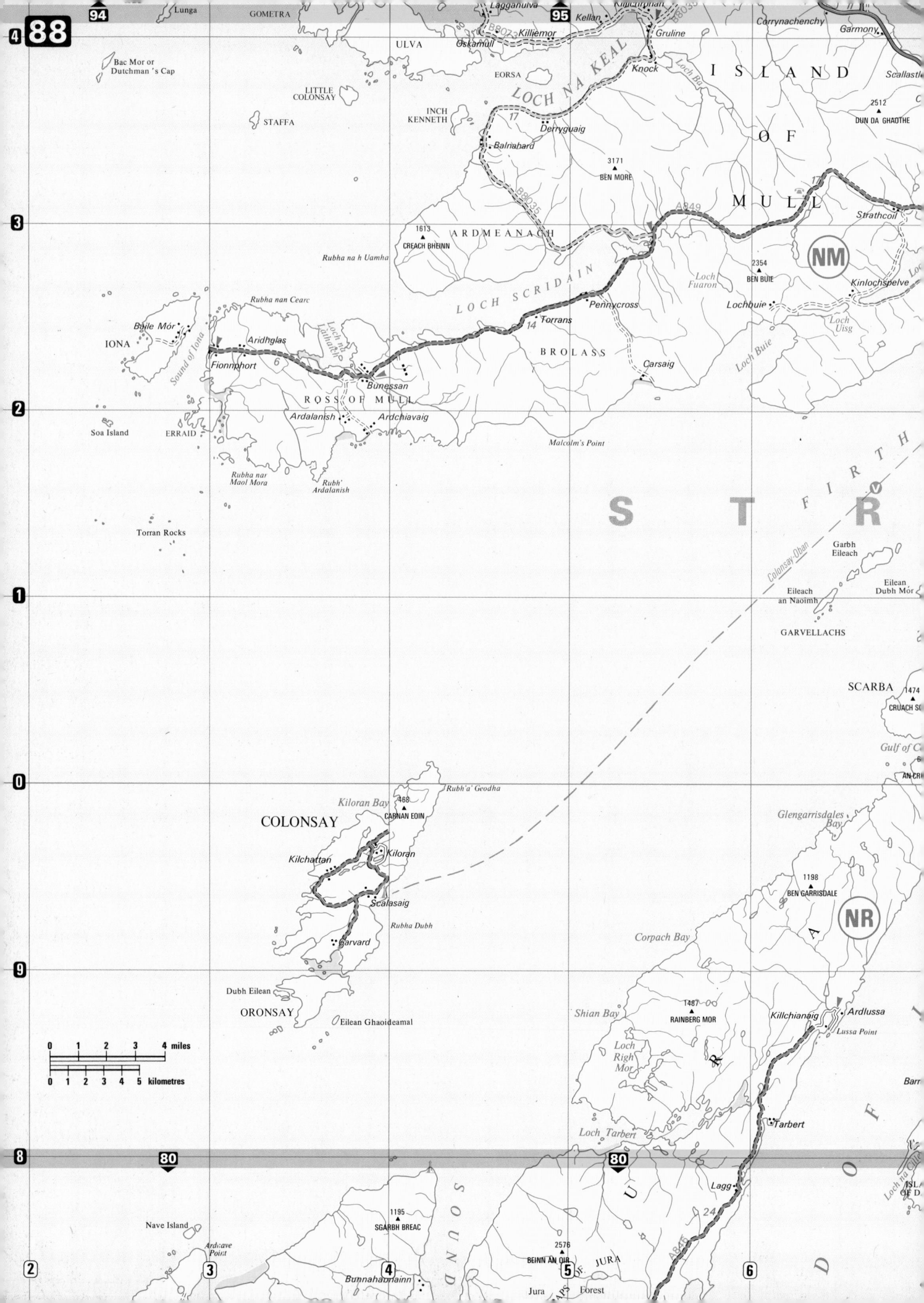

94

GOMETRA

Lunga

Lagganulva

95 Kellan

Killiemor

Kilchurphan

Corrynachenchy

Garmony

ULVA

Oskamull

Gruline

Scallastle

2512
DUN DA GHAOTHE

LITTLE
COLONSAY

EORSA

Knock

ISLAND

Bac Mor or
Dutchman's Cap

STAFFA

INCH
KENNETH

B807

LOCH NA KEAL

17

Derryguaig

Balnahard

B8035

OF

Loch Bà

A849

17

MULL

Strathcoil

3171
BEN MORE

3

1613
CREACH BHEINN

ARDMEANACH

NM

Rubha na h Uamha

2354
BEN BUIE

Kinlochspelve

Rubha nan Cearc

Loch Scridain

Loch
Fuaron

Lochbuie

Loch
Uisg

IONA

Baile Mór

Aridhglas

Pennycross

14

Torrans

Loch na Làthaich

Sound of Iona

6

Fionnphort

Bunessan

Carsaig

BROLASS

Loch Buie

2

Soa Island

ERRAID

ROSS OF MULL

Ardalanish

Ardchiavaig

Malcolm's Point

S

T

FIRTH

R

Rubha nar
Maol Mora

Rubh'
Ardalanish

Colonsay-Oban

Garbh
Eileach

Eilean
Dubh Mór

Torran Rocks

1

Eileach
an Naoimh

GARVELLACHS

SCARBA

1474
CRUACH SC

Gulf of C

AN-CR

0

Rubh'a' Geodha

Kiloran Bay

Glengarrisdales
Bay

468
CARNAN EOIN

COLONSAY

Kilchattan

Kiloran

1198
BEN GARRISDALE

NR

A

Scalasaig

Rubha Dubh

Corpach Bay

9

Garvard

1487
RAINBERG MOR

Killchianaig

Ardlussa

Dubh Eilean

Shian Bay

R

Lussa Point

ORONSAY

Eilean Ghaoideamal

Loch
Righ
Mor

0   1   2   3   4 miles

Loch Tarbert

Tarbert

0 1 2 3 4 5 kilometres

Barr

8

80

80

U

Lagg

Nave Island

1195
SGARBH BREAC

SOUND

OF JURA

24

A846

Ardskave
Point

OF D

Bunnahabhainn

2576
BEINN AN OIR

ISL
OF D

2

3

4

Jura   Forest

5

6

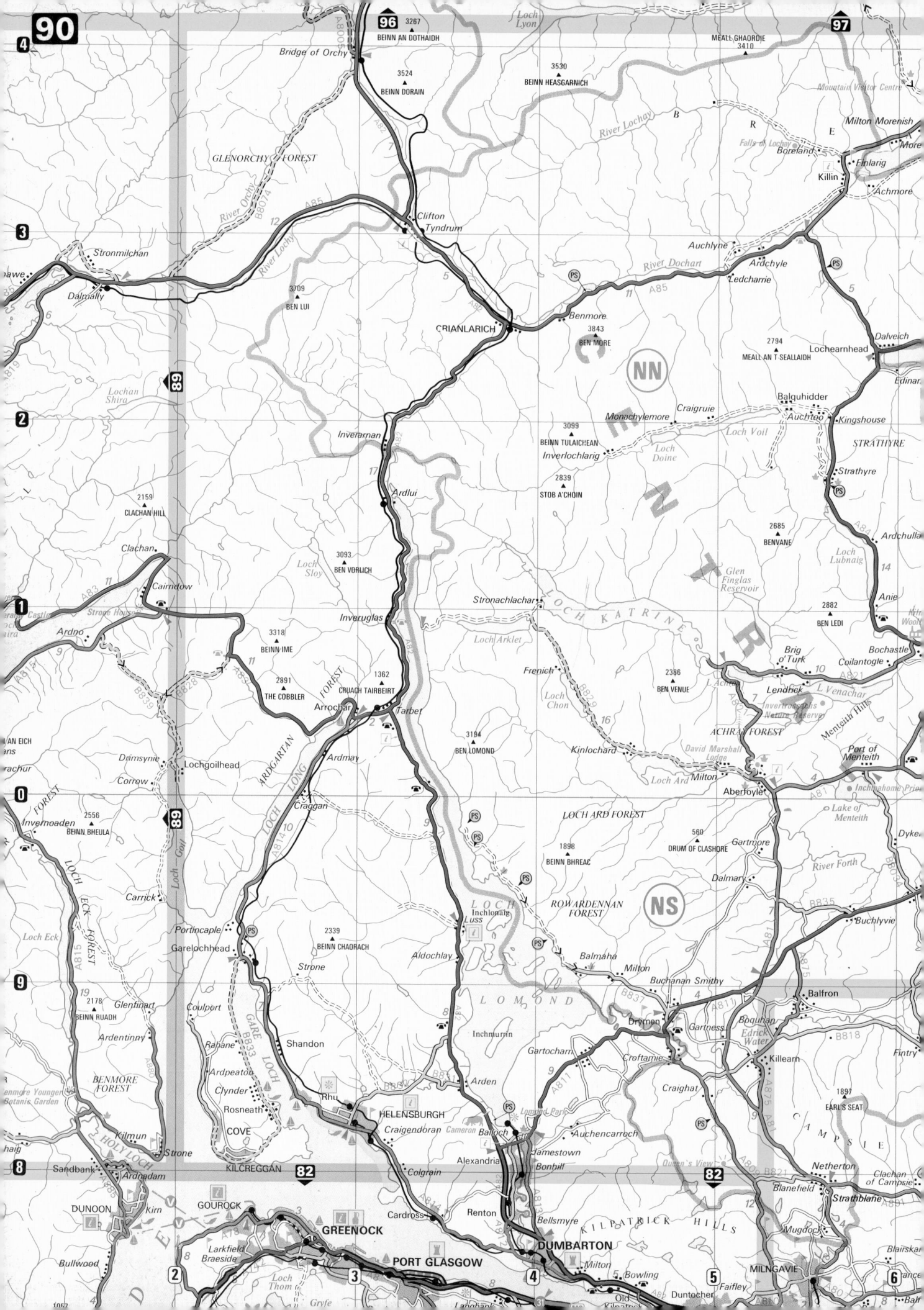

Lorraine & Paul Doherty
20 Cameron Crescent
Kippen
0786 870348
07732 86528
A811

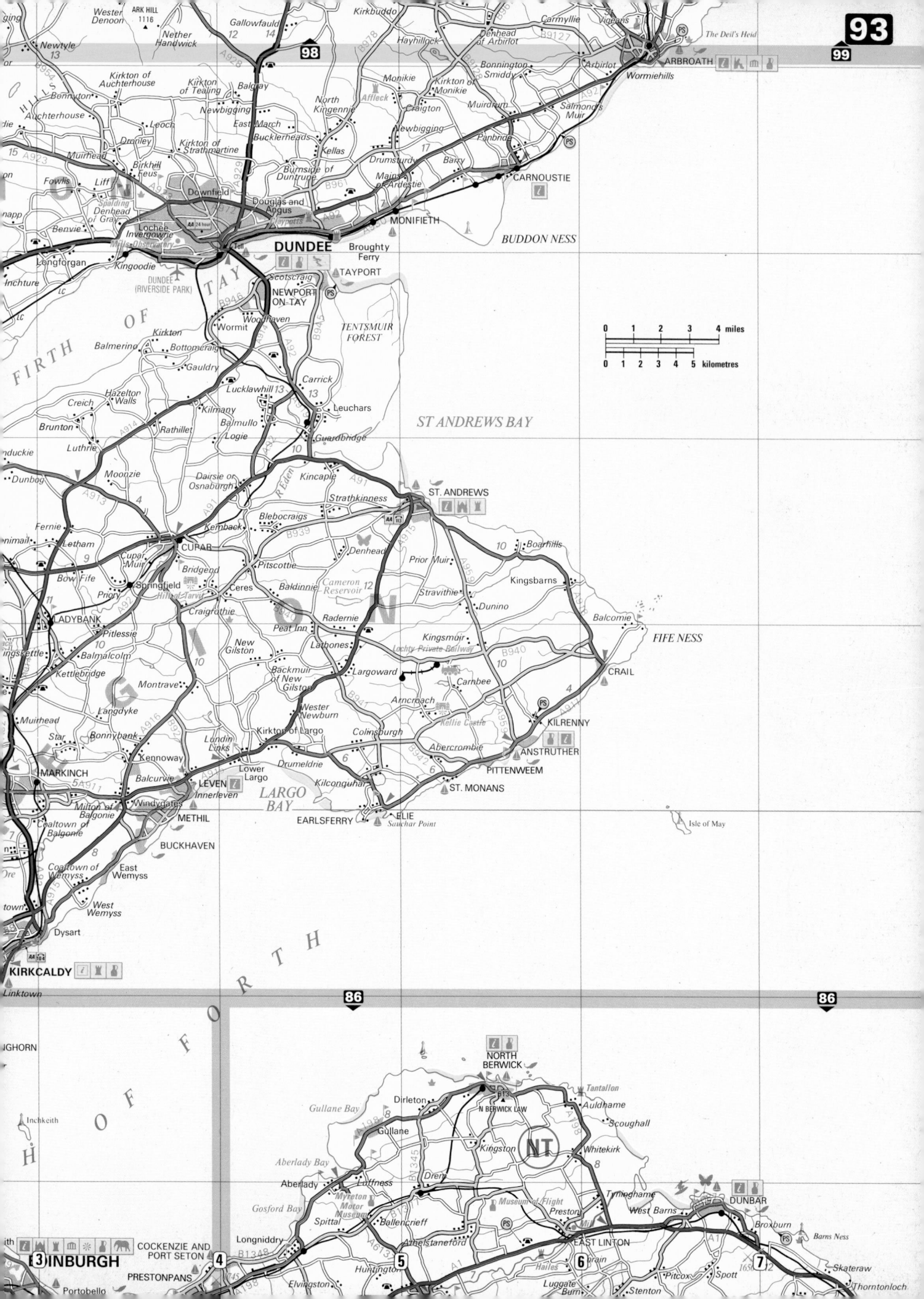

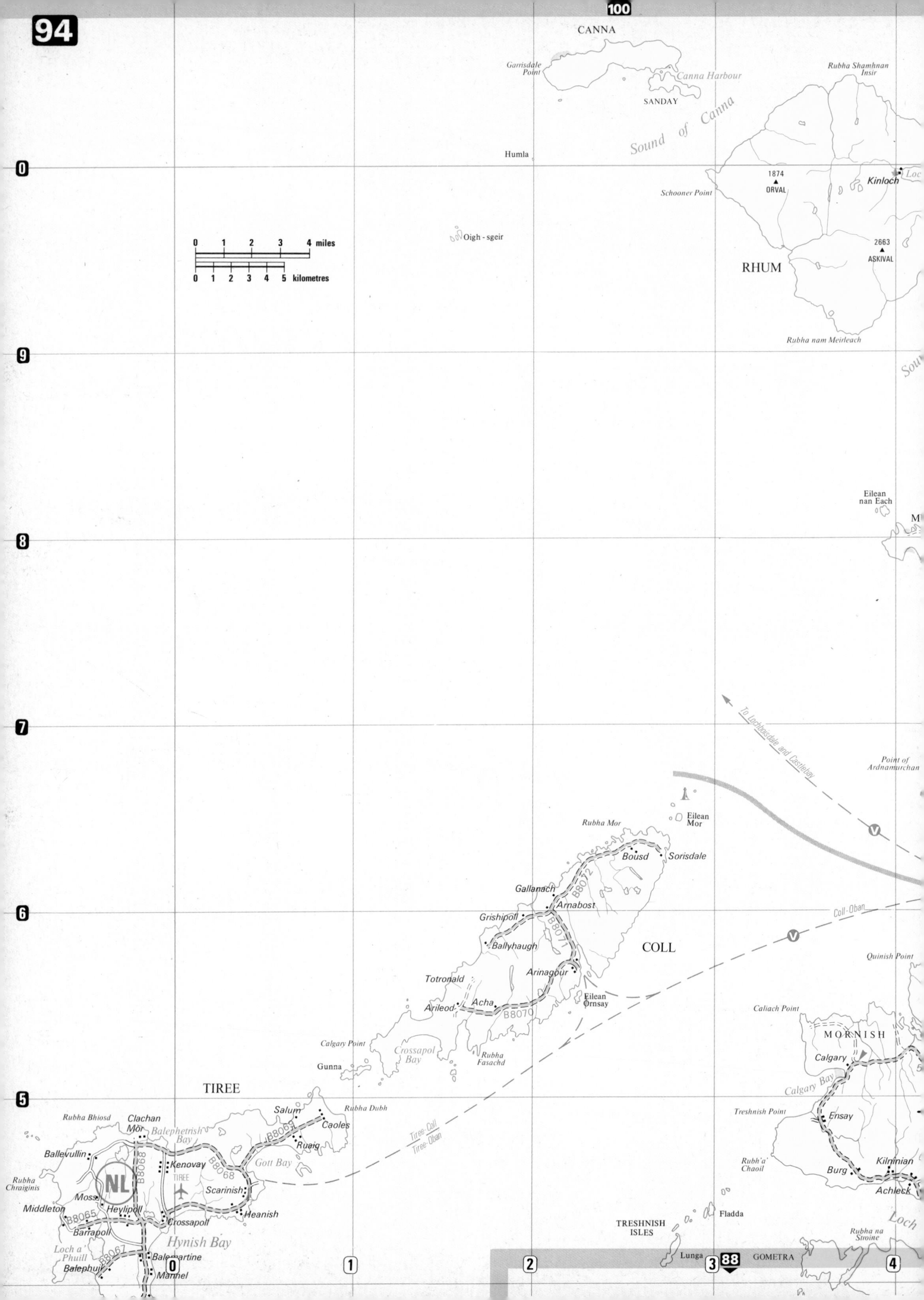

CANNA

Garrisdale Point

Canna Harbour

Rubha Shamhnan Insir

SANDAY

Sound of Canna

Humla

Schooner Point

1874 ▲ ORVAL

Kinloch

Loc

0

Oigh - sgeir

2663 ▲ ASKIVAL

0   1   2   3   4 miles

RHUM

0   1   2   3   4   5 kilometres

9

Rubha nam Meirleach

Sou

Eilean nan Each

8

M

7

To Lochboisdale and Castlebay

Point of Ardnamurchan

V

Rubha Mor

Eilean Mor

6

Bousd • Sorisdale

Gallanach

Arnabost

Coll - Oban

Grishipoll

B8072

Ballyhaugh

B8071

COLL

V

Quinish Point

Totronald

Arinagour

Arileod Acha

B8070

Eilean Ornsay

Caliach Point

MORNISH

Calgary Point

Crossapol Bay

Rubha Fasachd

Calgary

Gunna

Calgary Bay

5

TIREE

Salum

Rubha Dubh

Treshnish Point

Ensay

Rubha Bhiosd Clachan Mòr

Caoles

Tiree - Coll

Tiree - Oban

Balephetrish Bay

B8065

Ruaig

Ballevullin

B8068

Kenovay

B8068

Gott Bay

Rubh'a Chaoil

Burg

Kilninian

NL

TIREE

Scarinish

Rubha Chraiginis

Moss

Achieck

Middleton Heylipoll

Heanish

0

B8065

Barrapoll

Crossapoll

TRESHNISH ISLES

Fladda

Rubha na Stroine

Loch a' Phuill

B8067

Balemartine

Hynish Bay

Lunga

88

GOMETRA

Loch

Balephuil

Mannel

1

2

3

4

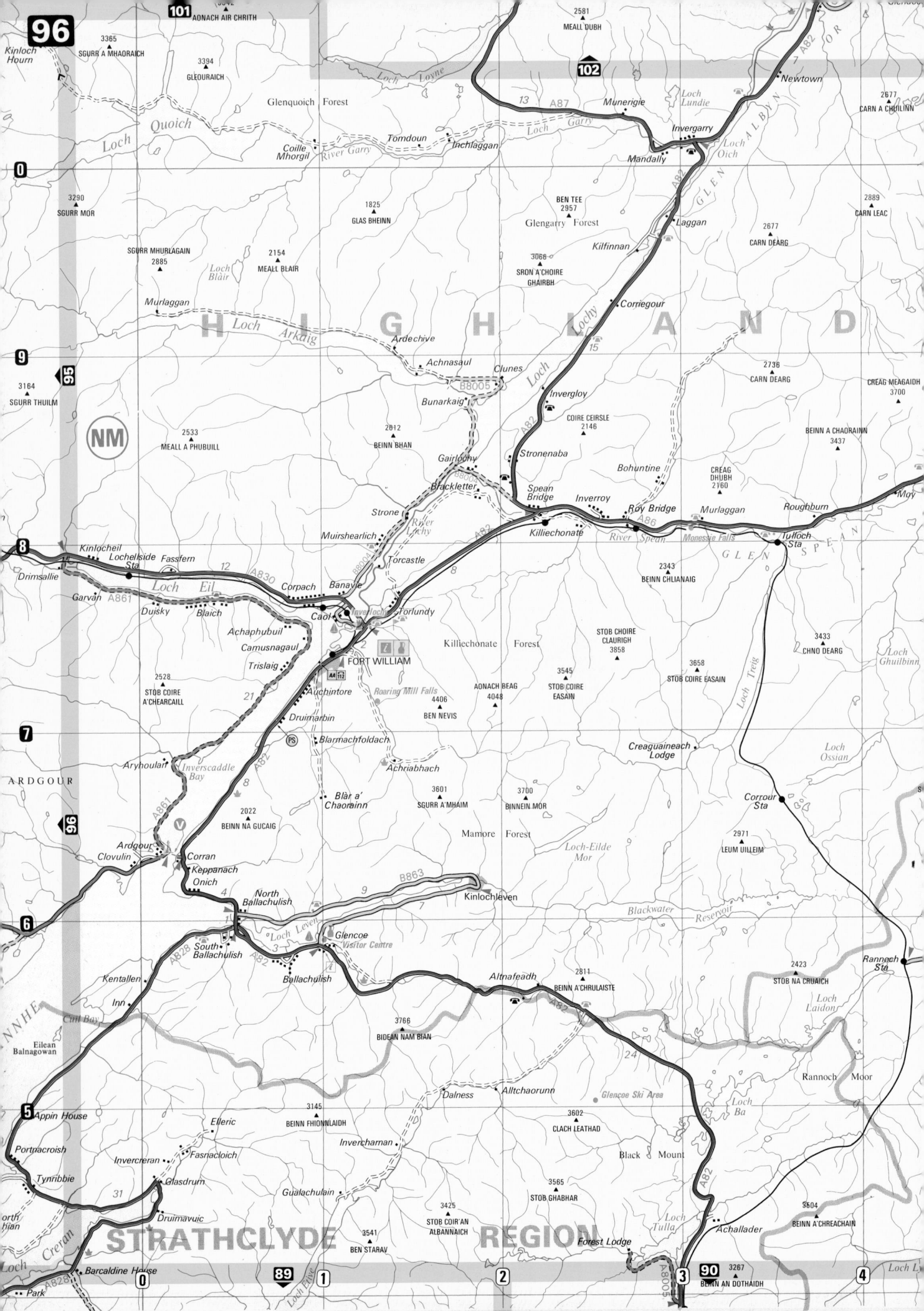

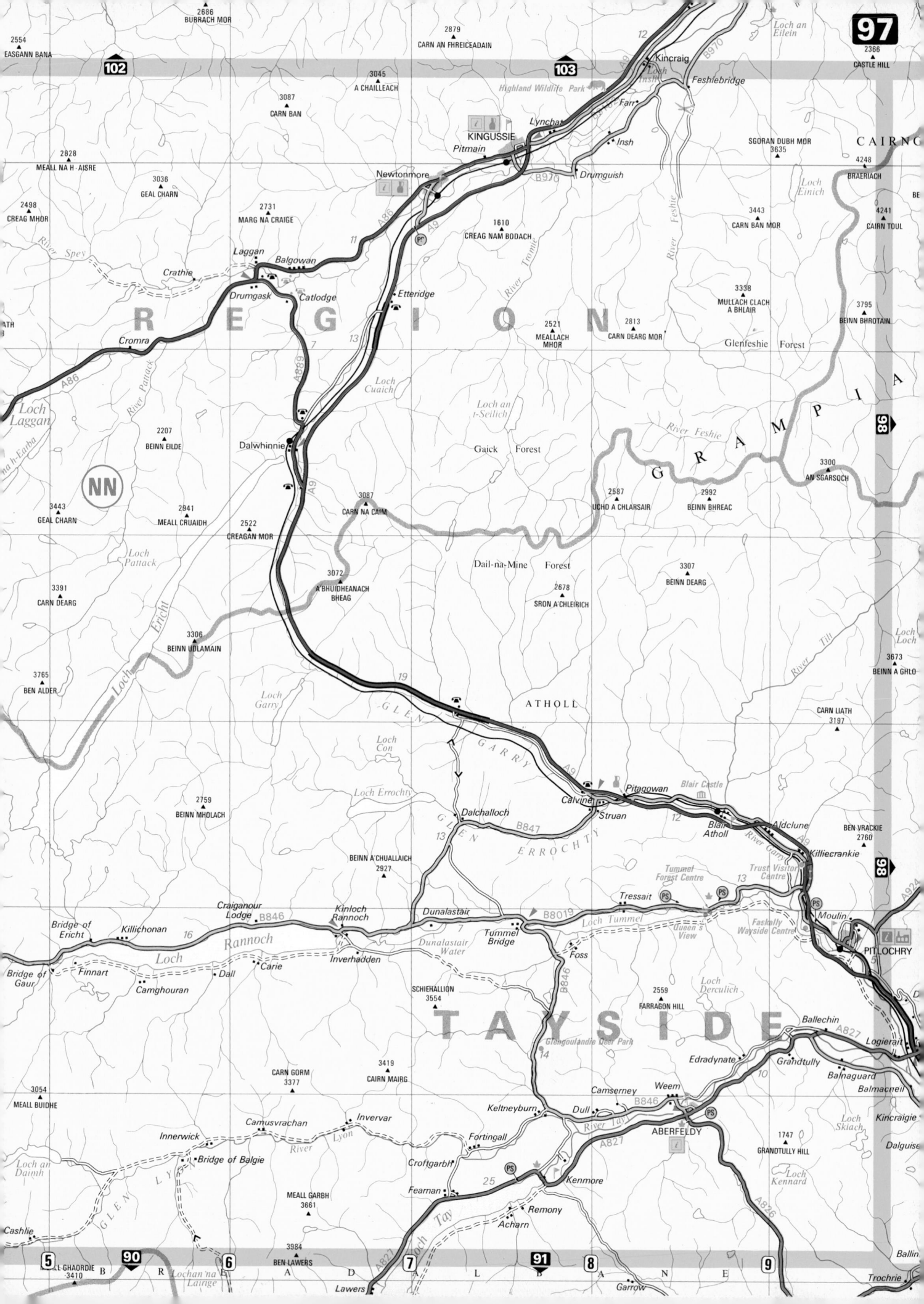

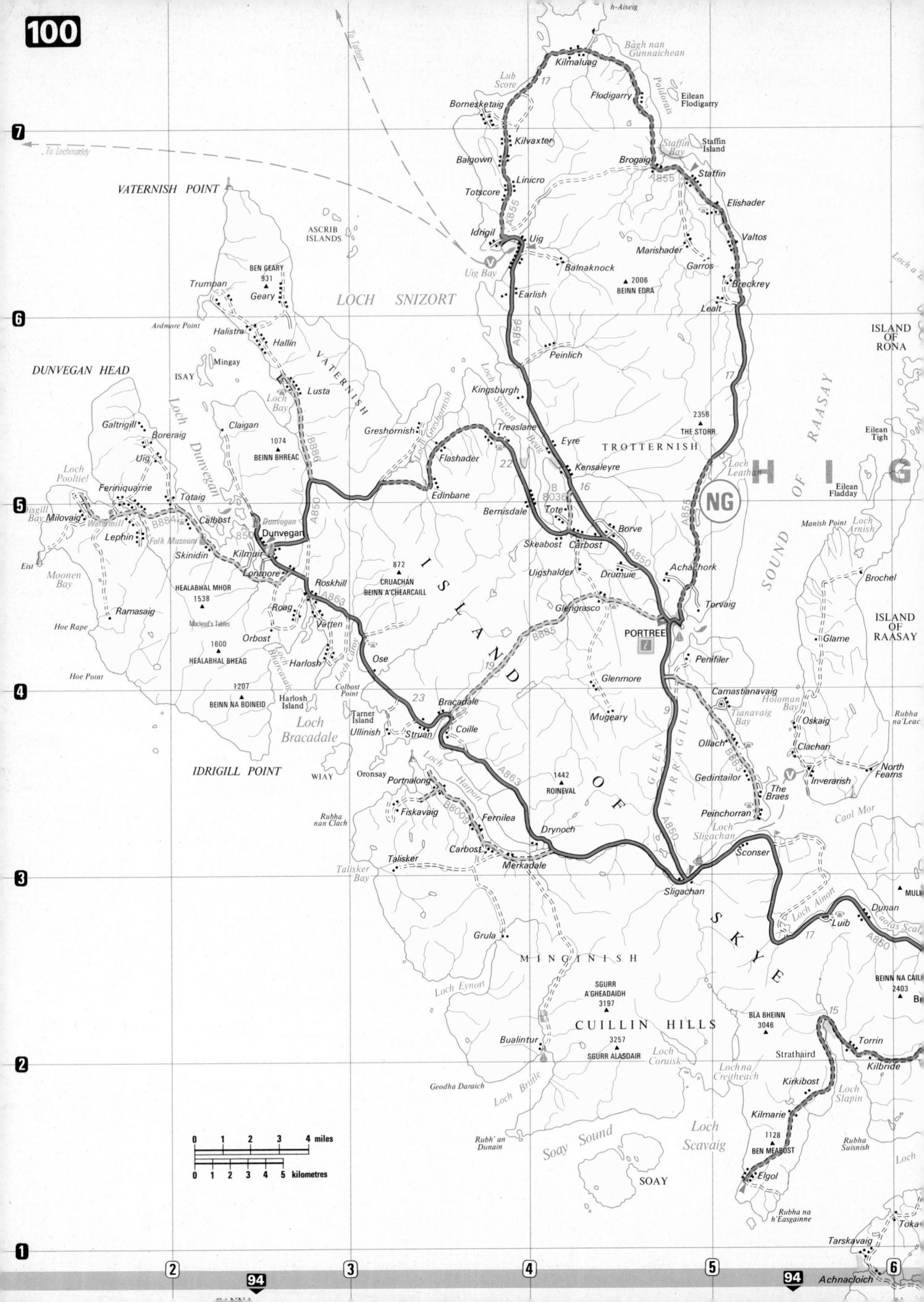

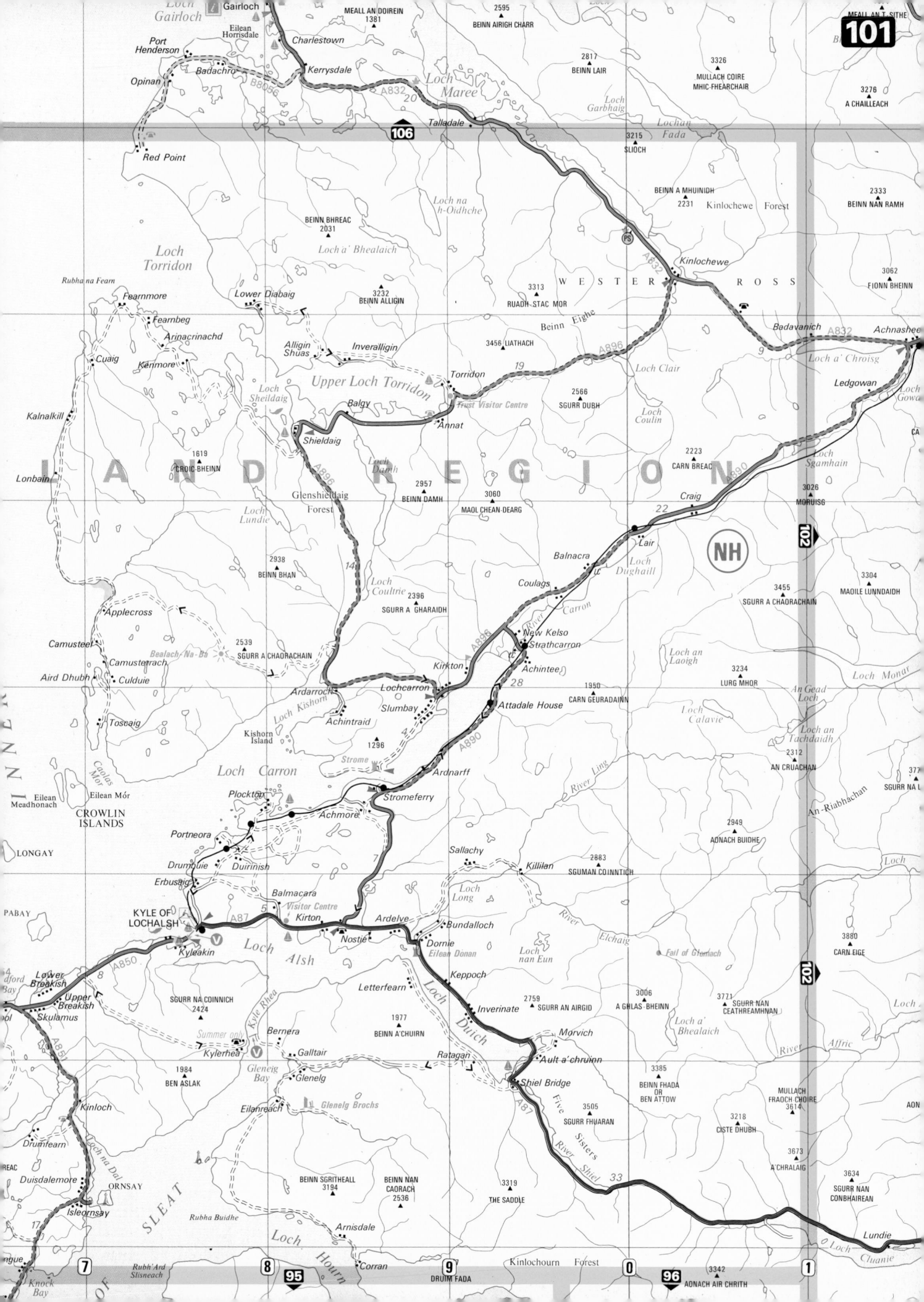

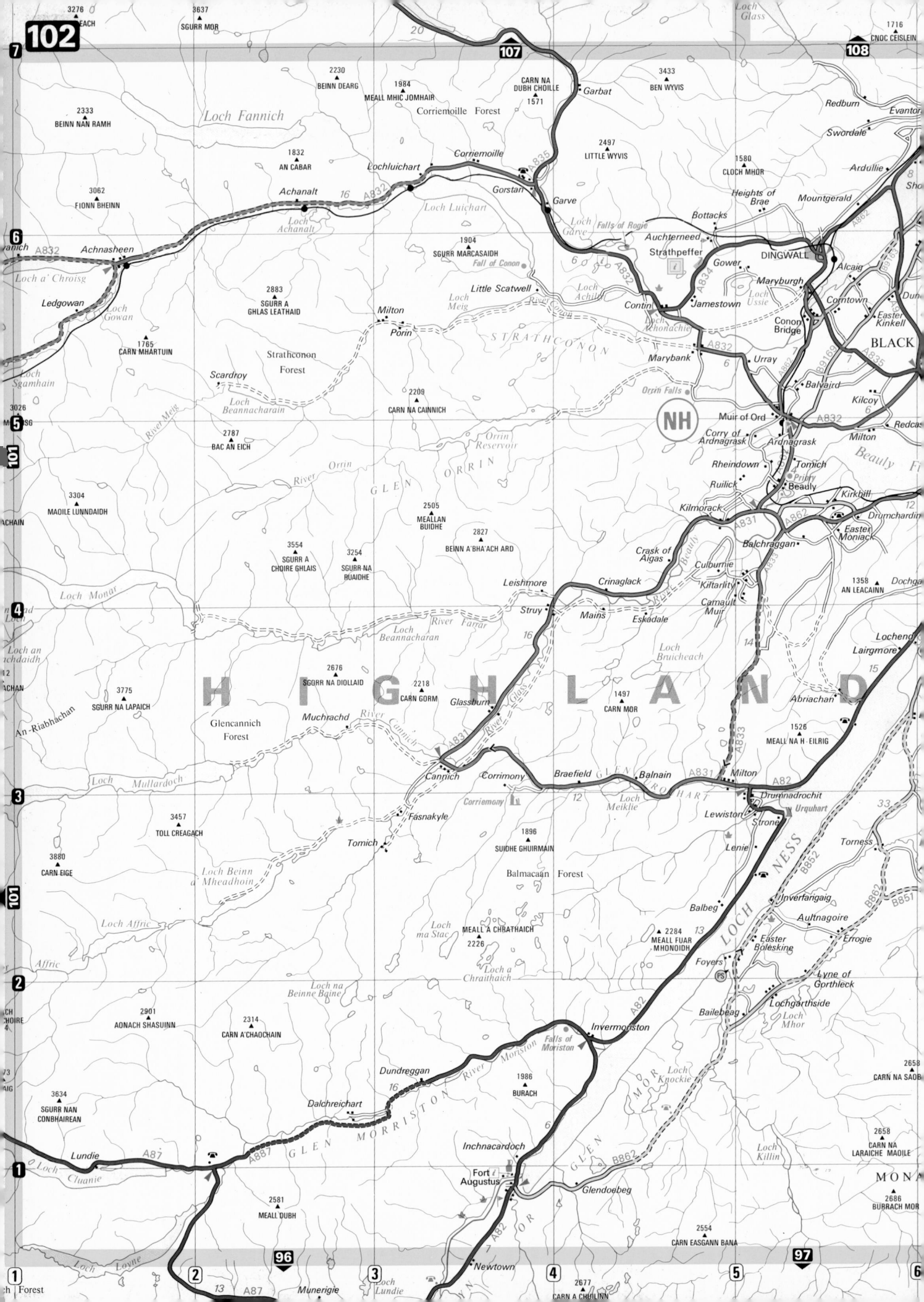

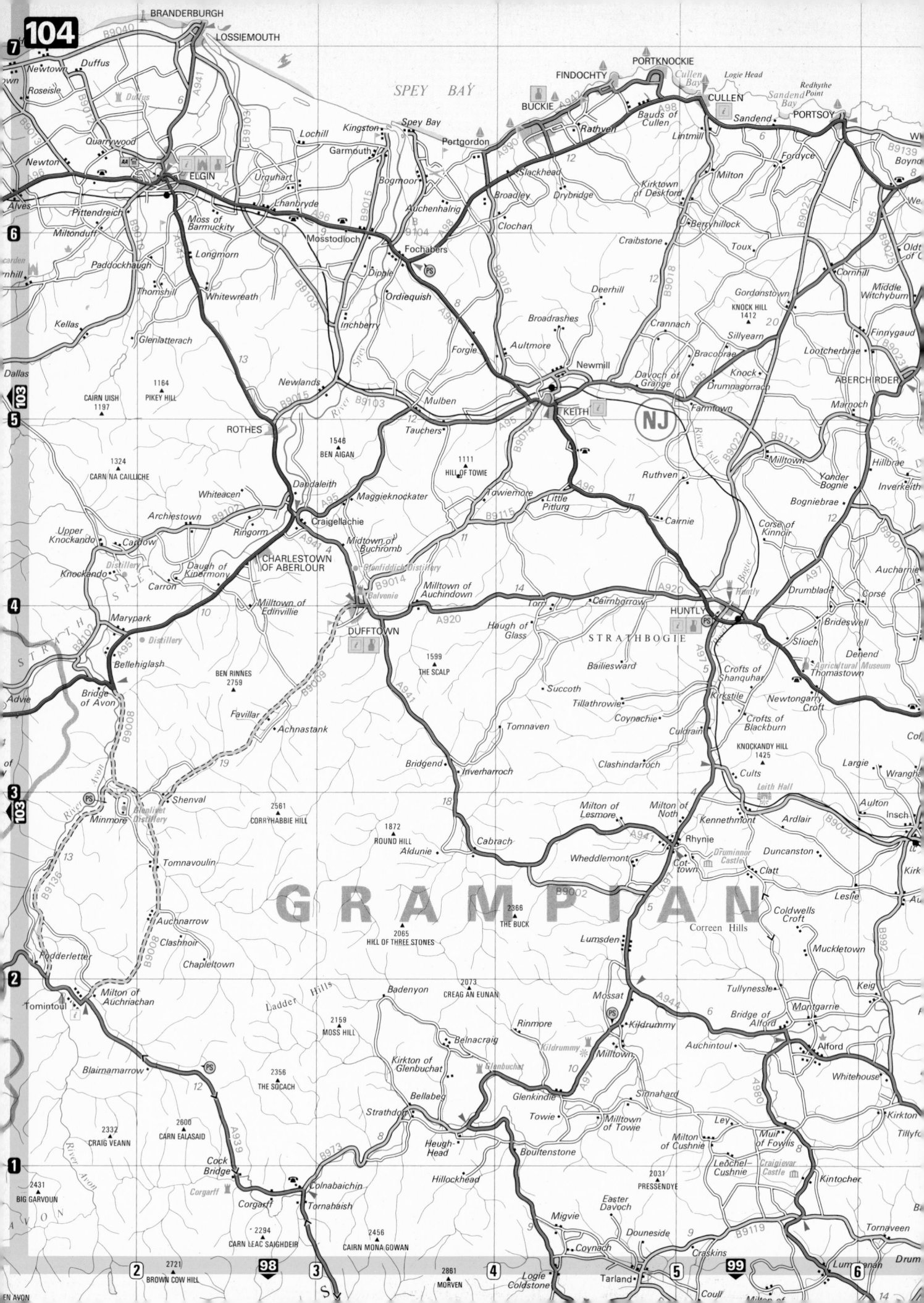

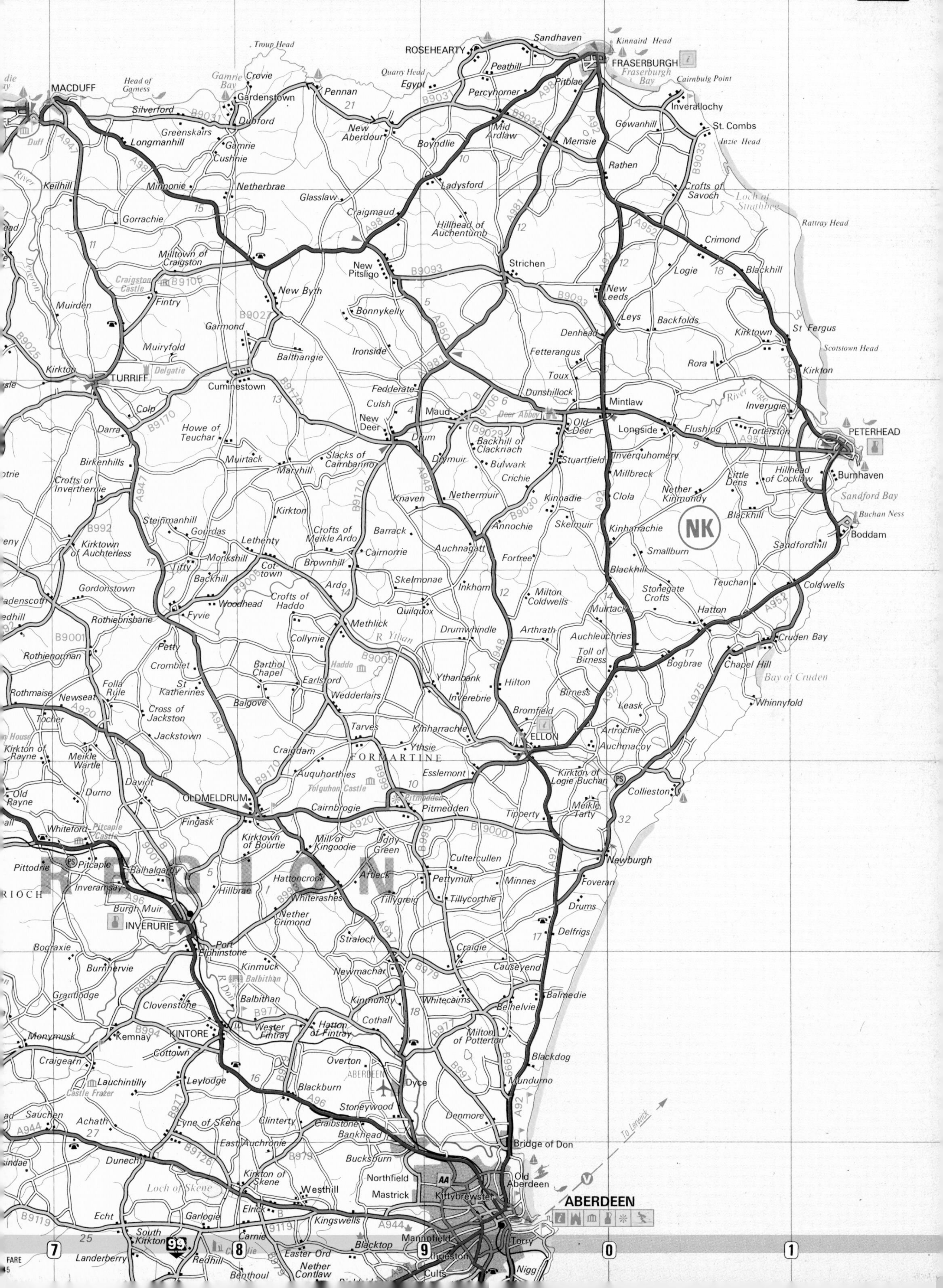

MACDUFF
ROSEHEARTY
FRASERBURGH
Fraserburgh Bay
Sandhaven
Kinnaird Head
Cairnbulg Point
Inverallochy
St. Combs
Inzie Head
Gowanhill
Memsie
Rathen
Crofts of Savoch
Loch of Strathbeg
Rattray Head
Crimond
Logie
Blackhill
New Leeds
Leys
Backfolds
Kirktown
St Fergus
Scotstown Head
Kirkton
Denhead
Fetterangus
Toux
Rora
Dunshillock
Mintlaw
River Ugie
Inverugie
PETERHEAD
Old Deer
Longside
Flushing
Torterston
Stuartfield
Inverquhomery
Millbreck
Little Dens
Hillhead of Cocklaw
Burnhaven
Nether Kinmundy
Clola
Sandford Bay
Buchan Ness
Boddam
NK
Blackhill
Sandfordhill
Smallburn
Kinharrachie
Kinnadie
Skelmuir
Blackhill
Teuchan
Coldwells
Stonegate Crofts
Hatton
Muirtack
Milton Coldwells
Arthrath
Auchleuchries
Cruden Bay
Bogbrae
Chapel Hill
Bay of Cruden
Toll of Birness
Birness
Leask
Whinnyfold
Bromfield
Artrochie
Auchmacoy
ELLON
Kirkton of Logie Buchan
Collieston
Esslemont
Tipperty
Meikle Tarty
Newburgh
Culterculen
Minnes
Foveran
Drums
Delfrigs
Causeyend
Balmedie
Belhelvie
Blackdog
Murcar
Bridge of Don
Old Aberdeen
ABERDEEN
To Lerwick

MACDUFF
Head of Garness
Gamrie Bay
Troup Head
Crovie
Gardenstown
Pennan
Quarry Head
Egypt
Peathill
Percyhorner
Pitblae
Silverford
Dubford
Greenskairs
Longmanhill
Gamrie
Cushnie
New Aberdour
Boyndlie
Mid Ardlaw
Netherbrae
Glasslaw
Ladysford
Keilhill
Gorrachie
Minnonie
Muiryfold
Milltown of Craigston
Craigston Castle
New Byth
New Pitsligo
Craigmaud
Hillhead of Auchentumb
Strichen
Muirden
Fintry
Bonnykelly
Ironside
B9093
New Leeds
TURRIFF
Delgatie
Cuminestown
Fedderate
Culsh
Maud
Deer Abbey
Colp
Howe of Teuchar
Darra
New Deer
Drum
Backhill of Clacknach
Crichie
Birkenhills
Crofts of Inverthernie
Muirtack
Maryhill
Slacks of Cairnbanno
Drymuir
Bulwark
Steinmanhill
Gourdas
Kirkton
Crofts of Meikle Ardo
Knaven
Nethermuir
Annochie
Fortree
Kirkton of Auchterless
Lethenty
Monkshill
Cairnorrie
Barrack
Auchnagatt
Tifty
Backhill
Brownhill
Ardo
Cottown
Skelmonae
Inkhorn
Gordonstown
Woodhead
Crofts of Haddo
Quilquox
Drumwhindle
Rothiebrisbane
Fyvie
Collynie
Methlick
Petty
Cromblet
Barthol Chapel
Haddo
Earlsford
Ythanbank
Inverebrie
Hilton
Rothienorman
St Katherines
Wedderlairs
Newseat
Folla Rule
Balgove
Rothmaise
Tocher
Cross of Jackston
Tarves
Kinharrachie
FORMARTINE
Jackstown
Craigdam
Ythsie
Meikle Wartle
Daviot
Durno
Auquhorthies
Tolquhon Castle
Esslemont
Old Rayne
OLDMELDRUM
Cairnbrogie
Pitmedden
Whiteford
Pitcaple Castle
Fingask
Kirktown of Bourtie
Mill of Kingoodie
Udny Green
Tipperty
Pitcaple
Balhalgardy
Hattoncrook
Hillbrae
Whiterashes
Tillygreig
Tillycorthie
Inveramsay
Burgh Muir
INVERURIE
Nether Crimond
Straloch
Craigie
Bogfixie
Burnhervie
Port Elphinstone
Kinmuck
Newmachar
Whitecairns
Grantlodge
Balbithan
Kinmundy
Cothall
Clovenstone
Kemnay
KINTORE
Wester Fintray
Hatton of Fintray
Milton of Potterton
Monymusk
Cottown
Craigearn
Leylodge
Overton
Blackburn
Dyce
Lauchintilly
Castle Fraser
Stoneywood
Denmore
Lyne of Skene
Clinterty
Craibstone
Bankhead
Sauchen
Achath
Dunecht
East Auchronie
Kirkton of Skene
Buckburn
Echt
Kirkton of Skene
Westhill
Northfield
Mastrick
Kittybrewster
AA
Loch of Skene
Blacktop
Kingswells
Mannofield
Torry
Nigg
Landerberry
Redhill
Easter Ord
Nether Contlaw
Cults
South Kirkton
Benthoul
Garlogie
Elrick
REGION

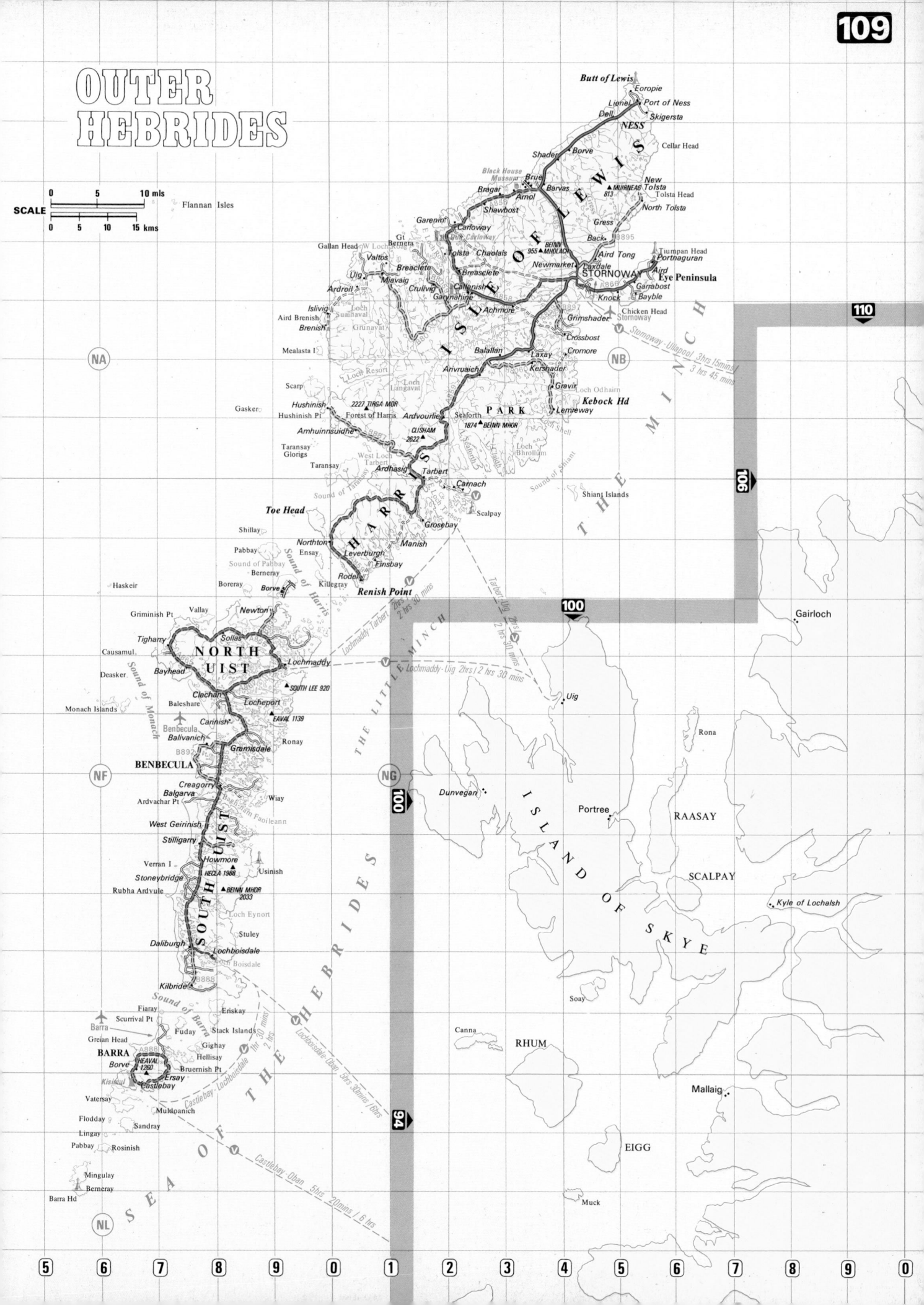

OUTER HEBRIDES

SCALE

0 5 10 mls

0 5 10 15 kms

Flannan Isles

Butt of Lewis
Eoropie
Lionel — Port of Ness
Dell — Skigersta
NESS
Cellar Head
Shader — Borve
New Tolsta
MUIRNEAG 813
Tolsta Head
North Tolsta
Black House Museum
Bragar — Bru
Barvas
Amol
Garenin
Shawbost
Gress
Back
B895
Carloway
Dun Carloway
Tolsta — Chaolais
BEINN MHOLACH 955
Aird Tong
Newmarket
STORNOWAY
Eye Peninsula
Tiumpan Head
Portnaguran
Aird
Garrabost
Bayble
Knock
Chicken Head
Stornoway
Gt Bernera
Valtos
Breaclete
Miavaig
Uig
Breasclete
Callanish
Ardroil
Crulivig
Garynahine
Achmore
Islivig
Aird Brenish
Brenish
Loch Suainaval
Grunavat
Balallan
Grimshader
Crossbost
Cromore
Mealasta I
Laxay
Kershader
Arivruaich
Scarp
Loch Resort
Loch Langavat
Gravir
Loch Odhairn
Gasker
Hushinish
Hushinish Pt
2227 TIRGA MOR
Forest of Harris
Ardvourlie
Seaforth
PARK
Kebock Hd
Lemreway
Amhuinnsuidhe
CLISHAM 2622
1874 BEINN MHOR
Taransay
Glorigs
Taransay
Sound of Taransay
Ardhasig
Tarbert
West Loch Tarbert
HARRIS
Carnach
Toe Head
Scalpay
Grosebay
Shiant Islands
Shillay
Northton
Ensay
Manish
Pabbay
Ensay
Bernera
Leverburgh
Finsbay
Haskeir
Boreray
Borve
Rodel
Killegray
Renish Point
Sound of Pabbay
Sound of Harris
Newton
Griminish Pt
Vallay
Tigharry
Sollas
Causamul
NORTH UIST
Bayhead
Lochmaddy
Deasker
SOUTH LEE 920
Monach Islands
Clachan
Locheport
Baleshare
Carinish
EAVAL 1139
Benbecula
Balivanich
Ronay
B892
Gramisdale
BENBECULA
Creagorry
Balgarva
Wiay
Ardvachar Pt
Bagh nam Faoileann
West Geirinish
Stilligarry
SOUTH UIST
Verran I
Howmore
Stoneybridge
HECLA 1988
Usinish
Rubha Ardvule
BEINN MHOR 2033
Loch Eynort
Daliburgh
Stuley
Lochboisdale
A888
Loch Boisdale
Kilbride
Fiaray
Eriskay
Scurrival Pt
Fuday
Stack Islands
Barra
Gighay
Greian Head
Hellisay
BARRA
Bruernish Pt
Borve
HEAVAL 1260
Ersay
Castlebay
Vatersay
Muldoanich
Kisimul
Floddday
Sandray
Lingay
Pabbay
Rosinish
Mingulay
Berneray
Barra Hd

THE MINCH

Gairloch

Dunvegan

Uig

Rona

Portree

RAASAY

ISLAND OF SKYE

SCALPAY

Kyle of Lochalsh

Soay

Canna

RHUM

Mallaig

EIGG

Muck

SEA OF THE HEBRIDES

Stornoway - Ullapool 3hrs 15mins / 3 hrs 45 mins
Tarbert-Uig 2hrs / 2 hrs 30 mins
Lochmaddy-Tarbert 2hrs 30 mins
Lochmaddy-Uig 1hr 2 hrs 30 mins
Castlebay Lochboisdale 1hr 30 mins
Lochboisdale-Oban 5hrs 30mins / 6hrs
Castlebay-Oban 5hrs 20mins / 6 hrs

THE LITTLE MINCH

NA NB NF NG NL

100 94 106 110

5 6 7 8 9 0 1 2 3 4 5 6 7 8 9 0

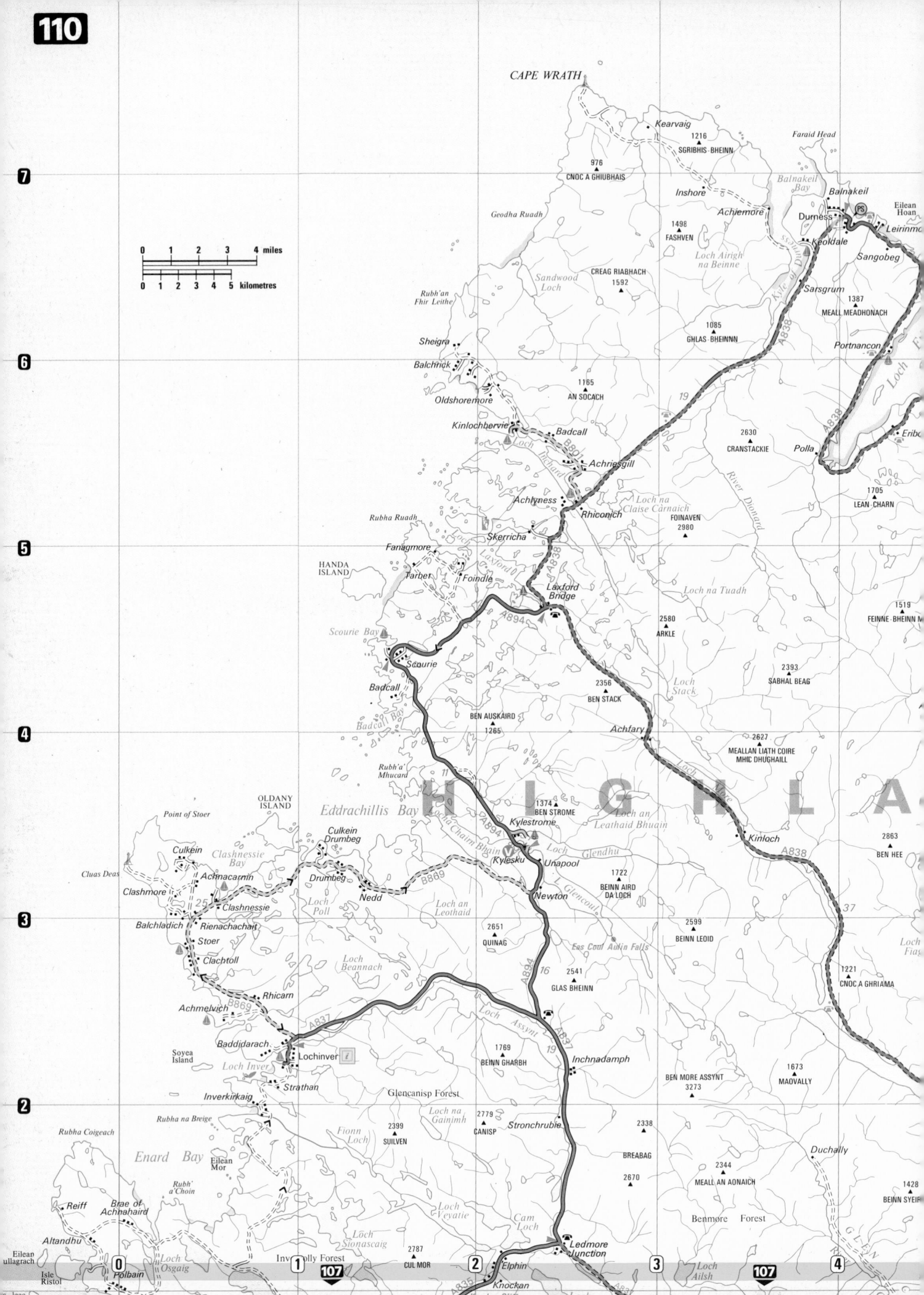

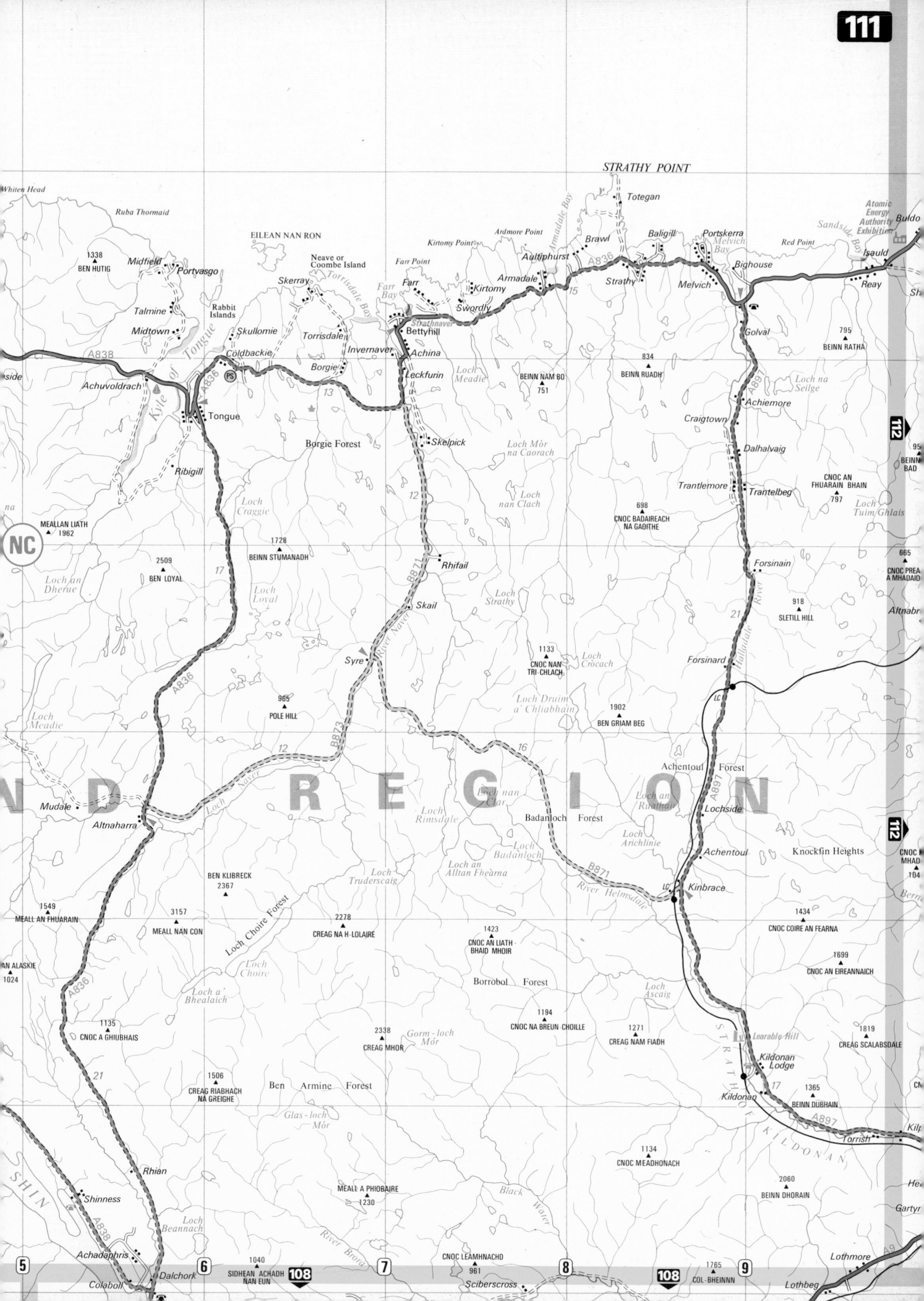

STRATHY POINT

Whiten Head

Ruba Thormaid

EILEAN NAN RON

Neave or
Coombe Island

1338
BEN HUTIG
Midfield
Portvasgo

Talmine

Midtown

Skerray

Rabbit
Islands

Skullomie

Torrisdale

Torrisdale Bay

Farr Point

Farr
Bay

Kirtomy Point

Ardmore Point

Armadale Bay

Totegan

Brawl

Aultiphurst

Armadale

Kirtomy

Swordly

Bettyhill

Baligill

Strathy

Portskerra

Melvich
Bay

Bighouse

Melvich

Red Point

Sandside Bay

Atomic
Energy
Authority
Exhibition

Buldo

Isauld

Reay

795
BEINN RATHA

Achuvoldrach

Coldbackie

Tongue

A836

PS

Invernaver

Achina

Borgie

Leckfurin

A838

Ribigill

Borgie Forest

Skelpick

Loch
Meadie

BEINN NAM BO
751

834

BEINN RUADH

Golval

A897

Achiemore

Craigtown

Dalhalvaig

112

BEINN
BAD

95

MEALLAN LIATH
1962

NC

Loch an
Dhérue

Loch
Craggie

1728
BEINN STUMANADH

Loch
Loval

2509
BEN LOYAL

17

Rhifail

B871

Skail

Loch Mór
na Caorach

Loch
nan Clach

Loch
Strathy

CNOC BADAIREACH
NA GAOITHE
698

Trantlemore

Trantelbeg

797

CNOC AN
FHUARAIN BHAIN

Loch
Tuim Ghlais

Forsinain

CNOC PREA
A MHADAID
665

Altnabr

965
POLE HILL

Syre

River Naver

B873

12

16

1133
CNOC NAN
TRI-CHLACH

Loch
Crocach

1902
BEN GRIAM BEG

918
SLETILL HILL

Forsinard

LC

Hallidale River

21

Loch
Meadie

Mudale

Altnaharra

A836

Loch Naver

REGION

Loch nan
Clar

Loch
Rimsdale

Badanloch Forest

Loch an
Ruadha

Achentoul Forest

Lochside

Achentoul

Knockfin Heights

112

CNOC
MHAD
104

Berri

BEN KLIBRECK
2367

Loch
Truderscaig

Loch
Badanloch

Loch an
Alltan Fheàrna

Loch
Arichlinie

B871

River Helmsdale

Kinbrace

LC

1549
MEALL AN FHUARAIN

3157
MEALL NAN CON

Loch Choire Forest

2278
CREAG NA H-LOLAIRE

Loch
Choire

1423
CNOC AN LIATH-
BHAID MHOIR

Borrobol Forest

Loch
Ascaig

1434
CNOC COIRE AN FEARNA

1699
CNOC AN EIREANNAICH

AN ALASKIE
1024

Loch a
Bhealaich

1135
CNOC A GHIUBHAIS

A836

2338
CREAG MHOR

Gorm-loch
Mòr

1194
CNOC NA BREUN-CHOILLE

1271
CREAG NAM FIADH

Learable Hill

Kildonan
Lodge

1819
CREAG SCALABSDALE

1506
CREAG RIABHACH
NA GREIGHE

Ben Armine Forest

Glas-loch
Mòr

STRATH OF KILDONAN

Kildonan

1365
BEINN DUBHAIN

A897

21

Rhian

SHIN

Shinness

Loch
Beannach

MEALL A PHIOBAIRE
1230

1134
CNOC MEADHONACH

Black
Water

2060
BEINN DHORAIN

Torrish

Kilp

A897

He

Gartyr

Achadaphris

A838

Colaboll

Dalchork

1040
SIDHEAN ACHADH
NAN EUN

108

CNOC LEAMHNACHD
961

Sciberscross

108

1765
COL-BHEINNN

9

Lothmore

Lothbeg

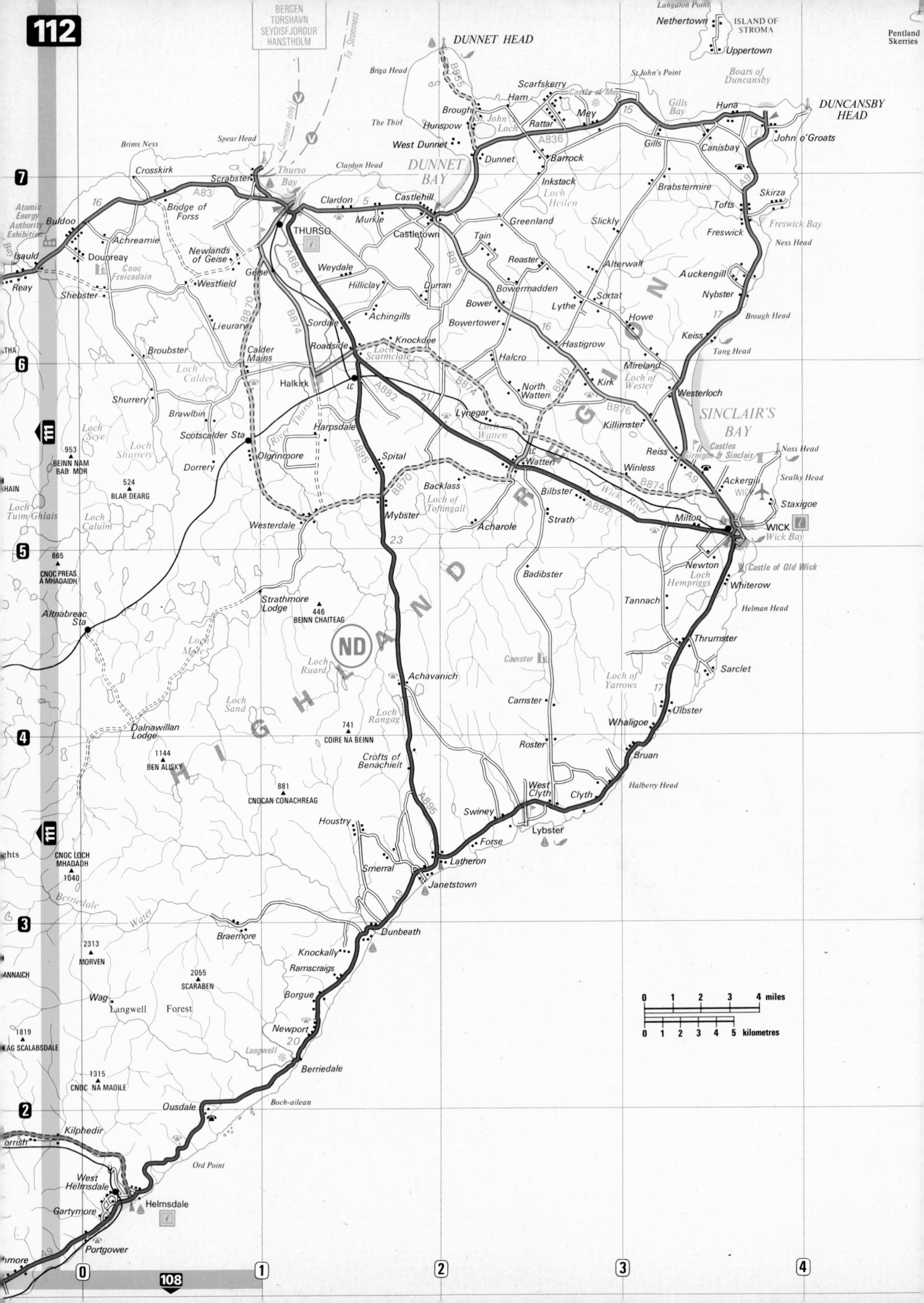

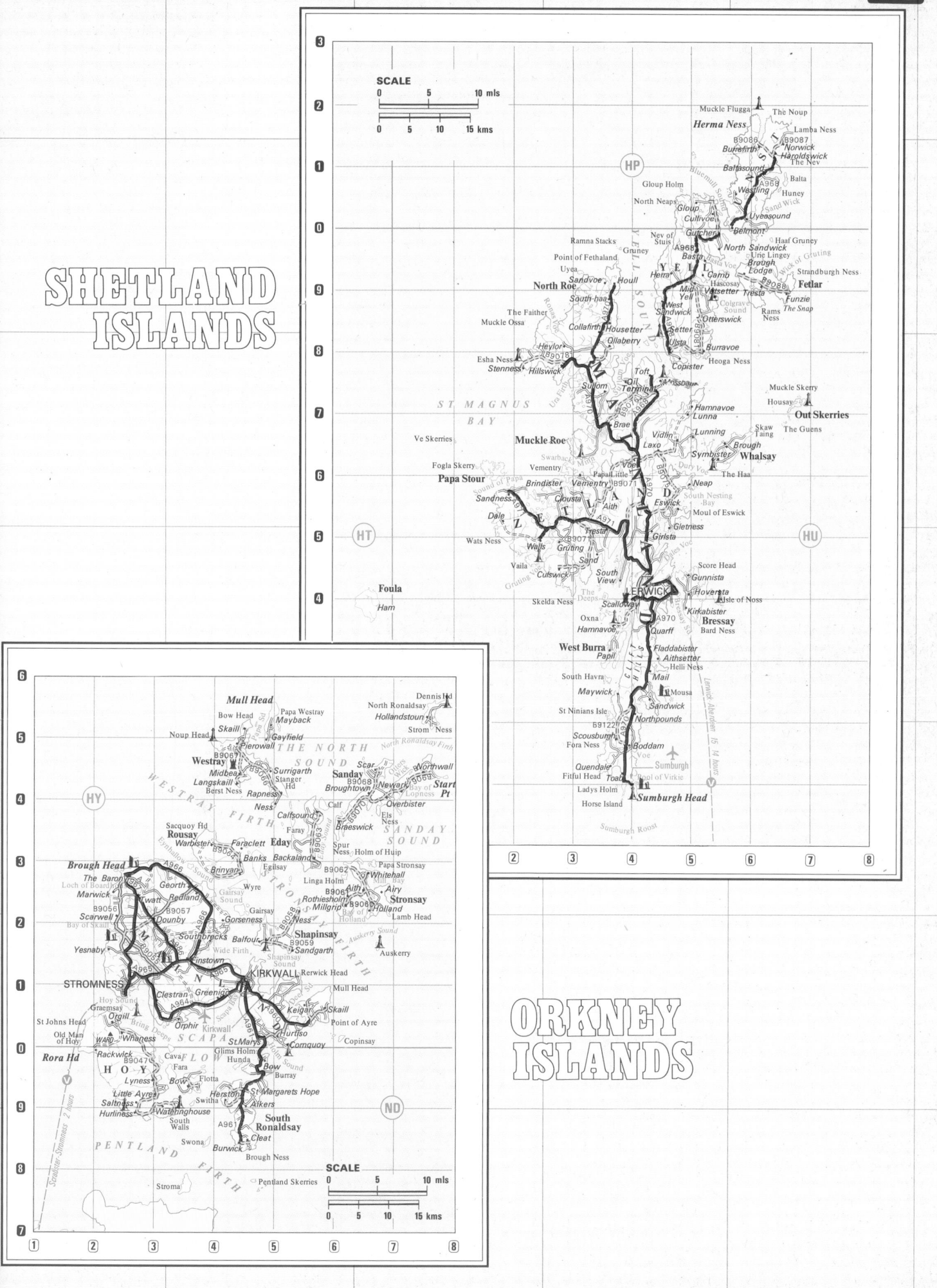

Motorway Maps

The maps on the following pages depict the principal motorways in Great Britain and are arranged in easy-to-follow strips. Enlarged details of many motorway junctions have been included to help the driver approach these without hesitation. The motorway guide opposite gives an overall picture of the system and enables the driver to plan extended use of motorways.

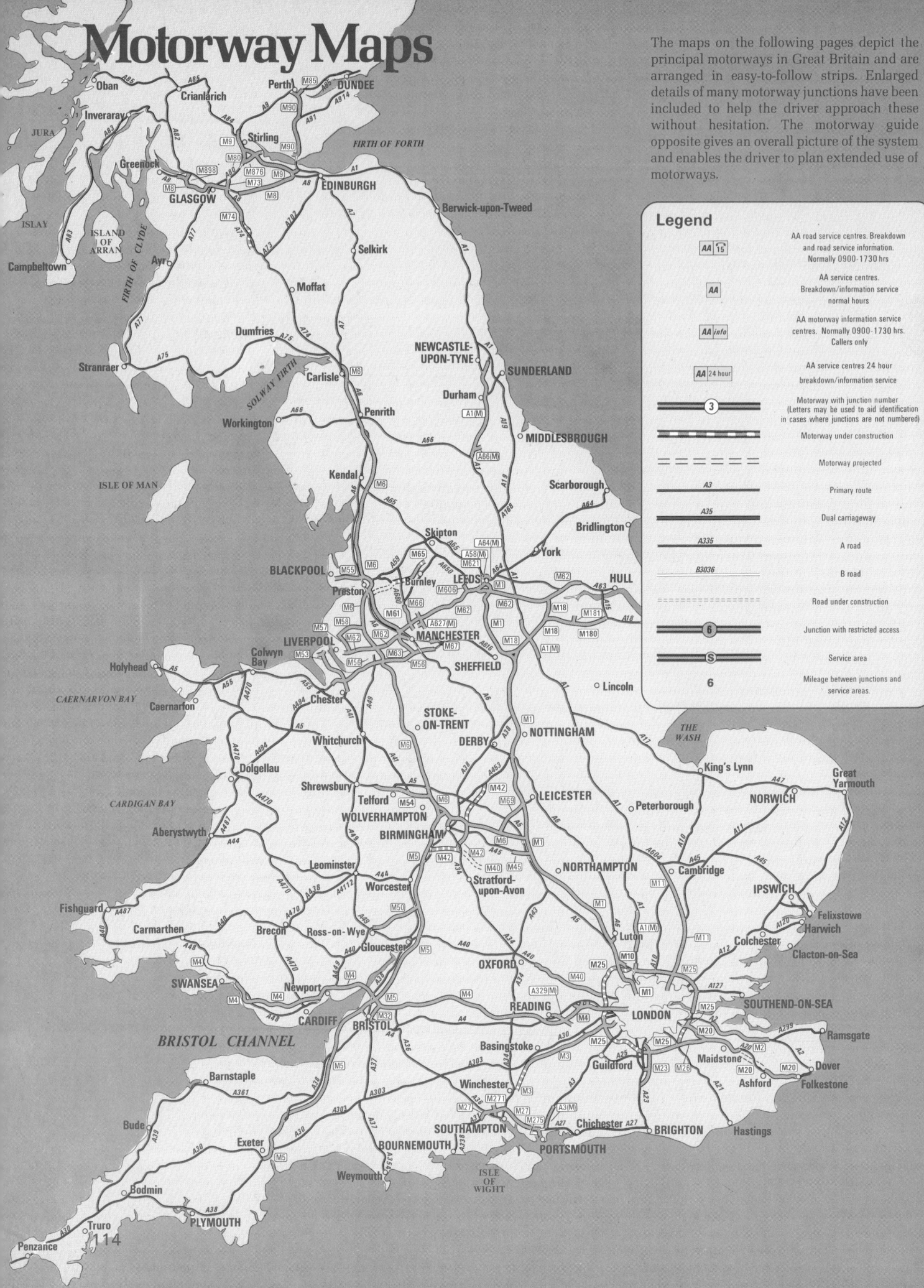

Legend

AA 15	AA road service centres. Breakdown and road service information. Normally 0900-1730 hrs
AA	AA service centres. Breakdown/information service normal hours
AA info	AA motorway information service centres. Normally 0900-1730 hrs. Callers only
AA 24 hour	AA service centres 24 hour breakdown/information service
3	Motorway with junction number (Letters may be used to aid identification in cases where junctions are not numbered)
	Motorway under construction
	Motorway projected
A3	Primary route
A35	Dual carriageway
A335	A road
B3036	B road
	Road under construction
6	Junction with restricted access
S	Service area
6	Mileage between junctions and service areas.

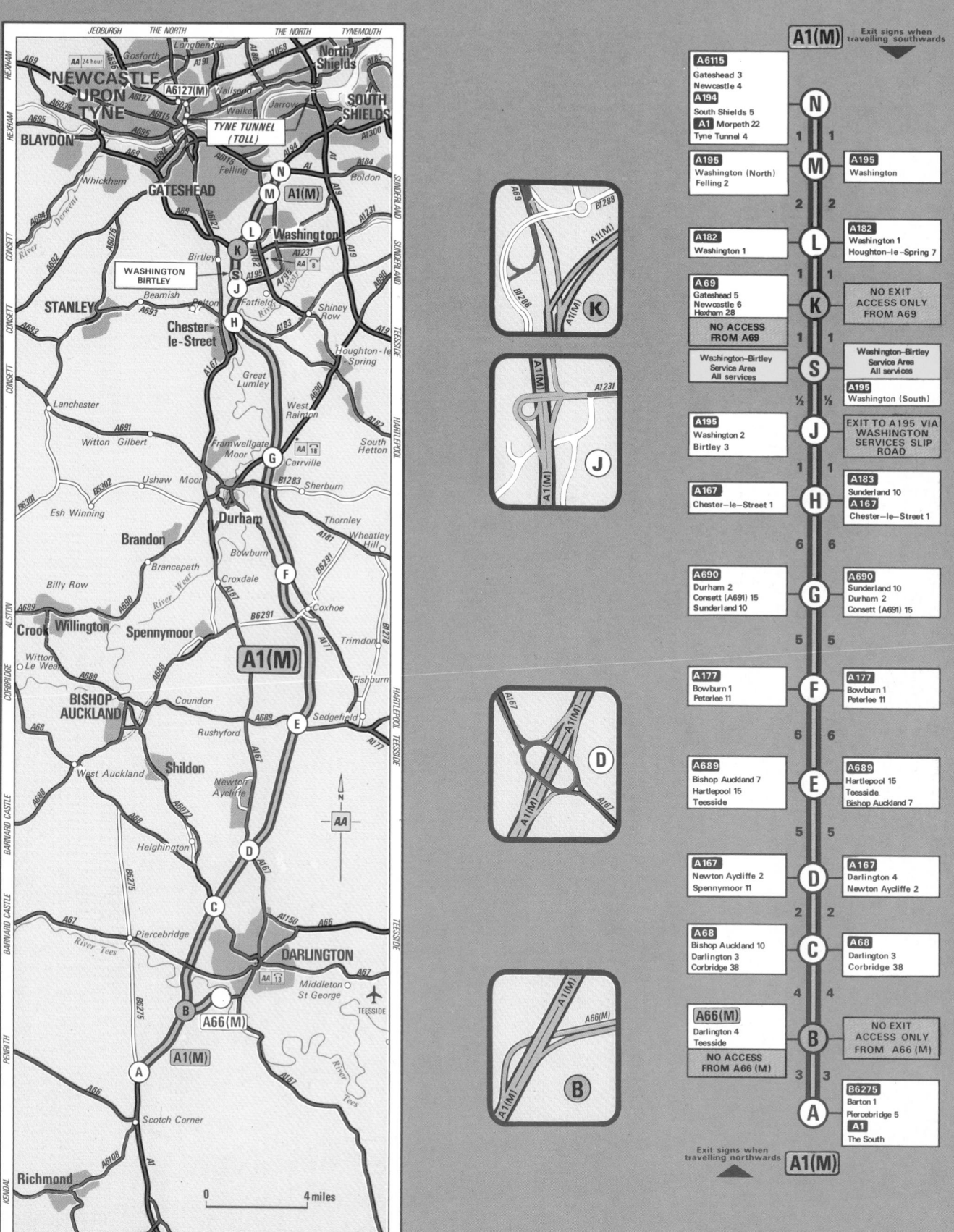

A1(M)

N

A6115
Gateshead 3
Newcastle 4
A194
South Shields 5
A1 Morpeth 22
Tyne Tunnel 4

1 | 1

M

A195
Washington (North)
Felling 2

A195
Washington

2 | 2

L

A182
Washington 1

A182
Washington 1
Houghton-le-Spring 7

1 | 1

K

A69
Gateshead 5
Newcastle 6
Hexham 28
NO ACCESS
FROM A69

NO EXIT
ACCESS ONLY
FROM A69

1 | 1

S

Washington-Birtley
Service Area
All services

Washington-Birtley
Service Area
All services
A195
Washington (South)

½ | ½

J

A195
Washington 2
Birtley 3

EXIT TO A195 VIA
WASHINGTON
SERVICES SLIP
ROAD

1 | 1

H

A167
Chester-le-Street 1

A183
Sunderland 10
A167
Chester-le-Street 1

6 | 6

G

A690
Durham 2
Consett (A691) 15
Sunderland 10

A690
Sunderland 10
Durham 2
Consett (A691) 15

5 | 5

F

A177
Bowburn 1
Peterlee 11

A177
Bowburn 1
Peterlee 11

6 | 6

E

A689
Bishop Auckland 7
Hartlepool 15
Teesside

A689
Hartlepool 15
Teesside
Bishop Auckland 7

5 | 5

D

A167
Newton Aycliffe 2
Spennymoor 11

A167
Darlington 4
Newton Aycliffe 2

2 | 2

C

A68
Bishop Auckland 10
Darlington 3
Corbridge 38

A68
Darlington 3
Corbridge 38

4 | 4

B

A66(M)
Darlington 4
Teesside
NO ACCESS
FROM A66 (M)

NO EXIT
ACCESS ONLY
FROM A66 (M)

3 | 3

A

B6275
Barton 1
Piercebridge 5
A1
The South

SOUTH MIMMS-HATFIELD-BALDOCK A1(M)

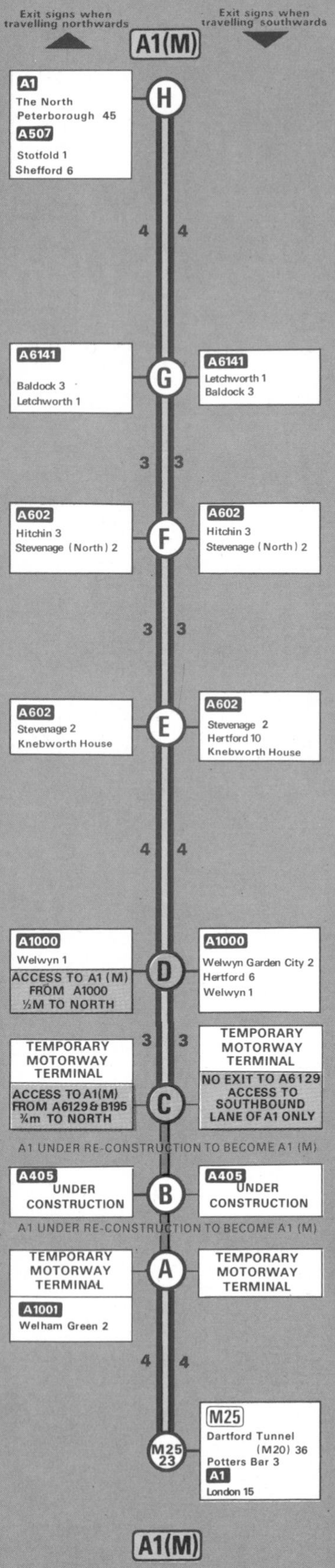

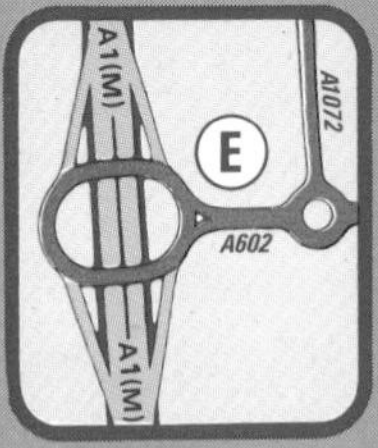

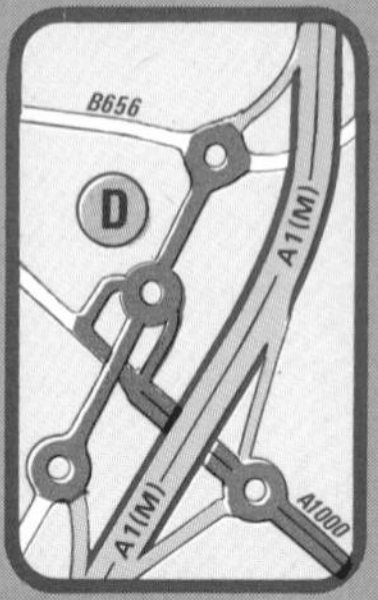

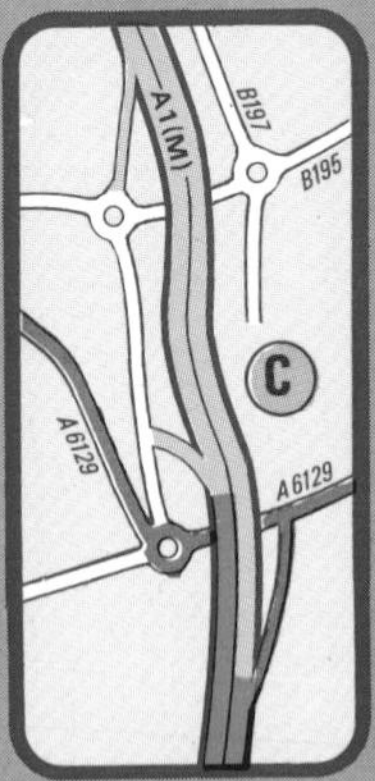

Exit signs when travelling northwards
Exit signs when travelling southwards
A1(M)
H
A1 The North Peterborough 45
A507 Stotfold 1 Shefford 6
4 4
G
A6141 Baldock 3 Letchworth 1
A6141 Letchworth 1 Baldock 3
3 3
F
A602 Hitchin 3 Stevenage (North) 2
A602 Hitchin 3 Stevenage (North) 2
3 3
E
A602 Stevenage 2 Knebworth House
A602 Stevenage 2 Hertford 10 Knebworth House
4 4
D
A1000 Welwyn 1
ACCESS TO A1 (M) FROM A1000 ½M TO NORTH
A1000 Welwyn Garden City 2 Hertford 6 Welwyn 1
3 3
C
TEMPORARY MOTORWAY TERMINAL
ACCESS TO A1(M) FROM A6129 & B195 ¾m TO NORTH
TEMPORARY MOTORWAY TERMINAL
NO EXIT TO A6129 ACCESS TO SOUTHBOUND LANE OF A1 ONLY
A1 UNDER RE-CONSTRUCTION TO BECOME A1 (M)
B
A405 UNDER CONSTRUCTION
A405 UNDER CONSTRUCTION
A1 UNDER RE-CONSTRUCTION TO BECOME A1 (M)
A
TEMPORARY MOTORWAY TERMINAL
A1001 Welham Green 2
TEMPORARY MOTORWAY TERMINAL
4 4
M25 23
M25 Dartford Tunnel (M20) 36 Potters Bar 3
A1 London 15
A1(M)

H
A1
A507
A1(M)
A507

E
A1(M)
A1072
A602
A1(M)

D
B656
A1(M)
A1(M)
A1000

C
A1(M)
B197
B195
A6129
A6129

THE NORTH
HUNTINGDON
CAMBRIDGE
NEWMARKET
Biggleswade
Royston
0
4 miles
BEDFORD
Henlow
A507
Stotfold
H
A1(M)
BALDOCK
Letchworth
G
Buntingford
Cottered
LUTON
Hitchin
F
Walkern
STEVENAGE
E
AA
Whitwell
Knebworth House
Knebworth
Watton-at-Stone
Kimpton
Codicote
Welwyn
D
A1(M)
Wheathampstead
WARE
HERTFORD
Welwyn Garden City
C
TEMPORARY MOTORWAY TERMINAL
Sandridge
Essendon
St. Albans
B
HATFIELD
A
Colney Heath
Welham Green
Brookmans Park
A1(M)
Cheshunt
Cuffley
M25
22
Potters Bar
24
M25
25
23
Shenley
Radlett
South Mimms
Barnet
Cockfosters
Enfield
Borehamwood
Elstree
M1
4
S
Whetstone
Southgate
Edmonton
Mill Hill
Stanmore
Edgware
Finchley
Wood Green
Muswell Hill
2
Hendon
Kingsbury
Golders Green
1
Harrow
Wembley
LONDON
Holloway
N. CIRCULAR RD.
WEST END
WEST END
CITY

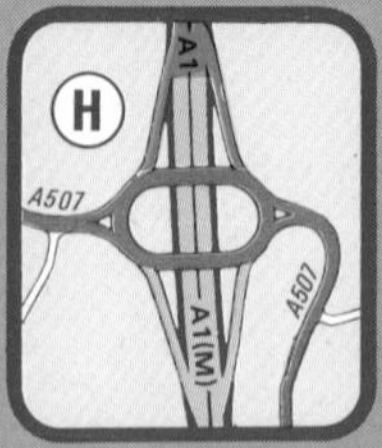

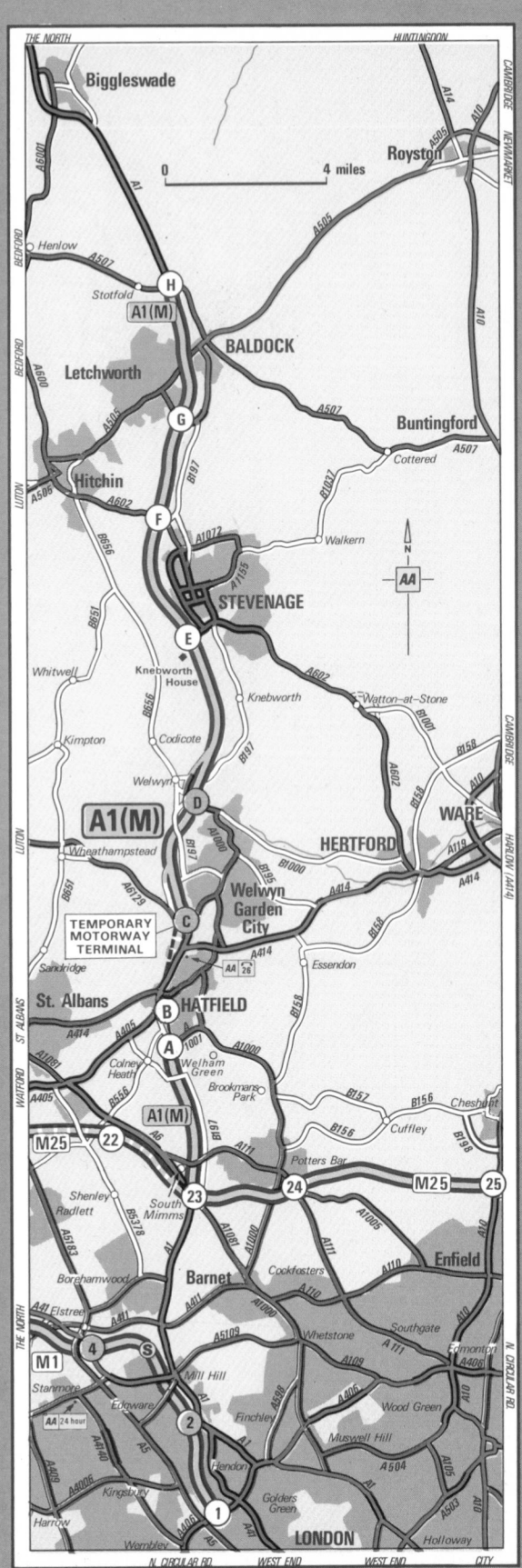

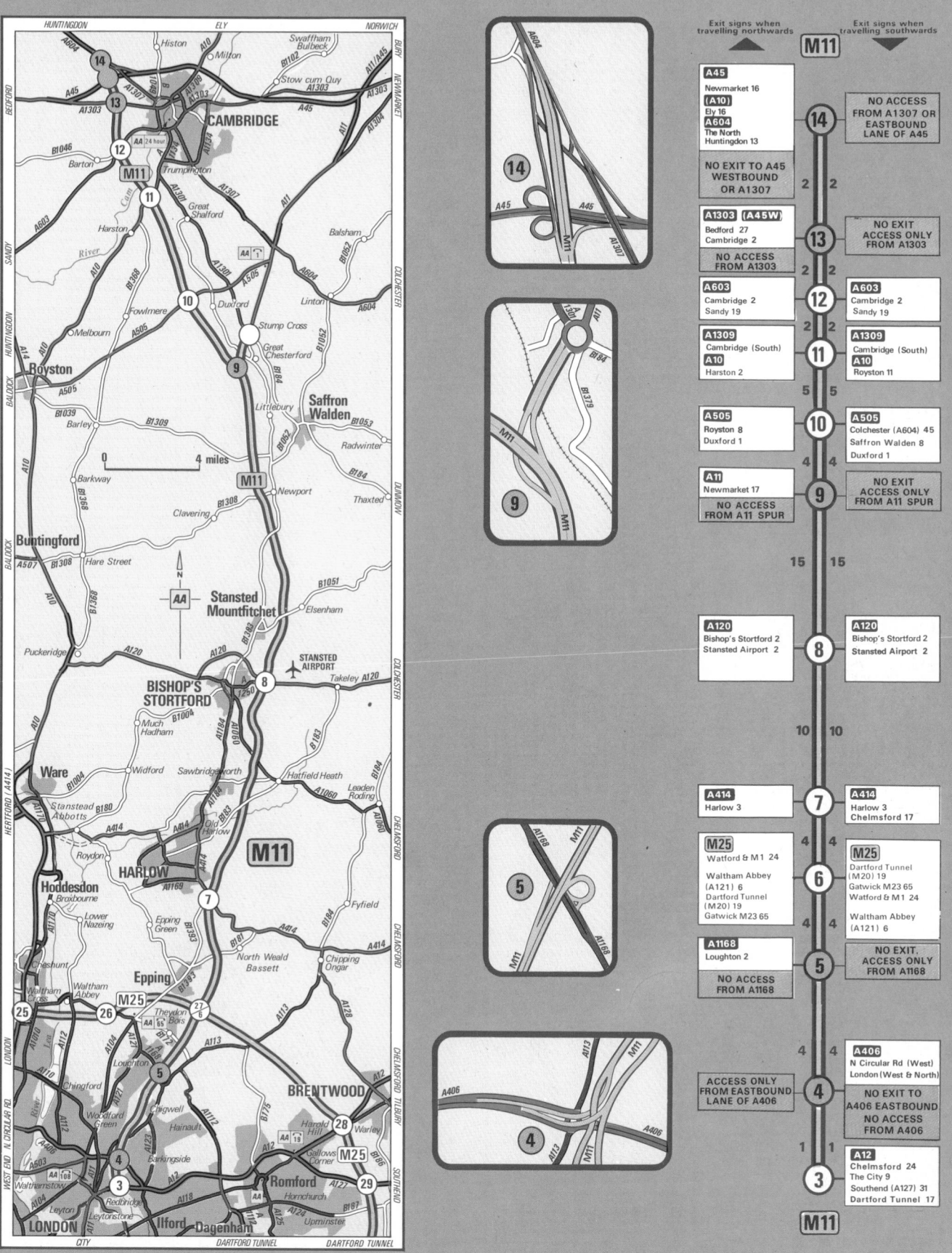

Exit signs when travelling northwards · M11 · Exit signs when travelling southwards

A45
Newmarket 16
(A10)
Ely 16
A604
The North
Huntingdon 13

14

NO ACCESS
FROM A1307 OR
EASTBOUND
LANE OF A45

2 | 2

NO EXIT TO A45
WESTBOUND
OR A1307

A1303 (A45W)
Bedford 27
Cambridge 2
NO ACCESS
FROM A1303

13

NO EXIT
ACCESS ONLY
FROM A1303

2 | 2

A603
Cambridge 2
Sandy 19

12

A603
Cambridge 2
Sandy 19

2 | 2

A1309
Cambridge (South)
A10
Harston 2

11

A1309
Cambridge (South)
A10
Royston 11

5 | 5

A505
Royston 8
Duxford 1

10

A505
Colchester (A604) 45
Saffron Walden 8
Duxford 1

4 | 4

A11
Newmarket 17
NO ACCESS
FROM A11 SPUR

9

NO EXIT
ACCESS ONLY
FROM A11 SPUR

15 | 15

A120
Bishop's Stortford 2
Stansted Airport 2

8

A120
Bishop's Stortford 2
Stansted Airport 2

10 | 10

A414
Harlow 3

7

A414
Harlow 3
Chelmsford 17

4 | 4

M25
Watford & M1 24

Waltham Abbey
(A121) 6
Dartford Tunnel
(M20) 19
Gatwick M23 65

6

M25
Dartford Tunnel
(M20) 19
Gatwick M23 65
Watford & M1 24

Waltham Abbey
(A121) 6

4 | 4

A1168
Loughton 2
NO ACCESS
FROM A1168

5

NO EXIT.
ACCESS ONLY
FROM A1168

4 | 4

ACCESS ONLY
FROM EASTBOUND
LANE OF A406

4

A406
N Circular Rd (West)
London (West & North)

NO EXIT TO
A406 EASTBOUND
NO ACCESS
FROM A406

1 | 1

3

A12
Chelmsford 24
The City 9
Southend (A127) 31
Dartford Tunnel 17

M11

117

LONDON–MILTON KEYNES M1

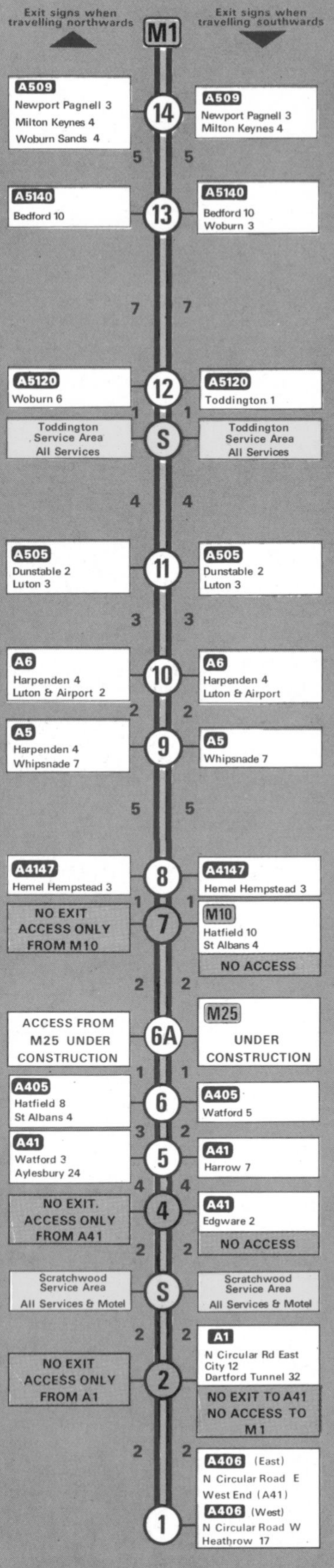

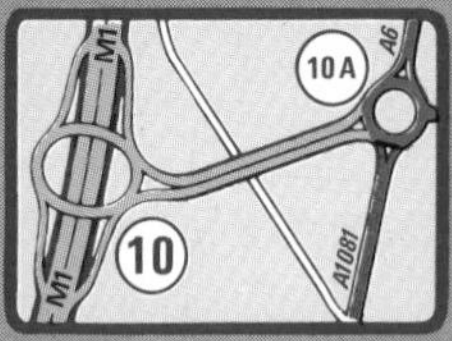

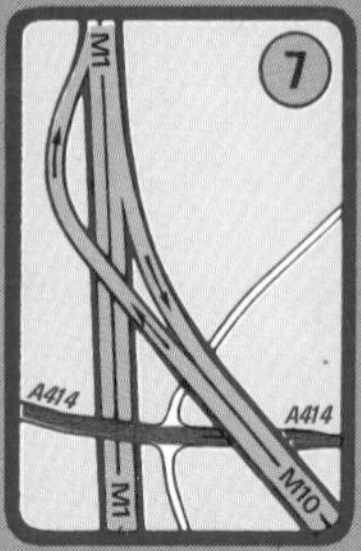

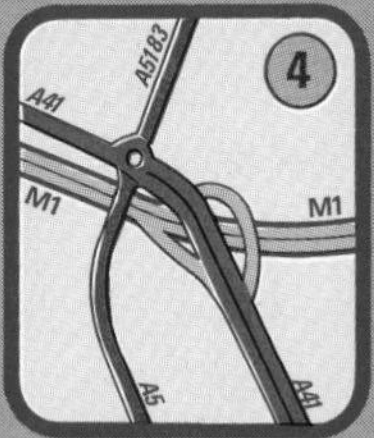

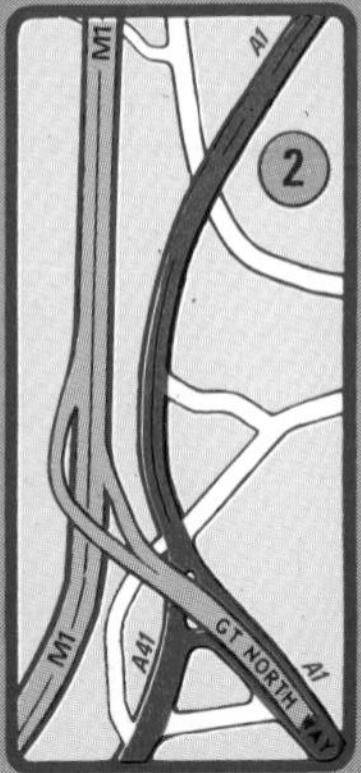

Exit signs when travelling northwards
M1
Exit signs when travelling southwards
A509 Newport Pagnell 3 Milton Keynes 4 Woburn Sands 4
14
A509 Newport Pagnell 3 Milton Keynes 4
5 5
A5140 Bedford 10
13
A5140 Bedford 10 Woburn 3
7 7
A5120 Woburn 6
12
A5120 Toddington 1
1 1
Toddington Service Area All Services
S
Toddington Service Area All Services
4 4
A505 Dunstable 2 Luton 3
11
A505 Dunstable 2 Luton 3
3 3
A6 Harpenden 4 Luton & Airport 2
10
A6 Harpenden 4 Luton & Airport
2 2
A5 Harpenden 4 Whipsnade 7
9
A5 Whipsnade 7
5 5
A4147 Hemel Hempstead 3
8
A4147 Hemel Hempstead 3
1 1
NO EXIT ACCESS ONLY FROM M10
7
M10 Hatfield 10 St Albans 4
NO ACCESS
2 2
ACCESS FROM M25 UNDER CONSTRUCTION
6A
M25 UNDER CONSTRUCTION
1 1
A405 Hatfield 8 St Albans 4
6
A405 Watford 5
3 2
A41 Watford 3 Aylesbury 24
5
A41 Harrow 7
4 4
NO EXIT. ACCESS ONLY FROM A41
4
A41 Edgware 2
NO ACCESS
2 2
Scratchwood Service Area All Services & Motel
S
Scratchwood Service Area All Services & Motel
2 2
NO EXIT ACCESS ONLY FROM A1
2
A1 N Circular Rd East City 12 Dartford Tunnel 32
NO EXIT TO A41 NO ACCESS TO M1
2 2
A406 (East) N Circular Road E West End (A41)
A406 (West) N Circular Road W Heathrow 17
1

M1
A5130
14
A509
M1

M1
10A
A6
10
M1
A1081

M1
7
A414
A414
M1
M10

A41
A5183
4
M1
M1
A5
A41

M1
A1
2
M1
A41
GT NORTH RD
A1

THE NORTH
BEDFORD
MILTON KEYNES
Kempston
0 4 miles
M1
A421
Woburn Sands
Aspley Guise
Bletchley
A507
Ampthill
Woburn
Clophill
Flitwick
Leighton Buzzard
Toddington
TODDINGTON
Barton in the Clay
B655
DUNSTABLE
LUTON
A505
Whipsnade
Markyate
LUTON
Redbourn
Harpenden
HEMEL HEMPSTEAD
Wheathampstead
A1(M)
M10
King's Langley
M25
ST ALBANS
London Colney
Hatfield
A405 to become M25
A1(M)
WATFORD
Radlett
Potters Bar
Oxhey
Bushey
Borehamwood
M25
Northwood
Elstree
SCRATCHWOOD
Stanmore
Barnet
Harrow
Edgware
Cockfosters
Whetstone
Wembley
Finchley
Southgate
Brent
Golders Green
LONDON
Southall
A40(M)
M4
Ealing
M41
Holloway
Marble Arch
A307 A205
A4
WEST END
CITY

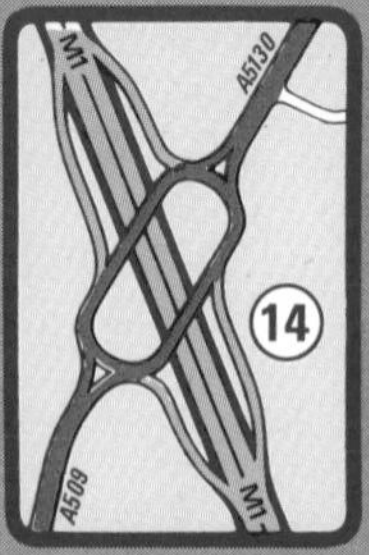

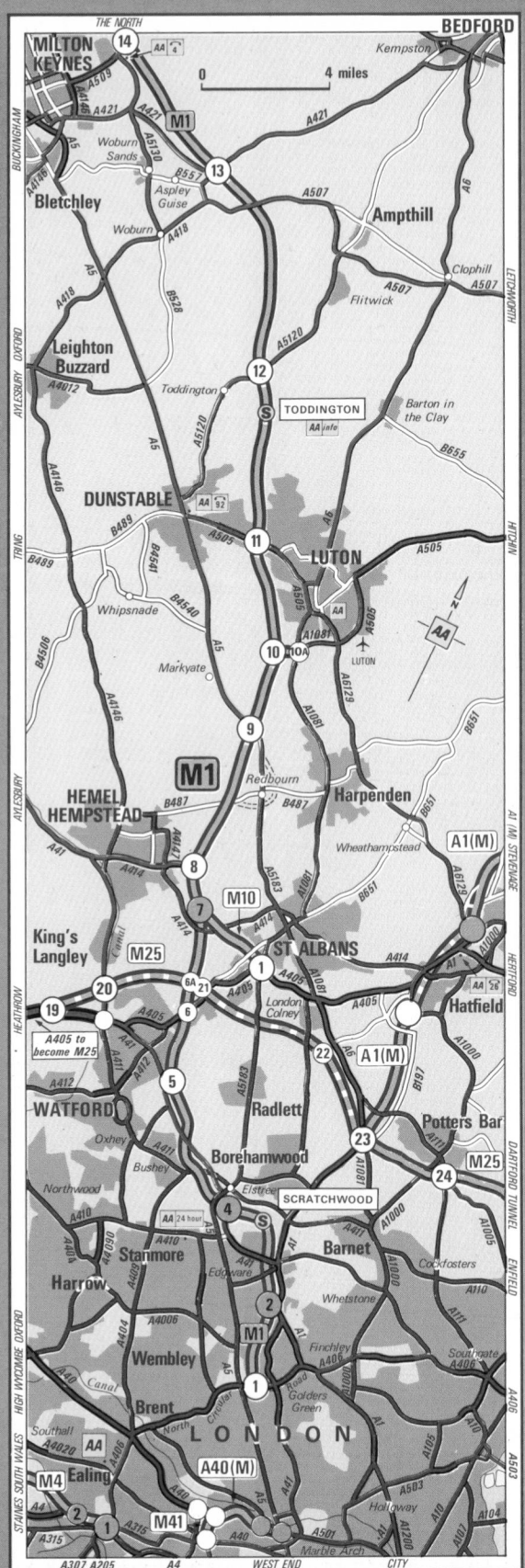

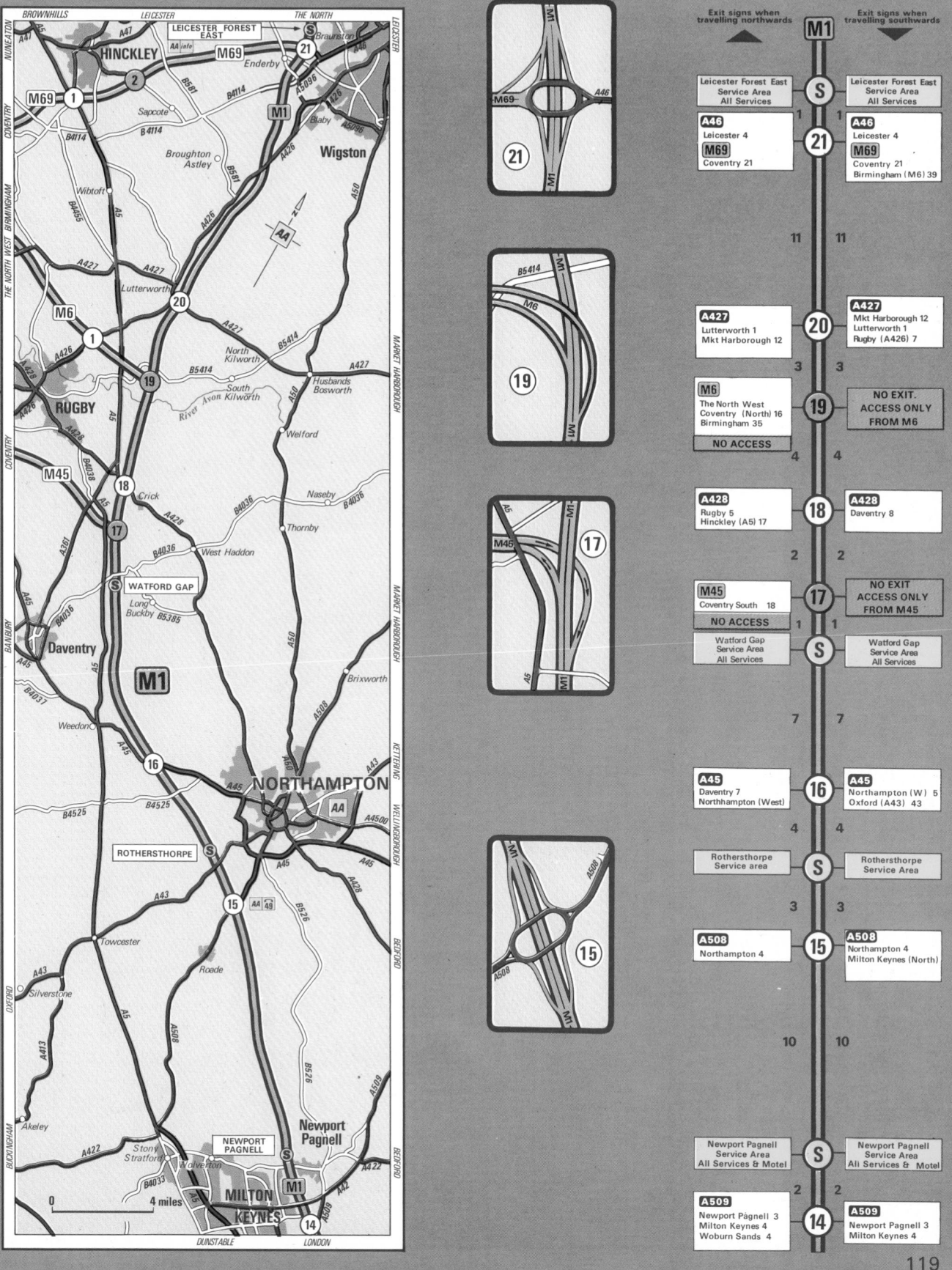

LEICESTER–BOLSOVER M1

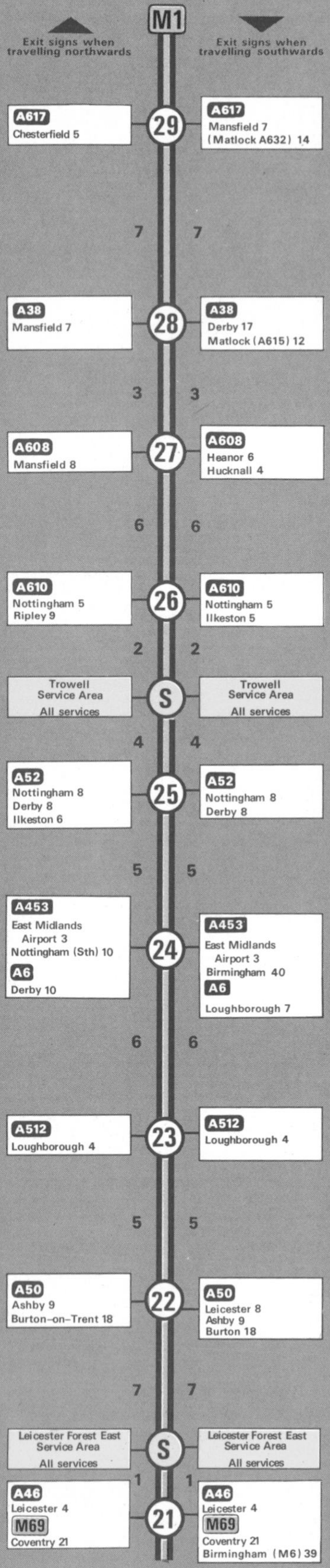

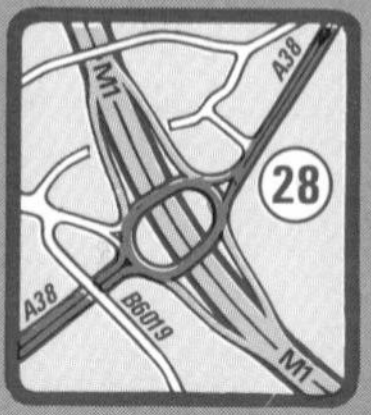

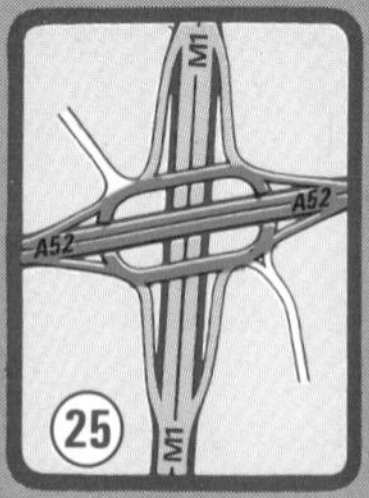

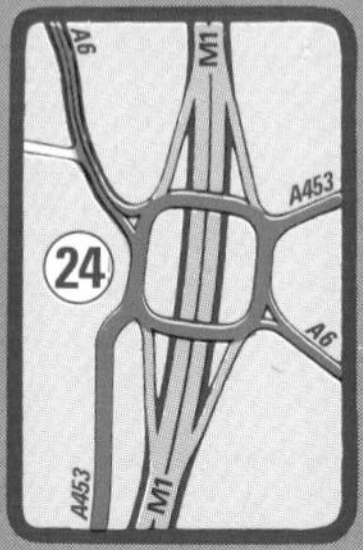

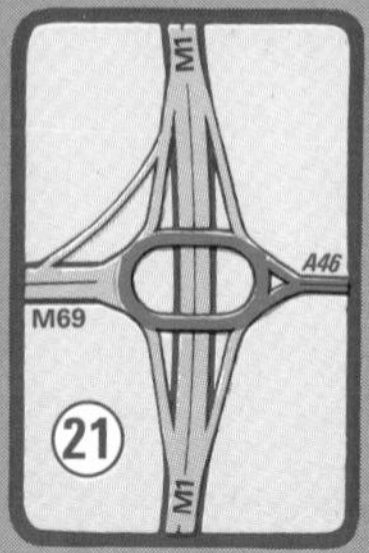

M1
Exit signs when travelling northwards
Exit signs when travelling southwards
A617 Chesterfield 5
29
A617 Mansfield 7 (Matlock A632) 14
7
7
A38 Mansfield 7
28
A38 Derby 17 Matlock (A615) 12
3
3
A608 Mansfield 8
27
A608 Heanor 6 Hucknall 4
6
6
A610 Nottingham 5 Ripley 9
26
A610 Nottingham 5 Ilkeston 5
2
2
Trowell Service Area All services
S
Trowell Service Area All services
4
4
A52 Nottingham 8 Derby 8 Ilkeston 6
25
A52 Nottingham 8 Derby 8
5
5
A453 East Midlands Airport 3 Nottingham (Sth) 10 A6 Derby 10
24
A453 East Midlands Airport 3 Birmingham 40 A6 Loughborough 7
6
6
A512 Loughborough 4
23
A512 Loughborough 4
5
5
A50 Ashby 9 Burton-on-Trent 18
22
A50 Leicester 8 Ashby 9 Burton 18
7
7
Leicester Forest East Service Area All services
S
Leicester Forest East Service Area All services
1
1
A46 Leicester 4 M69 Coventry 21
21
A46 Leicester 4 M69 Coventry 21 Birmingham (M6) 39

29
M1
A617
A6175
A617
M1

M1
A38
28
A38
B6019
M1

M1
A52
A52
25
M1

A6
M1
A453
24
A6
A453
M1

M1
A46
M69
21
M1

THE NORTH
WORKSOP
CHESTERFIELD
Bolsover
Warsop
29
M1
MANSFIELD
SUTTON IN ASHFIELD
KIRKBY IN ASHFIELD
28
ALFRETON
Ripley
27
HUCKNALL
Eastwood
HEANOR
26
ARNOLD
ILKESTON
TROWELL
NOTTINGHAM
Stapleford
BEESTON
25
LONG EATON
Castle Donington
EAST MIDLANDS
24
Kegworth
M1
Hathern
Shepshed
LOUGHBOROUGH
23
COALVILLE
22
0
4 miles
Markfield
Ibstock
LEICESTER
Groby
LEICESTER FOREST EAST
21
M69
Wigston
COVENTRY
LONDON
DERBY
BURTON-ON-TRENT
GRANTHAM
MELTON MOWBRAY
NEWARK
PETERBOROUGH
MARKET HARBOROUGH

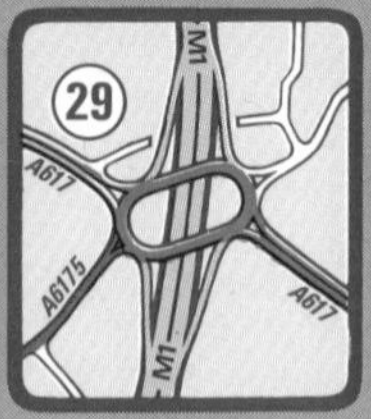

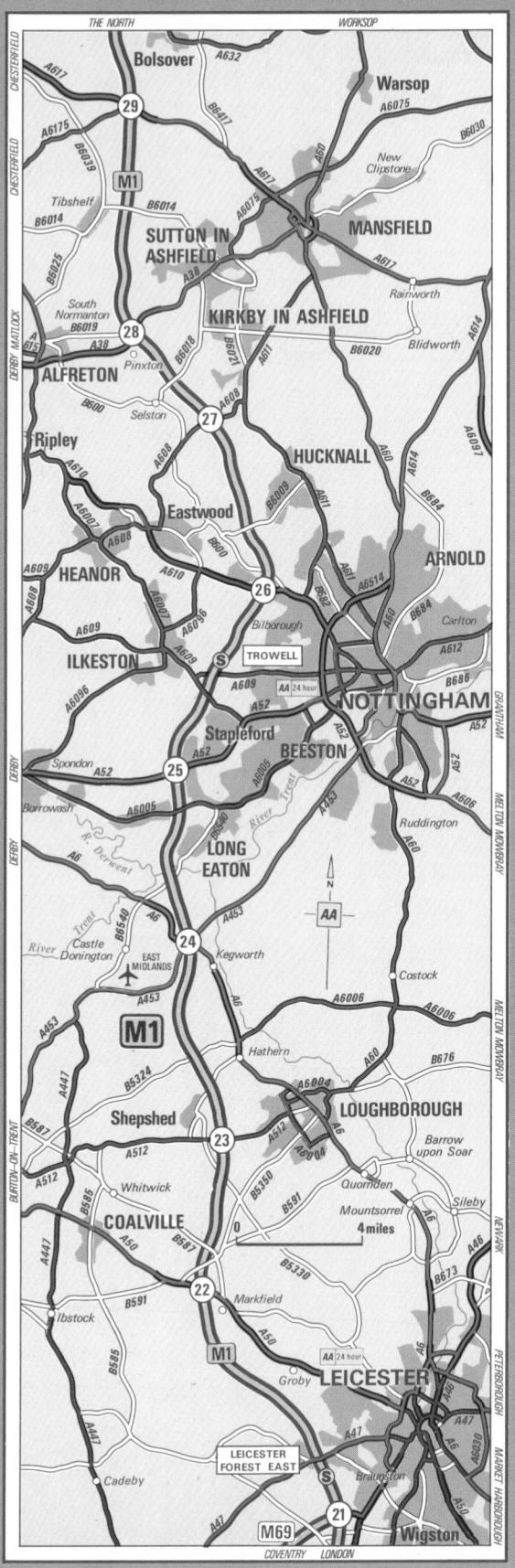

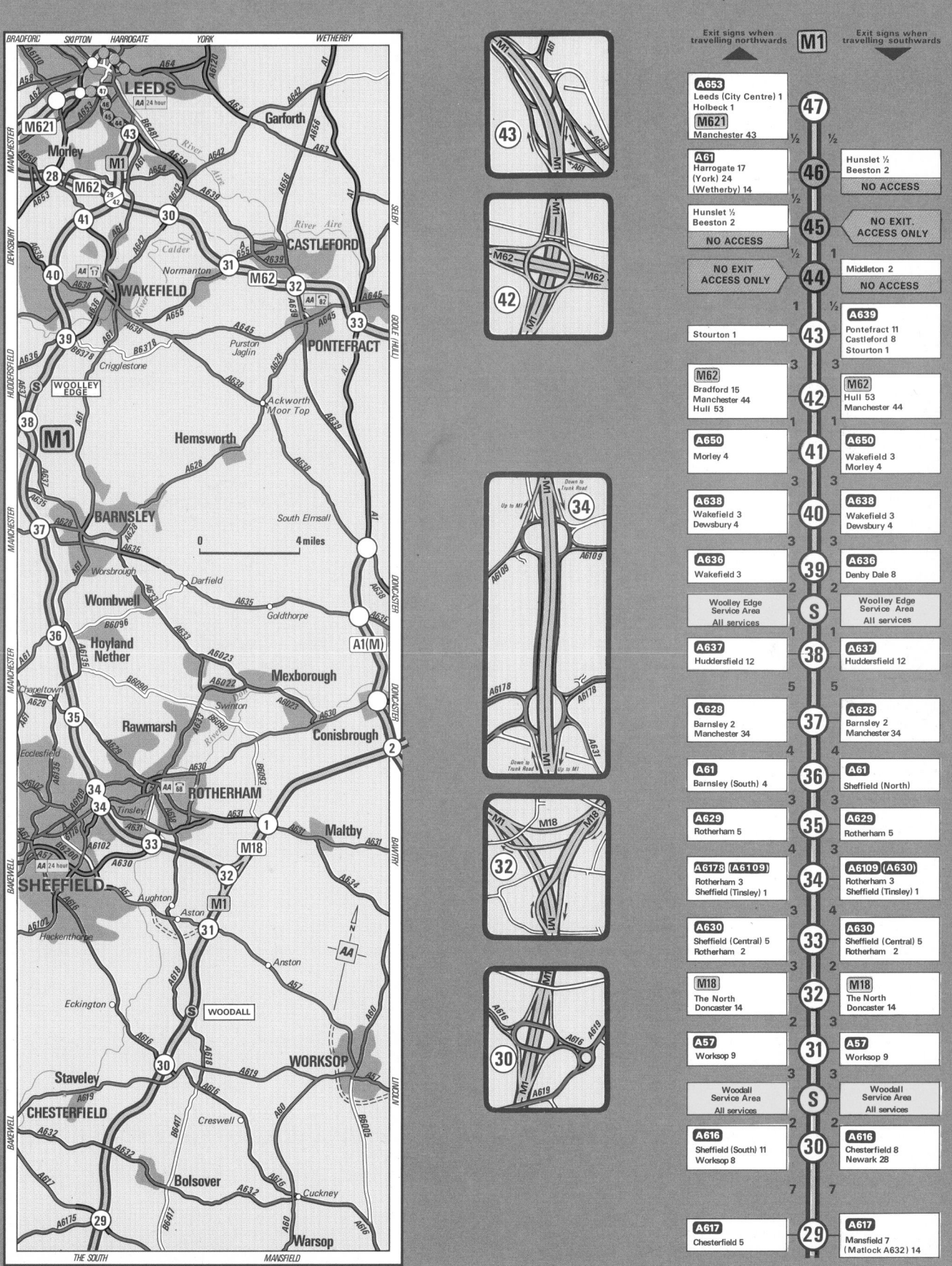

Exit signs when travelling northwards ▲ M1 Exit signs when travelling southwards ▼

Northwards	Jct	Southwards
A653 Leeds (City Centre) 1 Holbeck 1 / **M621** Manchester 43	47	
½		½
A61 Harrogate 17 (York) 24 (Wetherby) 14	46	Hunslet ½ Beeston 2 — NO ACCESS
½		½
Hunslet ½ Beeston 2 — NO ACCESS	45	NO EXIT. ACCESS ONLY
½		
NO EXIT ACCESS ONLY	44	Middleton 2 — NO ACCESS
1		½
Stourton 1	43	**A639** Pontefract 11 Castleford 8 Stourton 1
3		3
M62 Bradford 15 Manchester 44 Hull 53	42	**M62** Hull 53 Manchester 44
1		1
A650 Morley 4	41	**A650** Wakefield 3 Morley 4
3		3
A638 Wakefield 3 Dewsbury 4	40	**A638** Wakefield 3 Dewsbury 4
3		3
A636 Wakefield 3	39	**A636** Denby Dale 8
2		2
Woolley Edge Service Area — All services	S	Woolley Edge Service Area — All services
1		1
A637 Huddersfield 12	38	**A637** Huddersfield 12
5		5
A628 Barnsley 2 Manchester 34	37	**A628** Barnsley 2 Manchester 34
4		4
A61 Barnsley (South) 4	36	**A61** Sheffield (North)
3		3
A629 Rotherham 5	35	**A629** Rotherham 5
A6178 (A6109) Rotherham 3 Sheffield (Tinsley) 1	34	**A6109 (A630)** Rotherham 3 Sheffield (Tinsley) 1
A630 Sheffield (Central) 5 Rotherham 2	33	**A630** Sheffield (Central) 5 Rotherham 2
M18 The North Doncaster 14	32	**M18** The North Doncaster 14
2		2
A57 Worksop 9	31	**A57** Worksop 9
3		3
Woodall Service Area — All services	S	Woodall Service Area — All services
2		2
A616 Sheffield (South) 11 Worksop 8	30	**A616** Chesterfield 8 Newark 28
7		7
A617 Chesterfield 5	29	**A617** Mansfield 7 (Matlock A632) 14

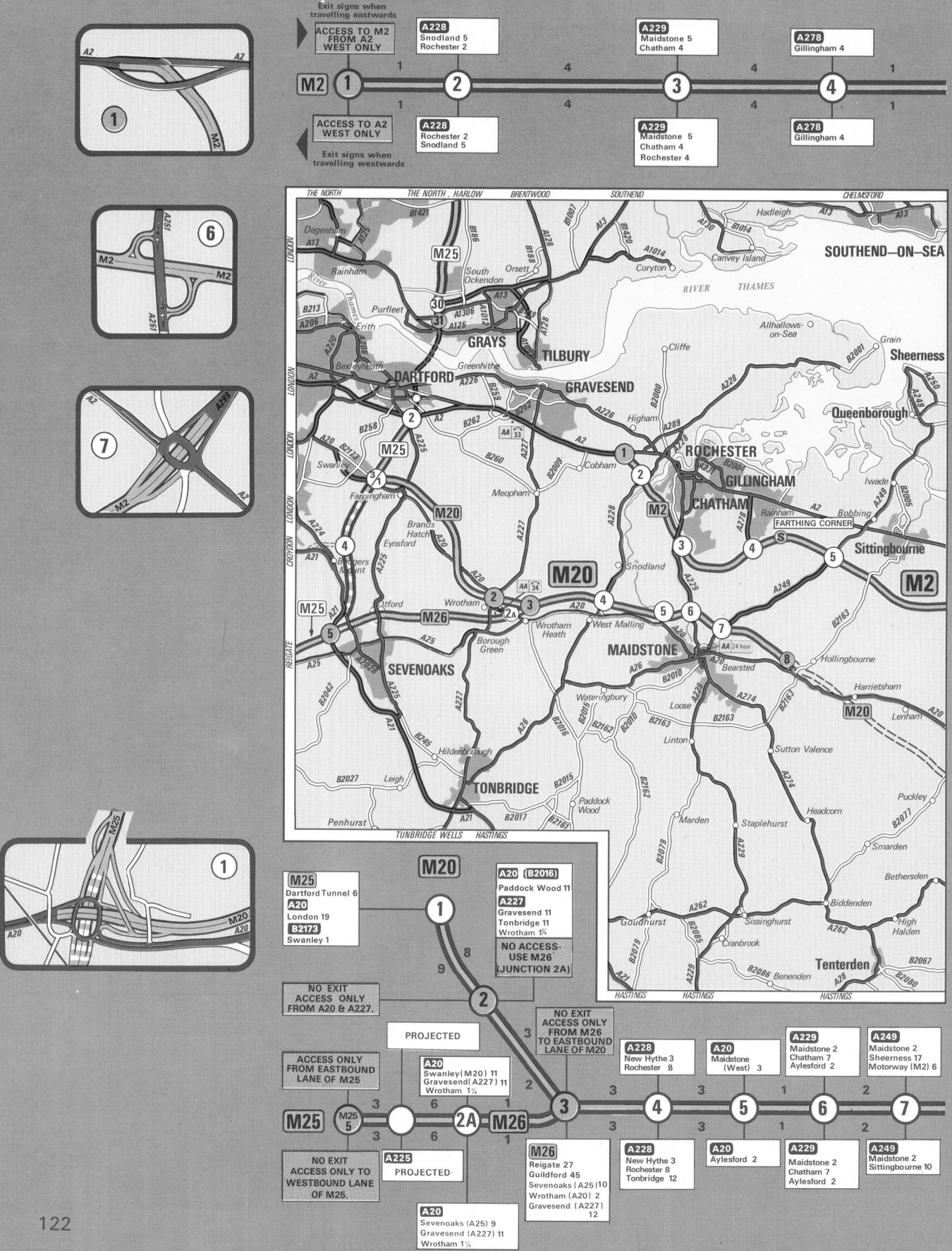

ACCESS TO M2
FROM A2
WEST ONLY

Exit signs when
travelling eastwards

A228
Snodland 5
Rochester 2

A229
Maidstone 5
Chatham 4

A278
Gillingham 4

M2 — 1 — 1 — 2 — 4 — 3 — 4 — 4 — 1

ACCESS TO A2
WEST ONLY

Exit signs when
travelling westwards

A228
Rochester 2
Snodland 5

A229
Maidstone 5
Chatham 4
Rochester 4

A278
Gillingham 4

THE NORTH · THE NORTH, HARLOW · BRENTWOOD · SOUTHEND · CHELMSFORD

SOUTHEND-ON-SEA

M25

RIVER THAMES

Dagenham · Rainham · Purfleet · Erith · GRAYS · TILBURY · Cliffe · Allhallows-on-Sea · Grain · Sheerness

Bexleyheath · DARTFORD · Greenhithe · GRAVESEND · Higham · ROCHESTER · GILLINGHAM · Queenborough · Iwade

Swanley · Cobham · CHATHAM · FARTHING CORNER · Bobbing · Sittingbourne

M20 · Meopham · Snodland · Rainham

Brands Hatch · Eynsford · Bridgers Mount · Farningham

M25 · Otford · Wrotham · M26 · Wrotham Heath · West Malling · MAIDSTONE · AA 24 hour · Hollingbourne · Harrietsham · Lenham

SEVENOAKS · Borough Green · Wateringbury · Loose · Bearsted · M20

Hildenborough · Linton · Sutton Valence · Headcorn · Puckley

TONBRIDGE · Paddock Wood · Marden · Staplehurst · Smarden · Bethersden

Penhurst · TUNBRIDGE WELLS · HASTINGS · Goudhurst · Cranbrook · Benenden · Sissinghurst · High Halden · Tenterden

M2

M20

M25
Dartford Tunnel 6
A20
London 19
B2173
Swanley 1

M20 (B2016)
Paddock Wood 11
A227
Gravesend 11
Tonbridge 11
Wrotham 1¾
**NO ACCESS-
USE M26
(JUNCTION 2A)**

1 — 8 — 9 — 2

NO EXIT
ACCESS ONLY
FROM A20 & A227.

PROJECTED

ACCESS ONLY
FROM EASTBOUND
LANE OF M25.

A20
Swanley (M20) 11
Gravesend (A227) 11
Wrotham 1¼

NO EXIT
ACCESS ONLY
FROM M26
TO EASTBOUND
LANE OF M20

A228
New Hythe 3
Rochester 8

A20
Maidstone
(West) 3

A229
Maidstone 2
Chatham 7
Aylesford 2

A249
Maidstone 2
Sheerness 17
Motorway (M2) 6

M25 — M25 5 — 2A — M26 — 3 — 4 — 5 — 6 — 7

NO EXIT
ACCESS ONLY TO
WESTBOUND LANE
OF M25.

A225 PROJECTED

M26
Reigate 27
Rochester 8
Sevenoaks (A25) 10
Wrotham (A20) 2
Gravesend (A227) 12

A228
New Hythe 3
Tonbridge 12

A20
Aylesford 2

A229
Maidstone 2
Chatham 7
Aylesford 2

A249
Maidstone 2
Sittingbourne 10

A20
Sevenoaks (A25) 9
Gravesend (A227) 11
Wrotham 1¼

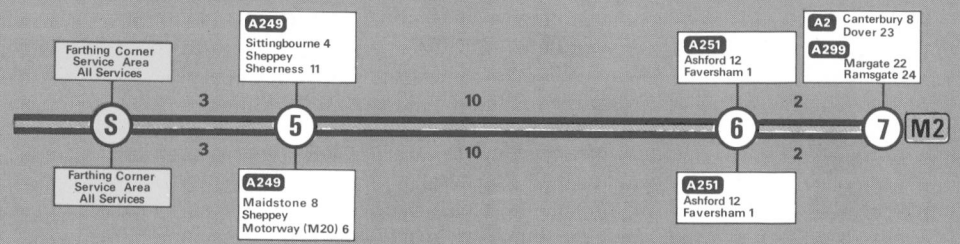

Farthing Corner Service Area All Services

A249 Sittingbourne 4 Sheppey Sheerness 11

A251 Ashford 12 Faversham 1

A2 Canterbury 8 Dover 23

A299 Margate 22 Ramsgate 24

S — 3 — 5 — 10 — 6 — 2 — 7 M2

S — 3 — 5 — 10 — 6 — 2 — 7

Farthing Corner Service Area All Services

A249 Maidstone 8 Sheppey Motorway (M20) 6

A251 Ashford 12 Faversham 1

Map

N AA

NORTH SEA

Minster-in-Sheppey

B2008 Eastchurch B2231 Leysdown

The Swale

MARGATE

Westgate on Sea A256 B2052 B2049 Broadstairs

HERNE BAY Birchington A28 B2190 B2050

WHITSTABLE B2205 A299 Herne Sarre A253 RAMSGATE AA

A299 A291 Upstreet A28 Minster A256 B2048

A2 Faversham B2040 Hersden B2046 A257 Wingham Ash Sandwich

Ospringe AA 29 Dunkirk A2 Sturry CANTERBURY A2050 A257 Eastry A256

M2 6 7 A290

Chartham A252 Bridge A2 B2046 A256

B2071 Challock A28 Barham A258 DEAL Walmer

Charing A252 B2068 B2065 A260 Temple Ewell Kingsdown

M20 9 Elham A260 Densole B2060 St Margarets Bay

ASHFORD 10 A20 Lyminge Alkham DOVER AA

Great Chart A2070 Sellindge Hawkinge A20 AA

A2042 A20 STRAIT OF DOVER

Woodchurch Ham Street B2067 Newingreen A261 Cheriton FOLKESTONE AA

Lympne Sandgate

B2069 A259 Hythe

HASTINGS NEW ROMNEY

11 12 13

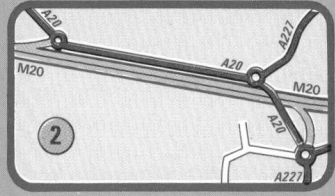

A20 A227 M20 A20 M20

2

A227

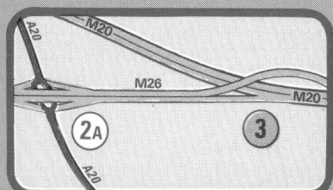

A20 M20 M20 M26 M20

2A A20 **3**

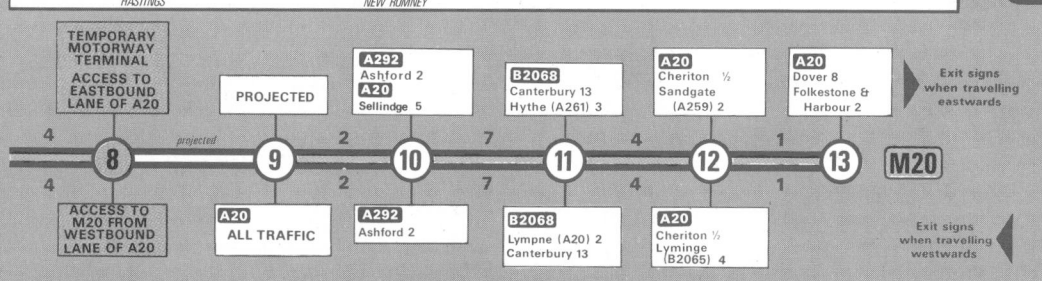

TEMPORARY MOTORWAY TERMINAL ACCESS TO EASTBOUND LANE OF A20

PROJECTED

A292 Ashford 2 **A20** Sellindge 5

B2068 Canterbury 13 Hythe (A261) 3

A20 Cheriton ½ Sandgate (A259) 2

A20 Dover 8 Folkestone & Harbour 2

Exit signs when travelling eastwards

4 — 8 — projected — 9 — 2 — 10 — 7 — 11 — 4 — 12 — 1 — 13 M20

4 — 8 — 9 — 2 — 10 — 7 — 11 — 4 — 12 — 1 — 13

ACCESS TO M20 FROM WESTBOUND LANE OF A20

A20 ALL TRAFFIC

A292 Ashford 2

B2068 Lympne (A20) 2 Canterbury 13

A20 Cheriton ½ Lyminge (B2065) 4

Exit signs when travelling westwards

A228 **6** M20 M20 A229

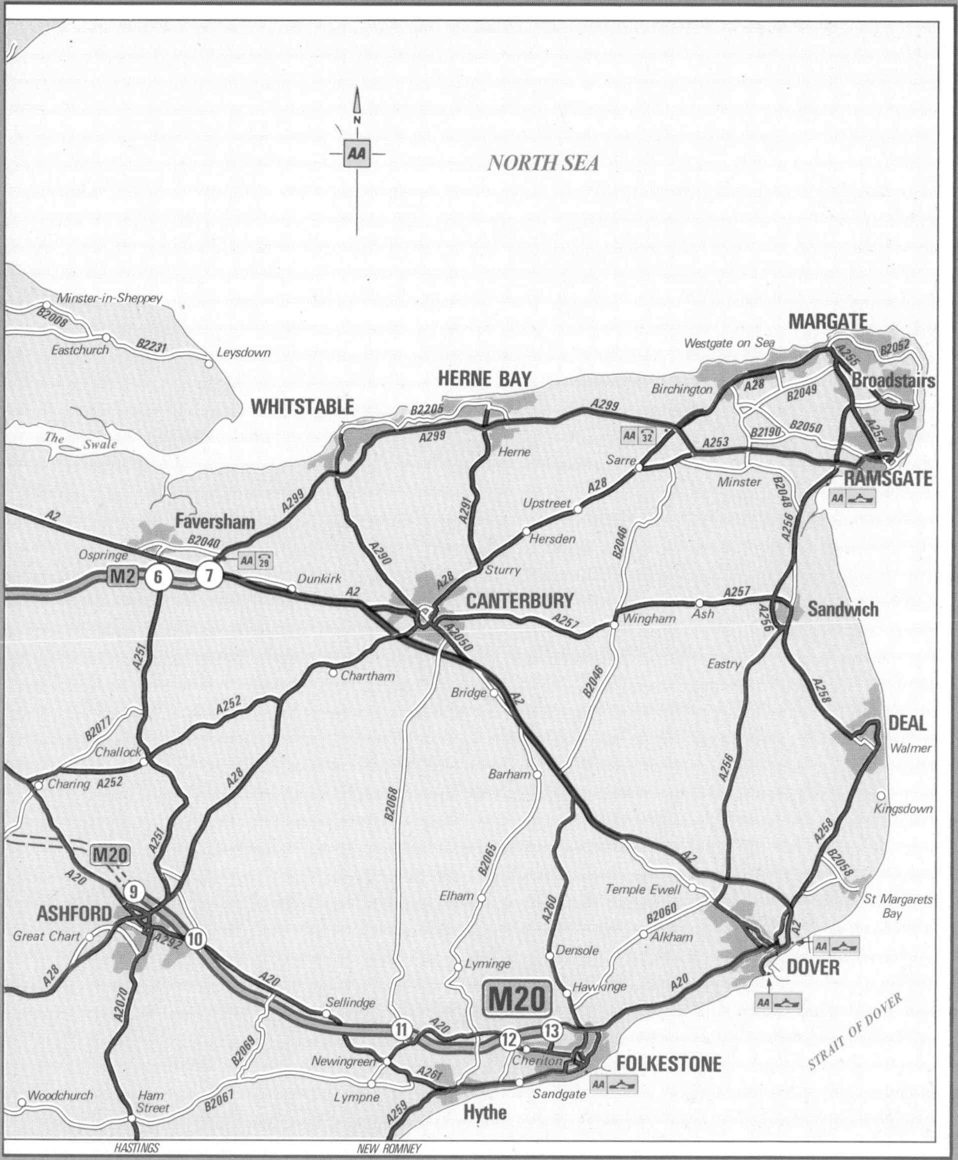

LONDON–BASINGSTOKE–SOUTHAMPTON M3

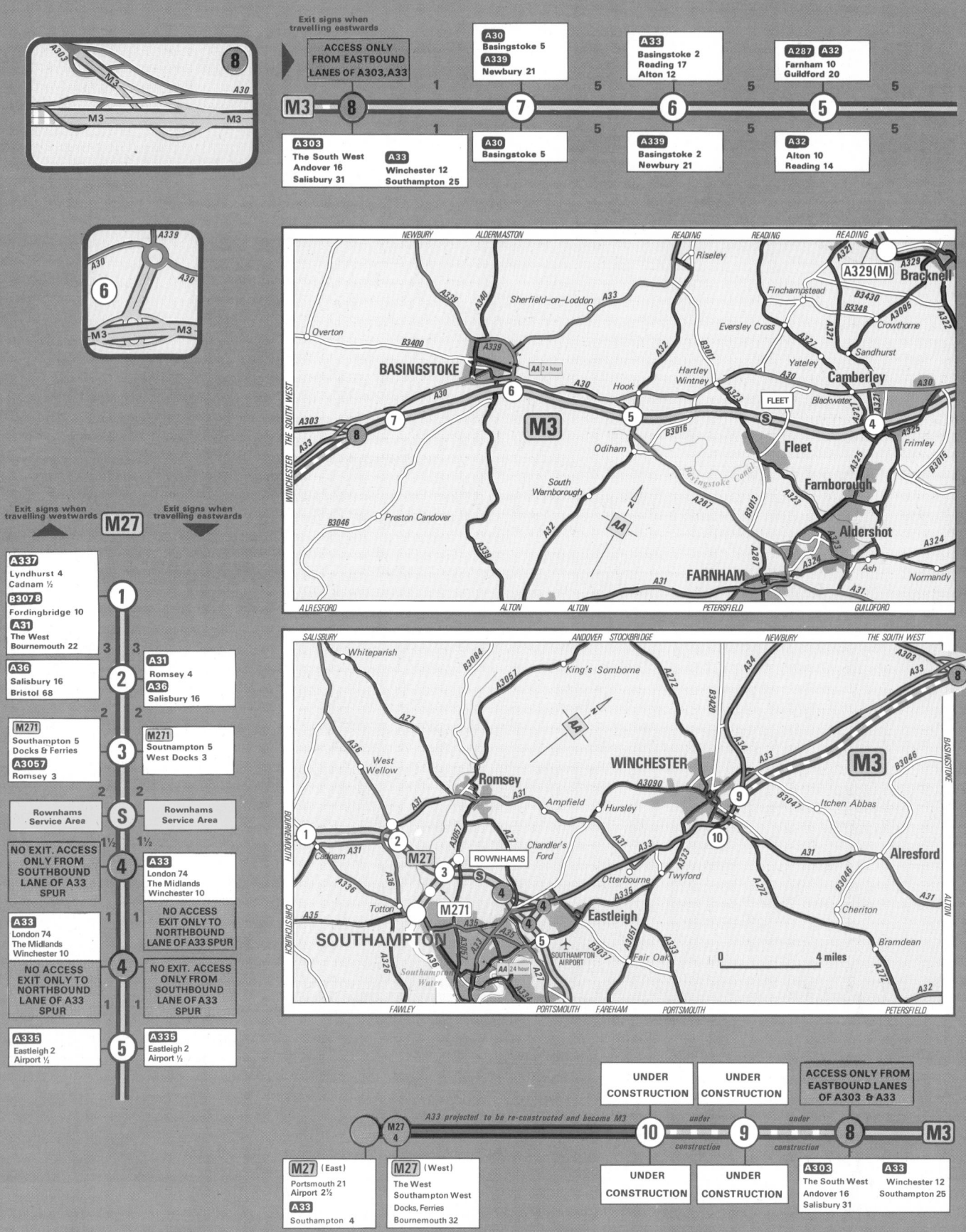

8

| M3 | 8 | 7 | 6 | 5 |

Exit signs when travelling eastwards

ACCESS ONLY FROM EASTBOUND LANES OF A303, A33

A30
Basingstoke 5
A339
Newbury 21

A33
Basingstoke 2
Reading 17
Alton 12

A287 A32
Farnham 10
Guildford 20

A303
The South West
Andover 16
Salisbury 31
A33
Winchester 12
Southampton 25

A30
Basingstoke 5

A339
Basingstoke 2
Newbury 21

A32
Alton 10
Reading 14

6

M27

Exit signs when travelling westwards / Exit signs when travelling eastwards

A337
Lyndhurst 4
Cadnam ½
B3078
Fordingbridge 10
A31
The West
Bournemouth 22

1

A36
Salisbury 16
Bristol 68

2

A31
Romsey 4
A36
Salisbury 16

M271
Southampton 5
Docks & Ferries
A3057
Romsey 3

3

M271
Southampton 5
West Docks 3

Rownhams Service Area **S** Rownhams Service Area

NO EXIT. ACCESS ONLY FROM SOUTHBOUND LANE OF A33 SPUR

4

A33
London 74
The Midlands
Winchester 10

A33
London 74
The Midlands
Winchester 10

NO ACCESS EXIT ONLY TO NORTHBOUND LANE OF A33 SPUR

NO ACCESS EXIT ONLY TO NORTHBOUND LANE OF A33 SPUR

4

NO EXIT. ACCESS ONLY FROM SOUTHBOUND LANE OF A33 SPUR

A335
Eastleigh 2
Airport ½

5

A335
Eastleigh 2
Airport ½

UNDER CONSTRUCTION UNDER CONSTRUCTION ACCESS ONLY FROM EASTBOUND LANES OF A303 & A33

A33 projected to be re-constructed and become M3

| M27 4 | **10** | under construction | **9** | under construction | **8** | M3 |

M27 (East)
Portsmouth 21
Airport 2½
A33
Southampton 4

M27 (West)
The West
Southampton West
Docks, Ferries
Bournemouth 32

UNDER CONSTRUCTION UNDER CONSTRUCTION

A303
The South West
Andover 16
Salisbury 31
A33
Winchester 12
Southampton 25

124

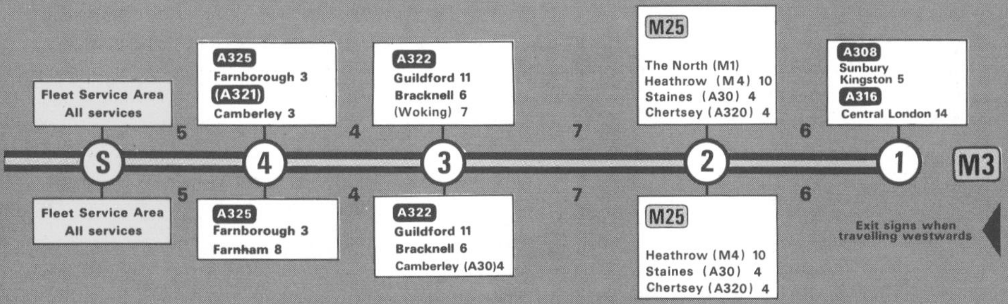

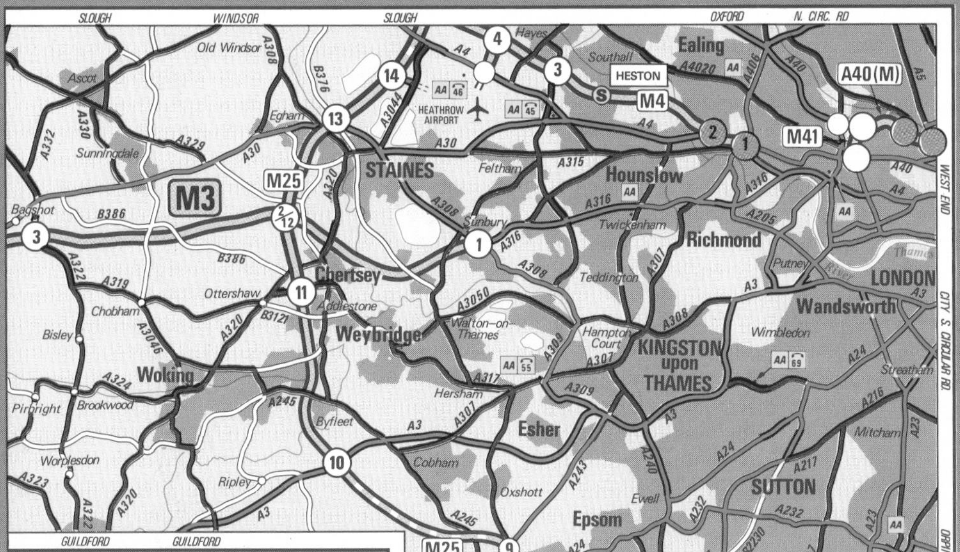

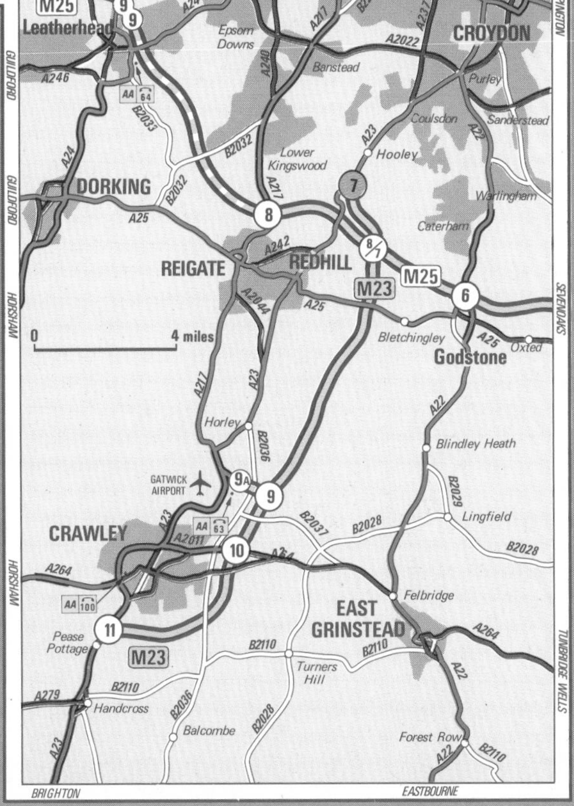

M3 junction strip (top)

| Fleet Service Area
All services | A325
Farnborough 3
(A321)
Camberley 3 | A322
Guildford 11
Bracknell 6
(Woking) 7 | M25
The North (M1)
Heathrow (M4) 10
Staines (A30) 4
Chertsey (A320) 4 | A308
Sunbury
Kingston 5
A316
Central London 14 |

S — 5 — **4** — 4 — **3** — 7 — **2** — 6 — **1**   M3

| Fleet Service Area
All services | A325
Farnborough 3
Farnham 8 | A322
Guildford 11
Bracknell 6
Camberley (A30) 4 | M25
Heathrow (M4) 10
Staines (A30) 4
Chertsey (A320) 4 | ◀ Exit signs when
travelling westwards |

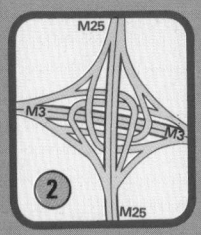

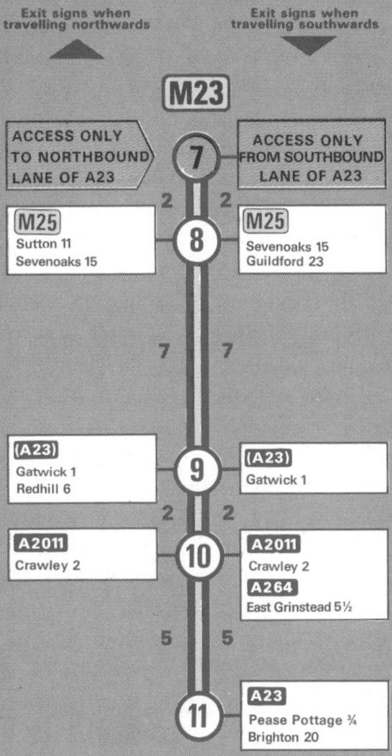

Selected Junctions on M23

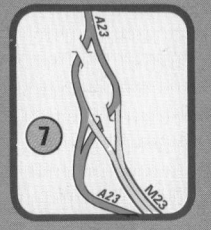

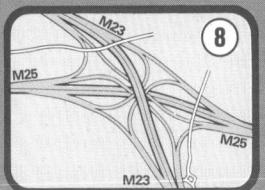

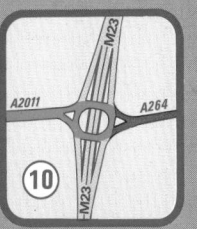

HOOLEY–PEASE POTTAGE

Exit signs when travelling northwards ▲   Exit signs when travelling southwards ▲

M23

| ACCESS ONLY TO NORTHBOUND LANE OF A23 | **7** | ACCESS ONLY FROM SOUTHBOUND LANE OF A23 |

2 — 2

| M25
Sutton 11
Sevenoaks 15 | **8** | M25
Sevenoaks 15
Guildford 23 |

7 — 7

| (A23)
Gatwick 1
Redhill 6 | **9** | (A23)
Gatwick 1 |

2 — 2

| A2011
Crawley 2 | **10** | A2011
Crawley 2
A264
East Grinstead 5½ |

5 — 5

| **11** | A23
Pease Pottage ¾
Brighton 20 |

Map

SLOUGH · WINDSOR · SLOUGH · OXFORD · N. CIRC. RD

Old Windsor · Hayes · Southall · Ealing · HESTON · A40(M) · A5
Ascot · Egham · HEATHROW AIRPORT · M4 · WEST END
Sunningdale · STAINES · Feltham · Hounslow · M41
Bagshot · M3 · M25 · Chertsey · Sunbury · Twickenham · Richmond · LONDON · Wandsworth · CITY S CIRCULAR RD
Chobham · Ottershaw · Addlestone · Walton-on-Thames · Hampton Court · KINGSTON upon THAMES · Wimbledon · Streatham
Bisley · Weybridge · Hersham · Putney
Woking · Brookwood · Byfleet · Esher · Epsom · SUTTON · Mitcham · ORPINGTON
Pirbright · Ripley · Cobham · Oxshott · Ewell · CROYDON · Purley · Sanderstead
Wormbledon · Leatherhead · Epsom Downs · Banstead · Coulsdon · SEVENOAKS
GUILDFORD · Lower Kingswood · Hooley · Warlingham · Caterham
DORKING · REIGATE · REDHILL · M25 · Godstone · Oxted · TUNBRIDGE WELLS
HORSHAM · Bletchingley
Horley · Blindley Heath · Lingfield
GATWICK AIRPORT · CRAWLEY · EAST GRINSTEAD · Felbridge
Pease Pottage · Turners Hill · Forest Row
Handcross · Balcombe
BRIGHTON · EASTBOURNE

0   4 miles

125

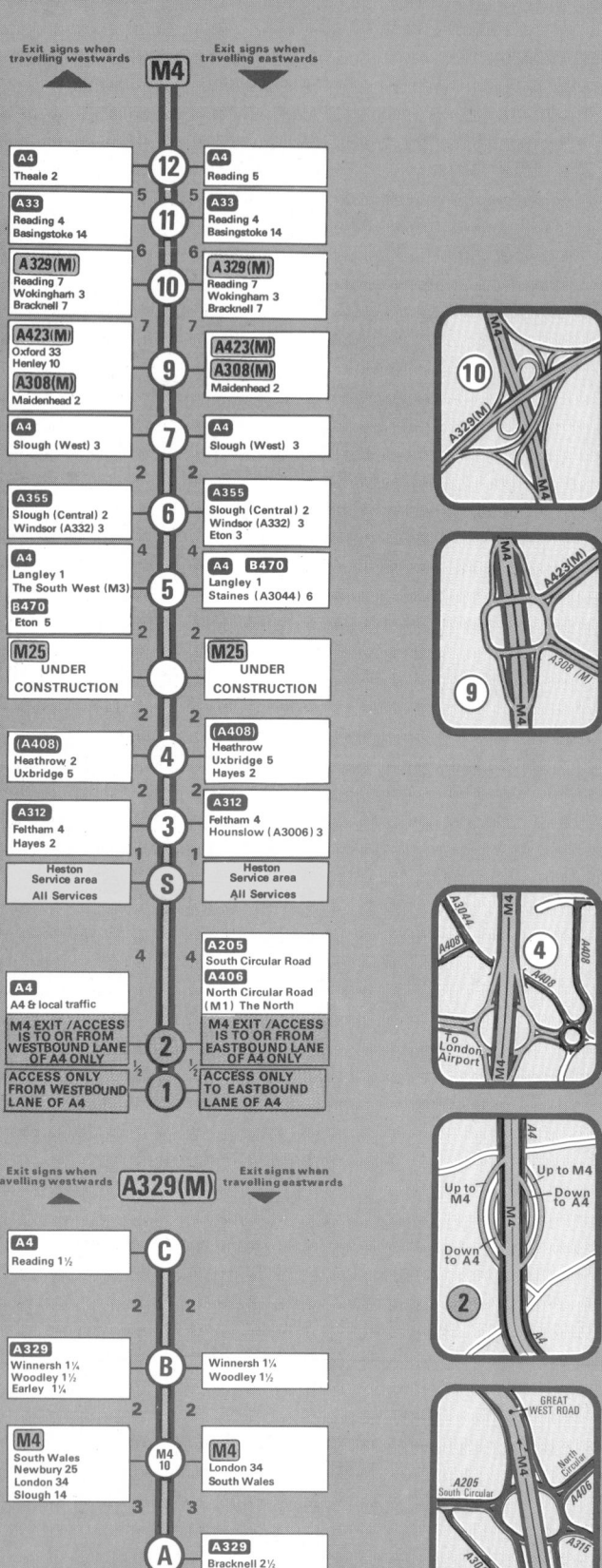

M4

Westwards	Jct	Eastwards
A4 Theale 2	12	**A4** Reading 5
A33 Reading 4 Basingstoke 14	11	**A33** Reading 4 Basingstoke 14
A329(M) Reading 7 Wokingham 3 Bracknell 7	10	**A329(M)** Reading 7 Wokingham 3 Bracknell 7
A423(M) Oxford 33 Henley 10 **A308(M)** Maidenhead 2	9	**A423(M)** **A308(M)** Maidenhead 2
A4 Slough (West) 3	7	**A4** Slough (West) 3
A355 Slough (Central) 2 Windsor (A332) 3	6	**A355** Slough (Central) 2 Windsor (A332) 3 Eton 3
A4 Langley 1 The South West (M3) **B470** Eton 5	5	**A4** **B470** Langley 1 Staines (A3044) 6
M25 UNDER CONSTRUCTION	○	**M25** UNDER CONSTRUCTION
(A408) Heathrow 2 Uxbridge 5	4	**(A408)** Heathrow Uxbridge 5 Hayes 2
A312 Feltham 4 Hayes 2	3	**A312** Feltham 4 Hounslow (A3006) 3
Heston Service area All Services	S	Heston Service area All Services
		A205 South Circular Road **A406** North Circular Road (M1) The North
A4 A4 & local traffic M4 EXIT /ACCESS IS TO OR FROM WESTBOUND LANE OF A4 ONLY	2	M4 EXIT /ACCESS IS TO OR FROM EASTBOUND LANE OF A4 ONLY
ACCESS ONLY FROM WESTBOUND LANE OF A4	1	ACCESS ONLY TO EASTBOUND LANE OF A4

A329(M)

Westwards	Jct	Eastwards
A4 Reading 1½	C	
A329 Winnersh 1¼ Woodley 1½ Earley 1¼	B	Winnersh 1¼ Woodley 1½
M4 South Wales Newbury 25 London 34 Slough 14	M4 10	**M4** London 34 South Wales
	A	**A329** Bracknell 2½ Wokingham 1½

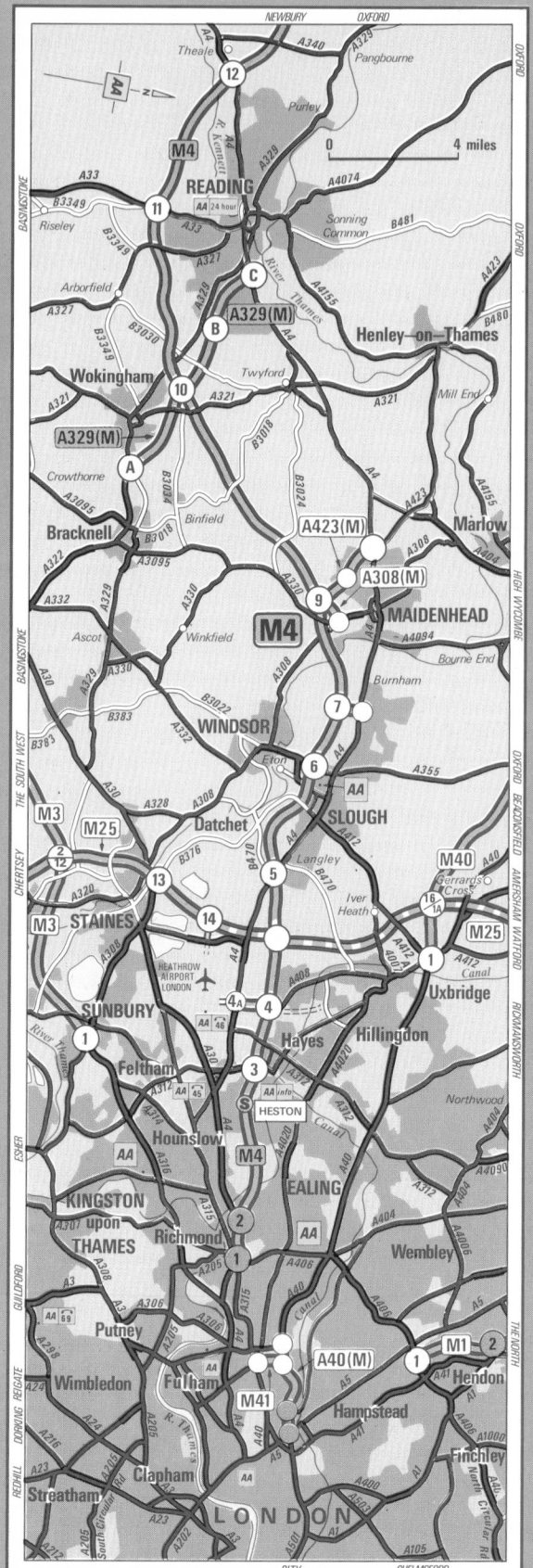

126

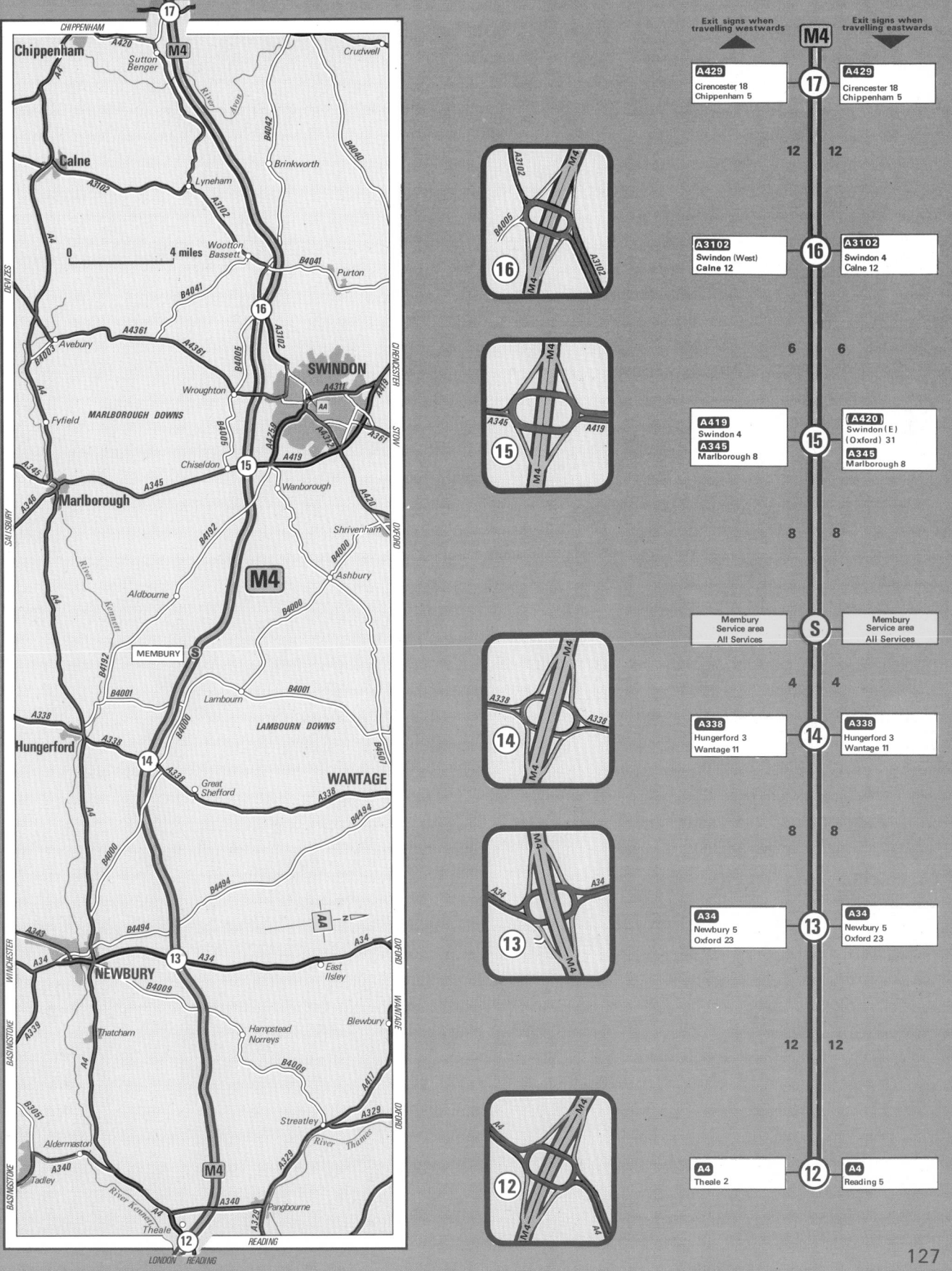

CHIPPENHAM

Chippenham
A420
Sutton
Benger
Crudwell

A4

Calne
A3102
Lyneham
Brinkworth

A4042
B4040

DEVIZES

0   4 miles

A3102
Wootton
Bassett
B4041
Purton

B4041

A4361
Avebury
A4361
A4005
A3102
SWINDON
A4311

B4005
Wroughton

CIRENCESTER

STOW

Fyfield
MARLBOROUGH DOWNS
A4259
AA
A4312
A361

A345
Chiseldon
15
A419
A345
Wanborough

A346
Marlborough
B4192
A420
Shrivenham

River Kennet
B4005
B4000
Ashbury

OXFORD

A345
Aldbourne
B4000
M4

B4192
MEMBURY
S
B4001
Lambourn
B4001
LAMBOURN DOWNS
B4507

A4
B4000
WANTAGE

A338
Hungerford
A338
Great
Shefford
A338
B4494

A4
B4000
B4494

A343
B4494
A34
OXFORD

13
A34
WANTAGE

WINCHESTER
A34
NEWBURY
East
Ilsley

BASINGSTOKE
A339
Thatcham
B4009
Hampstead
Norreys
Blewbury

A4
B4009
A417
OXFORD

B3051
Streatley
A329
River Thames

Aldermaston
A340
M4
A329
Pangbourne

Tadley
A340
A4
River Kennet
Theale
12
READING

LONDON   READING

Exit signs

Exit signs when travelling westwards ▲   M4   Exit signs when travelling eastwards ▼

Westwards		Eastwards
A429 Cirencester 18 Chippenham 5	17	**A429** Cirencester 18 Chippenham 5
12		12
A3102 Swindon (West) Calne 12	16	**A3102** Swindon 4 Calne 12
6		6
A419 Swindon 4 **A345** Marlborough 8	15	**(A420)** Swindon (E) (Oxford) 31 **A345** Marlborough 8
8		8
Membury Service area All Services	S	Membury Service area All Services
4		4
A338 Hungerford 3 Wantage 11	14	**A338** Hungerford 3 Wantage 11
8		8
A34 Newbury 5 Oxford 23	13	**A34** Newbury 5 Oxford 23
12		12
A4 Theale 2	12	**A4** Reading 5

127

Exit signs when travelling westwards ▲

Exit signs when travelling eastwards ▲

[M4]

Westward	Jct	Eastward
A48(M) Cardiff 9 NO ACCESS FROM A48 (M)	29	NO EXIT. ACCESS ONLY FROM A48 (M)
A48 Newport 2 **A467** Caerphilly 10	28	**A48** Newport 2
B4591	27	**B4591**
A4042 Cwmbran 4 Newport (Centre) 1	26	**A4042** Cwmbran 4 Newport (Centre) 1
B4596 Caerleon 2	25	**B4596** Caerleon 2
A455 **A48** Newport (East) **A449** Monmouth 20	24	**A449** Midlands (M50) Monmouth 20 **A48** Newport 4
B4245 Magor 1	23	**B4245** Magor 1
A466 **(A48)** Chepstow 2	22	**A466** Chepstow 2 Gloucester (A48) 30
SEVERN BRIDGE TOLLBOOTHS	21	SEVERN BRIDGE TOLLBOOTHS
Aust Service area All Services & Picnic area **A403** Avonmouth 9	21	Aust Service area All Services & Picnic area **A403** Avonmouth 9
M5 South West Bristol (West) Midlands	20	**M5** Bristol 8 South West Midlands Airport 20
M32 Bristol 6	19	**M32** Bristol 6
A46 Bath 11 Stroud 20	18	**A46** Bath 11 Stroud 20
Leigh Dalamere Service area All Services	S	Leigh Delamere Service area All Services
A429 Cirencester 18 Chippenham 5	17	**A429** Cirencester 18 Chippenham 5

(distances between junctions, westward / eastward):
2, 1, 2/2, 1, 3/3, 4/4, 8/8, 3/3, 5/5, 3/3, 7/7, 9/9, 2/2

Junction diagrams: 27, 26, 21, 20, 19

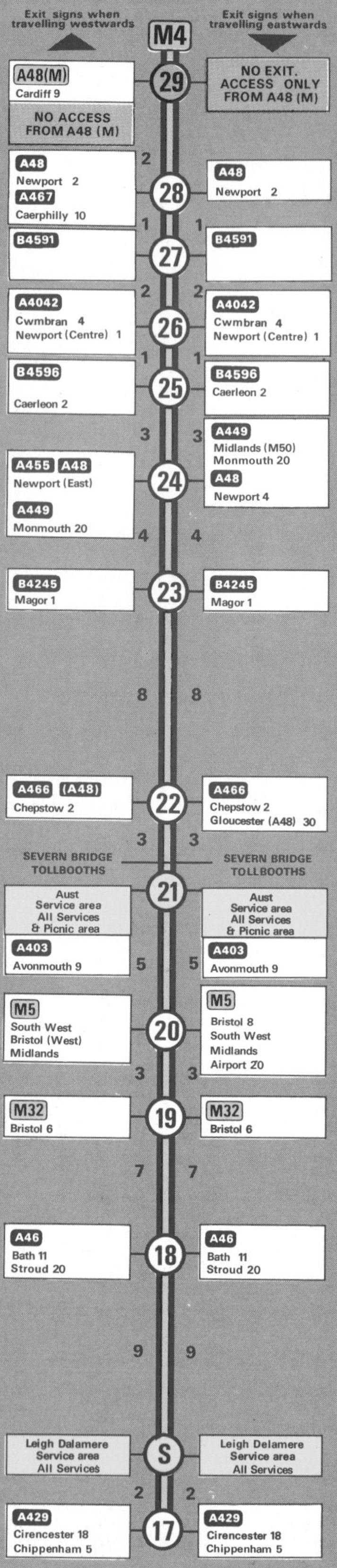

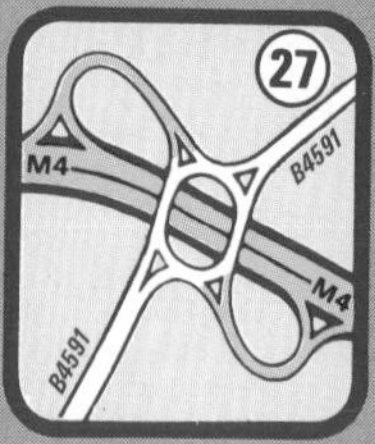

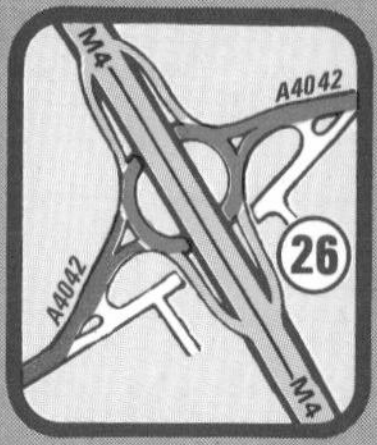

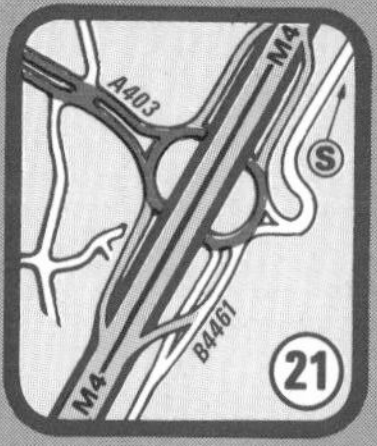

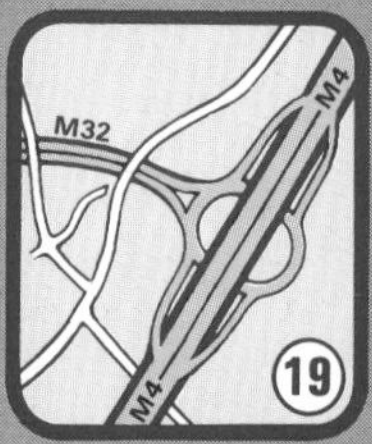

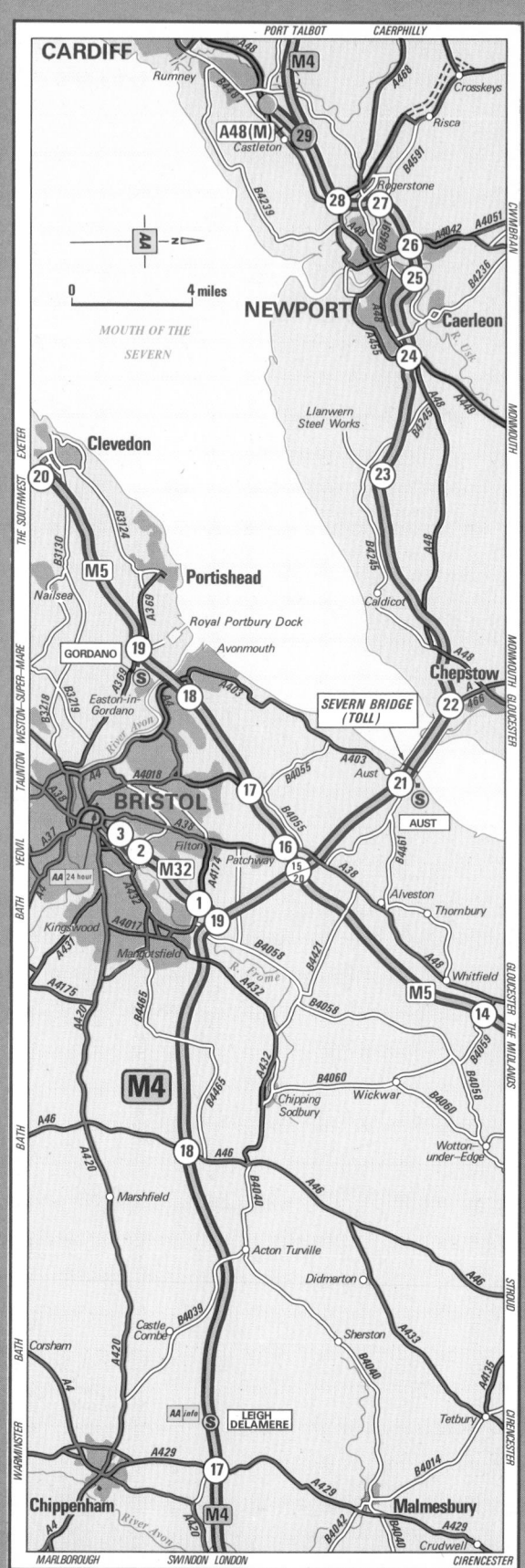

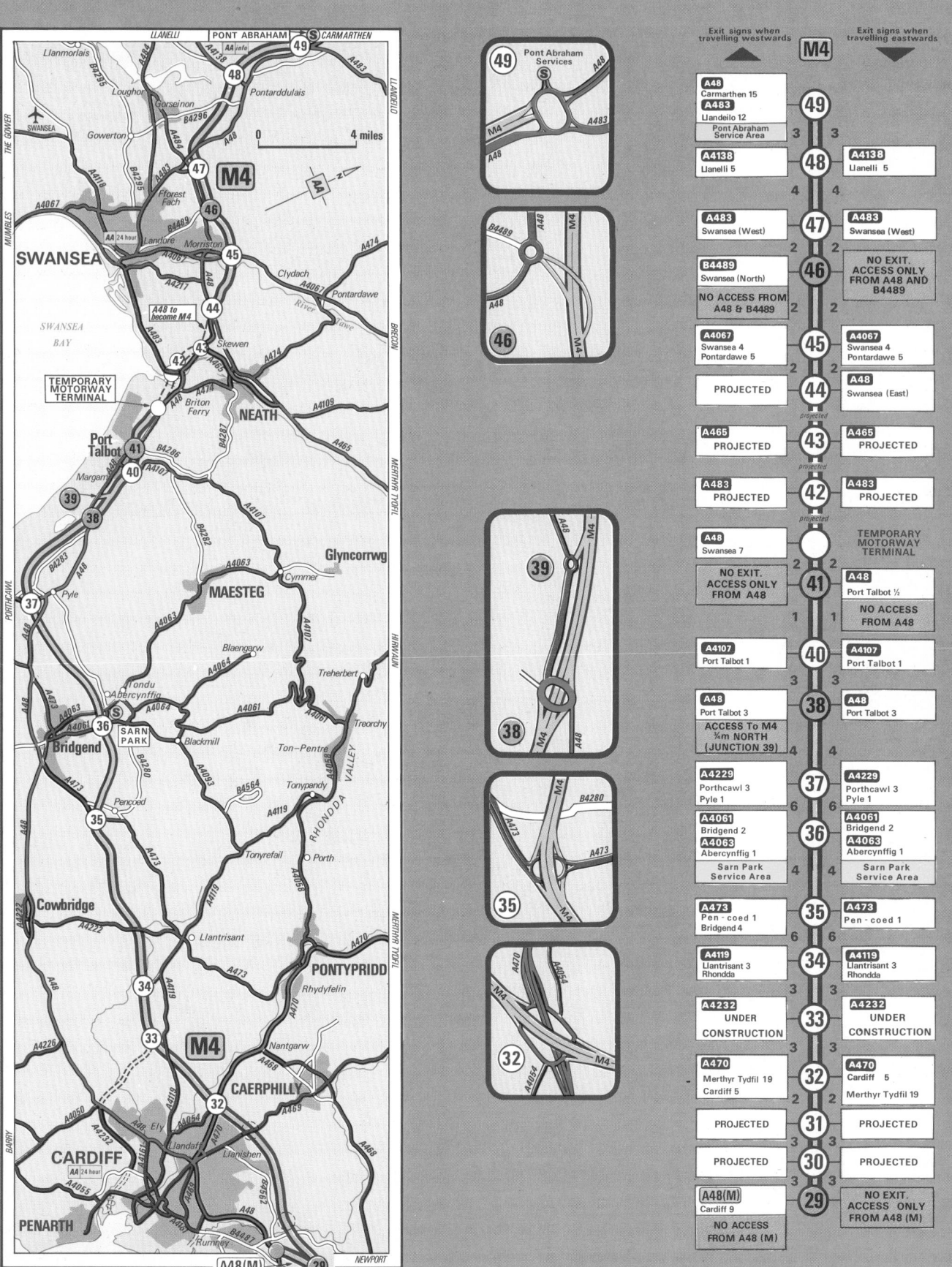

Exit signs when travelling westwards ▲ M4 Exit signs when travelling eastwards ▼

	Junction	
A48 Carmarthen 15 / **A483** Llandeilo 12 / Pont Abraham Service Area	49	
A4138 Llanelli 5	48	**A4138** Llanelli 5
A483 Swansea (West)	47	**A483** Swansea (West)
B4489 Swansea (North) NO ACCESS FROM A48 & B4489	46	NO EXIT. ACCESS ONLY FROM A48 AND B4489
A4067 Swansea 4 Pontardawe 5	45	**A4067** Swansea 4 Pontardawe 5
PROJECTED	44	**A48** Swansea (East)
A465 PROJECTED	43	**A465** PROJECTED
A483 PROJECTED	42	**A483** PROJECTED
A48 Swansea 7 NO EXIT. ACCESS ONLY FROM A48	TEMPORARY MOTORWAY TERMINAL / 41	**A48** Port Talbot ½ NO ACCESS FROM A48
A4107 Port Talbot 1	40	**A4107** Port Talbot 1
A48 Port Talbot 3 ACCESS To M4 ¾m NORTH (JUNCTION 39)	38	**A48** Port Talbot 3
A4229 Porthcawl 3 Pyle 1	37	**A4229** Porthcawl 3 Pyle 1
A4061 Bridgend 2 **A4063** Abercynffig 1 Sarn Park Service Area	36	**A4061** Bridgend 2 **A4063** Abercynffig 1 Sarn Park Service Area
A473 Pen-coed 1 Bridgend 4	35	**A473** Pen-coed 1
A4119 Llantrisant 3 Rhondda	34	**A4119** Llantrisant 3 Rhondda
A4232 UNDER CONSTRUCTION	33	**A4232** UNDER CONSTRUCTION
A470 Merthyr Tydfil 19 Cardiff 5	32	**A470** Cardiff 5 Merthyr Tydfil 19
PROJECTED	31	PROJECTED
PROJECTED	30	PROJECTED
A48(M) Cardiff 9 NO ACCESS FROM A48 (M)	29	NO EXIT. ACCESS ONLY FROM A48 (M)

129

BIRMINGHAM–CHELTENHAM M5   ROSS SPUR M50

Exit signs when travelling northwards ▲   M5   Exit signs when travelling southwards ▼

M6
London (M1) 120
Birmingham (NE,N)
The North West
Wolverhampton 10
Walsall 5
8

8

2   3

A41
Birmingham (NW)
West Bromwich 1
1
A41
Birmingham (NW)
West Bromwich 1

3   3

A4123
Dudley 3
Wolverhampton 6
2
A4123
Birmingham (West)
Dudley 3

3   3

A456
Birmingham
(West & Central)
3
A456
Kidderminster 11

1   1

Frankley
Service Area
All Services
S
Frankley
Service Area
All Services

4   4

A38
Birmingham (SW) 10
A491
Stourbridge 9
4
A38
Birmingham (SW) 10
Bromsgrove 3

7   7

A38
Bromsgrove 5
Droitwich 2
5
A38
Droitwich 2

6   6

A449
Kidderminster 15
Worcester (North) 4
6
A4538
Evesham 14
A449
Worcester (North) 4

3   3

A44
Worcester (South) 3
Evesham 13
7
A44
Evesham 13
Worcester (South) 3

8   8

Strensham
Service Area
All Services
S
Strensham
Service Area
All Services

1   1

M50
South Wales
Ross 23
8
M50
South Wales
Ross 23

4   4

A438
Evesham 11
Tewkesbury 2
9
A438
Evesham 11
Tewkesbury 2

5   5

NO EXIT.
ACCESS ONLY
FROM A4019
10
A4019
Cheltenham 4
NO ACCESS
FROM A4019

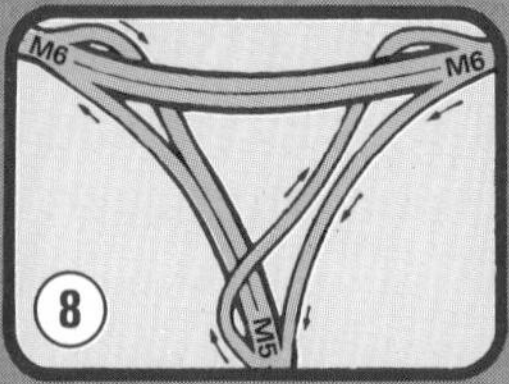

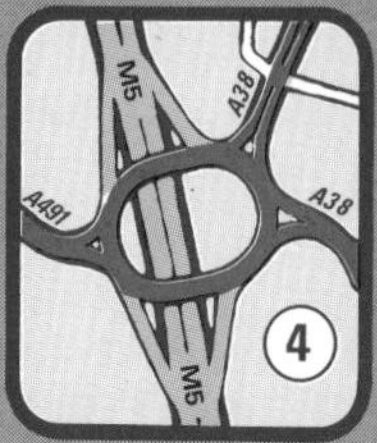

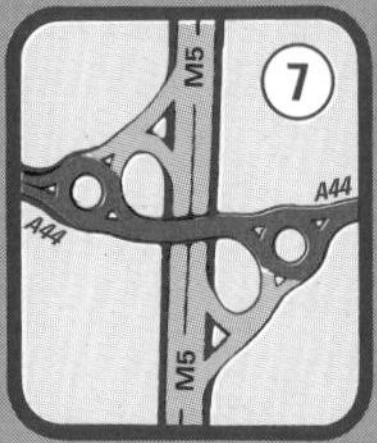

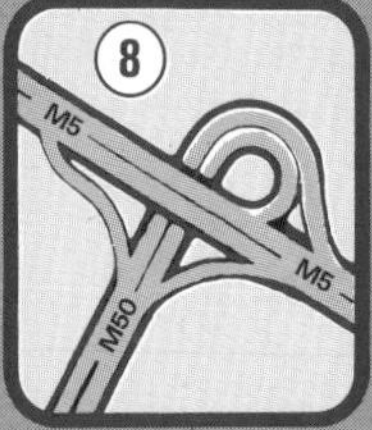

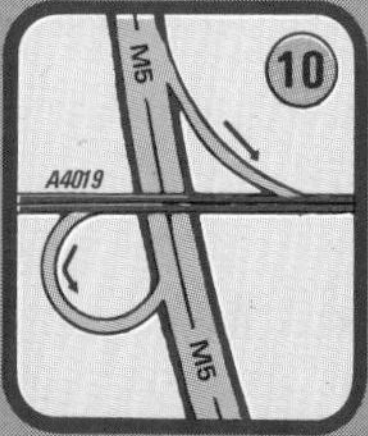

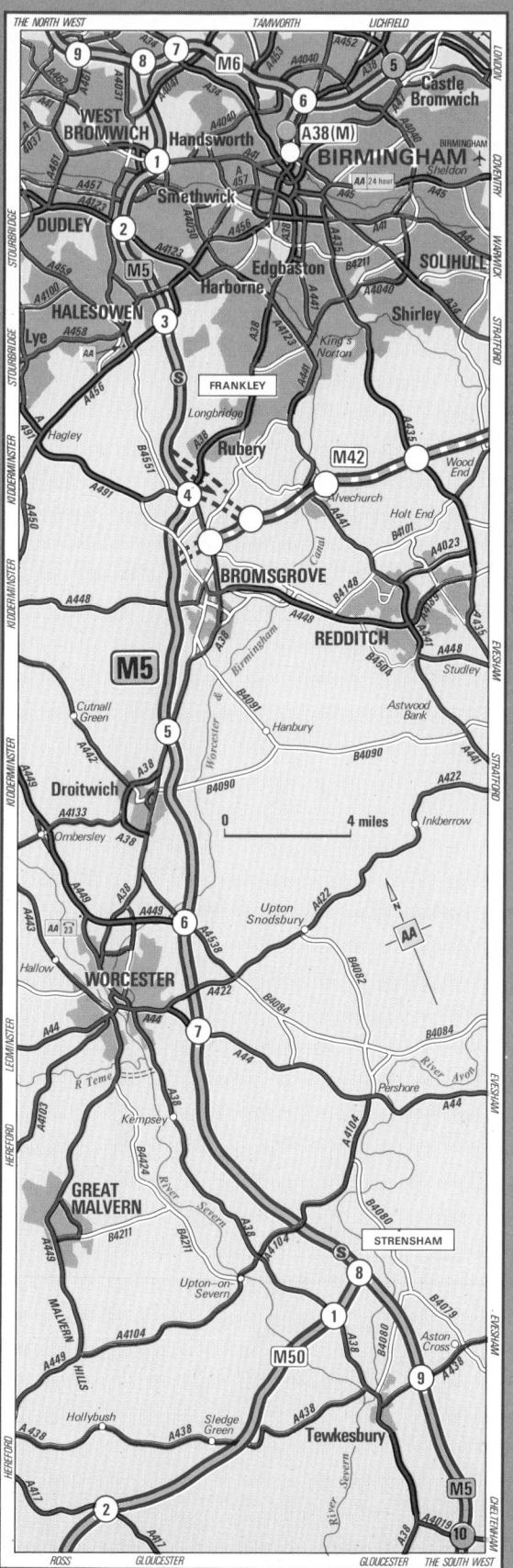

130

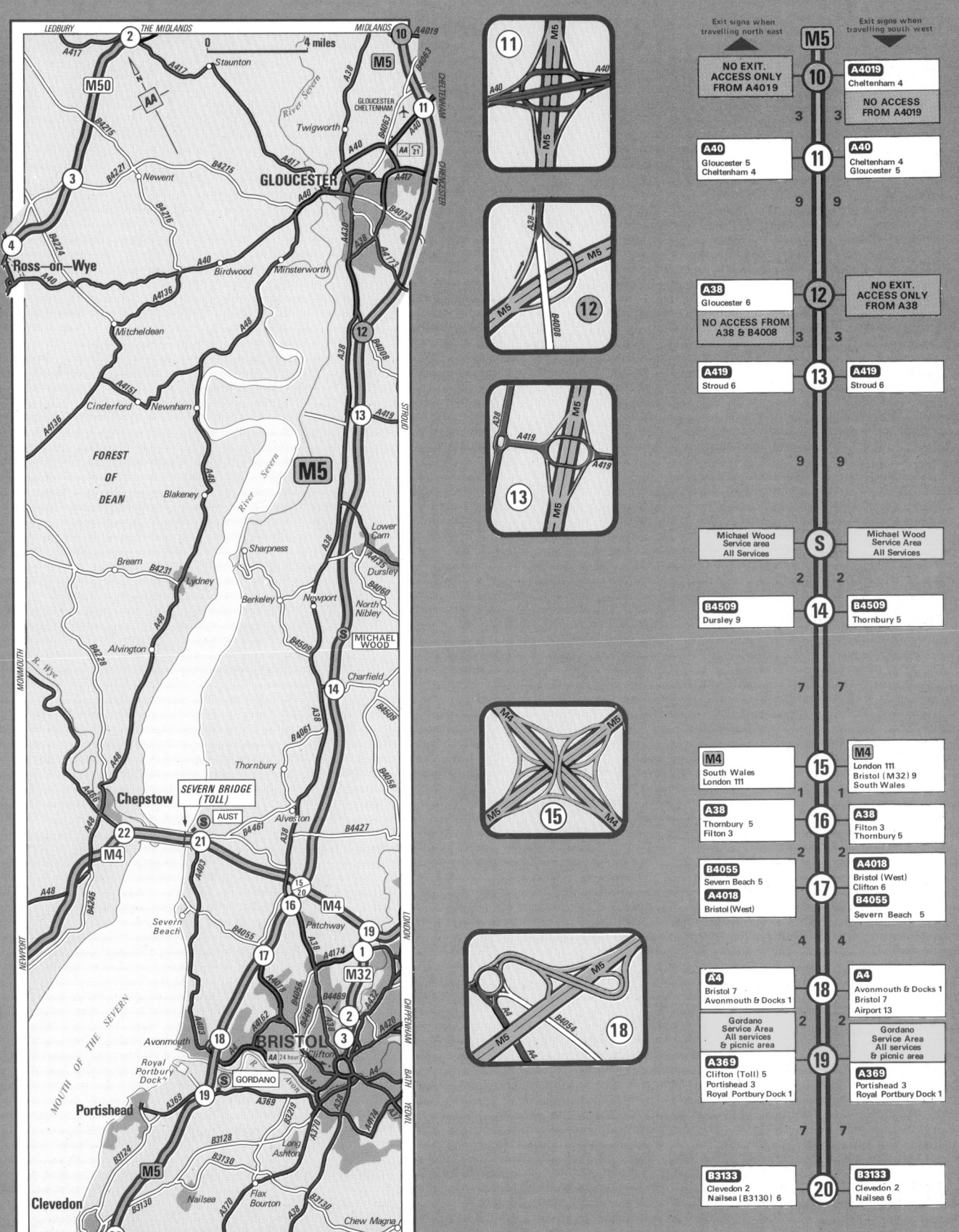

Map labels (left map):

LEDBURY · THE MIDLANDS · MIDLANDS · A4019
2 · THE MIDLANDS · 10
A417 · M50 · Staunton · A4063 · M5
A4221 · River Severn · Twigworth · GLOUCESTER CHELTENHAM
3 · Newent · B4215 · A417 · A40 · A38 · 11
A4216 · GLOUCESTER · A417 · AA 21
4 · A4224 · Ross-on-Wye · A40 · Birdwood · Minsterworth
A4136 · Mitcheldean · A48 · A38 · A4151 · Cinderford · Newnham · 12 · A4008
FOREST OF DEAN · A48 · River Severn · 13 · A419 · STROUD
Blakeney · M5 · Lower Cam
Bream · B4231 · Lydney · Sharpness · Dursley · A4135 · A4060
Berkeley · Newport · North Nibley
Alvington · A48 · B4509 · S · MICHAEL WOOD
MONMOUTH · R. Wye · Charfield · 14 · A38 · B4509
B4228 · A4061
Thornbury · B4058
Chepstow · SEVERN BRIDGE (TOLL) · Alveston · B4427
22 · 21 · S · AUST · B4461 · A38
M4 · A403 · 15 · 20 · M4 · 16
A48 · B4246 · B4055 · Patchway · 19
Severn Beach · 17 · A4174 · 1 · M32 · LONDON · CHIPPENHAM · BATH · YEOVIL
NEWPORT · A4078 · B4056 · B4469 · A432 · 2 · 3 · A420
18 · Avonmouth · BRISTOL · A4 · Clifton · AA 24 hour
Royal Portbury Dock · S · GORDANO · A4
MOUTH OF THE SEVERN · A369 · 19 · A369 · A4174
Portishead · B3124 · B3128 · B3130 · Long Ashton
M5 · Nailsea · A370 · Flax Bourton · B3130 · Chew Magna
Clevedon · B3130 · 20
THE SOUTH WEST · WESTON-S-MARE · TAUNTON

0 ———— 4 miles
N · AA

Junction diagrams:

11 · A40 · M5 · A40 · M5
12 · A38 · M5 · M5 · B4008
13 · A38 · M5 · A419 · A419 · M5
15 · M4 · M5 · M5 · M4
18 · M5 · A4 · M5 · B4054

Exit signs table:

Exit signs when travelling north east		Exit signs when travelling south west
	M5	
NO EXIT. ACCESS ONLY FROM A4019	10	**A4019** Cheltenham 4
		NO ACCESS FROM A4019
3		3
A40 Gloucester 5 Cheltenham 4	11	**A40** Cheltenham 4 Gloucester 5
9		2
A38 Gloucester 6	12	**NO EXIT. ACCESS ONLY FROM A38**
NO ACCESS FROM A38 & B4008 3		3
A419 Stroud 6	13	**A419** Stroud 6
9		9
Michael Wood Service area All Services	S	Michael Wood Service area All Services
2		2
B4509 Dursley 9	14	**B4509** Thornbury 5
7		7
M4 South Wales London 111	15	**M4** London 111 Bristol (M32) 9 South Wales
1		1
A38 Thornbury 5 Filton 3	16	**A38** Filton 3 Thornbury 5
2		2
B4055 Severn Beach 5 **A4018** Bristol (West)	17	**A4018** Bristol (West) Clifton 6 **B4055** Severn Beach 5
4		4
A4 Bristol 7 Avonmouth & Docks 1	18	**A4** Avonmouth & Docks 1 Bristol 7 Airport 13
2		2
Gordano Service Area All services & picnic area **A369** Clifton (Toll) 5 Portishead 3 Royal Portbury Dock 1	19	Gordano Service Area All services & picnic area **A369** Portishead 3 Royal Portbury Dock 1
7		7
B3133 Clevedon 2 Nailsea (B3130) 6	20	**B3133** Clevedon 2 Nailsea 6

131

CLEVEDON–WATERLOO CROSS M5

Exit signs when travelling north east ▲

Exit signs when travelling south west ▼

M5

20

B3133	B3133
Clevedon 2	Clevedon 2
Nailsea (B3130) 6	Nailsea 6

6   6

21

A370	A370
Weston-super-Mare 5	Weston-Super-Mare 5
Bristol South 17	

7   7

Brent Knoll (W)	Rest Area	Brent Knoll (E)
Rest Area		Rest Area

3   3

22

A38	A38
Weston-super-Mare 9	Highbridge 2
Burnham-on-Sea 3	Burnham-on-Sea 3
Bristol (South) 24	
Airport 17	

5   5

23

A38	A38
Highbridge 5	Bridgwater 4
(A39)	(A39)
Glastonbury 14	Glastonbury 14
Wells 20	Wells 20

5   5

24

A38	(A39)
Bridgwater 2	Minehead 28
Minehead 28	

7   7

25

A358	A358
Taunton 2	Taunton 2
Yeovil 24	Yeovil 24
	Barnstaple 52
	Honiton 20

5   5

S

Taunton Deane	Taunton Deane
Service Area	Service Area
All Services	All Services

2   2

26

A38	A38
Wellington 2	Wellington 2
Taunton 6	

8   8

27

A373	A373
Tiverton 7	Tiverton 7
Wellington 8	Barnstaple 40
	(B3181)
	Willand 3

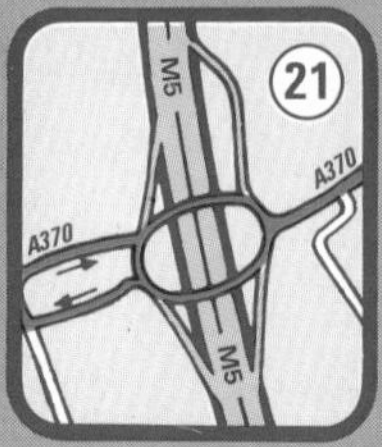

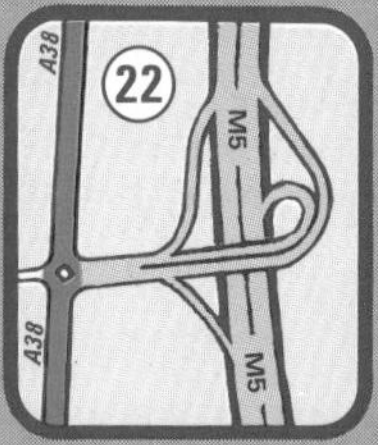

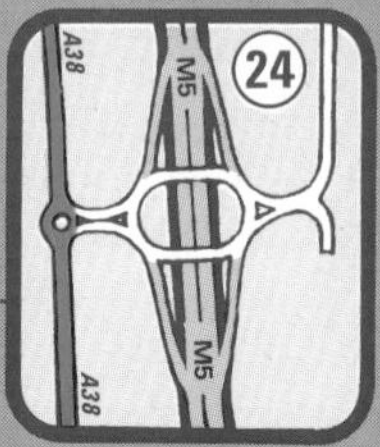

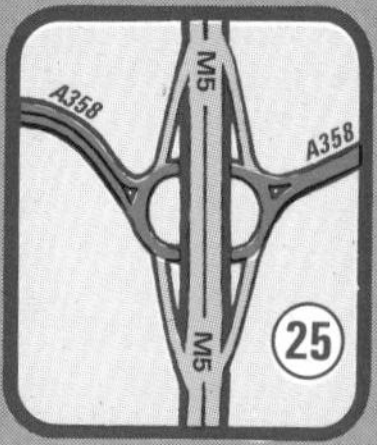

21

22

24

25

25

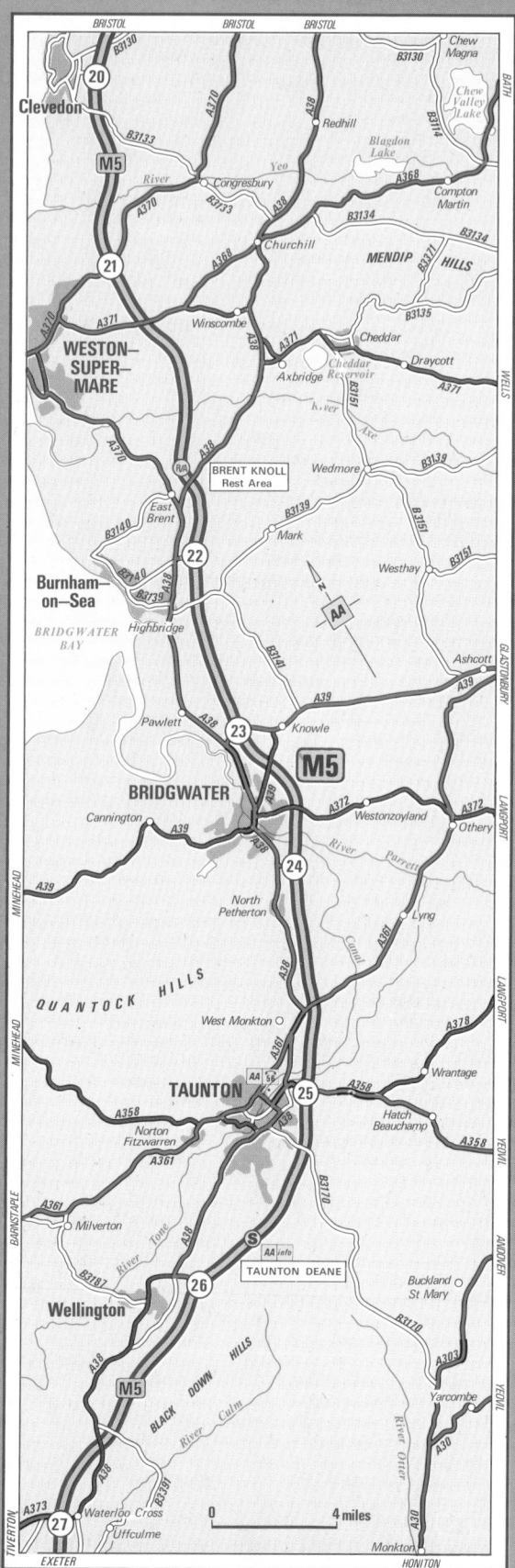

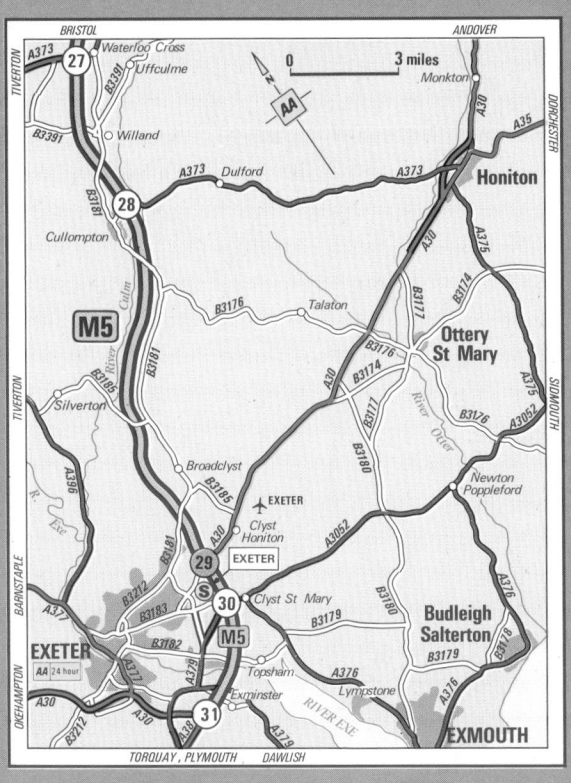

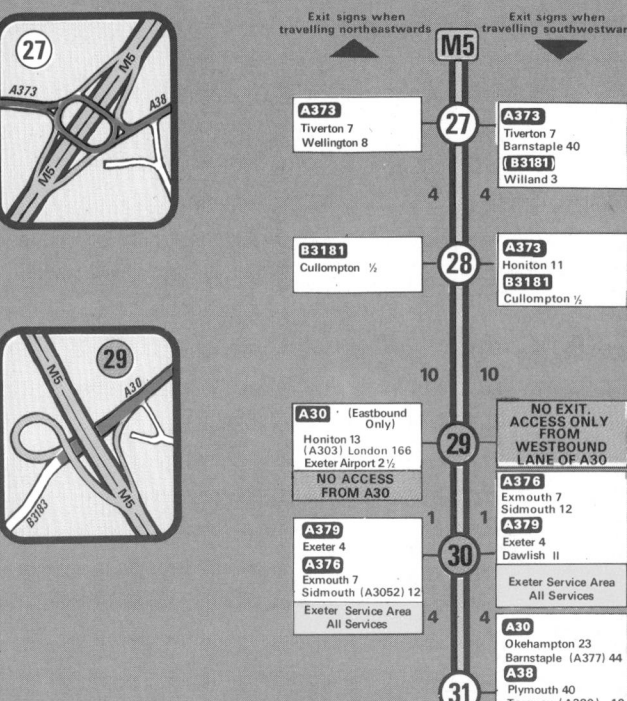

Exit signs when travelling northeastwards ▲ | M5 | ▼ Exit signs when travelling southwestwards

Exit signs when travelling northeastwards		Exit signs when travelling southwestwards
A373 Tiverton 7 Wellington 8	**27**	**A373** Tiverton 7 Barnstaple 40 **(B3181)** Willand 3
	4	
B3181 Cullompton ½	**28**	**A373** Honiton 11 **B3181** Cullompton ½
	10 10	
A30 (Eastbound Only) Honiton 13 (A303) London 166 Exeter Airport 2½ **NO ACCESS FROM A30**	**29**	**NO EXIT. ACCESS ONLY FROM WESTBOUND LANE OF A30** **A376** Exmouth 7 Sidmouth 12
	1 1	
A379 Exeter 4 **A376** Exmouth 7 Sidmouth (A3052) 12 Exeter Service Area All Services	**30**	**A379** Exeter 4 Dawlish 11 Exeter Service Area All Services
	4 4	
	31	**A30** Okehampton 23 Barnstaple (A377) 44 **A38** Plymouth 40 Torquay (A380) 19

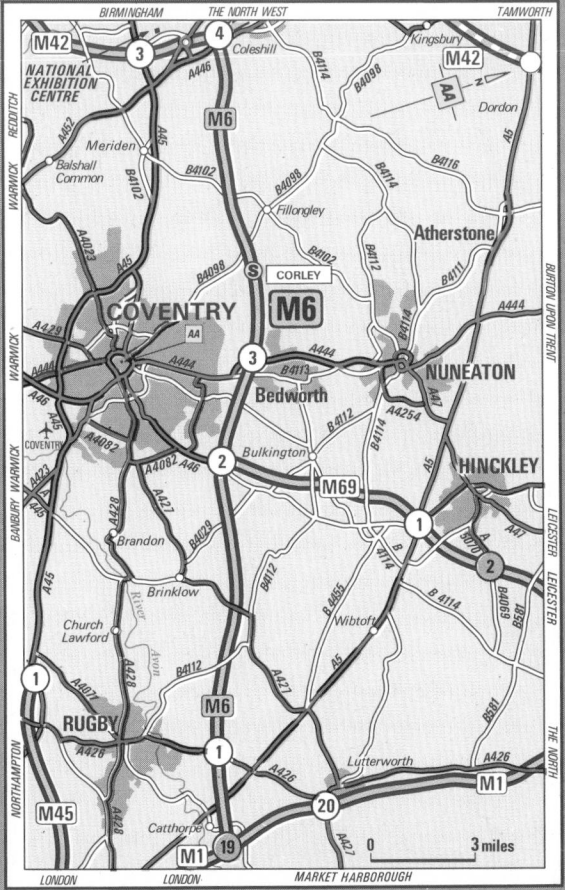

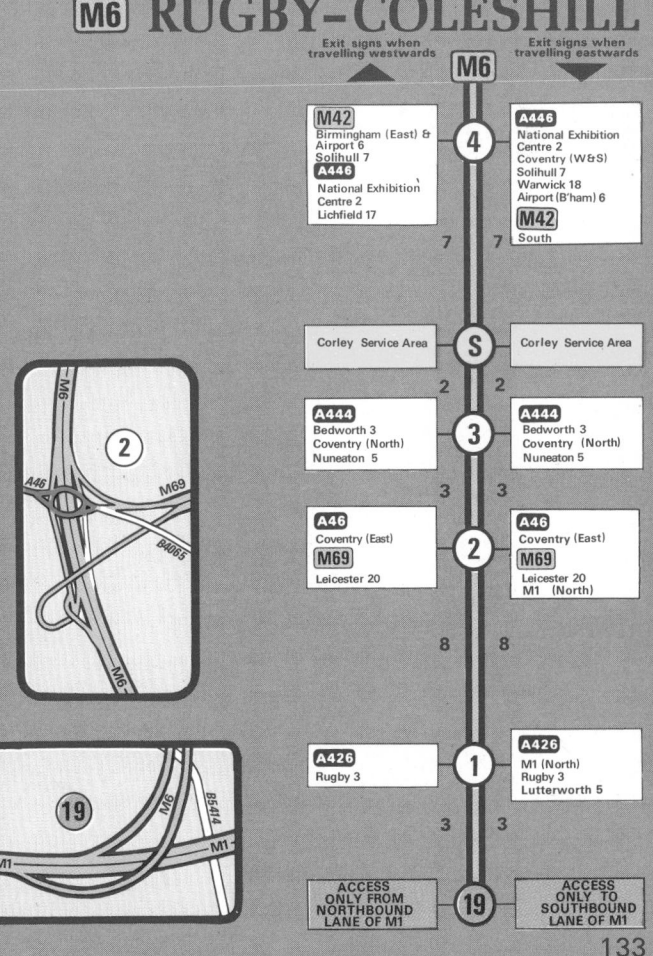

Exit signs when travelling westwards		Exit signs when travelling eastwards
M42 Birmingham (East) & Airport 6 Solihull 7 **A446** National Exhibition Centre 2 Lichfield 17	**4**	**A446** National Exhibition Centre 2 Coventry (W&S) Solihull 7 Warwick 18 Airport (B'ham) 6 **M42** South
	7 7	
Corley Service Area	**S**	Corley Service Area
	2 2	
A444 Bedworth 3 Coventry (North) Nuneaton 5	**3**	**A444** Bedworth 3 Coventry (North) Nuneaton 5
	3 3	
A46 Coventry (East) **M69** Leicester 20	**2**	**A46** Coventry (East) **M69** Leicester 20 M1 (North)
	8 8	
A426 Rugby 3	**1**	**A426** M1 (North) Rugby 3 Lutterworth 5
	3 3	
ACCESS ONLY FROM NORTHBOUND LANE OF M1	**19**	**ACCESS ONLY TO SOUTHBOUND LANE OF M1**

Exit signs when travelling westwards ▲

Exit signs when travelling eastwards ▼

M6

S — Keele Service Area | Keele Service Area

3 | 3

A500 Stoke (South) 3 Newcastle 2 — **15** — **A500** Stoke (South) 3 Stone 8 Eccleshall 10

11 | 11

A34 Eccleshall 6 Stone 6 Stafford ((North) 3 — **14** — **A34** Stafford (North) 3

5 | 5

A449 Stafford 3 — **13** — **A449** Stafford (South) 3

6 | 6

A5 Telford 16 — **12** — **A5** Telford 16 Cannock 4 Wolverhampton 9

3 | 3

A460 Cannock 3 — **11** — **A460** Wolverhampton 7

S — Hilton Park Service Area | Hilton Park Service Area

1 | 1

M54 North Wales Wolverhampton 6 Telford 18 **NO ACCESS FROM M54** — **10A** — **NO EXIT. ACCESS ONLY FROM M54**

4 | 4

A454 Walsall 2 Wolverhampton 5 — **10** — **A454** Walsall 2

A461 Wednesbury 2 — **9** — **A461** Wednesbury 2

3 | 3

M5 The South West Birmingham (NW. W & SW) West Bromwich 4 — **8** — **M5** The South West Birmingham (NW.W&SW) West Bromwich 4

1 | 1

A34 Birmingham (North) Walsall 4 — **7** — **A34** Birmingham (North & NE)

4 | 4

A38(M) Birmingham (Central) 3 **A38** Birmingham (NE) — **6** — **A38(M)** Birmingham (Central) 4 **A38** Birmingham (NE) Lichfield 14

3 | 3

A452 Birmingham (NE) Sutton Coldfield 5 **NO ACCESS FROM A452** — **5** — **NO EXIT. ACCESS ONLY FROM A452**

2 | 2

ACCESS FROM M42 UNDER CONSTRUCTION — ◯ — **M42** **UNDER CONSTRUCTION**

3 | 3

M42 Birmingham (East) & Airport 6 Solihull 7 **A446** National Exhibition Centre 2 Lichfield 17 — **4** — **A446** National Exhibition Centre 2 Coventry (W&S) Solihull 7 Warwick 18 Airport (B' ham) 6 **M42** South

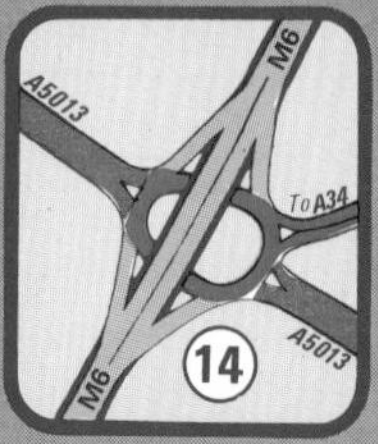

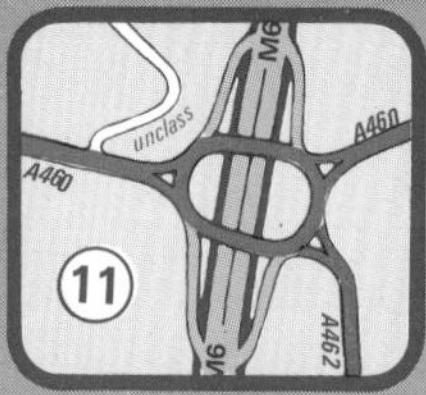

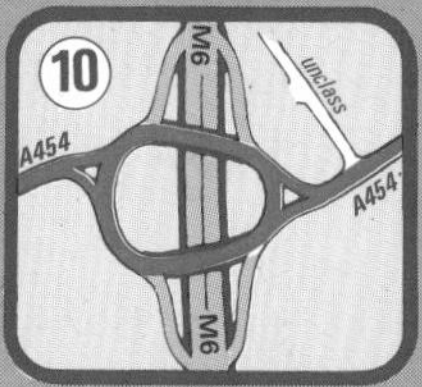

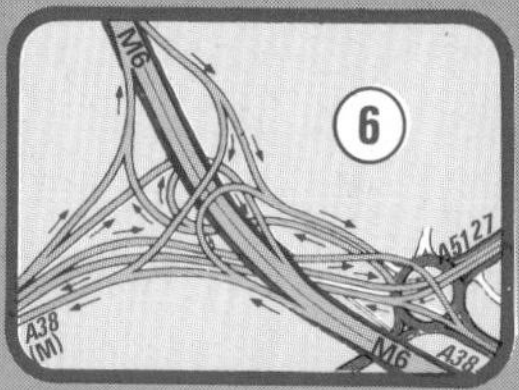

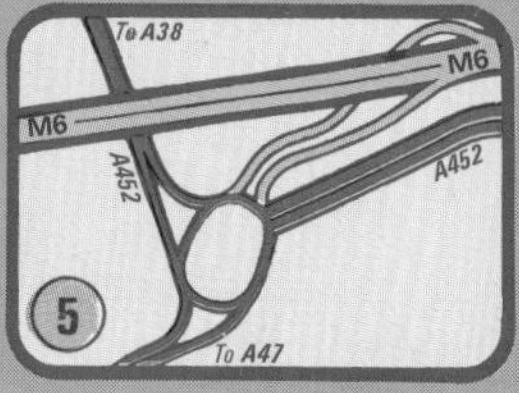

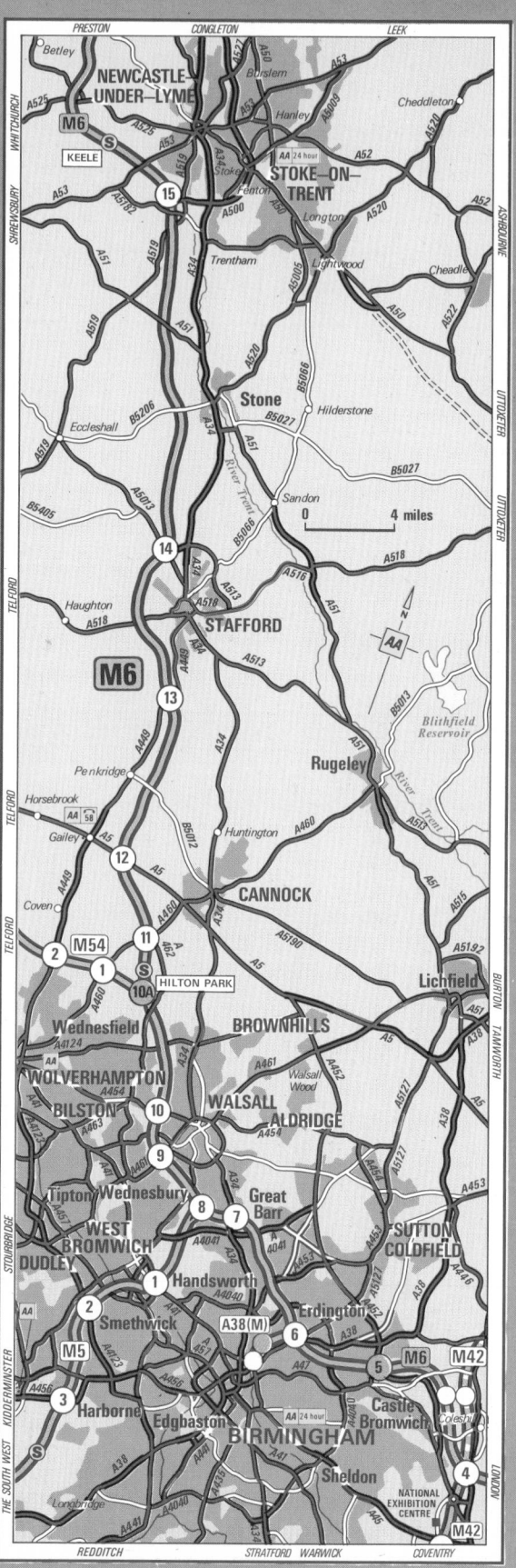

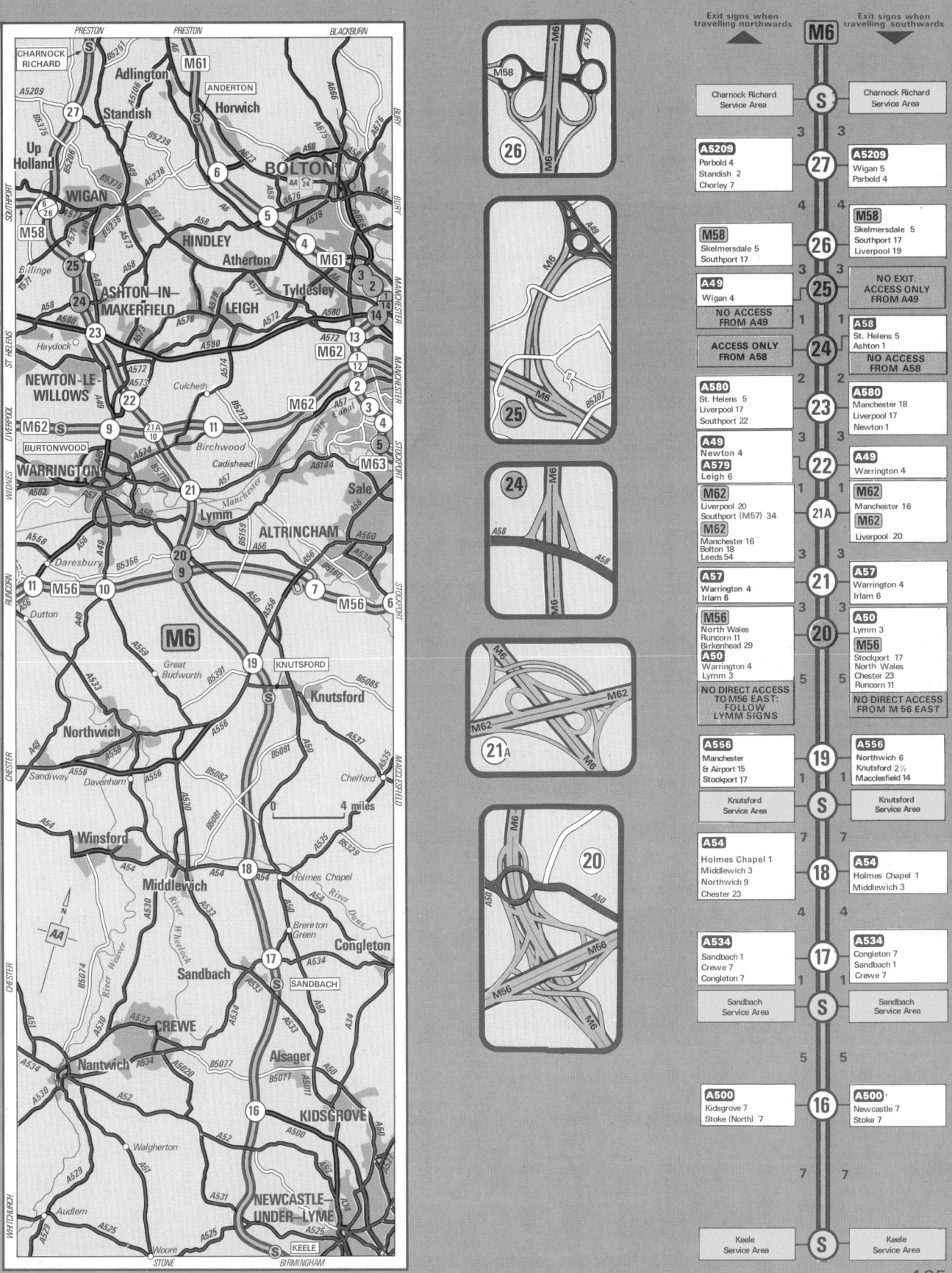

The following text appears along the right-hand strip diagram (exit signs):

Exit signs when travelling northwards ◄ **M6** ► **Exit signs when travelling southwards**

Northbound	Junction	Southbound
Charnock Richard Service Area	S	Charnock Richard Service Area
3		3
A5209 Parbold 4, Standish 2, Chorley 7	27	A5209 Wigan 5, Parbold 4
4		4
M58 Skelmersdale 5, Southport 17	26	M58 Skelmersdale 5, Southport 17, Liverpool 19
3		3
A49 Wigan 4 — NO ACCESS FROM A49	25	NO EXIT. ACCESS ONLY FROM A49
1		1
ACCESS ONLY FROM A58	24	A58 St. Helens 5, Ashton 1 — NO ACCESS FROM A58
2		2
A580 St. Helens 5, Liverpool 17, Southport 22	23	A580 Manchester 18, Liverpool 17, Newton 1
3		3
A49 Newton 4, A579 Leigh 6	22	A49 Warrington 4
1		1
M62 Liverpool 20, Southport (M57) 34; M62 Manchester 16, Bolton 18, Leeds 54	21A	M62 Manchester 16; M62 Liverpool 20
3		3
A57 Warrington 4, Irlam 6	21	A57 Warrington 4, Irlam 6
3		3
M56 North Wales, Runcorn 11, Birkenhead 29; A50 Warrington 4, Lymm 3 — NO DIRECT ACCESS TO M56 EAST: FOLLOW LYMM SIGNS	20	A50 Lymm 3; M56 Stockport 17, North Wales, Chester 23, Runcorn 11 — NO DIRECT ACCESS FROM M56 EAST
5		5
A556 Manchester & Airport 15, Stockport 17	19	A556 Northwich 6, Knutsford 2½, Macclesfield 14
1		1
Knutsford Service Area	S	Knutsford Service Area
7		7
A54 Holmes Chapel 1, Middlewich 3, Northwich 9, Chester 23	18	A54 Holmes Chapel 1, Middlewich 3
4		4
A534 Sandbach 1, Crewe 7, Congleton 7	17	A534 Congleton 7, Sandbach 1, Crewe 7
1		1
Sandbach Service Area	S	Sandbach Service Area
5		5
A500 Kidsgrove 7, Stoke (North) 7	16	A500 Newcastle 7, Stoke 7
7		7
Keele Service Area	S	Keele Service Area

Junction detail insets: 26, 25, 24, 21A, 20

Exit signs when travelling northwards ▲

Exit signs when travelling southwards ▼

M6

Northbound	Jct	Southbound
S NO ACCESS NORTHWARDS	**S**	Killington Lake Service Area Limited catering facilities
	7 / 7	
A591 South Lakes Kendal 8 Barrow 33 / **A65** Kirkby Lonsdale 7	**36**	**A65** Skipton 39 Kirkby Lonsdale 7 / **A591** Barrow 33
	4 / 4	
Burton Service Area Limited catering facilities	**S**	NO ACCESS SOUTHWARDS
	3 / 3	
A6 Carnforth 3 Morecambe 9	**35**	**A6** Carnforth 3 Morecambe 9
	4 / 4	
A683 Lancaster 2 Kirkby Lonsdale 15 Morecambe 6	**34**	**A683** Lancaster 2
	6 / 6	
A6 Lancaster (South) 5	**33**	**A6** Fleetwood 25 Garstang 6
	2 / 2	
Forton Service Area	**S**	Forton Service Area
	11 / 11	
M55 Blackpool 16 Fleetwood 20 / **A6** Garstang 9	**32**	**M55** Blackpool 16 / **A6** Preston 4
	4 / 4	
A59 Preston 3 Blackburn 7 Clitheroe 15	**31**	**A59** Preston 3 Blackburn 7
	2 / 2	
NO EXIT ACCESS ONLY FROM M61	**30**	**M61** Leeds 62 Bolton 18 Manchester 28 / NO ACCESS FROM M61
	1 / 1	
A6 Preston 4 Lytham St Annes 19	**29**	**A6** Chorley 5 Manchester 27
	2 / 2	
B5256 Leyland 1	**28**	**B5256** Leyland 2
	5 / 5	
Charnock Richard Service Area All Services & Motel	**S**	Charnock Richard Service Area All Services & Motel

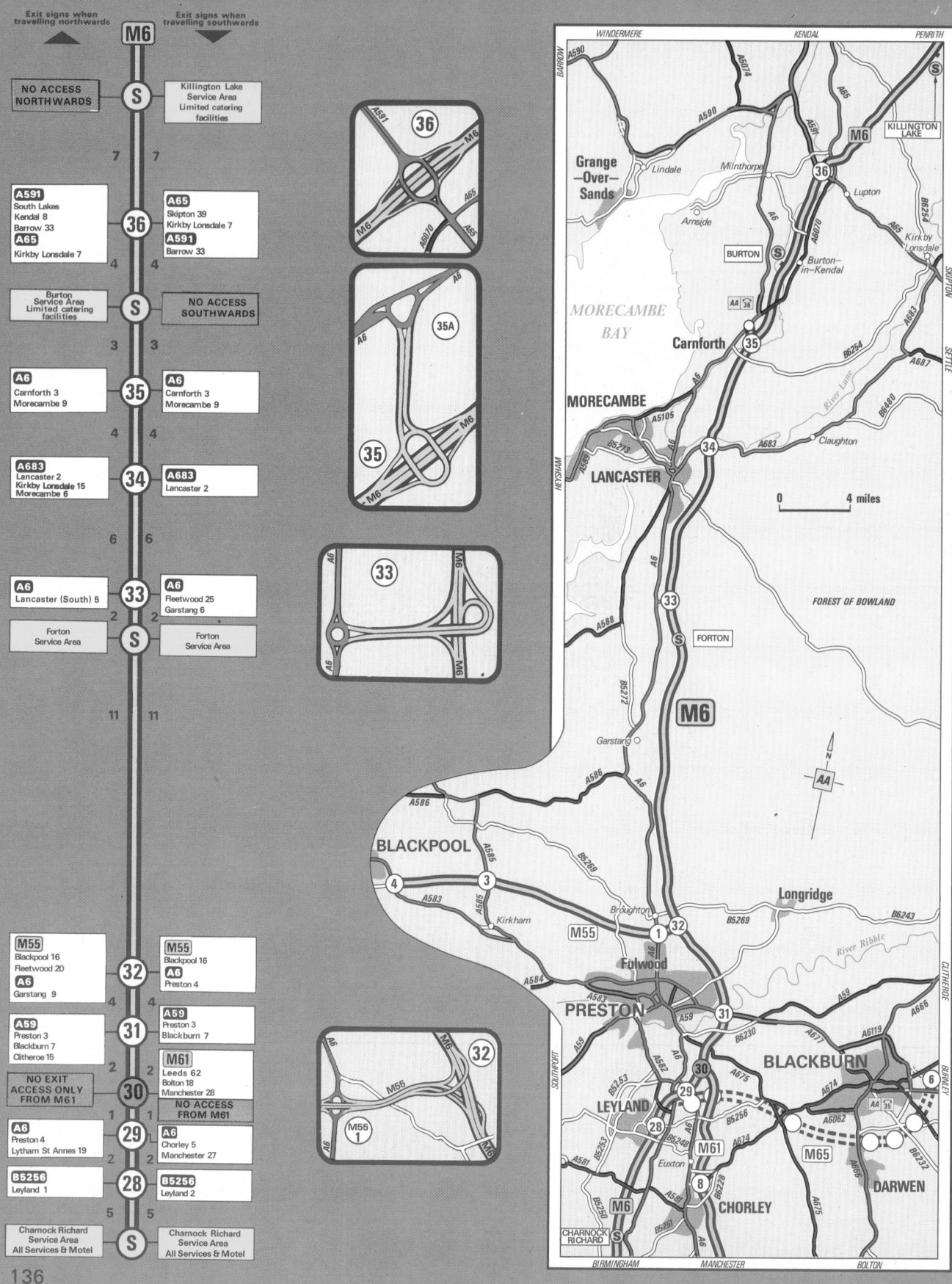

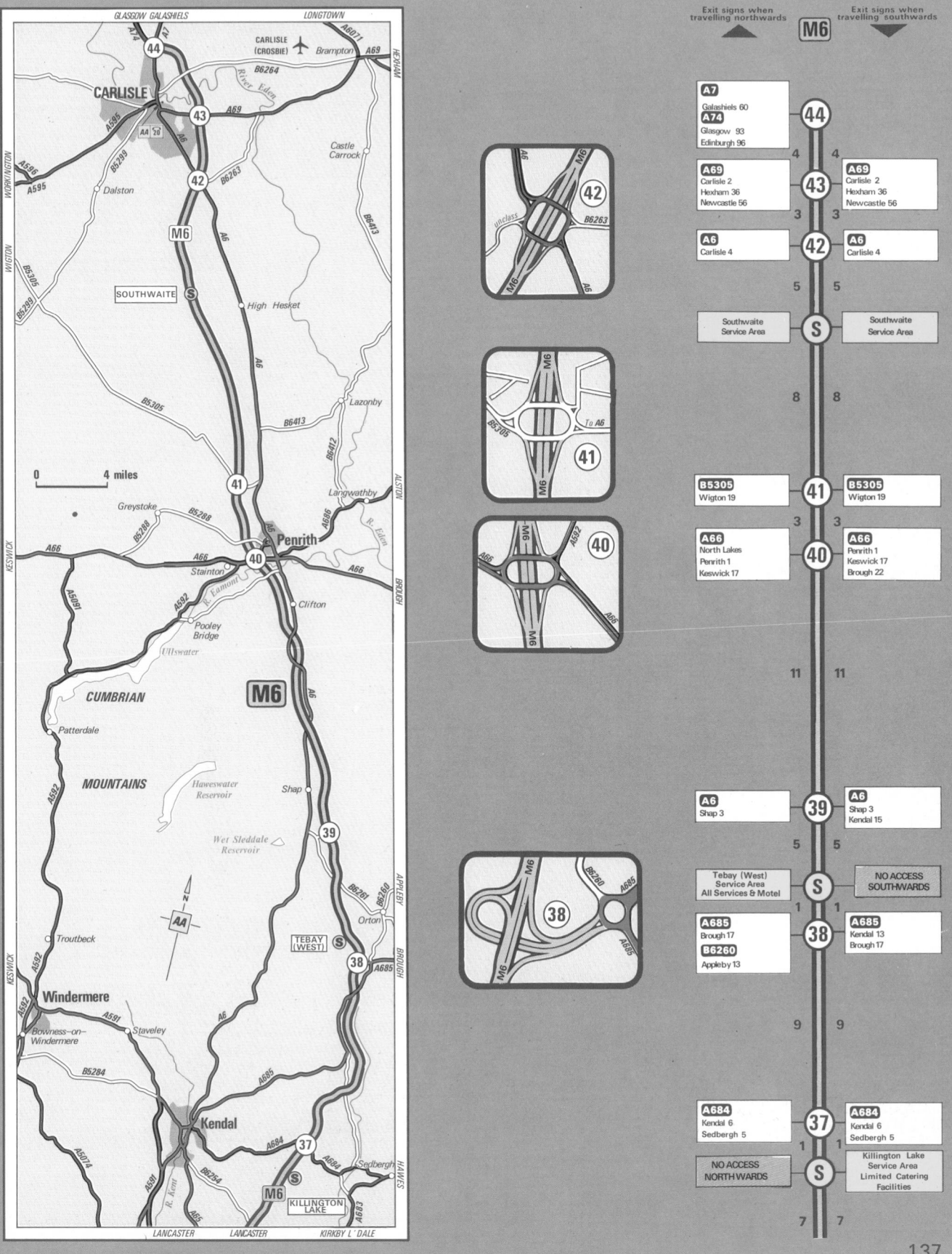

Exit signs when travelling northwards

Exit signs when travelling southwards

M6

A7 Galashiels 60 A74 Glasgow 93 Edinburgh 96	44	
4		4
A69 Carlisle 2 Hexham 36 Newcastle 56	43	A69 Carlisle 2 Hexham 36 Newcastle 56
3		3
A6 Carlisle 4	42	A6 Carlisle 4
5		5
Southwaite Service Area	S	Southwaite Service Area
8		8
B5305 Wigton 19	41	B5305 Wigton 19
3		3
A66 North Lakes Penrith 1 Keswick 17	40	A66 Penrith 1 Keswick 17 Brough 22
11		11
A6 Shap 3	39	A6 Shap 3 Kendal 15
5		5
Tebay (West) Service Area All Services & Motel	S	NO ACCESS SOUTHWARDS
1		1
A685 Brough 17 B6260 Appleby 13	38	A685 Kendal 13 Brough 17
9		9
A684 Kendal 6 Sedbergh 5	37	A684 Kendal 6 Sedbergh 5
1		1
NO ACCESS NORTHWARDS	S	Killington Lake Service Area Limited Catering Facilities
7		7

137

LONDON ORBITAL MOTORWAY M25

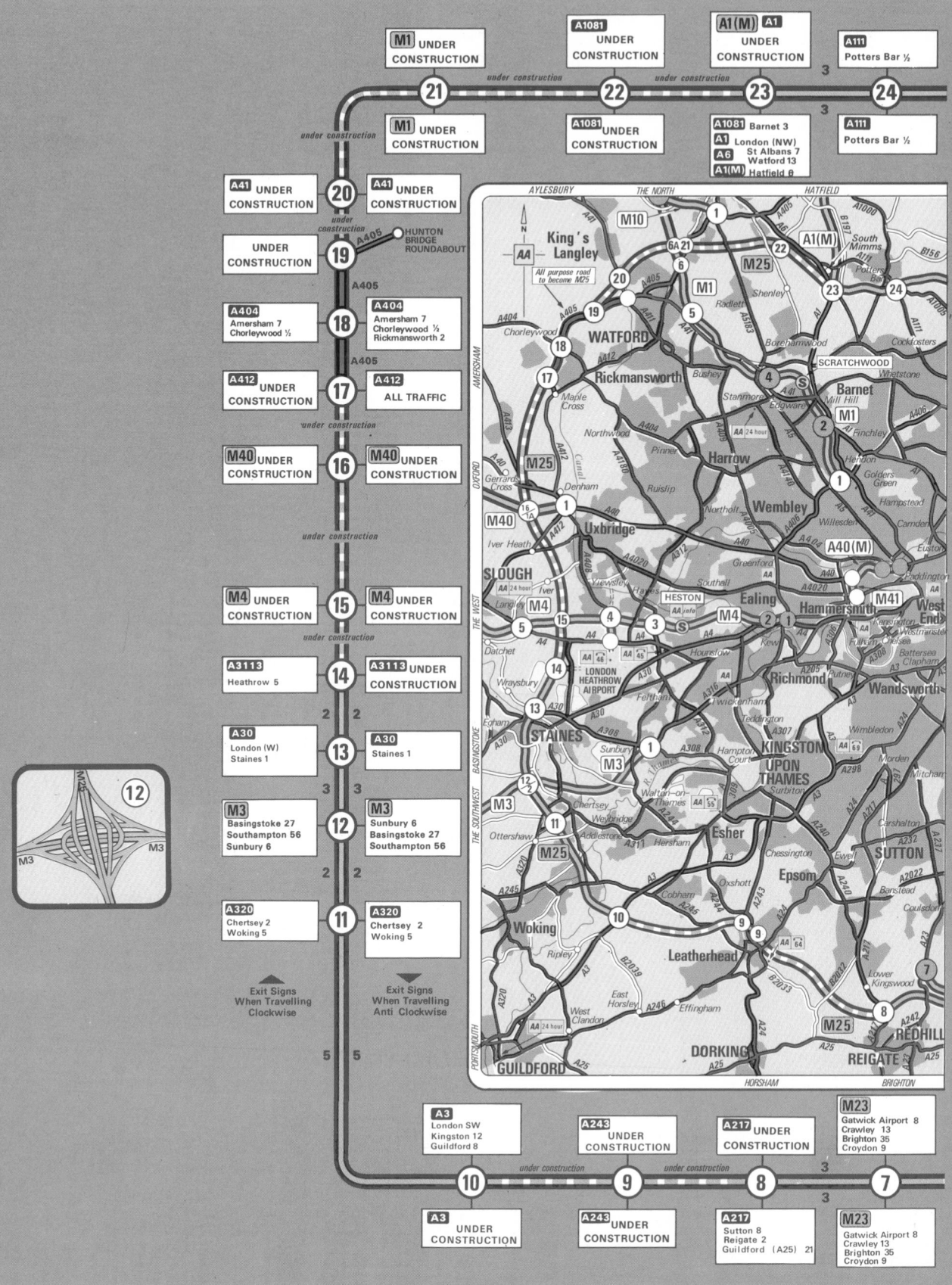

M1 UNDER CONSTRUCTION

A1081 UNDER CONSTRUCTION

A1(M) **A1** UNDER CONSTRUCTION

A111 Potters Bar ½

(21) under construction (22) under construction (23) (24)

M1 UNDER CONSTRUCTION

A1081 UNDER CONSTRUCTION

A1081 Barnet 3
A1 London (NW)
A6 St Albans 7
Watford 13
A1(M) Hatfield θ

A111 Potters Bar ½

A41 UNDER CONSTRUCTION

(20) **A41** UNDER CONSTRUCTION

UNDER CONSTRUCTION   (19) HUNTON BRIDGE ROUNDABOUT

A405

A404 Amersham 7
Chorleywood ½

(18) **A404** Amersham 7
Chorleywood ½
Rickmansworth 2

A405

A412 UNDER CONSTRUCTION

(17) **A412** ALL TRAFFIC

M40 UNDER CONSTRUCTION

(16) **M40** UNDER CONSTRUCTION

M4 UNDER CONSTRUCTION

(15) **M4** UNDER CONSTRUCTION

A3113 Heathrow 5

(14) **A3113** UNDER CONSTRUCTION

A30 London (W)
Staines 1

(13) **A30** Staines 1

M3 Basingstoke 27
Southampton 56
Sunbury 6

(12) **M3** Sunbury 6
Basingstoke 27
Southampton 56

A320 Chertsey 2
Woking 5

(11) **A320** Chertsey 2
Woking 5

Exit Signs When Travelling Clockwise

Exit Signs When Travelling Anti Clockwise

(12) M25 / M3 / M3

A3 London SW
Kingston 12
Guildford 8

A243 UNDER CONSTRUCTION

A217 UNDER CONSTRUCTION

M23 Gatwick Airport 8
Crawley 13
Brighton 35
Croydon 9

(10) under construction (9) under construction (8) (7)

A3 UNDER CONSTRUCTION

A243 UNDER CONSTRUCTION

A217 Sutton 8
Reigate 2
Guildford (A25) 21

M23 Gatwick Airport 8
Crawley 13
Brighton 35
Croydon 9

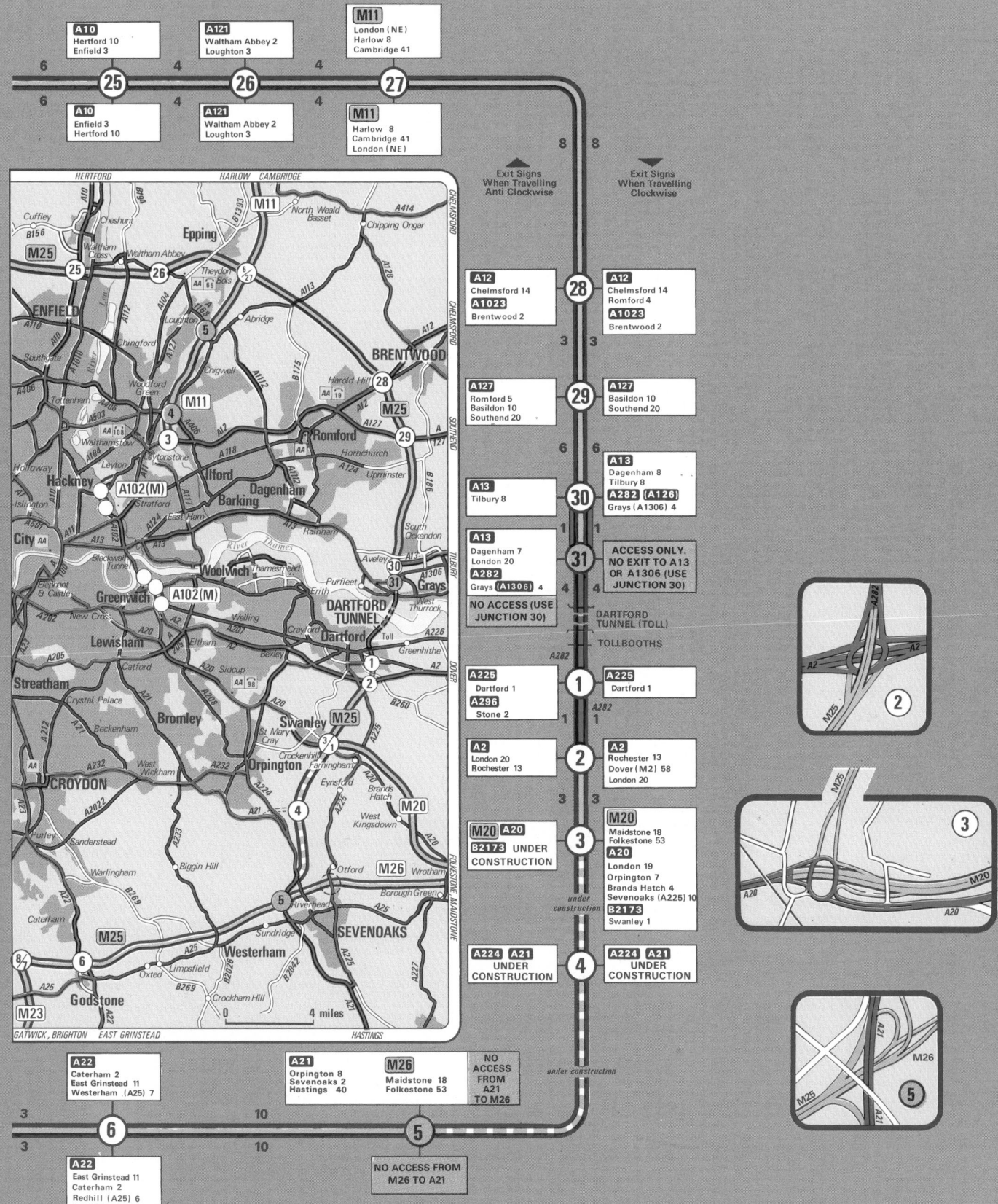

A10
Hertford 10
Enfield 3

6   **25**   4

A121
Waltham Abbey 2
Loughton 3

26   4

M11
London (NE)
Harlow 8
Cambridge 41

27

A10
Enfield 3
Hertford 10

6   4

A121
Waltham Abbey 2
Loughton 3

4

M11
Harlow 8
Cambridge 41
London (NE)

Exit Signs
When Travelling
Anti Clockwise

8   8

Exit Signs
When Travelling
Clockwise

A12
Chelmsford 14
A1023
Brentwood 2

28

A12
Chelmsford 14
Romford 4
A1023
Brentwood 2

3   3

A127
Romford 5
Basildon 10
Southend 20

29

A127
Basildon 10
Southend 20

6   6

A13
Dagenham 8
Tilbury 8
A282 (A126)
Grays (A1306) 4

A13
Tilbury 8

30

1   1

A13
Dagenham 7
London 20
A282
Grays (A1306) 4

NO ACCESS (USE
JUNCTION 30)

31

ACCESS ONLY.
NO EXIT TO A13
OR A1306 (USE
JUNCTION 30)

DARTFORD
TUNNEL (TOLL)

TOLLBOOTHS

A282

A225
Dartford 1
A296
Stone 2

1

A225
Dartford 1

A282

1   1

A2
London 20
Rochester 13

2

A2
Rochester 13
Dover (M2) 58
London 20

3   3

M20 A20
B2173 UNDER
CONSTRUCTION

3

M20
Maidstone 18
Folkestone 53
A20
London 19
Orpington 7
Brands Hatch 4
Sevenoaks (A225) 10
B2173
Swanley 1

under
construction

A224 A21
UNDER
CONSTRUCTION

4

A224 A21
UNDER
CONSTRUCTION

under construction

A22
Caterham 2
East Grinstead 11
Westerham (A25) 7

3   10

6

A21
Orpington 8
Sevenoaks 2
Hastings 40

M26
Maidstone 18
Folkestone 53

NO
ACCESS
FROM
A21
TO M26

10

5

3   10

A22
East Grinstead 11
Caterham 2
Redhill (A25) 6

NO ACCESS FROM
M26 TO A21

139

CADNAM–PORTSMOUTH M27

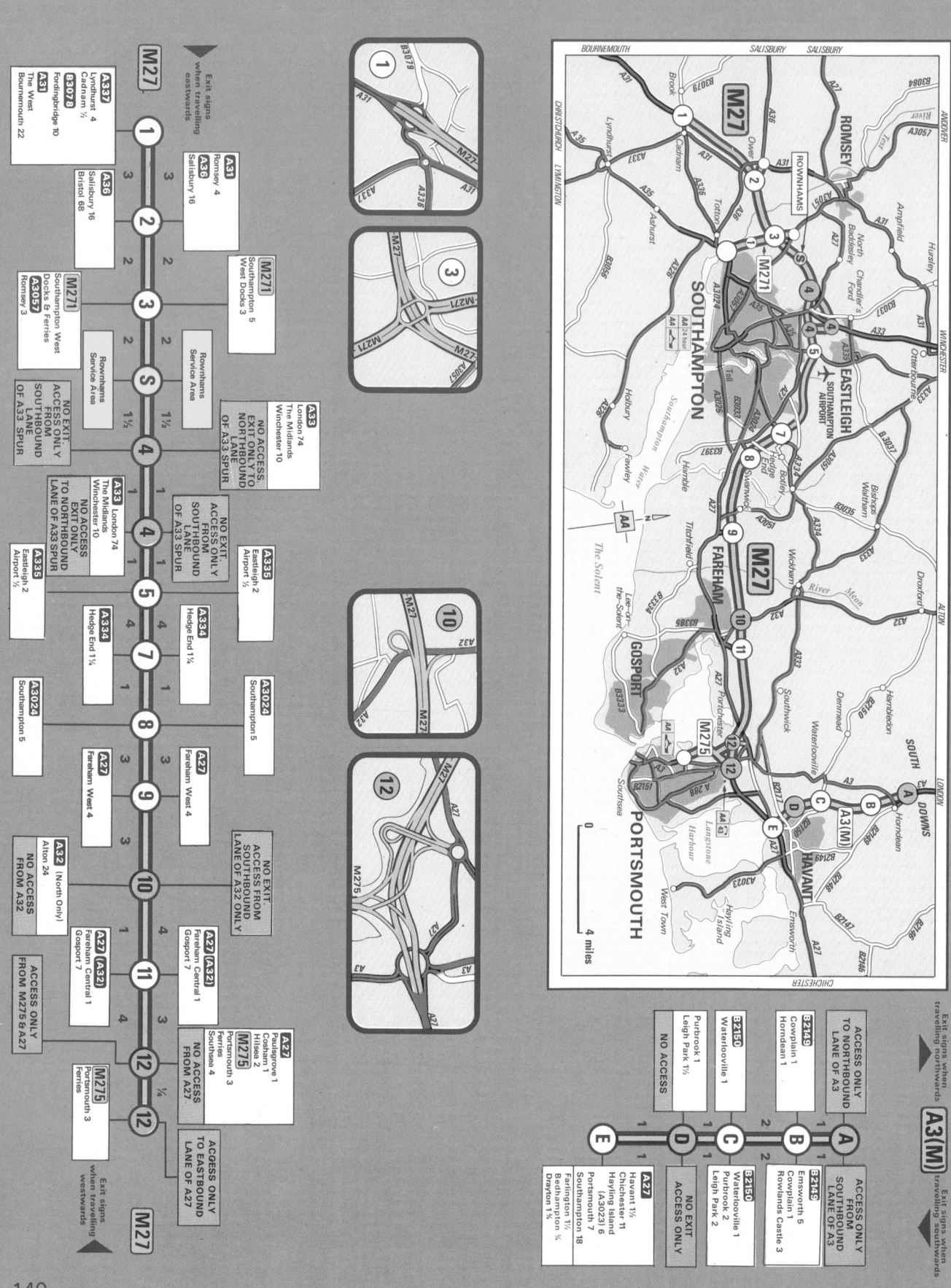

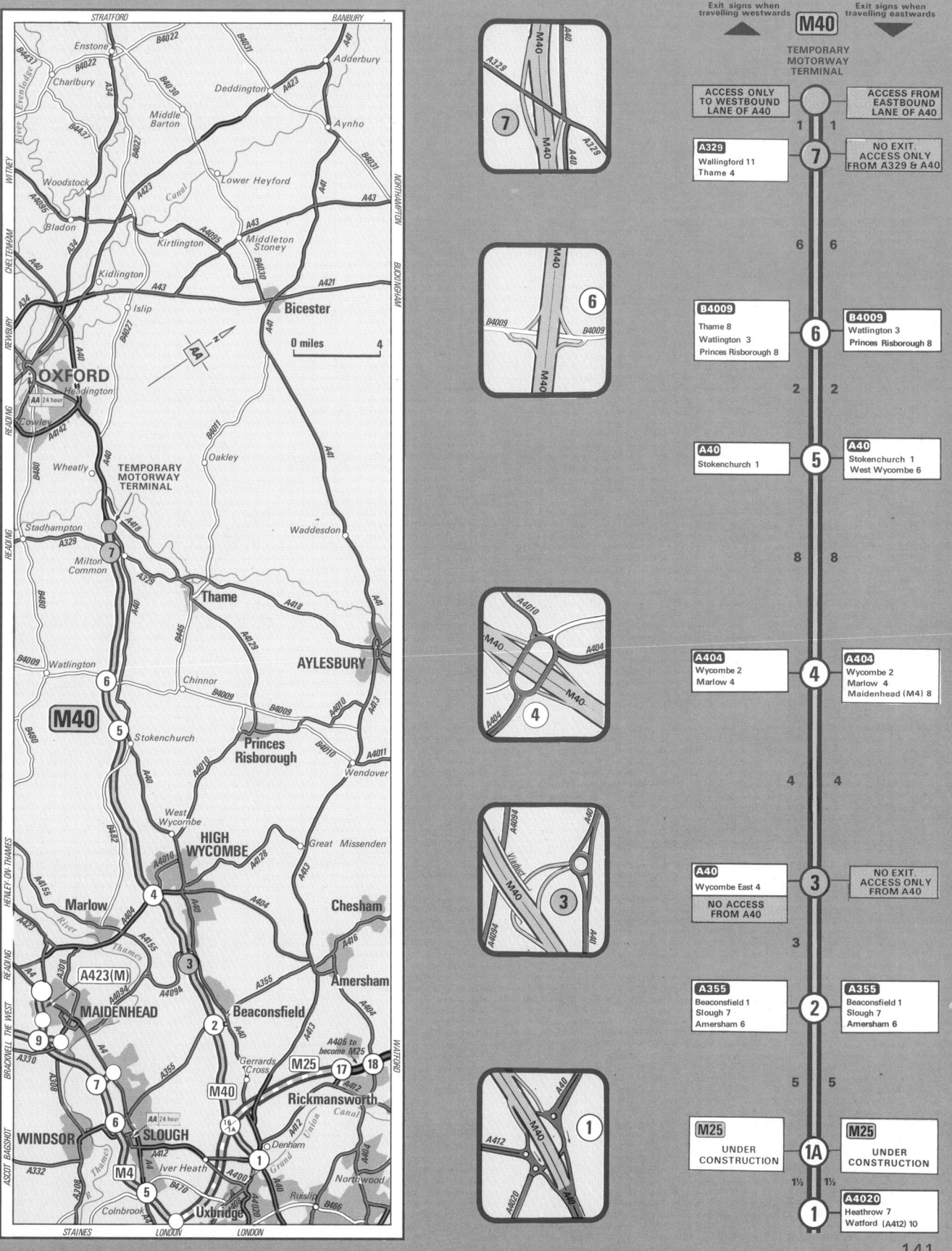

Exit signs when travelling northwards M42 Exit signs when travelling southwards

A453 A444
UNDER CONSTRUCTION

under construction

A5 UNDER CONSTRUCTION

A5 UNDER CONSTRUCTION

under construction

A446 A4097 UNDER CONSTRUCTION

A446 A4097 UNDER CONSTRUCTION

under construction

ACCESS FROM M6 UNDER CONSTRUCTION

M6 UNDER CONSTRUCTION

under construction

M6
The North West
Birmingham (North & Central)
Coventry 15
London (M1) 108
NO EXIT TO A446

4

ACCESS ONLY FROM M6 & A446

2   2

A45
National Exhibition Centre 1
Birmingham (E)
Airport (B'ham) 2
Coventry (S) 9
Lichfield (A446) 20

3

A45
National Exhibition Centre 1
Birmingham (E)
Airport (B'ham) 2
Coventry (S) 9

4   4

A41
Solihull 2
Warwick 12

2

A41
Warwick 12
Solihull 2

2   2

A34 UNDER CONSTRUCTION

1

A34
Redditch 12
Stratford 14

under construction

M40 PROJECTED

M40 PROJECTED

under construction

under construction

A435 UNDER CONSTRUCTION

A435 UNDER CONSTRUCTION

under construction

A441 UNDER CONSTRUCTION

A441 UNDER CONSTRUCTION

under construction

PROJECTED

PROJECTED

under construction

UNDER CONSTRUCTION

A38 UNDER CONSTRUCTION

Projected

M5 PROJECTED

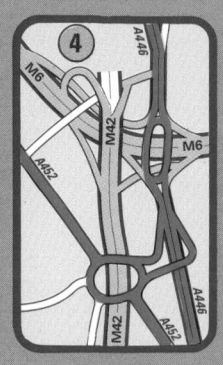

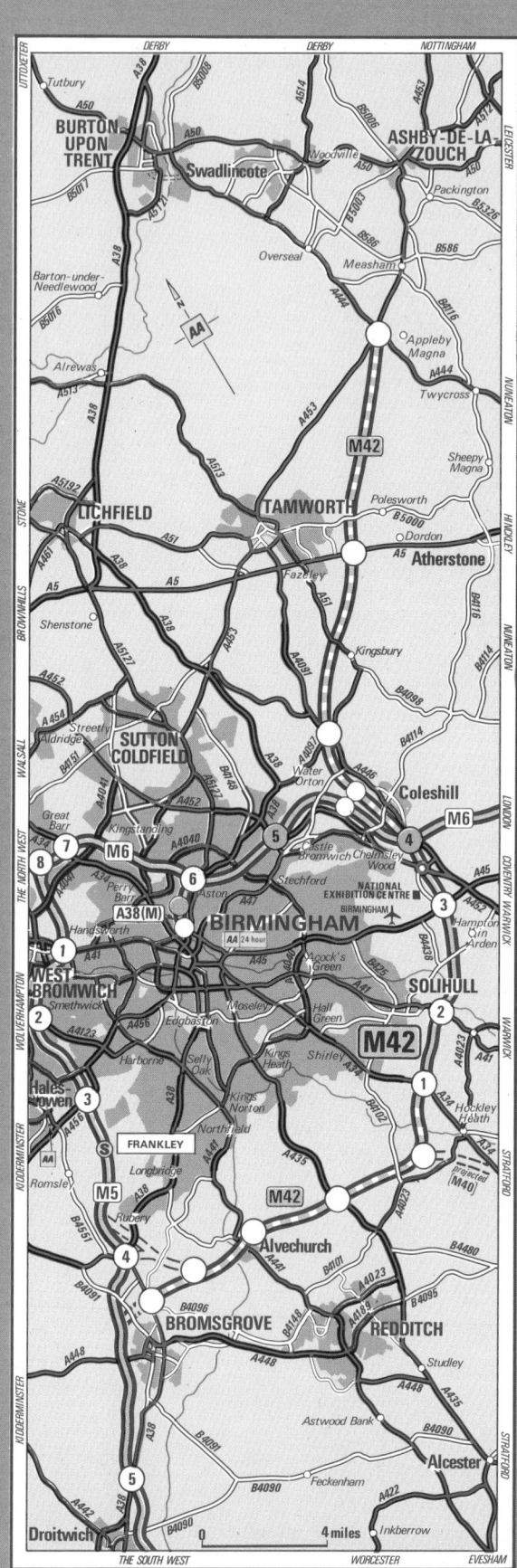

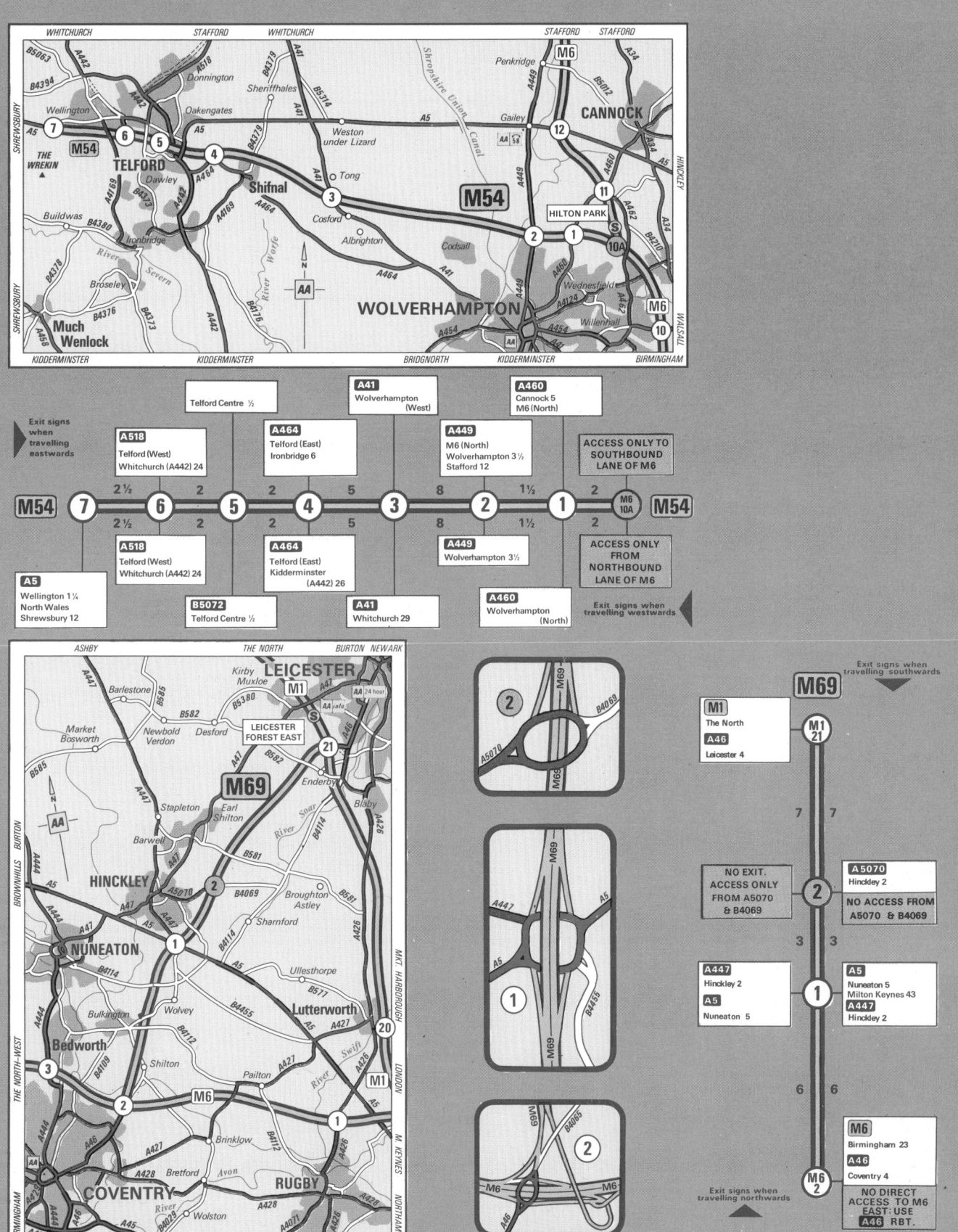

LIVERPOOL–HUDDERSFIELD M62

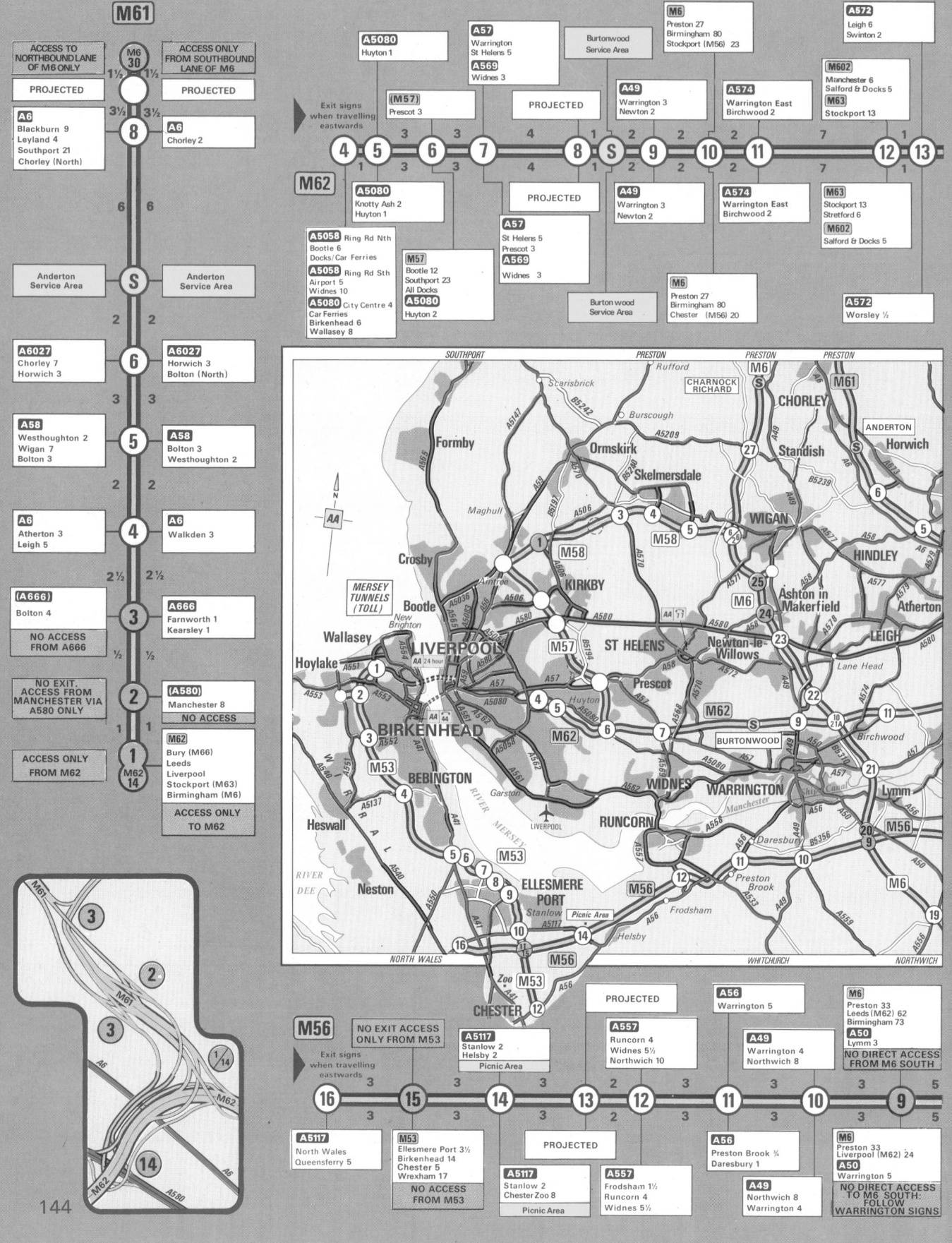

M61

ACCESS TO NORTHBOUND LANE OF M6 ONLY
PROJECTED

ACCESS ONLY FROM SOUTHBOUND LANE OF M6
PROJECTED

M6 30
1½   1½

8
3½   3½

A6
Blackburn 9
Leyland 4
Southport 21
Chorley (North)

A6
Chorley 2

6   6

Anderton Service Area

S

Anderton Service Area

2   2

A6027
Chorley 7
Horwich 3

6

A6027
Horwich 3
Bolton (North)

3   3

A58
Westhoughton 2
Wigan 7
Bolton 3

5

A58
Bolton 3
Westhoughton 2

2   2

A6
Atherton 3
Leigh 5

4

A6
Walkden 3

2½   2½

(A666)
Bolton 4

NO ACCESS FROM A666

3

A666
Farnworth 1
Kearsley 1

½   ½

NO EXIT. ACCESS FROM MANCHESTER VIA A580 ONLY

2

(A580)
Manchester 8
NO ACCESS

1   1

ACCESS ONLY FROM M62

M62 1 14

M62
Bury (M66)
Leeds
Liverpool
Stockport (M63)
Birmingham (M6)

ACCESS ONLY TO M62

M62 (eastbound exit signs)

Exit signs when travelling eastwards

A5080
Huyton 1

(M57)
Prescot 3

A57
Warrington
St Helens 5

A569
Widnes 3

PROJECTED

Burtonwood Service Area

A49
Warrington 3
Newton 2

A574
Warrington East
Birchwood 2

M6
Preston 27
Birmingham 80
Stockport (M56) 23

A572
Leigh 6
Swinton 2

M602
Manchester 6
Salford & Docks 5

M63
Stockport 13

4 5 6 7 8 S 9 10 11 12 13

4 1 3 1 3 1 3 4 1 1 2 2 1 2 7 1 1

A5080
Knotty Ash 2
Huyton 1

PROJECTED

A49
Warrington 3
Newton 2

A574
Warrington East
Birchwood 2

M63
Stockport 13
Stretford 6

M602
Salford & Docks 5

A5058 Ring Rd Nth
Bootle 6
Docks/Car Ferries
A5058 Ring Rd Sth
Airport 5
Widnes 10
A5080 City Centre 4
Car Ferries
Birkenhead 6
Wallasey 8

M57
Bootle 12
Southport 23
All Docks
A5080
Huyton 2

A57
St Helens 5
Prescot 3
A569
Widnes 3

Burton wood Service Area

M6
Preston 27
Birmingham 80
Chester (M56) 20

A572
Worsley ½

M56 (eastbound exit signs)

Exit signs when travelling eastwards

NO EXIT ACCESS ONLY FROM M53

A5117
Stanlow 2
Helsby 2
Picnic Area

A557
Runcorn 4
Widnes 5½
Northwich 10

PROJECTED

A56
Warrington 5

A49
Warrington 4
Northwich 8

M6
Preston 33
Leeds (M62) 62
Birmingham 73
A50
Lymm 3
NO DIRECT ACCESS FROM M6 SOUTH

16 15 14 13 12 11 10 9

3 3 2 3 2 2 2 2 3 5

A5117
North Wales
Queensferry 5

M53
Ellesmere Port 3½
Birkenhead 14
Chester 5
Wrexham 17
NO ACCESS FROM M53

A5117
Stanlow 2
Chester Zoo 8
Picnic Area

PROJECTED

A557
Frodsham 1½
Runcorn 4
Widnes 5½
Picnic Area

A56
Preston Brook ¾
Daresbury 1

A49
Northwich 8
Warrington 4

M6
Preston 33
Liverpool (M62) 24
A50
Warrington 5
NO DIRECT ACCESS TO M6 SOUTH: FOLLOW WARRINGTON SIGNS

Exit signs when travelling north-eastwards

Exit signs when travelling south-eastwards

M63 / M62 section

M62 / Warrington 13 / Liverpool 28 / Leeds 45 / Bolton 10 / Preston 29 / Bury 12 / **M602** / Salford & Docks 4

A57 / Irlam 3 / Eccles 2

B5214 / Barton Dock Estate

A5081 / Trafford Park 1 / Urmston 1

B5213 / Urmston ¾ / NO ACCESS FROM B5213 / PROJECTED

A56 / Altrincham 4 / Stretford 1

A6144 / Sale 1½

A5103 / Manchester 5 / NO EXIT TO A5103 SOUTH. NO ACCESS FROM A5103 NTH

A34 / Wilmslow 6 / Congleton 20 / **M56** / Warrington 18 / Chester 36 / Birmingham 82 / NO EXIT TO A34 NORTH. ACCESS ONLY FROM A34 SOUTH

NO EXIT. ACCESS ONLY FROM A560 SPUR

A560 / Cheadle 2 / **A5145** / Didsbury 3

PROJECTED / PROJECTED / PROJECTED / PROJECTED

M63 junctions (right column)

M63 — junctions 1 · 2 · 3 · 4 · 5 · 6 · 7 · 8 · 9 · 10 · 11 · 12 · 13 · 14 · 15 · 16

A57 / Irlam 3 / Eccles 2

B5214 / Barton Dock Estate / Urmston 1

A5081 / Trafford Park 1 / Stretford 2

NO EXIT ACCESS ONLY FROM B5213

PROJECTED

A56 / Stretford 1 / Manchester 4 / Sale 1 / Altrincham 4

A6144 / Sale 1½

A5103 / Wythenshawe 3 / (M56) / Manchester Airport 4 / Chester 36 / Birmingham (M6) 82 / NO EXIT TO A5103 NORTH. NO ACCESS FROM A5103 SOUTH

A34 / Cheadle 1 / Wilmslow 6 / Congleton 20 / NO EXIT / ACCESS TO/ FROM A34 NORTH

A560 / Cheadle 1 / NO ACCESS FROM A560 SPUR

A5145 / Stockport (Town Centre) ¾

A560 / Sheffield 34

PROJECTED / PROJECTED / PROJECTED

M62 / M66 section (top left)

M61 / Bolton 6 / Preston 26 / NO EXIT TO A580 / NO ACCESS FROM WESTBOUND LANE OF A580 / ACCESS ONLY FROM A666

A56 / Whitefield 1 / Salford 6

M66 / Manchester North 6 / Ashton-under-Lyne 11 / Bury 4 / Burnley 19 / Birch Service Area

A6046 / Heywood 1 / Middleton 2

A640 / Milnrow 1 / Shaw 2

A627(M) / Rochdale 3 / Oldham 4

A672 / Ripponden 6 / Sowerby Br. (A58) 9

A629 / Huddersfield 3 / Halifax 6

A640 / Huddersfield 4 / NO ACCESS FROM A640

M62

Junctions: 14 · 15 · 17 · 18 · S · 19 · 20 · 21 · 22 · 23 · 24

A666 / Swinton 2 / NO ACCESS FROM A666

A56 / Salford 6 Whitefield 1

M61 / Bolton 6 Preston 26 / **A580** / St Helens 18 / NO ACCESS FROM A580 NO EXIT TO EASTBOUND LANE OF A580

Birch Service Area

M66 / Manchester 6 / Bury 4 / Blackburn 20

A627(M) / Oldham 4 / Ashton 3 / Rochdale 3

A640 / Milnrow 1 / Shaw 2

A6046 / Middleton 2 / Heywood 1

A672 / Saddleworth 8

ACCESS ONLY FROM A640

A629 / Huddersfield 3 / Halifax 6

Exit signs when travelling westwards

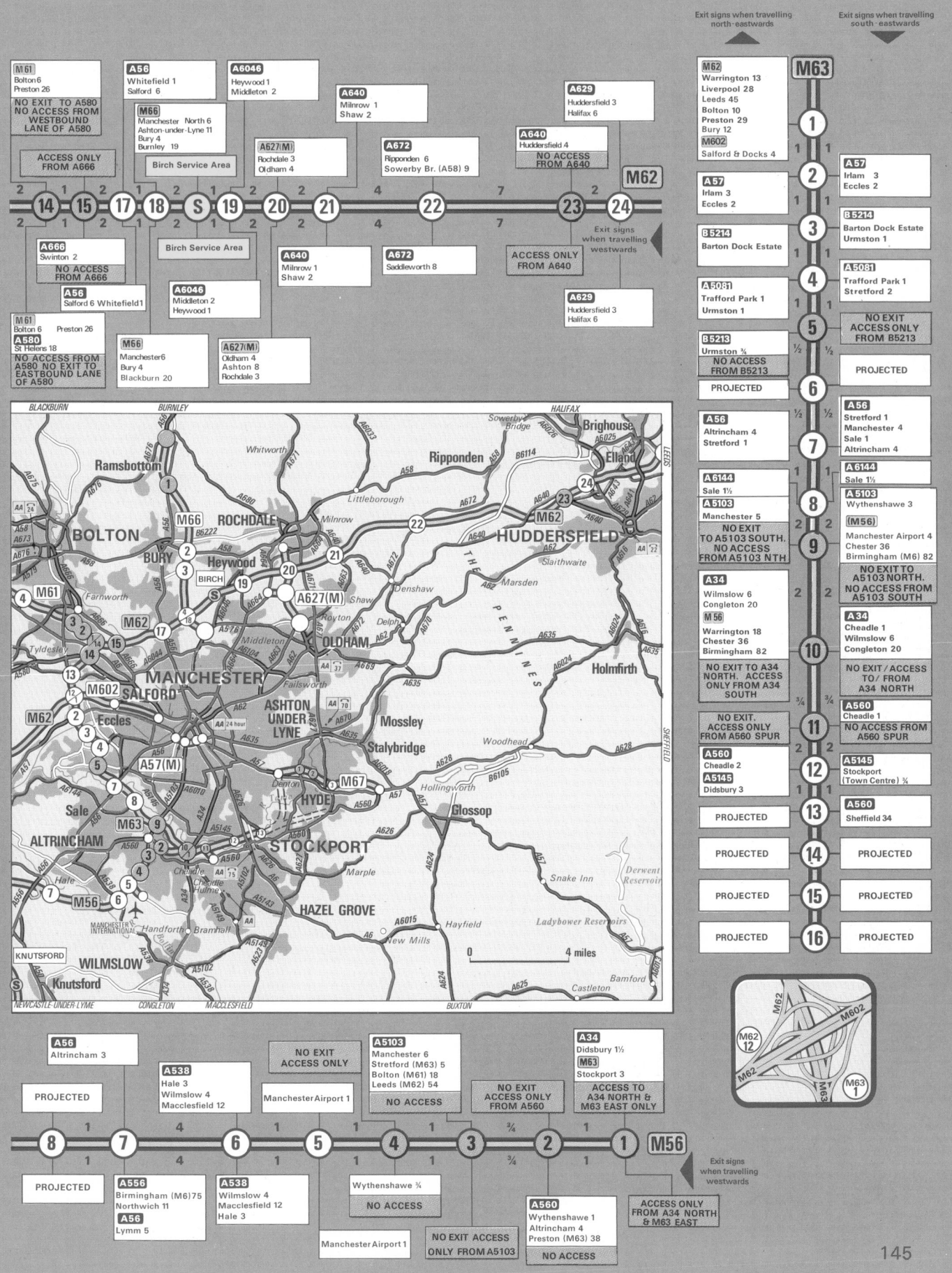

M56 section (bottom)

A56 / Altrincham 3

A538 / Hale 3 / Wilmslow 4 / Macclesfield 12

NO EXIT ACCESS ONLY

Manchester Airport 1

A5103 / Manchester 6 / Stretford (M63) 5 / Bolton (M61) 18 / Leeds (M62) 54 / NO ACCESS

NO EXIT ACCESS ONLY FROM A560

A34 / Didsbury 1½ / **M63** / Stockport 3 / ACCESS TO A34 NORTH & M63 EAST ONLY

Junctions: 8 · 7 · 6 · 5 · 4 · 3 · 2 · 1 **M56**

PROJECTED

A556 / Birmingham (M6) 75 / Northwich 11 / **A56** / Lymm 5

A538 / Wilmslow 4 / Macclesfield 12 / Hale 3

Wythenshawe ¾ / NO ACCESS

Manchester Airport 1

NO EXIT ACCESS ONLY FROM A5103

A560 / Wythenshawe 1 / Altrincham 4 / Preston (M63) 38 / NO ACCESS

ACCESS ONLY FROM A34 NORTH & M63 EAST

Exit signs when travelling westwards

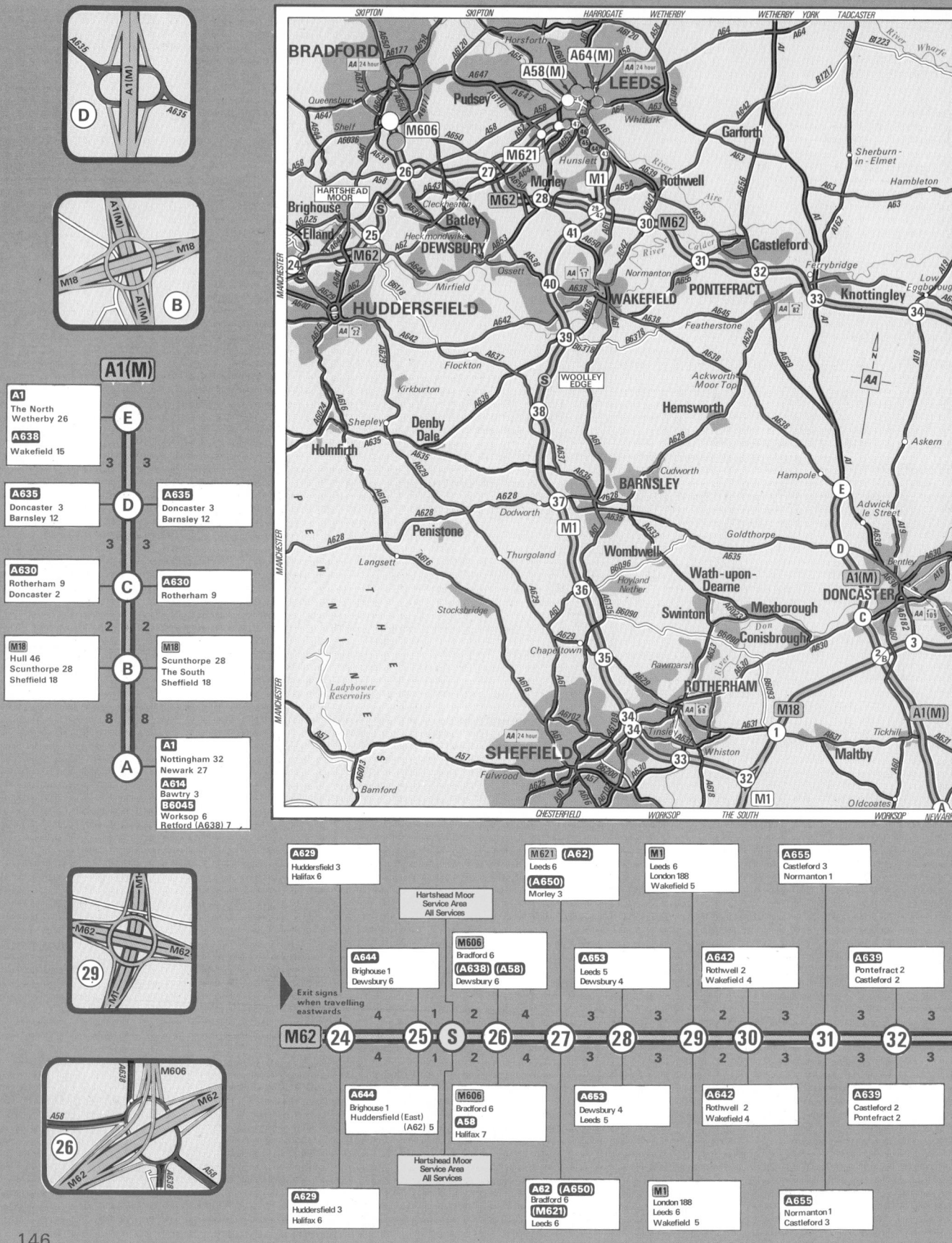

D
A635 / A1(M) / A635

B
A1(M) / M18 / M18 / A1(M)

A1(M)

A1 The North Wetherby 26	**E**	
A638 Wakefield 15		
	3	3
A635 Doncaster 3 Barnsley 12	**D**	**A635** Doncaster 3 Barnsley 12
	3	3
A630 Rotherham 9 Doncaster 2	**C**	**A630** Rotherham 9
	2	2
M18 Hull 46 Scunthorpe 28 Sheffield 18	**B**	**M18** Scunthorpe 28 The South Sheffield 18
	8	8
	A	**A1** Nottingham 32 Newark 27
		A614 Bawtry 3
		B6045 Worksop 6 Retford (A638) 7

29 M1 / M62 / M62 / M1

26 M606 / A638 / M62 / A58 / M62 / A58

Exit signs when travelling eastwards ▶

A629 Huddersfield 3 Halifax 6		Hartshead Moor Service Area All Services		M621 (A62) Leeds 6 (A650) Morley 3		M1 Leeds 6 London 188 Wakefield 5		A655 Castleford 3 Normanton 1
	A644 Brighouse 1 Dewsbury 6	M606 Bradford 6 (A638) (A58) Dewsbury 6		A653 Leeds 5 Dewsbury 4		A642 Rothwell 2 Wakefield 4		A639 Pontefract 2 Castleford 2

M62 — 24 — 25 — S — 26 — 27 — 28 — 29 — 30 — 31 — 32

(eastward) 4 1 2 4 3 2 3 3 3
(westward) 4 1 2 4 3 2 3 3 3

	A644 Brighouse 1 Huddersfield (East) (A62) 5	M606 Bradford 6 A58 Halifax 7		A653 Dewsbury 4 Leeds 5		A642 Rothwell 2 Wakefield 4		A639 Castleford 2 Pontefract 2

		Hartshead Moor Service Area All Services					

A629 Huddersfield 3 Halifax 6		A62 (A650) Bradford 6 (M621) Leeds 6		M1 London 188 Leeds 6 Wakefield 5		A655 Normanton 1 Castleford 3

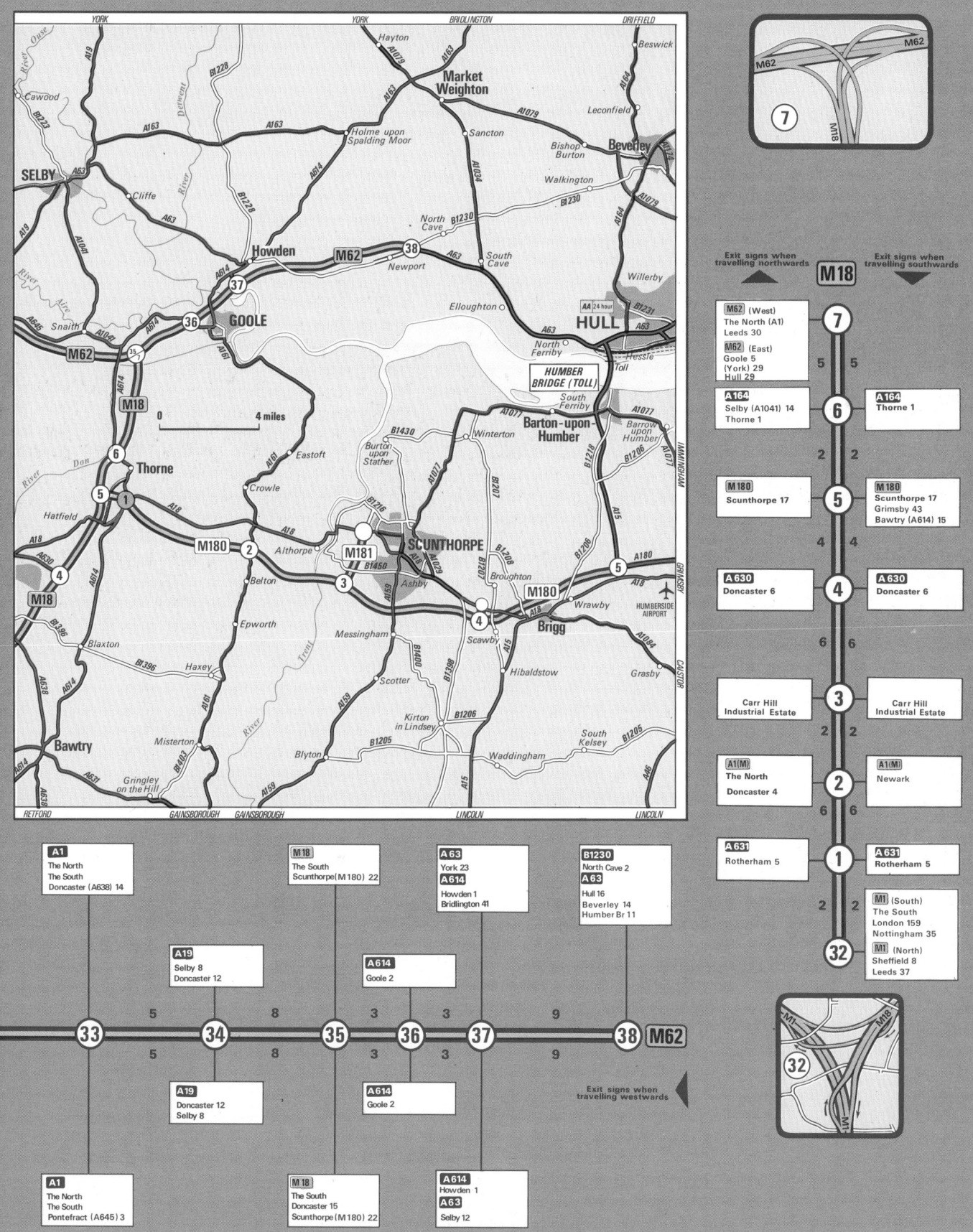

M18

Exit signs when travelling northwards — Exit signs when travelling southwards

7
- M62 (West) The North (A1) Leeds 30
- M62 (East) Goole 5 (York) 29 Hull 29

6
- A164 Selby (A1041) 14 Thorne 1
- A164 Thorne 1

5
- M180 Scunthorpe 17
- M180 Scunthorpe 17 Grimsby 43 Bawtry (A614) 15

4
- A630 Doncaster 6
- A630 Doncaster 6

3
- Carr Hill Industrial Estate
- Carr Hill Industrial Estate

2
- A1(M) The North Doncaster 4
- A1(M) Newark

1
- A631 Rotherham 5
- A631 Rotherham 5

32
- M1 (South) The South London 159 Nottingham 35
- M1 (North) Sheffield 8 Leeds 37

M62

33
- A1 The North The South Doncaster (A638) 14
- A1 The North The South Pontefract (A645) 3

34
- A19 Selby 8 Doncaster 12
- A19 Doncaster 12 Selby 8

35
- M18 The South Scunthorpe (M180) 22
- M18 The South Doncaster 15 Scunthorpe (M180) 22

36
- A614 Goole 2
- A614 Goole 2

37
- A63 York 23 A614 Howden 1 Bridlington 41
- A614 Howden 1 A63 Selby 12

38
- B1230 North Cave 2 A63 Hull 16 Beverley 14 Humber Br 11

Exit signs when travelling westwards

147

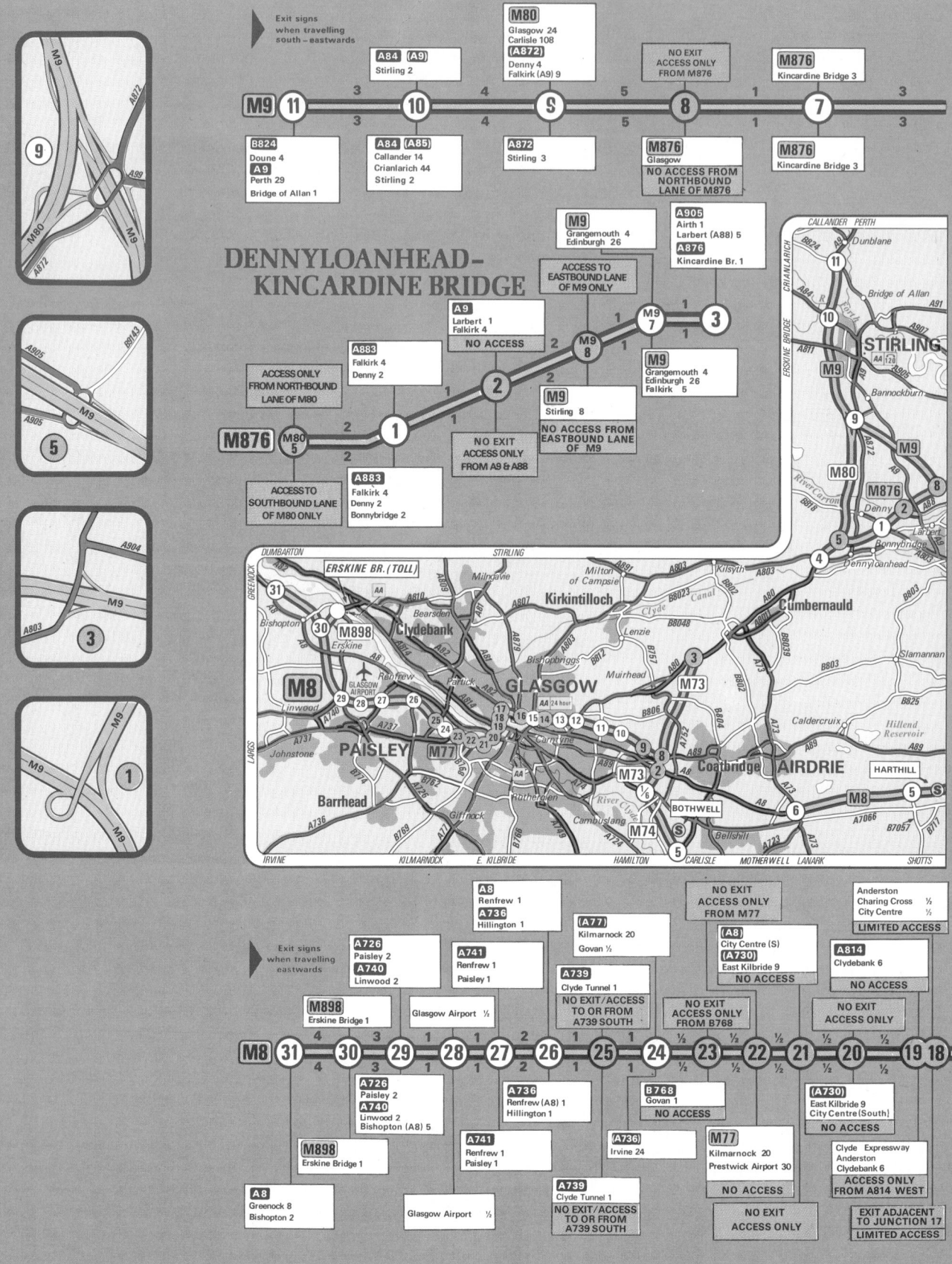

Exit signs when travelling south – eastwards

M9 | **11** | **10** | **9** | **8** | **7**

A84 (A9)
Stirling 2

M80
Glasgow 24
Carlisle 108
(A872)
Denny 4
Falkirk (A9) 9

NO EXIT
ACCESS ONLY
FROM M876

M876
Kincardine Bridge 3

B824
Doune 4
A9
Perth 29
Bridge of Allan 1

A84 (A85)
Callander 14
Crianlarich 44
Stirling 2

A872
Stirling 3

M876
Glasgow
NO ACCESS FROM
NORTHBOUND
LANE OF M876

M876
Kincardine Bridge 3

DENNYLOANHEAD– KINCARDINE BRIDGE

M9
Grangemouth 4
Edinburgh 26

A905
Airth 1
Larbert (A88) 5
A876
Kincardine Br. 1

ACCESS TO
EASTBOUND LANE
OF M9 ONLY

A9
Larbert 1
Falkirk 4
NO ACCESS

A883
Falkirk 4
Denny 2

M9 7
M9 8

M9 3

M9
Grangemouth 4
Edinburgh 26
Falkirk 5

ACCESS ONLY
FROM NORTHBOUND
LANE OF M80

M876 M80 5
M9 1

M9 2

M9
Stirling 8
NO ACCESS FROM
EASTBOUND LANE
OF M9

NO EXIT
ACCESS ONLY
FROM A9 & A88

ACCESS TO
SOUTHBOUND LANE
OF M80 ONLY

A883
Falkirk 4
Denny 2
Bonnybridge 2

ERSKINE BR. (TOLL)

M8 | **31** | **30** | **29** | **28** | **27** | **26** | **25** | **24** | **23** | **22** | **21** | **20** | **19** | **18**

Exit signs when travelling eastwards

A8
Renfrew 1
A736
Hillington 1

(A77)
Kilmarnock 20
Govan ½

NO EXIT
ACCESS ONLY
FROM M77

Anderston
Charing Cross ½
City Centre ½
LIMITED ACCESS

A726
Paisley 2
A740
Linwood 2

A741
Renfrew 1
Paisley 1

(A8)
City Centre (S)
(A730)
East Kilbride 9
NO ACCESS

A814
Clydebank 6
NO ACCESS

M898
Erskine Bridge 1

Glasgow Airport ½

A739
Clyde Tunnel 1
NO EXIT/ACCESS
TO OR FROM
A739 SOUTH

NO EXIT
ACCESS ONLY
FROM B768

NO EXIT
ACCESS ONLY

A726
Paisley 2
A740
Linwood 2
Bishopton (A8) 5

A736
Renfrew (A8) 1
Hillington 1

B768
Govan 1
NO ACCESS

(A730)
East Kilbride 9
City Centre (South)
NO ACCESS

M898
Erskine Bridge 1

A741
Renfrew 1
Paisley 1

(A736)
Irvine 24

M77
Kilmarnock 20
Prestwick Airport 30
NO ACCESS

Clyde Expressway
Anderston
Clydebank 6
ACCESS ONLY
FROM A814 WEST

A8
Greenock 8
Bishopton 2

Glasgow Airport ½

A739
Clyde Tunnel 1
NO EXIT/ACCESS
TO OR FROM
A739 SOUTH

NO EXIT
ACCESS ONLY

EXIT ADJACENT
TO JUNCTION 17
LIMITED ACCESS

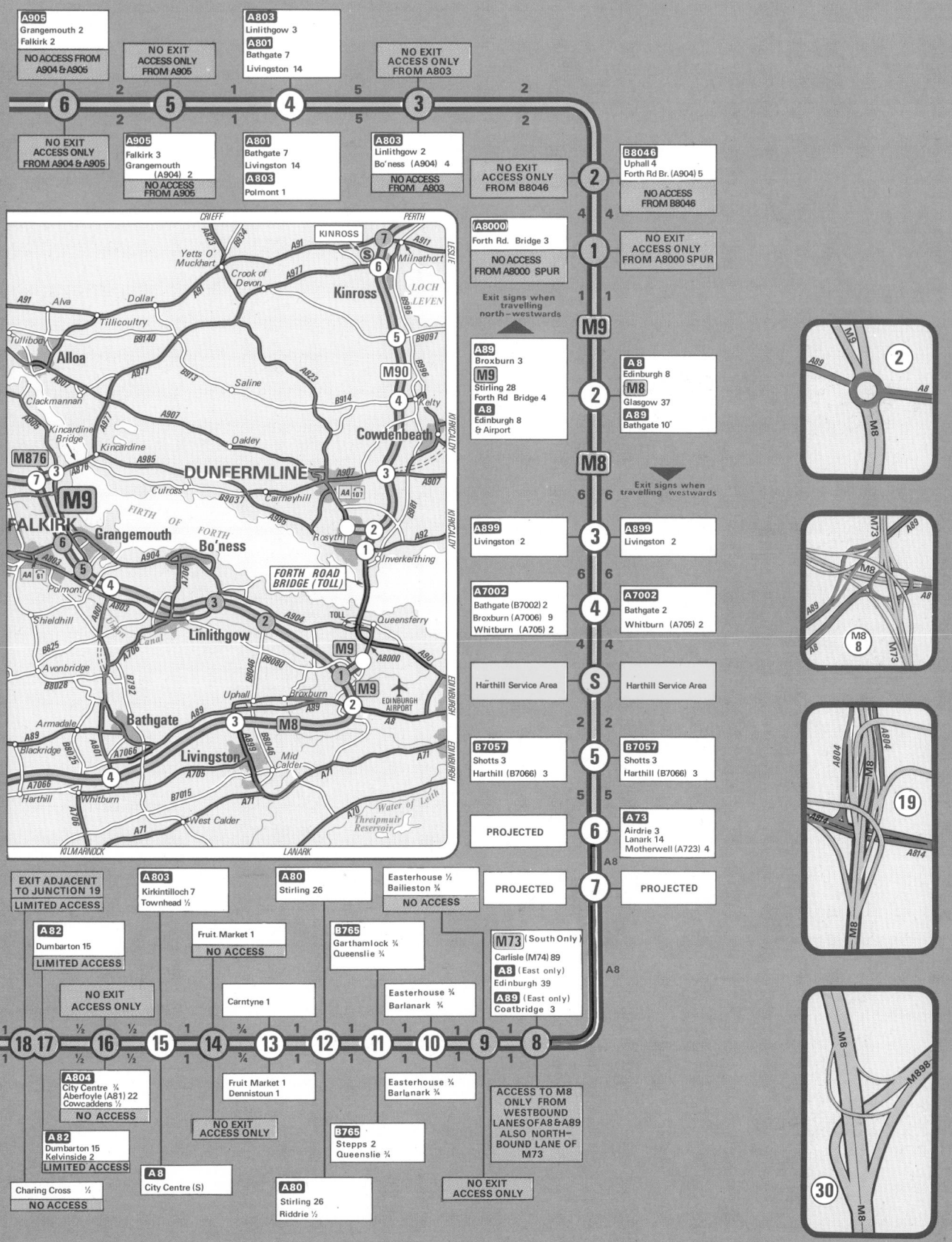

A905
Grangemouth 2
Falkirk 2
NO ACCESS FROM A904 & A905

A803
Linlithgow 3
A801
Bathgate 7
Livingston 14
NO EXIT ACCESS ONLY FROM A803

NO EXIT ACCESS ONLY FROM A905

NO EXIT ACCESS ONLY FROM A904 & A905

A905
Falkirk 3
Grangemouth (A904) 2
NO ACCESS FROM A905

A801
Bathgate 7
Livingston 14
A803
Polmont 1

A803
Linlithgow 2
Bo'ness (A904) 4
NO ACCESS FROM A803

B8046
Uphall 4
Forth Rd Br. (A904) 5
NO ACCESS FROM B8046

NO EXIT ACCESS ONLY FROM B8046

NO EXIT ACCESS ONLY FROM A8000 SPUR

A8000
Forth Rd. Bridge 3
NO ACCESS FROM A8000 SPUR

Exit signs when travelling north–westwards

A89
Broxburn 3
M9
Stirling 28
Forth Rd Bridge 4
A8
Edinburgh 8
& Airport

A8
Edinburgh 8
M8
Glasgow 37
A89
Bathgate 10

Exit signs when travelling westwards

A899
Livingston 2

A899
Livingston 2

A7002
Bathgate (B7002) 2
Broxburn (A7006) 9
Whitburn (A705) 2

A7002
Bathgate 2
Whitburn (A705) 2

Harthill Service Area

Harthill Service Area

B7057
Shotts 3
Harthill (B7066) 3

B7057
Shotts 3
Harthill (B7066) 3

PROJECTED

A73
Airdrie 3
Lanark 14
Motherwell (A723) 4

PROJECTED

PROJECTED

M73 (South Only)
Carlisle (M74) 89
A8 (East only)
Edinburgh 39
A89 (East only)
Coatbridge 3

EXIT ADJACENT TO JUNCTION 19
LIMITED ACCESS

A803
Kirkintilloch 7
Townhead ½

A80
Stirling 26

Easterhouse ½
Baillieston ¾
NO ACCESS

A82
Dumbarton 15
LIMITED ACCESS

Fruit. Market 1
NO ACCESS

B765
Garthamlock ¾
Queenslie ¾

NO EXIT ACCESS ONLY

Carntyne 1

Easterhouse ¾
Barlanark ¾

ACCESS TO M8 ONLY FROM WESTBOUND LANES OF A8 & A89 ALSO NORTH-BOUND LANE OF M73

A804
City Centre ¾
Aberfoyle (A81) 22
Cowcaddens ½
NO ACCESS

Fruit Market 1
Dennistoun 1

Easterhouse ¾
Barlanark ¾

A82
Dumbarton 15
Kelvinside 2
LIMITED ACCESS

NO EXIT ACCESS ONLY

B765
Stepps 2
Queenslie ¾

Charing Cross ½
NO ACCESS

A8
City Centre (S)

A80
Stirling 26
Riddrie ½

NO EXIT ACCESS ONLY

CENTRAL SCOTLAND M80 M73 M74

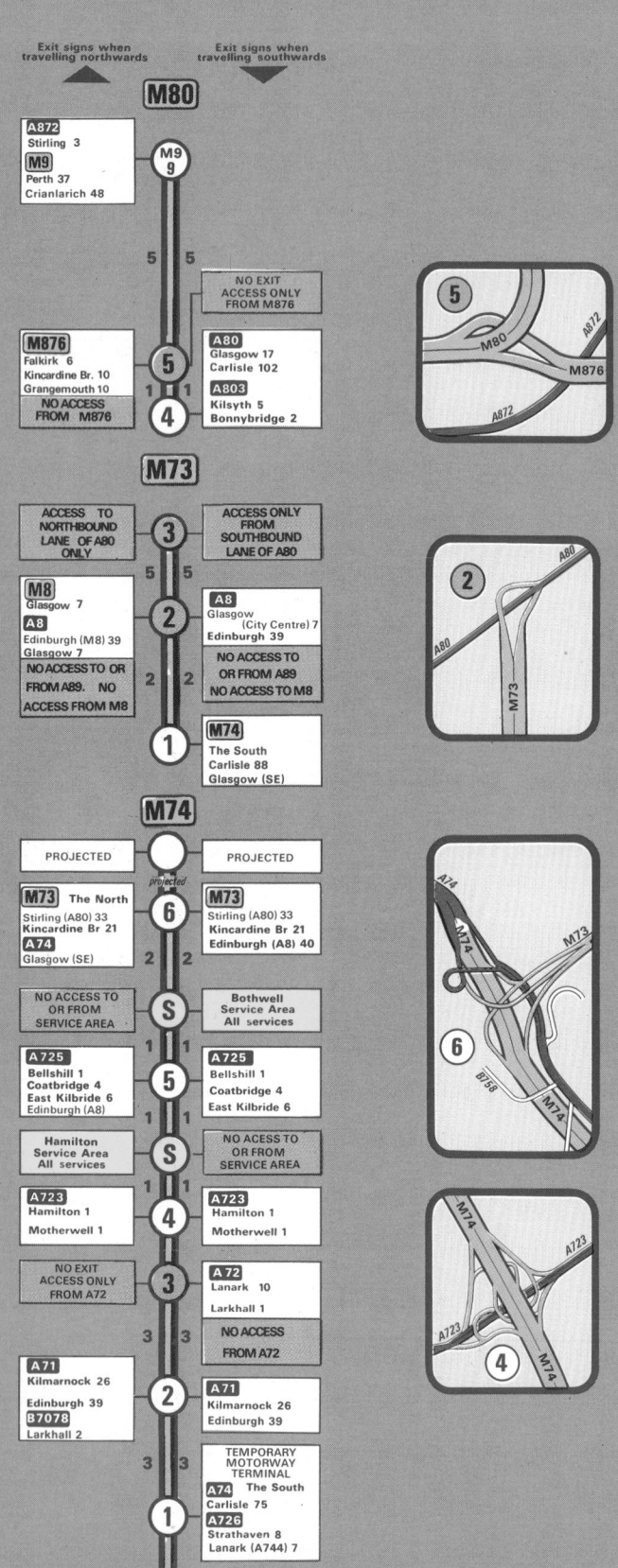

Exit signs when travelling northwards ▲   Exit signs when travelling southwards ▼

M80

A872
Stirling 3
M9
Perth 37
Crianlarich 48
— M9 9

5   5

NO EXIT
ACCESS ONLY
FROM M876

M876
Falkirk 6
Kincardine Br. 10
Grangemouth 10
NO ACCESS
FROM M876
— 5

A80
Glasgow 17
Carlisle 102
A803
Kilsyth 5
Bonnybridge 2
— 4

M73

ACCESS TO
NORTHBOUND
LANE OF A80
ONLY
— 3

ACCESS ONLY
FROM
SOUTHBOUND
LANE OF A80

5   5

M8
Glasgow 7
A8
Edinburgh (M8) 39
Glasgow 7
NO ACCESS TO OR
FROM A89. NO
ACCESS FROM M8
— 2

A8
Glasgow
(City Centre) 7
Edinburgh 39
NO ACCESS TO
OR FROM A89
NO ACCESS TO M8

2   2

— 1
M74
The South
Carlisle 88
Glasgow (SE)

M74

PROJECTED ○ PROJECTED

projected

M73 The North
Stirling (A80) 33
Kincardine Br 21
A74
Glasgow (SE)
— 6

M73 Stirling (A80) 33
Kincardine Br 21
Edinburgh (A8) 40

2   2

NO ACCESS TO
OR FROM
SERVICE AREA
— S

Bothwell
Service Area
All services

1   1

A725
Bellshill 1
Coatbridge 4
East Kilbride 6
Edinburgh (A8)
— 5

A725
Bellshill 1
Coatbridge 4
East Kilbride 6

1   1

Hamilton
Service Area
All services
— S

NO ACCESS TO OR
FROM
SERVICE AREA

1   1

A723
Hamilton 1
Motherwell 1
— 4

A723
Hamilton 1
Motherwell 1

1   1

NO EXIT
ACCESS ONLY
FROM A72
— 3

A 72
Lanark 10
Larkhall 1

3   3

NO ACCESS
FROM A72

A71
Kilmarnock 26
Edinburgh 39
B7078
Larkhall 2
— 2

A71
Kilmarnock 26
Edinburgh 39

3   3

— 1
TEMPORARY
MOTORWAY
TERMINAL
A74 The South
Carlisle 75
A726
Strathaven 8
Lanark (A744) 7

Under Construction

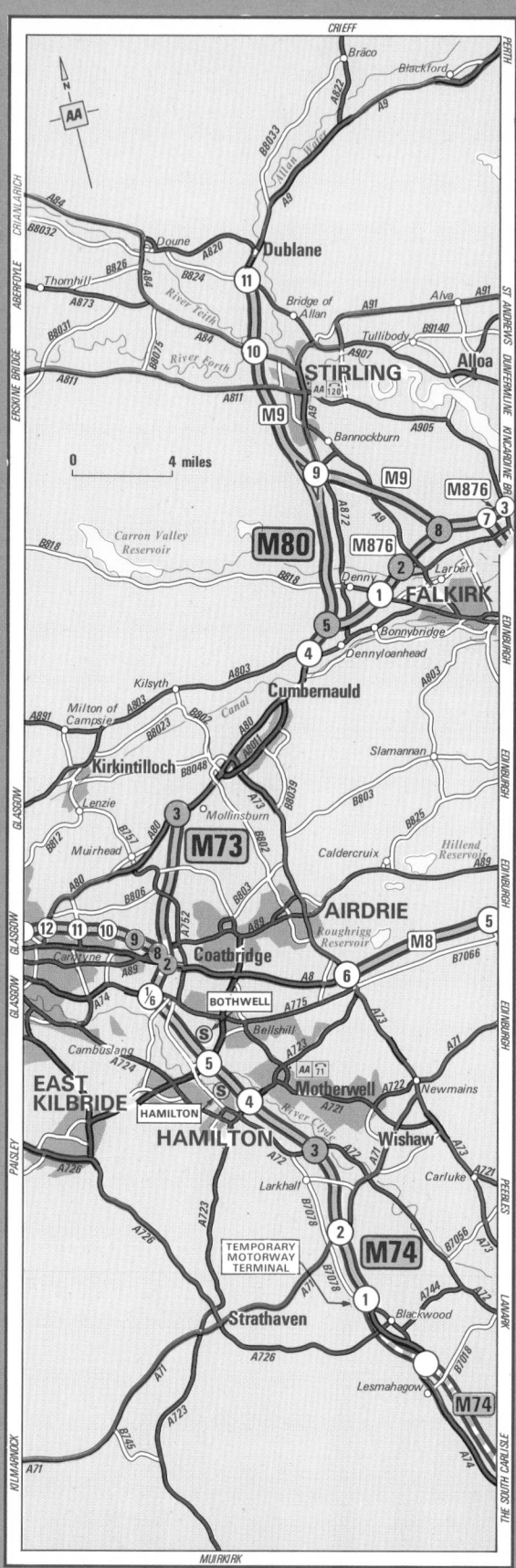

150

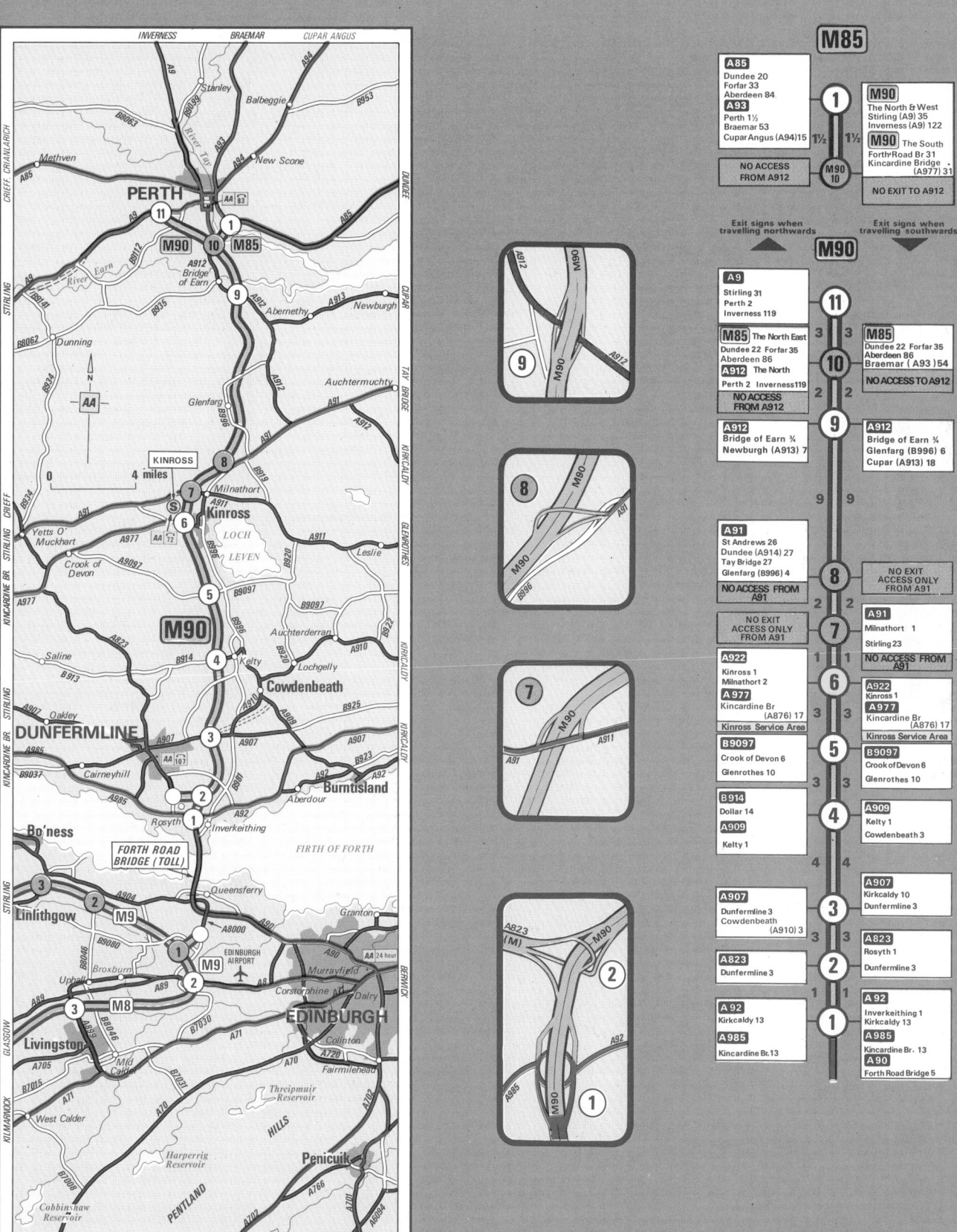

LEYLAND-COLNE M65

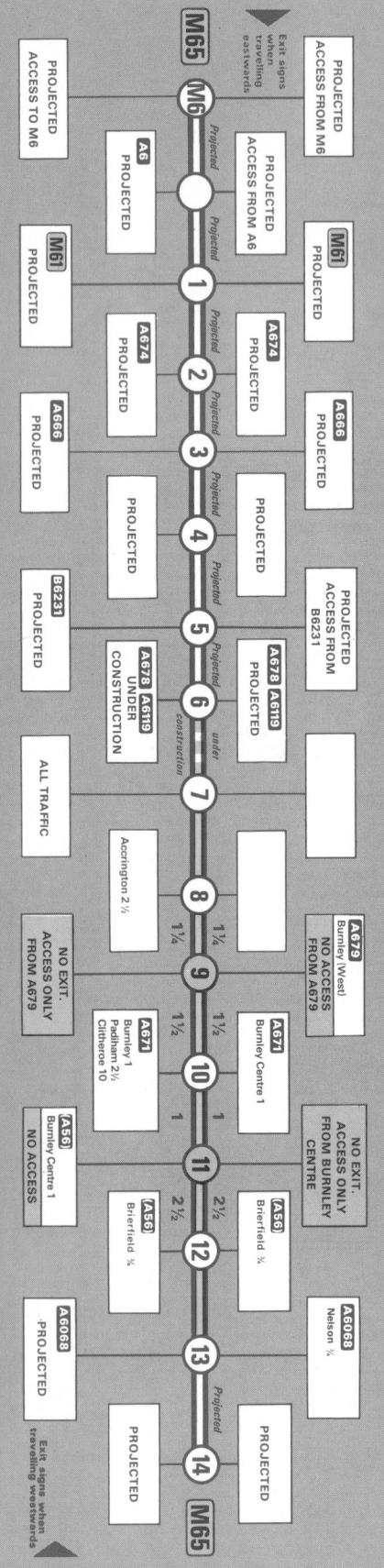

Exit signs when travelling eastwards ▼

M65

M6

PROJECTED ACCESS FROM M6

PROJECTED ACCESS TO M6 | PROJECTED

A6 PROJECTED | PROJECTED ACCESS FROM A6

M61 PROJECTED | **M61** PROJECTED — ①

A674 PROJECTED | **A674** PROJECTED — ②

A666 PROJECTED | **A666** PROJECTED — ③

PROJECTED — ④ | PROJECTED

B6231 PROJECTED — ⑤ | **A678 A619** PROJECTED | PROJECTED ACCESS FROM B6231

A678 A619 UNDER CONSTRUCTION — ⑥ | under construction

ALL TRAFFIC — ⑦

— ⑧ | Accrington 2¾

¼ 1¼

NO EXIT. ACCESS ONLY FROM A679 — ⑨ | **A679** Burnley (West) NO ACCESS FROM A679

1½ 1½

A671 Burnley 1 Padiham 2¾ Clitheroe 10 — ⑩ | **A671** Burnley Centre 1

1½ 1

A56 Burnley Centre 1 NO ACCESS — ⑪ | NO EXIT. ACCESS ONLY FROM BURNLEY CENTRE

1 2½

— ⑫ | **A56** Brierfield ¾ | **A56** Brierfield ¾

2½

A6068 PROJECTED — ⑬ | **A6068** Nelson ¾

Projected Projected

PROJECTED — ⑭ | PROJECTED

M65

Exit signs when travelling westwards ▲

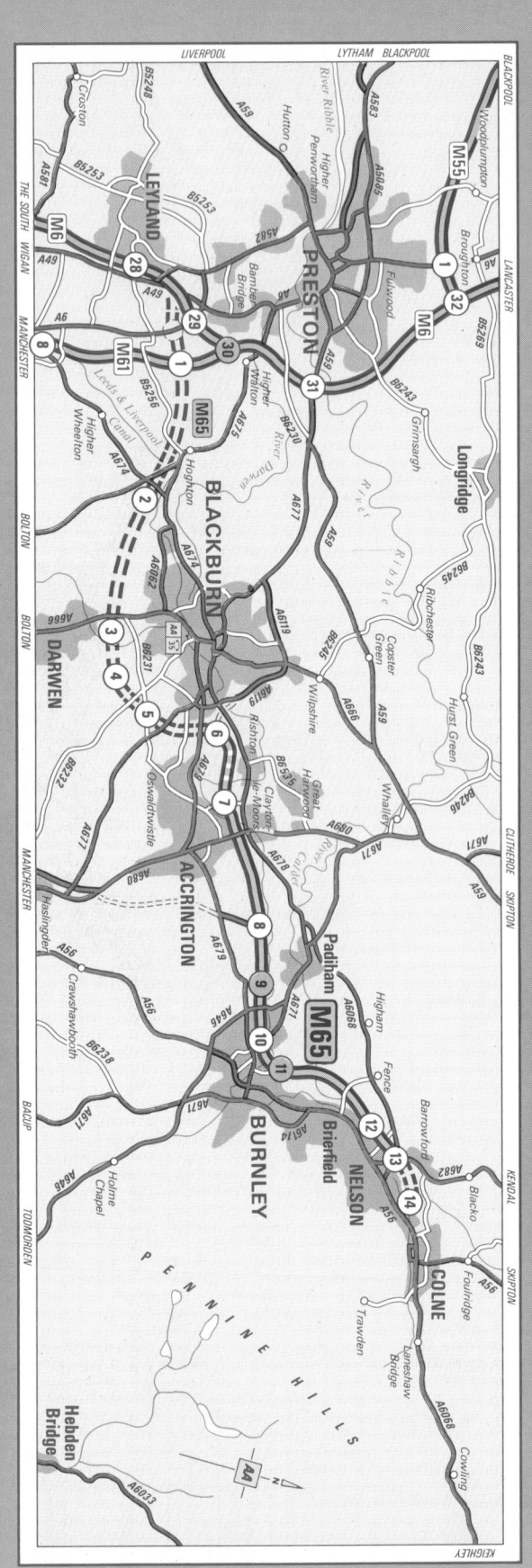

152

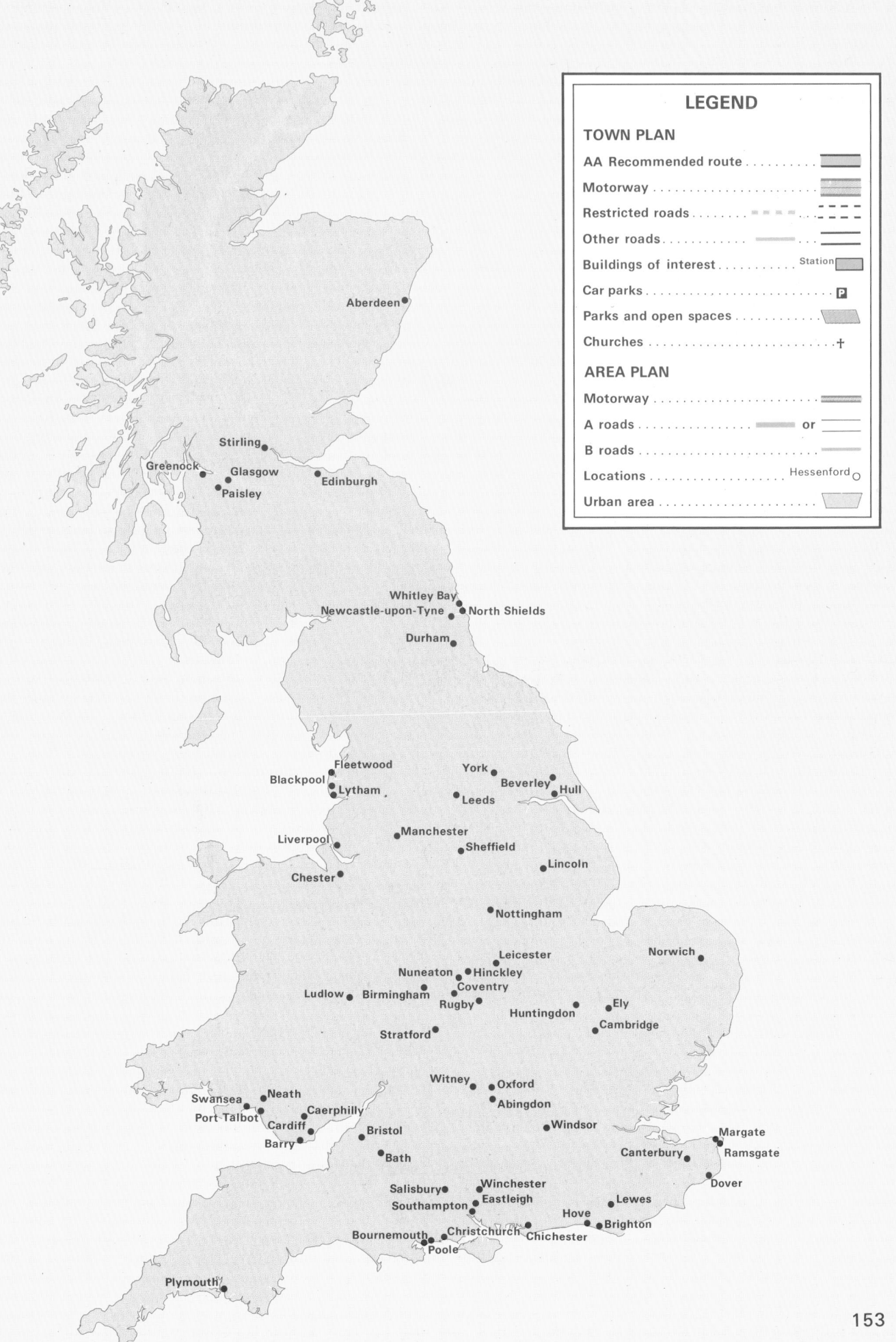

LEGEND

TOWN PLAN

AA Recommended route . . . .

Motorway . . . .

Restricted roads . . . .

Other roads . . . .

Buildings of interest . . . . Station

Car parks . . . . P

Parks and open spaces . . . .

Churches . . . . †

AREA PLAN

Motorway . . . .

A roads . . . . or

B roads . . . .

Locations . . . . Hessenford ○

Urban area . . . .

Aberdeen

Stirling
Greenock
Glasgow
Paisley
Edinburgh

Whitley Bay
Newcastle-upon-Tyne ● North Shields
Durham

Fleetwood
Blackpool
Lytham
York
Beverley Hull
Leeds

Liverpool
Manchester
Sheffield
Chester
Lincoln

Nottingham

Leicester
Norwich
Nuneaton ● Hinckley
Coventry
Ludlow ● Birmingham
Ely
Rugby
Huntingdon
Cambridge
Stratford

Witney
Oxford
Swansea ● Neath
Abingdon
Port Talbot
Caerphilly
Cardiff
Windsor
Barry
Bristol
Margate
Bath
Canterbury
Ramsgate
Dover
Winchester
Salisbury
Eastleigh
Lewes
Southampton
Hove
Bournemouth ● Christchurch ● Brighton
Poole ● Chichester
Plymouth

153

Aberdeen

Granite gives Aberdeen its especial character; but this is not to say that the city is a grim or a grey place, the granites used are of many hues – white, blue, pink and grey. Although the most imposing buildings date from the 19th century, granite has been used to dramatic effect since at least as early as the 15th century. From that time dates St Machar's Cathedral, originally founded in AD580,

but rebuilt several times, especially after a devasting fire started on the orders of Edward III of England in 1336. St Machar's is in Old Aberdeen, traditionally the ecclesiastical and educational hub of the city, while 'New' Aberdeen (actually no newer) has always been the commercial centre. Even that definition is deceptive, for although Old Aberdeen has King's College, founded in 1494, New Aberdeen has Marischal College, founded almost exactly a century later (but rebuilt in 1844)

and every bit as distinguished as a seat of learning. Both establishments functioned as independent universities until they were merged in 1860 to form Aberdeen University. The North Sea oil boom has brought many changes to the city, some of which threatened its character. But even though high-rise buildings are now common, the stately façades, towers and pillars of granite still reign supreme and Union Street remains one of the best thoroughfares in Britain.

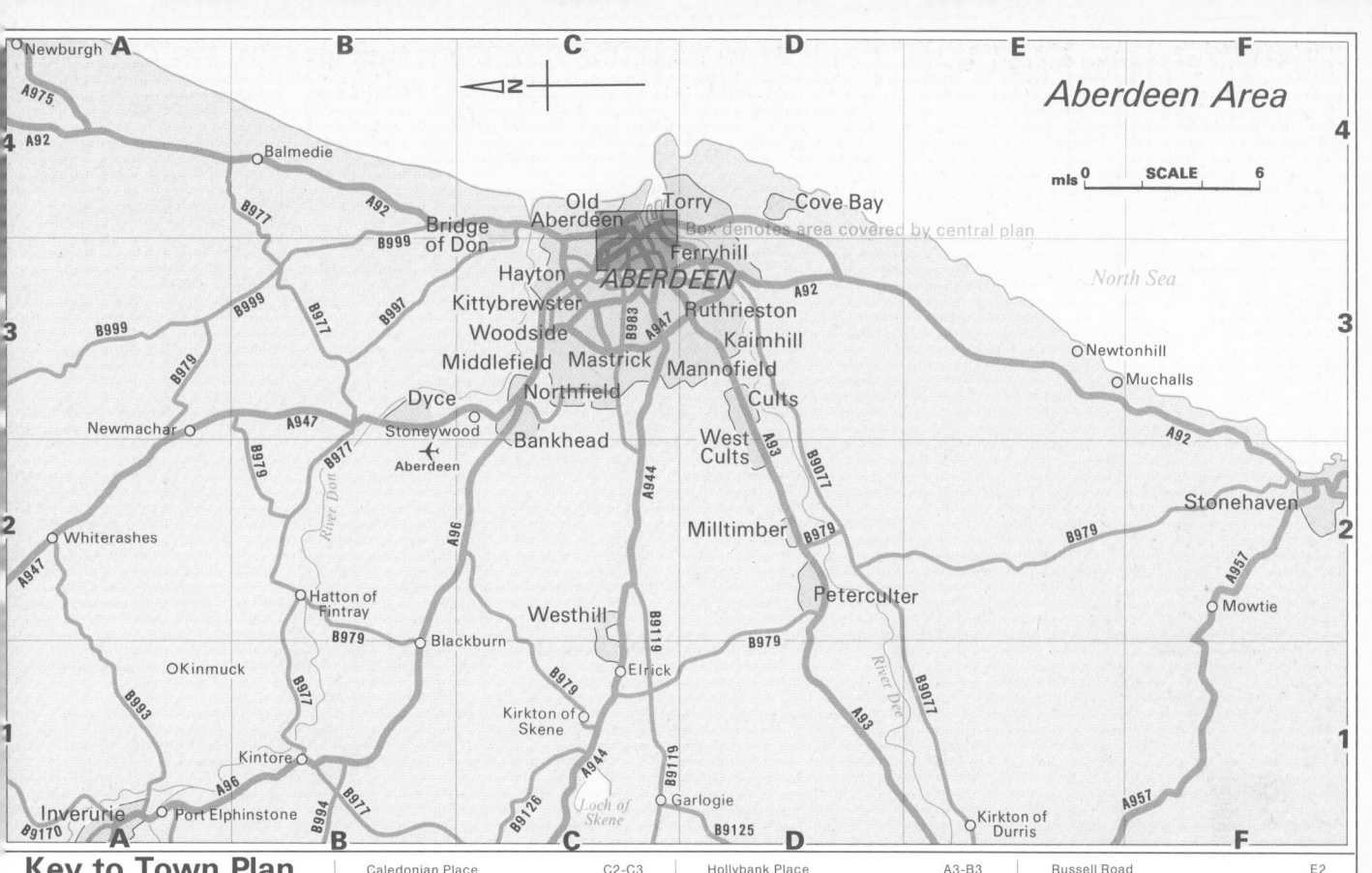

Key to Town Plan and Area Plan

Town Plan

A A Recommended roads	
Other roads	
Restricted roads	
Buildings of interest	Cinema
Car Parks	P
Parks and open spaces	
A A Service Centre	AA
Churches	†

Area Plan

A roads	
B roads	
Locations	Hattoncrook ○
Urban area	

Street Index with Grid Reference

Aberdeen

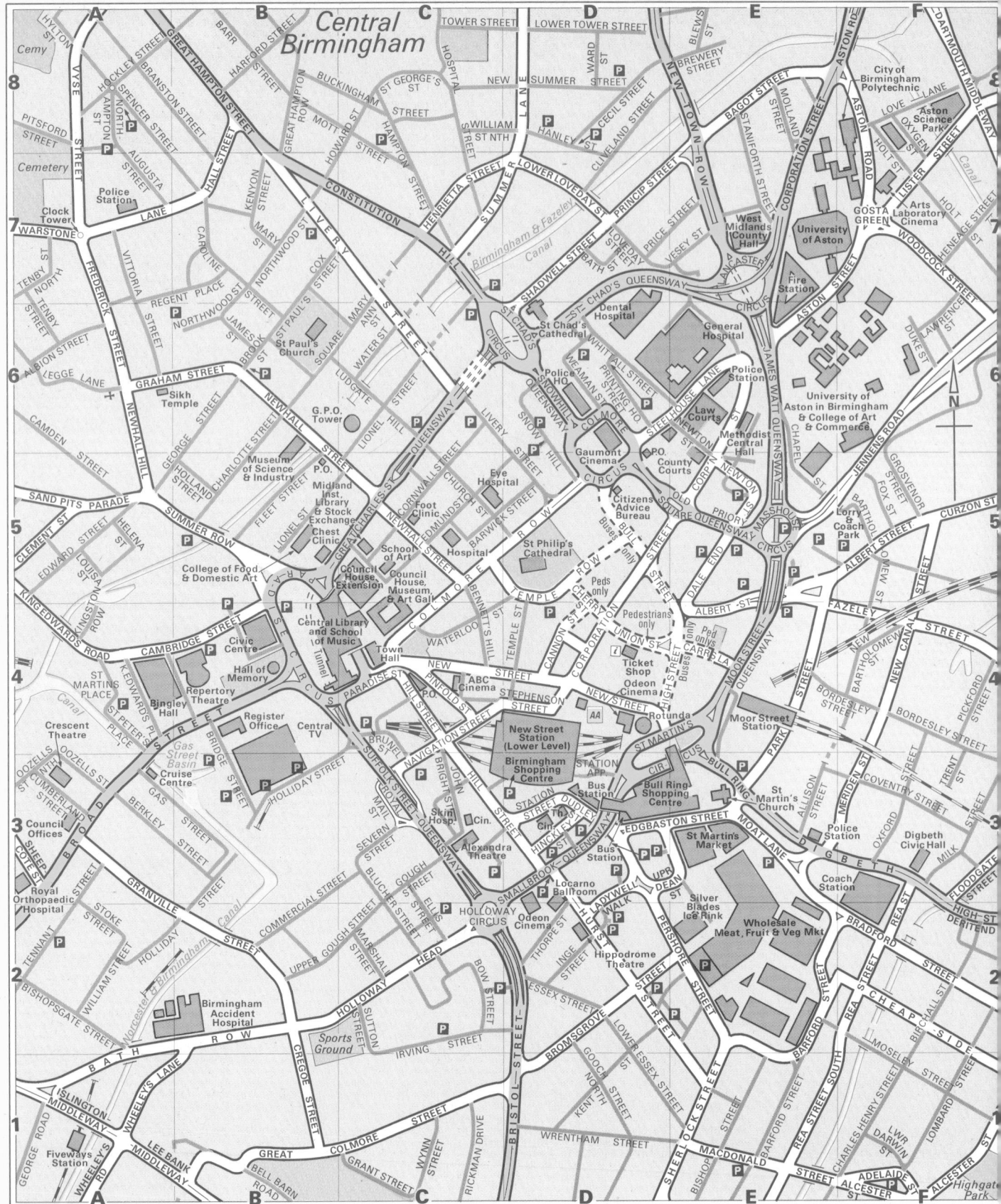

Birmingham

It is very difficult to visualise Birmingham as it was before it began the growth which eventually made it the second-largest city in England. When the Romans were in Britain it was little more than a staging post on Icknield Street. Throughout medieval times it was a sleepy agricultural centre in the middle of a heavily-forested region. Timbered houses clustered together round a green that was

eventually to be called the Bull Ring. But by the 16th century, although still a tiny and unimportant village by today's standards, it had begun to gain a reputation as a manufacturing centre. Tens of thousands of sword blades were made here during the Civil War. Throughout the 18th century more and more land was built on. In 1770 the Birmingham Canal was completed, making trade very much easier and increasing the town's development dramatically. All of that pales into near

insignificance compared with what happened in the 19th century. Birmingham was not represented in Parliament until 1832 and had no town council until 1838. Yet by 1889 it had already been made a city, and after only another 20 years it had become the second largest city in England. Many of Birmingham's most imposing public buildings date from the 19th century, when the city was growing so rapidly. Surprisingly, the city has more miles of waterway than Venice.

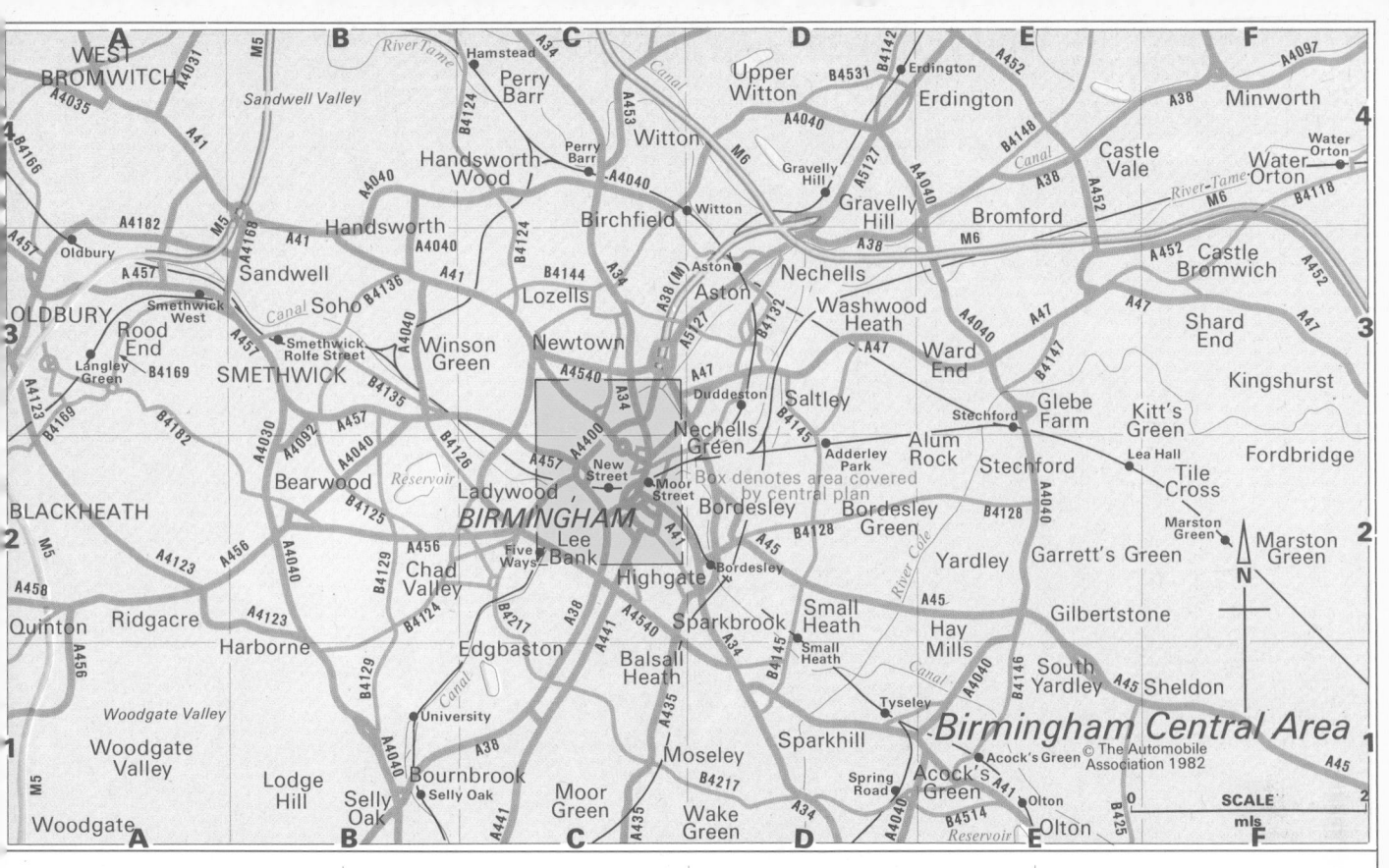

Key to Town Plan and Area Plan

Town Plan

AA Recommended roads
Restricted roads
Other roads
Buildings of interest   Station ▣
AA Service Centre   AA
Car Parks   P
Parks and open spaces
Churches   +

Area Plan

A roads
B roads
Locations   Meer End ○

Street Index with Grid Reference

Birmingham

Adelaide Street	F1
Albert Street	E4-E5-F5
Albion Street	A6
Alcester Street	F1
Allison Street	E3
Aston Road	E8-F8-F7
Aston Street	E6-F2-F7
Augusta Street	A7-A8
Bagot Street	E8
Barford Street	E1-E2-F2
Barr Street	B8
Bartholomew Street	F4-F5
Barwick Street	C5-D5
Bath Row	A1-A2-B2
Bath Street	D7
Bell Barn Road	B1
Bennett's Hill	C4-C5
Berkley Street	A3-B3
Birchall Street	F1-F2
Bishop Street	E1
Bishopsgate Street	A2
Blews Street	E8
Blucher Street	C2-C3
Bordesley Street	E4-F4-F3
Bow Street	C2
Bradford Street	E3-E2-F2
Branston Street	A8-B8-B7
Brewery Street	E8
Bridge Street	B3-B4
Bristol Street	C1-D1-D2-C2
Broad Street	A2-A3-A4-B4
Bromsgrove Street	D1-D2-E2
Brook Street	B6
Brunel Street	C3-C4
Buckingham Street	B8-C8
Bull Ring	E3
Bull Street	D5-E5-E4
Cambridge Street	A4-B4-B5

Camden Street	A5-A6
Cannon Street	D4
Caroline Street	B6-B7
Carrs Street	E4
Cecil Street	D8
Chapel Street	E5-E6
Charles Henry Street	F1
Charlotte Street	B5-B6
Cheapside	F1-F2
Cherry Street	D4-D5
Church Street	C6-C5-D5
Clement Street	A5
Cleveland Street	D7-D8-E8
Colmore Circus	D5-D6
Colmore Row	C4-C5-D5
Commercial Street	B2-B3-C3
Constitution Hill	B7-C7
Cornwall Street	C5-C6
Corporation Street	D4-D5-E5-E6-E7-E8
Coventry Street	E3-F3
Cox Street	B7
Cregoe Street	B1-B2
Cumberland Street	A3
Curzon Street	F5
Dale End	E4-E5
Dartmouth Middleway	F7-F8
Digbeth	E3-F3
Dudley Street	D3
Duke Street	F6
Edgbaston Street	D3-E3
Edmund Street	C5-D5
Edward Street	A5
Ellis Street	C2-C3
Essex Street	D2
Fazeley Street	E5-E4-F4
Fleet Street	B5
Floodgate Street	F3
Fox Street	F5
Frederick Street	A6-A7
Gas Street	A3-B3
George Road	A1
George Street	A5-B5-B6
Gooch Street North	D1-D2
Gosta Green	F7
Gough Street	C3
Graham Street	A6-B6
Grant Street	C1
Granville Street	A3-A2-B2
Great Charles St Queensway	B5-C5-C6
Great Colmore Street	B1-C1-D1
Great Hampton Row	B8
Great Hampton Street	A8-B8
Grosvenor Street	F5-F6
Hall Street	B7-B8
Hampton Street	C7-C8
Hanley Street	D7-D8
Helena Street	A5
Heneage Street	F7
Henrietta Street	C7-D7
High Street	D4-E4
High Street Deritend	F2-F3
Hill Street	C4-C3-D3
Hinckley Street	D3
Hockley Street	A8-B8
Holland Street	B5
Holliday Street	A2-B2-B3-C3-C4
Holloway Circus	C2-C3-D3-D2
Holloway Head	B2-C2
Holt Street	F7-F8
Hospital Street	C7-C8
Howard Street	B7-C7-C8
Hurst Street	D3-D2-E2-E1

Hylton Street	A8
Inge Street	D2
Irving Street	C2-D2
Islington Middleway	A1
James Street	B6
James Watt Queensway	E5-E6
Jennens Road	E5-F5-F6
John Bright Street	C3-C4
Kent Street	D1-D2
Kenyon Street	B7
King Edward's Place	A4
King Edward's Road	A4-A5
Kingston Row	A4
Ladywell Walk	D2-D3
Lancaster Circus	E6-E7
Lawrence Street	F6-F7
Lee Bank Middleway	A1-B1
Legge Lane	A6
Lionel Street	B5-C5-C6
Lister Street	F7-F8
Livery Street	B7-C7-C6-D6-D5
Lombard Street	F1-F2
Louisa Street	A5
Love Lane	F8
Loveday Street	D7
Lower Darwin Street	F1
Lower Essex Street	D2-D1-E1
Lower Loveday Street	D7
Lower Tower Street	D8
Ludgate Hill	B6-C6
Macdonald Street	E1-F1
Marshall Street	C2
Mary Street	B7
Mary Ann Street	C6-C7
Masshouse Circus	E5
Meriden Street	E3-F3
Milk Street	F3
Moat Lane	E3
Molland Street	E8
Moor Street Queensway	E4-E5
Moseley Street	E2-F2-F1
Mott Street	B8-C8-C7
Navigation Street	C3-C4
New Street	C4-D4
New Bartholomew Street	F4
New Canal Street	F4-F5
Newhall Hill	A5-A6
Newhall Street	B6-B5-C5
New Summer Street	C8-D8
Newton Street	E5
New Town Row	D8-E8-E7
Northampton Street	B6-B7
Northwood Street	B6-B7
Old Square	D5-D5
Oozells Street	A3-A4
Oozells Street North	A3-A4
Oxford Street	F3-F4
Oxygen Street	F7-F8
Paradise Circus	B4-B5
Paradise Street	C4
Park Street	E3-E4
Pershore Street	D3-D2-E2
Pickford Street	F4
Pinfold Street	C4
Pitsford Street	A8
Price Street	D7-E7
Princip Street	D7-E7-E8
Printing House Street	D6
Priory Queensway	E5
Rea Street	E2-F2-F3
Rea Street South	E1-F1-F2
Regent Place	A7-B7

Rickman Drive	C1
Royal Mail Street	C3
St Chad's Circus	C7-C6-D6
St Chad's Queensway	D6-D7-E7
St George's Street	C8
St Martin's Circus	D3-D4-E4-E3
St Martin's Place	A4
St Paul's Square	B7-B6-C6
St Peter's Place	A4
Sand Pits Parade	A5
Severn Street	C3
Shadwell Street	D6-D7
Sheepcote Street	A3
Sherlock Street	D1-E1-E2
Smallbrook Queensway	C3-D3
Snow Hill	D5-D6
Snow Hill Queensway	D6
Spencer Street	A8-A7-B7
Staniforth Street	E7-E8
Station Approach	D3
Station Street	D3
Steelhouse Lane	D6-E6
Stephenson Street	C4-D4
Stoke Street	A2-A3
Suffolk Street Queensway	B4-C4-C3
Summer Row	A5-B5
Summer Lane	C7-D7-D8
Sutton Street	C2
Temple Row	C5-D5
Temple Street	D4-D5
Tenby Street	A6-A7
Tenby Street North	A7
Tennant Street	A2-A3
Thorpe Street	D2-D3
Tower Street	C8-D8
Trent Street	F3-F4
Union Street	D4
Upper Dean Street	D3-E3
Upper Gough Street	B2-C2-C3
Vesey Street	D7-E7
Vittoria Street	A6-A7
Vyse Street	A7-A8
Ward Street	D8
Warford Street	B8
Warstone Lane	A7-B7
Water Street	C6
Waterloo Street	C4-C5-D5
Weaman Street	D6
Wheeley's Lane	A1-B1-B2
Wheeley's Road	A1
Whittall Street	D6-E6
William Street	A2
William Street North	C8-D8
Woodcock Street	F6-F7
Wrentham Street	D1-E1
Wynn Street	C1

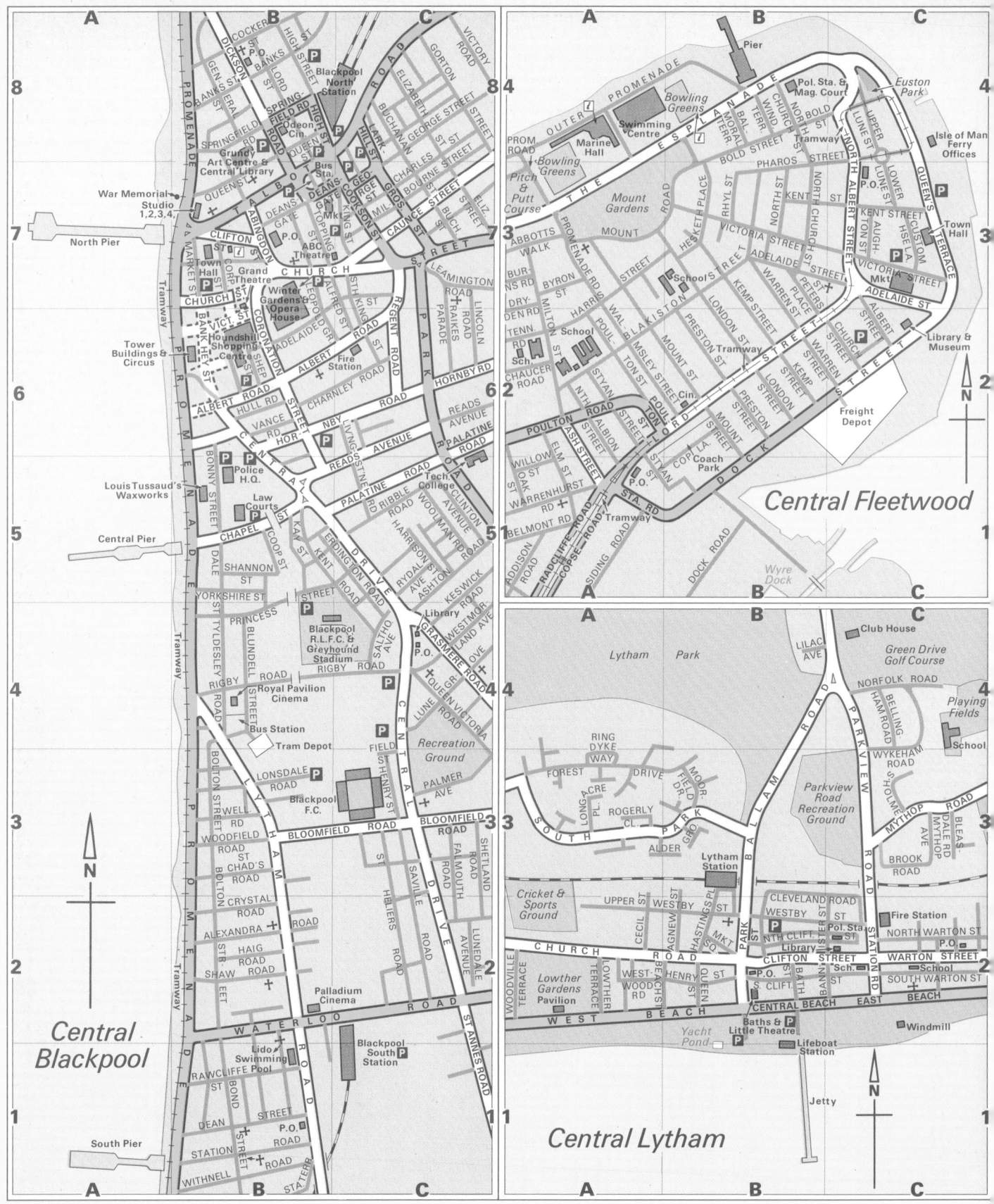

Blackpool

No seaside resort is regarded with greater affection than Blackpool. It is still the place where millions of North Country folk spend their holidays; its famous illuminations draw visitors from all over the world. It provides every conceivable kind of traditional holiday entertainment, and in greater abundance than any other seaside resort in Britain. The famous tower – built in the 1890s as a replica of the Eiffel Tower – the three piers, seven miles of promenade, five miles of illuminations, countless guesthouses, huge numbers of pubs, shops, restaurants and cafes play host to eight million visitors a year.

At the base of the tower is a huge entertainment complex that includes a ballroom, a circus and an aquarium. Other 19th-century landmarks are North Pier and Central Pier, the great Winter Gardens and Opera House and the famous trams that still run along the promenade – the only electric trams still operating in Britain. The most glittering part of modern Blackpool is the famous Golden Mile, packed with amusements, novelty shops and snack stalls. Every autumn it becomes part of the country's most extravagant light show – the illuminations – when the promenade is ablaze with neon representations of anything and everything from moon rockets to the Muppets. Autumn is also the time when Blackpool is a traditional venue for political party conferences.

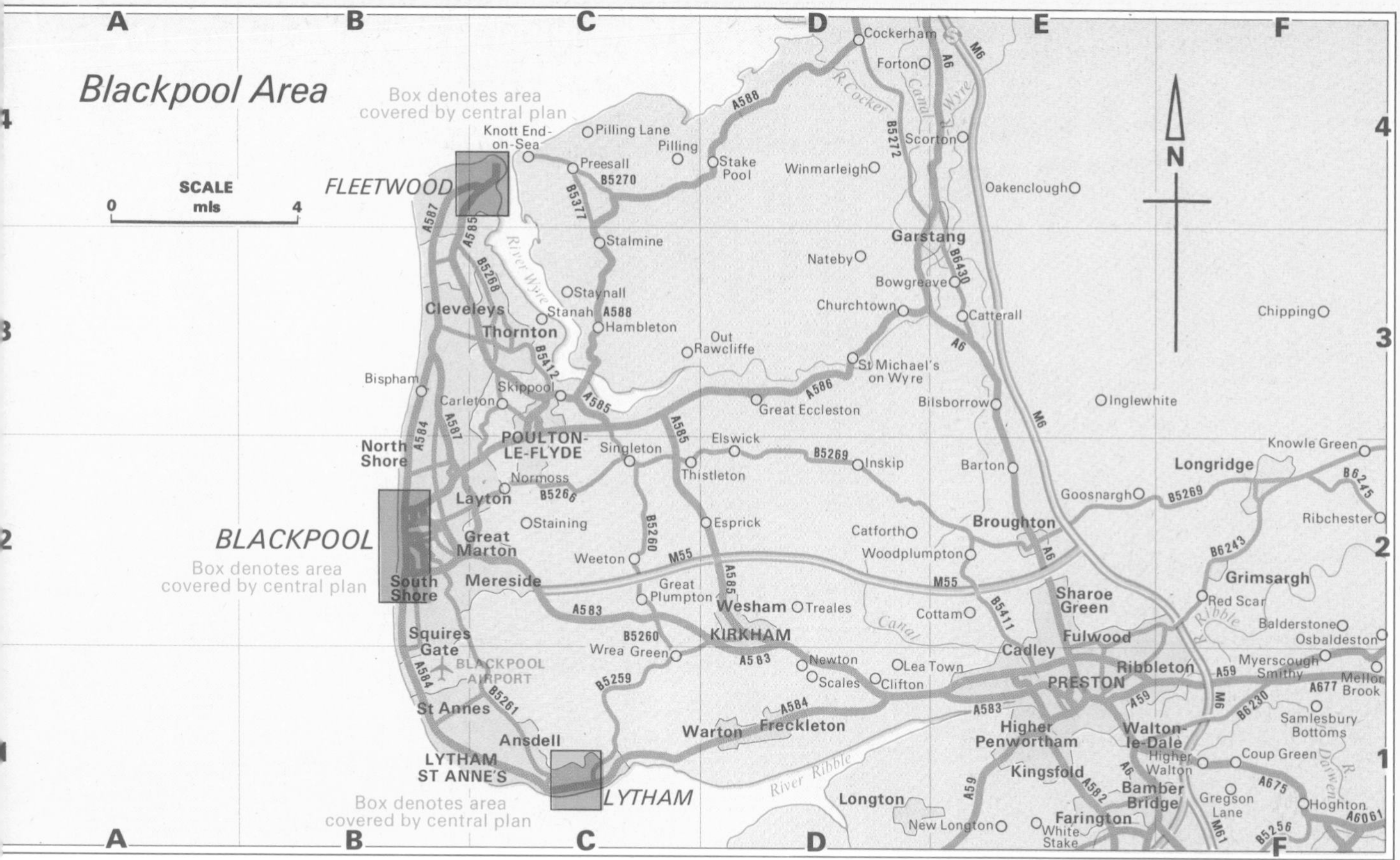

Blackpool Area

Box denotes area covered by central plan

SCALE
mls
0 — 4

FLEETWOOD

N

BLACKPOOL

Box denotes area covered by central plan

Box denotes area covered by central plan

LYTHAM

Map locations include: Cockerham, Forton, Pilling Lane, Pilling, Knott End-on-Sea, Preesall, Stake Pool, Winmarleigh, Scorton, Oakenclough, Stalmine, Garstang, Nateby, Bowgreave, Chipping, Cleveleys, Staynall, Stanah, Hambleton, Churchtown, Catterall, Thornton, Out Rawcliffe, St Michael's on Wyre, Bilsborrow, Inglewhite, Bispham, Carleton, Skippool, Knowle Green, North Shore, Poulton-le-Flyde, Singleton, Elswick, Thistleton, Inskip, Barton, Goosnargh, Longridge, Ribchester, Normoss, Layton, Staining, Esprick, Catforth, Woodplumpton, Broughton, Grimsargh, Red Scar, Balderstone, Osbaldeston, Blackpool, Great Marton, Mereside, Weeton, Great Plumpton, Wesham, Treales, Cottam, Sharoe Green, Fulwood, Cadley, Myerscough, Smithy, Mellor Brook, Squires Gate, Blackpool Airport, Wrea Green, Kirkham, Newton, Scales, Clifton, Lea Town, Preston, Ribbleton, St Annes, Warton, Freckleton, Higher Penwortham, Walton-le-Dale, Higher Walton, Coup Green, Samlesbury Bottoms, Ansdell, Lytham St Anne's, Lytham, Longton, Kingsfold, Bamber Bridge, Gregson Lane, Houghton, Farington, New Longton, White Stake

---

LEGEND

Town Plan
AA recommended route
Restricted roads
Other roads
Buildings of interest — School
Car parks — P
Parks and open spaces

Area Plan
A roads
B roads
Locations — Wrea Green ○
Urban area

Street Index with Grid Reference

Blackpool

Street	Grid
Abingdon Street	B7
Adelaide Street	B6-B7-C7
Albert Road	B6-C6
Alexandra Road	B2
Alfred Street	B7-C7-C6
Ashton Road	C4-C5
Bank Hey Street	B6-B7
Banks Street	B8
Bloomfield Road	B3-C3
Blundell Street	B4
Bolton Street	B2-B3-B4
Bond Street	B1-B2
Bonny Street	B5-B6
Buchanan Street	C7-C8
Caunce Street	C7-C8
Central Drive	B6-B5-C5-C4-C3-C2
Chapel Street	B5
Charles Street	C7-C8
Charnley Road	B6-C6
Church Street	B7-C7
Clifton Street	B7
Clinton Avenue	C5
Cocker Street	B8
Cookson Street	B8-B7-C7
Coop Street	B5
Coronation Street	B5-B6-B7
Corporation Street	B7
Crystal Road	B2
Dale Street	B4-B5
Deansgate	B7-C7
Dean Street	B1
Dickson Road	B7-B8
Erdington Road	B5-C5-C4
Elizabeth Street	C7-C8
Falmouth Road	C2-C3
Field Street	C3
General Street	B8
George Street	C7-C8
Gorton Street	C8
Grasmere Road	C4
Grosvenor Street	C7
Haig Road	B2
Harrison Street	C5
Henry Street	C3
High Street	B8
Hornby Road	B6-C6
Hull Road	B6
Kay Street	B5
Kent Road	B5-C5-C4
Keswick Road	C4-C5
King Street	C7
Larkhill Street	C8
Leamington Road	C7
Leopold Grove	B7-B6-C6
Lincoln Road	C6-C7
Livingstone Road	C5-C6
Lonsdale Road	B3
Lord Street	B8
Lunedale Avenue	C2
Lune Grove	C4
Lytham Road	B1-B2-B3-B4
Market Street	B7
Milbourne Street	C7-C8
Osbourne Road	B1
Palatine Road	B5-C5-C6
Palmer Avenue	C3
Park Road	C5-C6-C7
Princess Parade	A7-A8-B8-B7

Street	Grid
Princess Street	B4-B5-C5
Promenade	B1-B2-B3-B4-B5-B6-A6-A7-B7-B8
Queen Street	B7-B8
Queen Victoria Road	C3-C4
Raikes Parade	C6-C7
Rawcliffe Street	B1
Reads Avenue	B5-C5-C6
Regent Road	C6-C7
Ribble Road	C5
Rigby Road	B4-C4
Rydal Avenue	C5
St Annes Road	C1-C2
St Chad's Road	B3
St Heliers Road	C2-C3
Salthouse Avenue	C4
Saville Road	C2-C3
Shannon Street	B5
Shaw Road	B2
Sheppard Street	B6
Shetland Road	C2-C3
South King Street	C6-C7
Springfield Road	B8
Station Road	B1
Station Terrace	B1
Talbot Road	B7-B8-C8
Topping Street	B7
Tyldesley Road	B4
Vance Road	B6
Victoria Street	B6
Victory Road	C8
Waterloo Road	B2-C2
Wellington Road	B3
Westmorland Avenue	C4
Woodfield Road	B3
Woolman Road	C5
Yorkshire Street	B5

Fleetwood

Street	Grid
Abbotts Walk	A3
Adelaide Street	B3-C3-C2
Addison Road	A1
Albert Street	C2-C3
Ash Street	A1-A2
Aughton Street	C3
Balmoral Terrace	B4
Belmont Road	A1
Blakiston Street	A2-B2-B3
Bold Street	B4-C4
Burns Road	A3
Byron Street	A3

Street	Grid
Chaucer Road	A2
Church Street	C2
Cop Lane	A1-B1-B2
Copse Road	A1
Custom House Lane	C3
Dock Road	B1
Dock Street	B1-B2-C2
Dryder Road	A2-A3
Elm Street	A1-A2
Harris Street	A2-A3-B3
Hesketh Place	B3
Kemp Street	B2-B3
Kent Street	B2-B3
London Street	B2-B3
Lord Street	A1-A2-B2-C2-C3
Lower Lune Street	C3
Milton Street	A2-A3
Mount Road	A3-B3
Mount Street	A2-B2
North Albert Street	C3-C4
North Albion Street	A1-A2
North Church Street	B3-B4
North Street	B3
Oak Street	A1-A2
Outer Promenade	A4-B4
Pharos Street	B3-C3-C4
Poulton Road	A2
Poulton Street	A2
Preston Street	B2
Promenade Road	A3-A4
Queen's Terrace	C3-C4
Radcliffe Road	A1
Rhyl Street	B3
St Peters Place	B2-B3
Siding Road	A1
Station Road	A1
Styan Street	A2-A1-B1
Tennyson Road	A2
The Esplanade	A3-A4-B4
Upper Lune Street	C4
Victoria Street	B3-C3
Walmsley Street	A3-A2-B2
Warrenhurst Road	A1
Warren Street	B3-B2-C2
Willow Road	A1
Windsor Terrace	B4

Lytham

Street	Grid
Agnew Street	B2-B3
Alder Grove	A3-B3
Ballam Road	B2-B3-B4-C4
Bannister Street	C2
Bath Street	B2
Beach Street	B2
Bellingham Road	C4
Bleasdale Road	C3
Brook Road	C3
Cecil Street	A2-A3
Central Beach	B2-C2
Church Road	A2-B2
Cleveland Road	B3-C3
Clifton Street	B2-C2
East Beach	C2
Forest Drive	A3-B3
Hastings Place	B2-B3
Henry Street	C2
Lilac Avenue	B4
Longacre Place	A3
Lowther Terrace	A2
Market Square	B3
Moorfield Drive	B3
Mythop Avenue	C3
Mythop Road	C3
Norfolk Road	C4
North Clifton Street	B2-C2
North Warton Street	C2
Park Street	B2
Parkview Road	C2-C3-C4
Queen Street	B2
Ring Dyke Way	A3
Rogerly Close	A3
South Clifton Street	B2-C2
Southolme	C3
South Park	A3-B3
South Warton Street	C2
Station Road	C2
Upper Westby Street	A2-B2
Warton Street	C2
West Beach	A2-B2
Westby Street	B2-C2
Westwood Road	A2
Woodville Terrace	A2
Wykeham Road	C3-C4

BLACKPOOL

Three piers, seven miles of promenade packed with entertainments galore and seemingly endless sandy beaches spread out beneath Blackpool's unmistakable tower which stands 518ft high in Britain's busiest and biggest holiday resort.

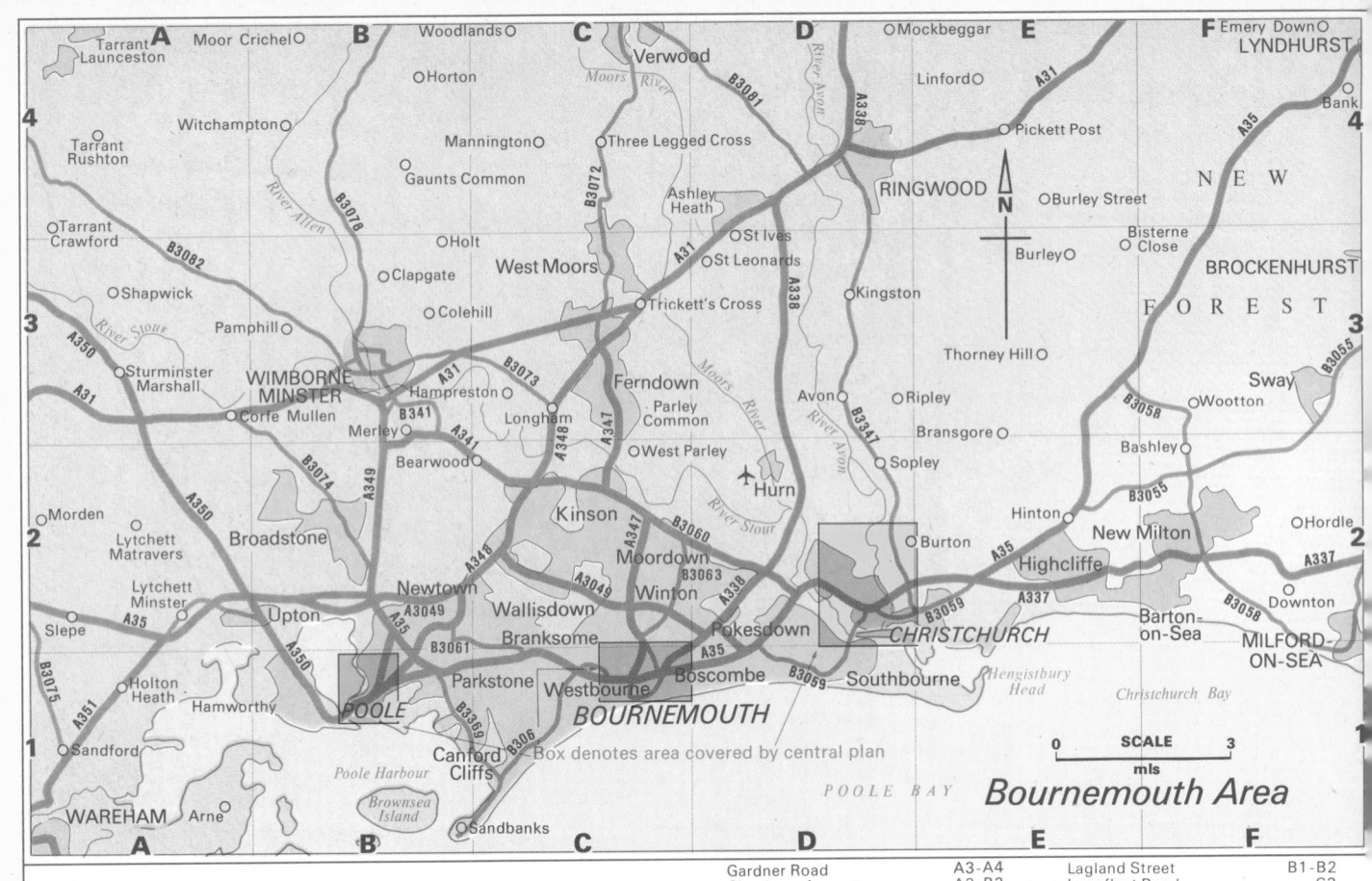

Box denotes area covered by central plan

Bournemouth Area

SCALE 0 — 3 mls

STREET INDEX – with grid reference

Bournemouth

Albert Road	C3
Avenue Road	B3-C3
Avenue West	A3
Bath Road	D2-E2-E3-E4-F4
Beacon Road	C1
Bodorgan Road	C4
Bourne Avenue	B3-C3
Braidley Road	B3-B4
Branksome Wood Road	A4
Cambridge Road	A2-A3
Central Drive	B4
Chine Crescent	A1-A2
Chine Crescent Road	A1-A2
Christchurch Road	F4
Cotlands Road	F4
Cranbourne Road	B2-C2
Crescent Road	A3-B3
Dean Park Crescent	C4-D4
Dean Park Road	C4
Durley Chine Road	A1-A2
Durley Gardens	A1
Durley Road	A1-A2-B1
East Overcliffe Drive	E2-F2-F3
Exeter Crescent	C2
Exeter Lane	C2-D2
Exeter Park Road	C2-D2
Exeter Road	C2-D2
Fir Vale Road	D3-D4
Gervis Place	C3-D3
Gervis Road	E3-F3
Glenfern Road	D3-E3-E4
Grove Road	E3-F3
Hahnemann Road	A1-B1-B2
Hinton Road	D2-D3-E2
Holdenhurst Road	F4
Lansdowne Road South	E4-F4
Lorne Park Road	E4
Madeira Road	D4-E4
Marlborough Road	A2
Meyrick Road	F3-F4
Norwich Avenue	A2-A3
Old Christchurch Road	D3-D4-E4-F4
Parsonage Road	D3-E3
Poole Hill	A2-B2

Priory Road	C1-C2
Richmond Hill	C3-C4
St Michael's Road	B2-B1-C1
St Peter's Road	D3-E3
St Stephen's Road	B3-B4-C4-C3
South Cliff Road	C1-D1
Stafford Road	E4
Suffolk Road	A3-B3
Surrey Road	A3
Terrace Road	B2-C2
The Triangle	B2-B3
Tregonwell Road	B2-C2-C1
Undercliffe Drive	D1-D2-E2-F2
Upper Hinton Road	D2-D3-E2
Upper Norwich Road	A2-B2
Upper Terrace Road	B2-C2
Wessex Way	A3-A4-B4-C4-D4-E4
West Cliff Gardens	B1-C1
West Cliff Promenade	B1-C1-D1
West Cliff Road	A1-B1
Westhill Road	A2-B2-B1
Westover Road	D2-D3
West Promenade	C1-D1
Wimborne Road	C4
Wootton Gardens	E3-E4
Yelverton Road	C3-D3

Christchurch

Albion Road	A4
Arcadia Road	A4
Arthur Road	B3
Avenue Road	A3-B3-B4
Avon Road West	A3-A4-B4
Bargates	B2-B3
Barrack Road	A3-B2-B3
Beaconsfield Road	B2-C3
Bridge Street	C2
Bronte Avenue	B4
Canberra Road	A4
Castle Street	B2-C2
Christchurch By-Pass	B2-C2-C3
Clarendon Road	A3-B3
Douglas Avenue	A2-B2
Endfield Road	A4
Fairfield	B3
Fairmile Road	A4-B4-B3
Flambard Avenue	B4

Gardner Road	A3-A4
Gleadowe Avenue	A2-B2
Grove Road East	A3-B3
Grove Road West	A3
High Street	B2
Iford Lane	A1
Jumpers Avenue	A4
Jumpers Road	A3-A4-B4
Kings Avenue	A2-B2
Manor Road	B2
Millhams Street	B2-C2
Mill Road	B3-B4
Portfield Road	A3-B3
Queens Avenue	B1
Quay Road	B1
St John's Road	A2
St Margarets Avenue	B1
Sopers Lane	B1-B2
South View Road	A1-B1
Stony Lane	C4-C3-C2
Stour Road	B3-B2-A1-A2
The Grove	A4
Tuckton Road	A1
Twynham Avenue	B2-B3
Walcott Avenue	A4-B4
Waterloo Place	C2
Wickfield Avenue	B1-B2
Wick Lane	A1-B1-B2
Willow Drive	A1-B1
Willow Way	A1-B1
Windsor Road	A3

Poole

Ballard Road	B1-C1
Church Street	A1
Dear Hay Lane	A2-B2
Denmark Road	C3
East Quay Road	B1
East Street	B1
Elizabeth Road	C3
Emerson Road	B1-B2
Esplanade	B3
Garland Road	C4
Green Road	B2-B1-C1
Heckford Road	C3-C4
High Street	A1-B1-B2
Hill Street	B2
Johns Road	C3-C4
Jolliffe Road	C4
Kingland Road	B2-C2
Kingston Road	C3-C4

Lagland Street	B1-B2
Longfleet Road	C3
Maple Road	C3-C4
Mount Pleasant Road	C2-C3
Newfoundland Drive	C1
New Orchard	A1-A2
North Street	B2
Old Orchard	B1
Parkstone Road	C3
Perry Gardens	B1
Poole Bridge	A1
St Mary's Road	C3
Seldown Lane	C2-C3
Shaftesbury Road	C3
Skinner Street	B1
South Road	B1
Stanley Road	B1
Sterte Avenue	A4-B4
Sterte Road	B2-B3-B4
Stokes Avenue	B4-C4
Strand Street	A1-B1
Tatnam Road	B4-C4
The Quay	A1-B1
Towngate Bridge	B2-B3
West Quay Road	A1-A2-B2
West Street	A1-A2-B2
Wimborne Road	B3-C3-C4

LEGEND

Town Plan
- AA Recommended route
- Other roads
- Restricted roads
- Buildings of interest — Town Hall
- AA Centre — AA
- Car Parks — P
- Parks and open spaces

Area Plan
- A roads
- B roads
- Locations — Ibsley○
- Urban area

Bournemouth

Until the beginning of the 19th century the landscape on which Bournemouth stands was open heath. Its rise began when a scattering of holiday villas were built by innovative trend-setters at a time when the idea of seaside holidays was very new. Soon a complete village had taken shape. In the next 50 years Bournemouth had become a major resort and its population catapulted to nearly 59,000.

Today's holidaymakers can enjoy Bournemouth's natural advantages – miles of sandy beaches, a mild climate and beautiful setting, along with a tremendous variety of amenities. These include some of the best shopping in the south – with shops ranging from huge departmental stores to tiny specialist places. Entertainments range from variety shows and feature films to opera, and the music of the world-famous Bournemouth Symphony Orchestra.

Poole has virtually been engulfed by the suburbs of Bournemouth, but its enormous natural harbour is still an attraction in its own right. At Poole Quay, some 15th-century cellars have been converted into a Maritime Museum, where the town's association with the sea from prehistoric times until the early 20th century is illustrated, and the famous Poole Pottery nearby offers guided tours of its workshops.

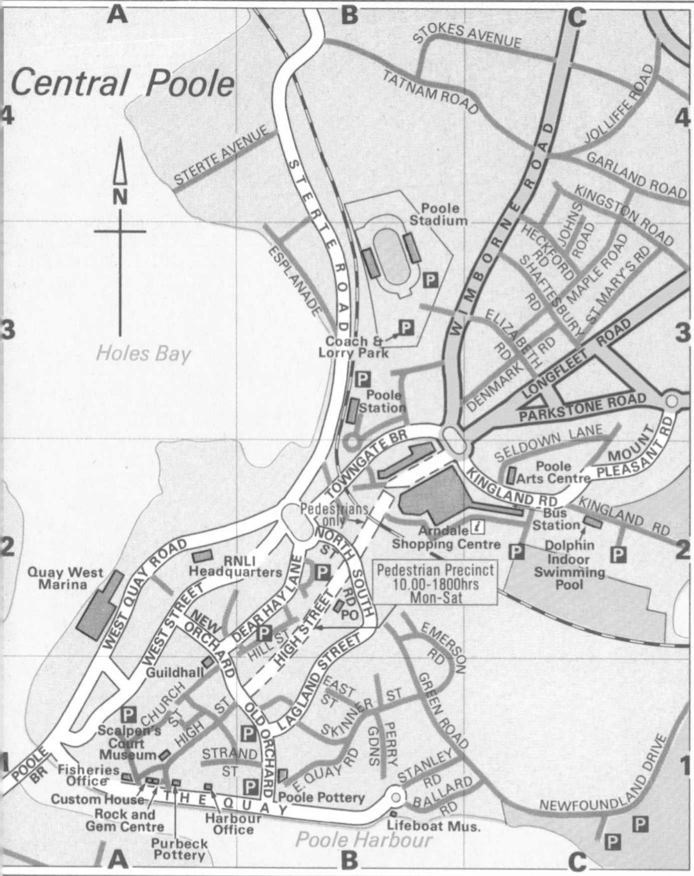

Central Poole

Holes Bay

STOKES AVENUE
TATNAM ROAD
JOLLIFFE ROAD
STERTE AVENUE
GARLAND ROAD
KINGSTON ROAD
WIMBORNE ROAD
HECKFORD ROAD
JOHNS ROAD
MAPLE ROAD
ST MARY'S RD
SHAFTESBURY RD
DENMARK RD
ELIZABETH RD
LONGFLEET ROAD
STERTE ROAD
ESPLANADE

Poole Stadium
Coach & Lorry Park
Poole Station
Poole Arts Centre
PARKSTONE ROAD
SELDOWN LANE
MOUNT PLEASANT RD
KINGLAND RD
Bus Station
Arndale Shopping Centre
Dolphin Indoor Swimming Pool
Pedestrian Precinct 10.00-1800hrs Mon-Sat
Pedestrians only
TOWNGATE BR
NORTH ST
SOUTH ST
DEAR HAY LANE
WEST QUAY ROAD
WEST STREET
NEW ORCHARD
HILL ST
HIGH ST
OLD ORCHARD
PO
Quay West Marina
RNLI Headquarters
Guildhall
CHURCH ST
Scalpen's Court Museum
STRAND ST
SKINNER ST
EAST ST
GREEN ROAD
PERRY GDNS
EMERSON RD
STANLEY RD
BALLARD
THE QUAY RD
Poole Pottery
POOLE BR
Fisheries Office
Custom House
Rock and Gem Centre
Purbeck Pottery
Harbour Office
Lifeboat Mus.
Poole Harbour
NEWFOUNDLAND DRIVE
THE QUAY

Central Christchurch

THE GROVE
FAIRMILE
WALCOTT A ALBION RD
FLAMBARD AVE
BRONTE AVE
ARCADIA RD
ENDFIELD ROAD
CANBERRA RD
JUMPERS AVE
GARDNER RD
Christchurch Hospital
Cemetery
Fire Station
AVON RD WEST
GROVE RD WEST
GROVE RD EAST
PORTFIELD ROAD
MILL ROAD
BARRACK ROAD
CLARENDON RD
ARTHUR RD
Station
FAIR-FIELD
Beaconsfield RD
CHRISTCHURCH BY-PASS
RIVER
STONY LANE
AVON
STOUR ROAD
MANOR ROAD
GLEADOWE AVE
ST JOHNS RD
KINGS AVENUE
TWYNHAM AVE
Police Station
Law Court
Rec. Grnd
PO
Library
DOUGLAS AVENUE
SOPERS LANE
HIGH ST
CASTLE ST
BRIDGE ST
WATER-LOO PL.
SOUTH VIEW ROAD
WICKFIELD AVE
WICK LANE
MARGARETS AVENUE
QUAY ROAD
QUEENS AVE
Christchurch Priory and Church
Christchurch Quay
RIVER STOUR
Golf Course
River Stour
IFORD LANE
WILLOW DRIVE
WILLOW WAY
TUCKTON ROAD
WICK LA
WICK LANE

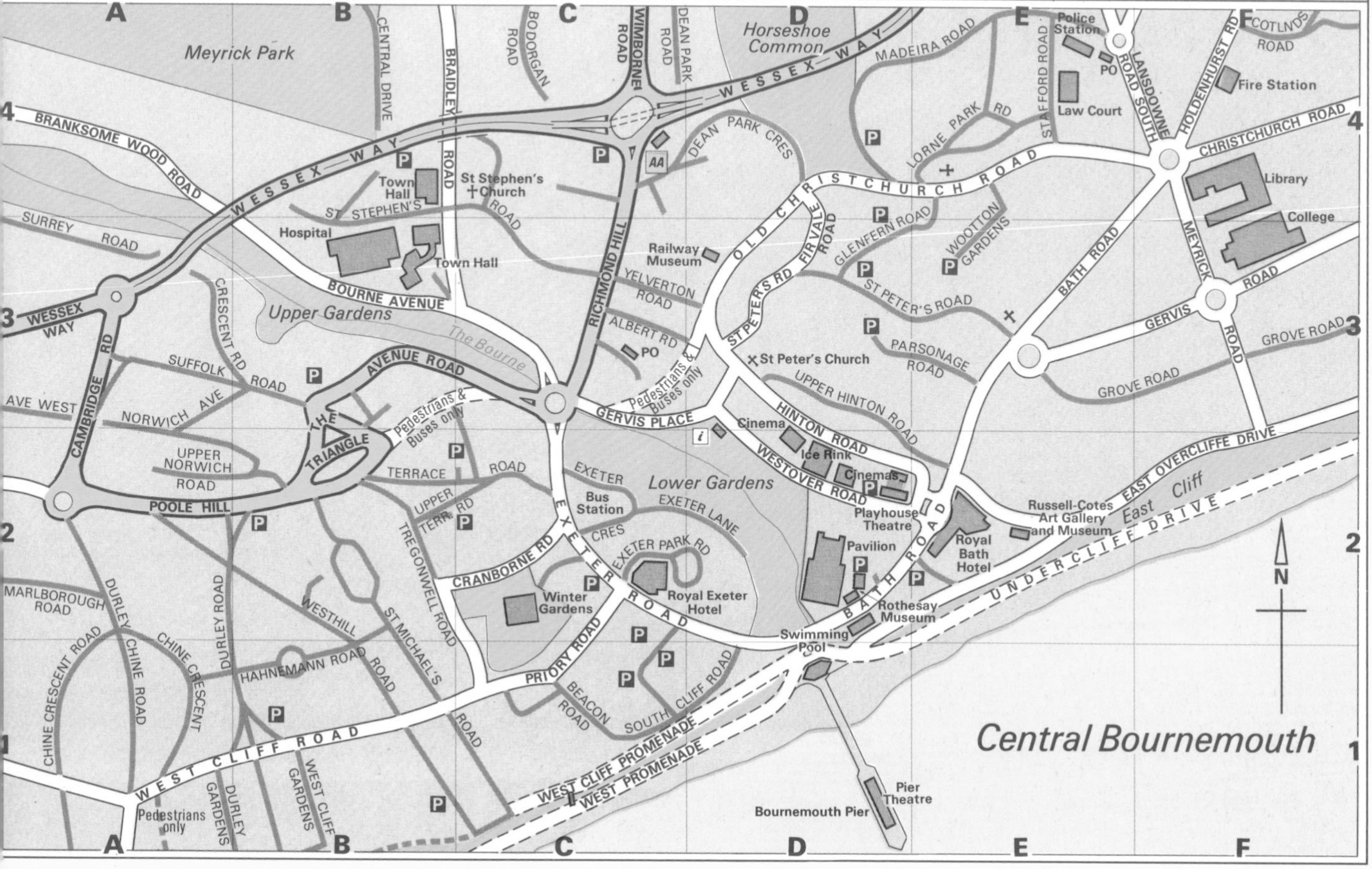

Central Bournemouth

Meyrick Park
CENTRAL DRIVE
BODORGAN ROAD
BRAIDLEY ROAD
WIMBORNE ROAD
DEAN PARK ROAD
Horseshoe Common
WESSEX WAY
MADEIRA ROAD
STAFFORD ROAD
Police Station
PO
Law Court
Fire Station
SCOTLNDS ROAD
HOLDENHURST RD
LANSDOWNE RD SOUTH
CHRISTCHURCH ROAD
BRANKSOME WOOD ROAD
SURREY ROAD
WESSEX WAY
Town Hall
St Stephen's Church
ST STEPHEN'S ROAD
Hospital
Town Hall
BOURNE AVENUE
Upper Gardens
The Bourne
RICHMOND HILL
Railway Museum
YELVERTON ROAD
DEAN PARK CRES
LORNE PARK RD
OLD CHRISTCHURCH ROAD
FIR VALE RD
GLENFERN ROAD
WOOTTON GARDENS
WNTON GARDENS
BATH ROAD
MEYRICK ROAD
Library
College
CHRISTCHURCH ROAD
GROVE ROAD
GERVIS ROAD
AA
CRESCENT RD
CAMBRIDGE RD
AVE WEST
SUFFOLK RD
NORWICH AVE
UPPER NORWICH ROAD
POOLE HILL
MARLBOROUGH ROAD
DURLEY ROAD
CHINE CRESCENT
CHINE CRESCENT ROAD
DURLEY CHINE ROAD
DURLEY CRESCENT
WESTHILL ROAD
HAHNEMANN ROAD
ST MICHAEL'S ROAD
TREGONWELL ROAD
CRANBORNE RD
WEST CLIFF ROAD
WEST CLIFF GARDENS
DURLEY GARDENS
Pedestrians only
THE TRIANGLE
AVENUE ROAD
Pedestrians & Buses only
TERRACE ROAD
UPPER TERRACE RD
EXETER RD
EXETER CRES
EXETER LANE
EXETER PARK RD
Bus Station
Lower Gardens
ALBERT RD
PO
Pedestrians & Buses only
GERVIS PLACE
Cinema
HINTON ROAD
St Peter's Church
ST PETER'S ROAD
PARSONAGE ROAD
UPPER HINTON ROAD
Ice Rink
Cinemas
WESTOVER ROAD
Playhouse Theatre
Pavilion
Royal Bath Hotel
Rothesay Museum
Russell-Cotes Art Gallery and Museum
East Cliff
EAST OVERCLIFFE DRIVE
UNDERCLIFF DRIVE
Winter Gardens
Royal Exeter Hotel
PRIORY ROAD
BEACON ROAD
SOUTH CLIFF ROAD
BATH ROAD
Swimming Pool
WEST CLIFF PROMENADE
WEST PROMENADE
WEST CLIFF ROAD
Pier Theatre
Bournemouth Pier

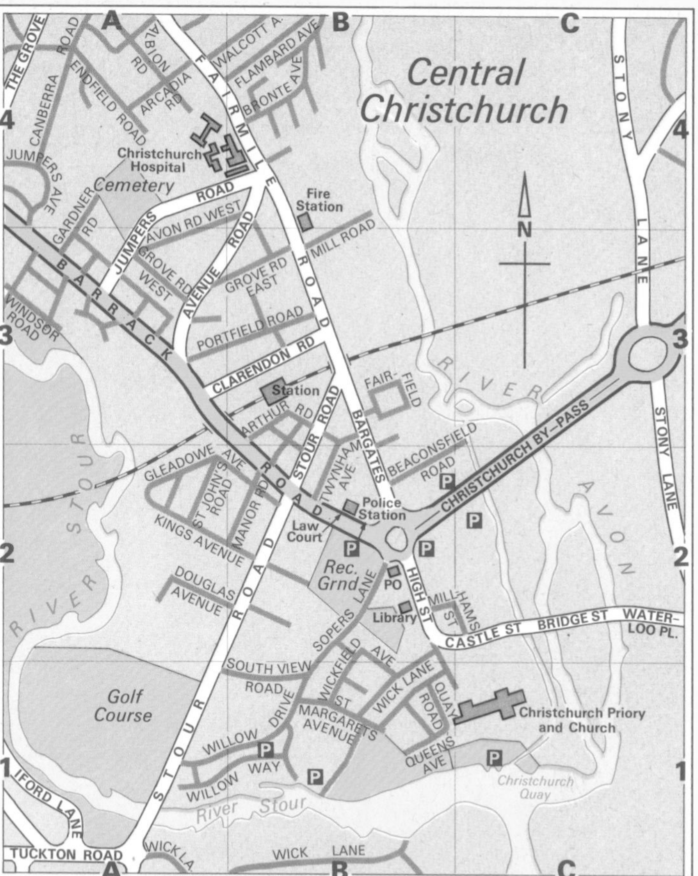

BOURNEMOUTH
The pier, safe sea-bathing, golden sands facing south and sheltered by steep cliffs, and plenty of amenities for the holiday maker make Bournemouth one of the most popular resorts on the south coast of England.

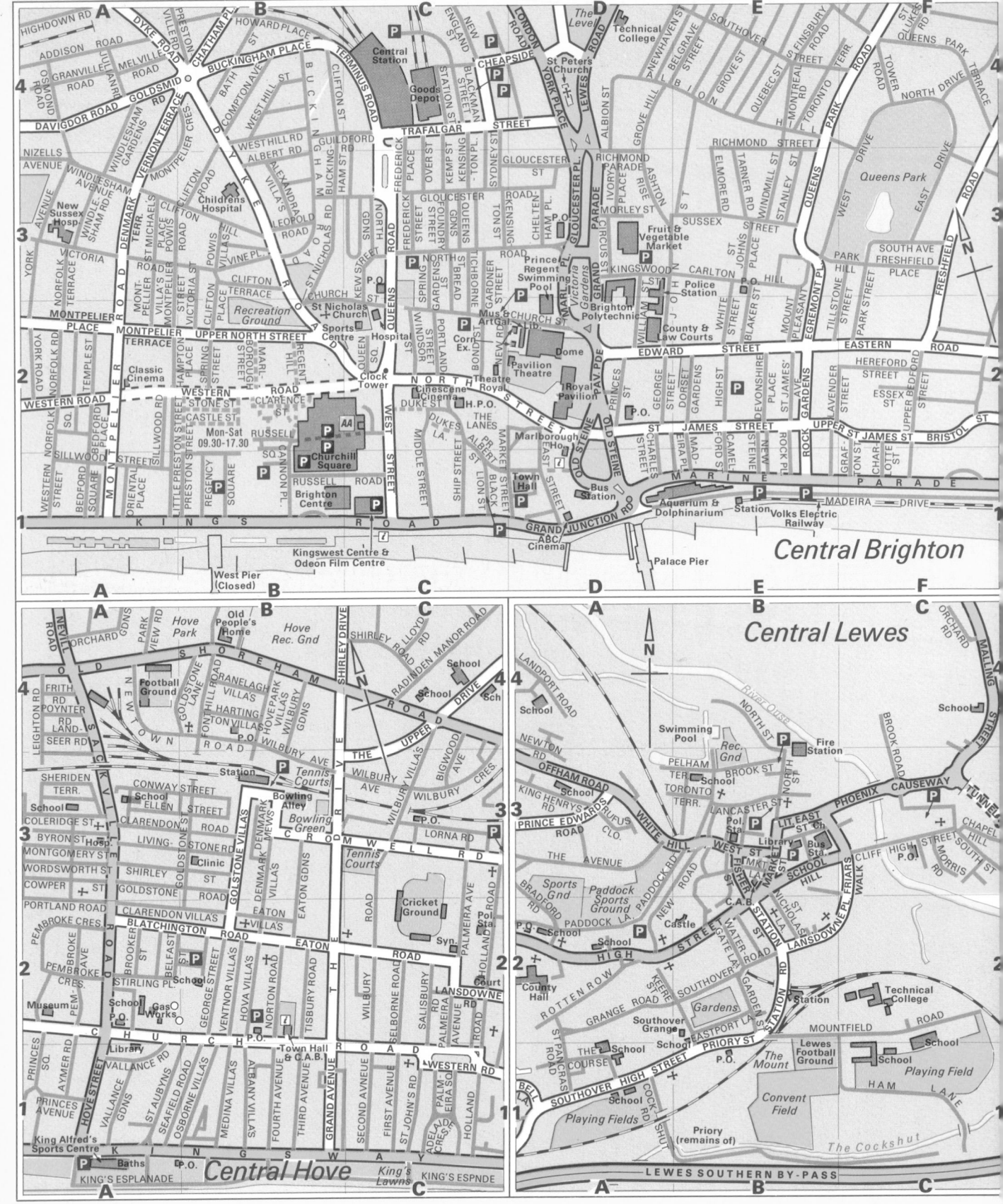

Brighton

Dr Richard Russell, from nearby Lewes, created the resort of Brighton almost singlehandedly. And he did it not by building houses or hotels, but by writing a book. His book, which praised the health-giving properties of sea-bathing and sea air, soon came to the attention of George, then Prince Regent and one day to become King George IV. He stayed at Brighthelmstone – as it was then known –

in 1783 and again in 1784. In 1786 the Prince rented a villa on the Steine – a modest house that was eventually transformed into the astonishing Pavilion. By 1800 – its popularity assured by royal patronage – the resort was described in a contemporary directory as 'the most frequented and without exception one of the most fashionable towns in the kingdom'.

Perhaps the description does not quite fit today, but Brighton is a perennially popular seaside

resort, as well as a shopping centre, university town and cultural venue. The Pavilion still draws most crowds, of course. Its beginnings as a villa are entirely hidden in a riot of Near Eastern architectural motifs, largely the creation of John Nash. Brighton's great days as a Regency resort *par excellence* are preserved in the sweeping crescents and elegant terraces, buildings which help to make it one of the finest townscapes in the whole of Europe.

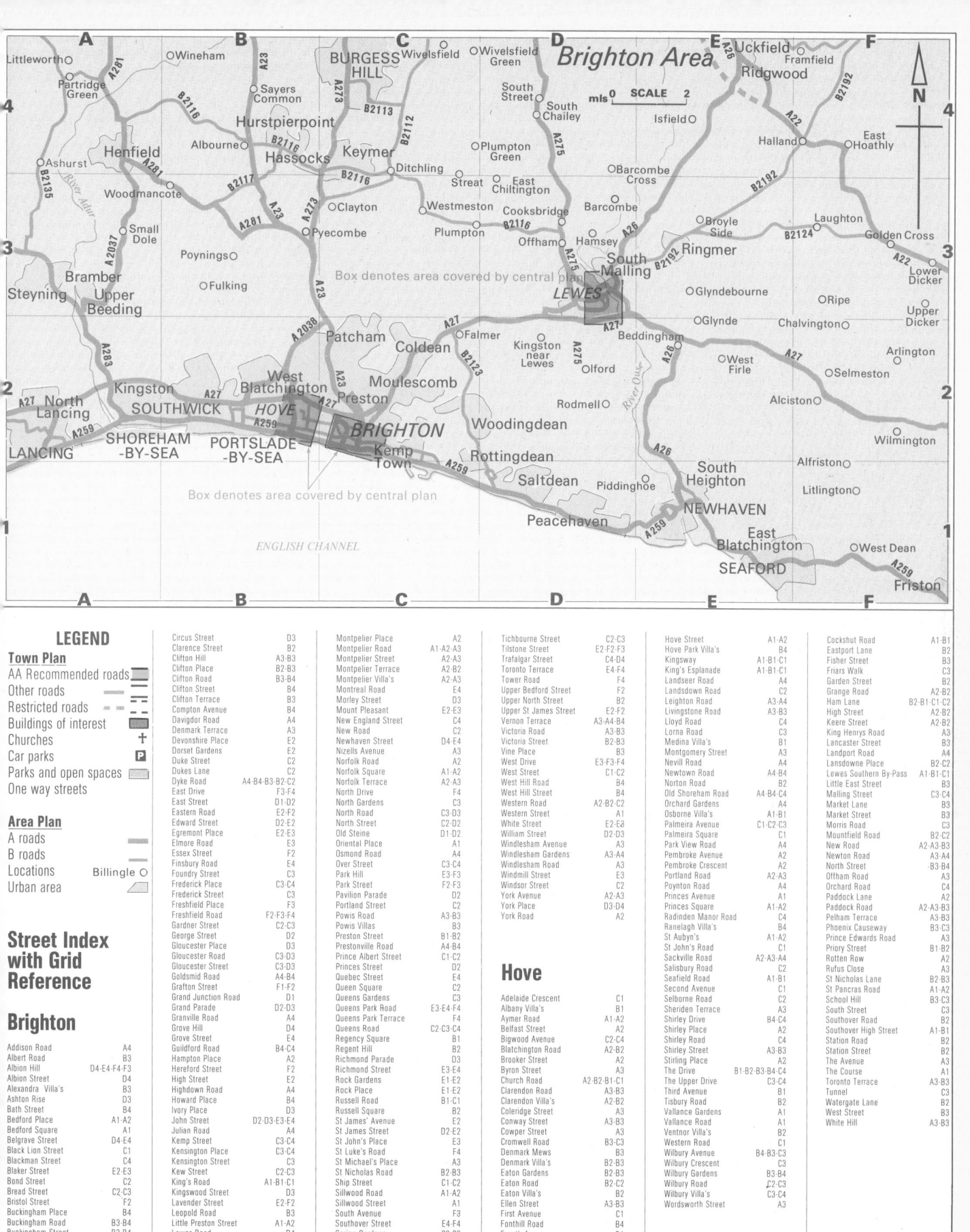

LEGEND

Town Plan

AA Recommended roads	▬▬
Other roads	▬
Restricted roads	┅┅
Buildings of interest	▨
Churches	+
Car parks	P
Parks and open spaces	▨
One way streets	

Area Plan

A roads	▬
B roads	▬
Locations	Billingle ○
Urban area	◢

Street Index with Grid Reference

Brighton

Addison Road	A4	Circus Street	D3
Albert Road	B3	Clarence Street	B2
Albion Hill	D4-E4-F4-F3	Clifton Hill	A3-B3
Albion Street	D4	Clifton Place	B2-B3
Alexandra Villa's	B3	Clifton Road	B3-B4
Ashton Rise	D3	Clifton Street	B4
Bath Street	B4	Clifton Terrace	B3
Bedford Place	A1-A2	Compton Avenue	B4
Bedford Square	A1	Davigdor Road	A4
Belgrave Street	D4-E4	Denmark Terrace	A3
Black Lion Street	C1	Devonshire Place	E2
Blackman Street	C4	Dorset Gardens	E2
Blaker Street	E2-E3	Duke Street	C2
Bond Street	C2	Dukes Lane	C2
Bread Street	C2-C3	Dyke Road	A4-B4-B3-B2-C2
Bristol Street	F2	East Drive	F3-F4
Buckingham Place	B4	East Street	D1-D2
Buckingham Road	B3-B4	Eastern Road	E2-F2
Buckingham Street	B3-B4	Edward Street	D2-E2
Camelford Street	E1-E2	Egremont Place	E2-E3
Cannon Place	B1-B2	Elmore Road	E3
Carlton Hill	E3	Essex Street	F2
Castle Street	B2	Finsbury Road	E4
Charles Street	D1-D2	Foundry Street	C3
Charlotte Street	F1-F2	Frederick Place	C3-C4
Chatham Place	B4	Frederick Street	C3
Cheapside	C4-D4	Freshfield Place	F3
Cheltenham Place	D3	Freshfield Road	F2-F3-F4
Church Street	B2-C2-D2	Gardner Street	C2-C3
		George Street	D2
		Gloucester Place	D3
		Gloucester Road	C3-D3
		Gloucester Street	C3-D3
		Goldsmid Road	A4-B4
		Grafton Street	F1-F2
		Grand Junction Road	D1
		Grand Parade	D2-D3
		Granville Road	A4
		Grove Hill	D4
		Grove Street	E4
		Guildford Road	B4-C4
		Hampton Place	A2
		Hereford Street	F2
		High Street	E2
		Highdown Road	A4
		Howard Place	B4
		Ivory Place	D3
		John Street	D2-D3-E3-E4
		Julian Road	A4
		Kemp Street	C3-C4
		Kensington Place	C3-C4
		Kensington Street	C3
		Kew Street	C2-C3
		King's Road	A1-B1-C1
		Kingswood Street	D3
		Lavender Street	E2-F2
		Leopold Road	B3
		Little Preston Street	A1-A2
		Lewes Road	D4
		London Road	D4
		Madeira Drive	D1-E1-F1
		Madeira Place	E1-E2
		Marine Parade	D1-E1-F1
		Market Street	C2-D2-D1
		Marlborough Place	D2-D3
		Marlborough Street	B2
		Melville Road	A4
		Middle Street	C1-C2
		Montpelier Crescent	A3-B3-B4

Montpelier Place	A2	Tichbourne Street	C2-C3
Montpelier Road	A1-A2-A3	Tilstone Street	E2-F2-F3
Montpelier Street	A2-A3	Trafalgar Street	C4-D4
Montpelier Terrace	A2-B2	Toronto Terrace	E4-F4
Montpelier Villa's	A2-A3	Tower Road	F4
Montreal Road	E4	Upper Bedford Street	F2
Morley Street	D3	Upper North Street	B2
Mount Pleasant	E2-E3	Upper St James Street	E2-F2
New England Street	C4	Vernon Terrace	A3-A4-B4
New Road	C2	Victoria Road	A3-B3
Newhaven Street	D4-E4	Victoria Street	B2-B3
Nizells Avenue	A3	Vine Place	B3
Norfolk Road	A2	West Drive	E3-F3-F4
Norfolk Square	A1-A2	West Street	C1-C2
Norfolk Terrace	A2-A3	West Hill Road	B4
North Drive	F4	West Hill Street	B4
North Gardens	C3	Western Road	A2-B2-C2
North Road	C3-D3	Western Street	A1
North Street	C2-D2	White Street	E2-E3
Old Steine	D1-D2	William Street	D2-D3
Oriental Place	A1	Windlesham Avenue	A3
Osmond Road	A4	Windlesham Gardens	A3-A4
Over Street	C3-C4	Windlesham Road	A3
Park Hill	E3-F3	Windmill Street	E3
Park Street	F2-F3	Windsor Street	C2
Pavilion Parade	D2	York Avenue	A1
Portland Street	C2	York Place	D3-D4
Powis Road	A3-B3	York Road	A2
Powis Villas	B3		
Preston Street	B1-B2		
Prestonville Road	A4-B4		
Prince Albert Street	C1-C2		
Princes Street	D2		
Quebec Street	E4		
Queen Square	C2		
Queens Gardens	C3		
Queens Park Road	E3-E4-F4		
Queens Park Terrace	F4		
Queens Road	C2-C3-C4		
Regency Square	B1		
Regent Hill	B2		
Richmond Parade	D3		
Richmond Street	E3-E4		
Rock Gardens	E1-E2		
Rock Place	E1-E2		
Russell Road	B1-C1		
Russell Square	B2		
St James's Avenue	E2		
St James Street	D2-E2		
St John's Place	E3		
St Luke's Road	F4		
St Michael's Place	A3		
St Nicholas Road	B2-B3		
Ship Street	C1-C2		
Sillwood Road	A1-A2		
Sillwood Street	A1		
South Avenue	F3		
Southover Street	E4-F4		
Spring Gardens	C2-C3		
Spring Street	B2		
Stanley Street	E3		
Station Street	C4		
Stone Street	B2		
Sussex Street	E3		
Sydney Street	C3-C4		
The Lanes	C2		
Tarner Road	E3		
Temple Street	A2		
Terminus Road	B4-C4		

Hove

Adelaide Crescent	C1	Hove Street	A1-A2
Albany Villa's	B1	Hove Park Villa's	B4
Aymer Road	A1-A2	Kingsway	A1-B1-C1
Belfast Street	A2	King's Esplanade	A1-B1-C1
Bigwood Avenue	C2-C4	Landseer Road	A4
Blatchington Road	A2-B2	Landsdown Road	C2
Brooker Street	A2	Leighton Road	A3-A4
Byron Street	A3	Livingstone Road	A3-B3
Church Road	A2-B2-B1-C1	Lloyd Road	C4
Clarendon Road	A3-B3	Lorna Road	C3
Clarendon Villa's	A2-B2	Medina Villa's	B1
Coleridge Street	A3	Montgomery Street	A3
Conway Street	A3-B3	Nevill Road	A4
Cowper Street	A3	Newtown Road	A4-B4
Cromwell Road	B3-C3	Norton Road	B2
Denmark Mews	B3	Old Shoreham Road	A4-B4-C4
Denmark Villa's	B2-B3	Orchard Gardens	A4
Eaton Gardens	B2-B3	Osborne Villa's	A1-B1
Eaton Road	B2	Palmeira Avenue	C1-C2-C3
Eaton Villa's	B2	Palmeira Square	C1
Ellen Street	A3-B3	Park View Road	A4
First Avenue	C1	Pembroke Avenue	A2
Fonthill Road	B4	Pembroke Crescent	A2
Fourth Avenue	B1	Portland Road	A2-A3
Frith Road	A4	Poynton Road	A4
George Street	B2	Princes Avenue	A1
Goldstone Lane	A4-B4	Princes Square	A1-A2
Goldstone Road	A3-B3	Radinden Manor Road	C4
Goldstone Street	B2-B3	Ranelagh Villa's	B4
Goldstone Villa's	B2-B3	St Aubyn's	A1-A2
Grand Avenue	B1	St John's Road	C1
Hartington Villas	A3	Sackville Road	A2-A3-A4
Holland Road	C1-C2-C3	Salisbury Road	C2
Hove Villa's	B2	Seafield Road	A1-B1
		Second Avenue	C1
		Selborne Road	C2
		Sheriden Terrace	A3
		Shirley Drive	B4-C4
		Shirley Place	A3
		Shirley Road	C4
		Shirley Street	A3-B3
		Stirling Place	A2
		The Drive	B1-B2-B3-B4-C4
		The Upper Drive	C3-C4
		Third Avenue	B1
		Tisbury Road	B2
		Vallance Gardens	A1
		Vallance Road	A1
		Ventnor Villa's	B2
		Western Road	C1
		Wilbur Avenue	B4-B3-C3
		Wilbur Crescent	C3
		Wilbury Gardens	B3-B4
		Wilbury Road	C2
		Wilbur Villa's	C3-C4
		Wordsworth Street	A3

Cockshut Road	A1-B1
Eastport Lane	B2
Fisher Street	B3
Friars Walk	C3
Garden Street	B2
Grange Road	A2-B2
Ham Lane	B2-B1-C1-C2
High Street	A2-B2
Keere Street	A2-B2
King Henrys Road	A3
Lancaster Street	B3
Landport Road	A3
Lansdowne Place	B2-C2
Lewes Southern By-Pass	A1-B1-C1
Little East Street	B3
Malling Street	C3-C4
Market Lane	B3
Market Street	B3
Morris Road	C3
Mountfield Road	B2-C2
New Road	A2-A3-B3
Newton Road	A3-A4
North Street	B3-B4
Offham Road	A3
Orchard Road	C4
Paddock Lane	A2
Paddock Road	A2-A3-B3
Pelham Terrace	A3-B3
Phoenix Causeway	B3-C3
Prince Edwards Road	A3
Priory Street	B1-B2
Rotten Row	A2
Rufus Close	A3
St Nicholas Lane	B2-B3
St Pancras Road	A1-A2
School Hill	B3-C3
South Street	C3
Southover Road	B2
Southover High Street	A1-B1
Station Road	B2
Station Street	B2
The Avenue	A3
The Course	A1
Toronto Terrace	A3-B3
Tunnel	C3
Watergate Lane	B2
West Street	B3
White Hill	A3-B3

Lewes

Bell Lane	A1
Bradford Road	A2-A3
Brook Road	C3-C4
Brook Street	B3
Chapel Hill	C3
Cliff High Street	C3

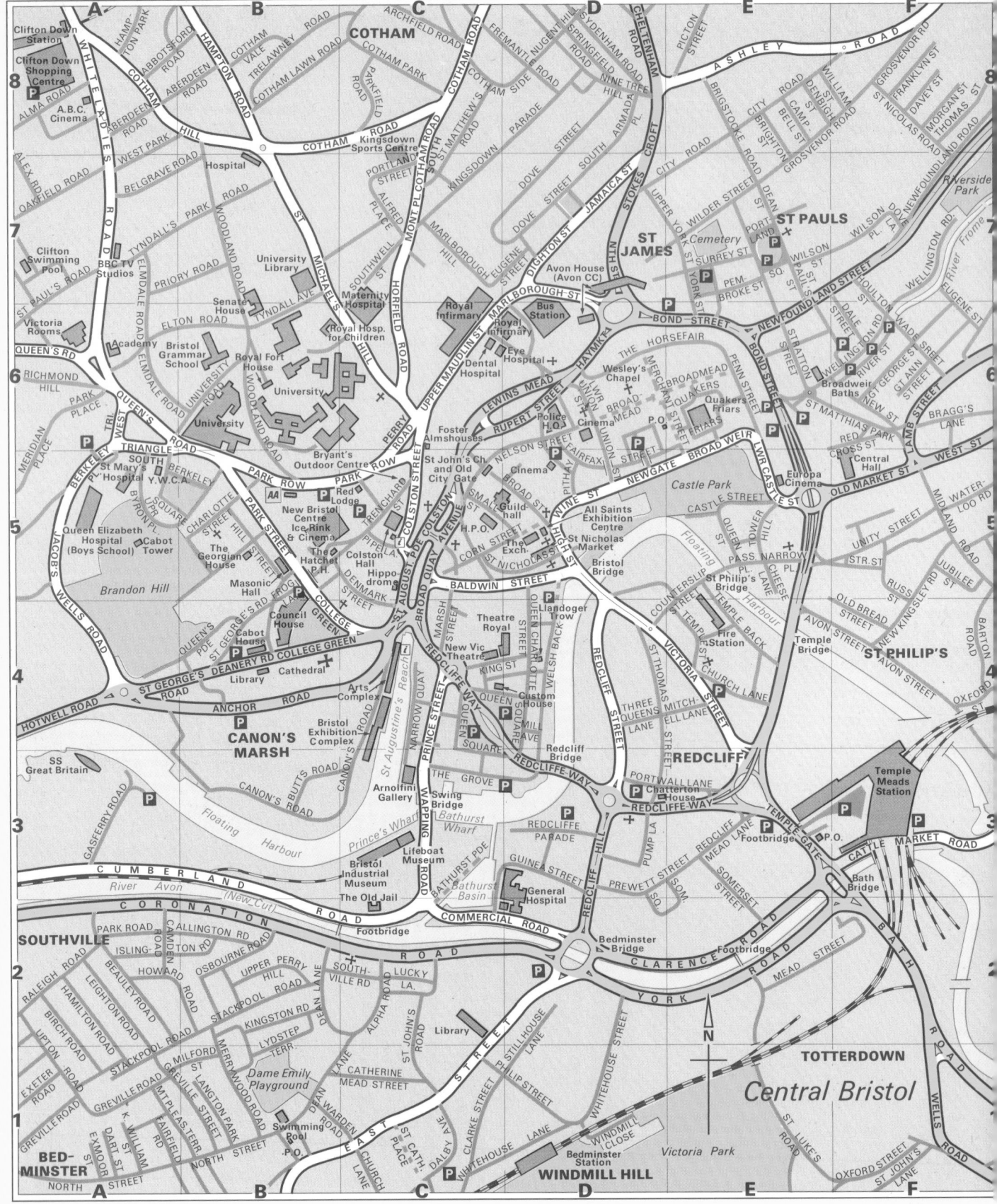

Bristol

One of Britain's most historic seaports, Bristol retains many of its visible links with the past, despite terrible damage inflicted during bombing raids in World War II. Most imposing is the cathedral, founded as an abbey church in 1140. Perhaps even more famous than the cathedral is the Church of St Mary Redcliffe. Ranking among the finest churches in the country, it owes much of

its splendour to 14th- and 15th-century merchants who bestowed huge sums of money on it.

The merchant families brought wealth to the whole of Bristol, and their trading links with the world are continued in today's modern aerospace and technological industries. Much of the best of Bristol can be seen in the area of the Floating Harbour – an arm of the Avon. Several of the old warehouses have been converted into museums, galleries and exhibition centres. Among them are

genuinely picturesque old pubs, the best-known of which is the Llandoger Trow. It is a timbered 17th-century house, the finest of its kind in Bristol. Further up the same street – King Street – is the Theatre Royal, built in 1766 and the oldest theatre in the country. In Corn Street, the heart of the business area, is a magnificent 18th-century corn exchange. In front of it are the four pillars known as the 'nails', on which merchants used to make cash transactions, hence 'to pay on the nail'.

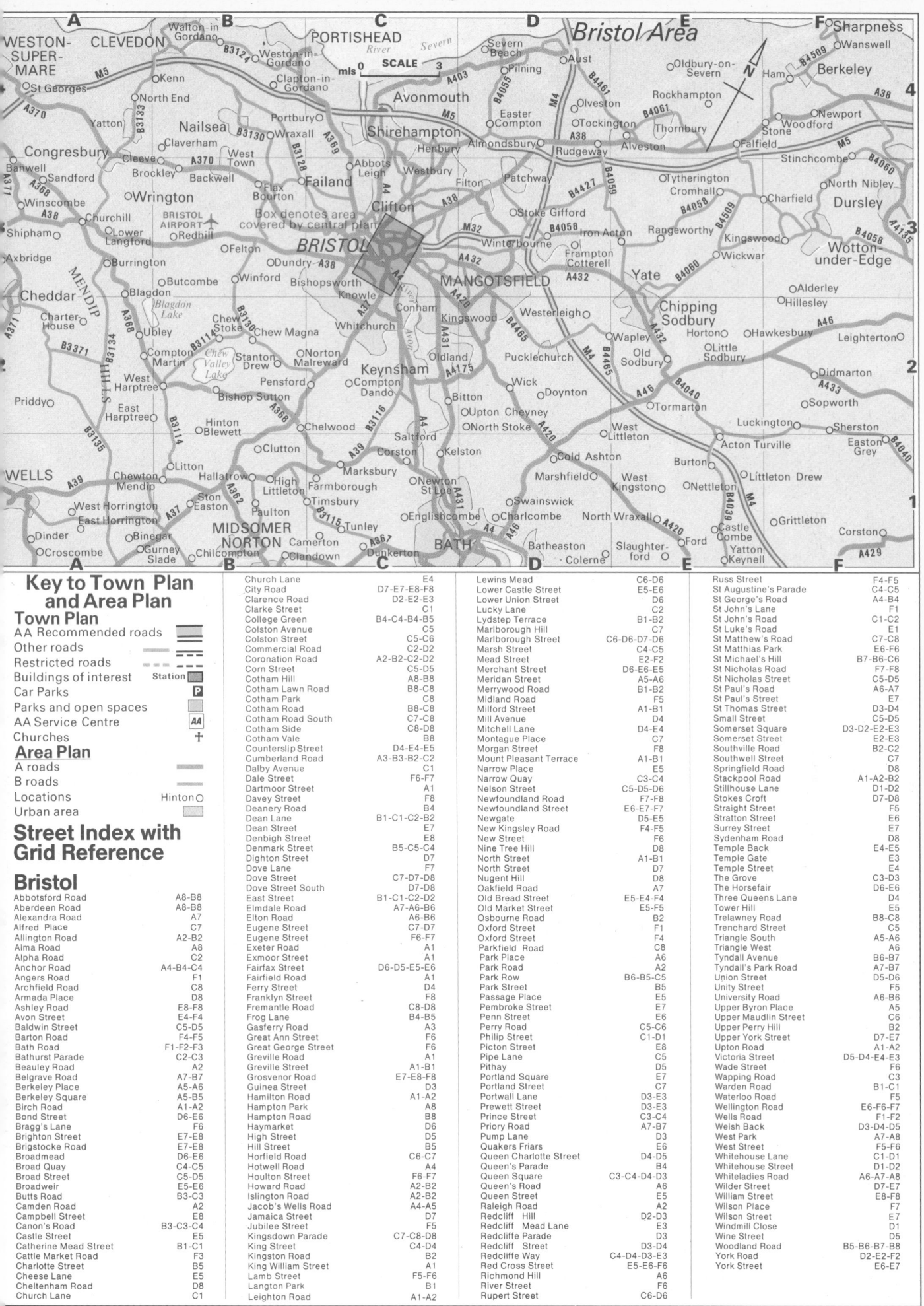

Bristol Area

Street Index with Grid Reference

Bristol

Abbotsford Road	A8-B8
Aberdeen Road	A8-B8
Alexandra Road	A7
Alfred Place	C7
Allington Road	A2-B2
Alma Road	A8
Alpha Road	C2
Anchor Road	A4-B4-C4
Angers Road	F1
Archfield Road	C8
Armada Place	D8
Ashley Road	E8-F8
Avon Street	E4-F4
Baldwin Street	C5-D5
Barton Road	F4-F5
Bath Road	F1-F2-F3
Bathurst Parade	C2-C3
Beauley Road	A2
Belgrave Road	A7-B7
Berkeley Place	A5-A6
Berkeley Square	A5-B5
Birch Road	A1-A2
Bond Street	D6-E6
Bragg's Lane	F6
Brighton Street	E7-E8
Brigstocke Road	E7-E8
Broadmead	D6-E6
Broad Quay	C4-C5
Broad Street	C5-D5
Broadweir	E5-E6
Butts Road	B3-C3
Camden Road	A2
Campbell Street	E8
Canon's Road	B3-C3-C4
Castle Street	E5
Catherine Mead Street	B1-C1
Cattle Market Road	F3
Charlotte Street	B5
Cheese Lane	E5
Cheltenham Road	D8
Church Lane	C1

Church Lane	E4
City Road	D7-E7-E8-F8
Clarence Road	D2-E2-E3
Clarke Street	C1
College Green	B4-C4-B4-B5
Colston Avenue	C5
Colston Street	C5-C6
Commercial Road	C2-D2
Coronation Road	A2-B2-C2-D2
Corn Street	C5-D5
Cotham Hill	A8-B8
Cotham Lawn Road	B8-C8
Cotham Park	C8
Cotham Road	B8-C8
Cotham Road South	C7-C8
Cotham Side	C8-D8
Cotham Vale	B8
Countership Street	D4-E4-E5
Cumberland Road	A3-B3-B2-C2
Dalby Avenue	C1
Dale Street	F6-F7
Dartmoor Street	A1
Davey Street	F8
Deanery Road	B4
Dean Lane	B1-C1-C2-B2
Dean Street	E7
Denbigh Street	E8
Denmark Street	B5-C5-C4
Dighton Street	D7
Dove Lane	F7
Dove Street	C7-D7-D8
Dove Street South	D7-D8
East Street	B1-C1-C2-D2
Elmdale Road	A7-A6-B6
Elton Road	A6-B6
Eugene Street	C7-D7
Eugene Street	F6-F7
Exeter Road	A1
Exmoor Street	A1
Fairfax Street	D6-D5-E5-E6
Fairfield Road	A1
Ferry Street	D4
Franklyn Street	F8
Fremantle Road	C8-D8
Frog Lane	B4-B5
Gasferry Road	A3
Great Ann Street	F6
Great George Street	F6
Greville Road	A1
Greville Street	A1-B1
Grosvenor Road	E7-E8-F8
Guinea Street	D3
Hamilton Road	A1-A2
Hampton Park	A8
Hampton Road	B8
Haymarket	D6
High Street	D5
Hill Street	B5
Horfield Road	C6-C7
Hotwell Road	A4
Houlton Street	F6-F7
Howard Road	A2-B2
Islington Road	A2-B2
Jacob's Wells Road	A4-A5
Jamaica Street	D7
Jubilee Street	F5
Kingsdown Parade	C7-C8-D8
King Street	C4-D4
Kingston Road	B2
King William Street	A1
Lamb Street	F5-F6
Langton Park	B1
Leighton Road	A1-A2

Lewins Mead	C6-D6
Lower Castle Street	E5-E6
Lower Union Street	D6
Lucky Lane	C2
Lydstep Terrace	B1-B2
Marlborough Hill	C7
Marlborough Street	C6-D6-D7-D6
Marsh Street	C4-C5
Mead Street	E2-F2
Merchant Street	D6-E6-E5
Meridan Street	A5-A6
Merrywood Road	B1-B2
Midland Road	F5
Milford Street	A1-B1
Mill Avenue	D4
Mitchell Lane	D4-E4
Montague Place	C7
Morgan Street	F8
Mount Pleasant Terrace	A1-B1
Narrow Place	E5
Narrow Quay	C3-C4
Nelson Street	C5-D5-D6
Newfoundland Road	F7-F8
Newfoundland Street	E6-E7-F7
Newgate	D5-E5
New Kingsley Road	F4-F5
New Street	F6
Nine Tree Hill	D8
North Street	A1-B1
North Street	D7
Nugent Hill	D8
Oakfield Road	A7
Old Bread Street	E5-E4-F4
Old Market Street	E5-F5
Osbourne Road	B2
Oxford Street	F1
Oxford Street	F4
Parkfield Road	C8
Park Place	A6
Park Road	A2
Park Row	B6-B5-C5
Park Street	B5
Passage Place	E5
Pembroke Street	E7
Penn Street	E6
Perry Road	C5-C6
Philip Street	C1-D1
Picton Street	E8
Pipe Lane	C5
Pithay	D5
Portland Square	E7
Portland Street	C7
Portwall Lane	D3-E3
Prewett Street	D3-E3
Prince Street	C3-C4
Priory Road	A7-B7
Pump Lane	D3
Quakers Friars	E6
Queen Charlotte Street	D4-D5
Queen's Parade	B4
Queen Square	C3-C4-D4-D3
Queen's Road	A6
Queen Street	E5
Raleigh Road	A2
Redcliff Hill	D2-D3
Redcliff Mead Lane	E3
Redcliffe Parade	D3
Redcliff Street	D3-D4
Redcliffe Way	C4-D4-D3-E3
Red Cross Street	E5-E6-F6
Richmond Hill	A6
River Street	F6
Rupert Street	C6-D6

Russ Street	F4-F5
St Augustine's Parade	C4-C5
St George's Road	A4-B4
St John's Lane	F1
St John's Road	C1-C2
St Luke's Road	E1
St Matthew's Road	C7-C8
St Matthias Park	E6-E7
St Michael's Hill	B7-B6-C6
St Nicholas Road	F7-F8
St Nicholas Street	C5-D5
St Paul's Road	A6-A7
St Paul's Street	E7
St Thomas Street	D3-D4
Small Street	C5-D5
Somerset Square	D3-D2-E2-E3
Somerset Street	E2-E3
Southville Road	B2-C2
Southwell Street	C7
Springfield Road	D8
Stackpool Road	A1-A2-B2
Stillhouse Lane	D1-D2
Stokes Croft	D7-D8
Straight Street	F5
Stratton Street	E6
Surrey Street	E7
Sydenham Road	D8
Temple Back	E4-E5
Temple Gate	E3
Temple Street	E4
The Grove	C3-D3
The Horsefair	D6-E6
Three Queens Lane	D4
Tower Hill	E5
Trelawney Road	B8-C8
Trenchard Street	C5
Triangle South	A5-A6
Triangle West	A6
Tyndall Avenue	B6-B7
Tyndall's Park Road	A7-B7
Union Street	D5-D6
Unity Street	F5
University Road	A6-B6
Upper Byron Place	A5
Upper Maudlin Street	C6
Upper Perry Hill	B2
Upper York Street	D7-E7
Upton Road	A1-A2
Victoria Street	D5-D4-E4-E3
Wade Street	F6
Wapping Road	C3
Warden Road	B1-C1
Waterloo Road	F5
Wellington Road	E6-F6-F7
Wells Road	F1-F2
Welsh Back	D3-D4-D5
West Park	A7-A8
West Street	F5-F6
Whitehouse Lane	C1-D1
Whitehouse Street	D1-D2
Whiteladies Road	A6-A7-A8
Wilder Street	D7-E7
William Street	E8-F8
Wilson Place	F7
Wilson Street	E7
Windmill Close	D1
Wine Street	D5
Woodland Road	B5-B6-B7-B8
York Road	D2-E2-F2
York Street	E6-E7

165

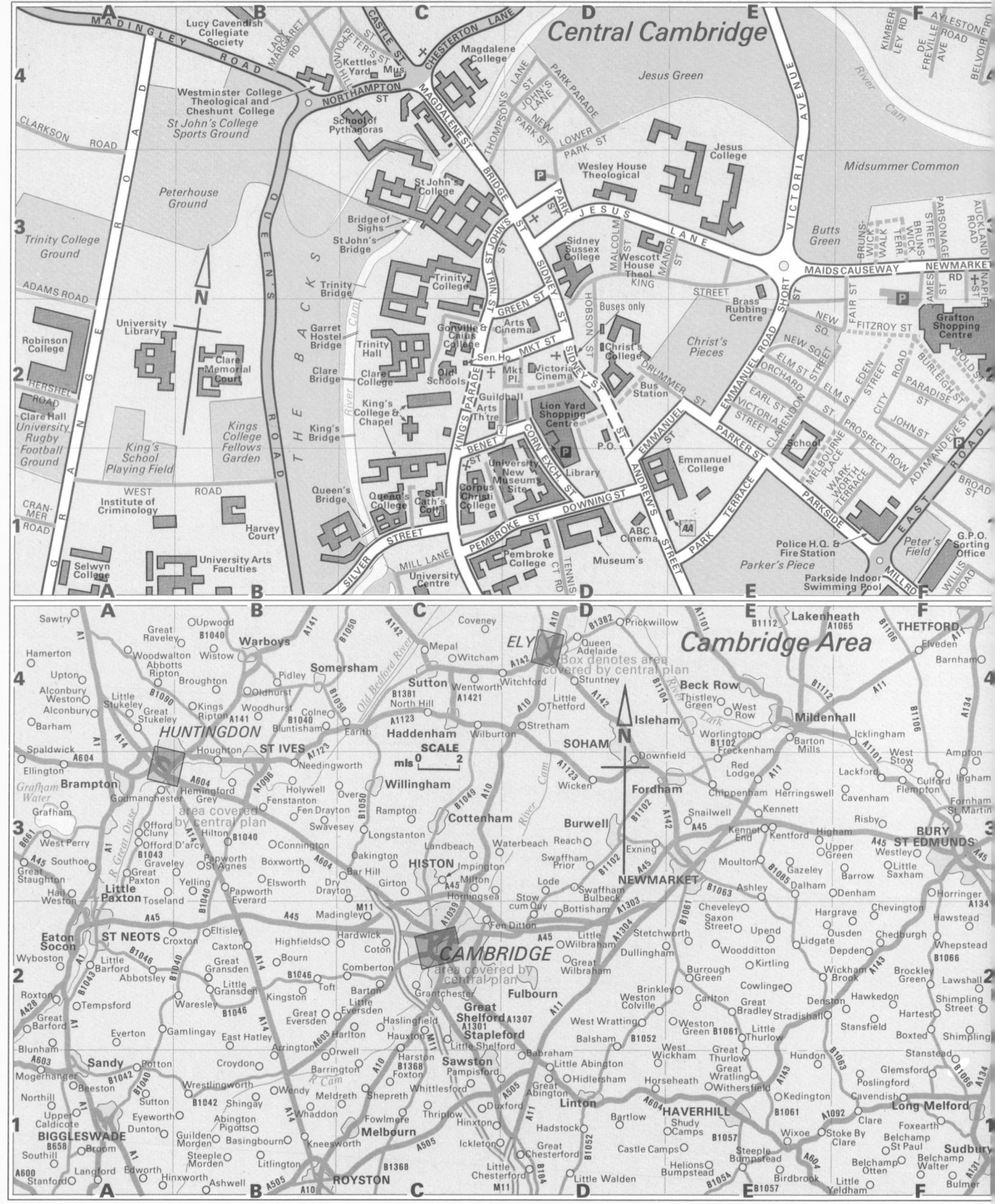

Cambridge

Few views in England, perhaps even in Europe, are as memorable as that from Cambridge's Backs towards the colleges. Dominating the scene, in every sense, is King's College Chapel. One of the finest Gothic buildings anywhere, it was built in three stages from 1446 to 1515.

No one would dispute that the chapel is Cambridge's masterpiece, but there are dozens of buildings here that would be the finest in any other town or city. Most are colleges, or are attached to colleges, and it is the university which permeates every aspect of Cambridge's landscape and life. In all there are 33 university colleges in the city, and nearly all have buildings and features of great interest. Cambridge's oldest church is St Bene't's, with a Saxon tower; its most famous is the Church of the Holy Sepulchre, one of only four round churches of its kind.

Huntingdon and **Ely** are both within easy driving distance of Cambridge. Oliver Cromwell and Samuel Pepys were pupils at Huntingdon Grammar School. The building is now a Cromwell museum. Ely also has strong Cromwellian connections – he and his family lived here for ten years. Ely's outstanding feature is the cathedral, a Norman foundation crowned by a stately octagonal lantern tower which contains the Stained Glass Museum.

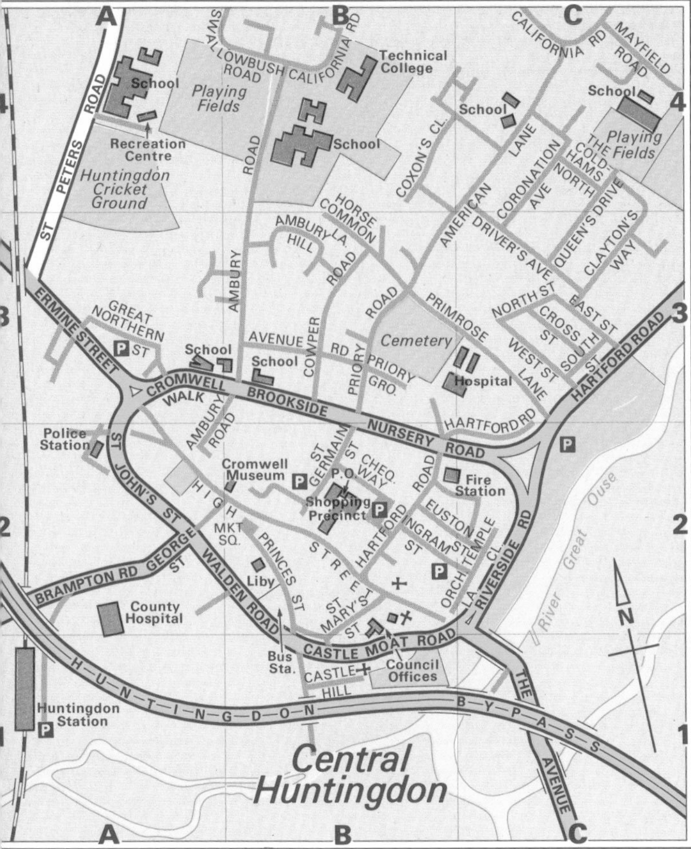

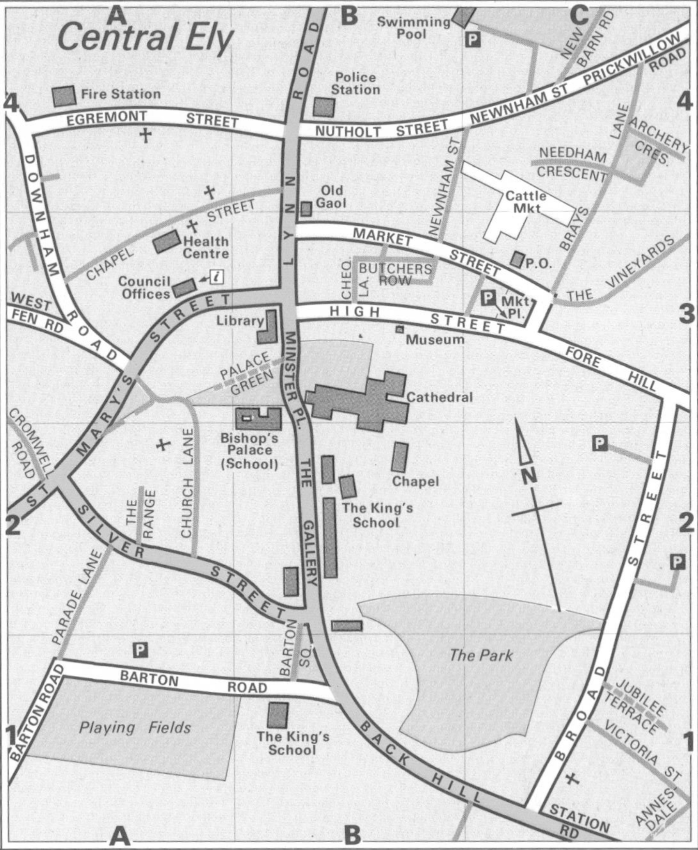

Central Huntingdon

(map labels) Swallowbush Road, California Road, Technical College, School, Playing Fields, Recreation Centre, Huntingdon Cricket Ground, St Peters Road, Ermine Street, Great Northern St, Ambury La Hill, Ambury Road, Horse Common, American Drivers Ave, Coronation Ave, North St, Queen's Drive, Clayton's Way, The Coldhams, Playing Fields, School, Cemetery, Primrose Lane, West St, South St, Cross Lane, Hospital, Priory Gro, Hartford Rd, Cowper Rd, Avenue Road, St Germain St, Cheq, P.O. Way, Euston, Cromwell Walk, Brookside, Nursery Road, Hartford Road, Police Station, Cromwell Museum, Ambury Road, High St, Shopping Precinct, Ingram Temple, Orch, La, Riverside Rd, Fire Station, P, Brampton Rd, George St, Walden Road, Princes St, St Mary's, Liby, County Hospital, Bus Sta., Castle Moat Road, Castle Hill, Council Offices, Huntingdon Station, H-U-N-T-I-N-G-D-O-N B-Y-P-A-S-S, The Avenue, River Great Ouse, N

Central Ely

(map labels) Swimming Pool, Police Station, New Barn Rd, Prickwillow Road, Fire Station, Egremont Street, Nutholt Street, Newnham St, Lane, Archery Cres., Needham Crescent, Cattle Mkt, Downham Road, Chapel St, Street, Health Centre, Old Gaol, Market Street, P.O., Brays Lane, The Vineyards, Council Offices, Library, Cheq La, Butchers Row, High Street, Mkt Pl, Fore Hill, West Fen Rd, St Mary's Street, Palace Green, Museum, Minster Pl, The Gallery, Cromwell Road, The Range, Church Lane, Silver Street, Bishop's Palace (School), Cathedral, Chapel, The King's School, Parade Lane, Barton Sq, Back Hill, The Park, Broad Street, Jubilee Terrace, Victoria St, Barton Road, Playing Fields, The King's School, Station Rd, Annesdale, N

Key to Town Plan and Area Plan

Town Plan
- AA Recommended roads
- Restricted roads
- Other roads
- Buildings of interest — College
- Car Parks — P
- Parks and open spaces
- Churches — †

Area Plan
- A roads
- B roads
- Locations — Haslingfield ○
- Urban area

Street Index with Grid Reference

Cambridge

Adam and Eve Street	F1-F2
Adams Road	A2-A3
Auckland Road	F3
Aylestone Road	F4
Belvoir Road	F4
Benet Street	C1-C2-D2
Bridge Street	C3-D3
Broad Street	F1
Brunswick Terrace	F3
Brunswick Walk	F3
Burleigh Street	F2
Castle Street	C4
Chesterton Lane	C4-D4
City Road	F2
Clarendon Street	E1-E2-F2
Clarkson Road	A3-A4
Corn Exchange Street	D1-D2
Cranmer Road	A1
De Freville Avenue	F4
Downing Street	D1
Drummer Street	D2-E2
Earl Street	E2
East Road	F1-F2
Eden Street	F2
Elm Street	E2-F2
Emmanuel Road	E2
Emmanuel Street	D1-D2-E2
Fair Street	F2-F3
Fitzroy Street	F2
Gold Street	F2
Grange Road	A1-A2-A3-A4
Green Street	C2-D2-D3
Hershel Road	A2
Hobson Street	D2-D3
James Street	F3
Jesus Lane	D3-E3
John Street	F2
Kimberley Road	F4
King's Parade	C1-C2
King Street	D2-D3-E3
Lady Margaret Road	B4
Lower Park Street	D3-D4
Madingley Road	A4-B4
Magdalene Street	C4
Maids Causeway	E3-F3
Malcolm Street	D3
Manor Street	D3-E3
Market Street	D2
Melbourne Place	E1-E2-F2
Mill Lane	C1
Mill Road	F1
Napier Street	F3
Newmarket Road	F3
New Park Street	D4
New Square	E2-F2
Northampton Street	B4-C4
Orchard Street	E2-F2
Paradise Street	F2
Parker Street	E1-E2
Park Parade	D4
Parkside	E1-F1
Park Street	D3
Park Terrace	E1
Parsonage Street	F3
Pembroke Street	C1-D1
Pound Hill	B4-C4
Prospect Row	F1-F2
Queens Road	B1-B2-B3-B4
St Andrew's Street	D2-D1-E1
St John's Street	C3-D3
St Peter's Street	B4-C4
Short Street	E2-E3
Sidney Street	D2-D3
Silver Street	B1-C1
Tennis Court Road	D1
Thompson's Lane	C3-C4-D4
Trinity Street	C2-C3
Victoria Avenue	E3-E4
Victoria Street	E2
Warkworth Terrace	F1
West Road	A1-B1
Willis Road	F1

Huntingdon

Ambury Hill	B3
Ambury Road	A2-A3-B3-B4
American Lane	B3-B4-C4
Avenue Road	B3
Brampton Road	A2
Brookside	B2-B3
California Road	B4-C4
Castle Hill	B1
Castle Moat Road	B1-B2
Chequers Way	B2
Clayton's Way	C3-C4
Coronation Avenue	C3-C4
Cowper Road	B3
Coxon's Close	B4
Cromwell Walk	A3-B3
Cross Street	C3
Driver's Avenue	C3-C4
East Street	C3
Ermine Street	A3
Euston Street	B2-C2
George Street	A2
Great Northern Street	A3
Hartford Road	B2-C2-C3
High Street	A2-B2
Horse Common Lane	B3
Huntingdon Bypass	A2-A1-B1-C1
Ingram Street	B2-C2
Market Square	B2
Mayfield Road	C4
North Street	C3
Nursery Road	B3-B2-C2
Orchard Lane	B2-C2
Primrose Lane	B3-C3
Princes Street	B2
Priory Grove	B3
Priory Road	B3
Queens Drive	C3-C4
Riverside Road	C2
St Germain Street	B2
St John's Street	A2-A3
St Mary's Street	B1-B2

Ely

Annesdale	C1
Archery Crescent	C4
Back Hill	B1-C1
Barton Road	A1-B1
Barton Square	B1-B2
Brays Lane	C3-C4
Broad Street	C1-C2-C3
Butchers Row	B3
Chapel Lane	A3-A4-B4
Chequers Lane	B3
Church Lane	A2-A3
Cromwell Road	A2-A3
Downham Road	A3-A4
Egremont Street	A4-B4
Fore Hill	C3
High Street	B3-C3
Jubilee Terrace	C1
Lynn Road	B3-B4
Market Street	B3-C3
Minster Place	B2-B3
Needham Crescent	C4
New Barn Road	C4
Newnham Street	B3-B4-C4
Nutholt Street	B4
Palace Green	A3-B3
Parade Lane	A1-A2
Prickwillow Road	C4
St Mary's Street	A2-A3-B3
Silver Street	A2-B2
Station Road	C1
The Gallery	B2
The Range	A2
The Vineyards	C3
Victoria Street	C1
West Fen Road	A3

Ely (left column continued)
St Peters Road	A3-A4
South Street	C3
Swallowbush Road	A4-B4
The Avenue	C1
The Coldhams North	C4
Temple Close	C2
Walden Road	A2-B2-B1
West Street	C3

CAMBRIDGE
Behind the gracious university college buildings beautiful lawns and gardens known as the Backs sweep down to the River Cam which, spanned by little bridges and shaded by willows, provides an idyllic setting for punting.

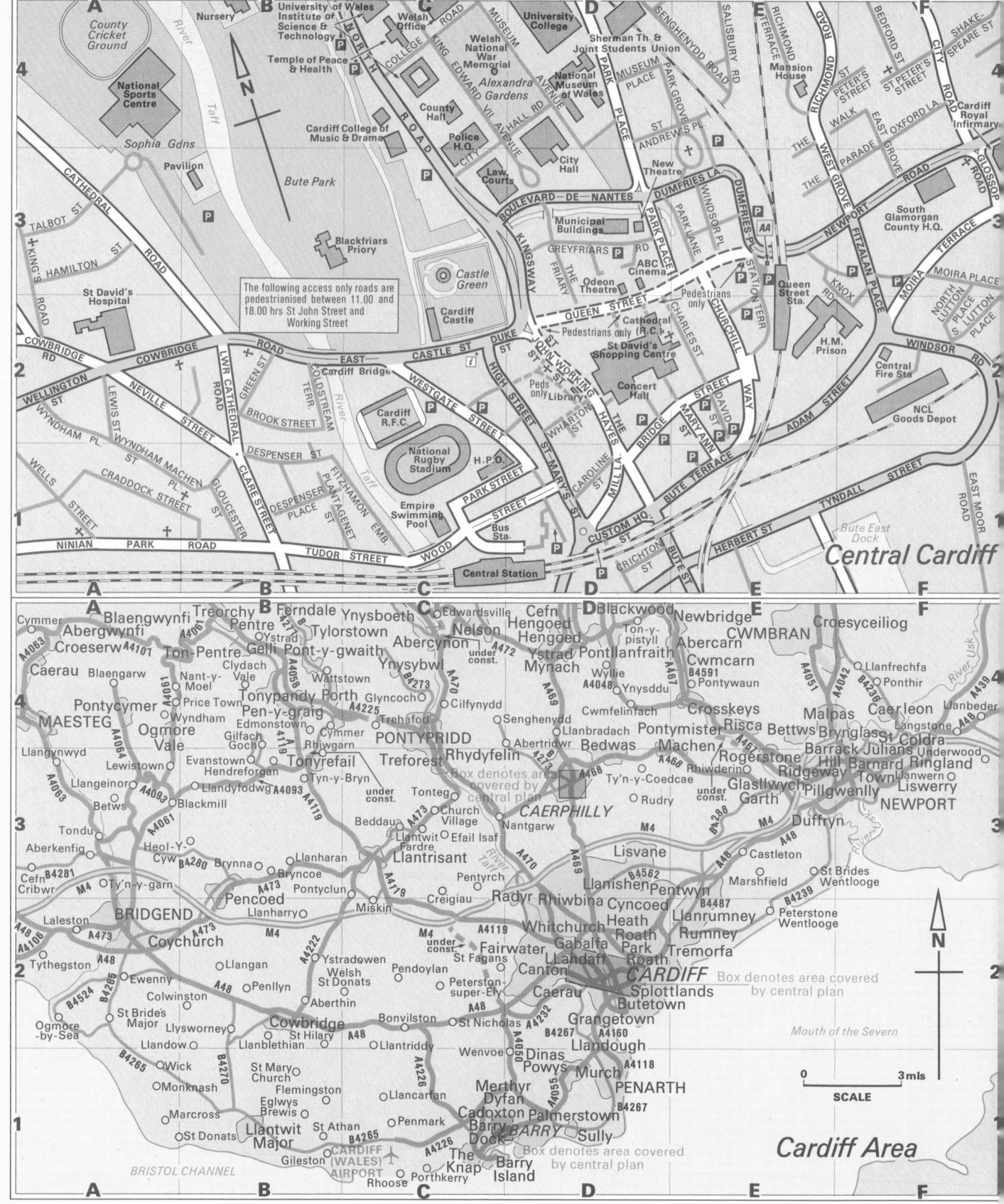

Cardiff

Strategically important to both the Romans and the Normans, Cardiff slipped from prominence in medieval times and remained a quiet market town in a remote area until it was transformed – almost overnight – by the effects of the Industrial Revolution. The valleys of South Wales were a principal source of iron and coal – raw materials which helped to change the shape and course of the 19th-century world. Cardiff became a teeming export centre; by the end of the 19th century it was the largest coal-exporting city in the world.

Close to the castle – an exciting place with features from Roman times to the 19th century – is the city's civic centre – a fine concourse of buildings dating largely from the early part of the 20th century. Among them is the National Museum of Wales – a superb collection of art and antiquities from Wales and around the world.

Barry has sandy beaches, landscaped gardens and parks, entertainment arcades and funfairs. Like Cardiff it grew as a result of the demand for coal and steel, but now its dock complex is involved in the petrochemical and oil industries.

Caerphilly is famous for two things – a castle and cheese. The cheese is no longer made here, but the 13th-century castle, slighted by Cromwell, still looms above its moat. No castle in Britain – except Windsor – is larger.

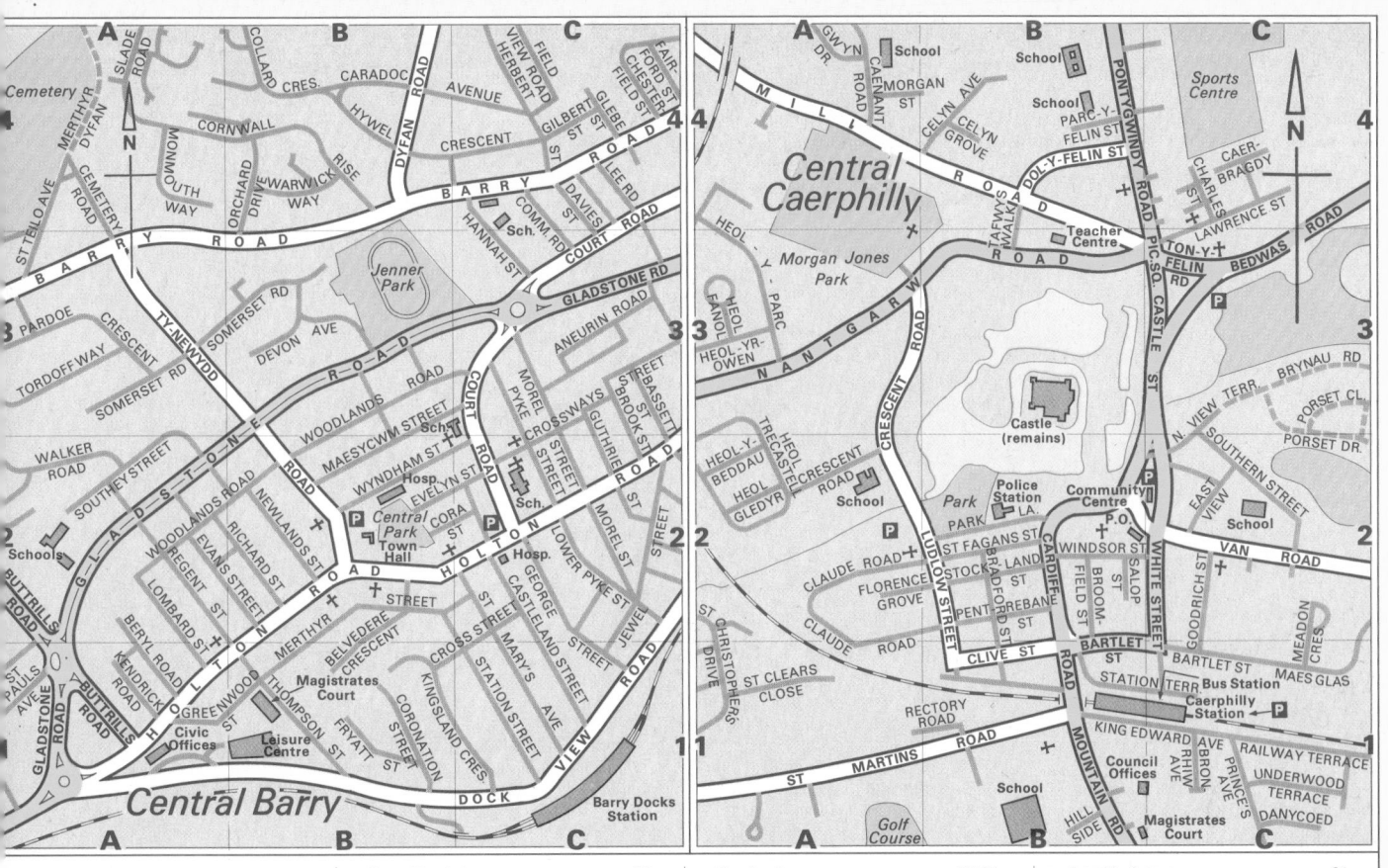

Street Index with Grid Reference

Cardiff

Adam Street	E1-E2-F2
Bedford Street	F4
Boulevard de Nantes	C3-D3
Bridge Street	D1-D2-E2
Brook Street	B2
Bute Street	D1-E1
Bute Terrace	D1-E1
Caroline Street	D1
Castle Street	C2
Cathedral Street	A4-A3-B3-B2
Central Square	D1
Charles Street	D2-E2
Churchill Way	E3-E2
City Hall Road	C3-C4-D4
City Road	F4
Clare Street	B1
College Road	C4
Cowbridge Road	A2
Cowbridge Road East	A2-B2-C2
Craddock Street	A1-B1
Crichton Street	D1
Custom House Street	D1
David Street	E2
Despenser Place	B1
Despenser Street	B1
Duke Street	C2-D2
Dumfries Place	D3-E3
Dumfries Place	E3
East Grove	F3-F4
East Moor Road	F1
Fitzalan Place	F3-F2
Fitzhamon Embankment	B1-C1
George VII Avenue	C4-C3
Glossop Road	F3
Gloucester Street	B1
Green Street	B2
Greyfriars Road	D3
Hamilton Street	A3
Herbert Street	E1
High Street	C2-D2
King's Road	A3-A2
Kingsway	C3-D3-D2
Knox Road	E3-F3-F2
Lewis Street	A2
Lower Cathedral Road	B2-B1
Machen Place	A1-B1
Mary Ann Street	D2-E2-E1
Millicent Street	D1-D2-E2
Mill Lane	D1
Moira Place	F3
Moira Terrace	F2-F3
Museum Avenue	C4-D4
Museum Place	D4
Neville Street	A2-B2-B1
Newport Road	E3-F3-F4
Ninian Park Road	A1-B1
North Lutton Place	F2-F3
North Road	B4-C4-C3
Oxford Lane	F4
Park Grove	D4-E4
Park Lane	D3-E3
Park Place	D4-D3-E3
Park Street	C1-D1
Plantaaenet Street	B1-C1
Queen Street	D2-D3
Richmond Road	E4
St Andrew's Place	D4-E4
St John Street	D2
St Mary's Street	D2-D1
St Peter's Street	E4-F4
Saisbury Road	E4
Senghenydd Road	D4-E4
Shakespeare Street	F4
South Lutton Place	F2-F3
Station Terrace	E3-E2
The Friary	D3-D2
The Hayes	D2-D1
The Parade	E3-F3
The Walk	E3-E4-F4
Talbot Street	A3
Tredegar Street	D1-E1
Tudor Street	B1-C1
Tyndall Street	E1-F1
Wellington Street	A2
Wells Street	A1
Westgate Street	C2-D2-D1
West Grove	E4-E3-F3
Wharton Street	D2
Windsor Place	E3
Windsor Road	F2
Wood Street	C1-D1
Working Street	D2
Wyndham Place	A2
Wyndham Street	A2-A1

Barry

Aneurin Road	C3
Barry Road	A3-A4-B3-B4-C4
Bassett Street	C3-C2
Belvedere Crescent	B1-B2
Beryl Road	A2-A1
Brook Street	C3-C2
Buttrills Road	A2-A1
Caradoc Avenue	B4-C4
Castleland Street	C2-C1
Cemetery Road	A4-A3
Chesterfield Street	C4
Collard Crescent	B4
Commercial Road	C4-C3
Cora Street	B2-C2
Cornwall Rise	A4-B4
Coronation Street	B1
Cross Street	B1-C1-C2
Crossways Street	C2-C3
Court Road	C2-C3-C4
Davies Street	C4-C3
Devon Avenue	B3
Dock View Road	B1-C1-C2
Dyfan Road	B4
Evans Street	A2-B2
Evelyn Street	B2-C2
Fairford Street	C4
Field View Road	C4
Fryatt Street	B1
George Street	C2-C1
Gilbert Street	C4
Gladstone Road	A1-A2-B2-B3-C3
Glebe Street	C4
Greenwood Street	A1-B1
Guthrie Street	C3-C2
Hannah Street	C4-C3
Herbert Street	C4
Holton Road	A1-B1-B2-C2
Hywel Crescent	B4-C4
Jewel Street	C1-C2
Kendrick Road	A1
Kingsland Crescent	B1-C1
Lee Road	C4
Lombard Street	A2-A1
Lower Pyke Street	C2
Maesycwm Street	B2-B3-C3
Merthyr Dyfan	A4
Merthyr Street	B1-B2-C2
Monmouth Way	A4
Morel Street	C3-C2
Newlands Street	B2
Orchard Drive	B3-B4
Pardoe Crescent	A3
Pyke Street	C3-C2
Regent Street	A2-B2
Richard Street	A2-B2
St Mary's Avenue	C2-C1
St Teilo Avenue	A1
Slade Road	A4
Somerset Road	A3-B3
Southey Street	A2-A3
Station Road	C1
Thompson Street	B1
Tordoff Way	A3
Ty-Newydd Road	A3-B3-B2
Walker Road	A2
Warwick Way	B4
Woodlands Road	A2-B2-B3-C3
Wyndham Street	B2-C2

Caerphilly

Bartlet Street	B1-B2-C1
Bedwas Road	C3-C4
Bradford Street	B2-B1
Broomfield Street	B2
Bronrhiw Avenue	C1
Brynau Road	C3
Caenant Road	A4
Caer Bragdy	C4
Cardiff Road	B2-B1
Castle Street	C3
Celyn Avenue	B4
Celyn Grove	B4
Charles Street	C4
Claude Road	A2-A1-B2
Clive Street	B1
Crescent Road	A2-A3-B3
Danycoed	C1
Dol-y-Felin Street	B4
East View	C2
Florence Grove	A2-B2
Goodrich Street	C1-C2
Gwyn Drive	A4
Heol Fanol	A3
Heol Gledyr	A2
Heol Trecastell	A3-A2
Hillside	B1
Heol-y-Beddau	A2
Hoel-y-Parc	A4-A3
Heol-yr-Owen	A3
King Edward Avenue	B1-C1
Lawrence Street	C3-C4
Ludlow Street	A2-B2
Maes Glas	C1
Meadon Crescent	C1-C2
Mill Road	A4-B4-B3
Morgan Street	A4-B4
Mountain Road	B1
Nantgarw Road	A3-B3
North View Terrace	C2-C3
Parc-y-Felin Street	B4
Park Lane	B2
Pentrebane Street	B2
Piccadilly Square	C3
Pontygwindy Road	B4-C4
Porset Close	C3
Porset Drive	C3-C2
Prince's Avenue	C1
Railway Terrace	C1
Rectory Road	A1-B1
St Christopher's Drive	A2-A1
St Clears Close	A1
St Fagans Street	B2
St Martins Road	A1-B1
Salop Street	B2
Southern Street	C3-C2
Station Terrace	B1-C1
Stockland Street	B2
Tafwys Walk	B3-B4
Ton-y-Felin Road	C3
Van Road	C2
White Street	C1-C2
Windsor Street	B2

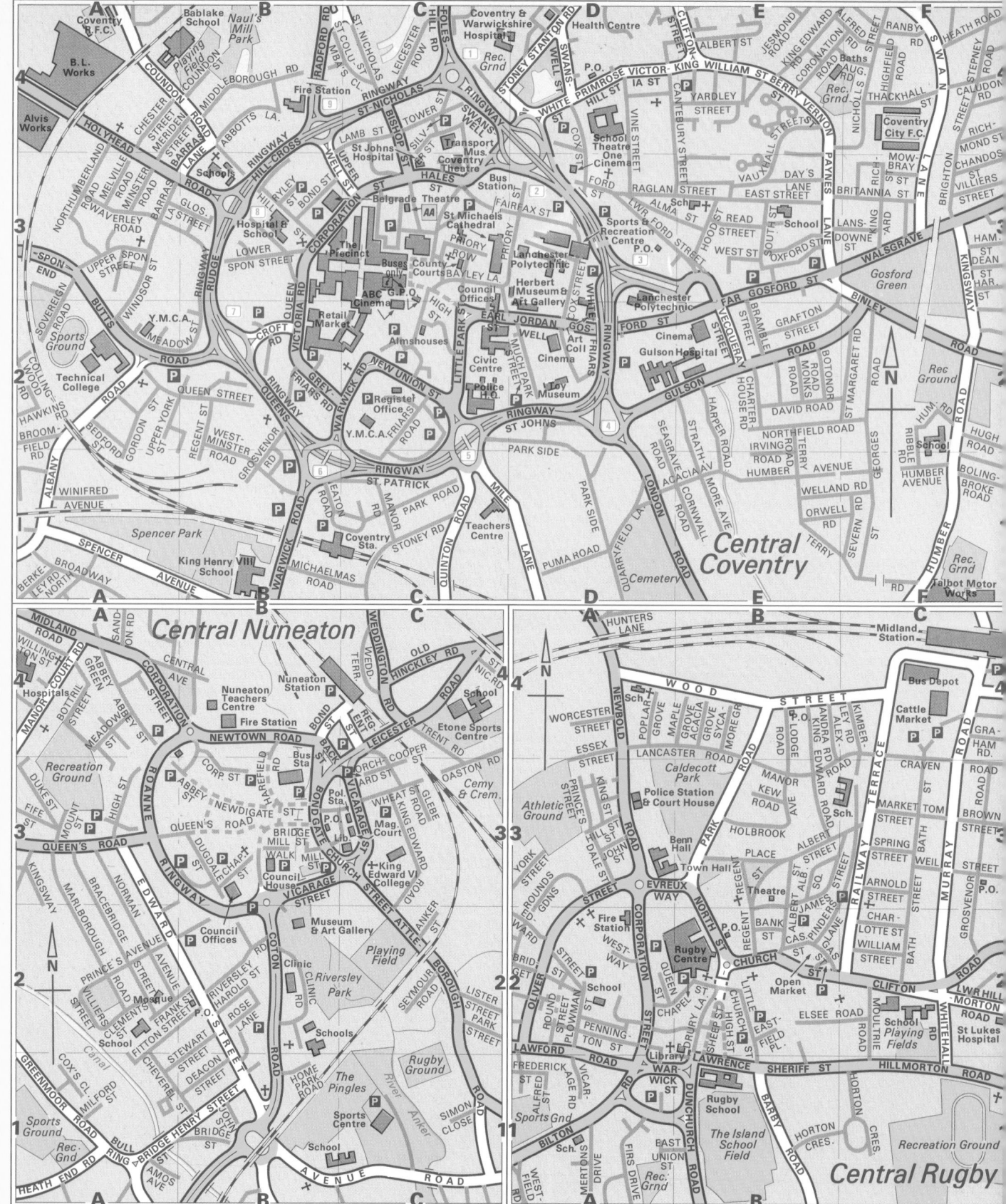

Coventry

Few British towns were as battered by the Blitz as Coventry. A raid in November 1940 flattened most of the city and left the lovely cathedral church a gaunt shell with only the tower and spire still standing. Rebuilding started almost immediately. Symbolising the creation of the new from the ashes of the old is Sir Basil Spence's cathedral, completed in 1962 beside the bombed ruins.

A few medieval buildings have survived intact in the city. St Mary's Guildhall is a finely restored 14th-century building with an attractive minstrels' gallery. Whitefriars Monastery now serves as a local museum. The Herbert Art Gallery and Museum has several collections. Coventry is an important manufacturing centre – most notably for cars – and it is also a university city with the fine campus of the University of Warwick some four miles from the centre.

Nuneaton is an industrial town to the north of Coventry with two distinguished old churches – St Nicholas' and St Mary's. Like Coventry it was badly damaged in the war and its centre has been rebuilt.

Rugby was no more than a sleepy market town until the arrival of the railway. Of course it did have the famous Rugby School, founded in 1567 and one of the country's foremost educational establishments. The railway brought industry – still the town's mainstay.

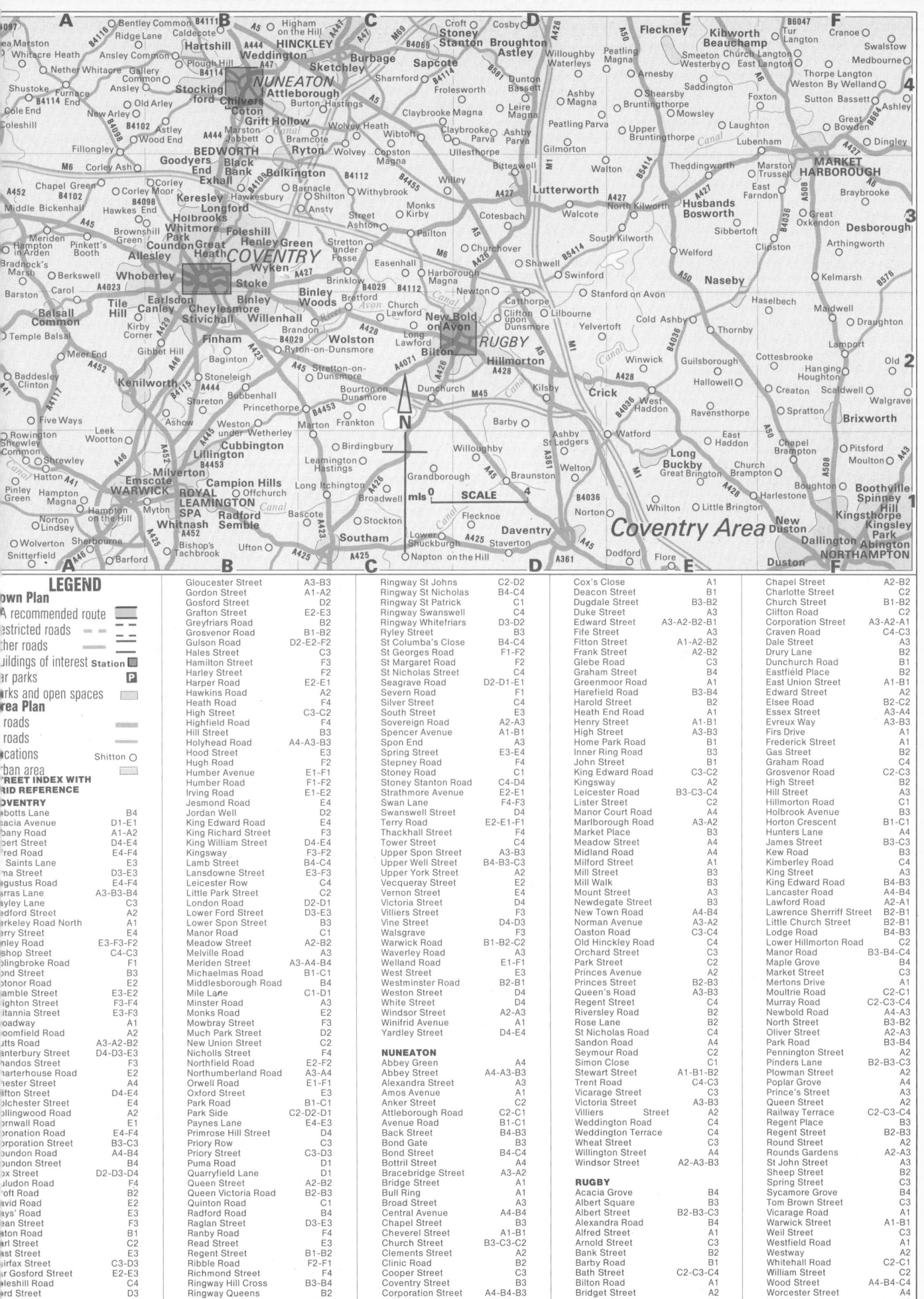

Coventry Area

SCALE

N

171

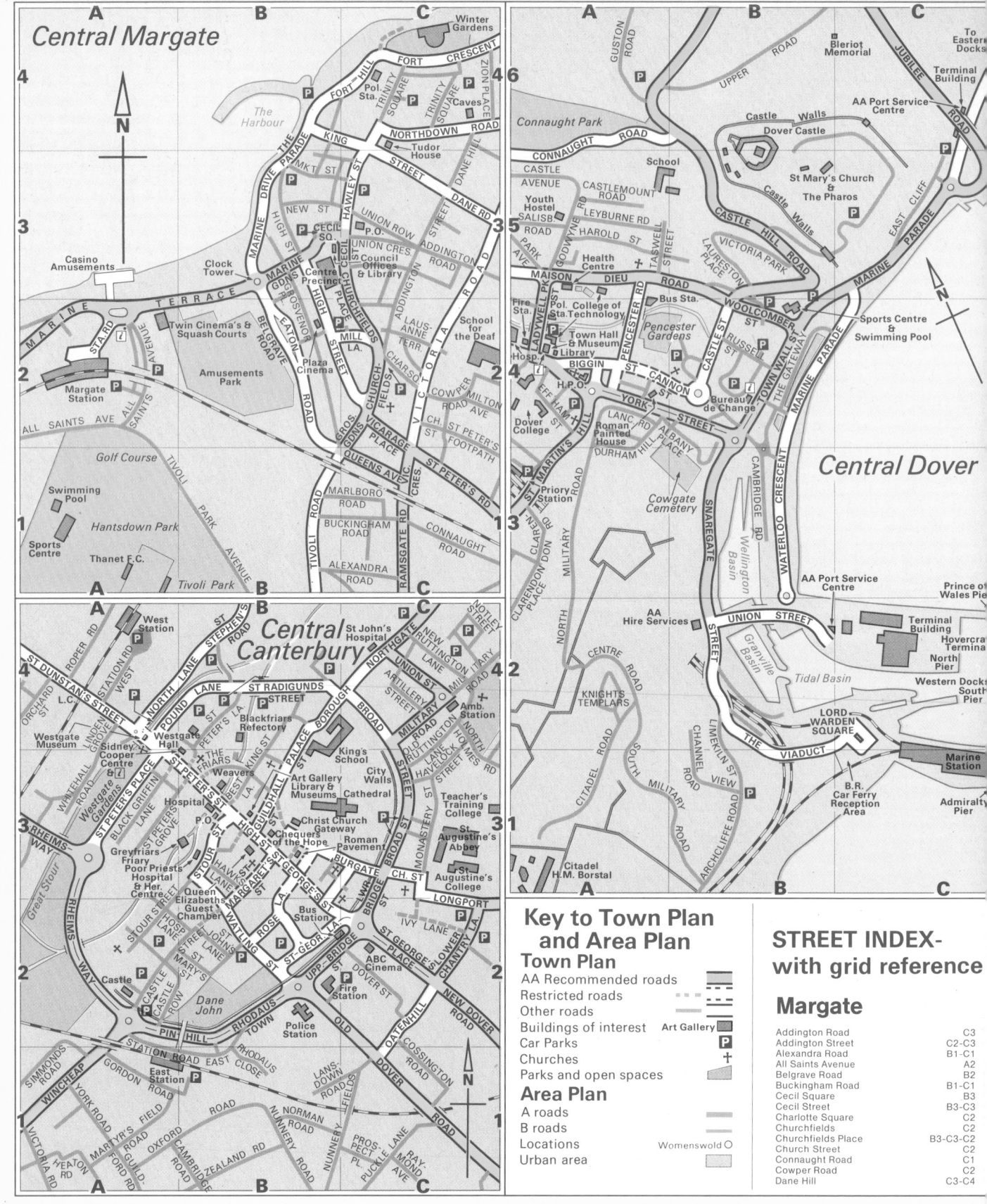

Central Margate

Central Dover

Central Canterbury

Key to Town Plan and Area Plan

Town Plan

AA Recommended roads	▬▬▬
Restricted roads	┄┄
Other roads	▬▬▬
Buildings of interest	Art Gallery
Car Parks	P
Churches	+
Parks and open spaces	◣

Area Plan

A roads	▬▬
B roads	▬▬
Locations	Womenswold ○
Urban area	▬

STREET INDEX— with grid reference

Margate

Addington Road	C3
Addington Street	C2-C3
Alexandra Road	B1-C1
All Saints Avenue	A2
Belgrave Road	B2
Buckingham Road	B1-C1
Cecil Square	B3
Cecil Street	B3-C3
Charlotte Square	C2
Churchfields	C2
Churchfields Place	B3-C3-C2
Church Street	C2
Connaught Road	C1
Cowper Road	C2
Dane Hill	C3-C4

Dover

Travellers tend to rush through Dover – it is one of the busiest passenger ports in England – and by so doing miss an exciting town with much of interest. Outstanding is the castle. Its huge fortifications have guarded the town since the 12th century, but within its walls are even older structures – a Saxon church and a Roman lighthouse called the Pharos. In the town itself, the town hall is housed within the walls of a 13th-century guest house called the Maison Dieu. The Roman Painted House in New Street consists of substantial remains of a Roman town house and include the best-preserved Roman wall paintings north of the Alps.

Canterbury is one of Britain's most historic towns. It is the seat of the Church in England, and has been so since St Augustine began his mission here in the 6th century. The cathedral is a priceless work of art containing many other works of art, including superb displays of medieval carving and stained glass. Ancient city walls – partly built on Roman foundations – still circle parts of the city, and a wealth of grand public buildings as well as charming private houses of many periods line the maze of lanes in the shadow of the cathedral.

Margate and **Ramsgate** both grew as commercial ports, but for many years they have specialised in catering for holidaymakers who like safe, sandy beaches and excellent facilities.

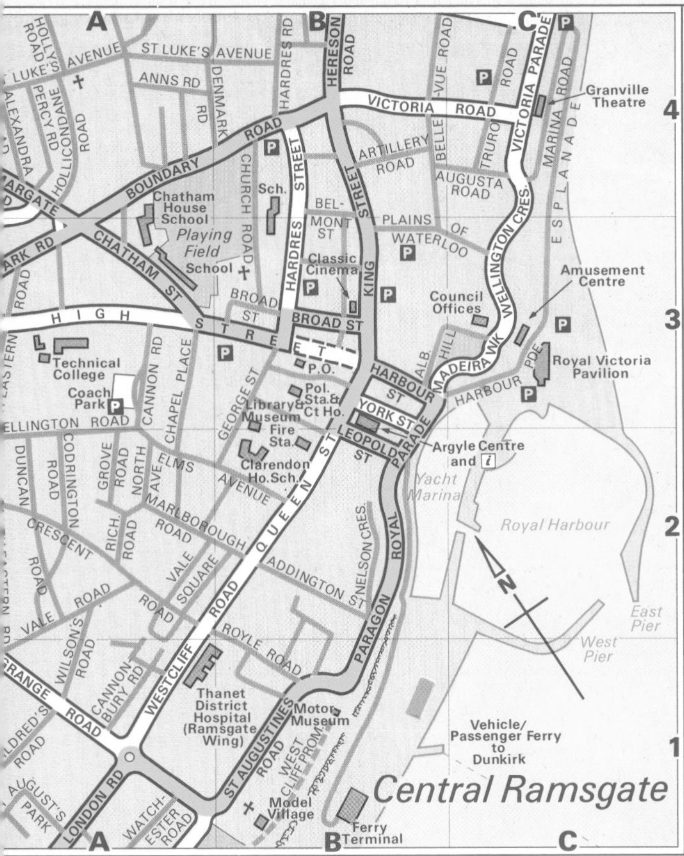
Central Ramsgate
A
B
C
4
3
2
1
Victoria Road
Boundary Road
Chatham Street
High Street
Broad Street
Harbour Parade
York Street
Leopold Street
Queen Street
Addington Street
Royle Road
Westcliff Road
London Rd
Grange Road
Vale Square
Marlborough Road
Ellington Road
Elms Ave
Chapel Place
Cannon Road
Grove Road
Codrington Road
Duncan Road
Crescent Road
Paragon Royal Parade
Nelson Cres.
St Augustines Road
West Cliff Prom.
Watchester Road
St August's Park
Wilson's Road
Cannonbury Rd
King Street
Hardres Street
Church Road
Belmont St
Plains of Waterloo
Artillery Road
Augusta Road
Belle Vue Road
Truro Road
Victoria Parade
Wellington Cres.
Madeira Walk
Esplanade
Marina Road
Hereson Road
Hardres Rd
Denmark Rd
Anns Rd
St Luke's Avenue
Hollicondane Road
Chatham House School
Playing Field
School
Sch.
Classic Cinema
Council Offices
Amusement Centre
Granville Theatre
Royal Victoria Pavilion
Technical College
Coach Park
Library & Museum
Pol. Sta. & Ct Ho.
Fire Sta.
Clarendon Ho. Sch.
P.O.
Argyle Centre and i
Yacht Marina
Royal Harbour
East Pier
West Pier
Thanet District Hospital (Ramsgate Wing)
Motor Museum
Model Village
Vehicle/ Passenger Ferry to Dunkirk
Ferry Terminal
N

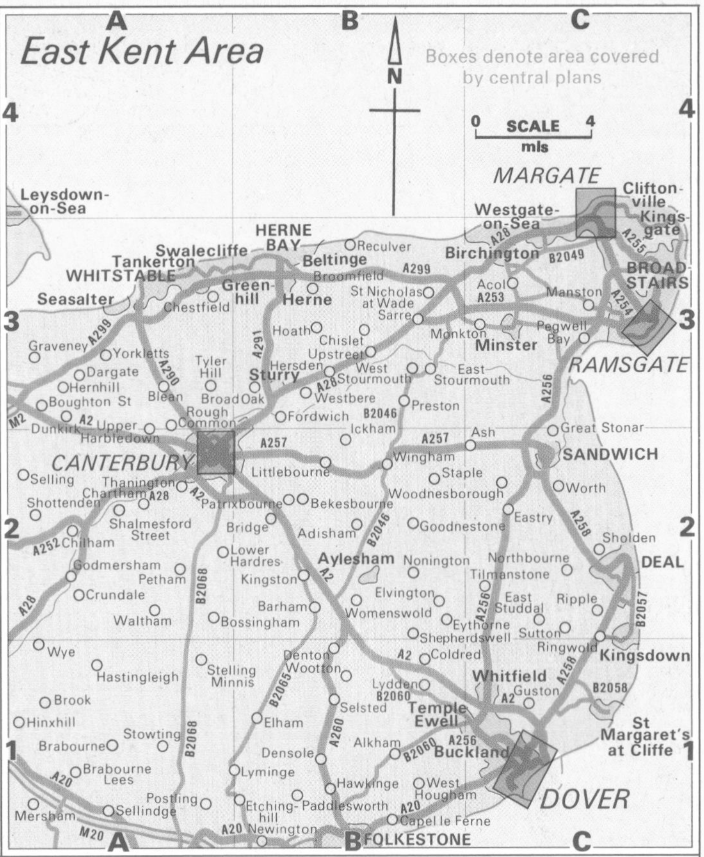
East Kent Area
A
B
C
4
3
2
1
N
Boxes denote area covered by central plans
SCALE
0
4
mls
MARGATE
Cliftonville
Kingsgate
Westgate-on-Sea
Birchington
BROADSTAIRS
RAMSGATE
Leysdown-on-Sea
HERNE BAY
Reculver
Swalecliffe
Tankerton
WHITSTABLE
Beltinge
Broomfield
Seasalter
Chestfield
Greenhill
Herne
St Nicholas at Wade
Sarre
Acol
Manston
Minster
Monkton
Pegwell Bay
Graveney
Yorkletts
Dargate
Hernhill
Boughton St
Tyler Hill
Blean
Sturry
Hoath
Chislet
Upstreet
Hersden
West Stourmouth
East Stourmouth
Westbere
Broad Oak
Rough Common
Fordwich
Preston
Ickham
Dunkirk
Upper Harbledown
CANTERBURY
Littlebourne
Wingham
Ash
Great Stonar
SANDWICH
Staple
Woodnesborough
Worth
Selling
Shottenden
Thanington
Chartham
Patrixbourne
Bekesbourne
Chilham
Shalmesford Street
Bridge
Adisham
Goodnestone
Eastry
Sholden
DEAL
Godmersham
Petham
Lower Hardres
Kingston
Aylesham
Nonington
Northbourne
Tilmanstone
Crundale
Barham
Elvington
Womenswold
East Studdal
Ripple
Waltham
Bossingham
Eythorne
Shepherdswell
Sutton
Ringwould
Kingsdown
Wye
Hastingleigh
Stelling Minnis
Denton
Wootton
Coldred
Whitfield
Lydden
Guston
Brook
Selsted
Temple Ewell
Hinxhill
Stowting
Elham
Alkham
Buckland
St Margaret's at Cliffe
Brabourne
Brabourne Lees
Densole
Lyminge
Hawkinge
West Hougham
DOVER
Mersham
Sellindge
Postling
Etching hill
Paddlesworth
Capel le Ferne
Newington
FOLKESTONE
M2
M20
A2
A20
A28
A252
A257
A253
A254
A255
A256
A258
A260
A290
A291
A299
B2046
B2049
B2058
B2060
B2065
B2068
A257

ane Road	C3
aton Road	B1-B2-B3
rt Crescent	C4
rt Hill	B4-C4
rosvenor Gardens	C1-C2
rosvenor Place	B2-B3
awley Street	C3
igh Street	B3-B2-C2
ng Street	B4-C4-C3
ausanne Terrace	C2
arine Drive	B3
arine Gardens	B3
arine Terrace	A2-A3-B3-B2
arket Street	B3-C3
arlborough Road	B1-C1
ill Lane	B2-C2
ilton Avenue	C2
ew Street	B3
orthdown Road	C4
ueens Avenue	C1
amsgate Road	C1
: Peter's Footpath	C1-C2
: Peter's Road	C1
ation Road	A2
e Parade	B3-B4
voli Park Avenue	A1-B1
voli Road	B1
inity Square	C4
nion Crescent	C3
nion Row	C3
carage Crescent	C1
carage Place	C1-C2
ctoria Road	C2-C3
on Place	C4

Canterbury

rtillery Street	C4
est Lane	B3
ack Griffin Lane	A3
orough	B4-C4
road Street	C4-C3
urgate	B3-C3
ambridge Road	A1-B1
astle Street	A2-B2
astle Row	A2-B2
hurch Street	C3
ossington Road	C2-C1
over Street	C2
Gordon Road	A1-B1
Guildford Road	A1
Guildhall Street	B3
Havelock Street	C3-C4
Hawks Lane	B3
Heaton Road	A1
High Street	B3
Hospital Lane	A2-B2
Ivy Lane	C2
King Street	B3-B4
Lansdown Road	B1-C1
Linden Grove	A3-A4
Longport	C3-C2
Lower Chantry Lane	C2
Martyr's Field Road	A1
Military Road	C4
Monastery Street	C3
New Dover Road	C2
New Ruttington Lane	C4
Norman Road	B1
Northgate	C4
North Holmes Road	C4-C3
North Lane	A4-B4
Notley Street	C4
Nunnery Fields	B1-C1
Nunnery Road	B1
Oatenhill	C1-C2
Old Dover Road	B2-C2-C1
Old Ruttington Lane	C3-C4
Orchard Street	A4
Oxford Road	A1-B1
Palace Street	B3-B4
Pin Hill	A2-B2
Pound Lane	A4-B4
Prospect Place	C1
Puckle Lane	C1
Raymond Avenue	C1
Rheims Way	A3-A2
Rhodaus Town	B2
Roper Road	A4
Rose Lane	B2-B3
St Dunstan's Street	A4
St Georges Lane	B2-C2
St George's Place	C2
St George's Street	B3-B2
St John's Lane	B2
St Mary's Street	A2-B2
St Peters Grove	A3-B3
St Peter's Lane	B4
St Peter's Place	A3
St Peter's Street	A3-B3
St Stephen's Road	B4
St Rudigunds Street	B4
Simmonds Road	A1-A2
Station Road East	A2-A1-B1
Station Road West	A4
Stour Street	A2-A3-B3
The Friars,	B3
Union Street	C4
Upper Bridge Street	B2-C2
Victoria Road	A1
Watling Street	B2
Whitehall Road	A3
Wincheap	A1-A2
York Road	A1
Zealand Road	B1

Dover

Albany Place	A4-B4-B3
Archcliffe Road	B1
Biggin Street	A4
Cambridge Road	B3
Cannon Street	A4-B4
Castle Avenue	A5
Castle Hill Road	B5
Castlemount Road	A5
Castle Street	B4
Centre Road	A2
Channel View Road	B2-B1
Citadel Road	A1-A2
Clarendon Place	A2-A3
Clarendon Road	A3
Connaught Road	A5-A6
Durham Hill	A4-A3
East Cliff	C5
Effingham Street	A4
Godwyne Road	A5
Guston Road	A6
Harold Street	A5
Jubilee Road	C6
Knights Templars	A2
Ladywell Park Road	A4-A5
Lancaster Road	A4
Laureston Place	B5
Leyburne Road	A5
Limekiln Street	B2-B1
Maison Dieu Road	A5-B5
Marine Parade	B4-C4-C5
North Military Road	A2-A3
Park Avenue	A5
Pencester Road	A4-A5
Russell Street	B4
St Martin's Hill	A3-A4
Salisbury Road	A5
Snaregate Street	B3-B2
South Military Road	A2-A1-B1
The Gateway	B4
The Viaduct	B2-B1
Taswell Street	A5
Town Hall Street	B4
Union Street	B2
Upper Road	A6-B6
Victoria Park	B5
Woolcomber Street	B4
York Street	A4-B4

Ramsgate

Addington Street	B2
Albion Hill	B3
Alexandra Road	A4
Anns Road	A4
Artillery Road	B4
Augusta Road	B4-C4
Belle Vue Road	B4
Belmont Street	B4
Boundary Road	A3-A4-B4
Broad Street	B3
Cannonbury Road	A1
Canon Road	A3
Chapel Place	A2-A3
Chatham Street	A3
Church Road	B3-B4
Codrington Road	A2
Crescent Road	A2
Denmark Road	A4-B4
Duncan Road	A2
Ellington Road	A2-A3
Elms Avenue	A2-B2
Esplanade	C3-C4
George Street	B2-B3
Grange Road	A1
Grove Road	A2
Harbour Parade	B3-C3
Harbour Street	B3
Hardres Street	B3-B4
Hereson Road	B4
High Street	A3-B3
Hollicondane Road	A4
Holly Road	A4
King Street	B3-B4
Leopold Street	B2-B3
London Road	A1
Madeira Walk	B3-C3
Margate Road	A3-A4
Marina Road	C4
Marlborough Road	A2-B2
Mildred's Road	A1
Nelson Crescent	B2
North Avenue	A2
Paragon Royal Parade	B1-B2-B3
Park Road	A3
Percy Road	A4
Plains of Waterloo	B3-C3
Queen Street	B2-B3
Richmond Road	A2
Royle Road	A2-B2-B1
St Augustines Road	A1-B1
St August's Park	A1
St Luke's Avenue	A4-B4
South Eastern Road	A1-A2-A3
Truro Road	C4
Vale Road	A1-A2
Vale Square	A2-B2
Victoria Parade	C4
Victoria Road	B4-C4
Watchester Road	A1
Wellington Crescent	C3-C4
West Cliff Promenade	B1
Westcliff Road	A1-A2-B2
Wilson's Road	A1-A2
York Street	B2-B3

DOVER
The famous White Cliffs of Dover provide exhilarating coastal walks with views out across the Channel. Paths to the north-east lead to Walmer and to the south-east, to Folkestone.

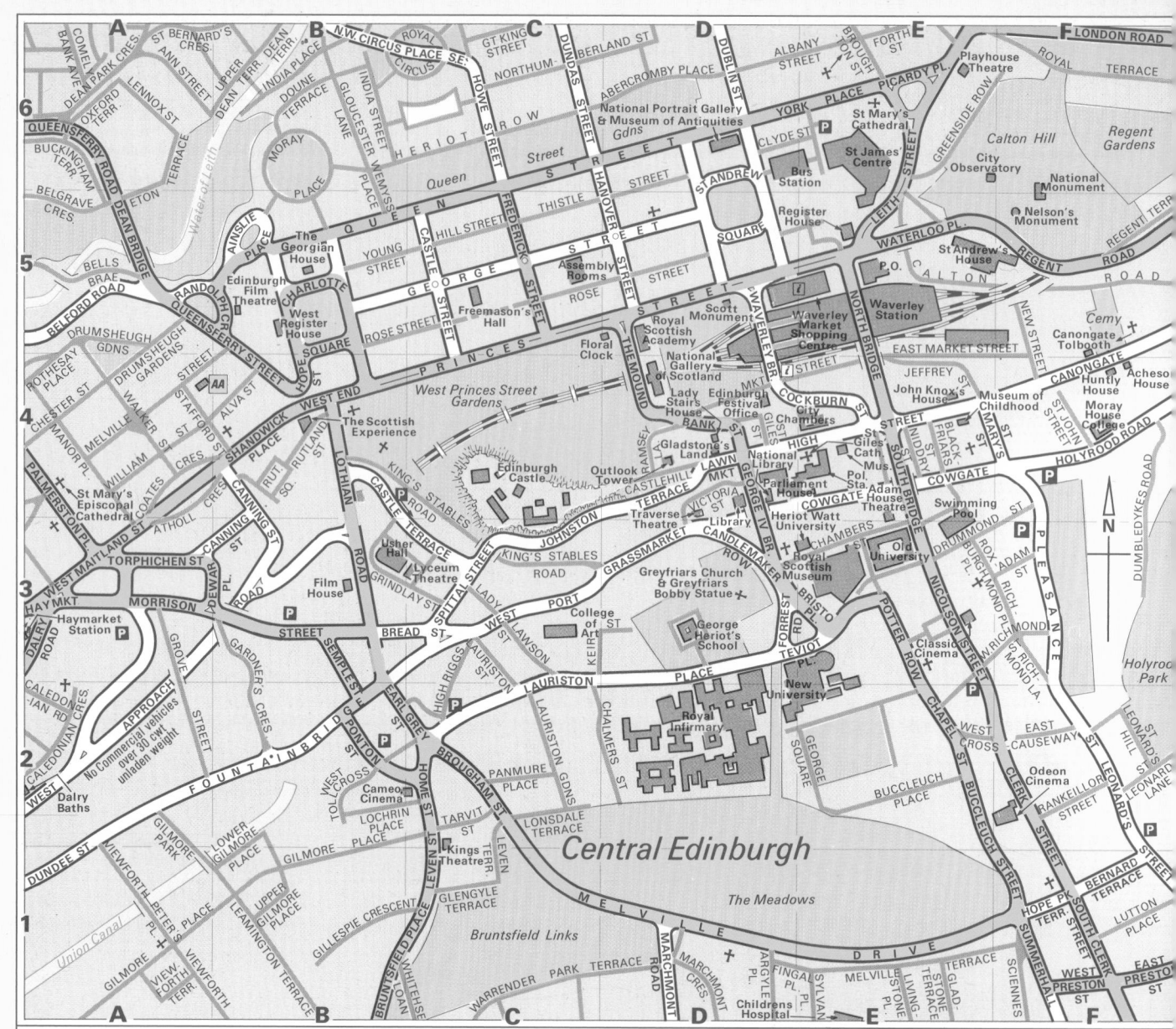

Key to Town Plan and Area Plan

Town Plan
A A Recommended roads
Other roads
Restricted roads
Buildings of intrest   Gallery
Car Parks   P
Parks and open spaces
A A Service Centre   AA
Churches   +

Area Plan
A roads
B roads
Locations   Newcraighall O
Urban area

Street Index with Grid Reference

Edinburgh

Edinburgh

Scotland's ancient capital, dubbed the "Athens of the North", is one of the most splendid cities in the whole of Europe. Its buildings, its history and its cultural life give it an international importance which is celebrated every year in its world-famous festival. The whole city is overshadowed by the craggy castle which seems to grow out of the rock itself. There has been a fortress here since the 7th century and most of the great figures of Scottish history have been associated with it. The old town grew up around the base of Castle Rock within the boundaries of the defensive King's Wall and, unable to spread outwards, grew upwards in a maze of tenements. However, during the 18th century new prosperity from the shipping trade resulted in the building of the New Town and the regular, spacious layout of the Georgian development makes a striking contrast with the old

hotch-potch of streets. Princes Street is the main east-west thoroughfare with excellent shops on one side and Princes Street Gardens with their famous floral clock on the south side.

As befits such a splendid capital city there are numerous museums and art galleries packed with priceless treasures. Among these are the famous picture gallery in 16th-century Holyroodhouse, the present Royal Palace, and the fascinating and unusual Museum of Childhood.

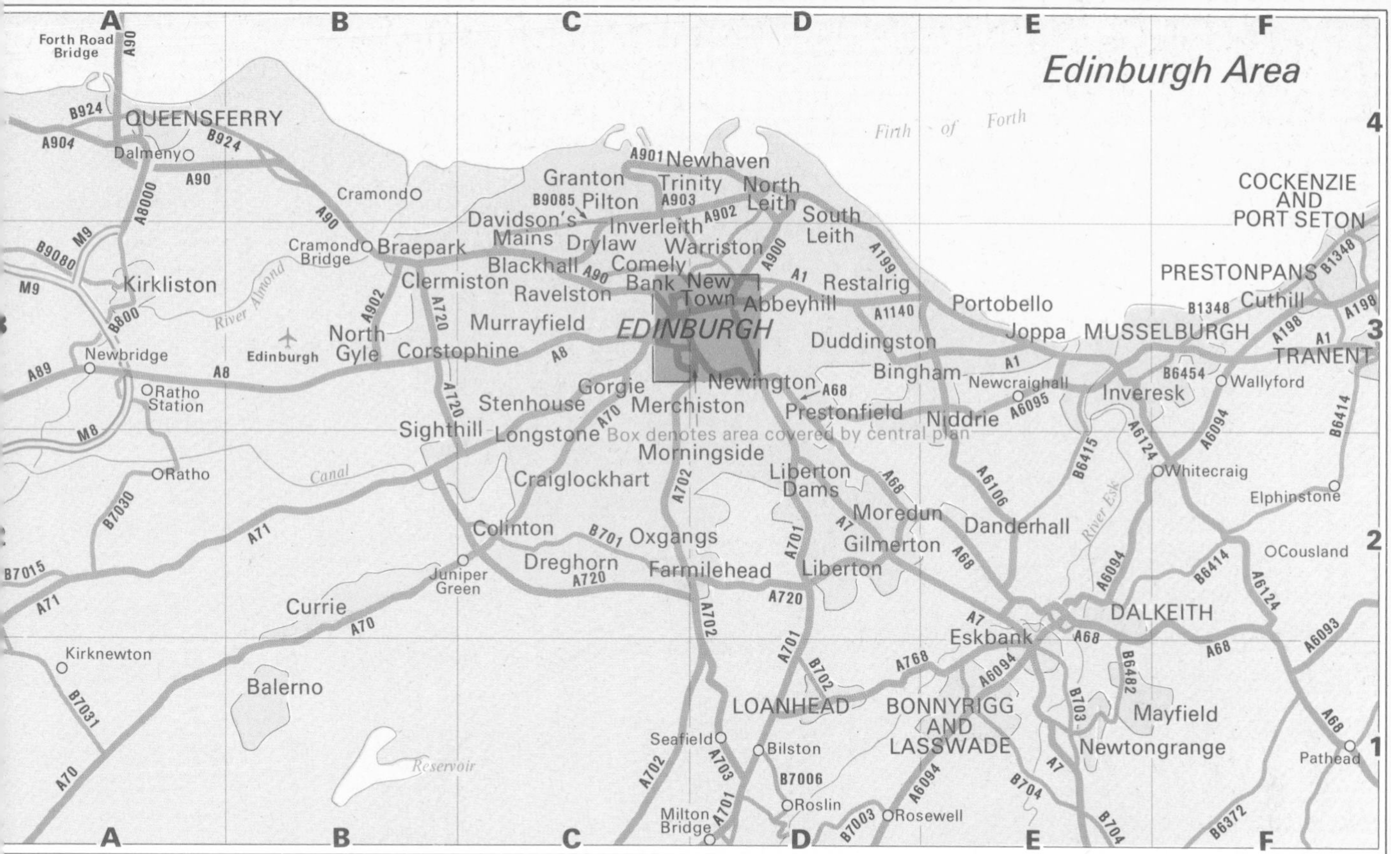

Edinburgh Area

Forth Road Bridge
QUEENSFERRY
Dalmeny
Cramond
Granton
Newhaven
Pilton
Trinity
North
Davidson's
Inverleith
Leith
Mains
Drylaw
Warriston
South
Braepark
Blackhall
Comely
Leith
Cramond Bridge
Clermiston
Ravelston
Bank
New
Restalrig
Kirkliston
North Gyle
Murrayfield
EDINBURGH
Abbeyhill
Portobello
Newbridge
Corstophine
Duddingston
Joppa
MUSSELBURGH
Ratho Station
Edinburgh
Gorgie
Newington
Bingham
Newcraighall
Inveresk
Ratho
Stenhouse
Merchiston
Prestonfield
Niddrie
Sighthill
Longstone
Box denotes area covered by central plan
Morningside
Liberton Dams
Moredun
Danderhall
Whitecraig
Elphinstone
Craiglockhart
Kirknewton
Colinton
Oxgangs
Gilmerton
Liberton
DALKEITH
Cousland
Juniper Green
Dreghorn
Farmilehead
Currie
Eskbank
Balerno
LOANHEAD
BONNYRIGG AND LASSWADE
Mayfield
Reservoir
Seafield
Bilston
Newtongrange
Pathead
Milton Bridge
Roslin
Rosewell

COCKENZIE AND PORT SETON
PRESTONPANS
Cuthill
TRANENT
Wallyford

Firth of Forth

Earl Grey Street	B2-C2	India Street	B6
East Cross Causeway	F2	Jeffrey Street	E4
East Market Street	E5-E4-F4-F5	Johnston Terrace	C3-C4-D4
East Preston Street	F1	Kier Street	C3-D3
Eton Terrace	A5-A6	King's Stables Road	B4-C4-C3
Fingal Place	D1-E1	Lady Lawson Street	C3
Forrest Road	D3	Lauriston Gardens	C2
Fountain Bridge	A2-B2-B3-C3	Lauriston Place	C2-C3-D3
Frederick Street	C5	Lauriston Street	C2-C3
Forth Street	E6	Lawn Market	D4
Gardeners Crescent	B2-B3	Leamington Terrace	A1-B1
George IV Bridge	D3-D4	Leith Street	E5-E6
George Square	E2	Lennox Street	A6
George Street	B5-C5-D5	Leven Street	C1-C2
Gillespie Crescent	B1-C1	Leven Terrace	C1-C2
Gilmore Park	A1-A2	Livingtone Place	E1
Gilmore Place	A1-B1-B2-C2	Lochrin Place	B2-C2
Gladstone Terrace	E1	London Road	F6
Glengyle Terrace	C1	Lonsdale Terrace	C2
Gloucester Lane	B6	Lothian Road	B3-B4
Grass Market	D3	Lower Gilmore Place	B1-B2
Great King Street	C6	Lutton Place	F1
Greenside Row	E6-F6	Manor Place	A4
Grindley Street	B3-C3	Marchmont Crescent	D1
Grove Street	A2-A3	Marchmont Road	D1
Hanover Street	C6-D6-D5	Market Street	D4-E4
Hay Market	A3	Melville Drive	C2-C1-D1-E1-F1
Heriot Row	B6-C6	Melville Street	A4-B4-B5
High Riggs	C2-C3	Melville Terrace	E1-F1
High Street	D4-E4	Moray Place	B5-B6
Holyrood Road	F4	Morriston Street	A3-B3
Home Street	C2	New Street	F4-F5
Hope Park Terrace	F1	Nicolson Street	E3-E2-F2
Hope Street	B4	Niddry Street	E4
Howe Street	C6	North Bridge	E4-E5
India Place	B6	North West Circus Place	B6
		Northumberland Street	C6-D6

Oxford Terrace	A6	South Bridge	E3-E4
Palmerston Place	A3-A4	South Clerk Street	F1
Panmure Place	C2	South East Circus Place	C6
Picardy Place	E6	Spittal Street	C3
Pleasance	F3-F4	Stafford Street	A4-B4
Ponton Street	B2-C2	Summerhall	F1
Potter Row	E2-E3	Sylvan Place	E1
Princes Street	B4-C4-C5-D5-E5	The Mound	D4-D5
Queen Street	B5-C5-C6-D6	Tarvit Street	C2
Queensferry Road	A5-A6	Teviot Place	D3-E3
Queensferry Street	A5-B5-B4	Thistle Street	C5-D5-D6
Ramsey Lane	D4	Torphichen Street	A3
Randolph Crescent	A5-B5	Upper Dean Terrace	B6
Rankeillor Street	F2	Upper Gilmore Place	B1
Regent Road	E5-F5	Victoria Street	D4
Regent Terrace	F5	Viewforth	A1-B1
Richmond Lane	F2-F3	Viewforth Terrace	A1
Richmond Place	E3-F3	Walker Street	A4-A5
Rose Street	B5-C5-D5	Warrender Park Terrace	C1-D1
Rothesay Place	A4-A5	Waterloo Place	E5
Roxbury Place	E3	Waverley Bridge	D4-D5
Royal Circus	B6-C6	Wemyss Place	B5-B6
Royal Terrace	E6-F6	West Approach Road	A2-A3-B3
Rutland Square	B4	West Cross-Causeway	E2
Rutland Street	B4	West End	B4
St Andrew Square	D5-D6	West Maitland Street	A3-A4
St Bernard's Crescent	A6-B6	West Port	C3
St Giles Street	D4	West Preston Street	F1
St John Street	F4	West Richmond Street	E3-F3
St Leonards Hill	F2	West Tollcross	B2
St Leonards Lane	F2	Whitehouse Loan	B1-C1
St Leonard's Street	F1-F2	William Street	A4
St Mary's Street	E4-F4	York Place	D6-E6
St Peter Place	A1	Young Street	B5-C5
Sciennes	F1		
Semples Street	B2-B3		
Shandwick Place	B4		

EDINBURGH
Holyrood Palace orginated as a guest house for the Abbey of Holyrood in the 16th century, but most of the present building was built for Charles II. Mary Queen of Scots was one of its most famous inhabitants.

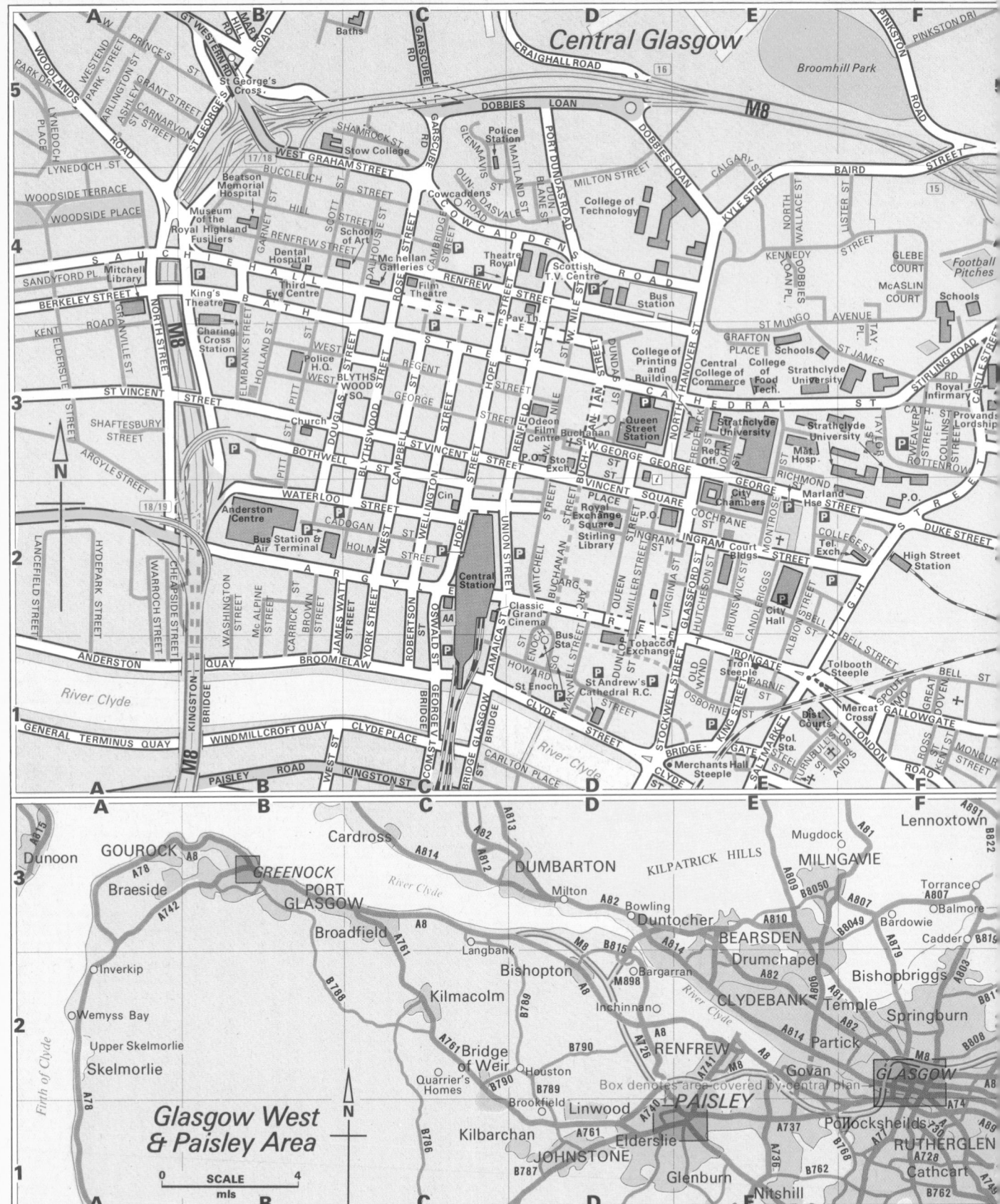

Glasgow

Although much of Glasgow is distinctly Victorian in character, its roots go back very many centuries. Best link with the past is the cathedral; founded in the 6th century, it has features from many succeeding centuries, including an exceptional 13th- century crypt. Nearby is Provand's Lordship, the city's oldest house. It dates from 1471 and is now a museum. Two much larger museums are to be found a little out of the centre – the Art Gallery and Museum contains one of the finest collections of paintings in Britain, while the Hunterian Museum, attached to the University, covers geology, archaeology, ethnography and more general subjects. On Glasgow Green is People's Palace – a museum of city life. Most imposing of the Victorian buildings are the City Chambers and City Hall which was built in 1841 as a concert hall but now houses the Scottish National Orchestra.

Paisley is famous for the lovely fabric pattern to which it gives its name. It was taken from fabrics brought from the Near East in the early 19th century, and its manufacture, along with the production of thread, is still important.

Greenock has been an important port and shipbuilding centre since as early as the 16th century. Its most famous son is James Watt, the inventor of steam power, born here in 1736. The town has numerous memorials to the great man.

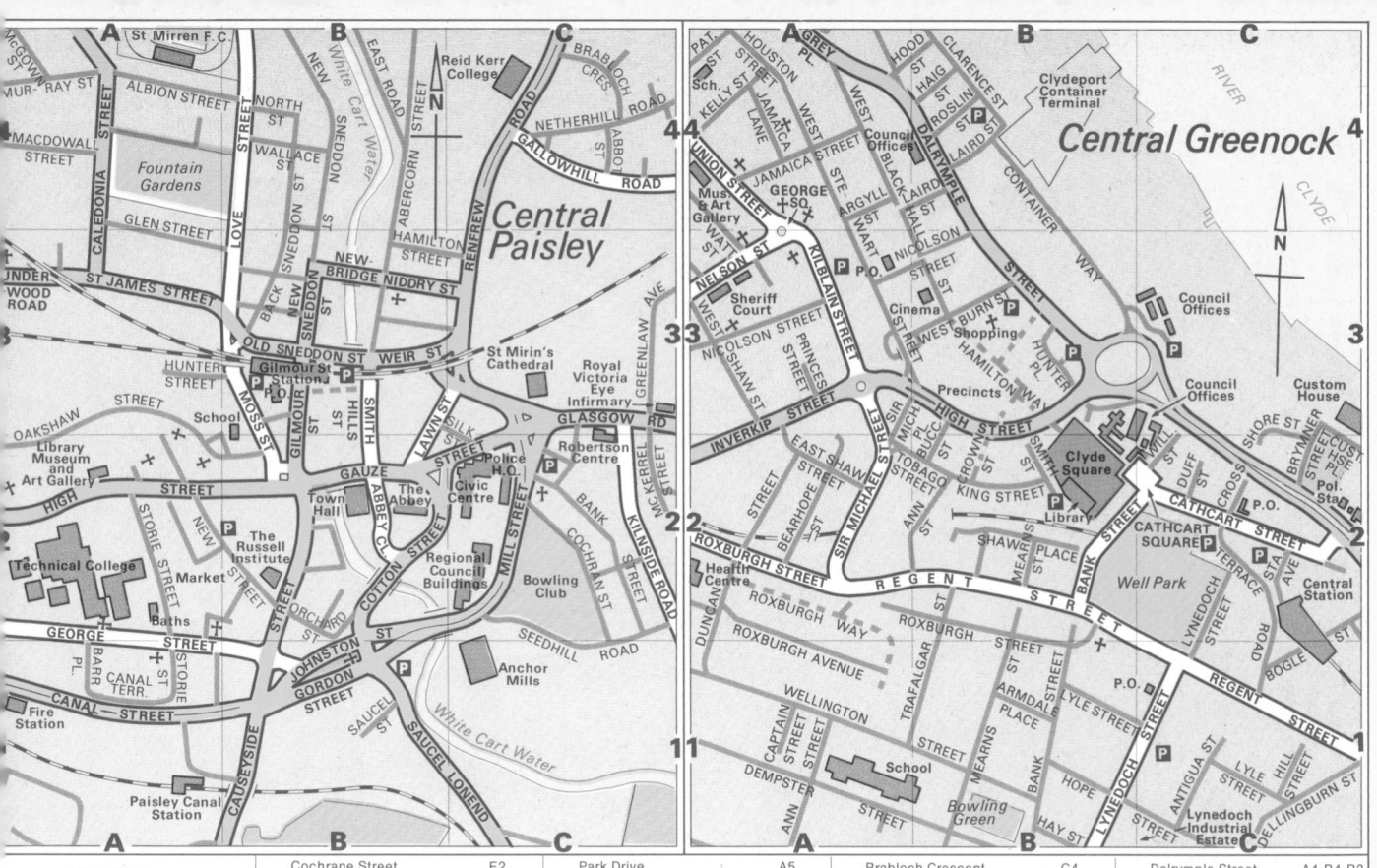

LEGEND

Town Plan

AA recommended route
Restricted roads
Other roads
Buildings of interest   Station
Car parks   P
Parks and open spaces

Area Plan

A roads
B roads
Locations   Garvock O
Urban area

Street Index with grid reference

Glasgow

Albion Street	E1-E2
Anderston Quay	A2-A1-B1
Argyle Street	A3-A2-B2-C2-D2-D1-E1
Arlington Street	A5
Ashley Street	A5
Baird Street	E4-E5-F5-F4
Balnian Street	B5
Bath Street	B4-C4-C3-D3
Bell Street	E2-E1-F1
Berkeley Street	A4
Blythswood Square	B3-C3
Blythswood Street	C2-C3
Bothwell Street	B3-C3-C2
Bridgegate	D1-E1
Bridge Street	C1
Broomielaw	B1-C1
Brown Street	B1-B2
Brunswick Street	E2
Buccleuch Street	B4-C4
Buchannan Street	D3-D4
Cadogan Street	B2-C2
Calgary Street	E4-E5-E4
Candleriggs	E1-E2
Cambridge Street	C4
Carlton Place	C1-D1
Carnarvon Street	A5-B5
Carrick Street	B1-B2
Castle Street	F3
Cathedral Street	D3-E3-F3
Cheapside Street	A1-A2
Clyde Place	B1-C1
Clyde Street	C1-D1-E1

Cochrane Street	E2
College Street	E2-F2
Collins Street	F3
Commerce Street	C1
Cowcaddens Road	C4-D4-E4
Craighall Road	C5-D5
Dalhousie Street	C4
Dobbies Loan	C5-D5-E5-E4-D4
Dobbies Loan Place	E4
Douglas Street	B3-C3
Duke Street	F2
Dunblane Street	D4-D5
Dundas Street	D3
Dunlop Street	D1
Elderslie Street	A3-A4
Elmbank Street	B3-B4
Gallowgate	E1-F1
Garscube Road	C4-C5
Garnet Street	B4
George V Bridge	C1
George Square	D3-E3-E2-D2
George Street	E3-E2-F2
Glasgow Bridge	C1
Glassford Street	E2
Glebe Court	F4
Grafton Place	E3
Grant Street	A5-B5
Granville Street	A3-A4
Great Dovenhill	F1
Great Western Road	A5-B5
High Street	E1-E2-F2-F3
Hill Street	B4-C4
Holland Street	B3-B4
Holm Street	C2
Hope Street	C2-C3-C4-D4
Howard Street	C1-D1
Hutcheson Street	E1-E2
Hyde Park Street	A1-A2
Ingram Street	D2-E2-F2
Irongate	E1
Jamaica Street	C1-C2-D2
James Watt Street	B1-B2-C2
John Street	E3
Kennedy Street	E4-F4
Kent Road	A3-A4
Kent Street	F1
King Street	E1
Kingston Bridge	B1
Kingston Street	B1-C1
Kyle Street	E4
Lister Street	F4
London Road	E1-F1
Lyndoch Place	A5
Lyndoch Street	A4-A5
McAlpine Street	B1-B2
McAslin Court	F4
Maryhill Road	B5
Maxwell Street	D1-D2
Miller Street	D2
Milton Street	D4-D5
Mitchell Street	D2
Moncur Street	F1
Montrose Street	E2-E3
New City Road	B5
North Street	A3-A4
North Frederick Street	E3
North Hannover Street	D3-E3-E4
North Wallace Street	E4
Old Wynd	E1
Osborne Street	E1
Oswald Street	C1-C2
Paisley Road	A1-B1

Park Drive	A5
Parliamentary Road	D3-E3
Parnie Street	E1
Pinkston Drive	F5
Pinkston Road	F5
Pitt Street	B2-B3-B4
Port Dundas Road	D4-D5
Queen Street	D2
Renfield Street	D4-D3-C3-C2-D2
Renfrew Street	B4-C4-C4
Richmond Street	E3-E2-F2
Robertson Street	C1-C2
Rose Street	C3-C4
Ross Street	F1
Rottenrow	F3
St Andrew's Square	E1-F1
St Enoch Square	D1-D2
St George's Road	A4-B4-B5
St James Road	E3-F3
St Mungo Avenue	E3-E4-F4
St Peter's Street	B5
St Vincent Place	D2-D3
St Vincent Street	A3-B3-C3-D3-D2
Saltmarket	E1
Sandyford Place	A4
Sauchiehall Street	A4-B4-C4-C3-D3
Scott Street	B4-C4
Shaftesbury Street	A3
Shamrock Street	B5-C5-C4
Spoutmouth	F1
Steel Street	E1
Stirling Road	F3
Stockwell Street	D1-E1
Taylor Place	F4
Taylor Street	F3
Turnbull Street	E1
Union Street	C2-D2
Virginia Street	D2-E2
Warroch Street	A1-A2
Washington Street	B1-B2
Waterloo Street	B2-C2
Weaver Street	F3
Wellington Street	C2-C3
West Street	B1
West Campbell Street	C2-C3
West George Street	B3-C3-D3
West Graham Street	B5-C5-C4
West Nile Street	D3-D4
West Prince's Street	A5-B5
West Regent Street	B3-C3-D3
Westend Park Street	A5
Windmill Croft Quay	B1
Woodlands Road	A4-A5
Woodside Place	A4
Woodside Terrace	A4
York Street	C1-C2

Paisley

Abbey Close	B2
Abbot Street	C4
Abercorn Street	B3-B4
Albion Street	A4-B4
Back Sneddon Street	B3-B4
Bank Street	C2
Barr Place	A1
Brabloch Crescent	C4
Caledonian Street	A3-A4
Canal Street	A1-B1
Canal Terrace	A1
Causeyside Street	A1-B1-B2
Cochran Street	C2
Cotton Street	B2
East Road	B4
Gauze Street	B2-C2-C3
George Street	A1-B1-B2-A2
Gilmour Street	B2-B3
Glasgow Road	C3
Glen Street	A4-A3-B3
Gordon Street	B1
Greenlaw Avenue	C3
Hamilton Street	B3-C3
High Street	A2-B2
Hunter Street	A3-B3
Johnstone Street	B1-B2
Kilnside Road	C2-C3
Lawn Street	B2-B3-C3
Love Street	B3-B4
Macdowall Street	A4
McGown Street	A4
McKerrel Street	C2-C3
Mill Street	C2
Moss Street	B2-B3
Murray Street	A4
Netherhill Road	C4
Newbridge	B3
New Sneddon Street	B3-B4
New Street	A2-B2
Niddry Street	B3-C3
North Street	B4
Oakshaw Street	A2-A3-B2
Old Sneddon Street	B3
Orchard Street	B2
Renfrew Road	C3-C4
St James Street	A3
Saucel Lonend	B1-C1
Saucel Street	B1
Seedhill Road	C1-C2
Silk Street	B3-C3-C2
Smith Hills Street	B2-B3
Storie Street	A1-A2
Underwood Road	A3
Wallace Street	B4
Wier Street	B3-C3

Dalrymple Street	A4-B4-B3
Dellingburn Street	C1
Dempster Street	A1-B1
Duff Street	C2
Duncan Street	A1-A2
East Shaw Street	A2-A3
George Square	A3-A4
Grey Place	A4
Haig Street	B4
Hamilton Way	B3
Hay Street	B1
High Street	A3-B3-B2
Hill Street	C1
Hood Street	A4-B4
Hope Street	B1-C1
Houston Street	A4
Hunter Place	B3
Inverkip Street	A2-A3
Jamaica Lane	A4
Jamaica Street	A4
Kelly Street	A4
Kilblain Street	A3
King Street	B2
Laird Street	A4-B4
Lyle Street	B1-C1
Lynedoch Street	B1-C1-C2
Mearns Street	B1-C1
Nelson Street	A3
Patrick Street	A4
Princes Street	A3
Regent Street	A2-B2-C2-C1
Roslin Street	B4
Roxburgh Avenue	A1-A2
Roxburgh Street	A2-B2-B1
Roxburgh Way	A1-A2
Shaw Place	B2
Sir Michael Place	A2-A3
Sir Michael Street	A2-A3
Smith Street	B2
Station Avenue	C2
Terrace Road	C1-C2
Tobago Street	A2-B2
Trafalgar Street	A1-B1-B2
Union Street	A4
Watt Street	A3-A4
Wellington Street	A1-B1
West Blackhall Street	A4-A3-B3
West Shaw Street	A3-B3
West Shaw Street	A3
West Stewart Street	A4-A3-B3
William Street	C2-C3

Greenock

Ann Street	A1
Ann Street	A2-B2
Antigua Street	C1
Argyll Street	A4
Armdale Place	B1
Bank Street	B1-B2-C2
Bearhope Street	A2
Bogle Street	C1-C2
Brymner Street	C2-C3
Buccleugh	B2-B3
Captain Street	A1
Cathcart Square	B2-C2
Cathcart Street	C2
Clarence Street	B4
Container Way	B3-B4
Cross Shore Street	C2-C3
Crown Street	B2
Custom House Place	C2-C3

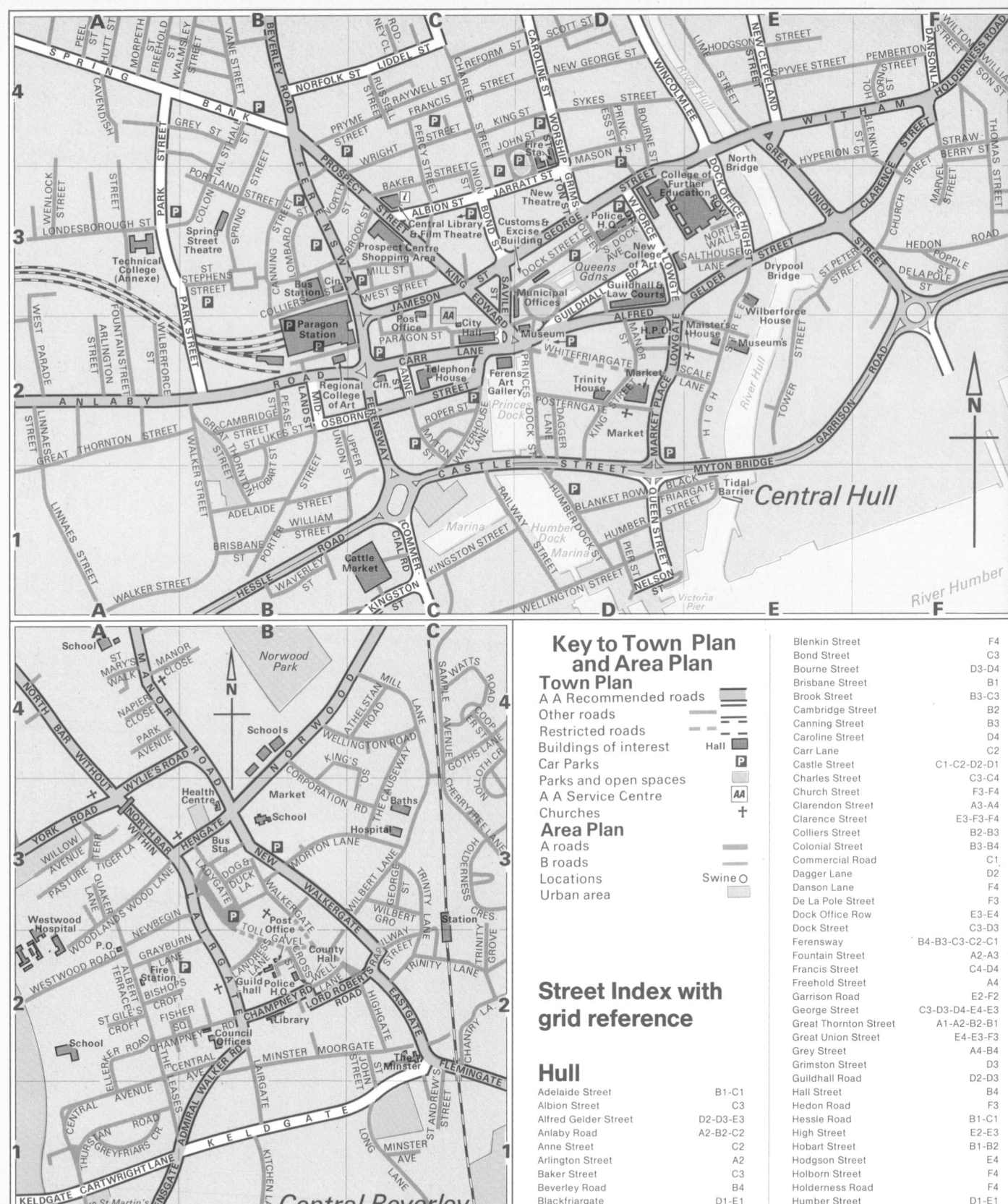

Key to Town Plan and Area Plan

Town Plan

A A Recommended roads	
Other roads	
Restricted roads	
Buildings of interest	Hall
Car Parks	P
Parks and open spaces	
A A Service Centre	AA
Churches	+

Area Plan

A roads	
B roads	
Locations	Swine ○
Urban area	

Street Index with grid reference

Hull

Adelaide Street	B1-C1
Albion Street	C3
Alfred Gelder Street	D2-D3-E3
Anlaby Road	A2-B2-C2
Anne Street	C2
Arlington Street	A2
Baker Street	C3
Beverley Road	B4
Blackfriargate	D1-E1
Blanket Row	D1
Blenkin Street	F4
Bond Street	C3
Bourne Street	D3-D4
Brisbane Street	B1
Brook Street	B3-C3
Cambridge Street	B2
Canning Street	B3
Caroline Street	D4
Carr Lane	C2
Castle Street	C1-C2-D2-D1
Charles Street	C3-C4
Church Street	F3-F4
Clarendon Street	A3-A4
Clarence Street	E3-F3-F4
Colliers Street	B2-B3
Colonial Street	B3-B4
Commercial Road	C1
Dagger Lane	D2
Danson Lane	F4
De La Pole Street	F3
Dock Office Row	E3-E4
Dock Street	C3-D3
Ferensway	B4-B3-C3-C2-C1
Fountain Street	A2-A3
Francis Street	C4-D4
Freehold Street	A4
Garrison Road	E2-F2
George Street	C3-D3-D4-E4-E3
Great Thornton Street	A1-A2-B2-B1
Great Union Street	E4-E3-F3
Grey Street	A4-B4
Grimston Street	D3
Guildhall Road	D2-D3
Hall Street	B4
Hedon Road	F3
Hessle Road	B1-C1
High Street	E2-E3
Hobart Street	B1-B2
Hodgson Street	E4
Holborn Street	E4
Holderness Road	F4
Humber Street	D1-E1
Humber Dock Street	D1

Hull

Officially Kingston-upon-Hull, this ancient port was specially laid out with new docks in 1293, on the decree of Edward I, and echoes of the town's past can be seen in the Town Docks Museum. The docks and the fishing industry are synonymous with Hull – it has Britain's busiest deep-sea fishing port – although flour-milling, vegetable oil extraction and petrochemical production are also important. The centre of Hull consists of broad streets and spacious squares and parks, such as Queen's Gardens, laid out on the site of what used to be Queen's Dock. The older part of the town which lies south-east of here between the docks and the River Hull is full of character, with a number of Georgian buildings and places of interest.

Beverley is one of England's most distinguished towns. Between its two principal buildings – the famous Minster and St Mary's Church – are medieval streets and pleasing market squares graced by redbrick Georgian houses built by the landed gentry of the East Riding during the town's heyday as a fashionable resort. The Minster's twin towers soar above the rooftops of the town as a constant reminder that here is one of the most beautiful pieces of Gothic architecture in Europe. The wealth of beauty and detail throughout is immense, but carving in both stone and wood is one of its most outstanding features.

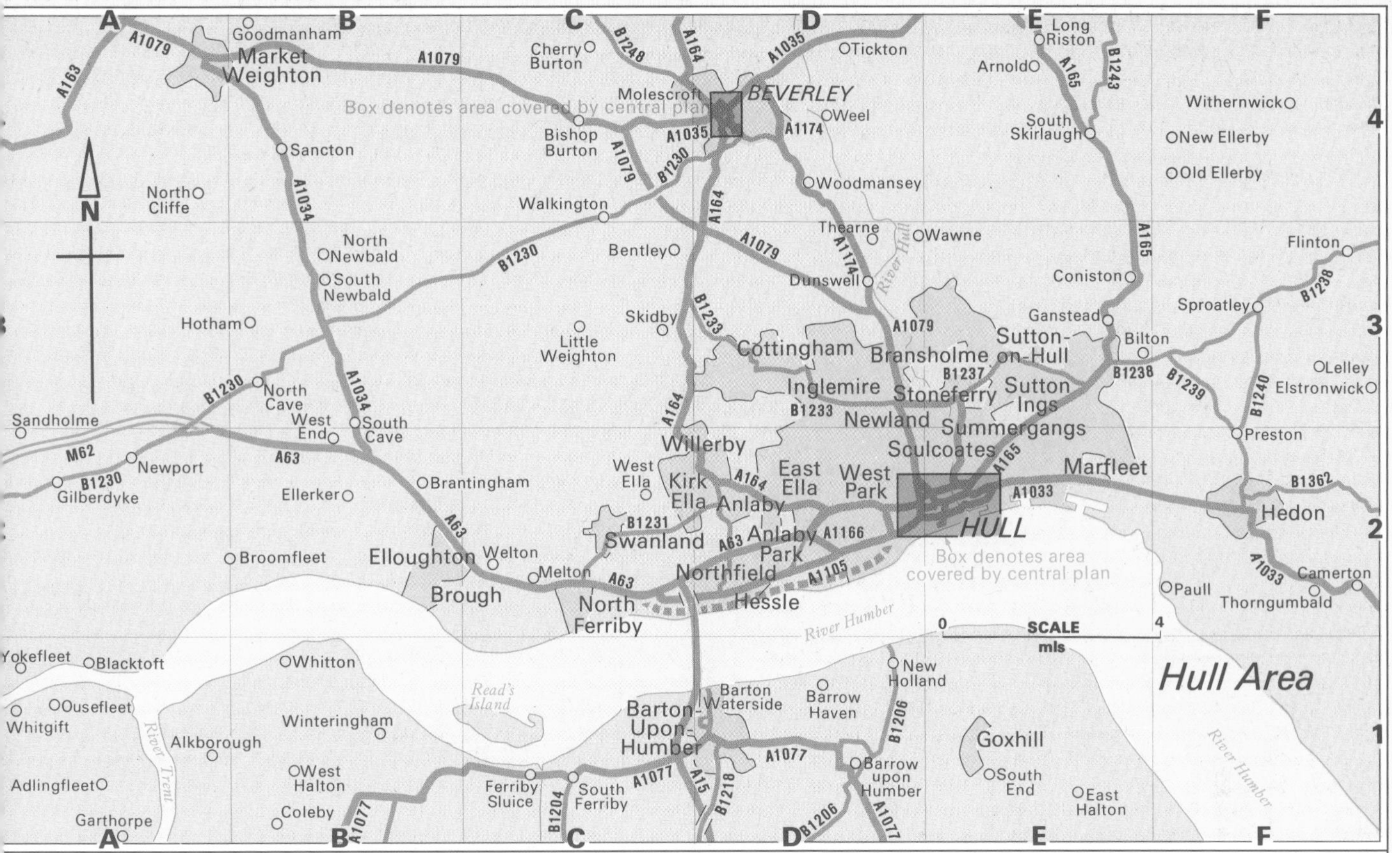

Hutt Street	A4
Hyperion Street	E3-E4-F4
Jameson Street	C2-C3
Jarrett Street	C3-D3
John Street	C4-D4
King Street	C4-D4
King Street	D2
King Edward Street	C3-C2-D2
Kingston Street	C1-D1
Liddel Street	C4
Lime Street	D4-E4
Lombard Street	B3
Linnaes Street	A1-A2
Londesborough Street	A3
Lowgate	D2-D3
Manor Street	D2
Market Place	D2
Marvel Street	F3-F4
Mason Street	D4
Midland Street	B2
Mill Street	C3
Morpeth Street	A4
Myton Bridge	E1-E2
Myton Street	C2
Nelson Street	D1
New Cleveland Street	E4
New George Street	D4
Norfolk Street	B4-C4
North Street	B3
North Walls	E3
Osborne Street	B2-C2
Paragon Street	C2
Park Street	B2-B3-A3-A4
Pease Street	B2
Peel Street	A4
Pemberton Street	F4
Percy Street	C3-C4
Pier Street	D1
Popple Street	F3
Porter Street	B1-B2
Portland Street	B3
Posterngate	D2
Princess Street	D4

Princes Dock Street	D2
Prospect Place	B4-B3-C3
Pryme Street	B4-C4
Queen Street	D1
Queens Dock Avenue	D3
Railway Street	C1-D1
Raywell Street	C4
Reform Street	C4-D4
Rodney Close	C4
Roper Street	C2
Russell Street	C4
St Lukes Street	B2
St Peter Street	E3-F3
St Stephens Street	B3
Salthouse Lane	E3
Saville Street	C2-C3
Scale Lane	D2-E2
Scott Street	D4
Spring Bank	A4-B4
Spring Street	B3-B4
Spyvee Street	E4-F4
Strawberry Street	F4
Sykes Street	D4
Thomas Street	F3-F4
Tower Street	E2-E3
Union Street	C3
Upper Union Street	B2-C2-C1
Vane Street	B4
Walker Street	A1-B1-B2
Walmesley Street	B4
Waterhouse Lane	C1-C2
Waverley Street	B1
Wellington Street	C1-D1
Wenlock Street	A3-A4
West Parade	A2-A3
West Street	C3
Whitefriar Gate	D2
Wilberforce Drive	D3
Wilberforce Street	A2
William Street	B1-C1
Williamson Street	F4
Wilton Street	F4
Wincolmlee	D4-E4

Witham	E4-F4
Worship Street	D3-D4
Wright Street	C3-C4

Beverley

Admiral Walker Road	A1-B1-B2
Albert Terrace	A2
Athelston Road	C4
Bishops Croft	A2-B2
Cartwright Lane	A1
Central Avenue	A1-A2-B2
Champney Road	A2-B2
Chantry Lane	C2
Cherrytree Lane	C3-C4
Cooper Street	C4
Corporation Road	B4-B3-C3
Cross Street	B2
Dog and Duck Lane	B3
Eastgate	C2
Ellerker Road	A1-A2
Flemingate	C1-C2
Fisher Square	A2-B2
George Street	C3
Goths Lane	C4
Grayburn Lane	A2-B2
Greyfriars Crescent	A1
Hengate	A3-B3
Highgate	C2
Holderness Crescent	C3
Keldgate	B1-C1
Keldgate Road	A1
Kings Square	B3-B4-C4-C3
Kitchen Lane	B1
Ladygate	B3
Lairgate	B1-B2-B3-A3
Landress Lane	B2
Long Lane	C1
Lord Roberts Road	B2-C2
Manor Close	A4-B4
Manor Road	A4-B4-B3

Mill Lane	C3-C4
Minster Avenue	C1
Minster Moorgate	B2-C2
Morton Lane	B3-C3
Napier Close	A4
New Walkergate	B3-C3-C2
Newbegin	A2-A3-B3
Nolloth Crescent	C3-C4
North Bar Within	A3
North Bar Without	A3-A4
Norwood	B3-B4-C4
Park Avenue	A4
Pasture Terrace	A3
Quaker Lane	A3
Queensgate	A1-B1
Railway Street	C2
St Andrew's Street	C1-C2
St Gile's Croft	A2
St John Street	C1-C2
St Mary's Walk	A4
Sample Avenue	C4
Sole Lane	A1
The Causeway	C3-C4
The Leases	A1-A2
Thurstan Road	A1
Tiger Lane	A3
Toll Gavel	B2-B3
Trinity Grove	C2-C3
Trinity Lane	C2-C3
Walkergate	B2-B3
Watts Road	C4
Well Lane	B2
Wellington Road	B4-C4
Westwood Road	A2
Wilbert Grove	C3
Wilbert Grove	C3
Wilbert Lane	B2-B3-C3
Willow Avenue	A3
Woodlands Wood Lane	A2-A3
Wylie's Road	A3-A4-B4
York Road	A3

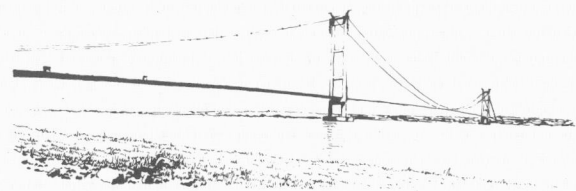

HULL
Schemes to cross the Humber estuary were first discussed over 100 years ago, but it was not until 1981 that the mammoth project was sucessfully completed. At 4626ft, the Humber Bridge has the longest main span in the world.

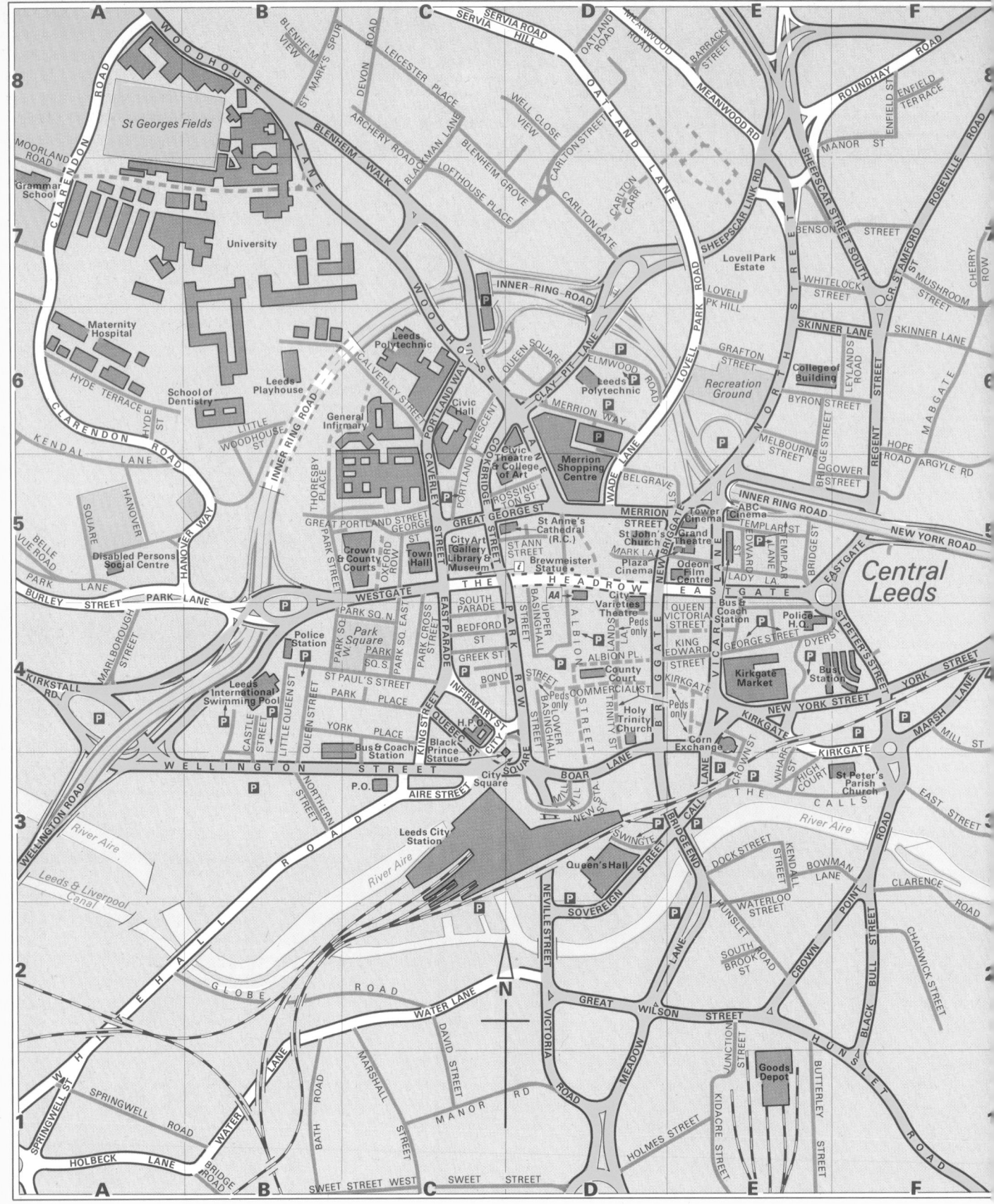

Leeds

In the centre of Leeds is its town hall – a monumental piece of architecture with a 225ft clock-tower. It was opened by Queen Victoria in 1858, and has been a kind of mascot for the city ever since. It exudes civic pride; such buildings could only have been created in the heyday of Victorian prosperity and confidence. Leeds' staple industry has always been the wool trade, but it

only became a boom town towards the end of the 18th century, when textile mills were introduced. Today, the wool trade and ready-made clothing (Mr Hepworth and Mr Burton began their work here) are still important, though industries like paper, leather, furniture and electrical equipment are prominent.

Across Calverley Street from the town hall is the City Art Gallery, Library and Museum. Its collections include sculpture by Henry Moore, who

was a student at Leeds School of Art. Nearby is the Headrow, Leeds' foremost shopping thoroughfare. On it is the City Varieties Theatre, venue for many years of the famous television programme 'The Good Old Days'. Off the Headrow are several shopping arcades, of which Leeds has many handsome examples. Leeds has a good number of interesting churches; perhaps the finest is St John's, unusual in that it dates from 1634, a time when few churches were built.

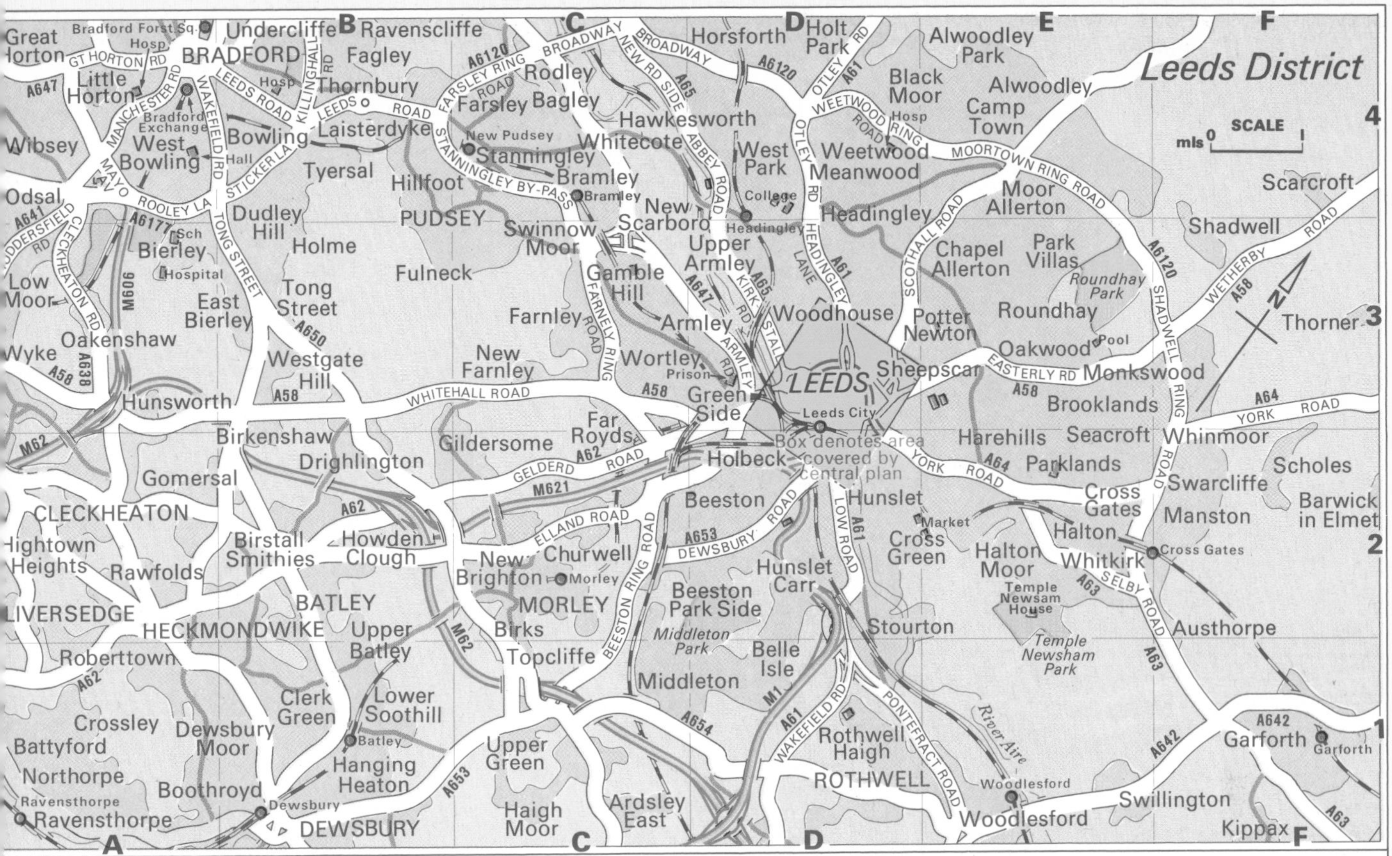

Leeds District

SCALE
mls 0

LEGEND

Town Plan

AA Recommended roads	
Other roads	
Restricted roads	
Buildings of interset	Museum
AA Service Centre	AA
Parks and open spaces	
Car Parks	P
Churches	†

District Plan

A roads	
B roads	
Stations	Kirkgate ●
Urban area	
Buildings of interest	Hospital

Street Index with Grid Reference

Leeds

Aire Street	C3
Albion Place	D4
Albion Street	D3-D4-D5
Archery Road	C7-C8
Argyle Road	F5
Barrack Street	E8
Bath Road	B1-B2
Bedford Street	C4
Belgrave Street	D5-E5
Belle Vue Road	A5
Benson Street	E7-F7
Black Bull Street	F1-F2-F3
Blackman Lane	C7-C8
Blenheim Grove	C8-C7-D7
Blenheim Walk	B8-C8-C7
Boar Lane	D3-D4
Bond Street	C4-D4
Bowman Lane	E3-F3
Bridge End	D3-E3
Bridge Road	B1
Bridge Street	E5-E6
Briggate	D3-D4-D5
Burley Street	A4-A5
Butterley Street	E1-E2
Byron Street	E6-F6
Call Lane	E3
Calverley Street	C5-C6
Carlton Carr	D7
Carlton Gate	D7
Carlton Street	D7-D8
Castle Street	B3-B4
Chadwick Street	F2
Chapeltown Road	E8
Cherry Row	F7
City Square	C3-C4-D4-D3
Clarence Road	F2-F3
Clarendon Road	A8-A7-A6-A5-B5
Clay Pit Lane	D6
Commercial Street	D4
Cookbridge Street	C5-C6-D6
Cross Stamford Street	F6-F7
Crown Street	E3-E4
Crown Point Road	E2-F2-F3
David Street	C1-C2
Devon Road	C8
Dock Street	E3
Dyer Street	E4-F4
East Parade	C4-C5
East Street	F3
Eastgate	E5-F5
Edward Street	E5
Elmwood Road	D6
George Street	C5
George Street	E4
Globe Road	A2-B2-C2
Gower Street	E5-F5
Grafton Street	E6
Great George Street	C5-D5
Great Portland Street	B5-C5-D5
Great Wilson Street	D2-E2
Greek Street	C4-D4
Hanover Square	A5
Hanover Way	A5-B5
High Court	E3
Holbeck Lane	A1-B1
Holmes Street	D1-E1
Hope Road	F5-F6
Hunslett Road	E3-E2-E1-F1-F2
Hyde Street	A6
Hyde Terrace	A6
Infirmary Street	C4-D4
Inner Ring Road	B5-B6-C6-C7-D7-D6-E6-E5-F5

Junction Street	E1-E2
Kendal Lane	A5-A6
Kendal Street	E3
Kidacre Street	E1
King Street	C3-C4
King Edward Street	D4-E4
Kirkgate	E4-E3-F3-F4
Kirkstall Road	A4
Lady Lane	E5
Lands Lane	D4-D5
Leicester Place	C8
Leylands Road	F6
Lisbon Street	B3-B4
Little Queen Street	B3-B4
Little Woodhouse Street	B6
Lofthouse Place	C7-D7
Lovell Park Hill	E7
Lovell Park Road	D6-E6-E7
Lower Basinghall Street	D3-D4
Mabgate	F6
Manor Road	C1-D1
Mark Lane	D5
Marlborough Street	A4
Marsh Lane	F4
Marshall Street	C1-C2
Meadow Lane	D1-D2-E2-E3
Meanwood Road	D8-E8
Melbourne Street	E6
Merrion Street	D5-E5
Merrion Way	D6
Mill Hill	D3
Mill Street	F4
Moorland Road	A7-A8
Mushroom Street	F6-F7
Neville Street	D2-D3
New Briggate	D5-E5
New Station Street	D3
New York Road	F5
New York Street	E4-F4
North Street	E5-E6-E7
Northern Street	B3
Oatland Lane	D8-D7-E7
Oatland Road	D8
Oxford Row	C5
Park Cross Street	C4-C5
Park Lane	A5-B5-B4
Park Place	B4-C4
Park Row	C4-C5-D5-D4
Park Square East	C4
Park Square North	B4-C4
Park Square South	C4
Park Square West	B4
Park Street	B5-C5
Portland Crescent	C5-C6

Portland Way	C6
Quebec Street	C3-C4
Queen Street	B3-B4
Queen Square	C6-D6
Queen Victoria Street	D4-E4
Regent Street	F5-F6
Roseville Road	F7-F8
Rossington Street	C5-D5
Roundhay Road	E8-F8
St Ann Street	C5-D5
St Paul's Street	B4-C4
St Peter's Street	E4-F4
Servia Hill	C8-D8
Servia Road	C8-D8
Sheepscar Link Road	E7-E8
Sheepscar Street North	E8
Sheepscar Street South	E8-E7-F7
Skinner Lane	E6-F6
South Brook Street	E2
South Parade	C4
Sovereign Street	D2-D3-E3
Springwell Road	A1-B1
Springwell Street	A1
Sweet Street	C1-D1
Sweet Street West	B1-C1
Swinegate	D3
The Calls	E3-F3
The Headrow	C5-D5
Templar Lane	E5
Templar Street	E5
Thoresby Place	B5-B6
Trinity Street	D4
Upper Basinghall Street	D4-D5
Vicar Lane	E4-E5
Victoria Road	D1-D2
Wade Lane	D5-D6
Water Lane	B1-B2-C2-D2
Waterloo Street	E2-E3
Well Cross View	D8
Wellington Road	A3
Wellington Street	A3-B3-C3
Westgate	B4-B5-C5-C4
Wharf Street	E3-E4
Whitehall Road	A1-A2-B2-B3-C3
Whitelock Street	E7-F7
Woodhouse Lane	A8-B8-B7-C7-C6-D6-D5
York Place	B4-C4
York Street	F4

LEEDS
Offices now occupy the handsome twin-towered Civic Hall which stands in Calverley Street in front of the new buildings of Leeds Polytechnic. This area of the city – the commercial centre – has been extensively redeveloped

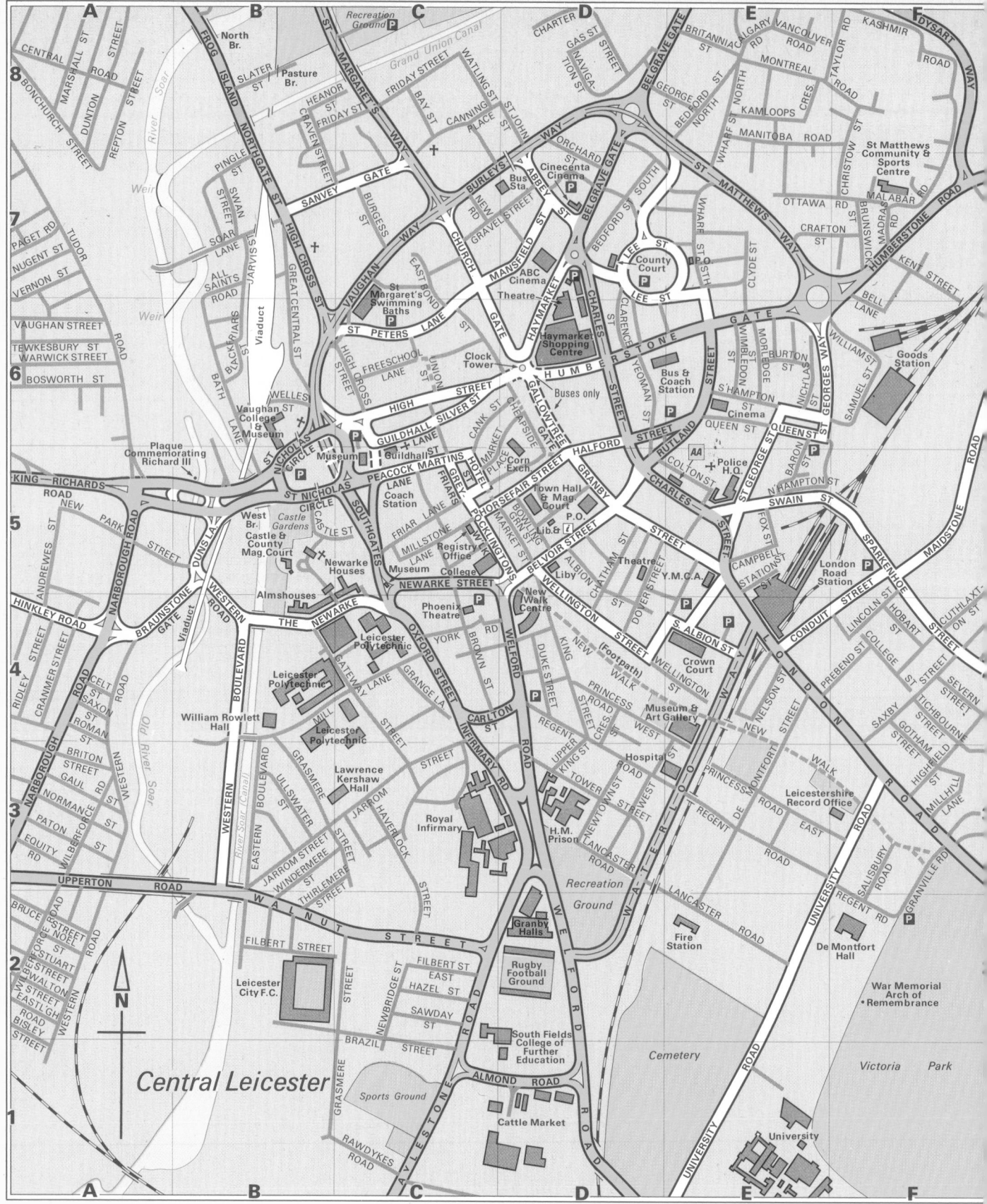

Leicester

A regional capital in Roman times, Leicester has retained many buildings from its eventful and distinguished past. Today the city is a thriving modern place, a centre for industry and commerce, serving much of the Midlands. Among the most outstanding monuments from the past is the Jewry Wall, a great bastion of Roman masonry. Close by are remains of the Roman baths and

several other contemporary buildings. Attached is a museum covering all periods from prehistoric times to 1500. Numerous other museums include the Wygston's House Museum of Costume, with displays covering the period 1769 to 1924; Newarke House, with collections showing changing social conditions in Leicester through four hundred years; and Leicestershire Museum and Art Gallery, with collections of drawings, paintings, ceramics, geology and natural history.

The medieval Guildhall has many features of interest, including a great hall, library and police cells. Leicester's castle, although remodelled in the 17th century, retains a 12th-century great hall. The Church of St Mary de Castro, across the road from the castle, has features going back at least as far as Norman times; while St Nicholas's Church is even older, with Roman and Saxon foundations. St Martin's Cathedral dates mainly from the 13th to 15th centuries and has a notable Bishop's throne.

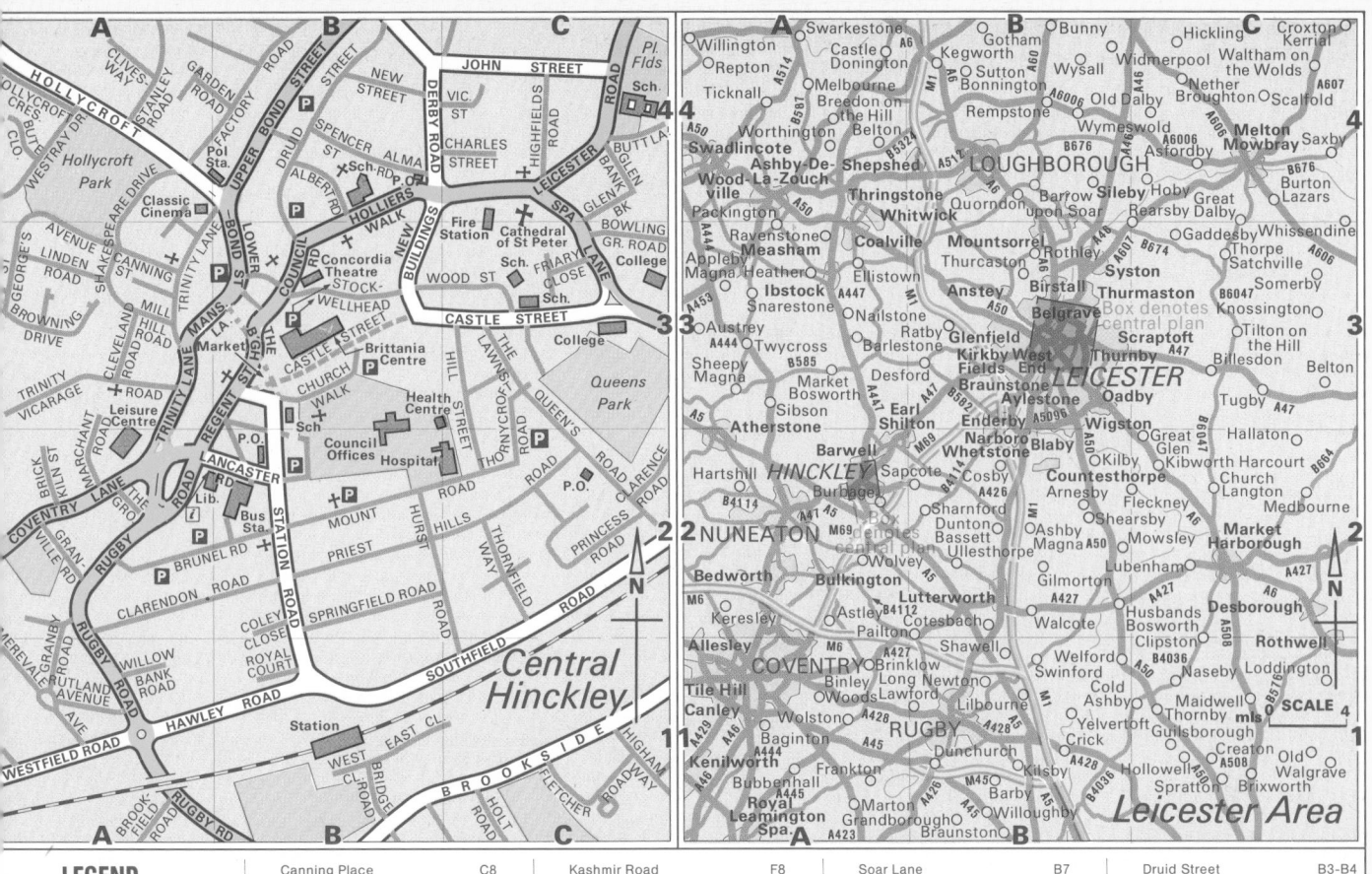

Central Hinckley

Leicester Area

Box denotes central plan

SCALE
0   4
mls

LEGEND

own Plan

A Recommended route

estricted roads

ther roads

uildings of interest

ar parks

arks and open spaces

Area Plan

. roads

. roads

ocations   Creaton○

urban area

Street Index with Grid Reference

Leicester

bbey Street	D7
lbion Street	D4-D5
ll Saints Road	B7
lmond Road	C1-D1
ndrewes Street	A4-A5
ylestone Road	C1-C2
aron Street	E5-E6
ath Lane	B5-B6
ay Street	C8
edford Street North	E8
edford Street South	D7
elgrave Gate	D7-D8-E8
ell Lane	F6-F7
elvoir Street	D5
isley Street	A1-A2
lackfriars Street	B6
onchurch Street	A7-A8
osworth Street	A6
owling Green Street	D5
raunstone Gate	A4-B4-B5
razil Street	C1-C2
ritannia Street	E8
riton Street	A3
rown Street	C4
ruce Street	A2
runswick Street	F7
urgess Street	C7
urleys Way	C7-D7-D8
urton Street	E6
algary Road	E8
ampbell Street	E5
ank Street	C6-D6

Canning Place	C8
Carlton Street	C4-D4
Castle Street	B5-C5
Celt Street	A4
Central Road	A8
Charles Street	D7-D6-D5-E5
Charter Street	D8
Chatham Street	D4-D5
Cheapside	D5-D6
Christow Street	F7-F8
Church Gate	C7-C6-D6
Clarence Street	D6-D7
Clyde Street	E6-E7
College Street	F4
Colton Street	D5-E5
Conduit Street	E4-F4-F5
Crafton Street	E7-F7
Cranmer Street	A4
Craven Street	B7-B8
Crescent Street	D4
Cuthlaxton Street	F4-F5
De Montfort Street	E3-E4
Dover Street	D4-D5
Duke Street	D4
Dunns Lane	B5
Dunton Street	A8
Dysart Way	F8
East Bond Street	C6-C7
Eastern Boulevard	B3-B4
Eastleigh Road	A2
Equity Road	A3
Filbert Street	B2-C2
Filbert Street East	C2
Fox Street	E5
Freeschool Lane	C6
Friar Lane	C5
Friday Street	B8-C8
Frog Island	B8
Gallowtree Gate	D6
Gas Street	D8
Gateway Street	B4-C4-C3
Gaul Street	A3
George Street	D8-E8
Gotham Street	F3-F4
Granby Street	D5-E5
Grange Lane	C4
Granville Road	F2-F3
Grasmere Street	B4-B3-C3-C2-C1-B1
Gravel Street	C7-D7
Great Central Street	B6-B7
Greyfriars	C5
Guildhall Lane	C6
Halford Street	D5-D6-E6
Haverlock Street	C2-C3
Haymarket	D6-D7
Hazel Street	C2
Heanor Street	B8-C8
High Cross Street	B7-B6-C6
Highfield Street	F3
High Street	C6-D6
Hinkley Road	A4
Hobart Street	F4
Horsefair Street	C5-D5
Hotel Street	C5
Humberstone Gate	D6-E6
Humberstone Road	F7
Infirmary Road	C4-C3-D3
Jarrom Street	B3-C3
Jarvis Street	B7
Kamloops Crescent	E8

Kashmir Road	F8
Kent Street	F7
King Richards Road	A5
King Street	D4
Lancaster Road	D3-E3-E2
Lee Street	D6-D7-E7
Lincoln Street	F4-F5
London Road	E5-E4-F4-F3
Madras Road	F7
Maidstone Road	F5-F6
Malabar Road	F7
Manitoba Road	E8
Mansfield Street	C7-D7
Market Place	C5-C6-D6
Market Street	D5
Marshall Street	A8
Morledge Street	E6
Mill Hill Lane	F3
Mill Lane	B4-C4
Millstone Lane	C5
Montreal Road	E8-F8
Narborough Road	A3-A4-A5
Navigation Street	D8
Nelson Street	E4
Newarke Street	C5
New Bridge Street	C2
New Park Street	A5-B5
New Road	C7
Newtown Street	D3
New Walk	D4-E4-E3-F3
Nicholas Street	E6
Noel Street	A2
Northampton Street	E5
Northgate Street	B7-B8
Norman Street	A3
Nugent Street	A7
Orchard Street	D7-D8
Ottawa Road	E7-F7
Oxford Street	C4
Paget Road	A7
Paton Street	A3
Peacock Lane	C5
Pingle Street	B7
Pocklingtons Walk	C5-D5
Prebend Street	E4-F4
Princess Road East	E3-F3
Princess Road West	D4
Queen Street	F4
Rawdykes Road	B1-C1
Regent Road	D4-D3-E3-F3-F2
Repton Street	A7-A8
Ridley Street	A4
Roman Street	A4
Rutland Street	D5-E5-E6
St George Street	E5-E6
St Georges Way	E6-F6
St John Street	D8
St Margaret's Way	B8-C8-C7
St Martins	C5
St Mathews Way	E6-E7
St Nicholas Circle	B6-B5-C5
St Peters Lane	C6
Salisbury Road	F2-F3
Samuel Stuart	F6
Sanvey Gate	B7-C7
Sawday Street	C2
Saxby Street	F4
Saxon Street	A4
Severn Street	F4
Silver Street	C6
Slater Street	B8

Soar Lane	B7
South Albion Street	E4
Southampton Street	E6
Southgates	C5
Sparkenhoe Street	F4-F5
Station Street	E5
Stuart Street	A2
Swain Street	E5-F5
Swan Street	B7
The Newarke	B4-C4
Taylor Road	E8-F8
Tewkesbury Street	A6
Thirlemere Street	B2-B3-C3
Tichbourne Street	F3-F4
Tower Street	E5
Tudor Road	A6-A7-A8
Ullswater Street	B3
Union Street	C6
University Road	E1-E2-E3-F3
Upper King Street	D3-D4
Upperton Road	A3-B3-B2
Vancouver Road	E8
Vaughan Way	C6-C7
Vaughan Street	A6
Vernon Street	A6-A7
Walnut Street	B3-B2-C2
Walton Street	A2
Warwick Street	A4
Waterloo Way	D2-D3-E3-E4
Watling Street	C8
Welford Road	D1-D2-D3-D4
Welles Street	B6
Wellington Street	D4-E4-D5
Western Boulevard	B3-B4
Western Road	A1-A2-A3-A4-B4-B5
West Street	D3-E3-E4
Wharf Street North	E7-E8
Wharf Street South	E7
Wilberforce Road	A2-A3
William Street	F6
Wimbledon Street	E6
Windermere Street	B2-B3-C3
Yeoman Street	D6
York Road	C4

Hinkley

Albert Road	B4
Alma Road	B4
Bowling Green Road	C3
Brick Kiln Street	A2
Bridge Road	B1
Brookfield Road	A1
Brookside	B1-C1
Browning Drive	A3
Brunel Road	A2-B2
Bute Close	A4
Butt Lane	C4
Canning Street	A3
Castle Street	B3-C3
Charles Street	C4
Church Walk	B3
Clarence Road	C2
Clarendon Road	A2-B2
Cleveland Road	A3
Clivesway	A4
Coley Close	B2
Council Road	B3
Coventry Lane	A2
Derby Road	B4

Druid Street	B3-B4
East Close	B1-C1
Factory Road	A4-B4
Fletcher Road	C1
Friary Close	C3
Garden Road	A4-B4
Glen Bank	C1
Granby Road	A1-A2
Granville Road	A2
Hawley Road	A1-B1
Higham Way	C1
Highfields Road	C4
Hill Street	C2-C3
Holliers Walk	B3-B4
Hollycroft	A4
Hollycroft Crescent	A4
Holt Road	C4
Hurst Road	B2-C2
John Street	C4
Lancaster Road	A2-B2
Leicester Road	C4
Linden Road	A3
Lower Bond Street	B3-B4
Mansion Lane	A3-B3
Marchant Road	A2-A3
Merevale Avenue	A1
Mill Hill Road	A3
Mount Road	B2-C2
New Buildings	B3-B4
New Street	B4
Priest Hills Road	B2-C2
Princess Road	C2
Queens Road	C2-C3
Regent Street	A2-A3-B3
Royal Court	
Rugby Road	A2-A1-B1
Rutland Avenue	A1
St George's Avenue	A3-A4
Shakespeare Drive	A3-A4
Southfield Road	B1-C1-C2
Spa Lane	C3-C4
Spencer Street	B4
Springfield Road	B2
Stanley Road	A4
Station Road	B1-B2
Stockwellhead	B3
The Borough	B3
The Grove	A2
The Lawns	C3
Thornfield Way	C4
Thornycroft Road	C2-C3
Trinity Lane	A2-A3-A4-B4
Trinity Vicarage Road	A3
Upper Bond Street	B4
Victoria Street	C4
West Close	B1
Westday Drive	A4
Westfield Road	A1
Willow Bank Road	A1
Wood Street	B3-C3

Central Liverpool

Liverpool

With a dockside frontage extending for something over seven miles, Liverpool is second only to London in pre-eminence as a port. Forming the centrepiece of the docks area are three monumental buildings – the Dock Board Offices, built in 1907 with a huge copper-covered dome; the Cunard Building, dating from 1912 and decorated with an abundance of ornamental carving; and best-known

of all, the world-famous Royal Liver Building, with the two 'liver birds' crowning its twin cupolas.

Some of the city's best industrial buildings have fallen into disuse in recent years, and have been preserved as monuments of the industrial age. One has become a maritime museum housing full-sized craft and a workshop where maritime crafts are demonstrated. Other museums and galleries include the Walker Art Gallery, with excellent collections of European painting and

sculpture; Liverpool City Libraries, one of the oldest and largest public libraries in Britain, with a vast collection of books and manuscripts; and Bluecoat Chambers, a Queen Anne building now used as a gallery and concert hall. Liverpool has two outstanding cathedrals: the Roman Catholic, completed in 1967 in an uncompromising controversial style; and the Protestant, constructed in the great tradition of Gothic architecture, but begun only in 1904.

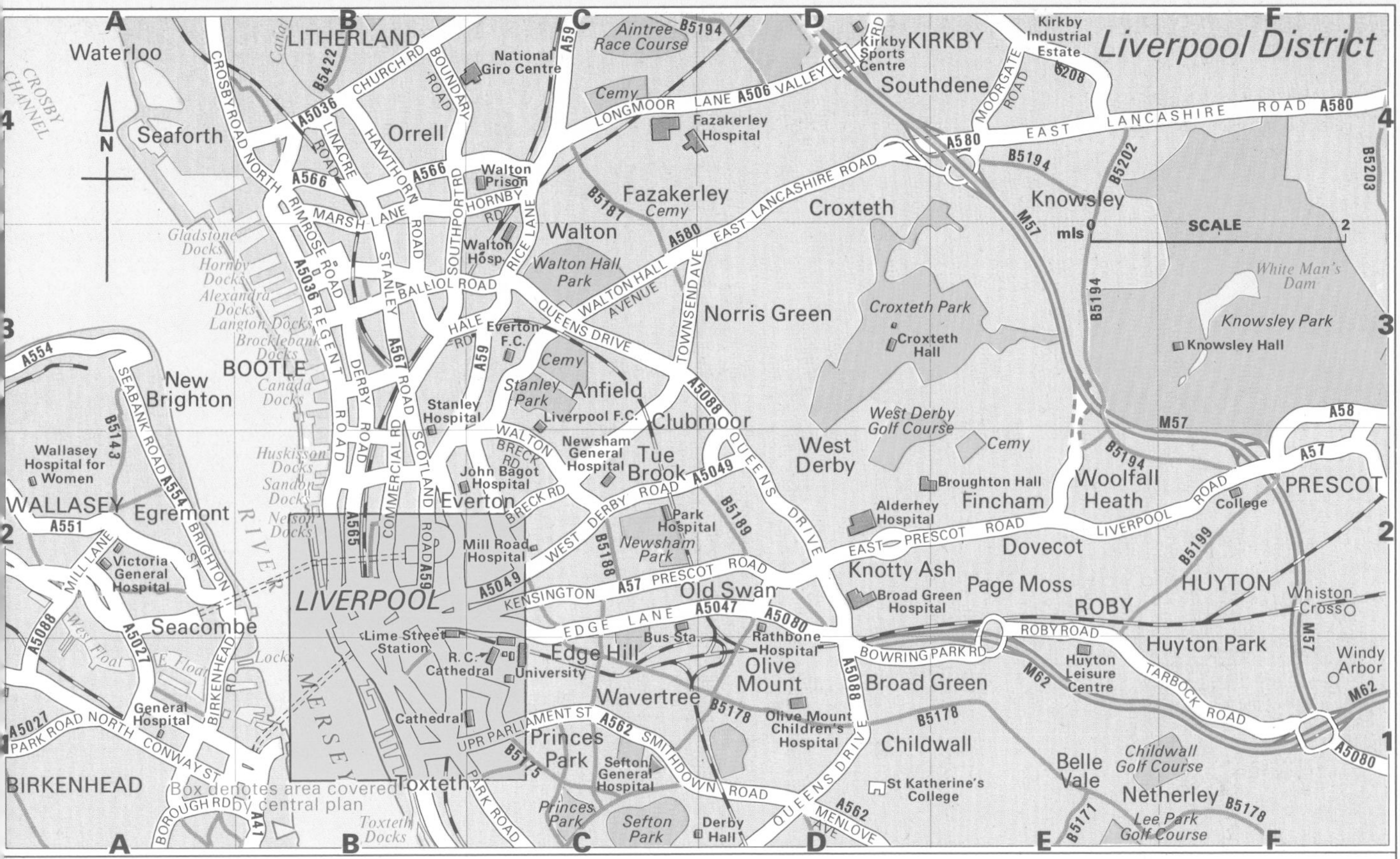

(Map of Liverpool District showing areas including Waterloo, Litherland, Bootle, New Brighton, Wallasey, Birkenhead, Seaforth, Orrell, Fazakerley, Walton, Croxteth, Norris Green, Anfield, Clubmoor, West Derby, Knowsley, Prescot, Huyton, Roby, Dovecot, Page Moss, Knotty Ash, Old Swan, Broad Green, Childwall, Wavertree, Toxteth, Liverpool, Edge Hill, etc. Major roads A580 East Lancashire Road, M57, M62, A59, A57, A562, etc. Scale shown 0–2 miles.)

Box denotes area covered by central plan

LEGEND

Town Plan

AA recommended route	
Restricted roads	
Other roads	
Buildings of interest	Castle
Car parks	P
Parks and open spaces	
AA Service Centre	AA

District Plan

A roads	
B roads	
Locations	Sefton ○

Street Index with Grid Reference

Liverpool

Addison Street	C6-D6
Arrad Street	F3-F4-F3
Bath Street	A6-B6-B5
Beaufort Street	D1
Bedford Street South	F2-F3
Berry Street	E3
Blackburn Place	E3-F3
Blackstock Street	C7-D7
Blenheim Street	C8-D8
Blundell Street	C2-D2
Bold Street	D4-D3-E3
Breck Road	F8
Brick Street	D1-D2
Brook Street	B5
Brownlow Hill	D4-E4-F4
Brow Side	E7-F7
Brunswick Road	F6
Brunswick Street	B4-C4
Burlington Street	B7-C7-C8-D8
Byrom Street	D6
Cambridge Street	F3
Canning Place	C3-C4
Canning Street	E2-F2
Carter Street	F1
Carver Street	E6-F6
Caryl Street	D1
Castle Street	C4-C5
Catherine Street	F2-F3
Chaloner Street	C2-C1-D1
Chatham Street	F3
Chapel Street	B5
Cheapside	C5
Chisenhale Street	B7-C7
Christian Street	D6-D7
Churchill Way North	C6-D6-D5
Church Street	C4-D4
Clarence Street	E4
Colquitt Street	D3-E3
Cook Street	C4
Cooper Street	D4
Copperas Hill	D4-E4-E5
Cornhill	C2-C3
Cotton Street	A8-B8
Crown Street	F4-F5
Dale Street	C5
Daulby Street	F5
Derby Square	C4
Devon Street	E6-F6
Dexter Street	E1
Dickson Street	A8-B8
Dryden Street	D8
Duke Street	C3-D3-E3
Earle Street	B5
Eldon Street	C7
Elliot Street	D4
Erskine Street	F6
Everton Brow	E7
Everton Road	F7-F8
Everton Terrace	E8-E7-F7
Falkner Street	E3-F3-F2
Fleet Street	D3-D4
Flint Street	D1
Fontenoy Street	D6
Fox Street	D7-E7
Freemasons' Row	C6
Gibson Street	F1
Gilbert Street	D3

Gill Street	E4-E5
Goree Piazza	B4
Grafton Street	D1
Great Crosshall Street	C6
Great George Street	E1-E2-E3
Great Homer Street	D7-D8
Great Howard Street	B6-B7-B8
Great Newton Street	E5-E4-F4
Hanover Street	C3-C4-D4
Hardman Street	E3
Hatton Garden	C5-C6
Henry Street	D3
Heyworth Street	F8
Hill Street	D1-E1
Hope Street	E2-E3-F3-F4
Hurst Street	C2-C3
Islington	E6-F6
Jamaica Street	D1-D2
James Street	B4-C4
Jordan Street	D1-D2
Juvenal Street	D7
Kempston Street	E5-F5-F6
Kent Street	D2-D3
Kepler Street	E8-F8
King Edward Street	B5-B6
Kingsway (Tunnel)	A6-A7-B7-C7
Kitchen Street	C2-D2
Landseer Road	F8
Langsdale Street	E6-F6
Leece Street	E3
Leeds Street	B6-C6
Limekiln Lane	C7-D7-D8
Lime Street	D4-D5
Liver Street	C3
London Road	D5-E5-F5
Lord Nelson Street	D5-E5
Lord Street	C4
Love Lane	B7-B8
Lydia Ann Street	D3
Mansfield Street	D6-E6
Mann Island	B4
Marybone	C6-D6
Mill Street	E1
Moss Street	F5-F6
Mount Pleasant	D4-E4-F4
Mount Street	E3
Myrtle Street	E3-F3
Naylor Street	C6-D6
Nelson Street	D2-D3-E3
Netherfield Road South	E7-F8
New Bird Street	D1-D2

New Islington	E6-F6
New Quay	B5
Nile Street	E2
North John Street	C4-C5
Norton Street	E5
Oil Street	A7-B7
Old Hall Street	B5-B6
Oriel Street	C6-C7-D7
Oxford Street	F3-F4
Pall Mall	B7-B6-C6-B5-C5
Paradise Street	C3-C4
Parker Street	D4
Park Lane	C3-D3-D2
Park Way	F1-F2
Parliament Street	D1-E1-E2
Paul Street	C7-D7
Pembroke Place	E5-F5
Percy Street	E2-F2
Porter Street	A7-B7
Prescot Street	F5-F6
Prince Edwin Street	E7-E8
Prince's Road	F1-F2
Queensway (Tunnel)	A3-A4-B4-C4-C5
Ranelagh Street	D4
Rathbone Street	E2-E3
Regent Street	A7-B7
Renshaw Street	D4-E4-E3
Richmond Row	D7-E7
Roberts Street	B6
Rodney Street	E3-E4
Roe Street	D5
Roscoe Street	E3-E4
Roscommon Street	D8-E8
Rose Place	D7-E7
Rose Vale	E8
Russell Street	E4-E5
St Anne Street	D7-D6-E6
St James's Place	E1
St James Road	E2-E1
St James's Street	D2-D1-E1
Salisbury Street	E7-E6-F6
Saltney Street	A8-B8
Sandon Street	F2
School Lane	C4-D4
Scotland Road	D6-D7-D8
Seel Street	D4-D3-E3
Sefton Street	D1
Seymour Street	E5
Shaw Street	E7-F7-F6
Silvester Street	C8-D8
Simpson Street	D1-D2

Slater Street	D3-D4
Soho Street	E6-E7
South John Street	C4
Sparling Street	C2-D2
Spencer Street	F7
Stanhope Street	D1-E1
Strand Street	B4-C4-C3
Tabley Street	C2-C3-D3
Tatlock Street	C8
Titchfield Street	C7-C8
Tithebarn Street	B5-C5-C6
The Strand	B4
Upper Duke Street	E3
Upper Hill Street	E1-F1
Upper Parliament Street	F2
Upper Pitt Street	D2
Upper Stanhope Street	E1-F1
Vauxhall Road	C6-C7-C8
Victoria Street	C4-C5-D5
Village Street	F7
Vine Street	F3
Wapping	C2-C3
Waterloo Road	A8-A7-B7-A6-B6
Water Street	B4-B5-C5
Whitechapel	C4-C5-D5
Wick Street	B7
Wilbraham Street	D8
William Brown Street	D5
William Henry Street	E6-E7-F7
Windsor Street	F1-F1
Wood Street	D4-D3-E3
York Street	C3-D3

LIVERPOOL
The Metropolitan Cathedral of Christ the King is one of Liverpool's most striking landmarks. Crowning the conical roof is a tower of stained glass which throws a pool of coloured light on to the altar below.

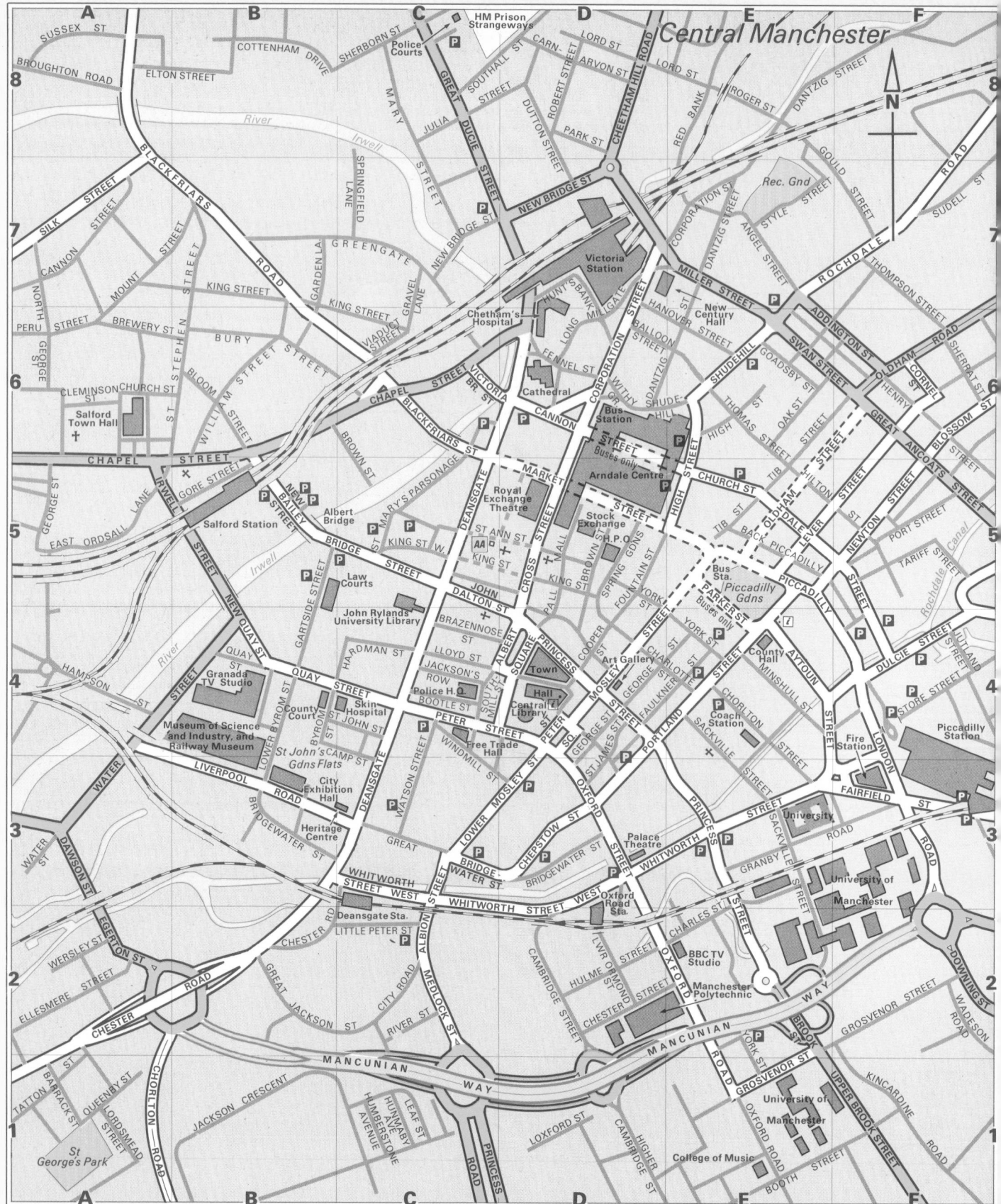

Manchester

The gigantic conurbation called Greater Manchester covers a staggering 60 square miles, reinforcing Manchester's claim to be Britain's second city. Commerce and industry are vital aspects of the city's character, but it is also an important cultural centre – the Hallé Orchestra has its home at the Free Trade Hall (a venue for many concerts besides classical music), there are several theatres, a library (the John Rylands) which houses one of the most important collections of books in the world, and a number of museums and galleries, including the Whitworth Gallery with its lovely watercolours.

Like many great cities it suffered badly during the bombing raids of World War II, but some older buildings remain, including the town hall, a huge building designed in Gothic style by Alfred Waterhouse and opened in 1877. Manchester Cathedral dates mainly from the 15th century and is noted for its fine tower and outstanding carved woodwork. Nearby is Chetham's Hospital, also 15th-century and now housing a music school. Much new development has taken place, and more is planned. Shopping precincts cater for the vast population, and huge hotels have provided services up to international standards. On the edge of the city is the Belle Vue centre, a large entertainments complex including concert and exhibition facilities, and a speedway stadium.

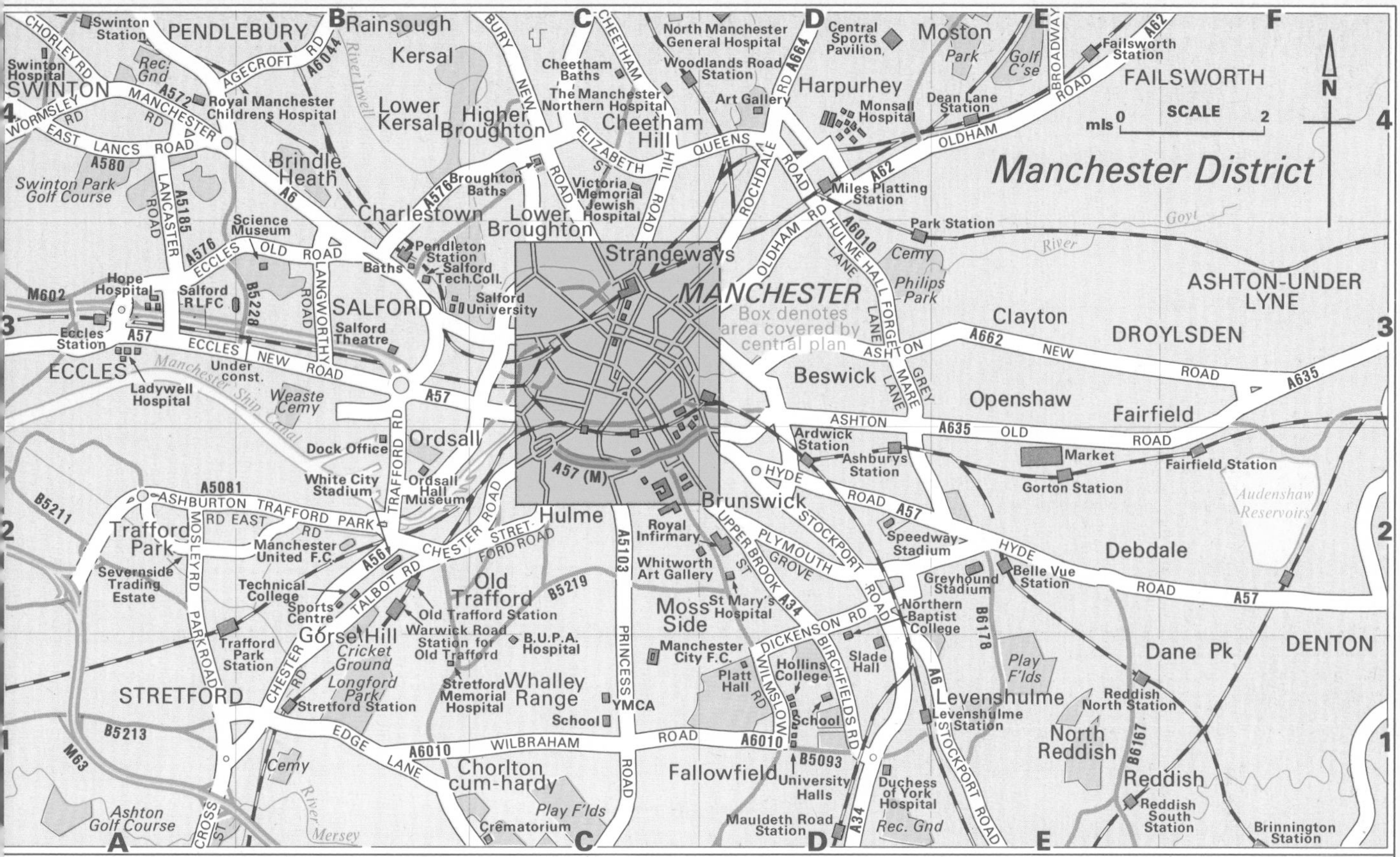

Manchester District map

(Map labels)

PENDLEBURY · Rainsough · Kersal · North Manchester General Hospital · Moston · Park · Golf C'se · Failsworth Station · FAILSWORTH

Swinton Station · Swinton Hospital · SWINTON · Rec. Grd · Agecroft · Cheetham · Cheetham Baths · Woodlands Road Station · Harpurhey · Monsall Hospital · Dean Lane Station · Broadway

Lower Kersal · Higher Broughton · Cheetham Hill · Art Gallery · Central Sports Pavilion · SCALE · mls 0 · 2 · N

Royal Manchester Childrens Hospital · Brindle Heath · Charlestown · Broughton Baths · Victoria Memorial Jewish Hospital · Lower Broughton · Manchester District

Science Museum · Pendleton Baths · Salford Tech. Coll. · Strangeways · MANCHESTER · Box denotes area covered by central plan · Miles Platting · Park Station · ASHTON-UNDER-LYNE

Hope Hospital · Salford RLFC · SALFORD · Salford University · Salford Theatre · Clayton · DROYLSDEN

Eccles Station · ECCLES · Under const. · Weaste Cemy · Ordsall · A57 · Beswick · Openshaw · Fairfield

Ladywell Hospital · Dock Office · White City Stadium · Ordsall Hall Museum · A57(M) · Hulme · Royal Infirmary · Ardwick Station · Ashburys Station · Market · Fairfield Station · Gorton Station · Audenshaw Reservoirs

Trafford Park · Manchester United F.C. · Old Trafford · Whitworth Art Gallery · Moss Side · St Mary's Hospital · Brunswick · Speedway Stadium · Greyhound Stadium · Belle Vue Station · Debdale · DENTON

Severnside Trading Estate · Technical College · Sports Centre · Gorse Hill · Old Trafford Station · Warwick Road Station for Old Trafford · B.U.P.A. · Manchester City F.C. · Platt Hall · Hollins College · Slade Hall · Northern Baptist College · Dane Pk

Trafford Park Station · Cricket Ground · Longford Park · Stretford Station · Whalley Range · YMCA · School · Levenshulme · Levenshulme Station · Reddish North Station · North Reddish

STRETFORD · Edge Lane · Chorlton cum-hardy · Wilbraham Road · Fallowfield · University Halls · Duchess of York Hospital · Reddish South Station · Brinnington Station · REDDISH

Cemy · Play F'lds · Crematorium · Mauldeth Road Station · Rec. Gnd · River Mersey

---

Key to Town Plan and Area Plan

Town Plan

- AA Recommended roads
- Other roads
- Restricted roads
- Buildings of interest — Baths
- Car parks — P
- Parks and open spaces
- Churches — †
- AA Service Centre — AA

District Plan

- A roads
- B roads

Street Index with Grid Reference

Manchester

Addington Street	E7-E6-F6
Albert Square	C4-D4
Albion Street	C2-C3
Angel Street	E7
Aytoun Street	E4-F4-F3-E3
Back Piccadilly	E5-F5-F4
Balloon Street	D6-E6
Barrack Street	A1
Blackfriars Road	A8-A7-B7-B6-C6
Blackfriars Street	C5-C6
Bloom Street	B6
Booth Street	E1-F1
Bootle Street	C4
Brazenose Street	C4-D4
Brewery Street	A6-B6
Bridge Street	B5-C5
Bridgewater Street	B3
Brook Street	E2
Broughton Road	A8
Brown Street	B6-C6-C5
Brown Street	D4-D5
Bury Street	B6-C6
Byrom Street	B4
Cambridge Street	D2
Camp Street	B4-C4-C3
Cannon Street	A7
Cannon Street	D6-D5-E5
Carnarvon Street	D8
Chapel Street	A6-A5-B5-B6-C6-D6
Charles Street	E2
Charlotte Street	D4-E4
Cheetham Hill Road	D7-D8
Chepstow Street	D3
Chester Road	A1-A2-B2-C2-C3
Chester Street	D2-E2
Chorlton Road	B2-A2-A1-B1
Chorlton Street	E3-E4
Church Street	A6-B6
Church Street	E5
City Road	C2
Cleminson Street	A6
Cooper Street	D4
Cornel Street	F6
Corporation Street	D6-D7-E7
Cottenham Drive	B8-C8
Cross Street	D4-D5-D6
Dale Street	E5-F5-F4
Dantzig Street	D6-E6-E7-E8-F8
Dawson Street	A3
Deansgate	C3-C4-C5-C6-D6
Downing Street	F2
Dulcie Street	F4
Dutton Street	D7-D8
East Ordsall Lane	A5
Egerton Street	A2
Ellesmere Street	A2
Elton Street	A8-B8
Fairfield Street	F3
Faulkner Street	D4-E4
Fennel Street	D6
Fountain Street	D4-D5
Garden Lane	B6-B7
Gartside Street	B4-B5
George Street	A5
George Street	D3-D4-E4
Goadsby Street	E6
Gore Street	B5
Gould Street	E8-E7-F7
Granby Road	E3-F3
Grape Street	B4
Gravel Lane	C6-C7
Great Ancoats Street	F5-F6
Great Bridgewater Street	C3-D3
Great Ducie Street	C8-C7-D7
Great Jackson Street	B2-C2
Greengate	B7-C7
Grosvenor Street	E1-E2-F2
Hampson Street	A4
Hanover Street	D7-D6-E6
Hardman Street	C4
Henry Street	F5-F6
High Street	E5-E6
Higher Cambridge Street	D1
Hilton Street	E5-F5
Hulme Street	D2
Humberstone Avenue	C1
Hunmaby Avenue	C1
Hunt's Bank	D6-D7
Irwell Street	A5-B5
Jackson Crescent	B1-C1
Jackson's Row	C4
John Dalton Street	C5-C4-D4-D5
Julia Street	C8-D8
Jutland Street	F4
Kincardine Road	F1-F2
King Street	A7-B7-B6-C6
King Street	C5-D5
King St West	C4
Leaf Street	C1
Lever Street	E5-F5-F6
Little Peter Street	B2-C2
Liverpool Road	A4-A3-B4-B3-C3
Lloyd Street	C4
London Road	F3-F4
Long Millgate	D6-D7
Lord Street	D8-E8
Lordsmead Street	A1
Lower Byrom Street	B3-B4
Lower Mosley Street	C3-D3-D4
Lower Ormond Street	D2
Loxford Street	D1
Mancunian Way	B2-B1-C2-C1-D1-D2-E2-F2
Market Street	C6-C5-D5-E5
Mary Street	C7-C8
Medlock Street	C2
Miller Street	D7-E7-E6
Minshull Street	E4
Mosley Street	D4-D5-E4-E5
Mount Street	A6-A7-B7
Newton Street	F5
New Bridge Street	C7-D7
North George Street	A6-A7
New Quay Street	B4-B5
Oak Street	E6
Oldham Road	F6-F7
Oldham Street	E5-E6-F6
Oxford Road	D2-E2-E1
Oxford Street	D4-D3-D2
Pall Mall	D4-D5
Park Street	D8
Parker Street	E4-E5
Peru Street	A6
Peter Street	C4-D4
Piccadilly	E5-E4-F4
Port Street	F5
Portland Street	D3-D4-E4-E5
Princess Street	D4-E4-D3-E3-E2
Quay Street	B4-C4
Queenby Street	A1
Red Bank	E7-E8
River Street	C2
Robert Street	D8
Rochdale Road	E7-F7-F8
Roger Street	E8
Sackville Street	E2-E3-E4
St Ann Street	C5-D5
St Mary's Parsonage	C5-C6
St James Street	D3-D4
St John Street	B4-C4
St Peter Square	D4
St Stephen Street	A6-B6-B7
Sherrat Street	F6
Sherborn Street	B8-C8
Shudehill	D6-E6
Silk Street	A7
Southall Street	C8-D8
Southmill Street	C4
Spring Gardens	D4-D5
Springfield Lane	C7-C8
Store Street	F4
Style Street	E7
Sudell Street	F7-F8
Sussex Street	A8
Swan Street	E6-F6
Tatton Street	A1
Tariff Street	F5
Thomas Street	E5-E6
Thompson Street	F6-F7
Tib Street	E5-E6-F6
Upper Brook Street	E2-E1-F1
Viaduct Street	C6
Victoria Bridge Street	C6-D6
Wadeson Road	F2
Water Street	A3-A4-B4
Watson Street	C3-C4
Wersley Street	A2
Whitworth Street	D3-E3
Whitworth Street West	B3-C3-C2-D2-D3
William Street	B6
Windmill Street	C4-C3-D3
Withy Green	D6
York Street	D5-D4-E4

MANCHESTER

The Barton Swing Bridge carries the Bridgewater Canal over the Manchester Ship Canal, which links Manchester with the sea nearly 40 miles away. Completed in 1894, the canal is navigable by vessels up to 15,000 tons.

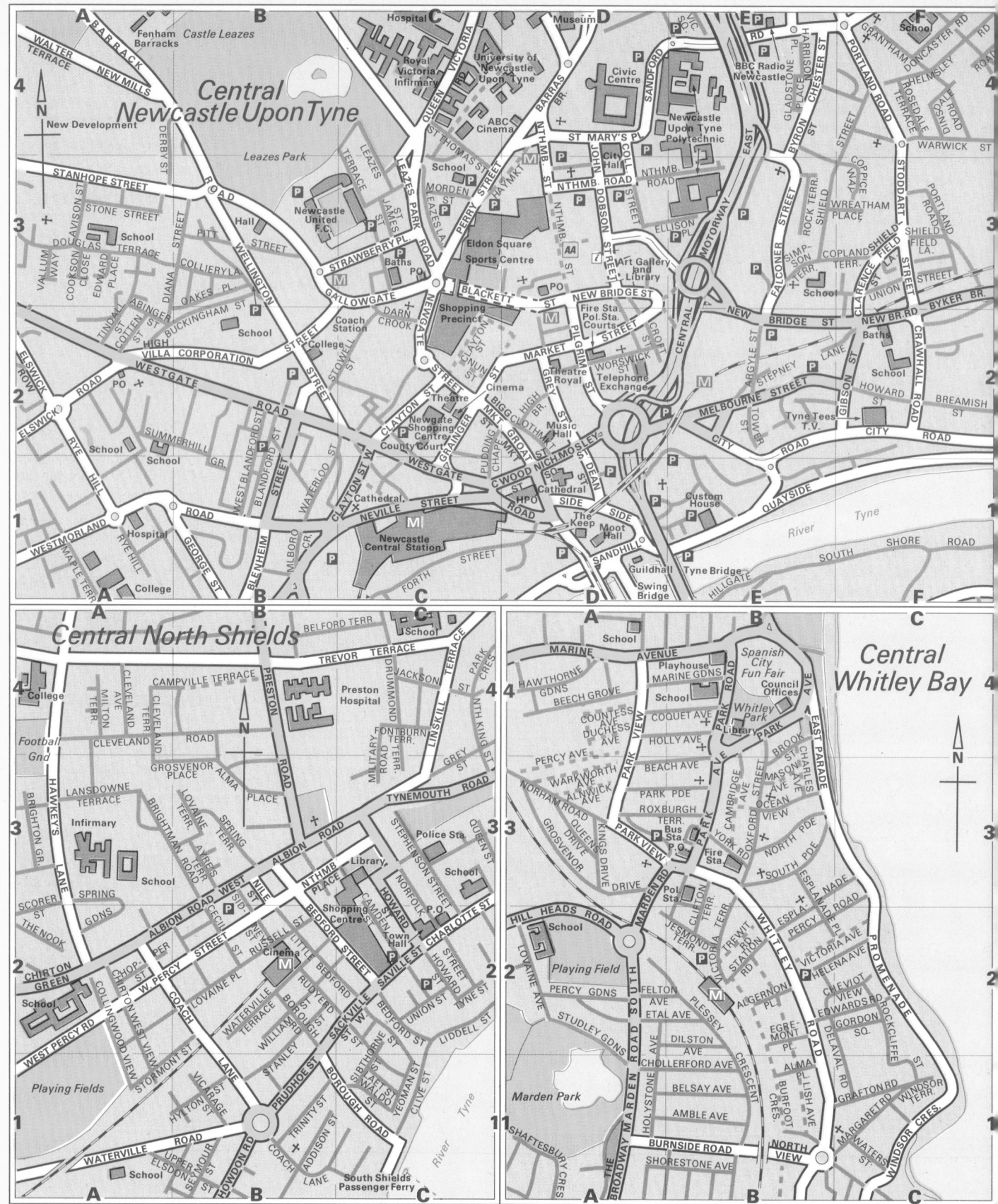

Newcastle

Six bridges span the Tyne at Newcastle; they all help to create a striking scene, but the most impressive is the High Level Bridge, built by Robert Stephenson in 1845-49 and consisting of two levels, one for the railway and one for the road. It is from the river that some of the best views of the city can be obtained. Grey Street is Newcastle's most handsome thoroughfare. It dates from the time, between 1835 and 1840, when much of this part of the city was replanned and rebuilt. Elegant façades curve up to Grey's Monument. Close to the Monument is the Eldon Centre, combining sports facilities and shopping centre to form an integrated complex which is one of the largest of its kind in Europe. Newcastle has many museums. The industrial background of the city is traced in the Museum of Science and Engineering, while the Laing Art Gallery and Museum covers painting, costumes and local domestic history. The Hancock Museum has an exceptional natural history collection and the John George Joicey Museum has period displays in a 17th-century almshouse. In Black Gate is one of Britain's most unusual museums – a collection of over 100 sets of bagpipes. Within the University precincts are three further museums. Of the city's open spaces, Town Moor is the largest. At nearly 1,000 acres it is big enough to feel genuinely wild.

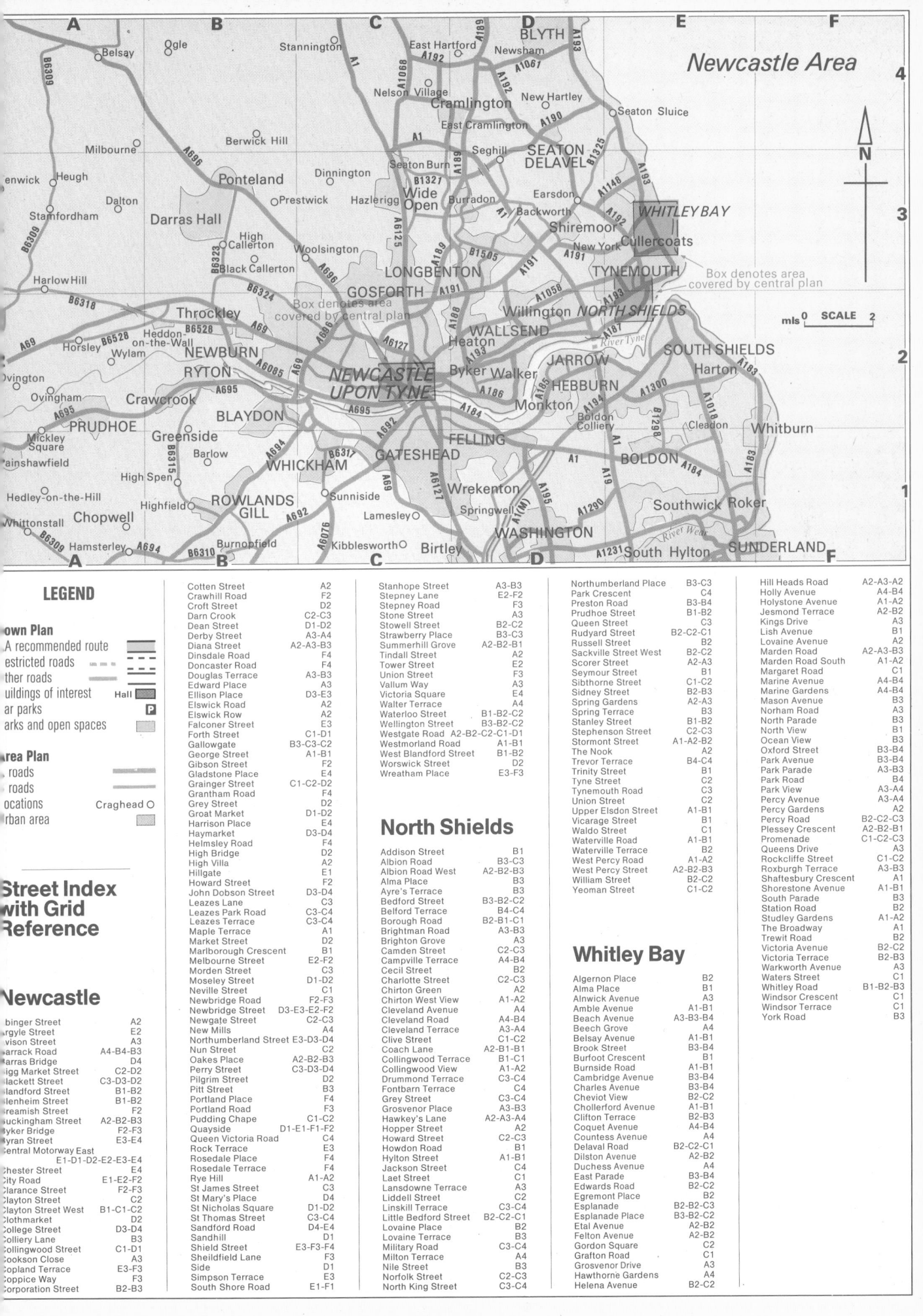

N

mls 0 SCALE 2

LEGEND

own Plan
- A recommended route
- restricted roads
- ther roads
- uildings of interest — Hall
- ar parks — P
- arks and open spaces

Area Plan
- roads
- roads
- ocations — Craghead O
- rban area

Street Index with Grid Reference

Newcastle

binger Street	A2
rgyle Street	E2
vison Street	A3
arrack Road	A4-B4-B3
arras Bridge	D4
igg Market Street	C2-D2
lackett Street	C3-D3-D2
landford Street	B1-B2
lenheim Street	B1-B2
reamish Street	F2
uckingham Street	A2-B2-B3
yker Bridge	F2-F3
yran Street	E3-E4
entral Motorway East	E1-D1-D2-E2-E3-E4
hester Street	E3
ity Road	E1-E2-F2
larance Street	F2-F3
layton Street	C2
layton Street West	B1-C1-C2
lothmarket	D2
ollege Street	D3-D4
olliery Lane	B3
ollingwood Street	C1-D1
ookson Close	A3
opland Terrace	E3-F3
oppice Way	F3
orporation Street	B2-B3

Cotten Street	A2
Crawhill Road	F2
Croft Street	D2
Darn Crook	C2-C3
Dean Street	D1-D2
Derby Street	A3-A4
Diana Street	A2-A3-B3
Dinsdale Road	F4
Doncaster Road	F4
Douglas Terrace	A3-B3
Edward Place	A3
Ellison Place	D3-E3
Elswick Road	A2
Elswick Row	A2
Falconer Street	E3
Forth Street	C1-D1
Gallowgate	B3-C3-C2
George Street	A1-B1
Gibson Street	F2
Gladstone Place	E4
Grainger Street	C1-C2-D2
Grantham Road	F4
Grey Street	D2
Groat Market	D1-D2
Harrison Place	E4
Haymarket	D3-D4
Helmsley Road	F4
High Bridge	D2
High Villa	A2
Hillgate	E1
Howard Street	F2
John Dobson Street	D3-D4
Leazes Lane	C3
Leazes Park Road	C3-C4
Leazes Terrace	C3-C4
Maple Terrace	A1
Market Street	D2
Marlborough Crescent	B1
Melbourne Street	E2-F2
Morden Street	C3
Moseley Street	D1-D2
Neville Street	C1
Newbridge Road	F2-F3
Newbridge Street	D3-E3-E2-F2
Newgate Street	C2-C3
New Mills	A4
Northumberland Street	E3-D3-D4
Nun Street	C2
Oakes Place	A2-B2-B3
Perry Street	C3-D3-D4
Pilgrim Street	D2
Pitt Street	B3
Portland Place	F4
Portland Road	F3
Pudding Chape	C1-C2
Quayside	D1-E1-F1-F2
Queen Victoria Road	C4
Rock Terrace	E3
Rosedale Place	F4
Rosedale Terrace	F4
Rye Hill	A1-A2
St James Street	C3
St Mary's Place	D4
St Nicholas Square	D1-D2
St Thomas Street	C3-C4
Sandford Road	D4-E4
Sandhill	D1
Shield Street	E3-F3-F4
Sheildfield Lane	F3
Side	D1
Simpson Terrace	E3
South Shore Road	E1-F1

Stanhope Street	A3-B3
Stepney Lane	E2-F2
Stepney Road	F3
Stone Street	A3
Stowell Street	B2-C2
Strawberry Place	B3-C3
Summerhill Grove	A2-B2-B1
Tindall Street	F4
Tower Street	E2
Union Street	F3
Vallum Way	A3
Victoria Square	E4
Walter Terrace	A4
Waterloo Street	B1-B2-C2
Wellington Street	B3-B2-C2
Westgate Road	A2-B2-C2-C1-D1
Westmorland Road	A1-B1
West Blandford Street	B1-B2
Worswick Street	D2
Wreatham Place	E3-F3

North Shields

Addison Street	B1
Albion Road	B3-C3
Albion Road West	A2-B2-B3
Alma Place	B3
Ayre's Terrace	B3
Bedford Street	B3-B2-C2
Belford Terrace	B4-C4
Borough Road	B2-B1-C1
Brightman Road	A3-B3
Brighton Grove	A3
Camden Street	C2-C3
Campville Terrace	A4-B4
Cecil Street	B2
Charlotte Street	C2-C3
Chirton Green	A2
Chirton West View	A1-A2
Cleveland Avenue	A4
Cleveland Road	A4-B4
Cleveland Terrace	A3-A4
Clive Street	C1-C2
Coach Lane	A2-B1-B1
Collingwood Terrace	B1-C1
Collingwood View	A1-A2
Drummond Terrace	C3-C4
Fontbarn Terrace	C4
Grey Street	C3-C4
Grosvenor Place	A3-B3
Hawkey's Lane	A2-A3-A4
Hopper Street	A2
Howard Street	C2-C3
Howdon Road	B1
Hylton Street	A1-B1
Jackson Street	C4
Laet Street	C1
Lansdowne Terrace	A3
Liddell Street	C2
Linskill Terrace	B2-C2-C1
Little Bedford Street	B2-C2-C1
Lovaine Place	B2
Lovaine Terrace	B3
Military Road	C3-C4
Milton Terrace	A4
Nile Street	B3
Norfolk Street	C2-C3
North King Street	C3-C4

Northumberland Place	B3-C3
Park Crescent	C4
Preston Road	B3-B4
Prudhoe Street	B1-B2
Queen Street	C3
Rudyard Street	B2-C2-C1
Russell Street	B2
Sackville Street West	B2-C2
Scorer Street	A2-A3
Seymour Street	B1
Sibthorne Street	C1-C2
Sidney Street	B2-B3
Spring Gardens	A2-A3
Spring Terrace	B3
Stanley Street	B1-B2
Stephenson Street	C2
Stormont Street	A1-A2-B2
The Nook	A2
Trevor Terrace	B4-C4
Trinity Street	B1
Tyne Street	C2
Tynemouth Road	C3
Union Street	C2
Upper Elsdon Street	A1-B1
Vicarage Street	B1
Waldo Street	C1
Waterville Road	A1-B1
Waterville Terrace	B2
West Percy Road	A1-A2
West Percy Street	A2-B2-B3
William Street	B2-C2
Yeoman Street	C1-C2

Whitley Bay

Algernon Place	B2
Alma Place	B1
Alnwick Avenue	A3
Amble Avenue	A1-B1
Beach Avenue	A3-B3-B4
Beech Grove	A4
Belsay Avenue	A1-B1
Brook Street	B3-B4
Burfoot Crescent	B1
Burnside Road	A1-B1
Cambridge Avenue	B3-B4
Charles Avenue	B3-B4
Cheviot View	B2-C2
Chollerford Avenue	A1-B1
Clifton Terrace	B2-B3
Coquet Avenue	A4-B4
Countess Avenue	A4
Delaval Road	B2-C2-C1
Dilston Avenue	A2-B2
Duchess Avenue	A4
East Parade	B3-B4
Edwards Road	B2-C2
Egremont Place	B2
Esplanade	B2-B3-C3
Esplanade Place	B3-B2-C2
Etal Avenue	A4
Felton Avenue	A2-B2
Gordon Square	C2
Grafton Road	C1
Grosvenor Drive	A3
Hawthorne Gardens	A4
Helena Avenue	B2-C2

Hill Heads Road	A2-A3-A2
Holly Avenue	A4-B4
Holystone Avenue	A1-A2
Jesmond Terrace	A2-B2
Kings Drive	A3
Lish Avenue	B1
Lovaine Avenue	A2
Marden Road	A2-A3-B3
Marden Road South	A1-A2
Margaret Road	C1
Marine Avenue	A4-B4
Marine Gardens	A4-B4
Mason Avenue	B3
Norham Road	A3
North Parade	B3
North View	B1
Ocean View	B3
Oxford Street	B3-B4
Park Avenue	B3-B4
Park Parade	A3-B3
Park Road	B4
Park View	A3-A4
Percy Avenue	A3-A4
Percy Gardens	A2
Percy Road	B2-C2-C3
Plessey Crescent	A2-B2-B1
Promenade	C1-C2-C3
Queens Drive	A3
Rockcliffe Street	C1-C2
Roxburgh Terrace	A3-B3
Shaftesbury Crescent	A1
Shorestone Avenue	A1-B1
South Parade	B3
Station Road	B2
Studley Gardens	A1-A2
The Broadway	A1
Trewit Road	B2
Victoria Avenue	B2-C2
Victoria Terrace	B2-B3
Warkworth Avenue	A3
Waters Street	C1
Whitley Road	B1-B2-B3
Windsor Crescent	C1
Windsor Terrace	C1
York Road	B3

Norwich

Fortunately the heart has not been ripped out of Norwich to make way for some bland precinct, so its ancient character has been preserved. Narrow alleys run between the streets – sometimes opening out into quiet courtyards, sometimes into thoroughfares packed with people, sometimes into lanes which seem quite deserted. It is a unique place, with something of interest on every corner.

The cathedral was founded in 1096 by the city's first bishop, Herbert de Losinga. Among its most notable features are the nave, with its huge pillars, the bishop's throne (a Saxon survival unique in Europe) and the cloisters with their matchless collection of roof bosses. Across the city is the great stone keep of the castle, set on a mound and dominating all around it. It dates from Norman times, but was refaced in 1834. The keep now forms part of Norwich Castle Museum –

an extensive and fascinating collection. Other museums are Bridewell Museum – collections relating to local crafts and industries within a 14th-century building – and Strangers' Hall, a genuinely 'old world' house, rambling and full of surprises, both in its tumble of rooms and in the things which they contain. Especially picturesque parts of the city are Elm Hill – a street of ancient houses; Tombland – with two gateways into the Cathedral Close; and Pull's Ferry – a watergate by the river.

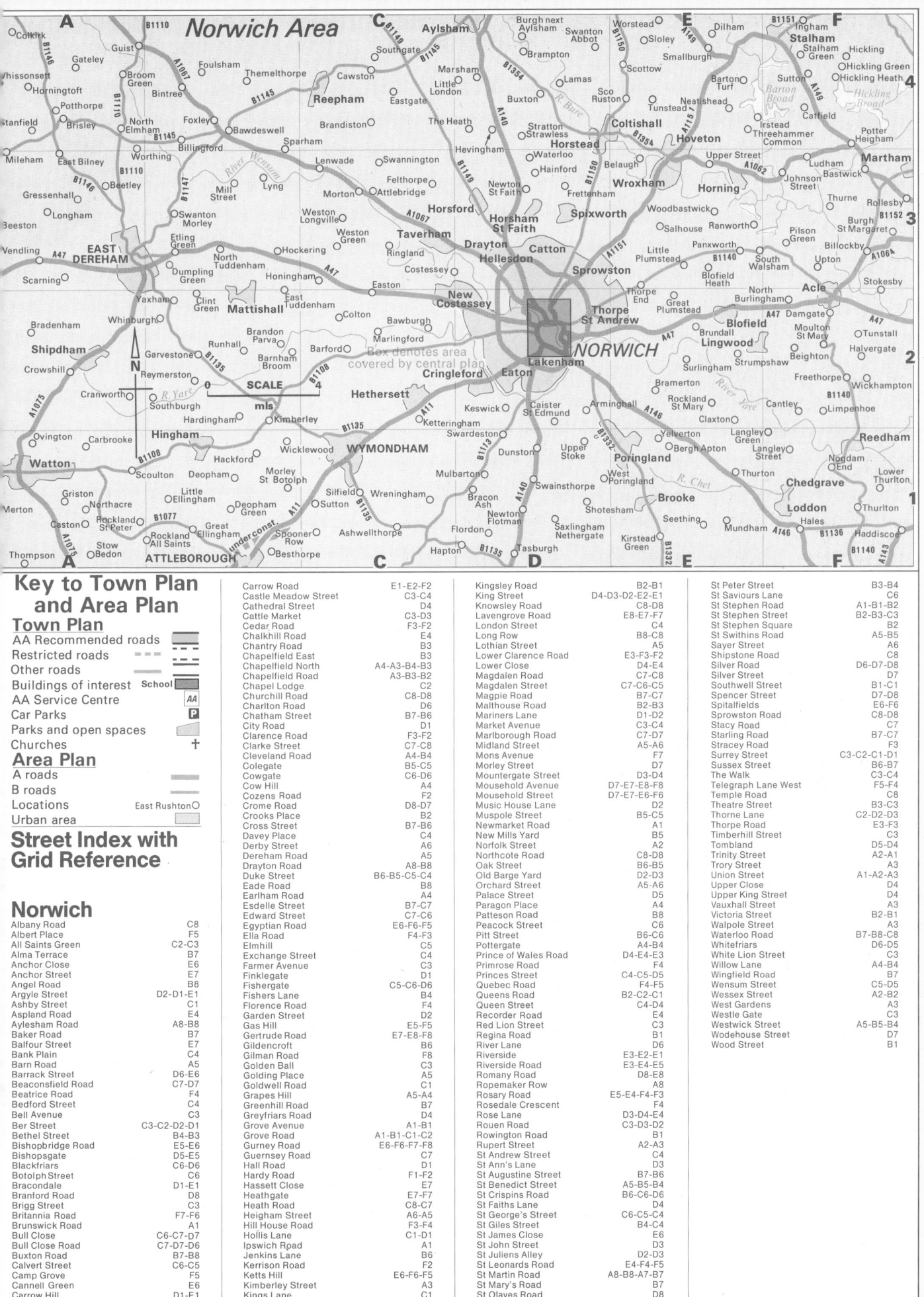

Norwich Area

Key to Town Plan and Area Plan

Town Plan
AA Recommended roads
Restricted roads
Other roads
Buildings of interest — School
AA Service Centre — AA
Car Parks — P
Parks and open spaces
Churches — +

Area Plan
A roads
B roads
Locations — East Rushton○
Urban area

Street Index with Grid Reference

Norwich

Albany Road	C8
Albert Place	F5
All Saints Green	C2-C3
Alma Terrace	B7
Anchor Close	E6
Anchor Street	E7
Angel Road	B8
Argyle Street	D2-D1-E1
Ashby Street	C1
Aspland Road	E4
Aylsham Road	A8-B8
Baker Road	B7
Balfour Street	E7
Bank Plain	C4
Barn Road	A5
Barrack Street	D6-E6
Beaconsfield Road	C7-D7
Beatrice Road	F4
Bedford Street	C4
Bell Avenue	C3
Ber Street	C3-C2-D2-D1
Bethel Street	B4-B3
Bishopbridge Road	E5-E6
Bishopsgate	D5-E5
Blackfriars	C6-D6
Botolph Street	C6
Bracondale	D1-E1
Branford Road	D8
Brigg Street	C3
Britannia Road	F7-F6
Brunswick Road	A1
Bull Close	C6-C7-D7
Bull Close Road	C7-D7-D6
Buxton Road	B7-B8
Calvert Street	C6-C5
Camp Grove	F5
Cannell Green	E6
Carrow Hill	D1-E1

Carrow Road	E1-E2-F2
Castle Meadow Street	C3-C4
Cathedral Street	D4
Cattle Market	C3-D3
Cedar Road	F3-F2
Chalkhill Road	E4
Chantry Road	B3
Chapelfield East	B3
Chapelfield North	A4-A3-B4-B3
Chapelfield Road	A3-B3-B2
Chapel Lodge	C2
Churchill Road	C8-D8
Charlton Road	D6
Chatham Street	B7-B6
City Road	D1
Clarence Road	F3-F2
Clarke Street	C7-C8
Cleveland Road	A4-B4
Colegate	B5-C5
Cowgate	C6-D6
Cow Hill	A4
Cozens Road	F2
Crome Road	D8-D7
Crooks Place	B2
Cross Street	B7-B6
Davey Place	C4
Derby Street	A6
Dereham Road	A5
Drayton Road	A8-B8
Duke Street	B6-B5-C5-C4
Eade Road	B8
Earlham Road	A4
Esdelle Street	B7-C7
Edward Street	C7-C6
Egyptian Road	E6-F6-F5
Ella Road	F4-F3
Elmhill	C5
Exchange Street	C4
Farmer Avenue	C3
Finklegate	D1
Fishergate	C5-C6-D6
Fishers Lane	B4
Florence Road	F4
Garden Street	D2
Gas Hill	E5-F5
Gertrude Road	E7-E8-F8
Gildencroft	B6
Gilman Road	F8
Golden Ball	C3
Golding Place	A5
Goldwell Road	C1
Grapes Hill	A5-A4
Greenhill Road	B7
Greyfriars Road	D4
Grove Avenue	A1-B1
Grove Road	A1-B1-C1-C2
Gurney Road	E6-F6-F7-F8
Guernsey Road	C7
Hall Road	D1
Hardy Road	F1-F2
Hassett Close	E7
Heathgate	E7-F7
Heath Road	C8-C7
Heigham Street	A6-A5
Hill House Road	F3-F4
Hollis Lane	C1-D1
Ipswich Road	A1
Jenkins Lane	B6
Kerrison Road	F2
Ketts Hill	E6-F6-F5
Kimberley Street	A3
Kings Lane	C1

Kingsley Road	B2-B1
King Street	D4-D3-D2-E2-E1
Knowsley Road	C8-D8
Lavengrove Road	E8-E7-F7
London Street	C4
Long Row	B8-C8
Lothian Street	A5
Lower Clarence Road	E3-F3-F2
Lower Close	D4-E4
Magdalen Road	C7-C8
Magdalen Street	C7-C6-C5
Magpie Road	B7-C7
Malthouse Road	B2-B3
Mariners Lane	D1-D2
Market Avenue	C3-C4
Marlborough Road	C7-D7
Midland Street	A5-A6
Mons Avenue	F7
Morley Street	D7
Mountergate Street	D3-D4
Mousehold Avenue	D7-E7-E8-F8
Mousehold Street	D7-E7-E6-F6
Music House Lane	D2
Muspole Street	B5-C5
Newmarket Road	A1
New Mills Yard	B5
Norfolk Street	A2
Northcote Road	C8-D8
Oak Street	B6-B5
Old Barge Yard	D2-D3
Orchard Street	A5-A6
Palace Street	D5
Paragon Place	A4
Patteson Road	B8
Peacock Street	C6
Pitt Street	B6-C6
Pottergate	A4-B4
Prince of Wales Road	D4-E4-E3
Primrose Road	F4
Princes Street	C4-C5-D5
Quebec Road	F4-F5
Queens Road	B2-C2-C1
Queen Street	C4-D4
Recorder Road	E4
Red Lion Street	C3
Regina Road	B1
River Lane	D6
Riverside	E3-E2-E1
Riverside Road	E3-E4-E5
Romany Road	D8-E8
Ropemaker Row	A8
Rosary Road	E5-E4-F4-F3
Rosedale Crescent	F4
Rose Lane	D3-D4-E4
Rouen Road	C3-D3-D2
Rowington Road	B1
Rupert Street	A2-A3
St Andrew Street	C4
St Ann's Lane	D3
St Augustine Street	B7-B6
St Benedict Street	A5-B5-B4
St Crispins Road	B6-C6-D6
St Faiths Lane	D4
St George's Street	C6-C5-C4
St Giles Street	B4-C4
St James Close	E6
St John Street	D3
St Julians Alley	D2-D3
St Leonards Road	E4-F4-F5
St Martin Road	A8-B8-A7-B7
St Mary's Road	B7
St Olaves Road	D8

St Peter Street	B3-B4
St Saviours Lane	C6
St Stephen Road	A1-B1-B2
St Stephen Street	B2-B3-C3
St Stephen Square	B2
St Swithins Road	A5-B5
Sayer Street	A6
Shipstone Road	C8
Silver Road	D6-D7-D8
Silver Street	D7
Southwell Street	B1-C1
Spencer Street	D7-D8
Spitalfields	E6-F6
Sprowston Road	C8-D8
Stacy Road	C7
Starling Road	B7-C7
Stracey Road	F3
Surrey Street	C3-C2-C1-D1
Sussex Street	B6-B7
The Walk	C3-C4
Telegraph Lane West	F5-F4
Temple Road	C8
Theatre Street	B3-C3
Thorne Lane	C2-D2-D3
Thorpe Road	E3-F3
Timberhill Street	C3
Tombland	D5-D4
Trinity Street	A2-A3
Trory Street	A3
Union Street	A1-A2-A3
Upper Close	D4
Upper King Street	D4
Vauxhall Street	A3
Victoria Street	B2-B1
Walpole Street	A3
Waterloo Road	B7-B8-C8
Whitefriars	D6-D5
White Lion Street	C3
Willow Lane	A4-B4
Wingfield Road	B7
Wensum Street	C5-D5
Wessex Street	A2-B2
West Gardens	A3
Westle Gate	C3
Westwick Street	A5-B5-B4
Wodehouse Street	D7
Wood Street	B1

191

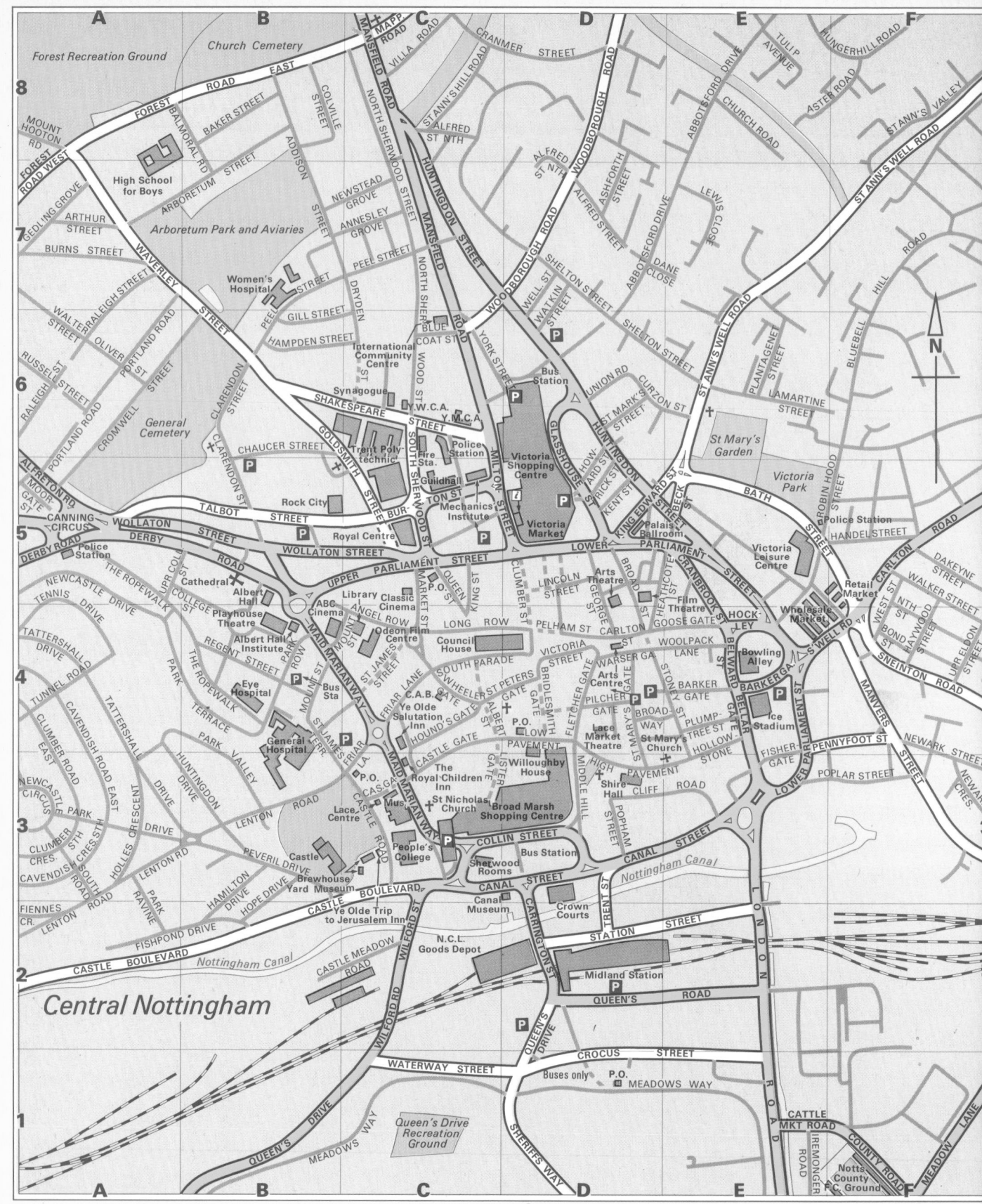

Nottingham

Hosiery and lace were the foundations upon which Nottingham's prosperity was built. The stockings came first – a knitting machine for these had been invented by a Nottinghamshire man as early as 1589 – but a machine called a 'tickler', which enabled simple patterns to be created in the stocking fabric, prompted the development of machine-made lace. The earliest fabric was produced in 1768, and an example from not much later than that is kept in the city's Castlegate Costume and Textile Museum. In fact, the entire history of lacemaking is beautifully explained in this converted row of Georgian terraces. The Industrial Museum at Wollaton Park has many other machines and exhibits tracing the development of the knitting industry, as well as displays on the other industries which have brought wealth to the city – tobacco, pharmaceuticals, engineering and printing. At Wollaton Hall is a natural history museum, while nearer the centre are the Canal Museum and the Brewhouse Yard Museum, a marvellous collection which shows items from daily life in the city up to the present day. Nottingham is not complete without mention of Robin Hood, the partly mythical figure whose statue is in the castle grounds. Although the castle itself has Norman foundations, the present structure is largely Victorian. It is now a museum.

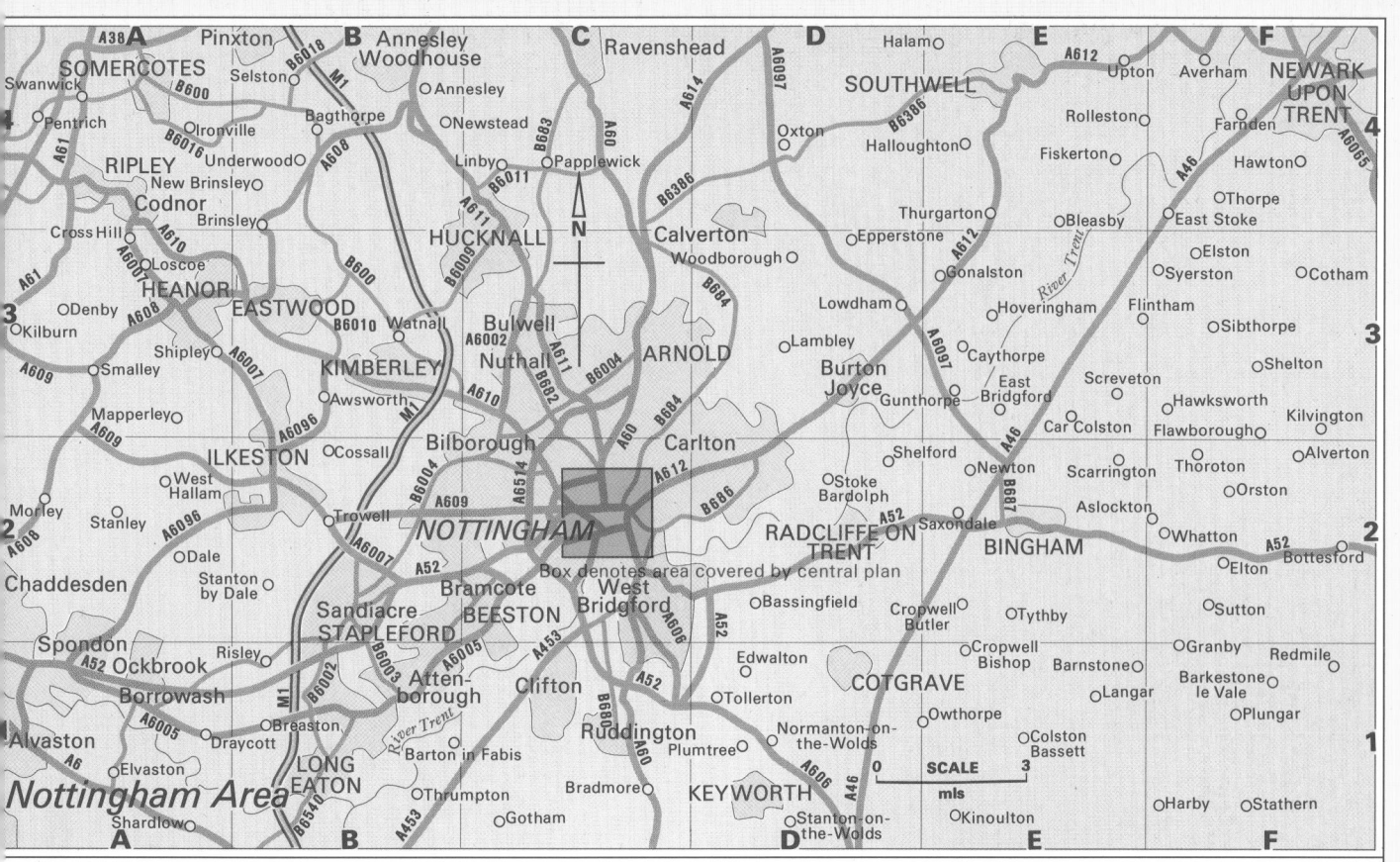

Nottingham Area

Key to Town Plan and Area Plan

Town Plan

AA Recommended roads
Restricted roads
Other roads
Buildings of interest   Theatre
Car Parks   P
Parks and open spaces
Churches   †

Area Plan

A roads
B roads
Locations   Bagthorpe○
Urban area

Street Index with Grid Reference

Nottingham

Abbotsford Drive	D7-E7-E8
Addison Street	B7-B8
Albert Street	C4
Alfred Street	D7
Alfred Street North	C8, D7-D8
Alfreton Road	A5-A6
Angel Row	B5-B4-C4
Annesley Grove	B7-C7
Ashforth Street	D7-D8
Aster Road	E8-F8
Arboretum Street	A7-B7-B8
Arthur Street	A7
Baker Street	B8
Balmoral Road	A8-B8-B7
Barker Gate	E4
Bath Street	E5-F5
Beck Street	E5
Bellargate	E4
Belward Street	E4
Bluebell Hill Road	F6-F7
Bluecoat Street	C6
Bond Street	F4
Bridlesmith Gate	D4
Broad Street	D4-D5
Broadway	D4-E4
Burns Street	A7
Burton Street	C5
Canal Street	C3-D3-E3

Canning Circus	A5
Carlton Road	F5
Carlton Street	D4
Carrington Street	D2-D3
Castle Boulevard	A2-B2-B3-C3
Castle Gate	C3-C4
Castle Market Road	E1-F1
Castle Meadow Road	B2-C2
Castle Road	C3
Cavendish Crescent South	A3
Cavendish Road East	A3-A4
Chaucer Street	B5-B6
Church Road	E8
Clarendon Street	B5-B6
Cliff Road	D3-E3
Clumber Crescent South	A3
Clumber Road East	A3-A4
Clumber Street	D4-D5
College Street	A5-B5-B4
Collin Street	C3-D3
Colville Street	B8
County Road	F1
Cranbrook Street	E4-E5
Cranmer Street	C8-D8
Crocus Street	D1-E1
Cromwell Street	A5-A6-B6
Curzon Street	D6-E6
Dane Close	D7-E7
Dakeyne Street	F5
Derby Road	A5-B5
Dryden Street	C6-C7
Fiennes Crescent	A2
Fishergate	E3-E4
Fishpond Drive	A2-B2
Fletcher Gate	D4
Forest Road East	A8-B8-C8
Forest Road West	A7-A8
Friar Lane	C3-C4
Gedling Grove	A7
George Street	D4-D5
Glasshouse Street	D5-D6
Gill Street	B6-C6
Goldsmith Street	B6-C6-C5
Goose Gate	D4-E4
Hamilton Drive	B2-B3
Hampden Street	B6-C6
Handel Street	E5-F5
Haywood Street	F4-F5
High Pavement	D4-D3-E3
Hockley	E4
Holles Crescent	A3
Hollowstone	E3-E4
Hope Drive	B2-B3
Hound's Gate	C4
Howard Street	D5-D6
Hungerhill Road	E8-F8

Huntingdon Drive	A4-A3-B3
Huntingdon Street	C8-C7-D7-D6-D5-E5
Huskisson Street	C6
Iremonger Road	E1
Kent Street	D5
King Edward Street	D5-E5
King Street	C4-C5
Lamartine Street	E6
Lenton Road	A2-A3-B3
Lewis Close	E7
Lincoln Street	D5
Lister Gate	C3-C4
London Road	E1-E2-E3
Long Row	C4-D4
Lower Parliament Street	D5-E5-E4-E3
Low Pavement	C4-D4
Maid Marion Way	B4-C4-C3
Mansfield Street	C6-C7-C8
Manvers Street	F3-F4
Mapperley Road	C8
Market Street	C4-C5
Meadow Lane	F1
Meadows Road	B1-C1-D1-E1
Middle Hill	D3-D4
Milton Street	C6-C5-D5
Moorgate Street	A5
Mount Hooton Road	A8
Mount Street	B4-C4
Newark Crescent	F3
Newark Street	F3-F4
Newcastle Circus	A3
Newcastle Drive	A4-A5
Newstead Grove	B7-C7
North Street	F4-F5
North Sherwood Street	C6-C7-C8
Oliver Street	A6
Park Drive	A3-B3
Park Ravine	A2-A3
Park Row	B4
Park Terrace	A4-B4
Park Valley	A4-B4-B3
Peel Street	B6-B7-C7
Pelham Street	D4
Pennyfoot Street	E4-F4
Peveril Street	B3
Pilcher Gate	D4
Plantagenet Street	E6
Plumptre Street	E4
Popham Street	D3
Poplar Street	E3-F3
Portland Road	A5-A6-A7
Queen's Drive	B1-C1, D1-D2
Queen's Road	D2-E2
Queen Street	C4-C5
Raleigh Street	A6-A7
Regent Street	B4

Rick Street	D5
Robin Hood Street	E5-F5-F6
Russell Street	A6
St Ann's Hill Road	C8
St Ann's Valley	F7-F8
St Ann's Well Road	E5-E6-E7-F7-F8
St James Street	C4
St James Terrace	B4-B3-C3
St Mark's Street	D6
St Peters Gate	C4-D4
Shakespeare Street	B6-C6
Shelton Street	D7-D6-E6
Sheriffs Way	D1
Sneinton Road	F4
South Parade	C4-D4
South Road	A3
South Sherwood Street	C5-C6
Southwell Road	E4-F4
Station Street	D2-E2
Stoney Street	D4-E4
Talbot Street	A5-B5-C5
Tattershall Drive	A4-A3-B3
Tennis Drive	A4-A5-A4
The Ropewalk	A5-A4-B4
Trent Street	D2-D3
Tulip Avenue	E8
Tunnel Road	A4
Union Road	D6
Upper College Street	A5-B5
Upper Eldon Street	F4
Upper Parliament Street	B5-C5-D5
Victoria Street	D4
Villa Road	C8
Walker Street	F4-F5
Walter Street	A6
Warser Gate	D4
Waterway Street	C1-D1
Watkin Street	D6-D7
Waverley Street	A8-A7-B7-B6
Wellington Street	D6-D7
West Street	F4-F5
Wheeler Gate	C4
Wilford Road	C1-C2
Wilford Street	C2-C3
Wollaton Street	A5-B5-C5
Woodborough Road	C6-C7-D7-D8
Woolpack Lane	D4-E4
York Street	C6-D6

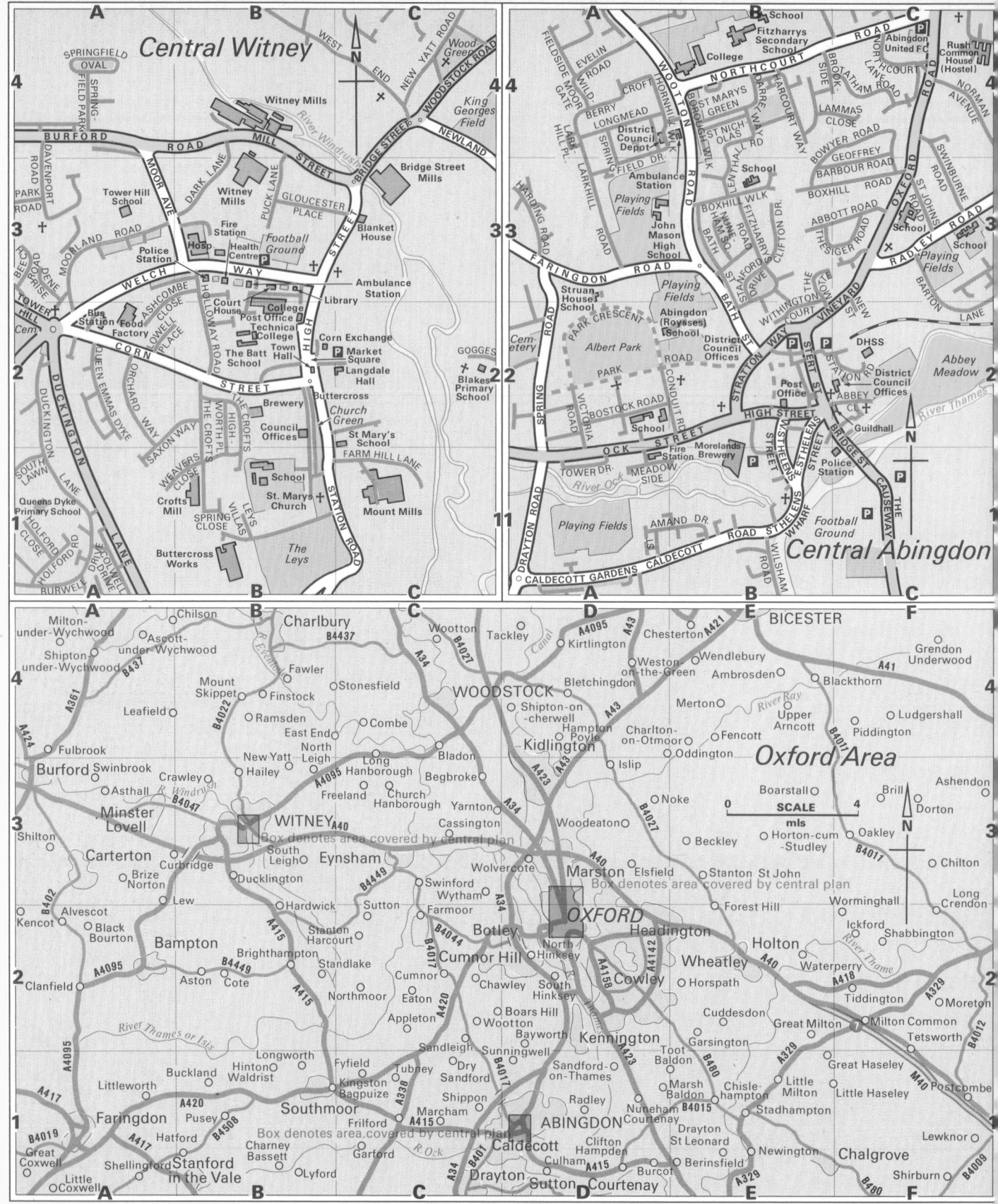

Central Witney

Springfield Oval
Springfield Park
Witney Mills
Tower Hill School
Witney Mills
Bridge Street Mills
Fire Station
Hosp
Football Ground
Blanket House
Police Station
Health Centre
Ambulance Station
Court House
College
Library
Post Office
Technical College
Corn Exchange
The Batt School
Town Hall
Market Square
Langdale Hall
Brewery
Buttercross
Council Offices
Church Green
St Mary's School
St. Marys Church
School
Crofts Mill
The Leys
Mount Mills
Buttercross Works
Queens Dyke Primary School
South Lawn
Bus Station
Food Factory
Blakes Primary School

Roads labelled: BURFORD ROAD, MILL STREET, BRIDGE STREET, WEST END, NEW YATT ROAD, WOODSTOCK ROAD, NEWLAND, GLOUCESTER PLACE, MOOR AVE, DARK LANE, PUCK LANE, HIGH STREET, WELCH WAY, CORN STREET, THE CROFTS, HIGH ST, WEAVERS CLOSE, SAXON WAY, SPRING CLOSE, LEYS VILLAS, STATION ROAD, FARM HILL LANE, DUCKLINGTON LANE, QUEEN EMMAS DYKE, ORCHARD WAY, MOORLAND ROAD, PARK ROAD, DAVENPORT ROAD, HOLLOWAY ROAD, ASHCOMBE CLOSE, LOWELL PLACE, WORTH PL, River Windrush, King Georges Field, Wood Green

Central Abingdon

School
Fitzharrys Secondary School
College
Abingdon United FC
Rush Common House (Hostel)
Ambulance Station
School
John Mason High School
Struan House School
Albert Park
Cemetery
Abingdon (Roysses) School
District Council Offices
Playing Fields
Post Office
District Council Offices
Abbey Meadow
School
Fire Station
Morelands Brewery
Guildhall
Police Station
Football Ground
Playing Fields
DHSS

Roads labelled: NORTHCOURT ROAD, WOOTTON ROAD, FARINGDON ROAD, OCK STREET, HIGH STREET, BRIDGE ST, STRATTON WAY, STATION RD, ST HELENS STREET, THE CAUSEWAY, SPRING ROAD, VICTORIA ROAD, BOSTOCK ROAD, CONDUIT ROAD, DRAYTON ROAD, CALDECOTT ROAD, CALDECOTT GARDENS, WILSHAM ROAD, AMAND DR, MEADOW SIDE, TOWER DR, River Ock, River Thames, BATH ST, STANFORD DRIVE, CLIFTON DR, BOXHILL ROAD, ABBOTT ROAD, BOWYER ROAD, GEOFFREY BARBOUR ROAD, RADLEY ROAD, OXFORD ROAD, ST JOHNS ROAD, SWINBURNE ROAD, NORMAN AVENUE, BARTON LANE, PARK CRESCENT, ALBERT PARK

Oxford Area

Milton-under-Wychwood, Ascott-under-Wychwood, Shipton-under-Wychwood, Chilson, Charlbury, Fawler, Finstock, Stonesfield, Wootton, Tackley, Kirtlington, Chesterton, BICESTER, Grendon Underwood, Mount Skippet, Leafield, Ramsden, Combe, Shipton-on-cherwell, Bletchingdon, Weston-on-the-Green, Wendlebury, Ambrosden, Blackthorn, WOODSTOCK, Hampton Poyle, Merton, Upper Arncott, Piddington, Ludgershall, East End, North Leigh, Bladon, Begbroke, Kidlington, Charlton-on-Otmoor, Fencott, Oddington, Islip, New Yatt, Hailey, Long Hanborough, Freeland, Church Hanborough, Yarnton, Cassington, Woodeaton, Noke, Beckley, Boarstall, Brill, Dorton, Oakley, Chilton, Ashendon, Fulbrook, Burford, Swinbrook, Crawley, Asthall, Minster Lovell, Shilton, Carterton, Curbridge, Brize Norton, Lew, Ducklington, WITNEY, South Leigh, Eynsham, Swinford, Wytham, Farmoor, Hardwick, Sutton, Stanton Harcourt, Wolvercote, Marston, Elsfield, Stanton St John, Forest Hill, Worminghall, Ickford, Shabbington, Long Crendon, Alvescot, Black Bourton, Bampton, Brighthampton, Aston, Cote, Standlake, Cumnor, OXFORD, Botley, North Hinksey, Cumnor Hill, Headington, Wheatley, Holton, Waterperry, Kencot, Clanfield, Northmoor, Eaton, Chawley, South Hinksey, Cowley, Horspath, Cuddesdon, Great Milton, Milton Common, Tetsworth, Appleton, Boars Hill, Wootton, Bayworth, Kennington, Garsington, Tiddington, Moreton, Longworth, Hinton Waldrist, Fyfield, Tubney, Dry Sandford, Sunningwell, Sandleigh, Toot Baldon, Marsh Baldon, Chislehampton, Little Milton, Great Haseley, Little Haseley, Postcombe, Buckland, Kingston Bagpuize, Frilford, Shippon, Radley, Sandford-on-Thames, Nuneham Courtenay, Stadhampton, Berinsfield, Newington, Chalgrove, Faringdon, Pusey, Littleworth, Hatford, Southmoor, Marcham, ABINGDON, Caldecott, Drayton, Clifton Hampden, Culham, Sutton Courtenay, Burcot, Shirburn, Lewknor, Great Coxwell, Little Coxwell, Shellingford, Stanford in the Vale, Charney Bassett, Garford, Lyford

Box denotes area covered by central plan

SCALE 0 — 4 mls

Oxford

From Carfax (at the centre of the city) round to Magdalen Bridge stretches High Street, one of England's best and most interesting thoroughfares. Shops rub shoulders with churches and colleges, alleyways lead to ancient inns and to a large covered market, and little streets lead to views of some of the finest architecture to be seen anywhere. Catte Street, beside St Mary's Church (whose lovely tower gives a panoramic view of Oxford), opens out into Radcliffe Square, dominated by the Radcliffe Camera, a great round structure built in 1749. Close by is the Bodleian Library, one of the finest collections of books and manuscripts in the world. All around are ancient college buildings. Close to Magdalen Bridge is Magdalen College, founded in 1448 and certainly not to be missed. Across the High Street are the Botanical Gardens, founded in 1621 and the oldest such foundation in England. Footpaths lead through Christ Church Meadow to Christ Church College and the cathedral. Tom Tower is the college's most notable feature; the cathedral is actually its chapel and is the smallest cathedral in England. Among much else not to be missed in Oxford is the Ashmolean Museum, whose vast collections of precious and beautiful objects from all over the world repay many hours of study; perhaps the loveliest treasure is the 9th-century Alfred Jewel.

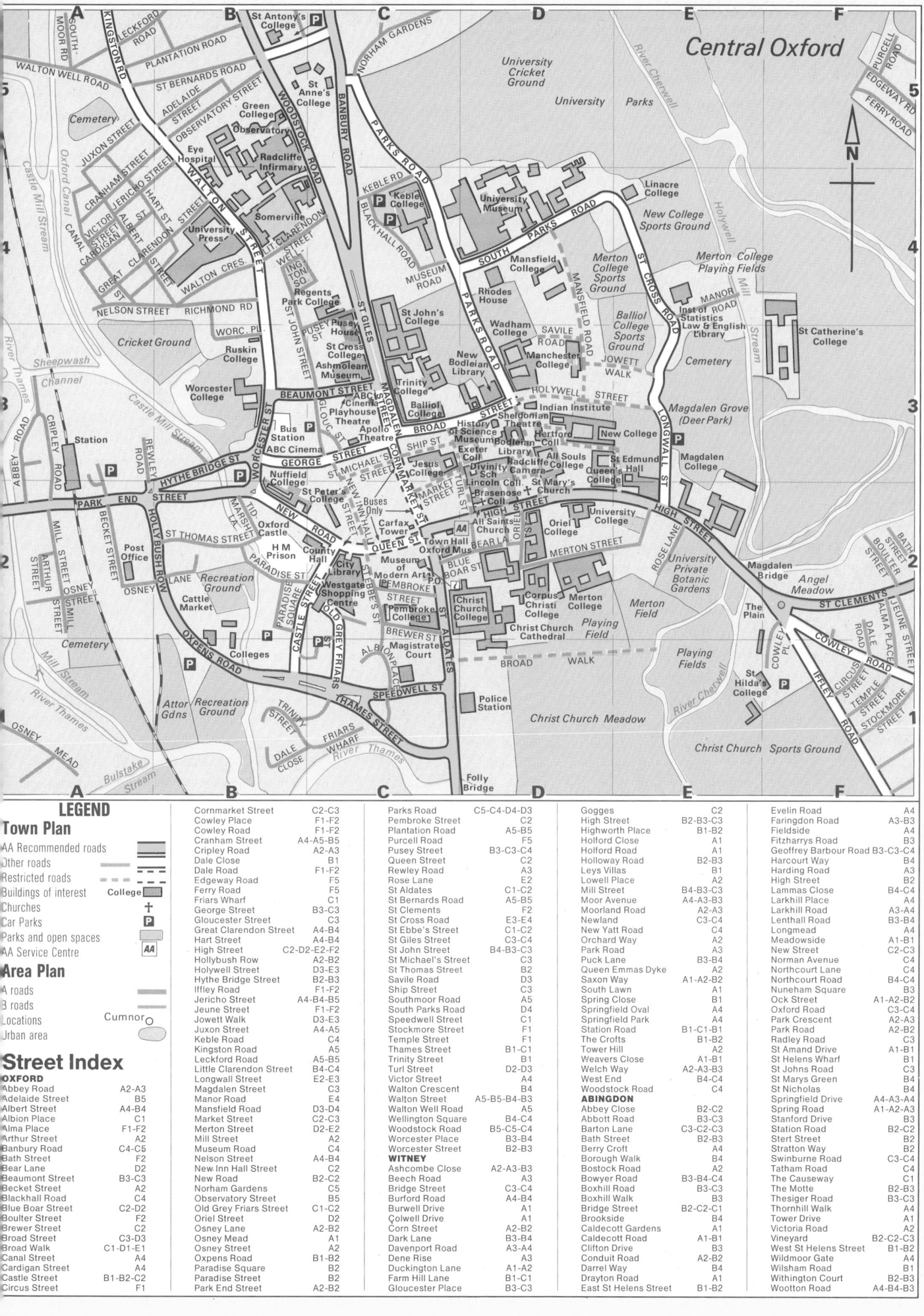

Central Oxford

LEGEND

Town Plan
AA Recommended roads
Other roads
Restricted roads
Buildings of interest — College
Churches — +
Car Parks — P
Parks and open spaces
AA Service Centre — AA

Area Plan
A roads
B roads
Locations — Cumnor
Urban area

Street Index

OXFORD

Abbey Road	A2-A3
Adelaide Street	B5
Albert Street	A4-B4
Albion Place	C1
Alma Place	F1-F2
Arthur Street	A2
Banbury Road	C4-C5
Bath Street	F2
Bear Lane	D2
Beaumont Street	B3-C3
Becket Street	A2
Blackhall Road	C4
Blue Boar Street	C2-D2
Boulter Street	F2
Brewer Street	C2
Broad Street	C3-D3
Broad Walk	C1-D1-E1
Canal Street	A4
Cardigan Street	A4
Castle Street	B1-B2-C2
Circus Street	F1
Cornmarket Street	C2-C3
Cowley Place	F1-F2
Cowley Road	F1-F2
Cranham Street	A4-A5-B5
Cripley Road	A2-A3
Dale Close	B1
Dale Road	F1-F2
Edgeway Road	F5
Ferry Road	F5
Friars Wharf	C1
George Street	B3-C3
Gloucester Street	C3
Great Clarendon Street	A4-B4
Hart Street	A4-B4
High Street	C2-D2-E2-F2
Hollybush Row	A2-B2
Holywell Street	D3-E3
Hythe Bridge Street	B2-B3
Iffley Road	F1-F2
Jericho Street	A4-B4-B5
Jeune Street	F1-F2
Jowett Walk	D3-E3
Juxon Street	A4-A5
Keble Road	C4
Kingston Road	A5
Leckford Road	A5-B5
Little Clarendon Street	B4-C4
Longwall Street	E2-E3
Magdalen Street	C3
Manor Road	E4
Mansfield Road	D3-D4
Market Street	C2-C3
Merton Street	D2-E2
Mill Street	A2
Museum Road	C4
Nelson Street	A4-B4
New Inn Hall Street	C2
New Road	B2-C2
Norham Gardens	C5
Observatory Street	B5
Old Grey Friars Street	C1-C2
Oriel Street	D2
Osney Lane	A2-B2
Osney Mead	A1
Osney Street	A2
Oxpens Road	B1-B2
Paradise Square	B2
Paradise Street	B2
Park End Street	A2-B2

Parks Road	C5-C4-D4-D3
Pembroke Street	C2
Plantation Road	A5-B5
Purcell Road	F5
Pusey Street	B3-C3-C4
Queen Street	C2
Rewley Road	A3
Rose Lane	E2
St Aldates	C1-C2
St Bernards Road	A5-B5
St Clements	F2
St Cross Road	E3-E4
St Ebbe's Street	C1-C2
St Giles Street	C3-C4
St John Street	B4-B3-C3
St Michael's Street	C3
St Thomas Street	B2
Savile Road	D3
Ship Street	C3
Southmoor Road	A5
South Parks Road	D4
Speedwell Street	C1
Stockmore Street	F1
Temple Street	F1
Thames Street	B1-C1
Trinity Street	B1
Turl Street	D2-D3
Victor Street	A4
Walton Crescent	B4
Walton Street	A5-B5-B4-B3
Walton Well Road	A5
Wellington Square	B4-C4
Woodstock Road	B5-C5-C4
Worcester Place	B3-B4
Worcester Street	B2-B3

WITNEY

Ashcombe Close	A2-A3-B3
Beech Road	A3
Bridge Street	C3-C4
Burford Road	A4-B4
Burwell Drive	A1
Colwell Drive	A1
Corn Street	A2-B2
Dark Lane	B3-B4
Davenport Road	A3-A4
Dene Rise	A3
Duckington Lane	A1-A2
Farm Hill Lane	B1-C1
Gloucester Place	B3-C3

Gogges	C2
High Street	B2-B3-C3
Highworth Place	B1-B2
Holford Close	A1
Holford Road	A1
Holloway Road	B2-B3
Leys Villas	B1
Lowell Place	A2
Mill Street	B4-B3-C3
Moor Avenue	A4-A3-B3
Moorland Road	A2-A3
Newland	C3-C4
New Yatt Road	C4
Orchard Way	A2
Park Road	A3
Puck Lane	B3-B4
Queen Emmas Dyke	B2
Saxon Way	A1-A2-B2
South Lawn	A1
Spring Close	B1
Springfield Oval	A4
Springfield Park	A4
Station Road	B1-C1-B1
The Crofts	B1-B2
Tower Hill	A2
Weavers Close	A1-B1
Welch Way	A2-A3-B3
West End	B4-C4
Woodstock Road	C4

ABINGDON

Abbey Close	B2-C2
Abbott Road	B3-C3
Barton Lane	C3-C2-C3
Bath Street	B2-B3
Berry Croft	A4
Borough Walk	B4
Bostock Road	A2
Bowyer Road	B3-B4-C4
Boxhill Road	B3-C3
Boxhill Walk	B3
Bridge Street	B2-C2-C1
Brookside	B4
Caldecott Gardens	A1
Caldecott Road	A1-B1
Clifton Drive	B3
Conduit Road	A2-B2
Darrel Way	B4
Drayton Road	A1
East St Helens Street	B1-B2

Evelin Road	A4
Faringdon Road	A3-B3
Fieldside	A4
Fitzharrys Road	B3
Geoffrey Barbour Road	B3-C3-C4
Harcourt Way	B4
Harding Road	A3
High Street	B2
Lammas Close	B4-C4
Larkhill Place	A4
Larkhill Road	A3-A4
Lenthall Road	B3-B4
Longmead	A4
Meadowside	A1-B1
New Street	C2-C3
Norman Avenue	C4
Northcourt Lane	C4
Northcourt Road	B4-C4
Nuneham Square	B3
Ock Street	A1-A2-B2
Oxford Road	C3-C4
Park Crescent	A2-A3
Park Road	A2-B2
Radley Road	C3
St Amand Drive	A1-B1
St Helens Wharf	B1
St Johns Road	C3
St Marys Green	B4
St Nicholas	B4
Springfield Drive	A4-A3-A4
Spring Road	A1-A2-A3
Stanford Drive	B3
Station Road	B2-C2
Stert Street	B2
Stratton Way	B2
Swinburne Road	C3-C4
Tatham Road	A2
The Causeway	C1
The Motte	B2-B3
Thesiger Road	B3-C3
Thornhill Walk	B2
Tower Drive	A1
Victoria Road	B2
Vineyard	B2-C2-C3
West St Helens Street	B1-B2
Wildmor Gate	A4
Wilsham Road	B1
Withington Court	B2-B3
Wootton Road	A4-B4-B3

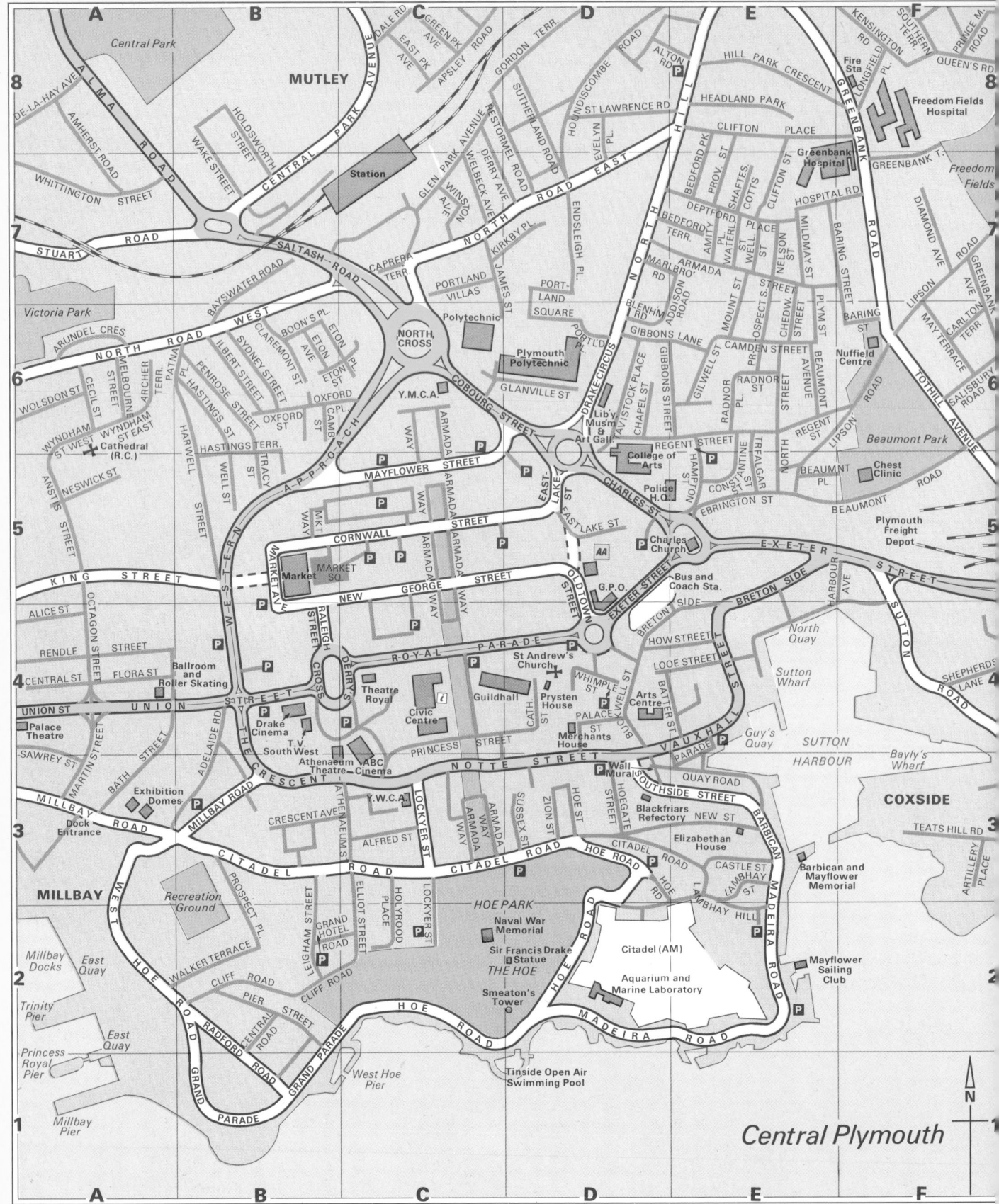

Central Plymouth

Plymouth

Ships, sailors and the sea permeate every aspect of Plymouth's life and history. Its superb natural harbour – Plymouth Sound – has ensured its importance as a port, yachting centre and naval base (latterly at Devonport) over many centuries. Sir Francis Drake is undoubtedly the city's most famous sailor. His statue stands on the Hoe – where he really did play bowls before tackling the Spanish Armada. Also on the Hoe are Smeaton's Tower, which once formed the upper part of the third Eddystone Lighthouse, and the impressive Royal Naval War Memorial. Just east of the Hoe is the Royal Citadel, an imposing fortress built in 1666 by order of Charles II. North is Sutton Harbour, perhaps the most atmospheric part of Plymouth. Here fishing boats bob up and down in a harbour whose quays are lined with attractive old houses, inns and warehouses. One of the memorials on Mayflower Quay just outside the harbour commemorates the sailing of the *Mayflower* from here in 1620. Plymouth's shopping centre is one of the finest of its kind, and was built after the old centre was badly damaged in World War II. Some buildings escaped destruction, including the Elizabethan House and the 500-year-old Prysten House. Next door is St Andrew's Church, with stained glass by John Piper.

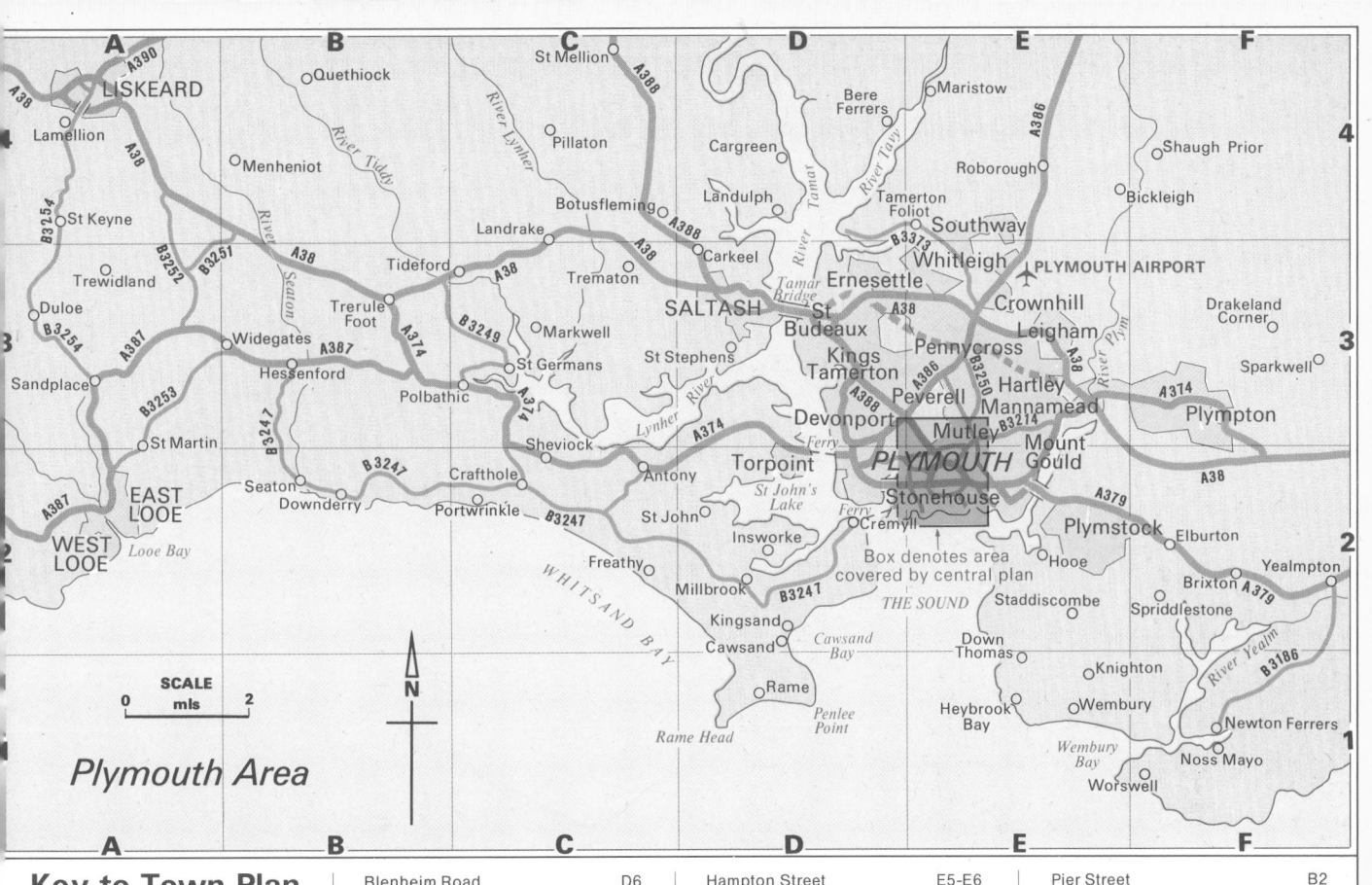

Plymouth Area

SCALE
0 mls 2

N

Key to Town Plan and Area Plan

Town Plan

AA Recommended roads
Other roads
Restricted roads
Buildings of interest
Car Parks   **P**
Parks and open spaces
AA Service Centre   **AA**

Area Plan

A roads
B roads
Locations   Sandplace O
Urban area

Street Index with Grid Reference

Plymouth

Addison Road	D6-D7-E7
Adelaide Road	B3-B4
Alfred Street	C3
Alice Street	A4
Alma Road	A8-A7-B7
Alton Road	D8-E8
Amherst Road	A7-A8
Amity Place	E7
Anstis Street	A5-A6
Apsley Road	C8
Archer Terrace	A6
Armada Street	D7-E7-F7
Armada Way	C3-C4-C5-C6
Artillery Place	F3
Arundel Crescent	A6
Athenaeum Street	C3
Barbican	E3
Baring Street	E7-F7-F6
Bath Street	A3-A4
Batter Street	D4-E4
Bayswater Road	B6-B7
Beaumont Avenue	E6
Beaumont Place	E5-F5
Beaumont Road	E5-F5-F6

Blenheim Road	D6
Boon's Place	B6
Breton Side	D4-E4-E5
Buckwell Street	D4
Cambridge Street	B6
Camden Street	E6
Caprera Terrace	C7
Carlton Terrace	F6
Castle Street	E3
Catherine Street	D4
Cecil Street	A6
Central Road	B2
Central Street	A4
Central Park Avenue	B7-B8-C8
Chapel Street	D6
Charles Street	D5
Chedworth Street	E6-E7
Citadel Road	B3-C3-D3-E3
Claremont Street	B6
Cliff Road	B2-C2
Clifton Place	E8-F8
Clifton Street	E7-E8
Cobourg Street	C6-D6
Constantine Street	E5-E6
Cornwall Street	B5-C5-D5
Crescent Avenue	B3-C3
Dale Road	C8
De-la-Hay-Avenue	A8
Deptford Place	D7-E7
Derry Avenue	C8-C7-D7
Derry's Cross	B4-C4
Diamond Avenue	F7
Drake Circus	D6
East Park Avenue	C8
Eastlake Street	D5
Ebrington Street	E5
Elliot Street	C2-C3
Endsleigh Place	D7
Eton Avenue	B6
Eton Place	B6-C6
Eton Street	B6-C6
Evelyn Place	D7-D8
Exeter Street	D4-D5-E5-F5
Flora Street	A4
Gibbons Lane	D6-E6
Gibbons Street	E6
Gilwell Street	E6
Glanville Street	C6-D6
Glen Park Avenue	C7-C8
Gordon Terrace	C8-D8
Grand Hotel Road	B2-C2
Grand Parade	B1-B2-C2
Great Western Road	B1-B2
Green Park Avenue	E3
Greenbank Avenue	F6-F7
Greenbank Road	F6-F7-F8-E8
Greenbank Terrace	F7-F8

Hampton Street	E5-E6
Harbour Avenue	E5-F5
Harwell Street	B5-B6
Hastings Street	B6
Hastings Terrace	B5-B6
Headland Park	E8
Hill Park Crescent	E8-F8
Hoe Road	C2-D2-D3
Hoe Street	D3
Hoegate Street	D3
Holdsworth Street	B7-B8
Holyrood Place	C2-C3
How Street	D4-E4
Hospital Road	E7-F7
Houndiscombe Road	D7-D8
Ilbert Street	B6
James Street	C6-C7
Kensington Road	F8
King Street	A5-B5
Kirkby Place	C7-D7
Lambhay Hill	E2-E3
Lambhay Street	E3
Leigham Street	B2-B3
Lipson Road	E5-E6-F6-F7
Lockyer Street	C2-C3
Longfield Place	F8
Looe Street	D4-E4
Madeira Road	D2-E2-E3
Marlborough Road	D7-E7
Market Avenue	B4-B5
Market Square	B5-C5
Market Way	B5
Martin Street	A3-A4
May Terrace	F6
Mayflower Street	B5-C5-C6-D5-D6
Melbourne Street	A6
Mildmay Street	E7
Millbay Road	A3-B3
Mount Street	E6-E7
Nelson Street	E7
Neswick Street	A5
New Street	D3-E3
New George Street	B4-B5-C5-D5
North Cross	C6
North Hill	D6-D7-E7-E8
North Road East	C7-D7-D8-E8
North Road West	A6-B6-B7-C7
North Street	E5-E6
Notte Street	C3-D3-D4
Octagon Street	A4-A5
Old Town Street	D4-D5
Oxford Place	B6-C6
Oxford Street	B6
Palace Street	D4
Parade	E3-E4
Patna Place	B6
Penrose Street	B6

Pier Street	B2
Portland Place	D6
Portland Square	D6-D7
Portland Villas	C7
Plym Street	E6-E7
Prince Maurice Road	F8
Princess Street	C3-C4-D4
Prospect Place	B2-B3
Prospect Street	E6-E7
Providence Street	E7-E8
Quay Road	D3-E3
Queen's Road	F8
Radford Road	B1-B2
Radnor Place	E6
Radnor Street	E6
Raleigh Street	B4
Regent Street	D6-E6-E6
Rendle Street	A4
Restormel Road	C8-D8-D7
Royal Parade	C4-D4
St Lawrence Road	D8-E8
Salisbury Road	F6
Saltash Road	B7-C7-C6
Sawrey Street	A3-A4
Shaftesbury Cottages	E7
Shepherds Lane	F4
Southern Terrace	F8
Southside Street	D3-E3
Stuart Road	A7-B7
Sussex Street	D3
Sutherland Road	D7-D8
Sutton Road	F4-F5
Syney Street	B6
Tavistock Place	D6
Teats Hill Road	F3
The Crescent	B4-B3-C3
Tothill Avenue	F5-F6
Tracy Street	B5
Trafalgar Street	E5-E6
Union Street	A4-B4
Vauxhall Street	D3-D4-E4
Wake Street	B7-B8
Walker Terrace	A2-B2
Waterloo Street	E7
Welbeck Avenue	C7
Well Street	B5
Well Street	E7
West Hoe Road	A3-A2-B3
Western Approach	B4-B5-B6-C6
Whimple Street	D4
Whittington Street	A7
Winston Lane	C7
Wolsdon Street	A6
Wyndham Street East	A6
Wyndham Street West	A6
Zion Street	D3

197

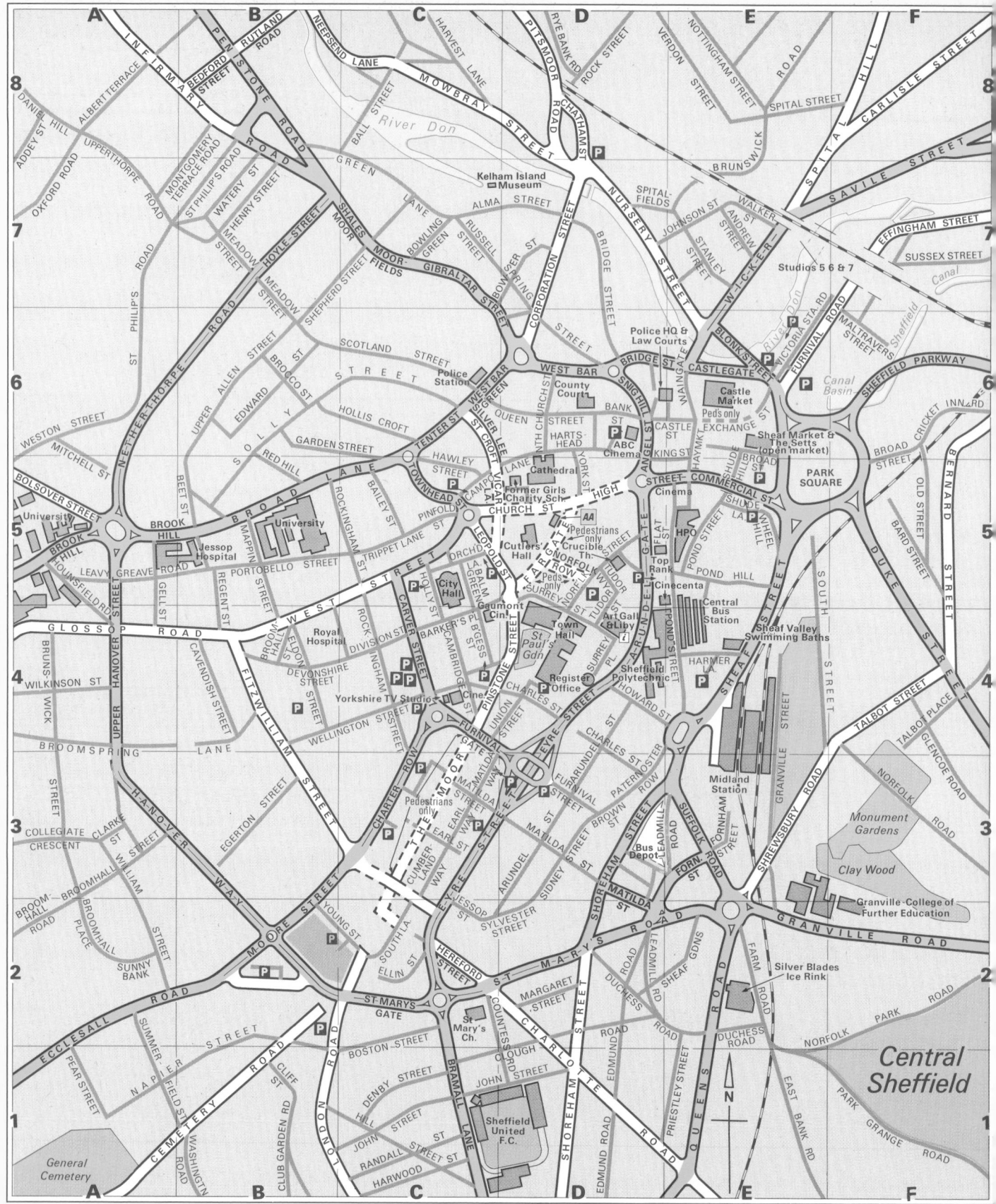

Sheffield

Cutlery – which has made the name of Sheffield famous throughout the world – has been manufactured here since at least as early as the time of Chaucer. The god of blacksmiths, Vulcan, is the symbol of the city's industry, and he crowns the town hall, which was opened in 1897 by Queen Victoria. At the centre of the industry, however, is Cutlers' Hall, the headquarters of the Company of Cutlers. This society was founded in 1624 and has the right to grant trade marks to articles of a sufficiently high standard. In the hall is the company's collection of silver, with examples of craftsmanship dating back every year to 1773. A really large collection of cutlery is kept in the city museum. Steel production, a vital component of the industry, was greatly improved when the crucible process was invented here in 1740. At Abbeydale Industrial Hamlet, 3½ miles south-west of the city centre, is a complete restored site open as a museum and showing 18th-century methods of steel production. Sheffield's centre, transformed since World War II, is one of the finest and most modern in Europe. There are no soot-grimed industrial eyesores here, for the city has stringent pollution controls and its buildings are carefully planned and set within excellent landscaping projects. Many parks are set in and around the city, and the Pennines are within easy reach.

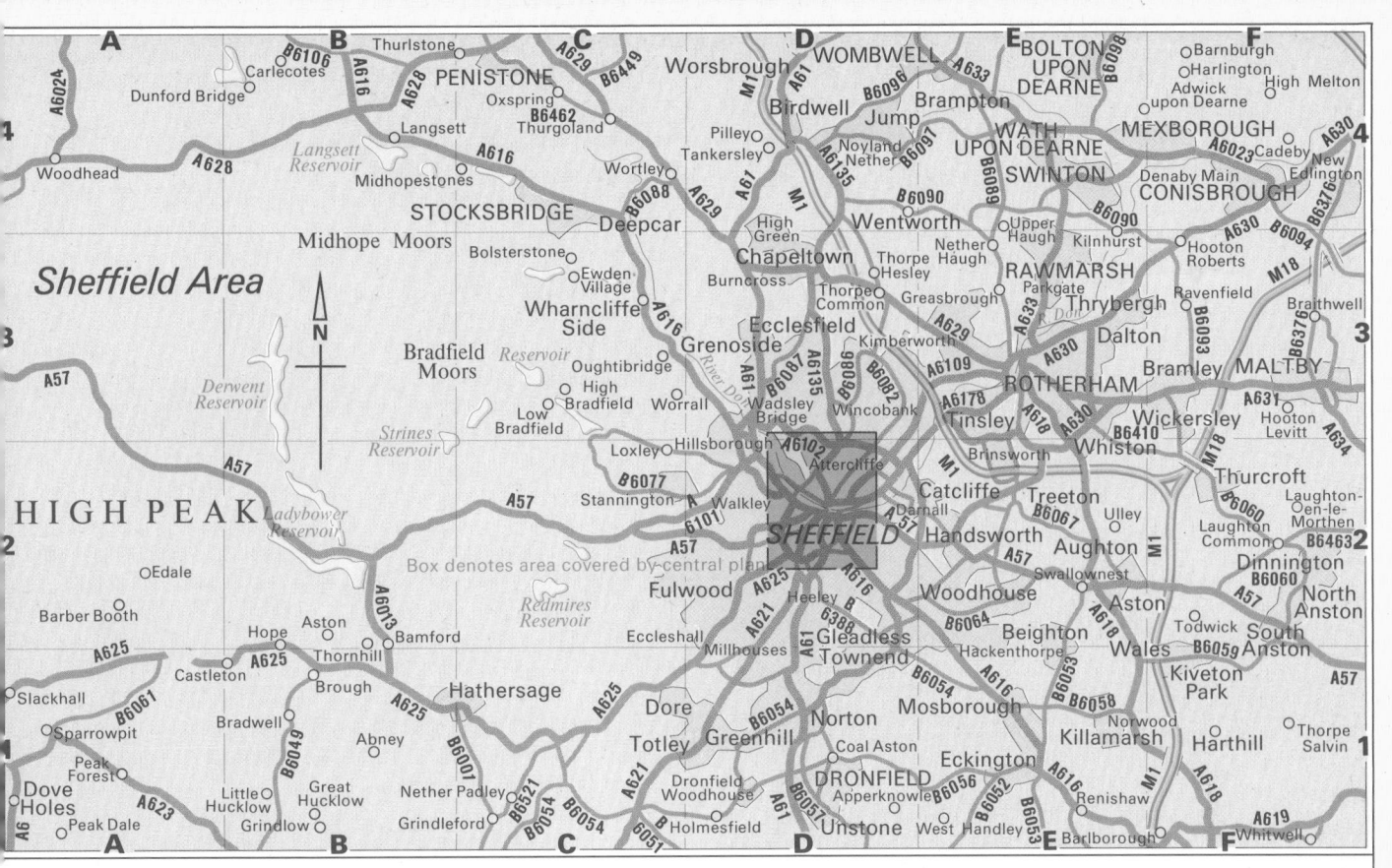

Sheffield Area

LEGEND

Town Plan

AA Recommended roads	
Other roads	
Restricted roads	
Buildings of interest	
AA Service Centre	AA
Car Parks	P
Parks and open spaces	

Area Plan

A roads	
B roads	
Locations	Oakworth O
Urban area	

Street Index with grid reference

Sheffield

Addey Street	A7-A8
Albert Terrace	A8
Alma Street	C7-D7
Andrew Street	E7
Angel Street	D5-D6
Arundel Gate	D4-D5
Arundel Street	C2-D2-D3-D4
Bailey Street	C5
Ball Street	C8
Balm Green	C4-C5
Bank Street	D6
Bard Street	F5
Barker's Pool	C4-C5-D5
Bedford Street	B8
Beet Street	B5
Bernard Street	F4-F5-F6
Blonk Street	E6
Bolsover Street	A5
Boston Street	C1-C2
Bower Street	C7-D7
Bowling Green	C7
Bramall Lane	C1-C2
Bridge Street	D7-D6-E6
Broad Lane	B5-C5-C6
Broad Street	E6.F5-F6
Brocco Street	B6
Brook Hill	A5-B5
Broomhall Place	A2
Broomhall Road	A2
Broomhall Street	A2-A3.B4
Broomspring Lane	A4-B4
Brown Street	D3

Brunswick Street	A3-A4
Brunswick Road	E7-E8
Burgess Street	C4
Cambridge Street	C4
Campo Lane	C5-D5-D6
Carlisle Street	F8
Carver Street	C4-C5
Castle Street	D6-E6
Castlegate	E6
Cavendish Street	B4
Cemetery Road	A1-B1-B2
Charles Street	D3-D4
Charlotte Road	C2-D2-D1-E1
Charter Row	C3-C4
Chatham Street	D7-D8
Church Street	C5-D5
Clarke Street	A3
Cliff Street	B1
Clough Road	C1-D1-D2
Club Garden Road	B1
Collegiate Crescent	A3
Commercial Street	E5
Corporation Street	D6-D7
Countess Road	C2-D2-D1
Cricket Inn Road	F6
Cumberland Way	C3
Daniel Hill	A8
Denby Street	C1
Devonshire Street	B4-C4
Division Street	C4
Duchess Road	D2-E2
Duke Street	F4-F5
Earl Street	C3
Earl Way	C3
East Bank Road	E1-E2
Ecclesall Road	A1-A2-B2
Edmund Road	D1-D2
Edward Street	B6
Effingham Street	F7
Egerton Street	B3
Eldon Street	B4
Ellin Street	C2
Eyre Street	C2-C3-D3-D4
Exchange Street	E6
Fargate	D5
Farm Road	E2
Fitzwilliam Street	B4-B3-C3
Flat Street	E5
Fornham Street	E3
Furnival Gate	C3-C4-D3-D4
Furnival Road	E6-F6-F7
Furnival Street	D3
Garden Street	B6-C6-C5
Gell Street	A4-A5
Gibraltar Street	C7-C6-D6
Glencoe Road	F3-F4
Glossop Road	A4-B4
Granville Road	E2-F2
Granville Street	E3-E4
Green Lane	B8-C8-C7
Hanover Way	A3-B3-B2
Harmer Lane	E4
Hartshead	D6
Harwood Street	C1
Harvest Lane	C8

Hawley Street	C5
Haymarket	E5-E6
Henry Street	B7
Hereford Street	C2
High Street	D5-E5
Hill Street	B1-C1
Hollis Croft	B6-C6
Holly Street	C4-C5
Hounsfield Road	A4-A5
Howard Street	D4-E4
Hoyle Street	B7
Infirmary Road	A8-B8 B7
Jessop Street	C2
John Street	C1-D1
Johnson Street	D7-E7
King Street	D5-E5-E6
Leadmill Road	D2-D3-E3
Leavy Greave Road	A5-B5
Lee Croft	C5-C6
Leopold Street	C5-D5
London Road	C1-B1-B2-C2
Maltravers Street	F6
Mappin Street	B4-B5
Margaret Street	D2
Matilda Street	C3-D3-D2
Matilda Way	C3
Meadow Street	B6-B7
Mitchell Street	A5-A6
Montgomery Terrace Road	A7-B7-B8
Moorfields	C7
Moore Street	B2-B3-C3
Mowbray Street	C8-D8-D7
Napier Street	A1-B1-B2
Neepsend Lane	B8-C8
Netherthorpe Road	A5-A6-B6-B7
Norfolk Park Road	E1-E2-F2
Norfolk Road	F3-F4
Norfolk Row	D5
Norfolk Street	D4-D5
North Church Street	D6
Nottingham Street	E8
Nursery Street	D7-E7-E6
Old Street	F5-F6
Orchard Lane	C5
Oxford Road	A7-A8
Park Grange Road	E1-F1
Park Square	E5-E6-F6-F5
Paternoster Row	D3-D4-E4
Pear Street	A1
Penistone Road	B7-B8
Pinfold Street	C5
Pinstone Street	C4-D4-D5
Pitsmoor Road	D8
Pond Hill	E5
Pond Street	E4-E5
Portobello Street	B5-C5
Priestley Street	D1-E1-E2
Queen Street	C6-D6
Queen's Road	E1-E2
Randall Street	C1
Regent Street	B4-B5
Rock Street	D8
Rockingham Street	B5-C5-C4

Russell Street	C7
Rutland Road	B8
Rye Bank Road	D8
St Mary's Gate	C2
St Mary's Road	C2-D2-E2-E3
St Philip's Road	A6-A7-B7-B8
Savile Street	E7-F7-F8
Scotland Street	B6-C6
Shales Moor	B7-C7
Sheaf Gardens	D2-E2
Sheaf Street	E4-E5
Sheffield Parkway	F6
Shepherd Street	B6-B7-C7
Shoreham Street	D1-D2-D3-E3
Shrewsbury Road	E3-E4-F3-F4
Shude Lane	E5
Shude Hill	E5-E6
Sidney Street	D3
Silver Street	C6
Snig Hill	D6
Solly Street	B5-B6-C6
South Lane	C2
South Street	E4-E5
Spital Hill	E7-E8-F8
Spital Street	E8-F8
Spitalfields	D7-E7
Spring Street	D6-D7
Stanley Street	E7
Suffolk Road	E3
Summerfield Street	A2-A1-B1
Sunny Bank	A2
Surrey Place	D4
Surrey Street	D4-D5
Sussex Street	F7
Sylvester Street	C2-D2
Talbot Place	F4
Talbot Street	F4
Tenter Street	C6
The Moor	C3-C4
Townhead Street	C5
Trippet Lane	C5
Tudor Street	D4-D5
Tudor Way	D5
Union Street	C4-D4
Upper Allen Street	B6
Upper Hanover Street	A3-A4-A5
Upperthorpe Road	A7-A8
Verdon Street	D8-E8
Vicar Lane	C5-D5
Victoria Station Road	E6-E7-F7
Waingate	E6
Walker Street	E7
Washington Road	B1
Watery Street	B7-B8
Wellington Street	B4-C4
West Bar	D6
West Bar Green	C6-D6
West Street	B4-B5-C5
Weston Street	A5-A6
Wheel Hill	E5
Wicker	E6-E7
Wilkinson Street	A4
William Street	A2-A3
York Street	D5-D6
Young Street	B2-C2

199

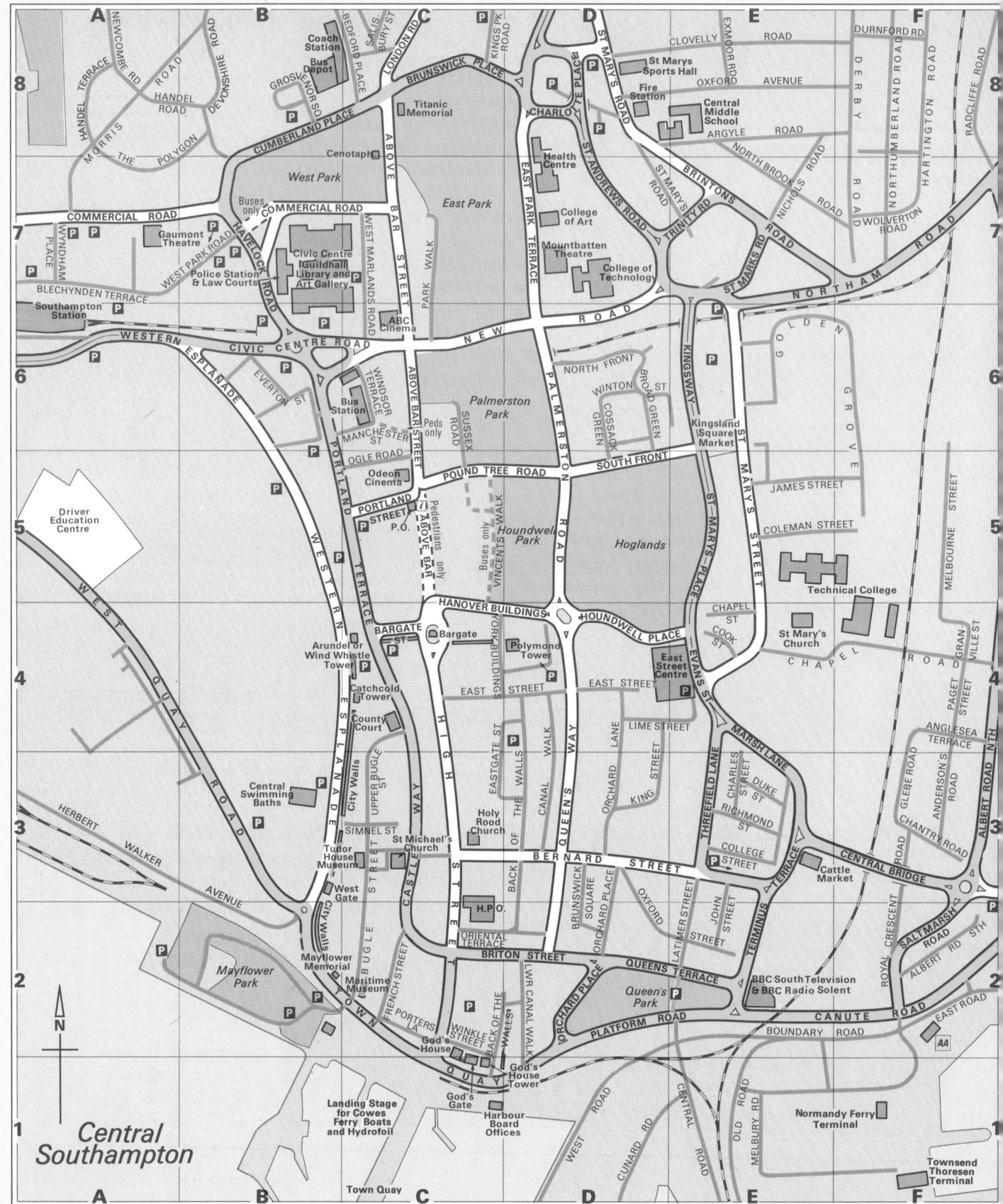

Southampton

In the days of the great ocean-going liners, Southampton was Britain's premier passenger port. Today container traffic is more important, but cruise liners still berth there. A unique double tide caused by the Solent waters, and protection from the open sea by the Isle of Wight, has meant that Southampton has always been a superb and important port. Like many great cities it was

devastated by bombing raids during World War II. However, enough survives to make the city a fascinating place to explore. Outstanding are the town walls, which stand to their original height in some places, especially along Western Esplanade. The main landward entrance to the walled town was the Bargate – a superb medieval gateway with a Guildhall (now a museum) on its upper floor. The best place to appreciate old Southampton is in and around St Michael's Square. Here is St Michael's

Church, oldest in the city and founded in 1070. Opposite is Tudor House Museum, a lovely gabled building housing much of interest. Down Bugle Street are old houses, with the town walls, pierced by the 13th-century West Gate, away to the right. At the corner of Bugle Street is the Wool House Maritime Museum, contained in a 14th-century warehouse. On the quayside is God's House Tower, part of the town's defences and now an archaeological museum.

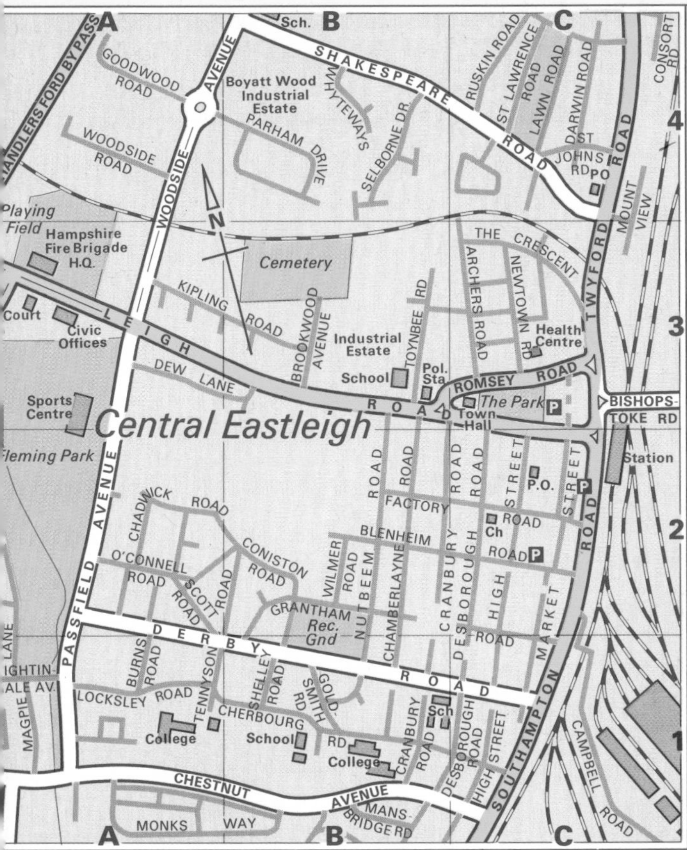

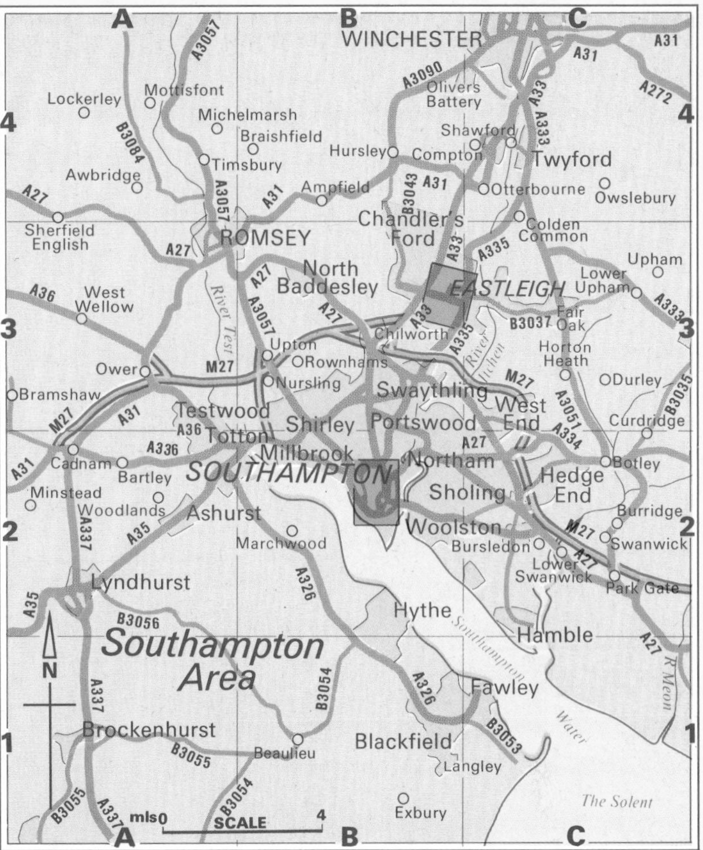

Map labels (Town Plan - Central Eastleigh):

Sch. · SHAKESPEARE RD · RUSKIN ROAD · ST LAWRENCE ROAD · LAWN ROAD · DARWIN ROAD · CONSORT RD
Goodwood Road · AVENUE · WHYTEWAYS · Boyatt Wood Industrial Estate · SELBORNE DR. · ST JOHNS RD PO · MOUNT VIEW · TWYFORD ROAD
Woodside Road · WOODSIDE · PARHAM DRIVE
Playing Field · Hampshire Fire Brigade H.Q. · KIPLING ROAD · BROOKWOOD AVENUE · Cemetery · THE CRESCENT · NEWTOWN RD · ARCHERS ROAD · Health Centre
Court · Civic Offices · LEIGH · DEW LANE · Industrial Estate · School · Pol. Sta. · ROMSEY ROAD · Town Hall · The Park · P · BISHOPSTOKE RD
Sports Centre · Central Eastleigh · P.O. · Station
Fleming Park · PASSFIELD AVENUE · CHADWICK ROAD · ROAD · FACTORY ROAD · P.O. · ROAD
LIGHTIN DALE AV · O'CONNELL ROAD · SCOTT · CONISTON ROAD · BLENHEIM ROAD · Ch · P
MAGPIE LANE · DERBY · BURNS RD · SHELLEY RD · GRANTHAM Rec. Gnd · WILMER ROAD · NUTBEEM ROAD · CHAMBERLAYNE · CRANBURY · DESBOROUGH · HIGH · STREET · MARKET STREET · SOUTHAMPTON · ROAD · CAMPBELL ROAD
LOCKSLEY ROAD · TENNYSON · GOLD · SMITH RD · Sch
CHERBOURG · College · School · RD · College
CHESTNUT AVENUE · MONKS WAY · MANS BRIDGE RD

Map labels (Area Plan - Southampton Area):

WINCHESTER · A31 · A31 · A272 · A3057 · A3090 · Oliver's Battery · A333 · A31 · A35
Lockerley · Mottisfont · Michelmarsh · Shawford · Twyford · Owslebury
B3084 · Braishfield · Hursley · Compton · Otterbourne · Golden Common
Awbridge · Timsbury · A31 · Ampfield · A3043 · A31 · Chandler's Ford · Lower Upham · Upham
Sherfield English · A27 · ROMSEY · North Baddesley · EASTLEIGH · A335 · Fair Oak · A333
A36 · West Wellow · A27 · Chilworth · B3037 · Horton Heath · Durley · B3035
Ower · M27 · Upton · Rownhams · Nursling · Swaythling · West End · Curdridge
Bramshaw · M27 · A31 · Testwood · Shirley · Portswood · Northam · Hedge End · Botley
Cadnam · Bartley · A336 · Totton · Millbrook · SOUTHAMPTON · Sholing · Burridge
Minstead · Woodlands · A35 · Ashurst · A337 · Woolston · Bursledon · Swanwick
Marchwood · Northam · M27 · Park Gate
Lyndhurst · A326 · B3056 · Southampton Area · Hythe · Hamble · A27 · R.Meon
A35 · N · A337 · B3054 · Fawley
Brockenhurst · B3055 · Beaulieu · Blackfield · Langley · Water · The Solent
B3055 · A331 · mls 0 · SCALE · 4 · Exbury

Key to Town Plan and Area Plan

Town Plan

A.A. Recommended roads
Other roads
Restricted roads
Buildings of interest — Cinema
A A Service Centre — AA
Car Parks — P
Parks and open spaces

Area Plan

A roads
B roads
Locations — Ower O
Urban Area

SOUTHAMPTON
Although liners still use Southampton's docks which handled all the great ocean-going passenger ships before the age of air travel replaced sea travel, the port is chiefly used by commercial traffic today.

Swansea

Like nearly all the towns in the valleys and along the coast of Glamorgan, Swansea grew at an amazing speed during the Industrial Revolution. Ironworks, non-ferrous metal smelting works and mills and factories of every kind were built to produce the goods which were exported from the city's docks. There had been a settlement here from very early times – the city's name is derived from Sweyn's Ea – Ea means island, and Sweyn was a Viking pirate who had a base here. Heavy industry is still pre-eminent in the area, but commerce is of increasing importance and the university exerts a strong influence. Hundreds of acres of parkland and open space lie in and around the city, and just to the west is the Gower, one of the most beautiful areas of Wales. The history of Swansea is traced in the Maritime, Industrial and Royal Institution of South Wales Museums, while the Glynn Vivian Art Gallery contains notable paintings and porcelain.

Neath and **Port Talbot** are, like Swansea, dominated by heavy industry. Neath was once a Roman station, and later had a castle and an abbey, ruins of which can still be seen. Port Talbot has been an industrial centre since 1770, when a copper-smelting works was built. Steelworks and petrochemical works stretch for miles around Swansea Bay.

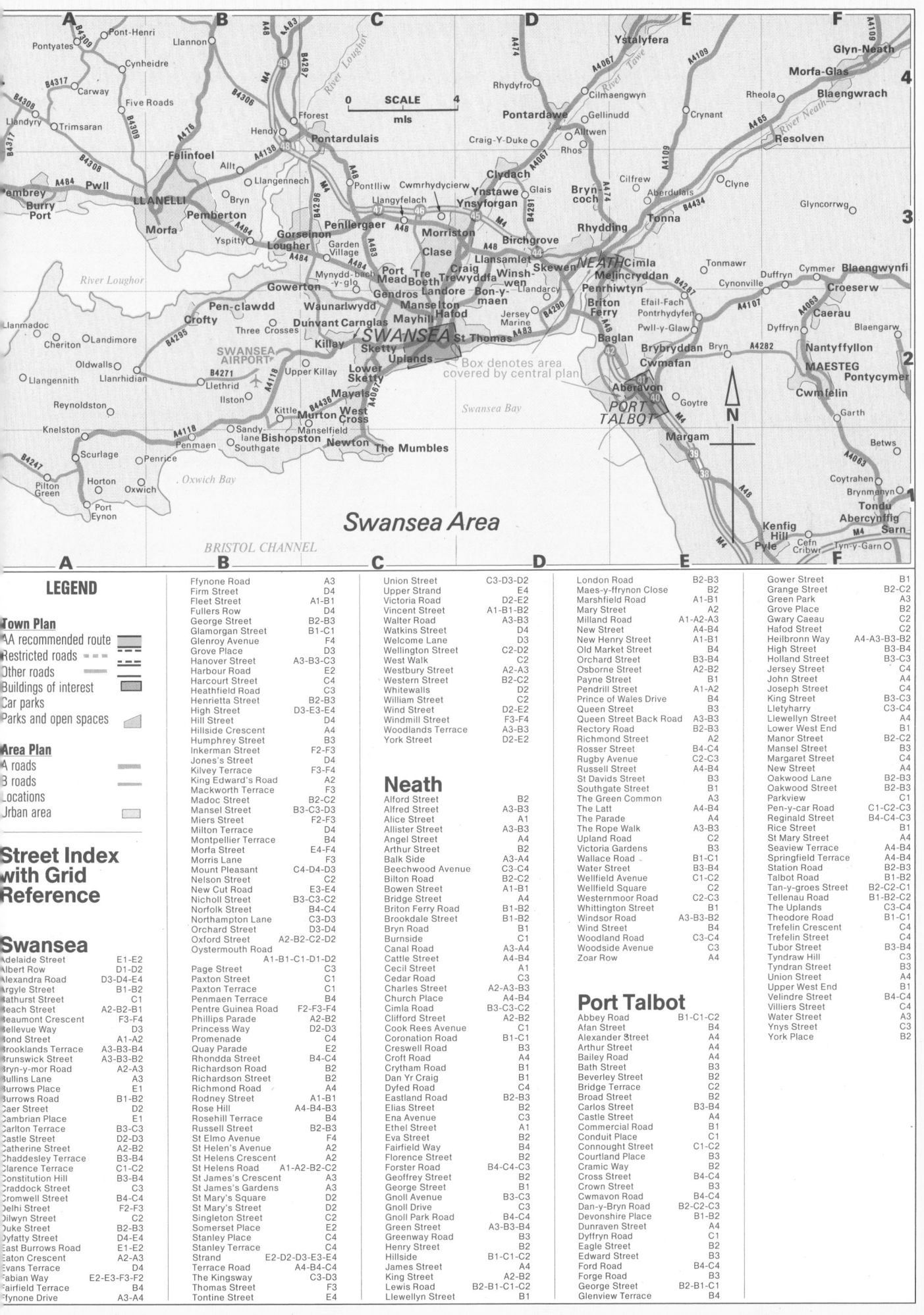

Swansea Area

BRISTOL CHANNEL

Box denotes area covered by central plan

LEGEND

Town Plan
- AA recommended route
- Restricted roads
- Other roads
- Buildings of interest
- Car parks
- Parks and open spaces

Area Plan
- A roads
- B roads
- Locations
- Urban area

Street Index with Grid Reference

Swansea

Adelaide Street	E1-E2
Albert Row	D1-D2
Argyle Street	B1-B2
Bathurst Street	C1
Beach Street	A2-B2-B1
Beaumont Crescent	F3-F4
Bellevue Way	D3
Bond Street	A1-A2
Brooklands Terrace	A3-B3-B4
Brunswick Street	A3-B3-B2
Bryn-y-mor Road	A2-A3
Bullins Lane	A3
Burrows Place	E1
Burrows Road	B1-B2
Caer Street	D2
Cambrian Place	E1
Carlton Terrace	B3-C3
Castle Street	D2-D3
Catherine Street	A2-B2
Chaddesley Terrace	B3-B4
Clarence Terrace	C1-C2
Constitution Hill	B3-B4
Craddock Street	C3
Cromwell Street	B4-C4
Delhi Street	F2-F3
Dilwyn Street	C2
Duke Street	B2-B3
Dyfatty Street	D4-E4
East Burrows Road	E1-E2
Eaton Crescent	A2-A3
Evans Terrace	D4
Fabian Way	E2-E3-F3-F2
Fairfield Terrace	B4
Ffynone Drive	A3-A4
Ffynone Road	A3
Firm Street	D4
Fleet Street	A1-B1
Fullers Row	D4
George Street	B2-B3
Glamorgan Street	B1-C1
Glenroy Avenue	F4
Grove Place	D3
Hanover Street	A3-B3-C3
Harbour Road	E2
Harcourt Street	C4
Heathfield Road	C3
Henrietta Street	B2-B3
High Street	D3-E3-E4
Hill Street	D4
Hillside Crescent	A4
Humphrey Street	B3
Inkerman Street	F2-F3
Jones's Street	D4
Kilvey Terrace	F3-F4
King Edward's Road	A2
Mackworth Terrace	F3
Madoc Street	B2-C2
Mansel Street	B3-C3-D3
Miers Street	F2-F3
Milton Terrace	D4
Montpellier Terrace	B4
Morfa Street	E4-F4
Morris Lane	F3
Mount Pleasant	C4-D4-D3
Nelson Street	C2
New Cut Road	E3-E4
Nicholl Street	B3-C3-C2
Norfolk Street	B4-C4
Northampton Lane	C3-D3
Orchard Street	D3-D4
Oxford Street	A2-B2-C2-D2
Oystermouth Road	A1-B1-C1-D1-D2
Page Street	C3
Paxton Street	C1
Paxton Terrace	C1
Penmaen Terrace	B4
Pentre Guinea Road	F2-F3-F4
Phillips Parade	A2-B2
Princess Way	D2-D3
Promenade	E2
Quay Parade	E2
Rhondda Street	B4-C4
Richardson Road	B2
Richardson Street	B2
Richmond Road	A4
Rodney Street	A1-B1
Rose Hill	A4-B4-B3
Rosehill Terrace	B4
Russell Street	B2-B3
St Elmo Avenue	F4
St Helen's Avenue	A2
St Helens Crescent	A2
St Helens Road	A1-A2-B2-C2
St James's Crescent	A3
St James's Gardens	A3
St Mary's Square	D2
St Mary's Street	D2
Singleton Street	C2
Somerset Place	E2
Stanley Place	C4
Stanley Terrace	C4
Strand	E2-D2-D3-E3-E4
Terrace Road	A4-B4-C4
The Kingsway	C3-D3
Thomas Street	F3
Tontine Street	E4
Union Street	C3-D3-D2
Upper Strand	E4
Victoria Road	D2-E2
Vincent Street	A1-B1-B2
Walter Road	A3-B3
Watkins Street	D4
Welcome Lane	D3
Wellington Street	C2-D2
West Walk	C2
Westbury Street	A2-A3
Western Street	B2-C2
Whitewalls	D2
William Street	C2
Wind Street	D2-E2
Windmill Street	F3-F4
Woodlands Terrace	A3-B3
York Street	D2-E2

Neath

Alford Street	B2
Alfred Street	A3-B3
Alice Street	A1
Allister Street	A3-B3
Angel Street	A4
Arthur Street	B2
Balk Side	A3-A4
Beechwood Avenue	C3-C4
Bilton Road	B2-C2
Bowen Street	A1-B1
Bridge Street	A4
Briton Ferry Road	B1-B2
Brookdale Street	B1-B2
Bryn Road	B1
Burnside	C1
Canal Road	A3-A4
Cattle Street	A4-B4
Cecil Street	A1
Cedar Road	C3
Charles Street	A2-A3-B3
Church Place	A4-B4
Cimla Road	B3-C3-C2
Clifford Street	A2-B2
Cook Rees Avenue	C1
Coronation Road	B1-C1
Creswell Road	B3
Croft Road	A4
Crytham Road	B1
Dan Yr Craig	B1
Dyfed Road	C4
Eastland Road	B2-B3
Elias Street	B2
Ena Avenue	C3
Ethel Street	A1
Eva Street	B2
Fairfield Way	B4
Florence Street	B2
Forster Road	B4-C4-C3
Geoffrey Street	B2
George Street	B1
Gnoll Avenue	B3-C3
Gnoll Drive	C3
Gnoll Park Road	B4-C4
Green Street	A3-B3-B4
Greenway Road	B3
Henry Street	B2
Hillside	B1-C1-C2
James Street	A4
King Street	A2-B2
Lewis Road	B2-B1-C1-C2
Llewellyn Street	B1
London Road	B2-B3
Maes-y-ffrynon Close	B2
Marshfield Road	A1-B1
Mary Street	A2
Milland Road	A1-A2-A3
New Street	A4-B4
New Henry Street	A1-B1
Old Market Street	B4
Orchard Street	B3-B4
Osborne Street	A2-B2
Payne Street	B1
Pendrill Street	A1-A2
Prince of Wales Drive	B4
Queen Street	B3
Queen Street Back Road	A3-B3
Rectory Road	B2-B3
Richmond Street	A2
Rosser Street	B4-C4
Rugby Avenue	C2-C3
Russell Street	A4-B4
St Davids Street	B3
Southgate Street	B1
The Green Common	A3
The Latt	A4-B4
The Parade	A4
The Rope Walk	A3-B3
Upland Road	C2
Victoria Gardens	B3
Wallace Road	B1-C1
Water Street	B3-B4
Wellfield Avenue	C1-C2
Wellfield Square	C2
Westernmoor Road	C2-C3
Whittington Street	B1
Windsor Road	A3-B3-B2
Wind Street	B4
Woodland Road	C3-C4
Woodside Avenue	C3
Zoar Row	A4

Port Talbot

Abbey Road	B1-C1-C2
Afan Street	B4
Alexander Street	A4
Arthur Street	A4
Bailey Road	A4
Bath Street	B3
Beverley Street	B2
Bridge Terrace	C2
Broad Street	B2
Carlos Street	B3-B4
Castle Street	A4
Commercial Road	B1
Conduit Place	C1
Connought Street	C1-C2
Courtland Place	B3
Cramic Way	B2
Cross Street	B4-C4
Crown Street	B3
Cwmavon Road	B4-C4
Dan-y-Bryn Road	B2-C2-C3
Devonshire Place	B1-B2
Dunraven Street	A4
Dyffryn Road	C1
Eagle Street	B2
Edward Street	B3
Ford Road	B4-C4
Forge Road	B2
George Street	B2-B1-C1
Glenview Terrace	B4
Gower Street	B1
Grange Street	B2-C2
Green Park	A3
Grove Place	B2
Gwary Caeau	C2
Hafod Street	C2
Heilbronn Way	A4-A3-B3-B2
High Street	B3-B4
Holland Street	B3-C3
Jersey Street	C4
John Street	A4
Joseph Street	C4
King Street	B3-C3
Lletyharry	C3-C4
Llewellyn Street	A4
Lower West End	B1
Manor Street	B2-C2
Mansel Street	B3
Margaret Street	C4
New Street	A4
Oakwood Lane	B2-B3
Oakwood Street	B2-B3
Parkview	C1
Pen-y-car Road	C1-C2-C3
Reginald Street	B4-C4-C3
Rice Street	B1
St Mary Street	A4
Seaview Terrace	A4-B4
Springfield Terrace	A4-B4
Station Road	B2-B3
Talbot Road	B1-B2
Tan-y-groes Street	B2-C2-C1
Tellenau Road	B1-B2-C2
The Uplands	C3-C4
Theodore Road	B1-C1
Trefelin Crescent	C4
Trefelin Street	C4
Tubor Street	B3-B4
Tyndraw Hill	C3
Tyndran Street	B3
Union Street	A4
Upper West End	B1
Velindre Street	B4-C4
Villiers Street	C4
Water Street	A3
Ynys Street	C3
York Place	B2

203

Tourist Plans

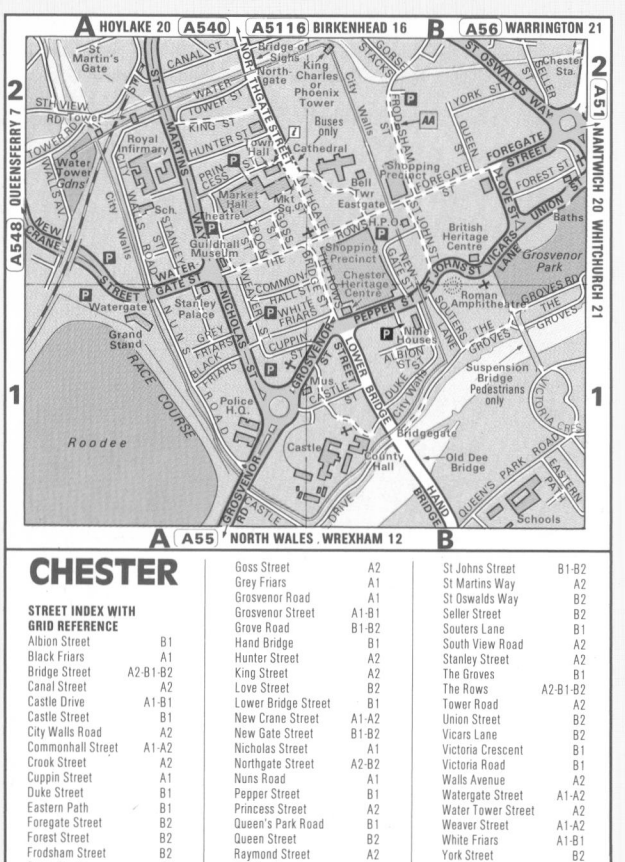

HOYLAKE 20 A540 | A5116 BIRKENHEAD 16 B | A56 WARRINGTON 21

CHESTER

STREET INDEX WITH GRID REFERENCE

Street	Grid	Street	Grid	Street	Grid
Albion Street	B1	Goss Street	A2	St Johns Street	B1-B2
Black Friars	A1	Grey Friars	A1	St Martins Way	A2
Bridge Street	A2-B1-B2	Grosvenor Road	A1	St Oswalds Way	B2
Canal Street	A2	Grosvenor Street	A1-B1	Seller Street	B2
Castle Drive	A1-B1	Grove Road	B1-B2	Souters Lane	B1
Castle Street	B1	Hand Bridge	B1	South View Road	A2
City Walls Road	A2	Hunter Street	A2	Stanley Street	A2
Commonhall Street	A1-A2	King Street	A2	The Groves	B2
Crook Street	A2	Love Street	B2	The Rows	A2-B1-B2
Cuppin Street	A1	Lower Bridge Street	B1	Tower Road	A2
Duke Street	B1	New Crane Street	A1-A2	Union Street	B2
Eastern Path	B1	New Gate Street	B1-B2	Vicars Lane	B2
Foregate Street	B2	Nicholas Street	A1	Victoria Crescent	B1
Forest Street	B2	Northgate Street	A2-B1	Victoria Road	B1
Frodsham Street	B2	Nuns Road	A1	Walls Avenue	A2
Gorse Stacks	B2	Pepper Street	B1	Watergate Street	A1-A2
		Princess Street	A2	Water Tower Street	A2
		Queen's Park Road	B1	Weaver Street	A1-A2
		Queen Street	B2	White Friars	A1-B1
		Raymond Street	A2	York Street	B2
		St John Street	B2		

A A55 NORTH WALES . WREXHAM 12 B

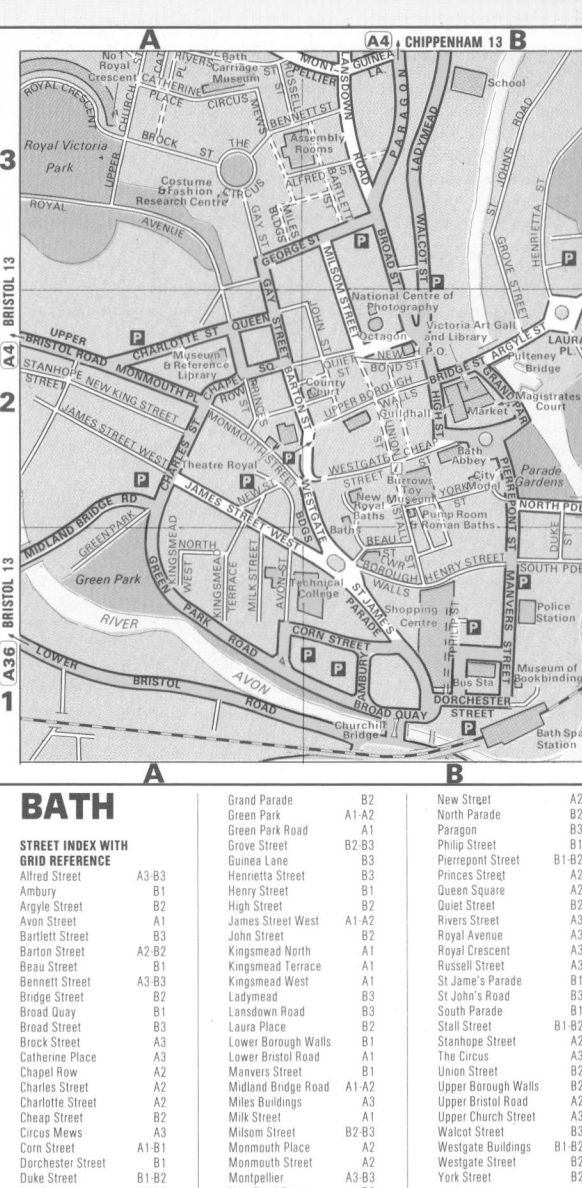

A4 CHIPPENHAM 13 B

BATH

STREET INDEX WITH GRID REFERENCE

Street	Grid	Street	Grid	Street	Grid
Alfred Street	A3-B3	Grand Parade	B2	New Street	A2
Ambury	B1	Green Park	A1-A2	North Parade	B2
Argyle Street	B2	Green Park Road	A1	Paragon	B3
Avon Street	A1	Grove Street	B2-B3	Philip Street	B1
Bartlett Street	B3	Guinea Lane	B3	Pierrepont Street	B1-B2
Barton Street	A2-B2	Henrietta Street	B3	Princes Street	A2
Beau Street	B1	Henry Street	B1	Queen Square	A2
Bennett Street	A3-B3	High Street	B2	Quiet Street	A2
Bridge Street	B2	James Street West	A1-A2	Rivers Street	A3
Broad Quay	B1	John Street	B2	Royal Avenue	A3
Broad Street	B3	Kingsmead North	A1	Royal Crescent	A3
Brock Street	A3	Kingsmead Terrace	A1	Russell Street	A3
Catherine Place	A3	Kingsmead West	A1	St Jame's Parade	B1
Chapel Row	A2	Ladymead	B3	St John's Road	B3
Charles Street	A2	Lansdown Road	B3	South Parade	B1
Charlotte Street	A2	Laura Place	B2	Stall Street	B1-B2
Cheap Street	B2	Lower Borough Walls	B1	Stanhope Street	A2
Circus Mews	A3	Lower Bristol Road	A1	The Circus	A3
Corn Street	A1-B1	Manvers Street	B1	Union Street	B2
Dorchester Street	B1	Midland Bridge Road	A1-A2	Upper Borough Walls	B2
Duke Street	B1-B2	Miles Buildings	A3	Upper Bristol Road	A3
Gay Street	A2-A3	Milk Street	A1	Upper Church Street	A3
George Street	A3-B3	Milsom Street	B2-B3	Walcot Street	B3
		Monmouth Place	A2	Westgate Buildings	B1-B2
		Monmouth Street	A2	Westgate Street	B2
		Montpellier	A3-B3	York Street	B2
		New Bond Street	B2		
		New King Street	A2		

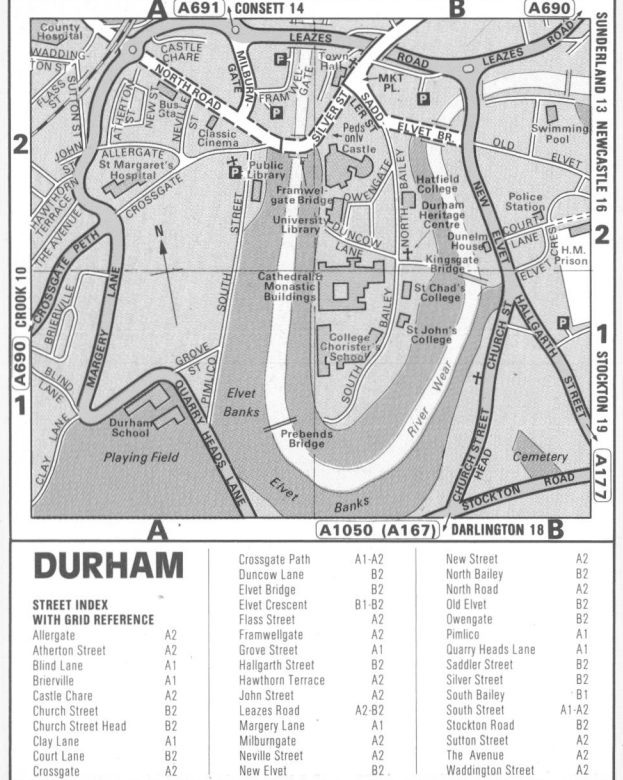

A A691 CONSETT 14 B A690

A A1050 (A167) DARLINGTON 18 B

DURHAM

STREET INDEX WITH GRID REFERENCE

Street	Grid	Street	Grid	Street	Grid
Allergate	A2	Crossgate Path	A1-A2	New Street	A2
Atherton Street	A2	Duncow Lane	B2	North Bailey	B2
Blind Lane	A1	Elvet Bridge	B2	North Road	A2
Brierville	A1	Elvet Crescent	B1-B2	Old Elvet	B2
Castle Chare	A2	Flass Street	A2	Owengate	B2
Church Street	B2	Framwellgate	A2	Pimlico	A1
Church Street Head	B2	Grove Street	A1	Quarry Heads Lane	A1
Clay Lane	A1	Halgarth Street	B2	Saddler Street	B2
Court Lane	B2	Hawthorn Terrace	A2	Silver Street	B2
Crossgate	A2	John Street	A2	South Bailey	B1
		Leazes Road	A2-B2	South Street	A1-A2
		Margery Lane	A1	Stockton Road	B1
		Milburngate	A2	Sutton Street	A2
		Neville Street	A2	The Avenue	A2
		New Elvet	B2	Waddington Street	A2

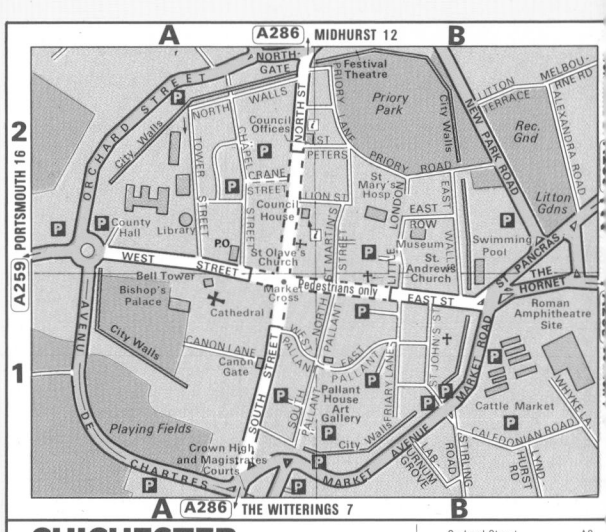

A A286 MIDHURST 12 B

A A286 THE WITTERINGS 7 B

CHICHESTER

STREET INDEX WITH GRID REFERENCE

Street	Grid	Street	Grid	Street	Grid
Alexandra Road	B2	Laburnum Grove	B1	Orchard Street	A2
Avenu de Chartres	A1	Lion Street	A2-B2	Priory Lane	B2
Caledonian Road	B1	Little London	B1-B2	Priory Road	B2
Canon Lane	A1	Litton Terrace	B2	St John's Street	B1
Chapel Street	A2	Lyndhurst Road	B2	St Martin's Street	B1-B2
Crane Street	A2	Market Avenue	B1	St Pancras	B1-B2
East Pallant	B1	Market Road	B1	St Peters	A2-B2
East Row	B1	Melbourne Road	B2	South Pallant	A1-B1
East Street	B1	New Park Road	B2	South Street	A1
East Street.	B1	Northgate	A2	Stirling Road	B1
East Walls	B2	North Pallant	B1	The Hornet	B1-B2
Friary Lane	B1	North Street	A2	Tower Street	A2
		North Walls	A2	West Pallant	A1
				West Street	A1-A2
				Whyke Lane	B2

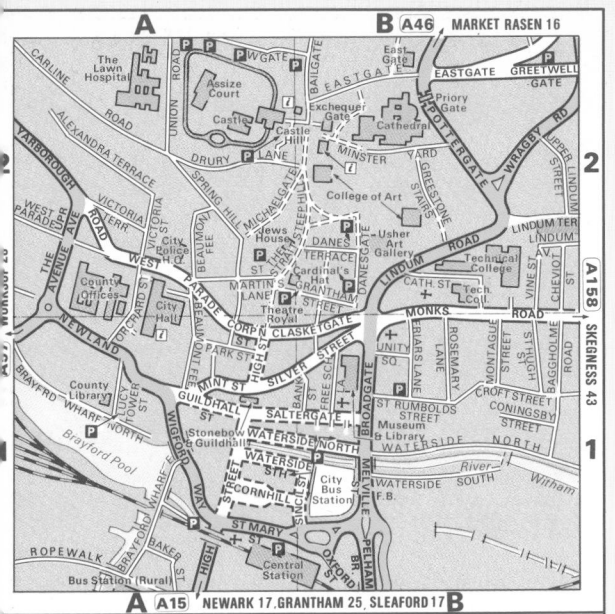

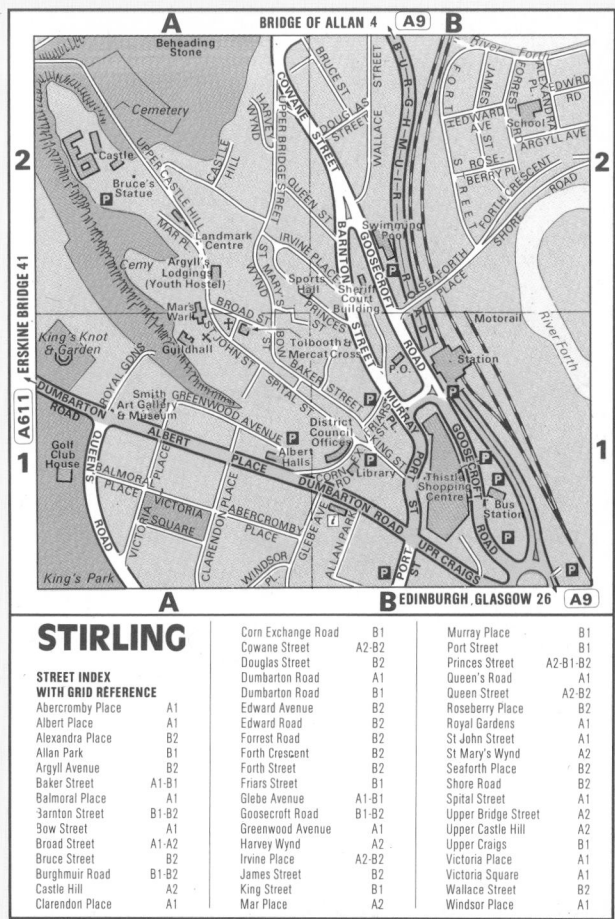

LINCOLN

STREET INDEX WITH GRID REFERENCE

Street	Grid	Street	Grid	Street	Grid
Alexandra Terrace	A2	Free School Lane	B1	St Martin's Lane	A2
Baggholme Road	B1	Friars Lane	B1	St Mary Street	A1
Bailgate	B2	Grantham Street	B2	St Rumbolds Street	B1
Baker Street	A1	Greestone Stairs	B2	Saltergate	A1-B1
Bank Street	B1	Greetwell Gate	B2	Silver Street	A1-B1
Beaumont Fee	A1-A2	Guildhall Street	A1	Sincil Street	B1
Brayford Wharf East	A1	High Street	A1	Spring Hill	A1
Brayford Wharf North	A1	Lindum Avenue	B2	Steep Hill	B2
Broadgate	B1	Lindum Road	B2	The Avenue	A1
Carline Road	A2	Lindum Terrace	B2	The Strait	A2-B2
Cathedral Street	B2	Lucy Tower Street	A1	Union Road	A2
Cheviot Street	B2	Melville Street	B1	Unity Square	A2
Clasketgate	A1-B1	Michaelgate	A2	Upper Avenue	A2
Coningsby Street	B1	Minster Yard	B2	Upper Lindum Street	B2
Cornhill	A1	Mint Street	A1	Victoria Street	A2
Corporation Street	A1	Monks Road	B1 B2	Victoria Terrace	A2
Croft Street	B1	Montague Street	B1	Vine Street	B2
Danesgate	B2	Newland	A1-A2	Waterside North	A1-B1
Danes Terrace	B2	Orchard Street	A1-A2	Waterside South	A1-B1
Drury Lane	A1	Oxford Street	B1	Westgate	A2
Eastgate	B2	Park Street	A1	West Parade	A2
		Pelham Bridge	B1	Wigford Way	A1
		Pottergate	B2	Wragby Road	B2
		Rope Walk	A1	Yarborough Road	A2
		Rosemary Lane	B1		
		St Hugh Street	B1		

LUDLOW

STREET INDEX WITH GRID REFERENCE

Street	Grid	Street	Grid	Street	Grid
Bell Lane	A1-A2	Gravel Hill	B3	Quarry Gardens	B3
Brand Lane	B2	High Street	A2	Raven Lane	A2
Broad Street	A2-B1-B2	Hillside	B3	St Johns Lane	B1
Bull Ring	B2	Julian Road	B3	St Johns Road	B1
Camp Lane	A1	King Street	A2-B2	St Julians Avenue	B3
Castle Square	A2	Linney	A2-A3	St Stephens Close	B2
Castle Street	A2	Lower Broad Street	B1	Silk Mill Lane	A1-B1
Church Street	A2	Lower Galdeford	B2	Springfield Close	B2
College Street	A2	Lower Mill Street	A1	Station Drive	A3-B3
Coronation Avenue	A3	Lower Raven Lane	A1-B1	Teme Avenue	B1
Corve Street	A3-B2-B3	Market Street	A2	Temeside	B1
Dinham	A2	Mill Street	A1-A2	Tower Street	B2
		Old Street	B1-B2	Upper Fee	B1
		Park Road	B1	Upper Galdeford	B2-B3
		Pepper Lane	A2	Upper Linney	A2
		Portcullis Lane	B2-B3		
		Poyner Road	B3		

STRATFORD

STREET INDEX WITH GRID REFERENCE

Street	Grid	Street	Grid	Street	Grid
Alcester Rd	A2	Henley St	A1-A2	Scholars Ln	A1
Arden St	A2	High St	A1	Shakespeare St	A1
Arthur Rd	A2	John St	B2	Sheep St	B1
Avenue Rd	B2	Kendall Av	A2-B2	Shipston Rd	B1
Banbury Rd	B1	Maidenhead Rd	B2	Southern Ln	A1-B1
Birmingham Rd	A1	Mansell St	A2	Swans Nest Ln	B1
Bridgefoot	B1	Market Pl	A1-A2	Tiddington Rd	B1
Bridge St	B1	Mayfield Av	B2	Tyler St	B2
Bridgeway	B1-B2	Mulberry St	A2-B2	Union St	B1
Broad St	A1	New Broad St	A1	Warwick Cres	B2
Bull St	A1	Old Town	A1	Warwick Road	B2
Chapel Ln	A1	Payton St	B2	Waterside	B1
Chapel St	A1	Percy St	B2	Welcombe Rd	B2
Chestnut Wk	A1	Rother St	A1	Wellesbourne Gr	A1-A2
Church St	A1	Rowley Cres	B2	West St	A1
Clopton Rd	A2	St Gregory's Rd	B2	Windsor St	A1
College Ln	A1	St Mary's Rd	B2	Wood St	A1
College St	A1	Sanctus St	A1		
Ely St	A1				
Evesham Pl	A1				
Great William St	A2-B2				
Greenhill St	A1				
Grove Rd	A1-A2				
Guild St	A2-B2				

STIRLING

STREET INDEX WITH GRID REFERENCE

Street	Grid	Street	Grid	Street	Grid
Abercromby Place	A1	Corn Exchange Road	B1	Murray Place	B1
Albert Place	A1	Cowane Street	A2-B2	Port Street	B1
Alexandra Place	B2	Douglas Street	B2	Princes Street	A2-B1-B2
Allan Park	A1	Dumbarton Road	A1	Queen's Road	A1
Argyll Avenue	B2	Dumbarton Road	B1	Queen Street	A2-B2
Baker Street	A1-B1	Edward Avenue	B2	Roseberry Place	A1
Balmoral Place	A1	Edward Road	B2	Royal Gardens	A1
Barnton Street	B1-B2	Forrest Road	B2	St John Street	B1
Bow Street	A1	Forth Crescent	B2	St Mary's Wynd	A2
Broad Street	A1-A2	Forth Street	B2	Seaforth Place	B2
Bruce Street	B2	Friars Street	B1	Shore Road	B2
Burghmuir Road	B1-B2	Glebe Avenue	A1-B1	Spital Street	A2
Castle Hill	A2	Goosecroft Road	B1-B2	Upper Bridge Street	A2
Clarendon Place	A1	Greenwood Avenue	A1	Upper Castle Hill	A2
		Harvey Wynd	A2	Upper Craigs	B1
		Irvine Place	A2-B2	Victoria Place	A1
		James Street	B2	Victoria Square	A1
		King Street	B1	Wallace Street	B2
		Mar Place	A2	Windsor Place	A1

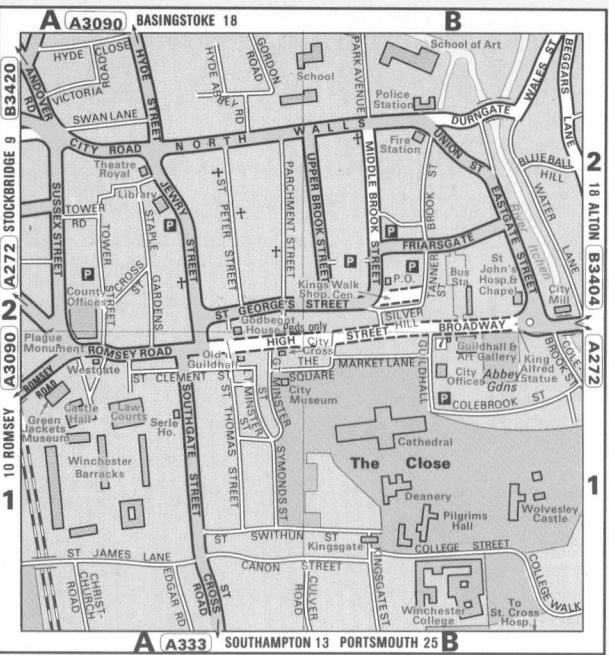

WINCHESTER

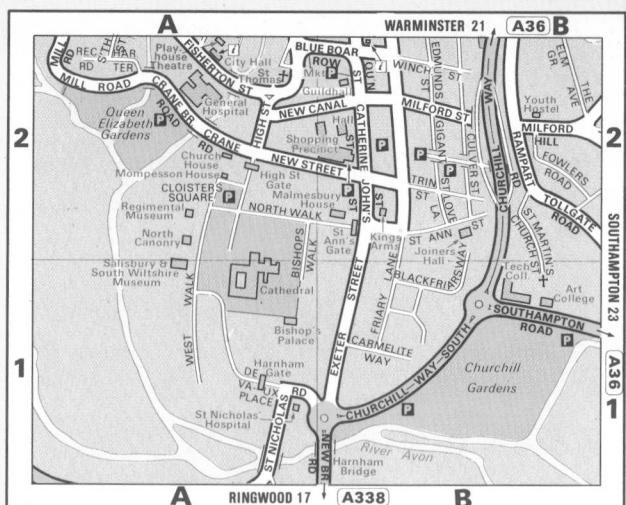

SALISBURY

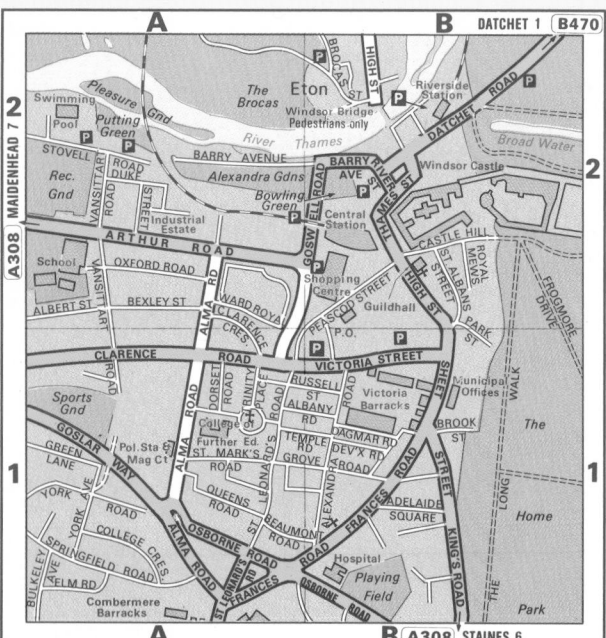

WINDSOR

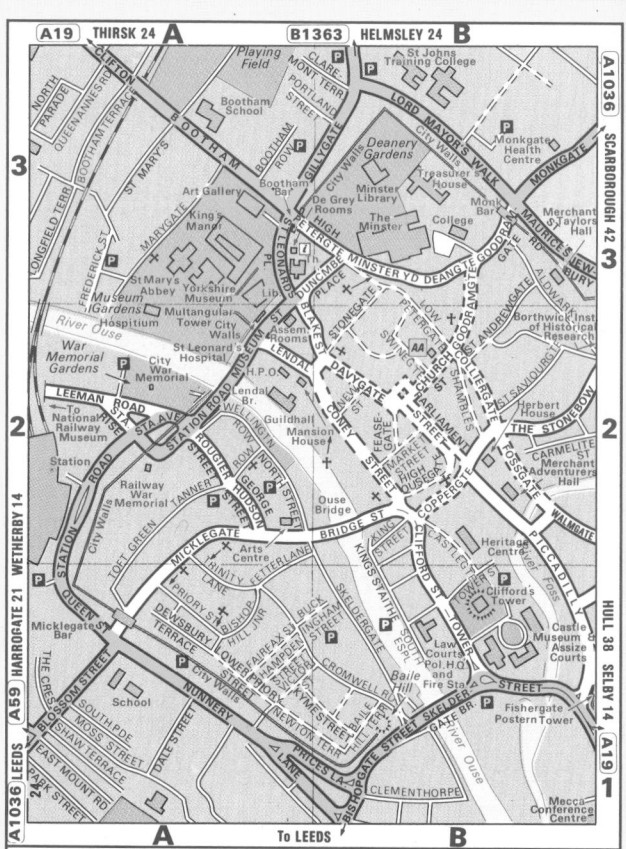

YORK

LONDON

London District

CHELMSFORD

Romford

Becontree

TILBURY

Beckton

Barking

A13

Erith

WELLING

ROCHESTER DOVER

SEVENOAKS MAIDSTONE

Sidcup Orpington

Orpington

Woolwich
Free Ferry
Weekdays 0600 - 2215hrs
Sundays 0740 - 2145hrs

Key to Inner London Maps

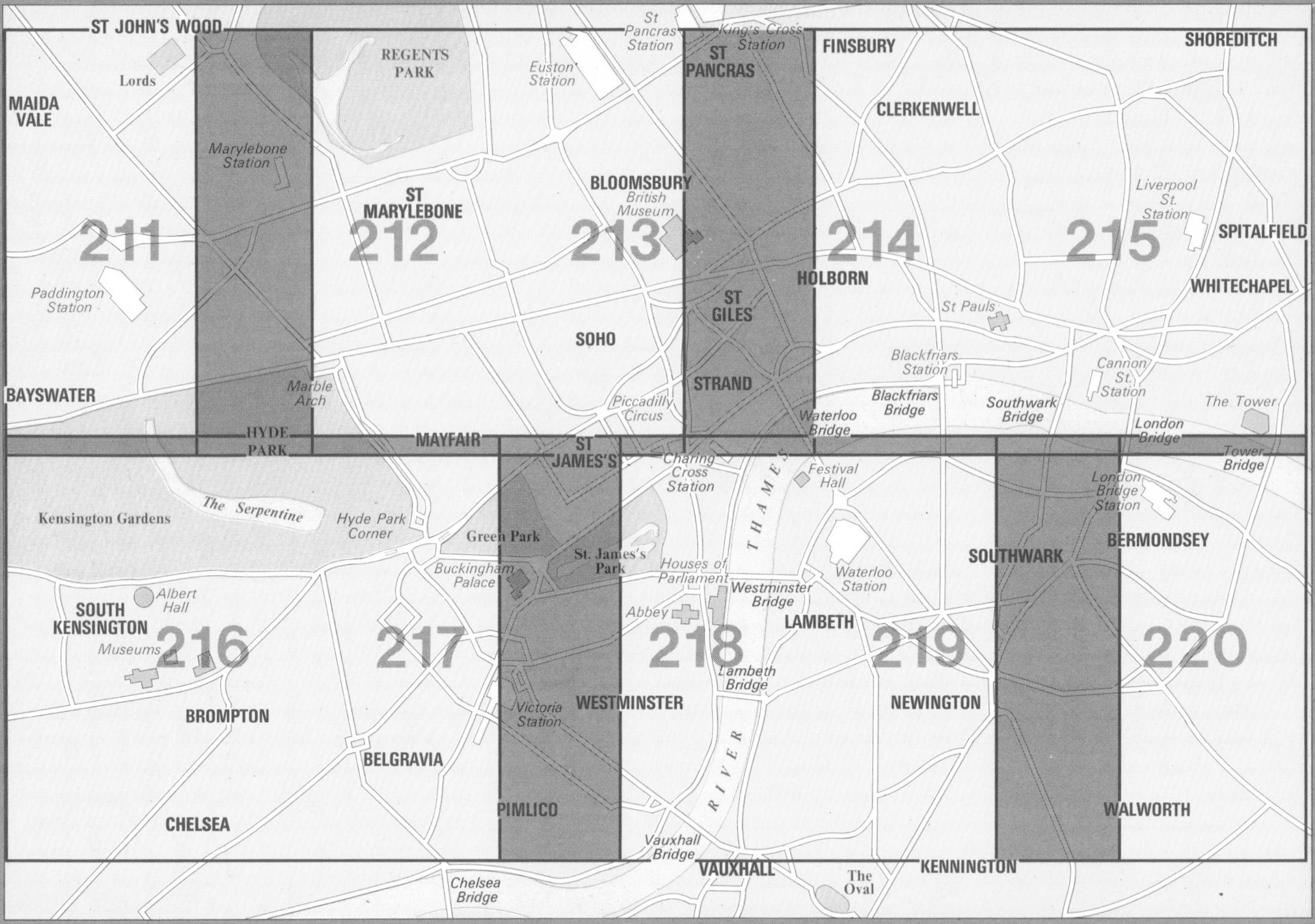

Map grid

ST JOHN'S WOOD				SHOREDITCH
Lords	REGENTS PARK	St Pancras Station	King's Cross Station	
MAIDA VALE		Euston Station	ST PANCRAS	FINSBURY
Marylebone Station			CLERKENWELL	Liverpool St. Station
211	ST MARYLEBONE **212**	BLOOMSBURY British Museum **213**	HOLBORN **214**	**215** SPITALFIELD
Paddington Station		SOHO	St Pauls	WHITECHAPEL
BAYSWATER	Marble Arch	ST GILES STRAND	Blackfriars Station	Cannon St. Station
		Piccadilly Circus	Blackfriars Bridge	Southwark Bridge
HYDE PARK	MAYFAIR	ST JAMES'S	Waterloo Bridge	London Bridge
Kensington Gardens	The Serpentine	Charing Cross Station	Festival Hall	Tower Bridge
Hyde Park Corner	Green Park	THAMES	Waterloo Station	London Bridge Station
SOUTH KENSINGTON Albert Hall	Buckingham Palace	St. James's Park	Westminster Bridge	SOUTHWARK BERMONDSEY
Museums **216**	**217**	Abbey **218** Houses of Parliament	LAMBETH **219**	**220**
BROMPTON		WESTMINSTER Lambeth Bridge	NEWINGTON	
	BELGRAVIA	Victoria Station		WALWORTH
CHELSEA		PIMLICO		
	Chelsea Bridge	Vauxhall Bridge	KENNINGTON	
		VAUXHALL The Oval		

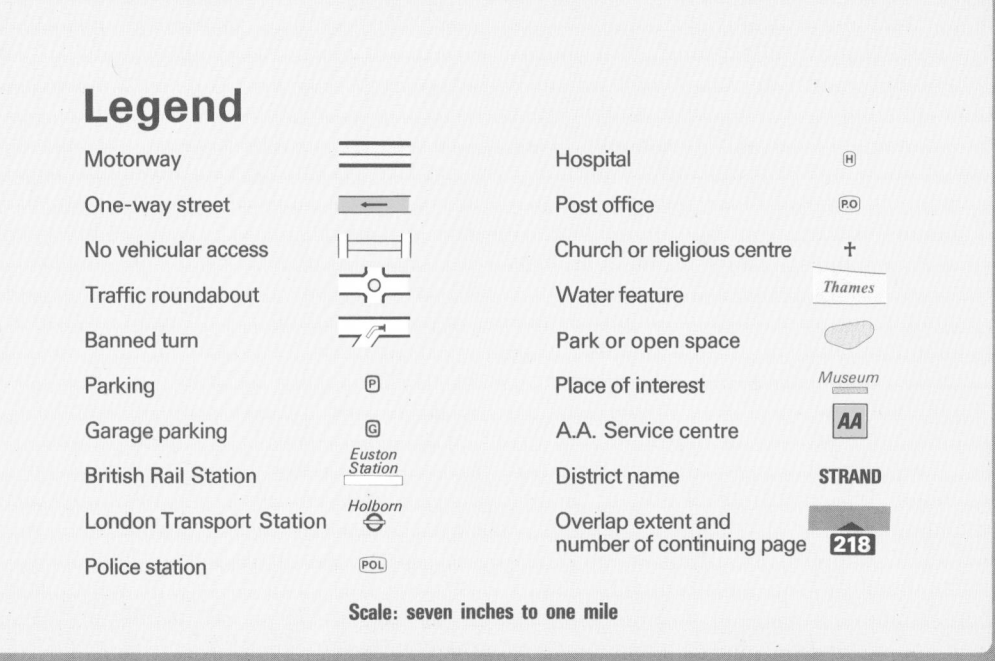

Legend

Motorway	≡≡≡		Hospital	Ⓗ
One-way street	←		Post office	P.O
No vehicular access	⊢⊣		Church or religious centre	†
Traffic roundabout	○		Water feature	*Thames*
Banned turn			Park or open space	
Parking	Ⓟ		Place of interest	*Museum*
Garage parking	Ⓖ		A.A. Service centre	**AA**
British Rail Station	Euston Station		District name	**STRAND**
London Transport Station	Holborn		Overlap extent and number of continuing page	**218**
Police station	POL			

Scale: seven inches to one mile

REGENTS PARK

A   B   C

REGENTS PARK

Nuffield Foundation

Ladbroke
Westmoreland
Hotel

London
Central
Mosque

St John's Hall
(Bedford Collage)

Boat
House

Boat
House

Open Air
Theatre

ALBANY STREET

CHESTER GATE

ST MARYLEBONE

Boating
Lake

Queen Mary's Gardens

Royal College
of Obstetricians
& Gynaecologists

Bedford
College

INNER CIRCLE

Royal College
of Physicians

CHESTER GATE

St ANDREW'S PLACE

211

Cockpit
Theatre

Rudolf
Steiner Hall

CLARENCE
GATE

Park
Square

Gt. Portland
Street

MARYLEBONE STATION

L.T.
Lost
Property
Office

Madam
Tussaud's

Royal Academy
of Music

Regents
Park

D   E   F

Harewood
Hotel

Marylebone

Planetarium
Times Centre

Baker St

London
Clinic

R.I.B.A.

Western
Ophthalmic
Hospital

Town
Hall

MARYLEBONE
CIRCUS

Polytechnic
of
Central London

Princess
Grace
Hospital

Screen on
Baker Street

Samaritan
Hospital

Seymour
Hall

Nat Heart
Hosp

G   H   J

Fitzroy
Nuffield
Hospital

Clifton Ford
Hotel

Wallace
Collection

Wigmore
Hall

Classic

Holiday
Inn

Portman
Intercontinental
Hotel

Home
House

Londoner
Hotel

New Mandeville
Hotel

Royal Coll of
Medicine

Bryanston
Court Hotel

PORTMAN
SQUARE

Churchill
Hotel

Selfridge
Hotel

Stratford
Court Hotel

Mostyn
Hotel

Portman Mews
South

Bond Street

Cumberland
Hotel

Mount Royal
Hotel

Odeon

OXFORD   STREET

Marble
Arch

Marble Arch

U.S.
Embassy

Claridges
Hotel

London Marriott
Hotel

Aeolian

K   L   M

MAYFAIR

OXFORD STREET

Oxford Street, where specially marked, is closed
to through traffic (except buses & taxis)
0700 hours – 1900 Monday – Saturday.

Britannia
Hotel

Grosvenor
House
Hotel

U.S.
Library

Connaught
Hotel

Mayfair
Theatre & Gate

Exit and Entrance to
Underground Car Park

217

BAYSWATER   ROAD

HYDE PARK

MAYFAIR

216

KENSINGTON

A

B

HYDE

C

The Long Water

Peter Pan

211

POL

BUCK HILL WALK

THE RING

Round Pond

Physical Energy

Serpentine Bridge

Norwegian / British Monument

SERPENTINE

ROAD

Boat House

Pier

Restaurant & Cafe

Lido

The Serpentine

KENSINGTON

Serpentine Gallery

GARDENS

THE DIAL WALK

THE FLOWER WALK

Albert Mem

ROTTEN

Kensington Palace

THE AVENUE

Royal Garden Hotel

NEW RIDE

CARRIAGE

THE

Knightsbridge Barracks

Bay

KENSINGTON

D

ROAD

KENSINGTON GORE

E

ALEXANDRA GATE

KENSINGTON

ROAD

KNIGHT

Kensington Palace Hotel

PALACE GATE

HYDE PARK GATE

QUEEN'S GATE

Princes Gate

PRINCE OF WALES GATE

RUTLAND GATE

Knights

ENNISMORE

TREVOR ST

RAPHAEL ST

Knightsbridge Fire Station

Kensington Court

De Vere Hotel

DE VERE GARDENS

PALACE GATE

Jay Mews

Royal Albert Hall

Royal Geographical Society

Royal School of Needlework

MONTPELIER SQUARE

TREVOR SQ

LANCELOT PL

P.O

Capital Hotel

Prince of Wales Hotel

Albert Place

Douro Place

CANNING PLACE

KENSINGTON GATE

QUEEN'S GATE MEWS

PRINCE CONSORT ROAD

Royal College of Music

PRINCE'S GARDENS

ENNISMORE GDNS

RUTLAND GDNS

MONTPELIER MEWS

MONTPELIER

F

HANS

BROMPTON PL

BASIL ST

Alban's Grove

VICTORIA GROVE

GLOUCESTER ROAD

LAUNCESTON PLACE

QUEEN'S GATE TERRACE

GORE STREET

Prince's Gardens

ENNISMORE GARDENS

ENNISMORE ST

BROMPTON

BEAUFORT GARDENS

COTTESMORE GDNS

Christ Church

PETERSHAM PLACE

Embassy House Hotel

Imperial College

ENNISMORE GARDENS MEWS

CHEVAL PLACE

OVINGTON SQUARE

WALTON PLACE

ELDON ROAD

KYNANCE MEWS

ELVASTON PL

PETERSHAM MEWS

QUEEN'S GATE PL

City & Guilds College

Brompton Oratory

BROMPTON SQUARE

OVINGTON SQUARE

LENNOX GARDENS

ORNWALL GARDENS

QUEEN'S GATE PLACE

Science Museum

Brompton Oratory

BROMPTON ROAD

EGERTON GDNS

OVINGTON STREET

HASKER STREET

CLABON

ORNWALL GARDENS

QUEENS GATE GDNS

British Museum of Natural History

Geological Museum

Victoria and Albert Museum

EXHIBITION ROAD

LENNOX GDNS MEWS

permarket

EMPEROR'S GATE

SOUTHWELL GDNS

Leicester Court Hotel

QUEENS GATE GDNS

QUEEN'S GATE MEWS

Baden-Powell House

CROMWELL

THURLOE PLACE

Rembrandt Hotel

EGERTON TERR

MILNER

GRENVILLE PLACE

Buckingham Hotel

Hosp

Tudor Court Hotel

CROMWELL GDNS

PLACE

THURLOE SQUARE

THURLOE ST

ALEXANDER PL

WALTON STREET

RAWLINGS STREET

MOORE STREET

ASHBURN GDNS

Milton Court Hotel

Stanhope Court Hotel

Eden Plaza Hotel

QUEENSBERRY PLACE

CROMWELL MEWS

THURLOE

SOUTH TERRACE

DONNE PLACE

FIRST STREET

HALSEY STREET

COLLINGHAM GARDENS

Forum Hotel

Gloucester Road

ASHBURN MEWS

STANHOPE GARDENS

HARRINGTON

ROAD

Norfolk Hotel

South Kensington

PELHAM STREET

PELHAM

CADOGAN

I

Gloucester Hotel

COLBECK MEWS

COURTFIELD GARDENS

ASHBURN PD

STANHOPE MEWS E

MANSON PLACE

SUMNER PLACE

ONSLOW SQUARE

PELHAM CRESCENT

SLOANE AVENUE

DRAYCOTT AVENUE

J

COLLINGHAM GARDENS

HARRINGTON GARDENS

Eden Hotel

CLAREVILLE ST

CLAREVILLE GROVE

Onslow Court Hotel

SUMNER PLACE

ONSLOW SQUARE

SYDNEY PLACE

LUCAN PLACE

ELYSTAN STREET

POL

PETYWARD

DRAYCOTT

WETHERBY PLACE

SOUTH KENSINGTON

GLEDHOW GARDENS

CRANLEY PLACE

BROMPTON ROAD

CRANLEY PLACE

ONSLOW GARDENS

ONSLOW

SYDNEY PLACE

IXWORTH PLACE

WHITEHEAD'S

P.O

ELYSTAN PLACE

BOLTON GARDENS

OLD

BROMPTON

ROAD

CRISSWELL PLACE

EVELYN GARDENS

ROLAND WAY

ROLAND GARDENS

CRANLEY GARDENS

Brompton Hosp

STEWARTS GROVE

SYDNEY STREET

CALE STREET

CALE STREET

ST LUKES STREET

ASTELL STREET

GODFREY STREET

MARKHAM STREET

MARKHAM SQUARE

BYWATER STREET

SMITH STREET

SOUTH KENSINGTON

FULHAM

ROAD

THE BOLTONS

PRIORY WALK

HARLEY GARDENS

THISTLE GROVE

ELM PARK GARDENS

SOUTH PARADE

Royal Marsden Hosp

CHELSEA SQUARE

Women's Hosp

DOVEHOUSE STREET

BRITTEN STREET

BURNSALL

Chelsea Cinema

CHELSEA

REDCLIFFE SQUARE

K

REDCLIFFE GARDENS

GILSTON ROAD

FULHAM

ROAD

ABC Cinema

ELM PARK ROAD

CHURCH

L

CHELSEA

Chelsea Fire Station

P.O

Chelsea Town Hall

KING'S ROAD

M

WELLINGTON SQUARE

REDCLIFFE MEWS

HARCOURT TERRACE

TREGUNTER ROAD

CARLYLE SQ

CARLYLE SQUARE

OAKLEY STREET

MANRESA ROAD

REDBURNE ST

SMITH TERRACE

TEDWORTH SQ

REDCLIFFE

THE LITTLE BOLTONS

The London Street Index

This map employs an arbitrary system of grid reference. Pages are identified by numbers and divided into twelve squares. Each square contains a blue letter; all references give the page number first, followed by the letter of the square in which a particular street can be found. Reference for Exhibition Road is *216 E*, meaning that the relevant map is on page *216* and that the street appears in the square designated E.

London Street Index

London Street Index

London Street Index

Principal Airports

Heathrow Airport, London *tel* 01-759 4321

The world's busiest International Airport, Heathrow lies just 16 miles of the capital and is well served by the surrounding road and Public Transport network. Access to the passenger terminals is via the Heathrow tunnel, which links the central area with the M4 or the A4 Bath Road. Heathrow central station is connected to the capital's underground network, linking the airport with central London in and about 45 minutes.

Aberdeen (Dyce)	Aberdeen (6m) (0224) 2331, 574281, 722331
Alderney	St Agnes (048 182) 2886, 2889, 2711
Barra	Island Foreshore, Barra (889 3181) 041
Bembridge	Sandown (098 387) 2511, (098 384) 2646
Benbecula	Benbecula, South Uist (0870) 2051
Biggin Hill	Biggin Hill (09594) 72277
Birmingham (Elmdon)	Birmingham (5½m) (021) 743 4272, 779 2537
Blackpool (Squires Gate)	Blackpool (2½m) (0253) 43061
Bournemouth (Hurn)	Bournemouth (5m); Christchurch (3m) (02016) 78646
Bristol (Lulsgate)	Bristol (7m) (027587) 4441
Campbeltown (Machrihanish)	Campbeltown (5m) (0586) 2571
Cambridge	Cambridge (1½m) (0223) 61133
Cardiff-Wales	Cardiff (10m) (0446) 710296
Carlise (Crosby)	Carlise (6m) (022873) 641
Compton Abbas	Shaftesbury (3m) Fontmell Magna 767
Coventry	Coventry (3m) (0203) 301717, 301792
Dundee	Dundee (0382) 69451
East Midlands	Derby (7m) (0332) 810621
Edinburgh	Edinburgh (5m) (031) 334 2351
Elstree	Watford, Herts (2½m) (01-953) 3502, 4411
Exeter	Exeter (4½m) (0392) 67433
Fairoaks	Woking, Surrey (2m) (099 05) 7300, 7700
Ford	Arundel (3m) (09064) 3094
Glasgow (Abbotsinch)	Glasgow (6m) (041) 887 1111
Glenforsa (Mull)	Salen, Isle of Mull, Aros 377
Gloucester/Cheltenham (Staverton)	
	Gloucester (4m); Cheltenham (4m) (0452) 713351, 712285
Goodwood	Chichester (2m) (0243) 83165, 82065
Guernsey	St Peter Port (2½m) (0481) 37766
Hawarden	Chester (4m) (0244) 24646
Humberside	Grimsby (10m); Scunthorpe (15m) (065 28) 456
Inverness (Dalcross)	Inverness (7m) (06676) 2280

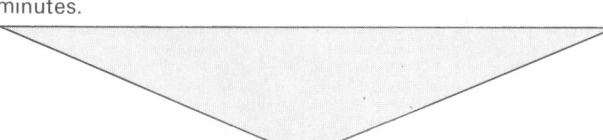

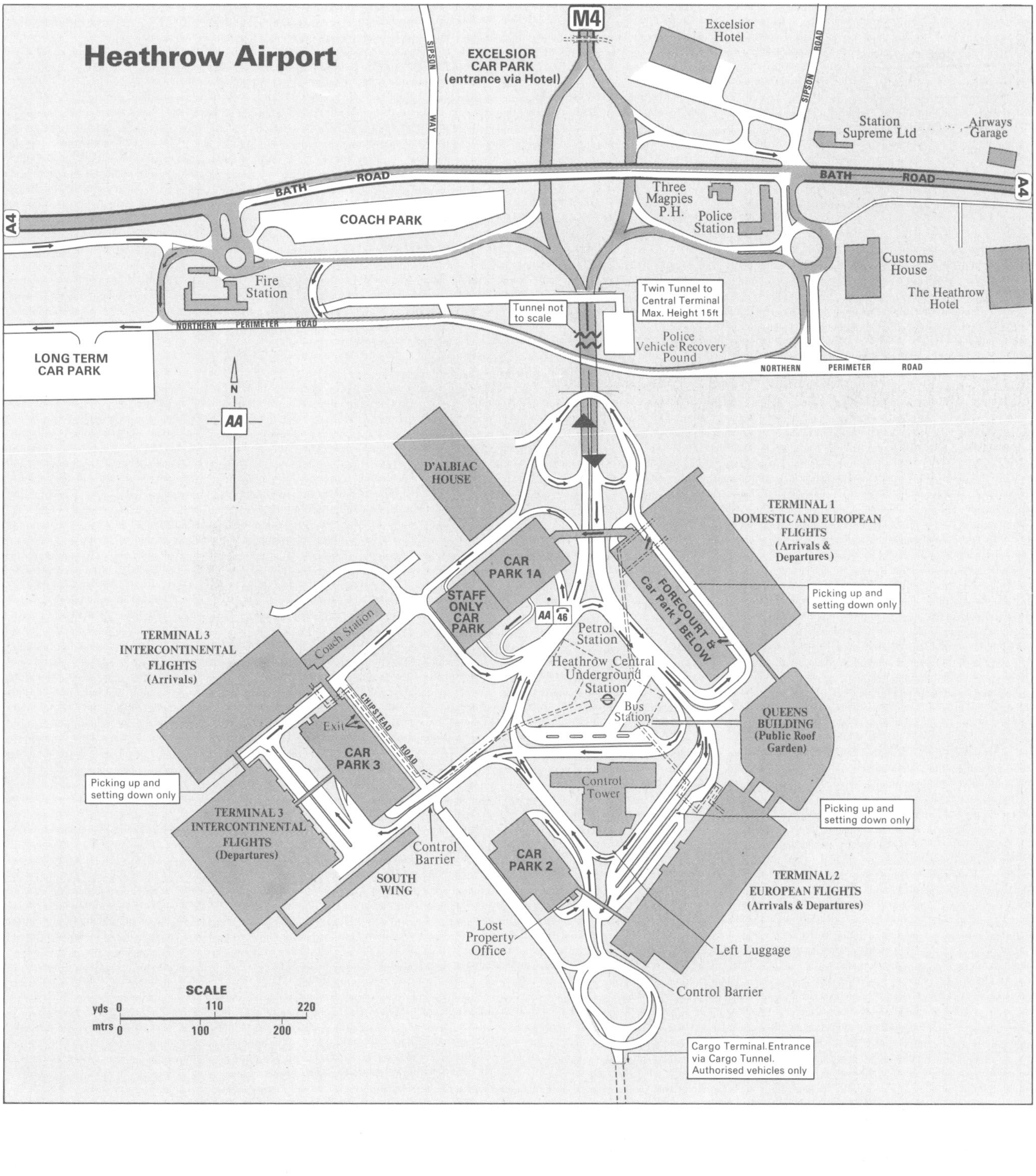

Heathrow Airport

EXCELSIOR CAR PARK (entrance via Hotel)

Excelsior Hotel

Station Supreme Ltd

Airways Garage

BATH ROAD

COACH PARK

Three Magpies P.H.

Police Station

Customs House

The Heathrow Hotel

Fire Station

Twin Tunnel to Central Terminal Max. Height 15ft

Tunnel not to scale

Police Vehicle Recovery Pound

NORTHERN PERIMETER ROAD

LONG TERM CAR PARK

N

AA

D'ALBIAC HOUSE

TERMINAL 1 DOMESTIC AND EUROPEAN FLIGHTS (Arrivals & Departures)

CAR PARK 1A

STAFF ONLY CAR PARK

Picking up and setting down only

FORECOURT & Car Park 1 BELOW

TERMINAL 3 INTERCONTINENTAL FLIGHTS (Arrivals)

Coach Station

AA 46

Petrol Station

Heathrow Central Underground Station

Bus Station

QUEENS BUILDING (Public Roof Garden)

Exit

CHRISTEAD ROAD

CAR PARK 3

Picking up and setting down only

TERMINAL 3 INTERCONTINENTAL FLIGHTS (Departures)

Control Barrier

SOUTH WING

Control Tower

CAR PARK 2

Picking up and setting down only

TERMINAL 2 EUROPEAN FLIGHTS (Arrivals & Departures)

Left Luggage

Lost Property Office

Control Barrier

SCALE
yds 0 — 110 — 220
mtrs 0 — 100 — 200

Cargo Terminal. Entrance via Cargo Tunnel. Authorised vehicles only

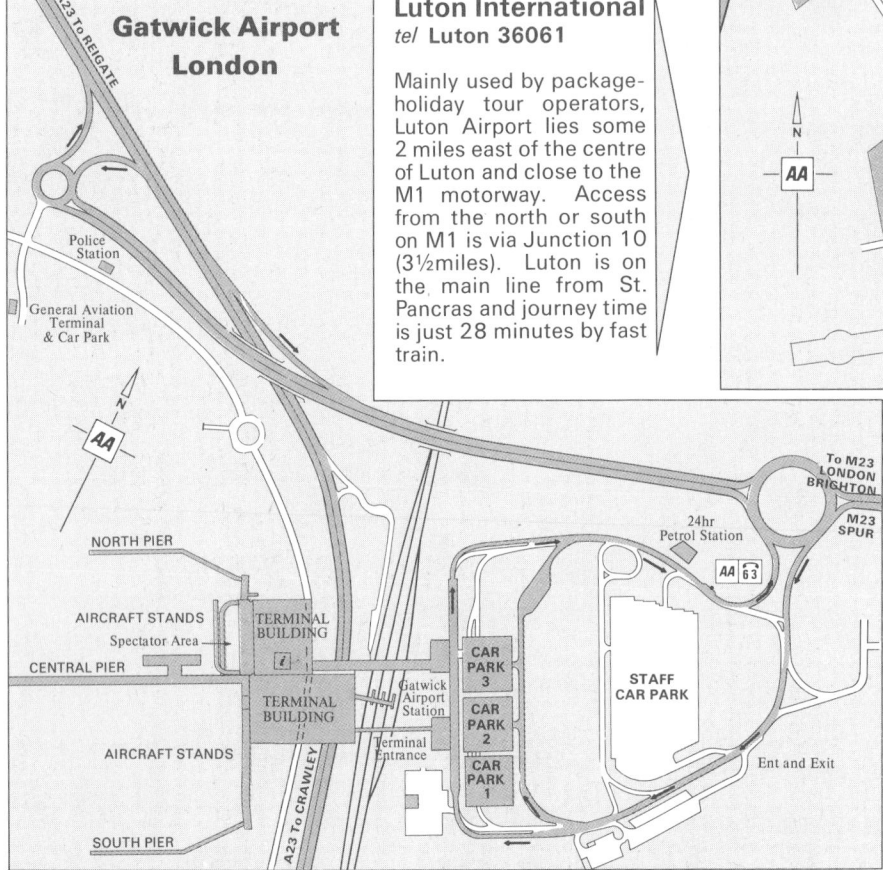

Manchester International Airport
tel 061-437 5233

The largest UK airport outside London, Manchester International Airport lies just 9 miles south of Manchester city centre, Access to the airport is via junction 5 on the M56 motorway, which is connected to the extensive national motorway network. The nearest railway station is Heald Green about 2 miles from the airport

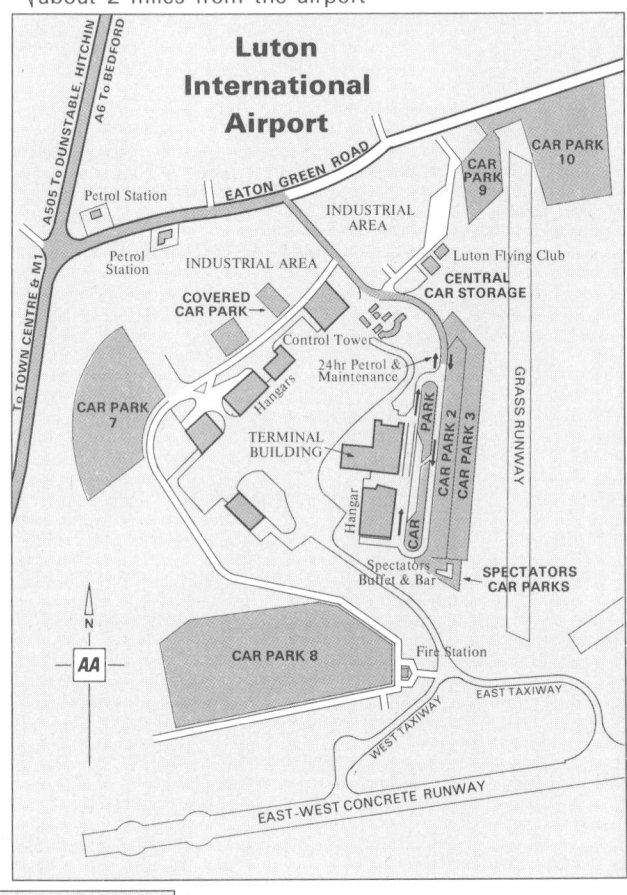

Luton International
tel Luton 36061

Mainly used by package-holiday tour operators, Luton Airport lies some 2 miles east of the centre of Luton and close to the M1 motorway. Access from the north or south on M1 is via Junction 10 (3½miles). Luton is on the main line from St. Pancras and journey time is just 28 minutes by fast train.

Gatwick Airport London
tel Crawley 28822

Most of the major airlines operate from Gatwick. It is also open to aircraft diverted from Heathrow, as well as the charter services of other airline companies. Access to Gatwick Airport is available from the M23 and A2... roads. There are ample parking facilities for both short and long stays. ... helicopter service links Gatwick with Heathrow in just 15 minutes, whilst fast rail services connect Gatwick Airport station with London (Victoria) in about 40 minutes.

Index to Atlas

The towns and villages shown on the main maps of this atlas are listed alphabetically in the index. To find a place in the atlas, use the reference numbers given with each placename. The relevant page number is given with the National Grid reference number, so that the place can be quickly and accurately pinpointed. The National Grid system is explained on page XIII.

Ardpeaton 228 Bartestree

Ardpeaton 90 NS 2185
Ardrishaig 89 NR 8585
Ardroil 109 NB 0432
Ardrossan 82 NS 2342
Ardshealach 95 NM 6967
Ardsley 59 SE 3805
Ardsley East 59 SE 3024
Ardslignish 95 NM 5661
Ardtalnaig 91 NN 7039
Ardullie 102 NH 5963
Ardvasar 95 NG 6303
Ardwell 68 NX 1045
Areley Kings 41 SO 8070
Argoed Mill 27 SN 9962
Aridhglas 88 NM 3123
Arinacrinachd 101 NG 7458
Arinagour 94 NM 2257
Arisaig 95 NM 6586
Arivruach 109 NB 2417
Arkendale 66 SE 3860
Arkesden 35 TL 4834
Arkholme 64 SD 5871
Arkley 21 TQ 2296
Arksey 60 SE 5706
Arkwright Town 53 SK 4270
Arlecdon 62 NY 0419
Arlesey 35 TL 1936
Arleston 41 SJ 6410
Arley (Ches.) 51 SJ 6780
Arley (Warw.) 43 SP 2890
Arlingham 32 SO 7010
Arlington (Devon) 6 SS 6140
Arlington (Glos.) 32 SP 1006
Arlington (E Susx) 13 TQ 5407
Armadale (Highld.) 111 NC 7864
Armadale (Lothian) 84 NS 9368
Armathwaite 71 NY 5046
Arminghall 47 TG 2504
Armitage 42 SK 0816
Armscote 33 SP 2444
Armthorpe 60 SE 6105
Arnabost 94 NM 2159
Arncliffe 65 SD 9371
Arncliffe Cote 65 SD 9470
Arncott 34 SP 6117
Arncroach 93 NO 5105
Arnesby 43 SP 6192
Arngask 92 NO 1310
Arnisdale 101 NG 8411
Arniston Engine 85 NT 3462
Arnol 109 NB 3148
Arnprior 90 NS 6194
Arnside 63 SD 4578
Arrad Foot 62 SD 3080
Arram 61 TA 0344
Arrathorne 65 SE 2093
Arreton 11 SZ 5386
Arrington 35 TL 3250
Arrochar 90 NN 2904
Arrow 32 SP 0856
Artafallie 102 NH 6249
Arthington 59 SE 2644
Arthingworth 44 SP 7581
Arthog 39 SH 6414
Arthrath 105 NJ 9636
Artrochie 105 NK 0032
Arundel 12 TQ 0107
Aryhoulan 96 NN 0168
Asby 62 NY 0620
Ascog 82 NS 1063
Ascot 20 SU 9168
Ascott-under-Wychwood 33 SP 2918
Asenby 66 SE 3975
Asfordby 44 SK 7018
Asfordby Hill 44 SK 7219
Asgarby (Lincs.) 55 TF 1145
Asgarby (Lincs.) 55 TF 3366
Ash (Kent) 21 TQ 5964
Ash (Kent) 15 TR 2958
Ash (Somer.) 9 ST 4720
Ash Bullayne 7 SS 7704
Ash Magna 51 SJ 5739
Ash Mill 7 SS 7823
Ash Priors 16 ST 1429
Ash Thomas 8 ST 0010
Ashampstead 19 SU 5676
Ashbocking 37 TM 1654
Ashbourne 52 SK 1846
Ashbrittle 8 ST 0521
Ashburton 5 SX 7569
Ashbury (Devon.) 6 SX 5097
Ashbury (Oxon.) 18 SU 2685
Ashby Folville 44 SK 7012
Ashby Magna 43 SP 5690
Ashby Parva 43 SP 5288
Ashby St. Ledgers 43 SP 5768
Ashby St. Mary 47 TG 3202
Ashby by Partney 55 TF 4266
Ashby cum Fenby 61 TA 2500
Ashby de la Launde 54 TF 0455
Ashby-de-la-Zouch 43 SK 3516
Ashchurch 32 SO 9233
Ashcombe 8 SX 9179
Ashcott 17 ST 4336
Ashdon 36 TL 5842
Asheldham 23 TL 9701
Ashen 36 TL 7442
Ashendon 34 SP 7014
Ashfield (Central) 91 NN 7803
Ashfield (Suff.) 37 TM 2062
Ashfield Green 37 TM 2673
Ashford (Derby.) 52 SK 1969
Ashford (Devon.) 6 SS 5335
Ashford (Kent) 15 TR 0142
Ashford (Surrey) 20 TQ 0671
Ashford Bowdler 40 SO 5170
Ashford Carbonel 40 SO 5270
Ashford Hill 19 SU 5562
Ashgill 84 NS 7849
Ashill (Devon) 8 ST 0811
Ashill (Norf.) 46 TF 8804
Ashill (Somer.) 8 ST 3217
Ashingdon 22 TQ 8693
Ashington (Northum.) 79 NZ 2687
Ashington (W Susx) 12 TQ 1315
Ashkirk 77 NT 4722
Ashleworth 32 SO 8125
Ashley (Cambs.) 36 TL 6961
Ashley (Ches.) 51 SJ 7784
Ashley (Devon.) 7 SS 6411
Ashley (Glos.) 18 ST 9394
Ashley (Hants.) 11 SU 3831
Ashley (Northants.) 44 SP 7991
Ashley (Staffs.) 51 SJ 7536
Ashley Green 34 SP 9705
Ashley Heath 10 SU 1105
Ashmansworth 19 SU 4156
Ashmansworthy 6 SS 3317
Ashmore 10 ST 9117
Ashorne 33 SP 3057
Ashover 53 SK 3463
Ashow 44 SP 3170
Ashperton 31 SO 6441
Ashprington 5 SX 8157
Ashreigney 6 SS 6213
Ashtead 21 TQ 1858
Ashton (Ches.) 50 SJ 5069
Ashton (Corn.) 2 SW 6028
Ashton (Devon.) 5 SX 8584
Ashton (Here. and Worc.) 30 SO 5164
Ashton (Northants.) 34 SP 7649
Ashton (Northants.) 45 TL 0588
Ashton Common 18 ST 8958
Ashton Keynes 18 SU 0494
Ashton under Hill 32 SO 9938
Ashton upon Mersey 51 SJ 7792
Ashton-in-Makerfield 57 SJ 5799
Ashton-under-Lyne 51 SJ 9399
Ashurst (Hants.) 11 SU 3310
Ashurst (Kent) 13 TQ 5038
Ashurst (W Susx) 12 TQ 1716
Ashurstwood 13 TQ 4236
Ashwater 6 SX 3895
Ashwell (Herts.) 35 TL 2639
Ashwell (Leic.) 44 SK 8613
Ashwellthorpe 47 TM 1397
Ashwick 17 ST 6447
Ashwicken 46 TF 7018
Askam in Furness 64 SD 2177
Askern 60 SE 5613
Askerswell 9 SY 5292
Askett 34 SP 8105
Askham (Cumbr.) 63 NY 5123
Askham (Notts.) 54 SK 7374
Askham Bryan 60 SE 5548
Askham Richard 60 SE 5347
Askrigg 65 SD 9491
Askwith 59 SE 1648
Aslackby 45 TF 0830
Aslacton 47 TM 1591
Aslockton 54 SK 7440
Aspatria 70 NY 1442
Aspenden 35 TL 3528
Asperton 34 SP 9436
Aspley Guise 34 SP 9436
Aspull 58 SD 6108
Asselby 60 SE 7127
Assington 36 TL 9338
Astbury 51 SJ 8461
Astcote 34 SP 6753
Asterley 40 SJ 3707
Asterton 40 SO 3991
Asthall 33 SP 2811
Asthall Leigh 33 SP 3012
Astley (Here. and Worc.) 41 SO 7867
Astley (Salop) 40 SJ 5218
Astley (Warw.) 43 SP 3189
Astley Abbots 41 SO 7096
Astley Cross 41 SO 8069
Astley Green 58 SJ 7099
Aston (Berks.) 20 SU 7884
Aston (Ches.) 61 SJ 5578
Aston (Ches.) 51 SJ 6046
Aston (Derby.) 52 SK 1883
Aston (Here. and Worc.) 40 SO 4571
Aston (Herts.) 35 TL 2722
Aston (Oxon.) 33 SP 3302
Aston (S Yorks.) 53 SK 4685
Aston (Salop) 40 SJ 5228
Aston (Salop) 41 SJ 6109
Aston (Staffs.) 41 SJ 7540
Aston (Staffs.) 41 SJ 9131
Aston (W Mids) 42 SP 0789
Aston Abbotts 34 SP 8420
Aston Botterell 41 SO 6284
Aston Cantlow 32 SP 1359
Aston Clinton 34 SP 8812
Aston Crews 29 SO 6723
Aston End 35 TL 2724
Aston Eyre 41 SO 6594
Aston Flamville 43 SP 4692
Aston Ingham 29 SO 6823
Aston Magna 33 SP 1935
Aston Rogers 40 SJ 3406
Aston Rowant 20 SU 7299
Aston Sandford 34 SP 7507
Aston Somerville 32 SP 0438
Aston Subedge 32 SP 1341
Aston Tirrold 19 SU 5586
Aston Upthorpe 19 SU 5586
Aston juxta Mondrum 51 SJ 6556
Aston le Walls 33 SP 4950
Aston on Clun 40 SO 3981
Aston-on-Trent 43 SK 4129
Astwick 35 TL 2138
Astwood 34 SP 9547
Astwood Bank 32 SP 0362
Aswarby (Lincs.) 54 TF 0639
Aswardby (Lincs.) 54 TF 3770
Atcham 40 SJ 5408
Athelington 37 TM 2170
Athelney 17 ST 3428
Athelstaneford 86 NT 5377
Atherington 6 SS 5923
Atherstone 43 SP 3097
Atherstone on Stour 33 SP 2050
Atherton 58 SD 6703
Atlow 53 SK 2248
Attenborough 53 SK 5134
Attleborough (Norf.) 47 TM 0495
Attleborough (Warw.) 43 SP 3790
Attlebridge 47 TG 1216
Atwick 67 TA 1850
Atworth 18 ST 8565
Aubourn 54 SK 9262
Auchagallon 81 NR 8934
Aucharnie 104 NJ 6341
Auchattie 99 NO 6994
Auchenblae 99 NO 7278
Auchenbrack 84 NS 7988
Auchencairn 69 NX 7951
Auchencarroch 90 NS 4182
Auchencrow 87 NT 8560
Auchendinny 85 NT 2561
Auchengray 85 NS 9953
Auchenhalrig 104 NJ 3661
Auchenheath 84 NS 8043
Auchentiber 82 NS 3647
Auchgourish 103 NH 9315
Auchindrain 89 NN 0303
Auchindrean 106 NH 1980
Auchininna 105 NJ 6446
Auchinleck (Strath.) 75 NS 5422
Auchinloch 84 NS 6670
Auchintore 96 NN 0972
Auchleuchries 105 NK 0136
Auchleven 104 NJ 6224
Auchlochan 84 NS 8037
Auchlyne 90 NN 5129
Auchmillan 75 NS 5129
Auchmithie 99 NO 6744
Auchmuirbridge 92 NO 2101
Auchnacree 98 NO 4663
Auchnagatt 105 NJ 9341
Auchronie 98 NO 4480
Auchterarder 91 NN 9312
Auchterderran 92 NT 2195
Auchterhouse 93 NO 3337
Auchtermuchty 92 NO 2311
Auchterneed 102 NH 4959
Auchtertool 92 NT 2190
Auchtoo 90 NN 5620
Auckengill 112 ND 3764
Auckley 60 SE 6501
Audenshaw 58 SJ 9196
Audlem 51 SJ 6543
Audley 51 SJ 7950
Aughton (Humbs.) 60 SE 7038
Aughton (Lancs.) 57 SD 3804
Aughton (Lancs.) 64 SD 5467
Aughton (S Yorks.) 53 SK 4586
Aughton Park 57 SD 4106
Auldearn 103 NH 9155
Aulden 30 SO 4654
Auldhame 86 NT 5984
Auldhouse 84 NS 6250
Ault-a-chrinn 101 NG 9420
Aultbea 106 NG 8789
Aultgrishan 106 NG 7485
Aultiphurst 111 NC 8065
Aultmore (Grampn.) 104 NJ 4053
Aultnagoire 102 NH 5423
Aulton 104 NJ 6028
Aundorach 103 NH 9716
Aunsby 54 TF 0438
Auquhorthies 105 NJ 8329
Aust 29 ST 5789
Austerfield 53 SK 6594
Austonley 59 SE 1207
Austrey 43 SK 2906
Austwick 65 SD 7668
Authorpe 55 TF 4080
Authorpe Row 55 TF 5373
Avebury 18 SU 0969
Aveley 21 TQ 5680
Avening 18 ST 8797
Averham 54 SK 7654
Aveton Gifford 5 SX 6947
Avielochan 103 NH 9016
Aviemore 103 NH 8912
Avington 19 SU 3767
Avoch 103 NH 6955
Avon 10 SZ 1498
Avon Dassett 33 SP 4150
Avonbridge 84 NS 9072
Avonmouth 29 ST 5177
Avonwick 5 SX 7158
Awbridge 11 SU 3323
Awkley 29 ST 5885
Awliscombe 8 ST 1301
Awre 32 SO 7008
Awsworth 53 SK 4843
Axbridge 17 ST 4254
Axford (Hants.) 19 SU 6043
Axford (Wilts.) 18 SU 2369
Axminster 8 SY 2998
Axmouth 8 SY 2591
Aylburton 29 SO 6101
Ayle 71 NY 7149
Aylesbeare 8 SY 0391
Aylesbury 34 SP 8213
Aylesby 61 TA 2007
Aylesford 14 TQ 7359
Aylesham 15 TR 2352
Aylestone 43 SK 5701
Aylmerton 47 TG 1839
Aylsham 47 TG 1926
Aylton 31 SO 6537
Aymestrey 30 SO 4265
Aynho 33 SP 5133
Ayot St. Lawrence 35 TL 1916
Ayot St. Peter 35 TL 2115
Ayr 75 NS 3321
Aysgarth 65 SE 0088
Ayside 62 SD 3983
Ayston 44 SK 8601
Aythorpe Roding 22 TL 5815
Ayton (Berwick.) 87 NT 9260
Ayton (N Yorks.) 67 SE 9884
Azerley 66 SE 2574

B

Babbinswood 40 SJ 3329
Babcary 17 ST 5628
Babel 27 SN 8235
Babell 50 SJ 1574
Babraham 35 TL 5150
Babworth 53 SK 6880
Back 109 NB 4840
Back of Keppoch 95 NM 6587
Backaland 113 HY 5630
Backbarrow 62 SD 3584
Backford 50 SJ 3971
Backhill of Clackriach 105 NJ 9347
Backies 108 NC 8302
Backmuir of New Gilston 93 NO 4308
Backwell 29 ST 4868
Backworth 79 NZ 2972
Bacon End 22 TL 6018
Baconsthorpe 47 TG 1237
Bacton (Here. and Worc.) 30 SO 3732
Bacton (Norf.) 47 TG 3434
Bacton (Suff.) 37 TM 0466
Bacup 58 SD 8622
Badachro 106 NG 7873
Badavanich 102 NH 1258
Badbury 18 SU 1980
Badby 33 SP 5559
Badcall (Highld.) 110 NC 1541
Badcall (Highld.) 110 NC 2355
Badcaul 106 NH 0191
Baddeley Green 51 SJ 9250
Baddesley Ensor 42 SP 2798
Baddidarach 110 NC 0923
Badenscoth 105 NJ 7038
Badenyon 104 NJ 3419
Badger 41 SO 7699
Badgers Mount 21 TQ 5061
Badgeworth (Glos.) 32 SO 9019
Badgworth (Somer.) 17 ST 3952
Badingham 37 TM 3067
Badlesmere 15 TR 0154
Badluarach 106 NG 9994
Badminton 18 ST 8082
Badrallach 106 NH 0691
Badsey 32 SP 0743
Badsworth 60 SE 4614
Badwell Ash 36 TL 9969
Bagby 66 SE 4680
Bagendon 32 SP 0006
Bagillt 50 SJ 2175
Baginton 43 SP 3474
Baglan 24 SS 7493
Bagley 40 SJ 4027
Bagnall 51 SJ 9250
Bagshot (Surrey) 20 SU 9163
Bagshot (Wilts.) 19 SU 3165
Bagthorpe (Norf.) 46 TF 7932
Bagthorpe (Notts.) 53 SK 4751
Bagworth 43 SK 4408
Bagwy Llydiart 29 SO 4427
Baildon 59 SE 1539
Baile Mor 88 NM 2824
Bailebeag 102 NH 5018
Baillieston 84 NS 6764
Bainbridge 66 SD 9390
Bainton (Cambs.) 45 TF 0906
Bairnkine 78 NT 6515
Baker Street 22 TQ 6381
Baker's End 35 TL 3917
Bakewell 53 SK 2168
Bala 49 SH 9236
Balallan 109 NB 2720
Balbeg 102 NH 4924
Balbeggie 92 NO 1629
Balbithan 105 NJ 7917
Balblair 103 NH 7066
Balchladich 110 NC 0330
Balchraggan 102 NH 5343
Balchrick 110 NC 1960
Balcombe 13 TQ 3130
Balcurvie 93 NO 3400
Baldersby 66 SE 3578
Balderstone 58 SD 6332
Balderton 54 SK 8151
Baldhu 2 SW 7743
Baldinnie 93 NO 4311
Baldock 35 TL 2434
Baldrine 56 SC 4281
Baldwin 57 SC 3581
Baldwin's Gate 51 SJ 7939
Baldwinholme 70 NY 3351
Bale 46 TG 0136
Balemartine 94 NL 9841
Balephuil 94 NL 9640
Balerno 85 NT 1666
Balfield 99 NO 5468
Balfour 113 HY 4716
Balfron 84 NS 5488
Balgarva 109 NF 7647
Balgaveny 105 NJ 6640
Balgavies 99 NO 5351
Balgedie 92 NO 1603
Balgove 105 NJ 8133
Balgowan 97 NN 6394
Balgown 100 NG 3868
Balgray 93 NO 4138
Balgrochan 84 NS 6278
Balhalgardy 105 NJ 7623
Balhary 98 NO 2646
Baligill 111 NC 8566
Balintore (Highld.) 108 NH 8675
Balintore (Tays.) 98 NO 2859
Balintraid 108 NH 7370
Balivanich 109 NF 7755
Balkeerie 98 NO 3244
Balkholme 60 SE 7828
Ball 40 SJ 3026
Ball Hill 19 SU 4263
Ballabeg 56 SC 2470
Ballacannell 56 SC 4382
Ballacarnane Beg 56 SC 3088
Ballachulish 96 NN 0758
Ballajora 56 SC 4790
Ballamodha 56 SC 2773
Ballantree 68 NX 0882
Ballasalla (I. of M.) 56 SC 2870
Ballater 98 NO 3695
Ballaugh 56 SC 3493
Ballchraggan 108 NH 7775
Ballechin 97 NN 9353
Ballencrieff 86 NT 4878
Ballevullin 94 NL 9546
Balliekine 81 NR 8739
Ballig 56 SC 2882
Ballinaby 80 NR 2267
Ballindean 93 NO 2529
Ballinger Common 34 SP 9103
Ballingham 31 SO 5731
Ballingry 92 NT 1797
Ballinluig 98 NN 9852
Ballintuim 98 NO 1054
Balloch (Highld.) 103 NH 7346
Balloch (Strath.) 90 NS 3981
Balloch (Tays.) 91 NN 8419
Balloch (Tays.) 98 NO 3557
Ballochan 99 NO 5290
Balls Cross 12 SU 9826
Ballsalla (I. of M.) 56 SC 3497
Ballygown 94 NM 4343
Ballygrant 80 NR 3966
Ballymichael 81 NR 9231
Balmacara 101 NG 8028
Balmaclellan 69 NX 6578
Balmacneil 98 NN 9850
Balmae 69 NX 6845
Balmaha 90 NS 4290
Balmalcolm 93 NO 3108
Balmedie 105 NJ 9617
Balmerino 93 NO 3525
Balmerlawn 11 SU 3003
Balmore 84 NS 6073
Balmullo 93 NO 4220
Balmungie 103 NH 7359
Balnacra 101 NG 9746
Balnaguard 97 NN 9451
Balnaguisich 108 NH 6771
Balnahard 88 NM 4534
Balnakeil 110 NC 3968
Balnaknock 100 NG 4162
Balnapaling 103 NH 7969
Balquhidder 90 NN 5320
Balsall Common 42 SP 2377
Balscote 33 SP 3841
Balsham 36 TL 5850
Baltasound (Unst) 113 HP 6208
Balterley 51 SJ 7550
Balthangie 105 NJ 8351
Baltonsborough 17 ST 5434
Balvaird 102 NH 5452
Balvicar 89 NM 7616
Bamburgh 87 NU 1834
Bamford 53 SK 2083
Bampton (Cumbr.) 63 NY 5118
Bampton (Devon.) 8 SS 9522
Bampton (Oxon.) 33 SP 3103
Banavie 96 NN 1177
Banbury 33 SP 4540
Banc-y-ffordd 26 SN 4037
Banchory 99 NO 6995
Banchory-Devenick 99 NJ 9101
Bancyfelin 25 SN 3218
Banff 105 NJ 6863
Bangor 48 SH 5872
Bangor-is-y-coed 50 SJ 3945
Banham 47 TM 0688
Bank 11 SU 2807
Bank Newton 65 SD 9152
Bank Street 31 SO 6362
Bankend (Dumf. and Galwy.) 70 NY 0268
Bankend (Strath.) 84 NS 8033
Bankfoot 92 NO 0635
Bankglen 76 NS 5912
Bankhead (Grampn.) 104 NJ 6608
Bankhead (Grampn.) 105 NJ 8910
Banks 113 HY 4331
Banks (Cumbr.) 71 NY 5664
Banks (Lancs.) 57 SD 3820
Bankshill 70 NY 1981
Banningham 47 TG 2129
Bannister Green 22 TL 6920
Bannockburn 91 NS 8190
Banstead 21 TQ 2559
Bantham 5 SX 6643
Banton 84 NS 7479
Banwell 17 ST 3959
Bapchild 15 TQ 9363
Bar Hill 35 TL 3864
Barassie 82 NS 3232
Baravulin 89 NM 9040
Barbaraville 108 NH 7471
Barber Booth 52 SK 1184
Barbon 63 SD 6282
Barbrook 7 SS 7147
Barby 43 SP 5470
Barcaldine 96 NM 9743
Barcheston 33 SP 2639
Barcombe 13 TQ 4214
Barcombe Cross 13 TQ 4216
Barden 65 SE 1493
Bardfield Saling 22 TL 6826
Bardney 55 TF 1169
Bardon Mill 71 NY 7764
Bardowie 84 NS 5873
Bardrainney 82 NS 3372
Bardsea 64 SD 3074
Bardsey 59 SE 3643
Bardsley 58 SD 9201
Bardwell 36 TL 9473
Barewood 30 SO 3856
Barford (Norf.) 47 TG 1107
Barford (Warw.) 33 SP 2660
Barford St. Martin 10 SU 0531
Barford St. Michael 33 SP 4332
Barfreston 15 TR 2650
Bargoed 28 SO 1500
Bargrennan 68 NX 3476
Barham (Cambs.) 45 TL 1375
Barham (Kent) 15 TR 2050
Barham (Suff.) 37 TM 1451
Barholm 45 TF 0811
Barkby 43 SK 6310
Barkestone-le-Vale 54 SK 7734
Barkham 20 SU 7866
Barking (Gtr London) 21 TQ 4785
Barking (Suff.) 37 TM 0653
Barkingside 21 TQ 4489
Barkisland 59 SE 0419
Barkston (Lincs.) 54 SK 9241
Barkston (N Yorks.) 60 SE 4936
Barkway 35 TL 3835
Barlaston 51 SJ 8938
Barlavington 12 SU 9716
Barlborough 53 SK 4777
Barlby 60 SE 6334
Barlestone 43 SK 4205
Barley (Herts.) 35 TL 4038
Barley (Lancs.) 58 SD 8240
Barleythorpe 44 SK 8409
Barling 23 TQ 9289
Barlow (Derby.) 53 SK 3474
Barlow (N Yorks.) 60 SE 6428
Barlow (Tyne and Wear) 72 NZ 1560
Barmby Moor 60 SE 7748
Barmby on the Marsh 60 SE 6828
Barmer 46 TF 8133
Barmouth 38 SH 6115
Barmpton 72 NZ 3118
Barmston 67 TA 1659
Barnack 45 TF 0705
Barnacle 43 SP 3884
Barnard Castle 72 NZ 0516
Barnard Gate 33 SP 4010
Barnardiston 36 TL 7148
Barnburgh 60 SE 4803
Barnby 47 TM 4789
Barnby Dun 60 SE 6109
Barnby Moor 53 SK 6684
Barnby in the Willows 54 SK 8552
Barnes 21 TQ 2276
Barnet 21 TQ 2496
Barnetby le Wold 61 TA 0509
Barney 46 TF 9932
Barnham (Suff.) 36 TL 8779
Barnham (W Susx) 12 SU 9604
Barnham Broom 47 TG 0807
Barnhead 99 NO 6657
Barnhill 104 NJ 1457
Barnhills 68 NW 9871
Barningham (Durham) 72 NZ 0810
Barningham (Suff.) 36 TL 9676
Barnoldby le Beck 61 TA 2303
Barnoldswick 58 SD 8746
Barns Green 12 TQ 1227
Barnsley (Glos.) 32 SP 0705
Barnsley (S Yorks.) 59 SE 3406
Barnstaple 6 SS 5533
Barnston (Essex) 22 TL 6519
Barnston (Mers.) 50 SJ 2783
Barnt Green 41 SP 0073
Barnton 51 SJ 6374
Barnwell All Saints 45 TL 0584
Barnwood 32 SO 8518
Barr 75 NX 2794
Barrachan 68 NX 3649
Barrack (Grampn) 105 NJ 8942
Barrapoll 94 NL 9542
Barras 99 NO 8580
Barrasford 78 NY 9273
Barregarrow 57 SC 3288
Barrhead 82 NS 5058
Barrhill (Strath.) 68 NX 2382
Barrington (Cambs.) 35 TL 3949
Barrington (Somer.) 9 ST 3918
Barripper 2 SW 6338
Barrmill 82 NS 3651
Barrow (Lancs.) 58 SD 7338
Barrow (Leic.) 44 SK 8815
Barrow (Salop) 41 SJ 6500
Barrow (Somer.) 17 ST 7231
Barrow (Suff.) 36 TL 7663
Barrow Gurney 29 ST 5267
Barrow Street 10 ST 8330
Barrow upon Humber 61 TA 0721
Barrow upon Soar 43 SK 5717
Barrow upon Trent 43 SK 3528
Barrow-in-Furness 64 SD 1969
Barrowby 54 SK 8736
Barrowden 44 SK 9400
Barrowford 58 SD 8538
Barry (S Glam.) 28 ST 1168
Barry (Tays) 93 NO 5334
Barry Island 28 ST 1166
Barsby 43 SK 6911
Barsham 47 TM 3989
Barston 42 SP 2078
Bartestree 31 SO 5641

Barthol Chapel 229 Blunham

Barthol Chapel 105 NJ 8134
Barthomley 51 SJ 7652
Bartley 11 SU 3012
Bartlow 36 TL 5845
Barton (Cambs.) 35 TL 4055
Barton (Ches.) 50 SJ 4454
Barton (Devon.) 8 SX 9067
Barton (Glos.) 32 SP 0925
Barton (Lancs.) 57 SD 5136
Barton (N Yorks.) 66 NZ 2208
Barton (Warw.) 32 SP 1051
Barton Bendish 46 TF 7105
Barton Hartshorn 34 SP 6431
Barton Mills 36 TL 7273
Barton Seagrave 44 SP 8877
Barton St. David 17 ST 5431
Barton Stacey 19 SU 4340
Barton Turf 47 TG 3522
Barton in Fabis 53 SK 5232
Barton in the Beans 43 SK 3906
Barton in the Clay 35 TL 0831
Barton on Sea 11 SZ 2493
Barton-Upon-Humber 61 TA 0222
Barton-le-Street 66 SE 7274
Barton-le-Willows 66 SE 7163
Barton-on-the-Heath 33 SP 2532
Barton-under-Needlewood 42 SK 1818
Barvas 109 NB 3649
Barway 45 TL 5475
Barwell 43 SP 4496
Barwick 9 ST 5513
Barwick in Elmet 59 SE 3937
Baschurch 40 SJ 4222
Bascote 33 SP 4063
Basford Green 51 SJ 9951
Bashall Eaves 58 SD 6943
Bashley 11 SZ 2496
Basildon (Berks.) 19 SU 6078
Basildon (Essex) 22 TQ 7189
Basingstoke 19 SU 6351
Baslow 53 SK 2572
Bason Bridge 17 ST 3445
Bassenthwaite 62 NY 2332
Bassett 11 SU 4116
Bassingbourn 35 TL 3344
Bassingfield 53 SK 6137
Bassingham 54 SK 9059
Bassingthorpe 44 SK 9628
Basta 113 HU 5295
Baston 45 TF 1114
Bastwick 47 TG 4217
Batcombe (Dorset.) 9 ST 6104
Batcombe (Somer.) 17 ST 6838
Bate Heath 51 SJ 6879
Bath 18 ST 7464
Bathampton 18 ST 7765
Bathealton 8 ST 0724
Batheaston 18 ST 7767
Bathford 18 ST 7866
Bathgate 85 NS 9768
Bathley 54 SK 7759
Bathpool 4 SX 2874
Batley 59 SE 2424
Batsford 33 SP 1834
Battersea 21 TQ 2876
Battisford 37 TM 0554
Battisford Tye 36 TM 0254
Battle (E Susx.) 14 TQ 7416
Battlefield 40 SJ 5117
Battlesbridge 22 TQ 7794
Battlesden 34 SP 9628
Battleton 16 SS 9127
Battramsley 11 SZ 3099
Baughurst 19 SU 5859
Baulking 19 SU 3190
Baumber 55 TF 2174
Baunton 32 SP 0204
Baverstock 10 SU 0231
Bawburgh 47 TG 1508
Bawdeswell 47 TG 0420
Bawdrip 17 ST 3339
Bawdsey 37 TM 3440
Bawtry 53 SK 6592
Baxenden 58 SD 7726
Baxterley 43 SP 2796
Bayble 109 NB 5231
Baydon 19 SU 2877
Bayford 35 TL 3108
Bayhead 109 NF 7468
Bayles 71 NY 7044
Baylham 37 TM 1051
Bayston Hill 40 SJ 4809
Bayton 41 SO 6973
Beachampton 34 SP 7737
Beachley 29 ST 5591
Beacon 8 ST 1705
Beacon End 23 TL 9524
Beacon's Bottom 20 SU 7895
Beaconsfield 20 SU 9490
Beadlam 66 SE 6584
Beadnell 87 NU 2329
Beaford 6 SS 5514
Beal (N Yorks.) 60 SE 5325
Beal (Northum.) 87 NU 0642
Bealings 37 TM 2348
Beaminster 9 ST 4801
Beamish 72 NZ 2253
Beamsley 65 SE 0752
Bean 21 TQ 5872
Beanacre 18 ST 9066
Beanley 79 NU 0818
Beare Green 12 TQ 1842
Bearley 33 SP 1760
Bearpark 72 NZ 2343
Bearsbridge 71 NY 7857
Bearsden 84 NS 5471
Bearsted 14 TQ 8055
Bearwood 10 SZ 0496
Beattock 77 NT 0702
Beauchamp Roding 22 TL 5809
Beauchief 53 SK 3381
Beaufort 28 SO 1611
Beaulieu 11 SU 3801
Beauly 102 NH 5246
Beaumaris 48 SH 6076
Beaumont (Cumbr.) 70 NY 3459
Beaumont (Essex) 23 TM 1725
Beausale 42 SP 2470
Beaworthy 6 SX 4699
Beazley End 22 TL 7428
Bebington 50 SJ 3384
Bebside 79 NZ 2881
Beccles 47 TM 4290
Becconsall 57 SD 4422
Beck Row 36 TL 6977
Beck Side 62 SD 2382
Beckbury 41 SJ 7601
Beckenham 21 TQ 3769
Beckermet 62 NY 0206
Beckfoot (Cumbr.) 70 NY 0949
Beckford 32 SO 9735
Beckhampton 18 SU 0868
Beckingham (Lincs.) 54 SK 8753
Beckingham (Notts.) 54 SK 7790
Beckington 18 ST 7951
Beckley (E Susx.) 14 TQ 8423
Beckley (Oxon) 33 SP 5611
Beckton 21 TQ 4381
Beckwithshaw 66 SE 2653
Becontree 21 TQ 4886
Bedale 66 SE 2688
Bedburn 72 NZ 1031
Beddau 28 ST 0585
Beddgelert 48 SH 5848
Beddingham 13 TQ 4408
Beddington 21 TQ 3165
Bedfield 37 TM 2266
Bedford 35 TL 0449
Bedhampton 12 SU 6906
Bedingfield 37 TM 1768
Bedlington 79 NZ 2581
Bedlinog 28 SO 0901
Bedmond 35 TL 0903
Bednall 41 SJ 9517
Bedrule 78 NT 6017
Bedstone 40 SO 3675
Bedwas 28 ST 1689
Bedworth 43 SP 3587
Beeby 43 SK 6608
Beech (Hants.) 11 SU 6938
Beech (Staffs.) 51 SJ 8538
Beech Hill 19 SU 6964
Beechingstoke 18 SU 0859
Beedon 19 SU 4877
Beeford 67 TA 1254
Beeley 53 SK 2667
Beelsby 61 TA 2001
Beenham 19 SU 5868
Beer 8 SY 2289
Beer Hackett 9 ST 5911
Beercrocombe 8 ST 3220
Beesby 55 TF 4680
Beeson 5 SX 8140
Beeston (Beds.) 35 TL 1648
Beeston (Ches.) 50 SJ 5358
Beeston (Norf.) 46 TF 9015
Beeston (Notts.) 53 SK 5336
Beeston (W Yorks.) 59 SE 2930
Beeston Regis 47 TG 1742
Beeswing 69 NX 8969
Beetham 63 SD 4979
Beetley 46 TF 9718
Begbroke 33 SP 4613
Begelly 24 SN 1107
Beguildy 40 SO 1979
Beighton (Norf.) 47 TG 3808
Beighton (S Yorks.) 53 SK 4483
Beith 82 NS 3454
Bekesbourne 15 TR 1955
Belaugh 47 TG 2818
Belbroughton 41 SO 9177
Belchamp Otten 36 TL 8041
Belchamp St. Paul 36 TL 7942
Belchamp Walter 36 TL 8240
Belchford 54 TF 2975
Belford 87 NU 1033
Belhelvie 105 NJ 9417
Bell Busk 65 SD 9056
Bellabeg 104 NJ 3513
Bellanoch 89 NR 7992
Bellaty 98 NO 2459
Belleau 55 TF 4078
Bellehiglash 104 NJ 1837
Bellerby 65 SE 1192
Belliehill 99 NO 5663
Bellingdon 34 SP 9405
Bellingham 78 NY 8383
Belloch 81 NR 6737
Bellochantuy 80 NR 6632
Bells Yew Green 13 TQ 6136
Bellsbank 75 NS 4804
Bellshill (Northum.) 87 NU 1230
Bellshill (Strath.) 84 NS 7360
Bellspool 85 NT 1635
Bellsquarry 85 NT 0465
Belmaduthy 103 NH 6556
Belmesthorpe 45 TF 0410
Belmont (Lancs.) 58 SD 6715
Belmont (Unst) 113 HP 5600
Belnacraig 104 NJ 3716
Belowda 3 SW 9661
Belper 53 SK 3447
Belsay 79 NZ 1078
Belses 78 NT 5725
Belsford 5 SX 7659
Belstead 37 TM 1341
Belston 75 NS 3820
Belstone 5 SX 6193
Belthorn 58 SD 7124
Beltoft 60 SE 8006
Belton (Humbs.) 60 SE 7806
Belton (Leic.) 43 SK 4420
Belton (Leic.) 44 SK 8101
Belton (Lincs.) 54 SK 9239
Belton (Norf.) 47 TG 4802
Belvedere 21 TQ 4978
Belvoir 54 SK 8133
Bembridge 11 SZ 6488
Bemersyde 86 NT 5933
Bempton 67 TA 1972
Benacre 47 TM 5184
Benenden 14 TQ 8033
Benholm 99 NO 8069
Benington (Herts.) 35 TL 3023
Benington (Lincs.) 55 TF 3946
Benllech 48 SH 5182
Benmore (Central) 90 NN 4125
Bennacott 4 SX 2991
Bennecarrigan 74 NR 9423
Benniworth 55 TF 2081
Benover 14 TQ 7048
Benson 19 SU 6191
Benthall (Northum.) 87 NU 2328
Benthall (Salop) 41 SJ 6602
Bentham 32 SO 9116
Bentley (Hants.) 12 SU 7844
Bentley (Humbs.) 61 TA 0135
Bentley (S Yorks.) 60 SE 5605
Bentley (Warw.) 43 SP 2895
Bentley Heath 42 SP 1676
Bentpath 77 NY 3190
Bentworth 19 SU 6640
Benvie 93 NO 3231
Benwick 45 TL 3490
Beoley 42 SP 0669
Beoraidbeg 95 NM 6793
Bepton 12 SU 8518
Berden 35 TL 4629
Bere Alston 4 SX 4466
Bere Ferrers 5 SX 4563
Bere Regis 10 SY 8494
Berea 24 SM 7929
Berepper 2 SW 6522
Bergh Apton 47 TG 3000
Berinsfield 19 SU 5696
Berkeley 29 ST 6899
Berkhamsted 34 SP 9907
Berkley 18 ST 8049
Berkswell 42 SP 2479
Bermondsey 21 TQ 3579
Bernisdale 100 NG 4050
Berrick Salome 19 SU 6293
Berriew 40 SJ 1801
Berrington (Northum.) 87 NU 0043
Berrington (Salop) 40 SJ 5206
Berrow 17 ST 2952
Berrow Green 32 SO 7458
Berry Hill 29 SO 5712
Berry Pomeroy 5 SX 8261
Berryhillock 104 NJ 5060
Berrynarbor 6 SS 5546
Bersham 50 SJ 3048
Bersted 12 SU 9300
Berwick 13 TQ 5105
Berwick Bassett 15 SU 0973
Berwick Hill 79 NZ 1775
Berwick St. James 10 SU 0739
Berwick St. John 10 ST 9421
Berwick St. Leonard 10 ST 9233
Berwick-upon-Tweed 87 NT 9953
Besford 32 SO 9144
Bessacarr 60 SE 6101
Bessels Leigh 33 SP 4501
Bessingham 47 TG 1636
Besthorpe (Norf.) 47 TM 0695
Besthorpe (Notts.) 54 SK 8264
Beswick 61 TA 0148
Betchworth 21 TQ 2149
Bethel 48 SH 5265
Bethersden 15 TQ 9240
Bethesda (Dyfed) 24 SN 0918
Bethesda (Gwyn.) 48 SH 6266
Bethlehem 25 SN 6825
Bethnal Green 21 TQ 3583
Betley 51 SJ 7548
Betsham 22 TQ 6071
Betteshanger 15 TR 3152
Bettiscombe 9 SY 3999
Bettisfield 50 SJ 4535
Betton (Salop) 51 SJ 6836
Bettws Bledrws 26 SN 5952
Bettws Cedewain 40 SO 1296
Bettws Evan 26 SN 3047
Bettws Gwerfil Goch 49 SJ 0346
Bettws Malpas 29 ST 3090
Bettws-Newydd 29 SO 3606
Bettyhill 111 NC 7061
Betws 25 SN 6311
Betws (Mid Glam.) 28 SS 9086
Betws Garmon 48 SH 5357
Betws-y-coed 49 SH 7956
Betws-yn-Rhos 49 SH 9073
Beulah (Dyfed) 26 SN 2846
Beulah (Powys) 27 SN 9251
Bevendean 13 TQ 3406
Bevercotes 53 SK 6972
Beverley 61 TA 0339
Beverston 18 ST 8693
Bevington 29 ST 6596
Bewaldeth 62 NY 2134
Bewcastle 71 NY 5674
Bewdley 41 SO 7875
Bewerley 65 SE 1564
Bewholme 67 TA 1650
Bexhill 14 TQ 7407
Bexley 21 TQ 4973
Bexwell 46 TF 6303
Beyton 36 TL 9363
Bibury 32 SP 1106
Bicester 33 SP 5822
Bickenhall 8 ST 2818
Bickenhill 42 SP 1882
Bicker 55 TF 2237
Bickerstaffe 57 SD 4404
Bickerton (Ches.) 50 SJ 5052
Bickerton (N Yorks.) 66 SE 4450
Bickington (Devon.) 6 SS 5332
Bickington (Devon.) 5 SX 7972
Bickleigh (Devon.) 8 SS 9407
Bickleigh (Devon.) 5 SX 5262
Bickleton 6 SS 5031
Bickley 21 TQ 4268
Bickley Moss 50 SJ 5448
Bicknacre 22 TL 7802
Bicknoller 16 ST 1039
Bicknor 14 TQ 8658
Bickton 10 SU 1412
Bicton (Salop) 40 SJ 4415
Bicton (Salop) 40 SO 2882
Bidborough 13 TQ 5643
Biddenden 14 TQ 8538
Biddenham 34 TL 0250
Biddestone 18 ST 8673
Biddisham 17 ST 3853
Biddlesden 34 SP 6340
Biddlestone 78 NT 9508
Biddulph 51 SJ 8857
Biddulph Moor 51 SJ 9057
Bideford 6 SS 4526
Bidford-on-Avon 32 SP 1052
Bielby 60 SE 7843
Bieldside 99 NJ 8702
Bierley 11 SZ 5077
Bierton 34 SP 8415
Bigbury 5 SX 6646
Bigbury-on-Sea 5 SX 6544
Bigby 61 TA 0507
Biggar (Cumbr.) 64 SD 1966
Biggar (Strath.) 85 NT 0437
Biggin (Derby.) 52 SK 1559
Biggin (Derby.) 53 SK 2548
Biggin (N. Yorks.) 60 SE 5434
Biggin Hill 21 TQ 4159
Biggleswade 35 TL 1944
Bighouse 111 NC 8964
Bighton 11 SU 6134
Bignor 12 SU 9814
Bilberry 4 SX 0159
Bilborough 53 SK 5241
Bilbrook 41 SJ 8703
Bilbrough 60 SE 5246
Bilbster 112 ND 2852
Bildeston 36 TL 9949
Billericay 22 TQ 6794
Billesdon 44 SK 7103
Billesley 32 SP 1456
Billingborough 55 TF 1134
Billinge 57 SD 5300
Billingford (Norf.) 46 TG 0120
Billingford (Norf.) 37 TM 1678
Billingham 73 NZ 4624
Billinghay 54 TF 1554
Billingley 59 SE 4304
Billingshurst 12 TQ 0825
Billingsley 41 SO 7085
Billington (Beds.) 34 SP 9422
Billington (Lancs.) 58 SD 7235
Billockby 47 TG 4213
Billy Row 72 NZ 1637
Bilsborrow 57 SD 5140
Bilsby 55 TF 4776
Bilsington 15 TR 0434
Bilsthorpe 53 SK 6560
Bilston (Lothian) 85 NT 2664
Bilston (W Mids) 41 SO 9496
Bilstone 43 SK 3606
Bilting 15 TR 0549
Bilton (Humbs.) 61 TA 1532
Bilton (N Yorks.) 66 SE 4750
Bilton (Northum.) 79 NU 2210
Bilton (Warw.) 43 SP 4873
Binbrook 55 TF 2093
Bincombe 9 SY 6884
Binegar 17 ST 6149
Binfield 20 SU 8471
Binfield Heath 20 SU 7478
Bingfield 79 NY 9772
Bingham 54 SK 7039
Bingham's Melcombe 9 ST 7701
Bingley 59 SE 1039
Binham 46 TF 9839
Binley (Hants.) 19 SU 4153
Binley (W Mids) 43 SP 3778
Binniehill 84 NS 8572
Binstead (Hants.) 12 SU 7741
Binstead (I. of W.) 11 SZ 5792
Binton 32 SP 1454
Bintree 46 TG 0123
Binweston 40 SJ 3004
Birch (Essex) 23 TL 9419
Birch (Gtr. Mches.) 58 SD 8507
Birch Green 23 TL 9418
Birch Vale 52 SK 0286
Bircham Newton 46 TF 7633
Bircham Tofts 46 TF 7732
Birchanger 22 TL 5122
Bircher 30 SO 4765
Birchgrove (S Glam.) 28 ST 1679
Birchgrove (W Glam.) 25 SS 7098
Birchington 15 TR 3069
Birchover 53 SK 2462
Bircotes 53 SK 6391
Bird End 42 SP 0193
Birdbrook 36 TL 7041
Birdham 12 SU 8200
Birdingbury 43 SP 4368
Birdlip 32 SO 9214
Birdsgreen 41 SO 7685
Birdston 84 NS 6575
Birdwell 59 SE 3401
Birdwood 32 SO 7318
Birgham 87 NT 7939
Birkenhead 50 SJ 3188
Birkenhills 105 NJ 7445
Birkenshaw (Strath.) 84 NS 6962
Birkenshaw (W Yorks.) 59 SE 2028
Birkhall 98 NO 3493
Birkhill Feus 93 NO 3433
Birkin 60 SE 5226
Birley 30 SO 4553
Birling (Kent) 14 TQ 6860
Birling (Northum.) 79 NU 2406
Birlingham 32 SO 9343
Birmingham 42 SP 0787
Birnam 98 NO 0341
Birness 105 NJ 9933
Birse 99 NO 5596
Birsemore 99 NO 5297
Birstall 43 SK 5809
Birstall Smithies 59 SE 2226
Birstwith 66 SE 2459
Birtley (Here. and Worc.) 40 SO 3669
Birtley (Northum.) 78 NY 8778
Birtley (Tyne and Wear) 72 NZ 2755
Birts Street 32 SO 7836
Bisbrooke 44 SP 8899
Bishampton 32 SO 9851
Bishop Auckland 72 NZ 2029
Bishop Burton 61 SE 9839
Bishop Middleham 72 NZ 3231
Bishop Monkton 66 SE 3266
Bishop Norton 54 SK 9892
Bishop Sutton 17 ST 5859
Bishop Thornton 66 SE 2663
Bishop Wilton 67 SE 7955
Bishop's Castle 40 SO 3288
Bishop's Caundle 9 ST 6912
Bishop's Cleeve 32 SO 9527
Bishop's Frome 31 SO 6648
Bishop's Itchington 33 SP 3857
Bishop's Nympton 7 SS 7523
Bishop's Offley 41 SJ 7729
Bishop's Stortford 22 TL 4821
Bishop's Sutton 11 SU 6031
Bishop's Tachbrook 33 SP 3161
Bishop's Tawton 6 SS 5630
Bishop's Waltham 11 SU 5517
Bishop's Wood (Staffs.) 41 SJ 8309
Bishopis Caundle 9 ST 6913
Bishopbriggs 84 NS 6070
Bishops Cannings 18 SU 0364
Bishops Lydeard 16 ST 1629
Bishopsbourne 15 TR 1852
Bishopsteignton 8 SX 9173
Bishopstoke 11 SU 4619
Bishopston 15 SS 5889
Bishopstone (Bucks.) 34 SP 8010
Bishopstone (E Susx) 13 TQ 4701
Bishopstone (Here. and Worc.) 30 SO 4143
Bishopstone (Wilts.) 10 SU 0625
Bishopstone (Wilts.) 18 SU 2483
Bishopswood (Somer.) 8 ST 2512
Bishopsworth 29 ST 5768
Bishopthorpe 60 SE 5947
Bishopton (Durham) 72 NZ 3621
Bishopton (Strath.) 82 NS 4371
Bishton 29 ST 3887
Bisley (Glos.) 32 SO 9005
Bisley (Surrey) 20 SU 9559
Bispham 57 SD 3139
Bissoe 2 SW 7741
Bisterne Close 11 SU 2202
Bitchfield 44 SK 9828
Bittadon 6 SS 5441
Bittaford 5 SX 6557
Bittering 46 TF 9317
Bitterley 40 SO 5577
Bitterne 11 SU 4513
Bitteswell 43 SP 5385
Bitton 29 ST 6769
Bix 20 SU 7285
Blaby 43 SP 5697
Black Bourton 33 SP 2804
Black Callerton 72 NZ 1769
Black Crofts 89 NM 9234
Black Dog (Devon) 7 SS 8009
Black Notley 22 TL 7620
Black Torrington 6 SS 4605
Blackacre 77 NY 0490
Blackadder 87 NT 8452
Blackawton 5 SX 8050
Blackborough 8 ST 0909
Blackborough End 46 TF 6614
Blackboys 13 TQ 5220
Blackbrook 51 SJ 7639
Blackburn (Grampn.) 105 NJ 8212
Blackburn (Lancs.) 58 SD 6827
Blackburn (Lothian) 85 NS 9865
Blackden Heath 51 SJ 7871
Blackdog (Grampn.) 105 NJ 9514
Blackfield 11 SU 4402
Blackford (Cumbr.) 70 NY 3962
Blackford (Somer.) 17 ST 6526
Blackford (Somer.) 17 ST 4147
Blackford (Tays.) 91 NN 8908
Blackfordby 43 SK 3318
Blackgang 11 SZ 4876
Blackhall Colliery 73 NZ 4539
Blackhaugh 86 NT 4238
Blackheath (Essex) 23 TM 0021
Blackheath (Surrey) 20 TQ 0346
Blackhill (Grampn.) 105 NK 0843
Blackland 18 SU 0168
Blackley 58 SD 8503
Blacklunans 98 NO 1560
Blackmill 28 SS 9386
Blackmoor 12 SU 7833
Blackmoor Gate 7 SS 6443
Blackmore 22 TL 6001
Blackmore End 36 TL 7430
Blackness 85 NT 0579
Blacknest 12 SU 7941
Blacko 58 SD 8541
Blackpill 25 SS 6290
Blackpool 57 SD 3035
Blackpool Gate 71 NY 5377
Blackridge 84 NS 8967
Blackrock (Gwent) 28 SO 2112
Blackrock (Islay) 80 NR 3063
Blackrod 58 SD 6110
Blackshaw 70 NY 0465
Blackstone 13 TQ 2416
Blackthorn 34 SP 6219
Blackthorpe 36 TL 9063
Blacktoft 60 SE 8424
Blacktop 105 NJ 8604
Blackwater (Corn.) 2 SW 7346
Blackwater (Hants.) 20 SU 8559
Blackwater (I. of W.) 11 SZ 5086
Blackwater (Suff.) 37 TM 5077
Blackwaterfoot 74 NR 8928
Blackwell (Derby.) 52 SK 1272
Blackwell (Here. and Worc.) 41 SO 9972
Blackwood (Gwent) 28 ST 1797
Blackwood (Strath.) 84 NS 7943
Blackwood Hill 51 SJ 9255
Blacon 50 SJ 3767
Bladnoch 68 NX 4254
Bladon 33 SP 4414
Blaenannerch 26 SN 2449
Blaenau Ffestiniog 49 SH 7045
Blaenavon 29 SO 2509
Blaenawey 29 SO 2919
Blaengarw 28 SS 9092
Blaengwrach 28 SN 8605
Blaengwynfi 28 SS 8996
Blaenplwyf 26 SN 5775
Blaenporth 26 SN 2648
Blaenrhondda 28 SS 9299
Blaenwaun 25 SN 2327
Blagdon (Avon) 17 ST 5059
Blagdon (Devon) 5 SX 8561
Blagdon Hill (Somerset) 8 ST 2118
Blaich 96 NN 0476
Blaina 28 SO 2008
Blair Atholl 97 NN 8765
Blair Drummond 91 NS 7398
Blairgowrie 98 NO 1745
Blairhall 85 NT 0089
Blairingone 91 NS 9896
Blairlogie 91 NS 8396
Blairskaith 84 NS 5975
Blaisdon 32 SO 7016
Blakebrook 41 SO 8077
Blakedown 41 SO 8778
Blakelaw 87 NT 7730
Blakemere 30 SO 3641
Blakeney (Glos.) 29 SO 6707
Blakeney (Norf.) 46 TG 0243
Blakenhall (Ches.) 51 SJ 7247
Blakenhall (W Mids) 41 SO 9297
Blakeshall 41 SO 8381
Blakesley 34 SP 6250
Blanchland 72 NY 9650
Bland Hill 65 SE 2053
Blandford Forum 10 ST 8806
Blandford St. Mary 10 ST 8805
Blanefield 84 NS 5579
Blankney 54 TF 0660
Blantyre 84 NS 6857
Blarghour 89 NM 9913
Blarmachfoldach 96 NN 0969
Blashford 10 SU 1406
Blaston 44 SP 8095
Blatherwycke 44 SP 9795
Blawith 62 SD 2888
Blaxhall 37 TM 3657
Blaxton 60 SE 6600
Blaydon 72 NZ 1863
Bleadon 17 ST 3456
Blean 15 TR 1260
Bleasby 54 SK 7049
Blebocraigs 93 NO 4214
Bleddfa 40 SO 2068
Bledington 33 SP 2422
Bledlow 34 SP 7802
Bledlow Ridge 20 SU 7998
Blegbie 86 NT 4861
Blencarn 63 NY 6331
Blencogo 70 NY 1947
Blencow 63 NY 4532
Blendworth 12 SU 7113
Blennerhasset 70 NY 1741
Bletchingdon 33 SP 5017
Bletchingley 21 TQ 3250
Bletchley (Bucks.) 34 SP 8733
Bletchley (Salop) 51 SJ 6233
Bletherston 24 SN 0721
Bletsoe 34 TL 0258
Blewbury 19 SU 5385
Blickling 47 TG 1728
Blidworth 53 SK 5855
Blindcrake 62 NY 1434
Blindley Heath 21 TQ 3645
Blisland 4 SX 0973
Bliss Gate 41 SO 7472
Blissford 10 SU 1713
Blisworth 34 SP 7253
Blo Norton 36 TM 0179
Blockley 32 SP 1634
Blofield 47 TG 3309
Blore 52 SK 1349
Bloxham 33 SP 4235
Bloxwich 42 SJ 9902
Bloxworth 10 SY 8894
Blubberhouses 65 SE 1655
Blue Anchor 16 ST 0343
Blue Bell Hill 14 TQ 7462
Blunderston 47 TM 5197
Blunham 35 TL 1551

Blunsdon St. Andrew 230 Brome Street

Blunsdon St. Andrew 18 SU 1389
Bluntisham 45 TL 3674
Blyborough 54 SK 9394
Blyford 37 TM 4276
Blymhill 41 SJ 8112
Blyth (Northum.) 79 NZ 3181
Blyth (Notts.) 53 SK 6287
Blyth Bridge 85 NT 1345
Blythburgh 37 TM 4575
Blythe Bridge 51 SJ 9541
Blyton 54 SK 8594
Bo'Ness 85 NS 9981
Boarhills 93 NO 5614
Boarhunt 11 SU 6008
Boarshead 13 TQ 5332
Boarstall 34 SP 6214
Boasley Cross 5 SX 5093
Boat of Garten 103 NH 9419
Boath 108 NH 5773
Bobbing 14 TQ 8865
Bobbington 41 SO 8090
Bobbingworth 22 TL 5305
Bocaddon 4 SX 1758
Bocking 22 TL 7623
Bocking Churchstreet 22 TL 7525
Boconnoc 4 SX 1460
Boddam (Grampn.) 105 NK 1342
Boddam (Shetld.) 113 HU 3915
Boddington 32 SO 8925
Bodedern 48 SH 3380
Bodelwyddan 49 SJ 0075
Bodenham (Here. and Worc.) 31 SO 5251
Bodenham (Wilts.) 10 SU 1626
Bodewryd 48 SH 3990
Bodfari 49 SJ 0970
Bodffordd 48 SH 4276
Bodfuan 48 SH 3237
Bodham Street 47 TG 1240
Bodiam 14 TQ 7826
Bodicote 33 SP 4537
Bodieve 3 SW 9973
Bodle Street Green 13 TQ 6514
Bodmin 4 SX 0767
Bodney 46 TL 8398
Bodorgan 48 SH 3867
Bog, The 40 SO 3597
Bogbrae 105 NK 0335
Bogend 82 NS 3932
Bogmoor 104 NJ 3562
Bogniebrae 104 NJ 5945
Bognor Regis 12 SZ 9399
Bograxie 105 NJ 7119
Bogside 84 NS 8353
Bogton 105 NJ 6751
Bogue 69 NX 6481
Bohortha 3 SW 8632
Bohuntine 96 NN 2882
Bojewyan 2 SW 3934
Bolam 72 NZ 1922
Bold Heath 50 SJ 5389
Boldon 72 NZ 3661
Boldon Colliery 72 NZ 3462
Boldre 11 SZ 3198
Boldron 72 NZ 0314
Bole 54 SK 7987
Bolehill 53 SK 2955
Boleside 86 NT 4933
Bolham Water 8 ST 1612
Bolingey 2 SW 7653
Bollington (Ches.) 57 SJ 7286
Bollington (Ches.) 51 SJ 9377
Bolney 13 TQ 2622
Bolnhurst 35 TL 0859
Bolshan 99 NO 6252
Bolsover 53 SK 4770
Bolsterstone 59 SK 2696
Bolstone 31 SO 5532
Boltby 66 SE 4886
Bolton (Cumbr.) 63 NY 6323
Bolton (Gtr Mches.) 58 SD 7108
Bolton (Humbs.) 67 SE 7752
Bolton (Lothian) 86 NT 5070
Bolton (Northum.) 79 NU 1013
Bolton Abbey 65 SE 0754
Bolton Percy 60 SE 5341
Bolton Upon Dearne 60 SE 4502
Bolton by Bowland 58 SD 7849
Bolton le Sands 64 SD 4867
Bolton-on-Swale 66 SE 2599
Boltonfellend 71 NY 4768
Boltongate 70 NY 2340
Bolventor 4 SX 1876
Bomere Heath 40 SJ 4719
Bonar-Bridge 108 NH 6191
Bonawe 89 NN 0133
Bonby 61 TA 0015
Boncath 26 SN 2038
Bonchester Bridge 78 NT 5811
Bondleigh 7 SS 6504
Bonehill 42 SK 1902
Bonhill 90 NS 3980
Boningale 41 SJ 8102
Bonjedward 78 NT 6523
Bonkle 84 NS 8356
Bonnington (Kent) 15 TR 0536
Bonnington (Lothian) 85 NT 1269
Bonnington Smiddy 93 NO 5739
Bonnybank 93 NO 3503
Bonnybridge 84 NS 8280
Bonnykelly 105 NJ 8553
Bonnyrigg 85 NT 3065
Bonnyton (Tays.) 93 NO 3338
Bonnyton (Tays.) 99 NO 6655
Bonsall 53 SK 2758
Bont 29 SO 3819
Bont Newydd (Gwyn.) 39 SH 7720
Bont-Dolgadfan 39 SH 8800
Bontddu 39 SH 6618
Bontgoch Elerch 39 SN 6886
Bontnewydd (Gwyn.) 48 SH 4859
Bontuchel 49 SJ 0857
Bonvilston 28 ST 0674
Booker 20 SU 8491
Booley 41 SJ 5725
Boosbeck 73 NZ 6516
Boot 62 NY 1700
Boothby Graffoe 54 SK 9859
Boothby Pagnell 54 SK 9730
Boothstown 58 SD 7200
Bootle (Cumbr.) 62 SD 1088
Bootle (Mers.) 50 SJ 3394
Boquhan 84 NS 5387
Boraston 41 SO 6170
Borden 14 TQ 8863
Bordley 65 SD 9465
Bordon 12 SU 7935
Boreham (Essex) 22 TL 7509
Boreham (Wilts.) 18 ST 8944
Boreham Street 13 TQ 6611
Borehamwood 21 TQ 1996
Boreland (Dumf. and Galwy.) 77 NY 1790
Boreraig 100 NG 1853
Borgie 111 NC 6759
Borgue (Dumf. and Galwy.) 69 NX 6248
Borgue (Highld.) 112 ND 1325
Borley 36 TL 8442
Bornesketaig 100 NG 3771
Borness 69 NX 6145
Borough Green 21 TQ 6057
Boroughbridge 66 SE 3966
Borras Head 50 SJ 3653
Borrowash 53 SK 4134
Borrowby 66 SE 4289
Borrowdale (Cumbr.) 62 NY 2514
Borth 38 SN 6089
Borthwickbrae 77 NT 4113
Borthwickshiels 77 NT 4315
Borve 109 NB 4055
Borve (Barra) 109 NF 6501
Borve (Island of Skye) 100 NG 4448
Borwick 64 SD 5273
Bosavern 2 SW 3730
Bosbury 31 SO 6943
Boscastle 4 SX 0990
Boscombe (Dorset) 10 SZ 1191
Boscombe (Wilts.) 11 SU 2038
Boscoppa 4 SX 0353
Bosham 12 SU 8004
Bosherton 24 SR 9694
Boskednan 2 SW 4434
Bosley 51 SJ 9165
Bossall 66 SE 7160
Bossiney 4 SX 0688
Bossingham 15 TR 1549
Bostock Green 51 SJ 6769
Boston 55 TF 3244
Boston Spa 59 SE 4245
Botallack 2 SW 3632
Botcheston 43 SK 4804
Botesdale 37 TM 0475
Bothal 79 NZ 2386
Bothamsall 53 SK 6773
Bothel 62 NY 1838
Bothenhampton 9 SY 4791
Botley (Bucks.) 34 SP 9802
Botley (Hants.) 11 SU 5112
Botley (Oxon.) 33 SP 4806
Botolphs 12 TQ 1909
Bottacks 102 NH 4860
Bottesford (Humbs.) 60 SE 9107
Bottesford (Leic.) 54 SK 8038
Bottisham 36 TL 5460
Bottomcraig 93 NO 3724
Bottoms 58 SD 9321
Botusfleming 4 SX 4061
Botwnnog 48 SH 2631
Boughrood 30 SO 1239
Boughspring 29 ST 5597
Boughton (Norf.) 46 TF 7002
Boughton (Northants.) 44 SP 7565
Boughton (Notts.) 53 SK 6768
Boughton Aluph 15 TR 0348
Boughton Green 14 TQ 7651
Boughton Lees 15 TR 0247
Boughton Malherbe 14 TQ 8849
Boughton Street 15 TR 0559
Boulby 73 NZ 7519
Bouldon 40 SO 5485
Boulmer 79 NU 2614
Boultham 54 SK 9568
Bourn 35 TL 3256
Bourne 45 TF 0920
Bourne End (Beds.) 34 SP 9644
Bourne End (Bucks.) 20 SU 8987
Bourne End (Herts.) 34 TL 0206
Bournebridge 21 TQ 5194
Bournemouth 10 SZ 0991
Bournes Green 30 SO 9104
Bournheath 41 SO 9474
Bournmoor 72 NZ 3051
Bournville 42 SP 0480
Bourton (Avon) 17 ST 3864
Bourton (Dorset) 17 ST 7630
Bourton (Oxon.) 18 SU 2387
Bourton (Salop) 41 SO 5996
Bourton on Dunsmore 43 SP 4370
Bourton-on-the-Hill 32 SP 1732
Bourton-on-the-Water 32 SP 1620
Bousd 94 NM 2563
Boveney 20 SU 9377
Boverton 28 SS 9868
Bovey Tracey 5 SX 8178
Bovingdon 35 TL 0103
Bovington Camp 10 SY 8389
Bow (Burray) (Ork) 113 ND 4897
Bow (Devon.) 7 SS 7201
Bow (Flotta) (Ork) 113 ND 3693
Bow Brickhill 34 SP 9034
Bow Street 38 SN 6284
Bow of Fife 93 NO 3112
Bowbank 63 NY 9423
Bowburn 72 NZ 3038
Bowcombe 11 SZ 4786
Bowd 8 SY 1190
Bowden (Borders) 86 NT 5530
Bowden (Devon.) 5 SX 8448
Bowden Hill 18 ST 9367
Bowdon 51 SJ 7586
Bower 112 ND 2463
Bowerchalke 10 SU 0122
Bowermadden 112 ND 2364
Bowers Gifford 22 TQ 7588
Bowershall 92 NT 0991
Bowertower 112 ND 2362
Bowes 72 NY 9913
Bowhill 77 NT 4227
Bowley 31 SO 5352
Bowlhead Green 12 SU 9138
Bowling 82 NS 4473
Bowling Bank 50 SJ 3948
Bowling Green 32 SO 8151
Bowmanstead 62 SD 3096
Bowmore 80 NR 3159
Bowness-on-Solway 70 NY 2262
Bowness-on-Windermere 62 SD 4097
Bowsden 87 NT 9941
Bowthorpe 47 TG 1709
Box (Glos.) 32 SO 8600
Box (Wilts.) 18 ST 8268
Boxbush 32 SO 7412
Boxford (Berks.) 19 SU 4271
Boxford (Suff.) 36 TL 9640
Boxgrove 12 SU 9007
Boxley 14 TQ 7759
Boxted (Suff) 36 TL 8251
Boxworth 35 TL 3464
Boyden Gate 15 TR 2264
Boylestone 52 SK 1835
Boyndie 104 NJ 6463
Boyndlie 105 NJ 9162
Boynton 67 TA 1368
Boysack 99 NO 6249
Boyton (Corn.) 4 SX 3192
Boyton (Suff.) 37 TM 3747
Boyton (Wilts.) 10 ST 9539
Bozeat 34 SP 9059
Braaid 56 SC 3176
Brabling Green 37 TM 2964
Brabourne 15 TR 1041
Brabourne Lees 15 TR 0840
Brabstermire 112 ND 3169
Bracadale 100 NG 3538
Braceborough 45 TF 0713
Bracebridge Heath 54 SK 9767
Braceby 54 TF 0135
Bracewell 58 SD 8648
Brackenfield 53 SK 3759
Brackletter 96 NN 1882
Brackley (Northants.) 33 SP 5837
Brackley (Strath.) 81 NR 7941
Bracknell 20 SU 8769
Braco 91 NN 8309
Bracobrae 104 NJ 5053
Bracon Ash 47 TM 1899
Bracora 95 NM 7192
Braconna 95 NM 7292
Bradbourne 53 SK 2052
Bradbury 72 NZ 3128
Bradda 56 SC 1970
Bradden 34 SP 6448
Braddock 4 SX 1662
Bradenham 20 SU 8297
Bradenstoke 18 SU 0079
Bradfield (Berks.) 19 SU 6072
Bradfield (Essex) 23 TM 1430
Bradfield (Norf.) 47 TG 2633
Bradfield (S Yorks.) 53 SK 2692
Bradfield Combust 36 TL 8957
Bradfield Green 51 SJ 6859
Bradfield St. Clare 36 TL 9057
Bradfield St. George 36 TL 9160
Bradford (Devon.) 6 SS 4207
Bradford (Northum.) 87 NU 1532
Bradford (W Yorks.) 59 SE 1633
Bradford Abbas 9 ST 5814
Bradford Leigh 18 ST 8362
Bradford Peverell 9 SY 6592
Bradford on Avon 18 ST 8260
Bradford-on-Tone 8 ST 1722
Brading 11 SZ 6087
Bradley (Derby.) 53 SK 2145
Bradley (Hants.) 19 SU 6341
Bradley (Here. and Worc.) 32 SO 9860
Bradley (Humbs.) 61 TA 2406
Bradley (N Yorks.) 65 SE 0380
Bradley (Staffs.) 41 SJ 8717
Bradley Green 32 SO 9861
Bradley in the Moors 52 SK 0541
Bradmore 53 SK 5831
Bradninch 8 SS 9903
Bradnop 52 SK 0155
Bradpole 9 SY 4794
Bradshaw 58 SD 7312
Bradstone 4 SX 3880
Bradwell (Bucks.) 34 SP 8339
Bradwell (Derby.) 52 SK 1781
Bradwell (Essex) 22 TL 8023
Bradwell (Norf.) 47 TG 5003
Bradwell Green 51 SJ 7563
Bradwell Grove 33 SP 2308
Bradwell Waterside 23 TL 9907
Bradwell-on-Sea 23 TM 0006
Bradworthy 6 SS 3213
Brae (Highld.) 106 NG 8185
Brae (Highld.) 103 NH 6662
Brae (Shetld.) 113 HU 3567
Brae of Achnahaird 110 NB 9913
Braedownie 98 NO 2875
Braefield 102 NH 4130
Braegrum 92 NO 0024
Braehead (Strath.) 84 NS 8134
Braehead (Strath.) 84 NS 9550
Braehead (Tays.) 99 NO 6852
Braehead (Wigtown.) 68 NX 4252
Braemar 98 NO 1592
Braemore 112 ND 0630
Braeside 82 NS 2375
Braeswick 113 HY 6037
Brafferton (Durham) 72 NZ 2921
Brafferton (N Yorks.) 66 SE 4370
Brafield-on-the-Green 34 SP 8158
Bragar 109 NB 2847
Bragbury End 35 TL 2621
Braidwood 84 NS 8448
Braigo 80 NR 2369
Brailes 33 SP 3139
Brailsford 53 SK 2541
Braintree 22 TL 7622
Braiseworth 37 TM 1371
Braishfield 11 SU 3725
Braithwaite 62 NY 2323
Braithwell 53 SK 5394
Bramber 12 TQ 1810
Bramcote 53 SK 5037
Bramdean 11 SU 6127
Bramerton 47 TG 2904
Bramfield (Herts.) 35 TL 2915
Bramfield (Suff.) 37 TM 4073
Bramford 37 TM 1246
Bramhall 51 SJ 8984
Bramham 59 SE 4242
Bramhope 59 SE 2443
Bramley (Hants.) 19 SU 6358
Bramley (S Yorks.) 53 SK 4892
Bramley (Surrey) 12 TQ 0044
Brampford Speke 8 SX 9298
Brampton (Cambs.) 45 TL 2170
Brampton (Cumbr.) 71 NY 5361
Brampton (Cumbr.) 63 NY 6723
Brampton (Lincs.) 54 SK 8479
Brampton (Norf.) 47 TG 2224
Brampton (S Yorks.) 59 SE 4101
Brampton (Suff.) 47 TM 4381
Brampton Abbotts 29 SO 6026
Brampton Ash 44 SP 7887
Brampton Bryan 40 SO 3672
Bramshall 52 SK 0633
Bramshaw 11 SU 2615
Bramshill 20 SU 7461
Bramshott 12 SU 8432
Bran End 22 TL 6525
Branault 95 NM 5369
Brancaster 46 TF 7743
Brancepeth 72 NZ 2238
Branchill 103 NJ 0852
Branderburgh 104 NJ 2371
Brandesburton 61 TA 1147
Brandeston 37 TM 2460
Brandiston 47 TG 1321
Brandon (Durham) 72 NZ 2439
Brandon (Lincs.) 54 SK 9048
Brandon (Northum.) 79 NU 0417
Brandon (Suff.) 46 TL 7886
Brandon (Warw.) 43 SP 4076
Brandon Bank 46 TL 6289
Brandon Creek 46 TL 6091
Brandon Parva 47 TG 0708
Brands Hatch 21 TQ 5764
Brandsby 66 SE 5872
Brane 2 SW 4028
Branscombe 8 SY 1988
Bransford 32 SO 7952
Bransgore 10 SZ 1897
Branston (Leic.) 54 SK 8029
Branston (Lincs.) 54 TF 0167
Branston (Staffs.) 42 SK 2221
Branstone 11 SZ 5583
Brant Broughton 54 SK 9154
Brantham 37 TM 1034
Branthwaite (Cumbr) 62 NY 0525
Brantingham 61 SE 9429
Branton 79 NU 0416
Branxholme 77 NT 4611
Branxton 87 NT 8937
Brassington 53 SK 2354
Brasted 21 TQ 4755
Brasted Chart 21 TQ 4653
Bratoft 55 TF 4765
Brattleby 54 SK 9480
Bratton 18 ST 9152
Bratton Clovelly 5 SX 4691
Bratton Fleming 7 SS 6437
Bratton Seymour 17 ST 6729
Braughing 35 TL 3925
Braunston (Leic.) 44 SK 8306
Braunston (Northants.) 43 SP 5366
Braunstone 43 SK 5502
Braunton 6 SS 4836
Brawby 67 SE 7378
Brawl 111 NC 8066
Brawlbin 112 ND 0757
Bray 20 SU 9079
Bray Shop 4 SX 3374
Braybrooke 44 SP 7684
Brayford 7 SS 6834
Brayton 60 SE 6030
Brazacott 4 SX 2691
Breachwood Green 35 TL 1522
Breaclete 109 NB 1537
Breadsall 53 SK 3639
Breadstone 32 SO 7000
Breage 2 SW 6128
Breakish 101 NG 6723
Bream 29 SO 6005
Breamore 10 SU 1517
Brean 17 ST 2955
Brearton 66 SE 3260
Breasclete 109 NB 2135
Breaston 53 SK 4533
Brechfa 26 SN 5230
Brechin 99 NO 5960
Breckles 46 TL 9594
Breckrey 100 NG 5061
Brecon 28 SO 0428
Bredbury 51 SJ 9292
Brede 14 TQ 8218
Bredenbury 31 SO 6058
Bredfield 37 TM 2653
Bredgar 14 TQ 8860
Bredhurst 14 TQ 7962
Bredon 32 SO 9236
Bredon's Norton 32 SO 9339
Bredwardine 30 SO 3344
Breedon on the Hill 43 SK 4022
Breich 85 NS 9560
Breighton 60 SE 7033
Breinton 30 SO 4739
Bremhill 18 ST 9873
Brenchley 14 TQ 6741
Brendon 7 SS 7648
Brenish 109 NA 9926
Brent 21 TQ 2084
Brent Eleigh 36 TL 9447
Brent Knoll 17 ST 3350
Brent Pelham 35 TL 4330
Brentford 21 TQ 1778
Brentwood 22 TQ 5993
Brenzett 15 TR 0027
Brereton 42 SK 0516
Brereton Green 51 SJ 7764
Brereton Heath 51 SJ 8064
Bressingham 47 TM 0780
Bretby 43 SK 2923
Bretford 43 SP 4277
Bretforton 32 SP 0943
Bretherton 57 SD 4720
Brettenham (Norf) 46 TL 9383
Brettenham (Suff.) 36 TL 9653
Bretton 50 SJ 3563
Brewham 17 ST 7136
Brewood 41 SJ 8808
Briantspuddle 10 SY 8193
Bricket Wood 35 TL 1301
Bricklehampton 32 SO 9842
Bride 56 NX 4501
Bridekirk 70 NY 1133
Bridell 26 SN 1742
Bridestowe 5 SX 5189
Brideswell 104 NJ 5739
Bridford 5 SX 8186
Bridge 15 TR 1854
Bridge End (Lincs.) 55 TF 1436
Bridge Green 35 TL 4636
Bridge Sollers 30 SO 4142
Bridge Street 36 TL 8749
Bridge Trafford 50 SJ 4471
Bridge of Alford 104 NJ 5617
Bridge of Allan 91 NS 7897
Bridge of Avon 104 NJ 1835
Bridge of Cally 98 NO 1351
Bridge of Canny 99 NO 6597
Bridge of Dee 69 NX 7360
Bridge of Don 105 NJ 9409
Bridge of Dye 99 NO 6585
Bridge of Earn 92 NO 1318
Bridge of Feugh 99 NO 7094
Bridge of Gairn 98 NO 3597
Bridge of Gaur 97 NN 5056
Bridge of Muchalls 99 NO 8991
Bridge of Orchy 90 NN 2939
Bridge of Weir 82 NS 3865
Bridgefoot 62 NY 0529
Bridgemary 11 SU 5702
Bridgend (Borders) 86 NT 5235
Bridgend (Dumf. and Galwy.) 77 NT 0708
Bridgend (Fife.) 93 NO 3911
Bridgend (Grampn.) 104 NJ 3731
Bridgend (Islay) 80 NR 3362
Bridgend (Lothian) 85 NT 0475
Bridgend (Mid Glam.) 28 SS 9079
Bridgend (Strath.) 89 NR 8592
Bridgend (Strath.) 84 NS 6970
Bridgend (Tays.) 92 NO 1224
Bridgend (Tays.) 99 NO 5368
Bridgend of Lintrathen 98 NO 2854
Bridgerule 6 SS 2803
Bridges 40 SO 3996
Bridgetown 16 SS 9233
Bridgeyate 29 ST 6873
Bridgham 46 TL 9686
Bridgnorth 41 SO 7193
Bridgtown 41 SJ 9808
Bridgwater 17 ST 3037
Bridlington 67 TA 1766
Bridport 9 SY 4692
Bridstow 29 SO 5824
Brierfield 58 SD 8436
Brierley (Glos.) 29 SO 6215
Brierley (Here. and Worc.) 30 SO 4956
Brierley (S Yorks.) 59 SE 4011
Brierley Hill 41 SO 9187
Brig o'Turk 90 NN 5306
Brigg 61 TA 0007
Brigham (Cumbr.) 62 NY 0830
Brigham (Humbs.) 67 TA 0753
Brighouse 59 SE 1423
Brighstone 11 SZ 4282
Brightgate 53 SK 2659
Brighthampton 33 SP 3803
Brightling 13 TQ 6821
Brightlingsea 23 TM 0816
Brighton (Corn.) 3 SW 9054
Brighton (E Susx) 13 TQ 3105
Brightons 84 NS 9277
Brightwalton 19 SU 4278
Brightwell (Oxon.) 19 SU 5790
Brightwell (Suff.) 37 TM 2543
Brightwell Baldwin 19 SU 6594
Brignall 72 NZ 0712
Brigsley 61 TA 2501
Brigsteer 63 SD 4889
Brigstock 44 SP 9485
Brill 34 SP 6513
Brilley 30 SO 2549
Brimfield 40 SO 5267
Brimington 53 SK 4073
Brimpsfield 32 SO 9312
Brimpton 19 SU 5564
Brind 60 SE 7430
Brindister 113 HU 2857
Brindle 57 SD 5924
Brindley Ford 51 SJ 8754
Brindley Heath 41 SJ 9914
Brineton 41 SJ 8013
Bringhurst 44 SP 8492
Brington 45 TL 0875
Briningham 46 TG 0334
Brinkhill 55 TF 3773
Brinkley 36 TL 6254
Brinklow 43 SP 4379
Brinkworth 18 SU 0184
Brinscall 58 SD 6321
Brinsley 53 SK 4548
Brinsop 30 SO 4344
Brinsworth 53 SK 4190
Brinton 46 TG 0335
Brinyan 113 HY 4327
Brisley 46 TF 9421
Brislington 29 ST 6170
Bristol 29 ST 5872
Briston 47 TG 0632
Britannia 58 SD 8821
Britford British Legion Village 14 TQ 7257
Briton Ferry 28 SS 7394
Britwell Salome 19 SU 6792
Brixham 5 SX 9255
Brixton 5 SX 5452
Brixton Deverill 10 ST 8638
Brixworth 44 SP 7470
Brize Norton 33 SP 2907
Broad Blunsdon 18 SU 1490
Broad Campden 32 SP 1537
Broad Chalke 10 SU 0325
Broad Green 32 SO 7656
Broad Haven 24 SM 8613
Broad Hill (Cambs.) 36 TL 5976
Broad Hinton 18 SU 1076
Broad Laying 19 SU 4362
Broad Marston 32 SP 1346
Broad Oak (Cumbr.) 62 SD 1194
Broad Oak (E Susx) 14 TQ 8320
Broad Oak (Here. and Worc.) 29 SO 4721
Broad Street 14 TQ 8356
Broad Town 18 SU 0977
Broadbottom 51 SJ 9993
Broadbridge 12 SU 8105
Broadbridge Heath 12 TQ 1431
Broadclyst 8 SX 9897
Broadford 100 NG 6423
Broadhaugh 77 NT 4509
Broadheath (Gtr Mches.) 51 SJ 7689
Broadheath (Here. and Worc.) 31 SO 6665
Broadheath (Here. and Worc.) 32 SO 8156
Broadhembury 8 ST 1004
Broadhempston 5 SX 8066
Broadley (Grampn.) 104 NJ 4161
Broadley (Gtr Mches.) 58 SD 8716
Broadley Common 35 TL 4207
Broadmayne 9 SY 7286
Broadmeadows 86 NT 4130
Broadmere 19 SU 6247
Broadoak (Dorset) 9 SY 4496
Broadoak (E Susx) 13 TQ 6022
Broadoak (Kent) 15 TR 1661
Broadrashes 104 NJ 4354
Broadstairs 15 TR 3967
Broadstone (Dorset) 10 SZ 0095
Broadstone (Salop) 40 SO 5389
Broadwas 32 SO 7555
Broadwater 12 TQ 1504
Broadway (Here. and Worc.) 32 SP 0937
Broadway (Somer.) 8 ST 3215
Broadwell (Glos.) 33 SP 2027
Broadwell (Oxon.) 33 SP 2503
Broadwell (Warw.) 33 SP 4565
Broadwell Lane End 29 SO 5811
Broadwey 9 SY 6683
Broadwindsor 9 ST 4302
Broadwood-Kelly 6 SS 6105
Broadwoodwidger 4 SX 4089
Brockbridge 11 SU 6118
Brockdam 79 NU 1624
Brockdish 37 TM 2179
Brockenhurst 11 SU 2902
Brocketsbrae 84 NS 8239
Brockford Street 37 TM 1166
Brockhall 34 SP 6362
Brockham 21 TQ 2049
Brockhampton (Here and worc.) 31 SO 5932
Brockholes 59 SE 1411
Brocklesby 61 TA 1311
Brockley 29 ST 4666
Brockley Green 36 TL 8254
Brockton (Salop) 40 SJ 3104
Brockton (Salop) 41 SJ 7103
Brockton (Salop) 40 SO 3285
Brockton (Salop) 41 SO 5793
Brockweir 29 SO 5301
Brockworth 32 SO 8916
Brocton 41 SJ 9619
Brodick 81 NS 0136
Brodsworth 60 SE 5007
Brogaig 109 NG 4768
Brogborough 34 SP 9638
Broken Cross (Ches.) 51 SJ 6872
Broken Cross (Ches.) 51 SJ 8973
Brokenborough 18 ST 9189
Bromborough 50 SJ 3582
Brome 37 TM 1376
Brome Street 37 TM 1576

romeswell
231
Carlton (N Yorks.)

omeswell 37 TM 3050
omfield (Cumb.) 70 NY 1746
omfield (Salop) 40 SO 4876
omham (Beds.) 34 TL 0051
omham (Wilts.) 18 ST 9665
omley Common 21 TQ 4266
ompton (Kent) 14 TQ 7668
ompton (N Yorks) 67 SE 9482
ompton (N Yorks.) 66 SE 3796
ompton Ralph 16 ST 0832
ompton Regis 16 SS 9531
ompton-on-Swale 65 SE 2199
omsash 29 SO 6424
omsgrove 41 SO 9570
omstead Heath 41 SJ 7917
omyard 31 SO 6554
omyard Downs 31 SO 6655
onaber 49 SH 7131
onant 27 SN 6467
onington 50 SJ 4839
onllys 30 SO 1435
onygarth 50 SJ 2636
rook (Hants.) 11 SU 2713
rook (Hants.) 11 SU 3428
rook (I. of W.) 11 SZ 3983
rook (Kent) 15 TR 0644
rook (Surrey) 12 SU 9338
rook Street 21 TQ 5792
rooke (Leic.) 44 SK 8405
rooke (Norf.) 47 TM 2999
rookfield 82 NS 4164
rookhouse 64 SD 5464
rookhouse Green 51 SJ 8061
rookland 15 TQ 9825
rookmans Park 35 TL 2404
rooks 40 SO 1499
rookthorpe 32 SO 8312
rookwood 20 SU 9557
room (Beds.) 35 TL 1743
room (Warw.) 32 SP 0953
room Hill (Dorset) 10 SU 0302
roome (Here. and Worc.) 41 SO 9078
roome (Norf.) 47 TM 3591
roome (Salop) 40 SO 3981
roomer's Corner 12 TQ 1221
roomfield (Essex) 22 TL 7010
roomfield (Kent) 14 TQ 8452
roomfield (Kent) 15 TR 2066
roomfield (Somer.) 16 ST 2231
roomfleet 60 SE 8727
roomhill (Northum.) 79 NU 2400
rora 108 NC 9003
roseley 41 SJ 6701
rothertoft 55 TF 2746
rotherton 60 SE 4825
rotton 73 NZ 6819
roubster 112 ND 0360
rough (Cumbr.) 63 NY 7914
rough (Derby.) 52 SK 1882
rough (Highld.) 112 ND 2273
rough (Humbs.) 61 SE 9326
rough (Notts.) 54 SK 8358
rough (Ork.) 113 HU 5666
rough Lodge 113 HU 5894
rough Sowerby 63 NY 7912
roughall 51 SJ 5641
Broughton (Borders) 85 NT 1136
Broughton (Bucks.) 34 SP 8940
Broughton (Cambs.) 45 TL 2878
Broughton (Clwyd) 50 SJ 3363
Broughton (Gtr Mches.) 58 SD 8201
Broughton (Hants.) 11 SU 3132
Broughton (Humbs.) 61 SE 9508
Broughton (Lancs.) 57 SD 5234
Broughton (Mid Glam.) 28 SS 9271
Broughton (N Yorks) 67 SE 7673
Broughton (N Yorks.) 65 SD 9451
Broughton (Northants.) 44 SP 8375
Broughton (Oxon.) 33 SP 4238
Broughton Astley 43 SP 5292
Broughton Gifford 18 ST 8763
Broughton Great (Cumbr.) 62 NY 0731
Broughton Hackett 32 SO 9254
Broughton Mills 62 SD 2290
Broughton Moor 62 NY 0533
Broughton Poggs 33 SP 2303
Broughton in Furness 62 SD 2087
Broughtown 113 HY 6540
Broughty Ferry 93 NO 4630
Brown Candover 11 SU 5839
Brown Edge 51 SJ 9053
Brown Head 74 NR 9025
Brownhill (Grampn.) 105 NJ 8640
Brownhills (W Mids) 42 SK 0405
Brownlow Heath 51 SJ 8360
Brownmuir 99 NO 7477
Brownston 5 SX 6952
Broxbourne 35 TL 3707
Broxburn (Lothian) 85 NT 0872
Broxburn (Lothian) 86 NT 6977
Broxted 22 TL 5727
Broxwood 30 SO 3654
Bruan 112 ND 3039
Brue 109 NB 3349
Bruera 50 SJ 4360
Bruichladdich 80 NR 2661
Bruisyard 37 TM 3266
Bruisyard Street 37 TM 3365
Brund 52 SK 1061
Brundall 47 TG 3208
Brundish 37 TM 2669
Brundish Street 37 TM 2671
Bruntingthorpe 43 SP 6090
Brunton (Fife) 93 NO 3220
Brunton (Northum.) 79 NU 2024
Brushford 16 SS 9225
Brushford Barton 7 SS 6707
Bruton 17 ST 6834
Bryanston 10 ST 8706
Brydekirk 70 NY 1870
Brymbo 50 SJ 2953
Bryn (Gtr Mches.) 57 SD 5600
Bryn (Salop) 40 SO 2985
Bryn (W Glam.) 28 SS 8192
Bryn Gates 57 SD 5901
Bryn-coch 25 SS 7499
Bryn-henllan 24 SN 0139
Bryn-y-maen (Clwyd) 49 SH 8376
Brynamman 25 SN 7114
Brynberian 26 SN 1035
Bryncae 28 SS 9983
Bryncethin 28 SS 9184
Bryncir 48 SH 4641
Bryncroes 48 SH 2231
Bryncrug 38 SH 6003
Bryneglwys 50 SJ 1447
Brynford 50 SJ 1774
Bryngwran 48 SH 3477
Bryngwyn (Gwent) 29 SO 3909
Bryngwyn (Powys) 30 SO 1849
Brynhoffnant 26 SN 3351
Brynmawr 28 SO 1911
Brynmenyn 28 SS 9084
Brynna 28 SS 9883
Brynrefail 48 SH 4786
Brynsadler 28 ST 0380
Brynsiencyn 48 SH 4867
Brynteg 48 SH 4982
Bualintur 100 NG 4020
Bubbenhall 43 SP 3672
Bubwith 60 SE 7136
Buccleuch 77 NT 3214
Buchanty 91 NN 9328
Buchlyvie 90 NS 5793
Buck's Cross 6 SS 3422
Buck's Mills 6 SS 3523
Buckabank 70 NY 3749
Buckden (Cambs.) 45 TL 1967
Buckden (N Yorks.) 65 SD 9477
Buckenham 47 TG 3505
Buckerell 8 ST 1200
Buckfast 5 SX 7367
Buckfastleigh 5 SX 7466
Buckhaven 93 NT 3598
Buckholm 86 NT 4838
Buckhorn Weston 9 ST 7524
Buckhurst Hill 21 TQ 4193
Buckie 104 NJ 4265
Buckingham 34 SP 6933
Buckland (Bucks.) 34 SP 8812
Buckland (Devon.) 55 SX 6743
Buckland (Glos.) 32 SP 0836
Buckland (Herts.) 35 TL 3533
Buckland (Kent) 15 TR 2942
Buckland (Oxon.) 19 SU 3497
Buckland (Surrey) 21 TQ 2250
Buckland Brewer 6 SS 4120
Buckland Common 34 SP 9306
Buckland Dinham 18 ST 7550
Buckland Filleigh 6 SS 4609
Buckland Monachorum 5 SX 4868
Buckland Newton 9 ST 6905
Buckland St. Mary 8 ST 2713
Buckland in the Moor 5 SX 7273
Buckland-Tout-Saints 5 SX 7546
Bucklebury 19 SU 5570
Bucklerheads 93 NO 4636
Bucklers Hard 11 SZ 4099
Bucklesham 37 TM 2442
Buckley 50 SJ 2764
Buckminster 44 SK 8722
Bucknall (Lincs.) 55 TF 1668
Bucknall (Staffs.) 51 SJ 9147
Bucknell (Oxon.) 33 SP 5525
Bucknell (Salop) 40 SO 3574
Bucks Green 12 TQ 0732
Bucks Hill 35 TL 0500
Bucks Horn Oak 12 SU 8142
Bucksburn 105 NJ 8909
Buckton (Here. and Worc.) 40 SO 3873
Buckton (Northum.) 87 NU 0838
Buckworth 55 TL 1476
Budbrooke 33 SP 2565
Budby 53 SK 6169
Bude 6 SS 2006
Budlake 8 SS 9700
Budle 87 NU 1534
Budleigh Salterton 8 SY 0682
Budock Water 2 SW 7832
Buerton 51 SJ 6843
Bugbrooke 34 SP 6757
Bugle 4 SX 0158
Bugthorpe 67 SE 7757
Builth Road 27 SO 0253
Builth Wells 27 SO 0351
Bulby 45 TF 0526
Buldoo 112 NC 9967
Bulford 18 SU 1643
Bulkeley 50 SJ 5254
Bulkington (Warw.) 43 SP 3986
Bulkington (Wilts.) 18 ST 9458
Bulkworthy 6 SS 3914
Bull Bay 48 SH 4395
Bulley 32 SO 7519
Bullwood 82 NS 1674
Bulmer (Essex) 36 TL 8440
Bulmer (N Yorks.) 66 SE 6967
Bulmer Tye 36 TL 8438
Bulphan 22 TQ 6385
Bulverhythe 14 TQ 7809
Bulwark 63 NJ 9447
Bulwell 53 SK 5345
Bulwick 44 SP 9694
Bumble's Green 35 TL 4005
Bunacaimb 95 NM 6588
Bunbury 51 SJ 5658
Bunchrew 102 NH 6145
Buncton 12 TQ 1413
Bundalloch 101 NG 8927
Bunessan 88 NM 3821
Bungay 47 TM 3389
Bunnahabhainn 80 NR 4173
Bunny 43 SK 5829
Buntingford 35 TL 3629
Bunwell 47 TM 1293
Burbage (Derby.) 52 SK 0472
Burbage (Leic.) 43 SP 4492
Burbage (Wilts.) 18 SU 2261
Burcombe (Wilts.) 10 SU 0630
Burcot 19 SU 5595
Bures 36 TL 9034
Burford 33 SP 2512
Burgess Hill 13 TQ 3118
Burgh (Suff.) 37 TM 2251
Burgh Castle 47 TG 4805
Burgh Heath 21 TQ 2458
Burgh Le Marsh 55 TF 5065
Burgh Muir 105 NJ 7622
Burgh St. Margaret 47 TG 4413
Burgh St. Peter 47 TM 4693
Burgh by Sands 70 NY 3259
Burgh next Aylsham 47 TG 2125
Burgh on Bain 55 TF 2186
Burghclere 19 SU 4660
Burghead 103 NJ 1168
Burghfield 19 SU 6668
Burghfield Common 19 SU 6466
Burghfield Hill 19 SU 6567
Burghill 30 SO 4744
Burghwallis 60 SE 5312
Burham 14 TQ 7262
Buriton 12 SU 7320
Burland 51 SJ 6153
Burlawn 3 SW 9970
Burleigh 20 SU 9070
Burlescombe 8 ST 0716
Burleston 10 SY 7794
Burley (Hants.) 11 SU 2103
Burley (Leic.) 44 SK 8810
Burley Street 11 SU 2004
Burley in Wharfdale 59 SE 1646
Burleydam 51 SJ 6042
Burlingjobb 30 SO 2558
Burlton 40 SJ 4526
Burmarsh 15 TR 1032
Burn 60 SE 5928
Burnage 51 SJ 8692
Burnaston 53 SK 2832
Burnby 60 SE 8346
Burneside 63 SD 5095
Burneston 66 SE 3084
Burnett 29 ST 6665
Burnfoot (Borders) 77 NT 4113
Burnfoot (Borders) 78 NT 5116
Burnfoot (Tays.) 91 NN 9804
Burnham (Berks. — Bucks.) 20 SU 9382
Burnham (Humbs.) 61 TA 0517
Burnham Beeches 20 SU 9585
Burnham Deepdale 46 TF 8044
Burnham Green 35 TL 2616
Burnham Market 46 TF 8342
Burnham Norton 46 TF 8243
Burnham Overy 46 TF 8442
Burnham Thorpe 46 TF 8541
Burnham-on-Crouch 23 TQ 9496
Burnham-on-Sea 17 ST 3049
Burnhaven 105 NK 1244
Burnhead 76 NX 8595
Burnhervie 105 NJ 7319
Burnhill Green 41 SJ 7800
Burnhope 72 NZ 1948
Burnhouse 82 NS 3850
Burniston 67 TA 0193
Burnley 58 SD 8332
Burnmouth 87 NT 9560
Burnopfield 72 NZ 1756
Burnside (Fife.) 92 NO 1607
Burnside (Lothian) 85 NT 0971
Burnside (Strath) 75 NS 5912
Burnside (Tays.) 99 NO 5050
Burnside of Duntrune 93 NO 4434
Burnt Yates 66 SE 2461
Burntisland 85 NT 2385
Burntwood 42 SK 0609
Burpham (Surrey) 20 TQ 0151
Burpham (W. Susx.) 12 TQ 0408
Burra Firth (Unst.) 113 HP 6113
Burradon (Northum.) 79 NT 9806
Burradon (Tyne and Wear) 79 NZ 2772
Burravoe (Shetld.) 113 HU 3666
Burravoe (Yell.) 113 HU 5280
Burrelton 92 NO 1936
Burridge 11 SU 5110
Burrill 66 SE 2387
Burringham 60 SE 8309
Burrington (Avon) 17 ST 4759
Burrington (Devon.) 6 SS 6316
Burrington (Here. and Worc.) 40 SO 4472
Burrough Green 36 TL 6355
Burrough on the Hill 44 SK 7510
Burrow Bridge 17 ST 3530
Burrowhill 20 SU 9763
Burry Port 25 SN 4400
Burscough 57 SD 4310
Burscough Bridge 57 SD 4411
Bursea 60 SE 8033
Burshill 61 TA 0948
Bursledon 11 SU 4809
Burslem 51 SJ 8749
Burstall 37 TM 0944
Burstock 9 ST 4202
Burston (Norf.) 47 TM 1383
Burston (Staffs.) 41 SJ 9330
Burstow 13 TQ 3141
Burstwick 61 TA 2228
Burtersett 65 SD 8989
Burton (Ches.) 50 SJ 3174
Burton (Ches.) 50 SJ 5063
Burton (Cumbr.) - in Kendal 64 SD 5276
Burton (Dorset) 10 SZ 1794
Burton (Dyfed) 24 SM 9805
Burton (Lincs.) 54 SK 9574
Burton (Northum.) 87 NU 1732
Burton (Somer.) 16 ST 1944
Burton (Wilts.) 18 ST 8179
Burton Agnes 67 TA 1063
Burton Bradstock 9 SY 4889
Burton Coggles 44 SK 9725
Burton Fleming 67 TA 0872
Burton Green (Clwyd) 50 SJ 3458
Burton Green (Warw.) 43 SP 2675
Burton Hastings 43 SP 4189
Burton Joyce 53 SK 6443
Burton Latimer 44 SP 9074
Burton Lazars 44 SK 7716
Burton Leonard 66 SE 3263
Burton Overy 43 SP 6798
Burton Pedwardine 55 TF 1142
Burton Pidsea 61 TA 2431
Burton Salmon 60 SE 4827
Burton in Lonsdale 64 SD 6572
Burton on the Wolds 43 SK 5921
Burton upon Stather 60 SE 8617
Burton upon Trent 42 SK 2423
Burtonwood 51 SJ 5692
Burwardsley 50 SJ 5156
Burwarton 41 SO 6185
Burwash 13 TQ 6724
Burwash Common 13 TQ 6423
Burwell (Cambs.) 36 TL 5866
Burwell (Lincs.) 55 TF 3579
Burwick (Shetld.) 113 HU 3940
Burwick (South Ronaldsay) 113 ND 4384
Bury (Cambs.) 45 TL 2883
Bury (Gtr. Mches.) 58 SD 8010
Bury (Somer.) 16 SS 9427
Bury (W. Susx.) 12 TQ 0113
Bury Green 35 TL 4521
Bury St. Edmunds 36 TL 8564
Burythorpe 67 SE 7964
Busbridge 12 SU 9842
Busby (Strath.) 84 NS 5856
Busby (Tays.) 92 NO 0327
Buscot 18 SU 2297
Bush Green 47 TM 2187
Bushbury 41 SJ 9202
Bushey 20 TQ 1395
Bushey Heath 21 TQ 1594
Bushley 32 SO 8734
Bushton 18 SU 0677
Butcher's Pasture 22 TL 6024
Butcombe 17 ST 5161
Butleigh 17 ST 5233
Butleigh Wootton 17 ST 5034
Butlers Marston 33 SP 3150
Butley 37 TM 3651
Butsfield 72 NZ 1044
Butt Green 51 SJ 6651
Buttercrambe 66 SE 7358
Butterknowle 72 NZ 1025
Butterleigh 8 SS 9708
Buttermere (Cumbr.) 62 NY 1717
Buttermere (Wilts.) 19 SU 3361
Buttershaw 59 SE 1329
Butterstone 98 NO 0646
Butterton 52 SK 0756
Butterwick (Humbs.) 60 SE 8305
Butterwick (Lincs.) 55 TF 3845
Butterwick (N. Yorks.) 66 SE 7377
Butterwick (N. Yorks.) 67 SE 9971
Buttington 40 SJ 2408
Buttock's Booth 34 SP 7864
Buttonoak 41 SO 7578
Buxhall 36 TM 0057
Buxted 13 TQ 4923
Buxton (Derby.) 52 SK 0673
Buxton (Norf.) 47 TG 2222
Buxton Heath 47 TG 1821
Bwlch 28 SO 1422
Bwlch-y-cibau 40 SJ 1717
Bwlch-y-ffridd 39 SO 0695
Bwlch-y-groes 26 SN 2436
Bwlch-y-sarnau 27 SO 0274
Bwlchgwyn 50 SJ 2653
Bwlchllan 27 SN 5758
Bwlchtocyn 38 SH 3126
Byers Green 72 NZ 2234
Byfield 33 SP 5153
Byfleet 20 TQ 0461
Byford 30 SO 3943
Bygrave 35 TL 2636
Byker 72 NZ 2763
Bylchau 49 SH 9762
Byley 51 SJ 7269
Bythorn 55 TL 0575
Byton 30 SO 3664
Byworth 12 SU 9921

C

Cabourne 61 TA 1301
Cabrach (Grampn.) 104 NJ 3826
Cadbury 8 SS 9105
Cadder 84 NS 6172
Caddington 35 TL 0619
Caddonfoot 86 NT 4534
Cade Street 13 TQ 6021
Cadeby (Leic.) 43 SK 4202
Cadeby (S Yorks.) 60 SE 5100
Cadeleigh 8 SS 9107
Cadgwith 2 SW 7214
Cadham 93 NO 2701
Cadishead 51 SJ 7091
Cadle 25 SS 6297
Cadley 18 SU 2066
Cadmore End 20 SU 7892
Cadnam 11 SU 2913
Cadney 61 TA 0103
Cadole 50 SJ 2062
Caeathro 48 SH 5061
Caehopkin 28 SN 8212
Caeo 27 SN 6739
Caerau (Mid Glam.) 28 SS 8594
Caerau (S Glam.) 28 ST 1375
Caerdeon 39 SH 6418
Caergeiliog 48 SH 3178
Caergwrle 50 SJ 3057
Caerleon 29 ST 3390
Caernarfon 48 SH 4862
Caerphilly 28 ST 1587
Caersws 39 SO 0392
Caerwent 29 ST 4790
Caerwys 50 SJ 1272
Caethle 38 SN 6099
Cairnbaan 89 NR 8390
Cairnbrogie 105 NJ 8527
Cairncross 87 NT 8963
Cairndow 89 NN 1810
Cairneyhill 85 NT 0486
Cairngaan 68 NX 1232
Cairngarroch (Dumf. and Galwy.) 68 NX 0649
Cairnhill (Grampn.) 105 NJ 6732
Cairnie 104 NJ 4945
Cairnorrie 105 NJ 8640
Cairnryan 68 NX 0668
Caister-on-Sea 47 TG 5212
Caistor 61 TA 1101
Caistor St. Edmund 47 TG 2303
Caistron 79 NT 9901
Calbourne 11 SZ 4286
Calcot 19 SU 6672
Caldbeck 62 NY 3239
Caldbergh 66 SE 0984
Caldecote (Cambs.) 45 TL 1488
Caldecote (Cambs.) 35 TL 3456
Caldecote (Herts.) 35 TL 2338
Caldecott (Leic.) 44 SP 8693
Caldecott (Northants.) 44 SP 9968
Calder Bridge 62 NY 0405
Calder Mains 112 ND 0959
Calder Vale 57 SD 5345
Calderbank 84 NS 7662
Calderbrook 58 SD 9418
Caldercruix 84 NS 8167
Caldermill 84 NS 6641
Caldicot 29 ST 4888
Caldwell 72 NZ 1613
Caldy 50 SJ 2285
Caledrhydiau 26 SN 4753
Calgary 94 NM 3751
Califer 103 NJ 0857
California (Central) 84 NS 9076
California (Norf.) 47 TG 5114
Calke 43 SK 3722
Callaly 79 NU 0509
Callander 91 NN 6208
Callanish 109 NB 2133
Callestick 2 SW 7750
Calligarry 95 NG 6203
Callington 4 SX 3669
Callow 30 SO 4934
Callow End 32 SO 8349
Callow Hill (Here. and Worc.) 41 SO 7473
Callow Hill (Wilts) 18 SU 0385
Callows Grave 41 SO 5966
Calmore 11 SU 3314
Calmsden 32 SP 0408
Calne 18 ST 9971
Calow 53 SK 4071
Calshot 11 SU 4701
Calstock 4 SX 4368
Calthorpe 47 TG 1831
Calthwaite 71 NY 4640
Calton (N Yorks.) 65 SD 9059
Calton (Staffs.) 52 SK 1050
Calveley 51 SJ 5958
Calver 53 SK 2374
Calver Hill 30 SO 3748
Calverhall 51 SJ 6037
Calverleigh 8 SS 9214
Calverley 59 SE 2036
Calvert 34 SP 6824
Calverton (Bucks) 34 SP 7938
Calverton (Notts.) 53 SK 6149
Calvine 97 NN 8066
Cam 29 ST 7599
Camastianavaig 100 NG 5039
Camb 113 HU 5293
Camber 15 TQ 9619
Camberley 20 SU 8760
Camblesforth 60 SE 6425
Cambo 79 NZ 0285
Cambois 79 NZ 3083
Camborne 2 SW 6440
Cambridge (Cambs.) 35 TL 4658
Cambus 91 NS 8593
Cambusbarron 91 NS 7792
Cambuskenneth 91 NS 8094
Cambuslang 84 NS 6459
Camden 21 TQ 2784
Camelford 4 SX 1083
Camelon 84 NS 8680
Camelsdale 12 SU 8932
Camerory 103 NJ 0231
Camerton (Avon) 17 ST 6857
Camerton (Cumbr.) 62 NY 0330
Camghouran 97 NN 5556
Cammachmore 99 NO 9295
Cammeringham 54 SK 9482
Camp, The 32 SO 9308
Campbelltown or Ardersier 103 NH 7854
Campbelton 74 NS 1950
Campbeltown 81 NR 7120
Campmuir 92 NO 2137
Campsall 60 SE 5313
Campsea Ashe 37 TM 3356
Campton 35 TL 1238
Camrose 24 SM 9220
Camserney 97 NN 8149
Camusteel 101 NG 7042
Camusterrach 101 NG 7141
Camusvrachan 97 NN 6248
Canada 11 SU 2817
Candlesby 55 TF 4567
Cane End 19 SU 6779
Canewdon 23 TQ 9094
Canford Bottom 10 SU 0300
Canford Cliffs 10 SZ 0689
Canisbay 112 ND 3472
Cann Common 10 ST 8920
Cannich 102 NH 3331
Cannington 17 ST 2539
Cannock 41 SJ 9710
Cannock Wood 42 SK 0412
Canon Bridge 30 SO 4341
Canon Frome 31 SO 6543
Canon Pyon 30 SO 4549
Canonbie 70 NY 3976
Canons Ashby 33 SP 5750
Canonstown 2 SW 5335
Canterbury 15 TR 1557
Cantley (Norf.) 47 TG 3704
Cantley (S Yorks) 60 SE 6202
Cantlop 40 SJ 5205
Canton 28 ST 1577
Cantraydoune 103 NH 7946
Cantraywood 103 NH 7748
Cantsfield 65 SD 6172
Canwick 54 SK 9869
Canworthy Water 4 SX 2291
Caol 96 NN 1076
Caoles 94 NM 0848
Capel 12 TQ 1740
Capel Bangor 39 SN 6580
Capel Betws Lleucu 27 SN 6058
Capel Carmel 38 SH 1628
Capel Coch 48 SH 4582
Capel Curig 49 SH 7258
Capel Cynon 26 SN 3849
Capel Dewi 26 SN 4542
Capel Garmon 49 SH 8155
Capel Gwyn (Dyfed) 25 SN 4622
Capel Gwyn (Gwyn) 48 SH 3575
Capel Gwynfe 25 SN 7222
Capel Hendre 25 SN 5911
Capel Isaac 25 SN 5982
Capel Iwan 26 SN 2836
Capel St. Mary 37 TM 0838
Capel le Ferne 15 TR 2439
Capel-y-ffin 30 SO 2531
Capenhurst 50 SJ 3673
Capernwray 64 SD 5372
Capheaton 79 NZ 0380
Cappercleuch 77 NT 2423
Capstone 14 TQ 7865
Capton 5 SX 8353
Caputh 92 NO 0940
Car Colston 54 SK 7142
Carbis Bay 2 SW 5339
Carbost (Island of Skye) 100 NG 3731
Carbost (Island of Skye) 100 NG 4248
Carbrooke 46 TF 9402
Carburton 53 SK 6173
Carcary 99 NO 6455
Carclew 2 SW 7838
Carcroft 60 SE 5409
Cardenden 92 NT 2195
Cardeston 40 SJ 3912
Cardiff 28 ST 1877
Cardigan 26 SN 1846
Cardington (Beds.) 35 TL 0847
Cardington (Salop) 40 SO 5095
Cardinham 4 SX 1268
Cardow 104 NJ 1942
Cardrona 85 NT 3038
Cardross (Strath.) 82 NS 3477
Cardurnock 70 NY 1758
Careby 44 TF 0216
Careston 99 NO 5260
Carew 24 SN 0403
Carew Cheriton 24 SN 0402
Carew Newton 24 SN 0404
Carey 31 SO 5631
Carfrae 86 NT 5769
Cargen 70 NX 9672
Cargenbridge 69 NX 9474
Cargill 92 NO 1536
Cargo 70 NY 3659
Cargreen 4 SX 4262
Carham 87 NT 7938
Carhampton 16 ST 0042
Carharrack 2 SW 7241
Carie (Tays.) 97 NN 6157
Carie (Tays.) 90 NN 6437
Carinish 109 NF 8159
Carisbrooke 11 SZ 4888
Cark 64 SD 3676
Carland Cross 2 SW 8454
Carlby 45 TF 0414
Carlecotes 59 SE 1703
Carleton (Cumbr.) 70 NY 4253
Carleton (Lancs.) 57 SD 3339
Carleton (N Yorks.) 58 SD 9749
Carleton Forehoe 47 TG 0805
Carleton Rode 47 TM 1192
Carlingcott 17 ST 6958
Carlisle 70 NY 3955
Carlops 85 NT 1656
Carloway 109 NB 2042
Carlton (Beds.) 34 SP 9555
Carlton (Cambs.) 36 TL 6453
Carlton (Cleve.) 72 NZ 3921
Carlton (Leic.) 43 SK 3905
Carlton (N Yorks.) 66 NZ 5004
Carlton (N Yorks.) 65 SE 0684
Carlton (N Yorks.) 66 SE 6086
Carlton (N Yorks.) 60 SE 6423

Cressage

234

Dowally

Cressage	41	SJ 5904
Cresselly	24	SN 0606
Cressing	22	TL 7920
Cresswell (Dyfed)	24	SN 0506
Cresswell (Northum.)	79	NZ 2993
Cresswell (Staffs.)	51	SJ 9739
Creswell	53	SK 5274
Cretingham	37	TM 2260
Crew Green	40	SJ 3215
Crewe (Ches.)	50	SJ 4253
Crewe (Ches.)	51	SJ 7055
Crewkerne	9	ST 4409
Crianlarich	90	NN 3825
Cribyn	26	SN 5251
Criccieth	48	SH 4938
Crich	53	SK 3554
Crichie	105	NJ 9544
Crichton	85	NT 3862
Crick (Northants.)	43	SP 5872
Crickadarn	27	SO 0942
Cricket St. Thomas	9	ST 3708
Crickheath	40	SJ 2923
Crickhowell	28	SO 2118
Cricklade	18	SU 0993
Cridling Stubbs	60	SE 5221
Crieff	91	NN 8621
Criggion	40	SJ 2915
Crigglestone	59	SE 3116
Crimond	105	NK 0556
Crimplesham	46	TF 6503
Crinaglack	102	NH 4240
Crinan	89	NR 7894
Cringleford	47	TG 1905
Crinow	24	SN 1214
Cripp's Corner	14	TQ 7821
Cripplesease	2	SW 5036
Croachy	103	NH 6527
Crockenhill	21	TQ 5067
Crockernwell	5	SX 7592
Crockerton	18	ST 8642
Crocketford or Ninemile Bar	69	NX 8272
Crockey Hill	60	SE 6246
Crockham Hill	21	TQ 4450
Crockleford Heath	23	TM 0426
Croes-y-mwyalch	29	ST 3092
Croeserw	28	SS 8695
Croesgoch	24	SM 8330
Croesyceiliog (Gwent)	25	SN 4016
Croesyceiliog (Gwent)	29	ST 3196
Croft (Ches.)	51	SJ 6393
Croft (Leic.)	43	SP 5195
Croft (Lincs.)	55	TF 5162
Croft-on-Tees	66	NZ 2909
Croftamie	90	NS 4786
Crofton	59	SE 3717
Crofty	25	SS 5295
Crogen	49	SJ 0237
Croggan	89	NM 7027
Croglin	71	NY 5747
Croick	106	NH 4591
Cromarty	103	NH 7866
Cromdale	103	NJ 0728
Cromer (Herts.)	35	TL 2928
Cromer (Norf.)	47	TG 2142
Cromford	53	SK 2956
Cromhall	29	ST 6990
Cromhall Common	29	ST 6989
Cromore	109	NB 4021
Cromra	97	NN 5489
Cromwell	54	SK 7961
Cronberry	76	NS 6022
Crondall	20	SU 7948
Cronk, The	56	SC 3495
Cronk-y-Voddy	56	SC 3086
Cronton	50	SJ 4988
Crook (Cumbr.)	63	SD 4694
Crook (Durham)	72	NZ 1635
Crook of Devon	92	NO 0300
Crookham (Berks.)	19	SU 5364
Crookham (Northum.)	87	NT 9138
Crookham Village	20	SU 7952
Crookhouse	86	NT 7627
Crooklands	63	SD 5383
Cropredy	33	SP 4646
Cropston	43	SK 5511
Cropthorne	32	SO 9944
Cropton	67	SE 7589
Cropwell Bishop	53	SK 6835
Cropwell Butler	53	SK 6837
Crosby (Cumbr.)	62	NY 0738
Crosby (I. of M.)	56	SC 3279
Crosby (Mers.)	50	SJ 3099
Crosby Garrett	65	NY 7309
Crosby Ravensworth	63	NY 6214
Croscombe	17	ST 5844
Cross (Somerset)	17	ST 4154
Cross Ash	29	SO 4019
Cross Green (Devon.)	4	SX 3888
Cross Green (Suff.)	36	TL 9952
Cross Hands	25	SN 5612
Cross Houses (Salop)	40	SJ 5307
Cross Inn (Dyfed)	26	SN 3957
Cross Inn (Dyfed)	26	SN 5464
Cross Inn (Mid Glam.)	28	ST 0583
Cross Lanes (Clwyd)	50	SJ 3746
Cross Lanes (N Yorks.)	66	SE 5264
Cross Street	37	TM 1876
Cross in Hand	13	TQ 5621
Cross of Jackston	105	NJ 7432
Crossaig	81	NR 8351
Crossapoll	94	NL 9943
Crossbost	109	NB 3924
Crosscanonby	62	NY 0739
Crossdale Street	47	TG 2239
Crossens	57	SD 3719
Crossford (Fife.)	85	NT 0686
Crossford (Strath.)	84	NS 8246
Crossgates (Fife.)	85	NT 1488
Crossgates (Powys)	27	SO 0865
Crossgill	64	SD 5562
Crosshill (Fife.)	92	NT 1796
Crosshill (Strath.)	75	NS 3206
Crosshouse (Strath.)	82	NS 3938
Crossings	71	NY 5177
Crosskeys (Gwent)	28	ST 2292
Crosskirk	112	ND 0370
Crosslanes (Salop.)	40	SJ 3218
Crosslee	77	NT 3018
Crossmichael	69	NX 7267
Crossmoor	57	SD 4438
Crossroads	99	NO 7594
Crossway	29	SO 4419
Crossway Green	41	SO 8368
Crosswell	26	SN 1236
Crosthwaite	63	SD 4491
Croston	57	SD 4818
Crostwick	47	TG 2515
Crostwight	47	TG 3329
Crouch Hill	9	ST 7010
Croughton	33	SP 5433
Crovie	105	NJ 8065
Crow Hill	29	SO 6326
Crowan	2	SW 6434
Crowborough	13	TQ 5130
Crowcombe	16	ST 1336
Crowfield (Northants.)	34	SP 6141
Crowfield (Suff.)	37	TM 1557
Crowhurst (E Susx)	14	TQ 7512
Crowhurst (Surrey)	21	TQ 3947
Crowland	45	TF 2310
Crowlas	2	SW 5133
Crowle (Here. and Worc.)	32	SO 9256
Crowle (Humbs.)	60	SE 7713
Crowmarsh Gifford	19	SU 6189
Crownhill	5	SX 4857
Crownthorpe	47	TG 0803
Crowthorne	20	SU 8464
Crowton	51	SJ 5774
Croxall	42	SK 1913
Croxdale	72	NZ 2636
Croxden	52	SK 0639
Croxley Green	20	TQ 0795
Croxton (Cambs.)	35	TL 2459
Croxton (Humbs.)	61	TA 0912
Croxton (Norf.)	46	TL 8786
Croxton (Staffs.)	51	SJ 7832
Croxton Kerrial	44	SK 8329
Croy (Highld.)	103	NH 7949
Croy (Strath.)	84	NS 7275
Croyde	6	SS 4439
Croydon (Cambs.)	35	TL 3149
Croydon (Gtr London)	21	TQ 3365
Cruckmeole	40	SJ 4309
Cruckton	40	SJ 4210
Cruden Bay	105	NK 0936
Crudgington	41	SJ 6317
Crudwell	18	ST 9592
Crug	40	SO 1872
Crugmeer	3	SW 9076
Crulivig	109	NB 1733
Crumlin	28	ST 2198
Crundale (Dyfed.)	24	SM 9718
Crundale (Kent)	15	TR 0749
Crunwear	24	SN 1810
Cruwys Morchard	7	SS 8712
Crux Easton	19	SU 4256
Crwbin	25	SN 4713
Crymmych	26	SN 1833
Crynant	28	SN 7095
Crystal Palace	21	TQ 3470
Cuaig	101	NG 7057
Cubbington	43	SP 3368
Cubert	2	SW 7857
Cublington	34	SP 8422
Cuckfield	13	TQ 3024
Cucklington	17	ST 7527
Cuckney	53	SK 5671
Cuddesdon	33	SP 5902
Cuddington (Bucks.)	34	SP 7311
Cuddington (Ches.)	51	SJ 5971
Cuddington Heath	50	SJ 4646
Cuddy Hill	57	SD 4937
Cudham	21	TQ 4459
Cudliptown	5	SX 5278
Cudworth (S Yorks.)	59	SE 3808
Cudworth (Somer.)	8	ST 3810
Cuffley	35	TL 3002
Culbo	103	NH 6360
Culbokie	102	NH 6059
Culburnie	102	NH 4941
Culcabock	103	NH 6844
Culcharry	103	NH 8650
Culcheth	51	SJ 6594
Culdrain	104	NJ 5133
Culduie	101	NG 7140
Culford	36	TL 8370
Culgaith	63	NY 6129
Culham	19	SU 5095
Culkein	110	NC 0333
Culkerton	18	ST 9296
Cullachie	103	NH 9720
Cullen	104	NJ 5166
Cullercoats	79	NZ 3571
Cullerlie	99	NJ 7603
Cullicudden	103	NH 6564
Cullingworth	59	SE 0636
Cullipool	89	NM 7313
Cullivoe	113	HP 5402
Culloch	91	NN 7818
Cullompton	8	ST 0207
Culmaily	108	NH 8099
Culmington	40	SO 4982
Culmstock	8	ST 1013
Culnacraig	106	NC 0603
Culrain	108	NH 5794
Culross	85	NS 9885
Culroy	75	NS 3114
Culsh (Grampn.)	105	NJ 8848
Culswick	113	HU 2745
Cultercullen	105	NJ 9124
Cults (Grampn.)	104	NJ 5331
Culverstone Green	14	TQ 6363
Culverthorpe	54	TF 0240
Culworth	33	SP 5447
Cumbernauld	84	NS 7676
Cumberworth	55	TF 5073
Cuminestown	105	NJ 8050
Cummersdale	70	NY 3952
Cummertrees	70	NY 1366
Cummingstown	103	NJ 1368
Cumnock	75	NS 5619
Cumnor	33	SP 4604
Cumrew	71	NY 5550
Cumwhinton	71	NY 4552
Cumwhitton	71	NY 5052
Cundall (N Yorks.)	66	SE 4272
Cunninghamhead	82	NS 3741
Cupar	93	NO 3714
Cupar Muir	93	NO 3613
Curbar	53	SK 2574
Curbridge (Hants.)	11	SU 5211
Curbridge (Oxon.)	33	SP 3208
Curdridge	11	SU 5313
Curdworth	42	SP 1892
Curland	8	ST 2716
Currie	85	NT 1867
Curry Mallet	8	ST 3221
Curry Rivel	9	ST 3824
Curtisden Green	14	TQ 7440
Cury	2	SW 6721
Cushnie	105	NJ 7962
Cushuish	16	ST 1930
Cusop	30	SO 2341
Cutiau	38	SH 6317
Cutnall Green	41	SO 8768
Cutsdean	32	SP 0830
Cutthorpe	53	SK 3473
Cuxham	19	SU 6695
Cuxton	14	TQ 7166
Cuxwold	61	TA 1701
Cwm (Clwyd)	49	SJ 0677
Cwm (Gwent)	28	SO 1805
Cwm (W Glam.)	25	SS 6895
Cwm Irfon	27	SN 8549
Cwm-Cewydd	39	SH 8713
Cwm-Llinau	39	SH 8407
Cwm-y-glo	48	SH 5562
Cwmafan	28	SS 7892
Cwmaman	28	SS 9999
Cwmbach (Dyfed)	25	SN 2525
Cwmbach (Mid Glam.)	28	SO 0201
Cwmbelan	39	SN 9481
Cwmbran	29	ST 2894
Cwmcarn	28	ST 2293
Cwmcarvan	29	SO 4707
Cwmcoy	26	SN 2941
Cwmdare	28	SN 9803
Cwmdu (Dyfed)	27	SN 6330
Cwmdu (Powys)	28	SO 1823
Cwmduad	26	SN 3731
Cwmfelin Boeth	24	SN 1919
Cwmfelin Mynach	24	SN 2324
Cwmffrwd	25	SN 4217
Cwmgwrach	28	SN 8605
Cwmisfael	25	SN 4915
Cwmllynfell	25	SN 7413
Cwmparc	28	SS 9496
Cwmpengraig	26	SN 3436
Cwmsychpant	26	SN 4746
Cwmtillery	28	SO 2105
Cwmyoy	29	SO 2923
Cwmystwyth	27	SN 7873
Cwrt-newydd	26	SN 4847
Cwrt-y-gollen	28	SO 2317
Cyffylliog	49	SJ 0557
Cymmer (Mid Glam.)	28	ST 0290
Cymmer (W Glam.)	28	SS 8696
Cynghardy	27	SN 8139
Cynwyd	49	SJ 0541
Cynwyl Elfed	25	SN 3727

D

Dacre (Cumbr.)	63	NY 4526
Dacre (N Yorks.)	65	SE 1960
Dacre Banks	65	SE 1961
Daddry Shield	63	NY 8937
Dadford	34	SP 6638
Dadlington	43	SP 4098
Dafen	25	SN 5201
Daffy Green	46	TF 9609
Dagenham	21	TQ 5084
Daglingworth	32	SO 9905
Dagnall	34	SP 9916
Dailly	75	NS 2701
Dairsie or Osnaburgh	93	NO 4117
Dalavich	89	NM 9612
Dalbeattie	69	NX 8361
Dalblair	76	NS 6419
Dalbog	99	NO 5871
Dalby	56	SC 2178
Dalcapon	98	NN 9755
Dalchalloch	97	NN 7264
Dalchenna	89	NN 0706
Dalchreichart	102	NH 2912
Dalcross	103	NH 7748
Dalderby	55	TF 2465
Dale (Derby.)	53	SK 4338
Dale (Dyfed)	24	SM 8005
Dale (Shetld.)	113	HU 1852
Dalelia	95	NM 7369
Dalgarven	82	NS 2945
Dalginross	91	NN 7721
Dalguise	98	NN 9947
Dalhalvaig	111	NC 8954
Dalham	36	TL 7261
Daliburgh	109	NF 7421
Dalkeith	85	NT 3367
Dall	97	NN 5956
Dallas	103	NJ 1252
Dalleagles	75	NS 5710
Dallinghoo	37	TM 2654
Dallington	13	TQ 6519
Dalmally	89	NN 1527
Dalmary	90	NS 5195
Dalmellington	75	NS 4705
Dalmeny	85	NT 1477
Dalmore (Highld.)	103	NH 6668
Dalnabreck	95	NM 7069
Dalnavie	108	NH 6483
Dalnawillan Lodge	112	ND 0341
Dalness	96	NN 1751
Dalqueich	92	NO 0704
Dalry	82	NS 2949
Dalrymple	75	NS 3514
Dalserf	84	NS 7950
Dalston	70	NY 3750
Dalswinton	69	NX 9385
Dalton (Dumf. and Galwy.)	70	NY 1173
Dalton (Lancs.)	57	SD 4907
Dalton (N Yorks.)	65	NZ 1108
Dalton (N Yorks.)	66	SE 4376
Dalton (N Yorks.)	53	SK 4593
Dalton (Northum.)	71	NY 9158
Dalton (Northum.)	79	NZ 1172
Dalton Piercy	73	NZ 4631
Dalton in Furness	64	SD 2374
Dalton-le-Dale	72	NZ 4047
Dalton-on-Tees	66	NZ 2908
Dalveich	90	NN 6124
Dalwhinnie	97	NN 6384
Dalwood	8	ST 2400
Damerham	10	SU 1015
Damgate	47	TG 4009
Damnaglaur	68	NX 1235
Danbury	22	TL 7805
Danby	66	NZ 7009
Danby Wiske	66	SE 3398
Dandaleith	104	NJ 2845
Danderhall	85	NT 3069
Dane End	35	TL 3321
Dane Hills	43	SK 5605
Danebridge	51	SJ 9665
Danehill	13	TQ 4027
Daren-felen	28	SO 2212
Darenth	21	TQ 5671
Daresbury	51	SJ 5782
Darfield	59	SE 4104
Dargate	15	TR 0861
Darite	4	SX 2569
Darlaston	41	SO 9796
Darlingscott	33	SP 2324
Darlington	72	NZ 2914
Darliston	51	SJ 5833
Darlochan	74	NR 6723
Darlton	54	SK 7773
Darowen	39	SH 8302
Darras Hall	79	NZ 1571
Darrington	60	SE 4919
Darsham	37	TM 4170
Dartford	21	TQ 5474
Dartington	5	SX 7862
Dartmeet	5	SX 6773
Dartmouth	5	SX 8751
Darton	59	SE 3110
Darvel	84	NS 5637
Darwen	58	SD 6922
Datchet	20	SU 9876
Datchworth	35	TL 2619
Dauntsey	18	ST 9882
Davenham	51	SJ 6570
Daventry	33	SP 5762
Davidstow	4	SX 1587
Davington	77	NT 2302
Daviot (Grampn.)	105	NJ 7528
Daviot (Highld.)	103	NH 7139
Davoch of Grange	104	NJ 4951
Dawley	41	SJ 6807
Dawlish	8	SX 9676
Dawlish Warren	8	SX 9778
Dawn	49	SH 8672
Dawsmere	55	TF 4430
Daylesford	33	SP 2425
Deal	15	TR 3752
Dean (Cumbr.)	62	NY 0725
Dean (Devon)	5	SX 7364
Dean (Hants.)	11	SU 5619
Dean (Somer.)	17	ST 6743
Dean Prior	5	SX 7363
Dean Row	51	SJ 8781
Deanburnhaugh	77	NT 3911
Deane	19	SU 5450
Deanland	10	ST 9918
Deanscale	62	NY 0926
Deanshanger	34	SP 7639
Deanston	91	NN 7101
Dearham	62	NY 0736
Debach	37	TM 2454
Debden	36	TL 5533
Debden Cross	36	TL 5832
Debenham	37	TM 1763
Dechmont	85	NT 0370
Deddington	33	SP 4631
Dedham	37	TM 0533
Deene	44	SP 9492
Deenethorpe	44	SP 9592
Deepcar	59	SK 2897
Deepcut	20	SU 9057
Deepdale (Cumbr.)	65	SD 7284
Deeping Gate	45	TF 1509
Deeping St. James	45	TF 1609
Deeping St. Nicholas	45	TF 2115
Deerhurst	32	SO 8729
Defford	32	SO 9143
Defynnog	28	SN 9227
Deganwy	49	SH 7779
Deighton (N Yorks.)	66	NZ 3801
Deighton (N Yorks.)	60	SE 6244
Deiniolen	48	SH 5863
Delabole	4	SX 0683
Delamere	51	SJ 5668
Dell	109	NB 4861
Delliefure	103	NJ 0731
Delph	59	SD 9807
Dembleby	54	TF 0437
Den, The	82	NS 3251
Denaby	60	SK 4899
Denbigh	49	SJ 0566
Denbury	5	SX 8268
Denby	53	SK 3946
Denby Dale	59	SE 2208
Denchworth	19	SU 3891
Denend	104	NJ 6038
Denford	44	SP 9976
Dengie	23	TL 9801
Denham (Bucks.)	20	TQ 0386
Denham (Suff.)	36	TL 7561
Denham (Suff.)	37	TM 1974
Denham Green	20	TQ 0388
Denhead (Fife.)	93	NO 4613
Denhead (Grampn.)	105	NJ 9952
Denhead of Arbirlot	99	NO 5543
Denhead of Gray	93	NO 3431
Denholm	78	NT 5718
Denholme	59	SE 0633
Denmead	11	SU 6511
Dennington	37	TM 2866
Denny	84	NS 8182
Dennyloanhead	84	NS 8180
Denshaw	59	SD 9710
Denside	99	NO 8095
Densole	15	TR 2141
Denston	36	TL 7652
Denstone	52	SK 0940
Dent	65	SD 7087
Denton (Cambs.)	45	TL 1487
Denton (Durham)	72	NZ 2118
Denton (E Susx.)	13	TQ 4502
Denton (Gtr. Mches.)	51	SJ 9295
Denton (Kent)	15	TR 2146
Denton (Lincs.)	54	SK 8632
Denton (N Yorks.)	59	SE 1448
Denton (Norf.)	47	TM 2887
Denton (Northants.)	34	SP 8357
Denton (Oxon.)	33	SP 5902
Denver	46	TF 6101
Denwick (Northum.)	79	NU 2014
Deopham	47	TG 0400
Deopham Green	47	TM 0499
Depden Green	36	TL 7756
Deptford (Gtr London)	21	TQ 3676
Deptford (Wilts.)	10	SU 0038
Derby	53	SK 3435
Derbyhaven	56	SC 2867
Deri	28	SO 1202
Derringstone	15	TR 2049
Derrington	41	SJ 8822
Derry Hill	18	ST 9670
Derrythorpe	60	SE 8208
Dersingham	46	TF 6830
Dervaig	94	NM 4351
Derwen	49	SJ 0650
Desborough	44	SP 8083
Desford	43	SK 4703
Detchant	87	NU 0836
Detling	14	TQ 7958
Deuddwr	40	SJ 2317
Devauden	29	ST 4899
Devil's Bridge	27	SN 7477
Devizes	18	SU 0061
Devonport	5	SX 4554
Devonside	91	NS 9296
Devoran	2	SW 7939
Dewlish	10	SY 7798
Dewsbury	59	SE 2422
Dhoon	56	SC 4586
Dhoor	56	SC 4396
Dhowin	56	NX 4101
Dial Post	12	TQ 1519
Dibden	11	SU 4108
Dibden Purlieu	11	SU 4106
Dickleburgh	47	TM 1682
Didbrook	32	SP 0531
Didcot	19	SU 5290
Diddington	45	TL 1965
Diddlebury	40	SO 5085
Didley	30	SO 4432
Didmarton	18	ST 8287
Didsbury	51	SJ 8490
Didworthy	5	SX 6862
Digby	54	TF 0754
Diggle	59	SE 0008
Dihewyd	26	SN 4855
Dilham	47	TG 332
Dilhorne	51	SJ 974
Dilston	72	NY 976
Dilton Marsh	18	ST 844
Dilwyn	30	SO 415
Dinas (Dyfed)	26	SN 013
Dinas (Dyfed)	25	SN 273
Dinas (Gwyn.)	48	SH 273
Dinas Powis	28	ST 157
Dinas-Mawddwy	39	SH 851
Dinchope	49	SO 458
Dinder	17	ST 574
Dinedor	31	SO 533
Dingley	44	SP 768
Dingwall	102	NH 545
Dinnet	98	NO 469
Dinnington (S Yorks.)	53	SK 538
Dinnington (Somer.)	9	ST 401
Dinnington (Tyne and Wear)	79	NZ 207
Dinorwic	48	SH 596
Dinton	10	SU 013
Dinwoodie Mains	77	NY 109
Dinworthy	6	SS 301
Dippen	81	NR 793
Dippin	74	NS 042
Dipple (Grampn.)	104	NJ 325
Dipple (Strath.)	75	NS 200
Diptford	5	SX 725
Dipton	72	NZ 155
Dirleton	86	NT 518
Discoed	30	SO 276
Diseworth	43	SK 452
Dishforth	66	SE 387
Disley	51	SJ 978
Diss	37	TM 117
Distington	62	NY 002
Ditcheat	17	ST 623
Ditchingham	47	TM 339
Ditchling	13	TQ 321
Dittisham	5	SX 865
Ditton (Ches.)	50	SJ 498
Ditton (Kent)	14	TQ 715
Ditton Green	36	TL 665
Ditton Priors	41	SO 608
Dixton (Glos.)	32	SO 983
Dixton (Gwent)	29	SO 511
Dobwalls	4	SX 216
Doccombe	5	SX 778
Dochgarroch	102	NH 614
Docking	46	TF 763
Docklow	31	SO 565
Dockray	62	NY 392
Doddinghurst	21	TQ 599
Doddington (Cambs.)	45	TL 409
Doddington (Kent)	15	TQ 935
Doddington (Lincs.)	54	SK 907
Doddington (Northum.)	87	NU 003
Doddington (Salop)	41	SO 617
Doddiscombsleigh	5	SX 858
Dodford (Here. and Worc.)	41	SO 927
Dodford (Northants.)	34	SP 616
Dodington (Avon)	29	ST 748
Dodleston	50	SJ 366
Dodworth	59	SE 310
Doe Lea	53	SK 456
Dog Village	8	SX 989
Dogdyke	55	TF 205
Dogmersfield	20	SU 785
Dol-for (Powys)	39	SH 800
Dolanog	39	SJ 061
Dolau	40	SO 136
Dolbenmaen	48	SH 504
Dolfach	27	SN 907
Dolfor (Powys)	40	SO 108
Dolgarrog	49	SH 776
Dolgellau	39	SH 721
Doll	108	NC 880
Dollar	91	NS 969
Dolphinholme	64	SD 515
Dolphinton	85	NT 104
Dolton	6	SS 571
Dolwen (Clwyd)	49	SH 887
Dolwen (Powys)	39	SH 970
Dolwyddelan	49	SH 735
Dolyhir	30	SO 245
Domgay	40	SJ 281
Doncaster	60	SE 580
Donhead St. Andrew	10	ST 912
Donhead St. Mary	10	ST 902
Donibristle	85	NT 168
Donington	55	TF 213
Donington on Bain	55	TF 238
Donisthorpe	43	SK 311
Donkey Town	20	SU 946
Donnington (Berks.)	19	SU 466
Donnington (Glos.)	33	SP 192
Donnington (Here. and Worc.)	32	SO 703
Donnington (Salop)	41	SJ 580
Donnington (Salop)	41	SJ 711
Donnington (W Susx.)	12	SU 850
Donyatt	8	ST 331
Doonfoot	75	NS 321
Dorchester (Dorset)	9	SY 699
Dorchester (Oxon.)	19	SU 579
Dordon	43	SK 260
Dore	53	SK 308
Dores	102	NH 593
Dorking	21	TQ 164
Dormans Lane	13	TQ 404
Dormanstown	73	NZ 582
Dormington	31	SO 584
Dorney	20	SU 937
Dornie	101	NG 882
Dornoch (Highld.)	108	NH 798
Dornock (Dumf. and Galwy.)	70	NY 236
Dorrery	112	ND 075
Dorridge	42	SP 177
Dorrington (Lincs.)	54	TF 075
Dorrington (Salop)	40	SJ 470
Dorsington	32	SP 134
Dorstone	30	SO 314
Dorton	34	SP 671
Dosthill	42	SP 219
Doublebois	4	SX 196
Dougarie	81	NR 883
Doughton	18	ST 879
Douglas (I. of M.)	56	SC 387
Douglas (Strath.)	84	NS 833
Douglas Hill	48	SH 606
Douglas and Angus	93	NO 433
Douglastown	98	NO 414
Doulting	17	ST 644
Dounby	113	HY 292
Doune (Tays.)	91	NN 720
Douneside	104	NJ 480
Dounie	108	NH 559
Dounreay	112	NC 996
Dousland	5	SX 536
Dove Holes	52	SK 07
Dovenby	62	NY 093
Dover	15	TR 314
Doverdale	32	SO 856
Doveridge	52	SK 113
Dowally	98	NO 00

owdeswell 235 Eldroth

owdeswell 32 SO 9919
owland 6 SS 5610
owlish Wake 8 ST 3712
own Ampney 18 SU 1097
own Hatherley 32 SO 8622
own St. Mary 7 SS 7404
ownderry 4 SX 3153
owne 21 TQ 4361
ownend (Berks.) 19 SU 4775
ownend (I. of W.) 11 SZ 5387
ownfield 93 NO 3833
owngate 4 SX 3772
ownham (Cambs.) 45 TL 5284
ownham (Essex) 22 TQ 7395
ownham (Lancs.) 58 SD 7844
ownham (Northum.) 87 NT 8633
ownham Market 46 TF 6003
ownhead 17 ST 6845
ownhill 3 SW 8669
ownholme 65 SE 1197
ownies 99 NO 9294
ownley 20 SU 8495
ownton (Hants.) 11 SZ 2693
ownton (Wilts.) 10 SU 1721
ownton on the Rock 40 SO 4273
owsby 45 TF 1129
oynton 29 ST 7173
affan 84 NS 7945
akeland Corner 5 SX 5758
akemyre 82 NS 2850
akes Broughton 32 SO 9248
aughton (N. Yorks.) 65 SE 0352
aughton (Northants.) 44 SP 7676
ax 60 SE 6726
aycote 43 SP 4469
aycott (Derby) 53 SK 4433
aycott (Glos.) 33 SP 1836
aycott (Somer.) 17 ST 4750
aycott in the Clay 42 SK 1528
aycott in the Moors 51 SJ 9840
ayton (Hants.) 11 SU 6605
ayton (Here. and Worc.) 41 SO 9076
ayton (Leic.) 44 SP 8392
ayton (Norf.) 47 TG 1713
ayton (Oxon.) 33 SP 4241
ayton (Oxon.) 19 SU 4794
ayton (Somer.) 9 ST 4024
ayton Bassett 42 SK 1900
ayton Parslow 34 SP 8428
ayton St. Leonard 19 SU 5996
efach (Dyfed) 26 SN 3538
efach (Dyfed) 26 SN 5045
efach (Dyfed) 25 SN 5213
eghorn 82 NS 3538
em 86 NT 5079
ewsteignton 5 SX 7391
by 55 TF 3874
ffield 18 SU 0799
ft 2 SW 4328
gg 62 SD 0698
ghlington 59 SE 2229
mnin 95 NM 5553
mpton 9 ST 4104
msallie 95 NM 9779
msynie 89 NN 1502
nkstone 36 TL 9661
nkstone Green 36 TL 9660
ointon 42 SK 0226
oitwich 32 SO 8962
on 92 NO 1415
onfield 53 SK 3578
onfield Woodhouse 53 SK 3278
ongan 75 NS 4418
onley 93 NO 3435
oxford 11 SU 6018
oylsden 58 SJ 9098
uid 49 SJ 0343
uidston 24 SM 8716
uimarbin 96 NN 0861
uimavuic 96 NN 0044
um (Grampn.) 105 NJ 8946
um (Tays.) 92 NO 0400
umbeg 110 NC 1232
umblade 104 NJ 5840
umbuie (Dumf. and Galwy.) 69 NX 5682
umbuie (Highld.) 101 NG 7730
umburgh 70 NY 2659
umchapel 84 NS 5270
umchardine 102 NH 5644
umclog 84 NS 6339
umeldrie 93 NO 4403
umelzier 85 NT 1333
umfearn 101 NG 6716
umgask 97 NN 6193
umgley 98 NO 4250
umguish 97 NN 7999
umhead 99 NO 6092
umlasie 104 NJ 6405
umlemble 74 NR 6619
umlithie 99 NO 7880
ummore 68 NX 1336
umnadrochit 102 NH 5029
umnagorrach 104 NJ 5252
umrash 69 NX 6871
umsturdy 93 NO 4935
umuie 100 NG 4546
umuillie 103 NH 9420
umwhindle 105 NJ 9236
unkendub 99 NO 6646
ury 50 SJ 2964
y Doddington 54 SK 8446
y Drayton 35 TL 3862
ybeck 63 NY 6615
ybridge (Grampn.) 104 NJ 4362
ybridge (Strath.) 82 NS 3536
ybrook 29 SO 6416
yhope 77 NT 2624
ymen 90 NS 4788
ymuir 105 NJ 9146
ynoch 100 NG 4031
ubford 105 NJ 7963
ubton 99 NO 5652
uck's Cross 35 TL 1156
uckington 50 SJ 4851
ucklington 33 SP 3507
uddingston 85 NT 2972
uddington 44 SK 9800
uddleswell 13 TQ 4628
uddo 87 NT 9342
uddon 50 SJ 5164
udleston Heath 50 SJ 3636
udley 41 SO 9390
uffield 53 SK 3443
uffryn 28 SS 8495
ufftown 104 NJ 3240
uffus 104 NJ 1668
ufton 63 NY 6925
uggleby 67 SE 8766
uirinish 101 NG 7831
uisdalemore 101 NG 6913
uisky 96 NN 0176
ukestown 28 SO 1410
ukinfield 58 SJ 9497
ulas (Gwyn.) 48 SH 4789
Dulcote 17 ST 5644
Dulford 8 ST 0606
Dull 97 NN 8049
Dullingham 36 TL 6357
Dulnain Bridge 103 NH 9924
Duloe (Beds.) 35 TL 1560
Duloe (Corn.) 4 SX 2358
Dulsie 103 NH 9341
Dulverton 16 SS 9127
Dulwich 21 TQ 3373
Dumbarton 82 NS 4075
Dumbleton 32 SP 0135
Dumfries 70 NX 9775
Dummer 19 SU 5845
Dun (Tays.) 99 NO 6659
Dunalastair 97 NN 7159
Dunan (Isle of Skye) 100 NG 5828
Dunan (Strath.) 82 NS 1571
Dunans 89 NS 0491
Dunball 17 ST 3140
Dunbar 86 NT 6878
Dunbeath 112 ND 1629
Dunbeg 89 NM 8734
Dunblane 91 NN 7801
Dunbog 93 NO 2817
Duncanston (Highld.) 102 NH 5956
Duncaston (Grampn.) 104 NJ 5826
Dunchurch 43 SP 4871
Duncote 34 SP 6750
Duncow 70 NX 9683
Duncrievie 92 NO 1309
Duncton 12 SU 9516
Dundee 93 NO 4030
Dundon 17 ST 4732
Dundonald 82 NS 3634
Dundraw 70 NY 2149
Dundreggan 102 NH 3114
Dundrennan 69 NX 7447
Dundry 29 ST 5566
Dunecht 105 NJ 7509
Dunfermiline 85 NT 0987
Dunford Bridge 59 SE 1502
Dunham 54 SK 8174
Dunham Town 51 SJ 7488
Dunham-on-the-Hill 50 SJ 4772
Dunhampton 41 SO 8466
Dunholme 54 TF 0279
Dunino 93 NO 5311
Dunipace 84 NS 8083
Dunk's Green 21 TQ 6152
Dunkeld 98 NO 0242
Dunkeswell 8 ST 1407
Dunkirk 15 TR 0758
Dunlappie 99 NO 5967
Dunley 41 SO 7869
Dunlop 82 NS 4049
Dunmore (Central.) 84 NS 8989
Dunmore (Strath.) 81 NR 7961
Dunnet 112 ND 2171
Dunnichen 99 NO 5048
Dunning 92 NO 0114
Dunnington (Humbs.) 67 TA 1551
Dunnington (N. Yorks.) 66 SE 6652
Dunnington (Warw.) 32 SP 0653
Dunnockshaw 58 SD 8127
Dunollie 89 NM 8532
Dunoon 82 NS 1777
Dunragit 68 NX 1557
Duns 87 NT 7853
Duns Tew 33 SP 4528
Dunsby 45 TF 1026
Dunscore 69 NX 8684
Dunscroft 60 SE 6409
Dunsden Green 20 SU 7477
Dunsfold 12 TQ 0036
Dunsford 5 SX 8089
Dunshelt 93 NO 2410
Dunshillock 105 NJ 9848
Dunsley 73 NZ 8511
Dunsmore 34 SP 8605
Dunstable 35 TL 0221
Dunstall 42 SK 1920
Dunstall Green 36 TL 7460
Dunstan 79 NU 2419
Dunster 16 SS 9943
Dunston (Lincs.) 54 TF 0663
Dunston (Norf.) 47 TG 2302
Dunston (Staffs.) 41 SJ 9217
Dunston (Tyne and Wear) 72 NZ 2263
Dunsville 60 SE 6407
Dunswell 61 TA 0735
Dunsyre 85 NT 0748
Dunterton 4 SX 3779
Duntisbourne Abbots 32 SO 9707
Duntisbourne Rouse 32 SO 9805
Duntish 9 ST 6906
Duntocher 82 NS 4972
Dunton (Beds.) 35 TL 2344
Dunton (Bucks.) 34 SP 8224
Dunton (Norf.) 46 TF 8730
Dunton Bassett 43 SP 5490
Dunton Green 21 TQ 5157
Dunton Wayletts 22 TQ 6590
Dunure 75 NS 2515
Dunvant 25 SS 5993
Dunvegan 100 NG 2548
Dunwich 37 TM 4770
Durdar 70 NY 4051
Durham 72 NZ 2742
Durisdeer 76 NS 8903
Durleigh 16 ST 2736
Durley (Hants.) 11 SU 5115
Durley (Wilts.) 18 SU 2364
Durley Street 11 SU 5217
Durnamuck 106 NH 0192
Durness 110 NC 4067
Durno 105 NJ 7128
Durran 108 ND 1863
Durrington (W Susx.) 12 TQ 1105
Durrington (Wilts.) 18 SU 1544
Dursley 29 ST 7597
Durston 17 ST 2828
Durweston 10 ST 8508
Duston 34 SP 7261
Duthil 103 NH 9324
Dutlas 40 SO 2077
Duton Hill 22 TL 6026
Dutton 51 SJ 5779
Duxford 35 TL 4846
Dwygyfylchi 49 SH 7377
Dwyran 48 SH 4466
Dyce 105 NJ 8812
Dyffryn 28 SS 8593
Dyffryn Ardudwy 38 SH 5822
Dyffryn Ceidrych 25 SN 7025
Dyffryn Cellwen 28 SN 8509
Dyke (Devon.) 6 SS 3123
Dyke (Grampn.) 103 NH 9858
Dyke (Lincs.) 45 TF 1022
Dykehead (Central) 90 NS 5997
Dykehead (Strath.) 84 NS 8759
Dykehead (Tays.) 98 NO 3860
Dykends 98 NO 2557
Dylife 39 SN 8594
Dymchurch 15 TR 1029
Dymock 32 SO 6931
Dyrham 29 ST 7375
Dysart 93 NT 3093
Dyserth 49 SJ 0579

E

Eagland Hill 57 SD 4345
Eagle 54 SK 8767
Eaglescliffe 72 NZ 4215
Eaglesfield (Cumbr.) 62 NY 0928
Eaglesfield (Dumf and Galwy.) 70 NY 2374
Eaglesham 84 NS 5751
Eairy 56 SC 2977
Eakring 53 SK 6762
Ealand 60 SE 7811
Ealing 21 TQ 1781
Eamont Bridge 63 NY 5228
Earby 58 SD 9046
Earcroft 58 SD 6824
Eardington 41 SO 7290
Eardisland 30 SO 4158
Eardisley 30 SO 3149
Eardiston (Here. and Worcs.) 41 SO 6968
Eardiston (Salop) 40 SJ 3725
Earith 45 TL 3875
Earl Shilton 43 SP 4697
Earl Soham 37 TM 2363
Earl Sterndale 52 SK 0967
Earl Stonham 37 TM 1158
Earl's Croome 32 SO 8642
Earl's Green 36 TM 0366
Earle 87 NT 9826
Earlestown 51 SJ 5795
Earlish 100 NG 3861
Earls Barton 34 SP 8563
Earls Colne 22 TL 8528
Earlsdon 43 SP 3177
Earlsferry 93 NO 4800
Earlsford 105 NJ 8334
Earlston (Borders) 86 NT 5738
Earlston (Strath.) 82 NS 4035
Earlswood 42 SP 1174
Earlswood Common 29 ST 4595
Earnley 12 SZ 8196
Earsdon 79 NZ 3272
Earshaig 76 NT 0402
Earsham 47 TM 3289
Earswick 66 SE 6157
Eartham 12 SU 9309
Easby 66 NZ 5708
Easdale (Strath.) 89 NM 7317
Easebourne 12 SU 8922
Easenhall 43 SP 4679
Easington (Bucks.) 34 SP 6810
Easington (Cleve.) 73 NZ 7418
Easington (Durham) 72 NZ 4143
Easington (Humbs.) 61 TA 3919
Easington (Northum.) 87 NU 1234
Easington (Oxon.) 19 SU 6697
Easington Lane 72 NZ 3646
Easingwold 66 SE 5269
Easole Street 15 TR 2652
Eassie and Nevay 98 NO 3345
East Aberthaw 28 ST 0367
East Allington 5 SX 7648
East Anstey 7 SS 8626
East Ashling 12 SU 8207
East Barkwith 55 TF 1681
East Barming 14 TQ 7254
East Barnet 21 TQ 2794
East Barsham 46 TF 9133
East Beckham 47 TG 1640
East Bedfont 20 TQ 1074
East Bergholt 37 TM 0734
East Bilney 46 TF 9519
East Blatchington 13 TQ 4800
East Boldre 11 SU 3700
East Bradenham 46 TF 9208
East Brent 17 ST 3452
East Bridge 37 TM 4566
East Bridgford 53 SK 6943
East Buckland 7 SS 6731
East Budleigh 8 SY 0684
East Burton 10 SY 8386
East Cairnbeg 99 NO 7076
East Calder 85 NT 0867
East Carleton (Norf.) 47 TG 1802
East Carlton (Northants.) 44 SP 8389
East Chaldon or Chaldon Herring 10 SY 7983
East Challow 19 SU 3988
East Chiltington 13 TQ 3715
East Chisenbury 18 SU 1352
East Clandon 20 TQ 0651
East Claydon 34 SP 7325
East Combe (Somer.) 16 ST 1631
East Cottingwith 60 SE 7042
East Coulston 18 ST 9454
East Cowes 11 SZ 5095
East Cowton 66 NZ 3103
East Cramlington 79 NZ 2876
East Creech 10 SY 9282
East Dean (E Susx.) 13 TV 5597
East Dean (Hants.) 11 SU 2726
East Dean (W Susx.) 12 SU 9013
East Dereham 46 TF 9913
East Down 6 SS 5941
East Drayton 54 SK 7775
East End (Avon) 29 ST 4770
East End (Dorset) 10 SY 9998
East End (Hants.) 19 SU 4161
East End (Hants.) 11 SZ 3697
East End (Herts.) 35 TL 4527
East End (Kent) 14 TQ 8335
East End (Oxon.) 33 SP 3914
East Farleigh 14 TQ 7353
East Farndon 44 SP 7185
East Ferry 60 SK 8199
East Garston 19 SU 3676
East Ginge 19 SU 4486
East Goscote 43 SK 6413
East Grafton 18 SU 2560
East Grimstead 11 SU 2227
East Grinstead 13 TQ 3938
East Guldeford 15 TQ 9321
East Haddon 43 SP 6668
East Hagbourne 19 SU 5388
East Halton 61 TA 1419
East Ham (Gtr London) 21 TQ 4283
East Hanney 19 SU 4192
East Hanningfield 22 TL 7601
East Hardwick 60 SE 4618
East Harling 46 TL 9986
East Harlsey 66 SE 4299
East Harptree 17 ST 5655
East Hartford 79 NZ 2679
East Harting 12 SU 7919
East Hatley 35 TL 2850
East Hauxwell 65 SE 1693
East Heckington 55 TF 1944
East Hedleyhope 72 NZ 1540
East Hendred 19 SU 4588
East Heslerton 67 SE 9276
East Hoathly 13 TQ 5216
East Horrington 17 ST 5846
East Horsley 20 TQ 0952
East Huntspill 17 ST 3444
East Hyde 35 TL 1317
East Ilsley 19 SU 4981
East Kennett 18 SU 1167
East Keswick 59 SE 3544
East Kilbride 84 NS 6354
East Kirkby 55 TF 3362
East Knighton 10 SY 8185
East Knoyle 10 ST 8830
East Lambrook 9 ST 4319
East Langdon 15 TR 3346
East Langton 44 SP 7292
East Langwell 108 NC 7206
East Lavington 12 SU 9416
East Layton 72 NZ 1609
East Leake 43 SK 5526
East Leigh (Devon.) 7 SS 6905
East Lexham 46 TF 8617
East Lilburn 79 NU 0423
East Linton 86 NT 5977
East Looe 4 SX 2553
East Lound 60 SK 7899
East Lulworth 10 SY 8581
East Mains 99 NO 6797
East Malling 14 TQ 7057
East March 93 NO 4436
East Marden 12 SU 8014
East Markham 54 SK 7472
East Marton 65 SD 9050
East Meon 11 SU 6822
East Mersea 23 TM 0414
East Molesey 21 TQ 1568
East Morden 10 SY 9194
East Morton 59 SE 1042
East Norton 44 SK 7800
East Oakley 19 SU 5749
East Ogwell 5 SX 8370
East Ord 87 NT 9851
East Panson 4 SX 3692
East Peckham 14 TQ 6649
East Pennard 17 ST 5937
East Poringland 47 TG 2701
East Portlemouth 5 SX 7438
East Prawle 5 SX 7736
East Preston 12 TQ 0702
East Putford 6 SS 3616
East Quantoxhead 16 ST 1343
East Rainton 72 NZ 3347
East Ravendale 61 TF 2399
East Raynham 46 TF 8825
East Rudham 46 TF 8228
East Runton 47 TG 1942
East Ruston 27 TG 3427
East Saltoun 86 NT 4767
East Shefford 19 SU 3974
East Sleekburn 79 NZ 2785
East Stoke (Dorset) 10 SY 8787
East Stoke (Notts.) 54 SK 7549
East Stour 10 ST 8022
East Stourmouth 15 TR 2662
East Stratton 19 SU 5440
East Studdal 15 TR 3149
East Taphouse 4 SX 1863
East Thirston 79 NZ 1999
East Tilbury 22 TQ 6877
East Tisted 12 SU 7032
East Torrington 55 TF 1483
East Tuddenham 47 TG 0811
East Tytherley 11 SU 2929
East Tytherton 18 ST 9674
East Village 7 SS 8405
East Wall 40 SO 5293
East Walton 46 TF 7416
East Wellow 11 SU 3020
East Wemyss 93 NT 3396
East Whitburn 84 NS 9665
East Wickham 21 TQ 4576
East Williamston 24 SN 0905
East Winch 46 TF 6916
East Wittering 12 SZ 7996
East Witton 65 SE 1486
East Woodhay 19 SU 4061
East Worldham 12 SU 7538
East Wretham 46 TL 9190
Eastbourne 13 TV 6199
Eastbury (Berks.) 19 SU 3477
Eastbury (Gtr London) 20 TQ 0991
Eastchurch 15 TQ 9871
Eastcombe (Glos.) 32 SO 8804
Eastcote (Gtr London) 20 TQ 1188
Eastcote (W Mids) 42 SP 1979
Eastcott (Corn.) 6 SS 2515
Eastcott (Wilts.) 18 SU 0255
Eastcourt 18 ST 9792
Eastend (Essex) 23 TQ 9492
Easter Ardross 108 NH 6373
Easter Balmoral 98 NO 2693
Easter Boleskine 102 NH 5122
Easter Compton 29 ST 5782
Easter Galcantray 103 NH 8147
Easter Kinkell 102 NH 5756
Easter Lednathie 98 NO 3363
Easter Moniack 102 NH 5543
Easter Muckovie 103 NH 7044
Easter Ord 99 NJ 8304
Eastergate 12 SU 9405
Eastern Green 43 SP 2780
Easterton 18 SU 0154
Eastertown 17 ST 3454
Eastfield (N Yorks.) 67 TA 0484
Eastfield (Strath.) 84 NS 7574
Eastfield (Strath.) 84 NS 8964
Eastfield Hall 79 NU 2206
Eastgate (Durham) 72 NY 9538
Eastgate (Norf.) 47 TG 1423
Eastham (Mers.) 50 SJ 3580
Easthampstead 20 SU 8667
Easthope 40 SO 5695
Easthorpe 23 TL 9121
Eastington (Glos.) 32 SO 7705
Eastington (Glos.) 32 SP 1213
Eastleach Martin 33 SP 1905
Eastleach Turville 33 SP 1905
Eastleigh (Hants.) 11 SU 4518
Eastling 15 TQ 9656
Eastney 11 SZ 6698
Eastnor 32 SO 7337
Eastoft 60 SE 8016
Easton (Cambs.) 45 TL 1371
Easton (Cumbr.) 70 NY 4372
Easton (Devon.) 5 SX 7288
Easton (Dorset) 9 SY 6871
Easton (Hants.) 11 SU 5132
Easton (I. of W.) 11 SZ 3485
Easton (Lincs.) 44 SK 9226
Easton (Norf.) 47 TG 1311
Easton (Somer.) 17 ST 5147
Easton (Suff.) 37 TM 2858
Easton Grey 18 ST 8787
Easton Maudit 34 SP 8858
Easton Royal 18 SU 2060
Easton on the Hill 44 TF 0004
Easton-in-Gordano 29 ST 5175
Eastrea 45 TL 2997
Eastriggs 70 NY 2465
Eastrington 60 SE 7929
Eastry 15 TR 3155
Eastville 55 TF 4057
Eastwell 44 SK 7728
Eastwick 35 TL 4311
Eastwood (Essex) 22 TQ 8588
Eastwood (Notts.) 53 SK 4646
Eastwood (W Yorks.) 58 SD 9625
Eathorpe 43 SP 3969
Eaton (Ches.) 51 SJ 5763
Eaton (Ches.) 51 SJ 8765
Eaton (Leic.) 44 SK 7929
Eaton (Norf.) 47 TG 2006
Eaton (Notts.) 54 SK 7077
Eaton (Oxon.) 33 SP 4403
Eaton (Salop) 40 SO 3789
Eaton (Salop) 40 SO 4989
Eaton Bishop 30 SO 4439
Eaton Bray 34 SP 9720
Eaton Constantine 41 SJ 5906
Eaton Hastings 18 SU 2698
Eaton Socon 35 TL 1658
Eaton upon Tern 41 SJ 6523
Ebberston 67 SE 8983
Ebbesborne Wake 10 ST 9824
Ebbw Vale (Gwent) 28 ST 2094
Ebchester 72 NZ 1055
Ebford 8 SX 9887
Ebrington 33 SP 1840
Ecchinswell 19 SU 5059
Ecclaw 86 NT 7568
Ecclefechan 70 NY 1974
Eccles (Borders) 87 NT 7641
Eccles (Gtr Mches) 58 SJ 7798
Eccles (Kent) 14 TQ 7260
Eccles Road 46 TM 0190
Ecclesfield 53 SK 3393
Eccleshall 41 SJ 8329
Ecclesmachan 85 NT 0573
Eccleston (Ches.) 50 SJ 4162
Eccleston (Lancs.) 57 SD 5216
Eccleston (Mers.) 50 SJ 4895
Eccup 59 SE 2842
Echt 105 NJ 7305
Eckford 78 NT 7125
Eckington (Derby) 53 SK 4379
Eckington (Here. and Worc.) 32 SO 9241
Ecton 34 SP 8263
Edale 52 SK 1285
Edburton 13 TQ 2311
Ediderton 108 NH 7184
Eddleston 85 NT 2447
Edenbridge 21 TQ 4446
Edenfield 58 SD 8019
Edenhall 63 NY 5632
Edenham 45 TF 0621
Edensor 53 SK 2469
Edenthorpe 60 SE 6206
Ederline 89 NM 8702
Edern 48 SH 2739
Edgbaston 42 SP 0684
Edgcott 34 SP 6722
Edge 40 SJ 3908
Edge End 29 SO 5913
Edgebolton 41 SJ 5721
Edgefield 47 TG 0934
Edgeworth 32 SO 9406
Edgmond 41 SJ 7119
Edgmond Marsh 41 SJ 7120
Edgton 40 SO 3885
Edgware 21 TQ 2091
Edgworth 58 SD 7416
Edinample 90 NN 6022
Edinbane 100 NG 3451
Edinburgh 85 NT 2674
Edingale 42 SK 2112
Edingley 53 SK 6655
Edingthorpe 47 TG 3132
Edington (Somer.) 17 ST 3939
Edington (Wilts.) 18 ST 9252
Edington Burtle 17 ST 3943
Edith Weston 44 SK 9205
Edithmead 17 ST 3249
Edlesborough 34 SP 9719
Edlingham 79 NU 1108
Edlington 55 TF 2371
Edmondbyers 72 NZ 0150
Edmondsham 10 SU 0611
Edmondsley 72 NZ 2348
Edmondthorpe 44 SK 8517
Edmonton 21 TQ 3493
Ednam 86 NT 7337
Edradynate 97 NN 8852
Edrom 87 NT 8255
Edstaston 50 SJ 5131
Edstone 33 SP 1761
Edwalton 53 SK 5935
Edwardstone 36 TL 9442
Edwinsford 27 SN 6334
Edwinstowe 53 SK 6266
Edworth 35 TL 2241
Edwyn Ralph 31 SO 6457
Edzell 99 NO 5968
Efail Isaf 28 ST 0884
Efailnewydd 48 SH 3536
Efenechtyd 50 SJ 1155
Effingham 20 TQ 1253
Efford 7 SS 8901
Egerton (Gtr Mches.) 58 SD 7014
Egerton (Kent) 14 TQ 9047
Eggington 34 SP 9525
Egginton 52 SK 2628
Egglescliffe 72 NZ 4213
Eggleston 72 NZ 0023
Egham 20 TQ 0171
Egleton 44 SK 8707
Eglingham 79 NU 1019
Egloshayle 4 SX 0071
Egloskerry 4 SX 2786
Eglwys-Brewis 28 ST 0168
Eglwysbach 49 SH 8070
Eglwyswrw 26 SN 1438
Egmanton 54 SK 7368
Egremont 62 NY 0110
Egton 67 NZ 8006
Egton Bridge 67 NZ 8005
Egypt 105 NJ 9166
Eilanreach 101 NG 8017
Eilean Darach 106 NH 1087
Elan Village 27 SN 9365
Elberton (Avon) 29 ST 6088
Elburton (Devon.) 5 SX 5353
Elcombe 18 SU 1280
Eldernell 45 TL 3298
Eldersfield 32 SO 7931
Elderslie 82 NS 4462
Eldroth 65 SD 7665

Eldwick 236 Forsto

Eldwick 59 SE 1240
Elford (Northum.) 87 NU 1830
Elford (Staffs.) 42 SK 1810
Elgin 104 NJ 2162
Elgol 100 NG 5214
Elham 15 TR 1744
Elie 93 NO 4900
Elim 48 SH 3584
Eling 11 SU 3612
Elishader 100 NG 5065
Elishaw 78 NY 8694
Elkesley 53 SK 6875
Elkstone 32 SO 9612
Elland 59 SE 1020
Ellastone 52 SK 1143
Ellemford 86 NT 7360
Ellen's Green 12 TQ 1035
Ellenhall 41 SJ 8426
Ellerbeck (N Yorks.) 66 SE 4396
Ellerby (Humbs.) 61 TA 1637
Ellerby (N Yorks.) 73 NZ 7914
Ellerdine Heath 41 SJ 6121
Ellerker 60 SE 9229
Ellerton (Humbs.) 60 SE 7039
Ellerton (Salop) 41 SJ 7126
Ellesborough 34 SP 8306
Ellesmere 50 SJ 3934
Ellesmere Port 50 SJ 4077
Ellingham (Norf.) 47 TM 3592
Ellingham (Northum.) 87 NU 1725
Ellingstring 65 SE 1783
Ellington (Northum.) 79 NZ 2792
Ellisfield 19 SU 6345
Ellistown 43 SK 4311
Ellon 105 NJ 9530
Ellough 47 TM 4486
Elloughton 61 SE 9428
Ellwood 29 SO 5808
Elm 45 TF 4607
Elm Park 21 TQ 5385
Elmbridge 41 SO 8967
Elmdon (Essex) 35 TL 4639
Elmdon (W Mids) 42 SP 1783
Elmdon Heath 42 SP 1580
Elmesthorpe 43 SP 4696
Elmhurst 42 SK 1112
Elmley Castle 32 SO 9841
Elmley Lovett 41 SO 8669
Elmore 32 SO 7715
Elmore Back 32 SO 7716
Elmscott 6 SS 2321
Elmsett 37 TM 0546
Elmstead Market 23 TM 0624
Elmsted Court 15 TR 1145
Elmstone 15 TR 2660
Elmstone Hardwicke 32 SO 9226
Elmswell 36 TL 9964
Elmton 53 SK 5073
Elphin 110 NC 2111
Elphinstone 85 NT 3970
Elrick 105 NJ 8206
Elrig 68 NX 3247
Elsdon 78 NY 9393
Elsecar 59 SE 3800
Elsenham 22 TL 5425
Elsfield 33 SP 5409
Elsham 61 TA 0312
Elsing 47 TG 0516
Elslack 58 SD 9349
Elsrickle 85 NT 0643
Elstead (Surrey) 12 SU 9043
Elsted (W Susx.) 12 SU 8119
Elston 54 SK 7548
Elstone 7 SS 6716
Elstow 35 TL 0547
Elstree 21 TQ 1895
Elstronwick 61 TA 2232
Elswick 57 SD 4138
Elsworth 35 TL 3163
Elterwater 62 NY 3204
Eltham 21 TQ 4274
Eltisley 35 TL 2759
Elton (Cambs.) 45 TL 0893
Elton (Ches.) 50 SJ 4575
Elton (Clev.) 72 NZ 4017
Elton (Derby) 53 SK 2261
Elton (Glos.) 29 SO 6914
Elton (Here. and Worc.) 40 SO 4571
Elton (Notts.) 54 SK 7638
Elvanfoot 76 NS 9517
Elvaston 53 SK 4132
Elveden 36 TL 8279
Elvingston 86 NT 4674
Elvington (Kent) 15 TR 2750
Elvington (N Yorks.) 60 SE 6947
Elwick (Cleve.) 73 NZ 4532
Elwick (Northum.) 87 NU 1136
Elworth 51 SJ 7361
Elworthy 16 ST 0835
Ely (Cambs.) 45 TL 5380
Ely (S Glam.) 28 ST 1476
Emberton 34 SP 8849
Embleton (Cumbr.) 62 NY 1630
Embleton (Northum.) 79 NU 2322
Embo 108 NH 8192
Emborough 17 ST 6151
Embsay 65 SE 0053
Emery Down 11 SU 2808
Emley 59 SE 2413
Emmer Green 20 SU 7177
Emmington 34 SP 7402
Emneth 45 TF 4807
Emneth Hungate 45 TF 5107
Empingham 44 SK 9408
Empshott 12 SU 7731
Emsworth 12 SU 7405
Enborne 19 SU 4365
Enchmarsh 40 SO 4996
End Moor 63 SD 5584
Enderby 43 SP 5399
Endon 51 SJ 9253
Enfield 21 TQ 3296
Enford 18 SU 1351
Engine Common 29 ST 6984
Englefield 19 SU 6272
Englefield Green 20 SU 9870
English Bicknor 29 SO 5815
English Frankton 40 SJ 4529
Englishcombe 17 ST 7162
Enham-Alamein 19 SU 3648
Enmore 16 ST 2335
Ennerdale Bridge 62 NY 0615
Enoch 76 NS 8801
Enochdhu 98 NO 0662
Ensbury 10 SZ 0896
Ensdon 40 SJ 4016
Ensis 6 SS 5626
Enstone 33 SP 3725
Enterkinfoot 76 NS 8504
Enville 40 SO 8286
Eoropie 109 NB 5156
Epperstone 53 SK 6548
Epping 35 TL 4602
Epping Green (Essex) 35 TL 4305
Epping Green (Herts.) 35 TL 2906
Epping Upland 35 TL 4404
Eppleby 72 NZ 1713
Epsom 21 TQ 2160
Epwell 33 SP 3540
Epworth 60 SE 7803
Erbistock 50 SJ 3541
Erbusaig 101 NG 7629
Erdington 42 SP 1291
Eredine 89 NM 9609
Eriboll 110 NC 4356
Ericstane 77 NT 0710
Eridge Green 13 TQ 5535
Erines 81 NR 8575
Eriswell 36 TL 7278
Erith 21 TQ 5177
Erlestoke 18 ST 9853
Ermington 5 SX 6353
Erpingham 47 TG 1831
Errogie 102 NH 5622
Errol 93 NO 2522
Ersary 109 NF 7100
Erskine 82 NS 4771
Ervie 68 NX 0067
Erwarton 37 TM 2234
Erwood 27 SO 0943
Eryholme 66 NZ 3208
Eryrys 50 SJ 2057
Escalls 2 SW 3627
Escrick 60 SE 6243
Esgairgeiliog 39 SH 7605
Esh 72 NZ 1944
Esh Winning 72 NZ 1942
Esher 20 TQ 1464
Eshott 79 NZ 2097
Eshton 65 SD 9356
Eskadale 102 NH 4539
Eskbank 85 NT 3266
Eskdale Green 62 NY 1400
Esprick 57 SD 4035
Essendine 44 TF 0412
Essendon 35 TL 2708
Essich 103 NH 6539
Essington 41 SJ 9603
Esslemont 105 NJ 9329
Eston 73 NZ 5518
Eswick 113 HU 4854
Etal 87 NT 9339
Etchilhampton 18 SU 0460
Etchingham 14 TQ 7126
Etchinghill (Kent) 15 TR 1639
Etchinghill (Staffs.) 42 SK 0218
Eton 20 SU 9678
Etteridge 97 NN 6892
Ettington 33 SP 2649
Etton (Humbs.) 61 SE 9743
Etton (Cambs.) 45 TF 1306
Ettrick 77 NT 2714
Ettrickbridge End 77 NT 3824
Etwall 53 SK 2732
Euston 36 TL 8978
Euxton 57 SD 5518
Evanton 102 NH 6066
Evedon 55 TF 0947
Evelix 108 NH 7690
Evenjobb 30 SO 2662
Evenley 33 SP 5834
Evenlode 33 SP 2229
Evenwood 72 NZ 1524
Evercreech 17 ST 6438
Everdon 33 SP 5957
Everingham 60 SE 8042
Everleigh 18 SU 1953
Everley 67 SE 9789
Eversholt 34 SP 9933
Evershot 9 ST 5704
Eversley 20 SU 7762
Eversley Cross 20 SU 7961
Everton (Beds.) 35 TL 2051
Everton (Hants) 11 SZ 2993
Everton (Notts.) 53 SK 6891
Evertown 70 NY 3576
Evesbatch 31 SO 6848
Evesham 32 SP 0344
Evington 43 SK 6203
Ewden Village 59 SK 2797
Ewell 21 TQ 2262
Ewell Minnis 15 TR 2643
Ewelme 19 SU 6491
Ewen 18 SU 0097
Ewenny 28 SS 9077
Ewerby 55 TF 1247
Ewesley 79 NZ 0592
Ewhurst (E Susx) 14 TQ 7924
Ewhurst (Surrey) 12 TQ 0940
Ewloe 50 SJ 3066
Eworthy 6 SX 4494
Ewshot 20 SU 8149
Ewyas Harold 29 SO 3828
Exbourne 6 SS 6002
Exbury 11 SU 4200
Exebridge 8 SS 9324
Exelby 66 SE 2986
Exeter 8 SX 9292
Exford 7 SS 8538
Exhall 32 SP 1055
Exminster 8 SX 9487
Exmouth 8 SY 0080
Exning 36 TL 6265
Exton (Devon) 8 SX 9886
Exton (Hants.) 11 SU 6121
Exton (Leic.) 44 SK 9211
Exton (Somer.) 16 SS 9233
Eyam 53 SK 2176
Eydon 33 SP 5450
Eye (Cambs.) 45 TF 2202
Eye (Here. and Worc.) 30 SO 4963
Eye (Suffolk) 37 TM 1473
Eyemouth 87 NT 9464
Eyeworth 35 TL 2545
Eyhorne Street 14 TQ 8354
Eyke 37 TM 3151
Eynesbury 35 TL 1859
Eynsford 21 TQ 5365
Eynsham 33 SP 4309
Eype 9 SY 4491
Eythorne 15 TR 2849
Eyton (Here. and Worc.) 30 SO 4761
Eyton (Salop) 40 SO 3687
Eyton upon the Weald Moors 41 SJ 6414

F

Faccombe 19 SU 3958
Faceby 66 NZ 4903
Faddiley 51 SJ 5752
Fadmoor 66 SE 6789
Faifley 82 NS 5073
Failand 29 ST 5272
Failford 75 NS 4526
Failsworth 58 SD 9002
Fair Oak (Hants.) 11 SU 4918
Fairbourne 38 SH 6113
Fairburn 60 SE 4727
Fairfield 41 SO 9475
Fairford 32 SP 1501
Fairlie 82 NS 2155
Fairlight 14 TQ 8612
Fairmile 8 SY 0997
Fairmilehead 85 NT 2567
Fairoak (Staffs.) 51 SJ 7632
Fairseat 14 TQ 6261
Fairstead (Essex) 22 TL 7616
Fairstead (Norf.) 47 TG 2723
Fairwarp 13 TQ 4626
Fairy Cross 6 SS 4024
Fakenham 46 TF 9229
Fala 86 NT 4361
Fala Dam 86 NT 4261
Falahill 85 NT 3956
Faldingworth 54 TF 0684
Falfield 29 ST 6893
Falkenham 37 TM 2939
Falkirk 84 NS 8880
Falkland 92 NO 2507
Falla 78 NT 7013
Fallin 91 NS 8391
Falmer 13 TQ 3508
Falmouth 2 SW 8032
Falstone 78 NY 7287
Fanagmore 110 NC 1750
Fangdale Beck 66 SE 5694
Fangfoss 67 SE 7653
Fanmore 94 NM 4244
Fans 86 NT 6140
Far Cotton 34 SP 7458
Faraclett 113 HY 4433
Farcet 45 TL 2094
Farden 41 SO 5776
Fareham 11 SU 5806
Farewell 42 SK 0811
Faringdon 19 SU 2895
Farington 57 SD 5425
Farlam 71 NY 5558
Farleigh 21 TQ 3660
Farleigh Hungerford 18 ST 7957
Farleigh Wallop 19 SU 6246
Farlesthorpe 55 TF 4774
Farley (Salop) 40 SJ 3808
Farley (Staffs.) 52 SK 0644
Farley (Wilts.) 11 SU 2229
Farley Green 20 TQ 0645
Farley Hill 20 SU 7564
Farleys End 32 SO 7615
Farlington 66 SE 6167
Farlow 41 SO 6380
Farmborough 17 ST 6560
Farmcote 32 SP 0629
Farmers 27 SN 6444
Farmington 32 SP 1315
Farmoor 33 SP 4407
Farmtown 104 NJ 5051
Farnborough (Berks.) 19 SU 4381
Farnborough (Gtr London) 21 TQ 4464
Farnborough (Hants.) 20 SU 8753
Farnborough (Warw.) 33 SP 4349
Farncombe 20 SU 9745
Farndish 34 SP 9263
Farndon (Ches.) 50 SJ 4154
Farndon (Notts.) 54 SK 7651
Farnell 99 NO 6255
Farnham (Dorset) 10 ST 9514
Farnham (Essex) 35 TL 4724
Farnham (N Yorks.) 66 SE 3460
Farnham (Suff.) 37 TM 3660
Farnham (Surrey) 20 SU 8446
Farnham Common 20 SU 9584
Farnham Green 35 TL 4625
Farnham Royal 20 SU 9682
Farningham 21 TQ 5566
Farnley 59 SE 2147
Farnley Tyas 59 SE 1612
Farnsfield 53 SK 6456
Farnworth (Ches.) 50 SJ 5187
Farnworth (Gtr Mches.) 58 SD 7305
Farr (Highld.) 111 NC 7163
Farr (Highld.) 103 NH 6833
Farr (Highld.) 97 NH 8203
Farringdon 8 SY 0191
Farrington Gurney 17 ST 6255
Farsley 59 SE 2135
Farthinghoe 33 SP 5339
Farthingstone 34 SP 6155
Farway 8 SY 1895
Fasnacloich 96 NN 0247
Fasque 99 NO 6475
Fassfern 96 NN 0278
Fatfield 72 NZ 3053
Fattahead 105 NJ 6657
Faugh 71 NY 5154
Fauldhouse 84 NS 9260
Faulkbourne 22 TL 7917
Faulkland 18 ST 7354
Fauls 51 SJ 5933
Faversham 15 TR 0161
Favillar 104 NJ 2734
Fawfieldhead 52 SK 0763
Fawkham Green 21 TQ 5865
Fawler 33 SP 3717
Fawley (Berks.) 19 SU 3981
Fawley (Bucks.) 20 SU 7586
Fawley (Hants.) 11 SU 4503
Fawley Chapel 29 SO 5829
Faxfleet 60 SE 8624
Faygate 13 TQ 2134
Fazeley 42 SK 2001
Fearby 65 SE 1981
Fearnan 97 NN 7244
Fearnhead 51 SJ 6290
Fearnmore 101 NG 7260
Featherstone (Staffs.) 41 SJ 9305
Featherstone (W Yorks.) 59 SE 4222
Feckenham 32 SP 0061
Fedderate 105 NJ 8949
Feering 22 TL 8720
Feetham 65 SD 9898
Felbridge 13 TQ 3739
Felbrigg 47 TG 2039
Felcourt 13 TQ 3841
Felden 35 TL 0404
Felindre (Dyfed) 25 SN 7027
Felindre (Powys) 40 SO 1681
Felinfach 27 SO 0933
Felinfoel 25 SN 5202
Felingwm Uchaf 25 SN 5024
Felixkirk 66 SE 4684
Felixstowe 37 TM 3034
Felkington 87 NT 9444
Felling 72 NZ 2762
Felmersham 34 SP 9957
Felmingham 47 TG 2529
Felpham 12 SZ 9599
Felsham 36 TL 9457
Felsted 22 TL 6720
Feltham 20 TQ 1072
Felthorpe 47 TG 1618
Felton (Avon) 29 ST 5165
Felton (Here. and Worc.) 31 SO 5748
Felton (Northum.) 79 NU 1800
Felton Butler 40 SJ 3917
Feltwell 46 TL 7190
Feltwell Anchor 46 TL 6789
Fen Ditton 35 TL 4860
Fen Drayton 45 TL 3468
Fen End 42 SP 2274
Fence 58 SD 8237
Fendike Corner 55 TF 4560
Feniscowles 58 SD 6425
Feniton 8 SY 1199
Fenny Bentley 52 SK 1750
Fenny Bridges 8 SY 1198
Fenny Compton 33 SP 4152
Fenny Drayton 43 SP 3597
Fenny Stratford 34 SP 8834
Fenrother 79 NZ 1792
Fenstanton 45 TL 3168
Fenton (Cambs.) 45 TL 3279
Fenton (Lincs.) 54 SK 8476
Fenton (Lincs.) 54 SK 8750
Fenton (Staffs.) 51 SJ 8944
Fenton Town 87 NT 9733
Fenwick (Northum.) 87 NU 0639
Fenwick (Northum.) 79 NZ 0572
Fenwick (S Yorks.) 60 SE 5916
Fenwick (Strath.) 82 NS 4643
Feochaig 74 NR 7714
Feock 2 SW 8238
Feolin Ferry 80 NR 4469
Feriniquarrie 100 NG 1750
Fern 99 NO 4861
Ferndale 28 SS 9997
Ferndown 10 SU 0700
Ferness 103 NH 9645
Fernham 19 SU 2991
Fernhill Heath 32 SO 8659
Fernhurst 12 SU 9028
Fernie 93 NO 3115
Fernilea 100 NG 3732
Fernilee 52 SK 0178
Ferrensby 66 SE 3660
Ferring 12 TQ 0902
Ferrybridge 60 SE 4824
Ferryden 99 NO 7156
Ferryhill 72 NZ 2832
Ferryside 25 SN 3610
Fersfield 47 TM 0682
Feshiebridge 97 NH 8504
Fetcham 21 TQ 1555
Fetterangus 105 NJ 9850
Fettercairn 99 NO 6573
Fewston 65 SE 1954
Ffairfach 25 SN 6220
Ffestiniog 49 SH 7042
Fforest 25 SN 5804
Ffostrasol 26 SN 3747
Ffrith 50 SJ 2855
Ffrwdgrech 28 SO 0227
Ffynnonddrain 25 SN 4021
Ffynnongroew 50 SJ 1382
Fiddes 99 NO 8181
Fiddington (Glos.) 32 SO 9231
Fiddington (Somer.) 16 ST 2140
Fiddlers Hamlet 35 TL 4701
Field 52 SK 0233
Field Broughton 62 SD 3881
Field Dalling 46 TG 0039
Field Head 43 SK 4909
Fifehead Magdalen 10 ST 7721
Fifehead Neville 9 ST 7610
Fifield (Berks.) 20 SU 9076
Fifield (Oxon.) 33 SP 2318
Figheldean 18 SU 1547
Filby 47 TG 4613
Filey 67 TA 1180
Filgrave 34 SP 8748
Filkins 33 SP 2304
Filleigh (Devon.) 7 SS 6628
Filleigh (Devon.) 7 SS 7410
Fillingham 54 SK 9485
Fillongley 43 SP 2787
Filton 29 ST 6079
Fimber 67 SE 8960
Finavon 99 NO 4957
Fincham 46 TF 6806
Finchampstead 20 SU 7963
Finchdean 12 SU 7312
Finchingfield 36 TL 6832
Finchley 21 TQ 2890
Findern 53 SK 3030
Findhorn 103 NJ 0464
Findo Gask 91 NO 0020
Findochty 104 NJ 4667
Findon (Grampn.) 99 NO 9397
Findon (W. Susx) 12 TQ 1208
Findon Mains 102 NH 6060
Finedon 44 SP 9272
Fingal Street 37 TM 2169
Fingask 105 NJ 7827
Fingest 20 SU 7791
Finghall 65 SE 1889
Fingringhoe 23 TM 0220
Finmere 34 SP 6333
Finnart 97 NN 5157
Finningham 37 TM 0669
Finningley 104 SK 6699
Finnygaud 104 NJ 6054
Finsbay 109 NG 0786
Finsbury 21 TQ 3282
Finstall 41 SO 9869
Finsthwaite 62 SD 3687
Finstock 33 SP 3516
Finstown 113 HY 3514
Fintry (Central) 84 NS 6186
Fintry (Grampn.) 105 NJ 7554
Fionnphort (Island of Mull) 88 NM 2923
Fir Tree 72 NZ 1334
Firbeck 53 SK 5688
Firgrove 58 SD 9113
Firsby 55 TF 4563
Fishbourne (I of W) 11 SZ 5592
Fishbourne (W Susx) 12 SU 8304
Fishburn 72 NZ 3632
Fishcross 91 NS 8995
Fisher's Pond 11 SU 4820
Fisherford 105 NJ 6635
Fisherstreet 12 SU 9531
Fisherton (Highld.) 103 NH 7451
Fisherton (Strath.) 75 NS 2717
Fishguard 24 SM 9637
Fishlake 60 SE 6513
Fishpool 58 SD 8009
Fishtoft 55 TF 3642
Fishtoft Drove 55 TF 3148
Fishtown of Usan 99 NO 7254
Fishwick 87 NT 9151
Fiskavaig 100 NG 3234
Fiskerton (Lincs.) 54 TF 0472
Fiskerton (Notts.) 54 SK 7351
Fittleton 18 SU 1449
Fittleworth 12 TQ 01
Fitton End 45 TF 43
Fitz 40 SJ 44
Fitzhead 16 ST 12
Fitzwilliam 59 SE 41
Five Ashes 13 TQ 55
Five Oak Green 13 TQ 64
Five Oaks 12 TQ 09
Five Roads 25 SN 49
Fivehead 8 ST 35
Flackwell Heath 20 SU 88
Fladbury 32 SO 99
Fladdabister 113 HU 43
Flagg 52 SK 13
Flamborough 67 TA 22
Flamstead 35 TL 08
Flansham 12 SU 96
Flasby 65 SD 94
Flash 52 SK 02
Flashader 100 NG 35
Flatt, The 71 NY 56
Flaunden 34 TL 01
Flawborough 54 SK 78
Flawith 66 SE 48
Flax Bourton 29 ST 50
Flaxby 66 SE 39
Flaxley 29 SO 69
Flaxpool 16 ST 14
Flaxton 66 SE 67
Fleckney 43 SP 64
Flecknoe 33 SP 51
Fleet (Hants.) 20 SU 80
Fleet (Lincs.) 45 TF 38
Fleet Hargate 45 TF 39
Fleetham 79 NU 19
Fleetwood 57 SD 32
Flemingston 28 ST 01
Flemington 84 NS 65
Flempton 36 TL 81
Fletching 13 TQ 43
Flexford 20 SU 93
Flimby 62 NY 02
Flimwell 14 TQ 71
Flint 50 SJ 24
Flint Mountain 50 SJ 23
Flintham 54 SK 74
Flinton 61 TA 21
Flitcham 46 TF 72
Flitton 35 TL 05
Flitwick 35 TL 03
Flixborough 60 SE 87
Flixton (Gtr Mches.) 51 SJ 74
Flixton (N Yorks.) 67 TA 04
Flixton (Suff.) 47 TM 31
Flockton 59 SE 23
Flodden 87 NT 92
Flodigarry 100 NG 46
Flookburgh 64 SD 36
Flordon 47 TM 18
Flore 34 SP 64
Flotterton 79 NT 99
Flowton 37 TM 08
Flushing (Corn.) 2 SW 80
Flushing (Grampn.) 105 NK 05
Flyford Flavell 32 SO 97
Fobbing 22 TQ 71
Fochabers 104 NJ 34
Fochriw 28 SO 10
Fockerby 60 SE 84
Fodderletter 104 NJ 14
Foel 39 SH 99
Foffarty 98 NO 41
Foggathorpe 60 SE 75
Fogo 87 NT 77
Foindle 110 NC 19
Folda 98 NO 19
Fole 52 SK 04
Foleshill 43 SP 35
Folke 9 ST 65
Folkestone 15 TR 23
Folkingham 54 TF 07
Folkington 13 TQ 56
Folksworth 45 TL 14
Folkton 67 TA 05
Folla Rule 105 NJ 73
Follifoot 66 SE 34
Folly Gate 6 SX 57
Fonthill Bishop 10 ST 93
Fonthill Gifford 10 ST 92
Fontmell Magna 10 ST 86
Fontwell 12 SU 94
Foolow 52 SK 19
Foots Cray 21 TQ 47
Forcett 72 NZ 17
Ford (Bucks.) 34 SP 77
Ford (Glos.) 32 SP 08
Ford (Northum.) 87 NT 94
Ford (Salop) 40 SJ 41
Ford (Staffs.) 52 SK 06
Ford (Strath.) 89 NM 86
Ford (W Susx) 12 TQ 00
Ford (Wilts.) 18 ST 84
Ford End 22 TL 67
Ford Street (Somer.) 8 ST 15
Fordcombe 13 TQ 52
Fordell 85 NT 15
Forden 40 SJ 22
Fordham (Cambs.) 36 TL 63
Fordham (Essex) 23 TL 92
Fordham (Norf.) 46 TL 61
Fordingbridge 10 SU 14
Fordon 67 TA 04
Fordoun 99 NO 74
Fordstreet (Essex) 23 TL 92
Fordwells 33 SP 30
Fordwich 15 TR 18
Fordyce 104 NJ 55
Foremark 43 SK 33
Forest Gate 21 TQ 40
Forest Green 12 TQ 12
Forest Head 71 NY 58
Forest Hill 33 SP 58
Forest Mill 91 NS 95
Forest Row 13 TQ 42
Forest Town 53 SK 56
Forestburn Gate 79 NZ 06
Forestfield 84 NS 85
Foreststide 12 SU 75
Forfar 98 NO 45
Forgandenny 92 NO 08
Forgie 104 NJ 39
Formby 57 SD 29
Forncett End 47 TM 14
Forncett St. Mary 47 TM 16
Forncett St. Peter 47 TM 16
Forneth 98 NO 09
Fornham All Saints 36 TL 83
Fornham St. Martin 36 TL 85
Forres 103 NJ 03
Forsbrook 51 SJ 96
Forse 112 ND 22
Forsinard 111 NC 88
Forstal, The 14 TQ 89
Forston 9 SY 66

ort Augustus 237 Great Altcar

rt Augustus 102 NH 3709
rt George 103 NH 7656
rt William 96 NN 1074
rter 98 NO 1864
rteviot 92 NO 0517
rth 84 NS 9453
rthampton 32 SO 8532
rtingall 97 NN 7447
rton 19 SU 4243
rton (Lancs.) 64 SD 4851
rton (Salop) 40 SJ 4216
rton (Somer.) 8 ST 3306
rton (Staffs.) 41 SJ 7521
rtree 105 NJ 9640
rtrie 105 NJ 6645
rtrose 103 NH 7256
rtuneswell 9 SY 6873
rty Hill 21 TQ 3398
rward Green 37 TM 1059
sbury 19 SU 3157
sdyke 55 TF 3133
ss 97 NN 7958
ss-y-ffin 26 SN 4460
ssebridge 32 SP 0811
ster Street 35 TL 4909
ston (Derby.) 52 SK 1831
ston (Lincs.) 54 SK 8542
ston on the Wolds 67 TA 1055
therby 55 TF 3191
theringhay 45 TL 0593
ul Mile 13 TQ 6215
ulden (Borders) 87 NT 9355
ulden (Norf.) 46 TL 7699
ulridge 58 SD 8942
ulsham 47 TG 0324
untainhall 86 NT 4349
ur Ashes 36 TM 0070
ur Crosses (Gwyn.) 48 SH 3939
ur Crosses (Powys) 39 SJ 0508
ur Crosses (Powys) 40 SJ 2718
ur Crosses (Staffs.) 41 SJ 9509
ur Elms 21 TQ 4648
ur Forks 16 ST 2336
ur Gotes 45 TF 4516
ur Lanes 2 SW 6838
ur Marks 11 SU 6634
ur Mile Bridge 48 SH 2778
ur Oaks (E Susx) 14 TQ 8624
ur Oaks (W Mids) 42 SP 1198
ur Oaks (W Mids) 42 SP 2480
ur Throws 14 TQ 7729
urlanes End 51 SJ 8059
urstones 71 NY 8967
vant 10 SU 0028
veran 105 NJ 9824
wey 4 SX 1251
wlis 93 NO 3133
wlis Wester 91 NN 9223
wlmere 35 TL 4245
wnhope 31 SO 5734
x Lane 20 SU 8557
xdale 56 SC 2878
xearth 36 TL 8344
xfield 62 SD 2085
xham 18 ST 9777
xhole (Corn.) 3 SW 9654
xholes (N Yorks.) 67 TA 0173
xley (Norf.) 47 TG 0321
xley (Wilts.) 18 ST 8985
xt 52 SK 0348
xton (Cambs.) 35 TL 4148
xton (Leic.) 44 SP 7090
xup 65 SD 8676
y 29 SO 5928
yers 102 NH 4921
ddon 3 SW 9158
dley 42 SK 1513
dswell 51 SJ 9831
isthorpe 67 TA 1561
mfield 13 TQ 4920
mingham Earl 47 TG 2702
mingham Pigot 47 TG 2703
mlingham 37 TM 2863
mpton (Dorset) 9 SY 6294
mpton (Lincs.) 55 TF 3239
mpton Cotterell 29 ST 6582
mpton Mansell 32 SO 9202
mpton West End 55 TF 3041
mpton on Severn 32 SO 7407
msden 37 TM 1959
mwellgate Moor 72 NZ 2644
nche 41 SO 8178
nkby 50 SJ 2486
nkley 41 SO 9980
nkton 43 SP 4270
nt 13 TQ 5835
serburgh 105 NJ 9966
ting Green 23 TM 0923
tton 11 SU 6600
athy 4 SX 3952
ckenham 36 TL 6672
ckleton 57 SD 4228
eby 44 SK 8020
eland 33 SP 4112
ethorpe 47 TG 4105
ethorpe Common 47 TG 4004
iston 55 TF 3743
mington 6 SS 5132
nchay 29 ST 6377
nchbeer 5 SX 6785
nsham 12 SU 8441
shfield 36 SD 2807
shford 18 ST 7860
shwater 11 SZ 3487
ssingfield 37 TM 2677
ston 37 TM 1739
swick 112 ND 3667
ttenham 47 TG 2417
uchie 93 NO 2806
ar's Gate 13 TQ 4933
day Bridge 45 TF 4605
daythorpe 67 SE 8759
ern Barnet 21 TQ 2892
esthorpe 54 TF 0683
eth 20 SU 7990
lford 19 SU 4497
lsham 19 SU 5373
mley 20 SU 8758
ndsbury 14 TQ 7369
ng 46 TF 7334
ngford 34 SP 6028
nsted 14 TQ 8957
nton-on-Sea 23 TM 2319
ockheim 99 NO 5949
sby on the Wreake 43 SK 6917
skney 55 TF 4555
ston (E Susx) 13 TV 5498
ston (Suff.) 37 TM 4160
tchley 53 SK 3553
th Bank 55 TF 3147
th Common 41 SO 6969
tham 11 SU 2413
thelstock 6 SS 4619
thville 55 TF 3250
Frittenden 14 TQ 8141
Fritton (Norf.) 47 TG 4700
Fritton (Norf.) 47 TM 2293
Fritwell 33 SP 5229
Frizington 62 NY 0316
Frocester 32 SO 7803
Frodesley 40 SJ 5101
Frodsham 50 SJ 5177
Froggatt 53 SK 2476
Froghall 52 SK 0247
Frogmore 20 SU 8360
Frolesworth 43 SP 5090
Frome 18 ST 7747
Frome St. Quintin 9 ST 5902
Fromes Hill 31 SO 6846
Fron (Gwyn.) 48 SH 3539
Fron (Powys) 40 SJ 2203
Fron (Powys) 30 SO 0865
Fron Cysyllte 50 SJ 2741
Fron-goch 49 SH 9039
Frosterley 72 NZ 0237
Froxfield 19 SU 2967
Froxfield Green 11 SU 7025
Fryerning 22 TL 6400
Fryton 66 SE 6875
Fulbeck 54 SK 9450
Fulbourn 35 TL 5256
Fulbrook 33 SP 2513
Fulford (N Yorks.) 60 SE 6149
Fulford (Somer.) 16 ST 2129
Fulford (Staffs.) 51 SJ 9438
Fulham 21 TQ 2576
Fulking 13 TQ 2411
Full Sutton 67 SE 7455
Fuller Street 22 TL 7415
Fuller's Moor 50 SJ 4953
Fullerton 11 SU 3739
Fulletby 55 TF 2973
Fullwood 82 NS 4450
Fulmer 20 SU 9985
Fulmodeston 46 TF 9931
Fulnetby 55 TF 0979
Fulstow 61 TF 3297
Fulwell 72 NZ 3959
Fulwood (Lancs.) 57 SD 5331
Fulwood (S Yorks.) 53 SK 3085
Funtington 12 SU 7908
Funtley 11 SU 5608
Funzie 113 HU 6689
Furnace 89 NN 0200
Furneux Pelham 35 TL 4327
Fyfett 8 ST 2314
Fyfield (Essex) 22 TL 5707
Fyfield (Glos.) 33 SP 2003
Fyfield (Hants.) 19 SU 2946
Fyfield (Oxon.) 19 SU 4298
Fyfield (Wilts.) 18 SU 1468
Fylingthorpe 67 NZ 9405
Fyvie 105 NJ 7637

G

Gabroc Hill 82 NS 4551
Gaddesby 43 SK 6813
Gaer 28 SO 1721
Gaerwen 48 SH 4871
Gagingwell 33 SP 4025
Gainford 72 NZ 1716
Gainsborough 54 SK 8189
Gainsford End 36 TL 7235
Gairloch 106 NG 8076
Gairlochy 96 NN 1784
Gairney Bank 92 NT 1299
Galashiels 86 NT 4936
Galby 43 SK 6901
Galgate 64 SD 4855
Galhampton 17 ST 6329
Gallatown 93 NT 2994
Galley Common 43 SP 3192
Galleyend 22 TL 7103
Galleywood 22 TL 7002
Gallowfauld 98 NO 4342
Galltair 101 NG 8120
Galmisdale 95 NM 4784
Galmpton (Devon) 5 SX 6940
Galmpton (Devon) 5 SX 8856
Galphay 66 SE 2572
Galston 82 NS 5036
Galtrigill 100 NG 1854
Gamblesby 63 NY 6039
Gamlingay 35 TL 2452
Gamrie 105 NJ 7962
Gamston (Notts.) 53 SK 6037
Gamston (Notts.) 54 SK 7076
Ganavan 89 NM 8632
Ganllwyd 39 SH 7224
Gannochy 99 NO 5970
Ganstead 61 TA 1434
Ganthorpe 66 SE 6870
Ganton 67 SE 9877
Garbhallt (Strath.) 89 NS 0295
Garboldisham 46 TM 0081
Gardenstown 105 NJ 7964
Gare Hill 18 ST 7840
Garelochhead 90 NS 2491
Garford 19 SU 4296
Garforth 59 SE 4033
Gargrave 65 SD 9354
Gargunnock 91 NS 7094
Garinin 109 NB 1944
Garlieston 69 NX 4746
Garlogie 105 NJ 7805
Garmond 105 NJ 8052
Garmony 88 NM 6741
Garmouth 104 NJ 3364
Garn 48 SH 2734
Garn-Dolbenmaen 48 SH 4944
Garnant 25 SN 6813
Garnett Bridge 63 SD 5299
Garnkirk 84 NS 6768
Garrabost 109 NB 5133
Garraron 89 NM 8008
Garras 2 SW 7023
Garreg 48 SH 6141
Garreg Bank 50 SJ 2811
Garrick 91 NN 8412
Garrigill 71 NY 7441
Garros 100 NG 4963
Garrow 91 NN 8240
Garsdon 18 ST 9687
Garshall Green 51 SJ 9633
Garsington 33 SP 5802
Garstang 57 SD 4945
Garston 50 SJ 4083
Garswood 50 SJ 5599
Gartcosh 84 NS 6968
Garth (Clwyd) 50 SJ 2542
Garth (I. of M.) 56 SC 3177
Garth (Mid Glam.) 28 SS 8690
Garth (Powys) 27 SN 9549
Garthbrengy 27 SO 0433
Gartheli 27 SN 5956
Garthmyl 40 SO 1999
Garthorpe (Humbs.) 60 SE 8419
Garthorpe (Leic.) 44 SK 8320
Gartmore 90 NS 5297
Gartness (Central) 90 NS 5086
Gartness (Strath.) 84 NS 7864
Gartocharn 90 NS 4286
Garton 61 TA 2635
Garton-on-the-Wolds 67 SE 9859
Gartymore 112 ND 0114
Garvald 86 NT 5870
Garvan 96 NM 9777
Garvard 88 NR 3691
Garve 102 NH 3961
Garvestone 46 TG 0207
Garvock 82 NS 2571
Garway 29 SO 4522
Garynahine 109 NB 2331
Gastard 18 ST 8868
Gasthorpe 46 TL 9780
Gatcombe 11 SZ 4885
Gate Burton 54 SK 8382
Gate Helmsley 66 SE 6955
Gatebeck 63 SD 5485
Gateforth 60 SE 5528
Gatehead 82 NS 3936
Gatehouse 78 NY 7988
Gatehouse of Fleet 69 NX 5966
Gatelawbridge 76 NX 9096
Gateley 46 TF 9624
Gatenby 66 SE 3287
Gateshead 72 NZ 2562
Gatesheath 50 SJ 4760
Gateside (Fife.) 92 NO 1809
Gateside (Strath.) 82 NS 3653
Gateside (Tays.) 98 NO 4344
Gathurst 57 SD 5307
Gatley 51 SJ 8387
Gattonside 86 NT 5435
Gatwick Airport - London 13 TQ 2841
Gauldry 93 NO 3723
Gaunt's Common 10 SU 0205
Gautby 55 TF 1772
Gavinton 87 NT 7652
Gawber 59 SE 3207
Gawcott 34 SP 6831
Gawsworth 51 SJ 8869
Gawthrop 63 SD 6987
Gawthwaite 62 SD 2784
Gay Street 12 TQ 0820
Gaydon 33 SP 3654
Gayfield 113 HY 4930
Gayhurst 34 SP 8446
Gayles 65 NZ 1207
Gayton (Mers.) 50 SJ 2680
Gayton (Norf.) 46 TF 7219
Gayton (Northants.) 34 SP 7054
Gayton (Staffs.) 41 SJ 9728
Gayton Thorpe 46 TF 7418
Gayton le Marsh 55 TF 4284
Gaywood 46 TF 6320
Gazeley 36 TL 7264
Geary 100 NG 2661
Gedding 36 TL 9457
Geddington 44 SP 8983
Gedintailor 100 NG 5235
Gedney 45 TF 4024
Gedney Broadgate 45 TF 4022
Gedney Drove End 45 TF 4629
Gedney Dyke 45 TF 4126
Gedney Hill 45 TF 3311
Geise 112 ND 1064
Geldeston 47 TM 3891
Gell 49 SH 8569
Gelli Gynan 50 SJ 1854
Gelligaer 28 ST 1397
Gellilydan 49 SH 6839
Gellioedd 49 SH 9344
Gelly 24 SN 0819
Gellyburn 92 NO 0939
Gellywen 25 SN 2723
Gelston 69 NX 7758
Genoch Mains 68 NX 1356
Gentleshaw 42 SK 0511
George Nympton 7 SS 7023
Georgeham 6 SS 4639
Georgetown 82 NS 4567
Georgia 2 SW 4836
Georth 113 HY 3626
Germansweek 4 SX 4394
Germoe 2 SW 5829
Gerrans 3 SW 8735
Gerrards Cross 20 TQ 0088
Gestingthorpe 36 TL 8138
Geuffordd 40 SJ 2114
Gibraltar 55 TF 5558
Gidea Park 21 TQ 5390
Gidleigh 5 SX 6788
Gifford 86 NT 5368
Giggleswick 65 SD 8163
Gilberdyke 60 SE 8329
Gilcrux 62 NY 1138
Gildersome 59 SE 2429
Gildingwells 53 SK 5585
Gileston 28 ST 0167
Gilfach 28 ST 1598
Gilfach Goch 28 SS 9890
Gilfachrheda 26 SN 4058
Gillamoor 66 SE 6890
Gilling East 66 SE 6176
Gilling West 65 NZ 1805
Gillingham (Dorset) 10 ST 8026
Gillingham (Kent) 14 TQ 7768
Gillingham (Norf.) 47 TM 4191
Gillow Heath 51 SJ 8858
Gills 112 ND 3172
Gilmerton (Lothian) 85 NT 2968
Gilmerton (Tays.) 91 NN 8823
Gilmorton 43 SP 5787
Gilsland 71 NY 6366
Gilsland Spa 71 NY 6367
Gilston 86 NT 4456
Gilwern 21 SO 2414
Gimingham 47 TG 2836
Gipping 37 TM 0763
Gipsey Bridge 55 TF 2850
Girlsta 113 HU 4351
Girsby 66 NZ 3508
Girthon 69 NX 6053
Girton (Cambs.) 35 TL 4262
Girton (Notts.) 54 SK 8266
Girvan 75 NX 1897
Gisburn 58 SD 8248
Gisleham 37 TM 5188
Gislingham 37 TM 0771
Gissing 47 TM 1485
Gittisham 8 SY 1398
Gladestry 30 SO 2355
Gladsmuir 86 NT 4573
Glais 25 SN 7000
Glaisdale 67 NZ 7705
Glamis 98 NO 3846
Glan-Conwy 49 SH 8352
Glan-Mule 40 SO 1690
Glan-y-don 50 SJ 1679
Glan-yr-afon (Gwyn.) 49 SH 9141
Glan-yr-afon (Gwyn.) 49 SJ 0242
Glanaber Terrace 49 SH 7547
Glanaman 25 SN 6713
Glandford 47 TG 0441
Glandwr (Dyfed) 24 SN 1928
Glangrwyne 28 SO 2316
Glanrhyd 26 SN 1442
Glanton 79 NU 0714
Glanton Pike 79 NU 0514
Glanvilles Wootton 9 ST 6708
Glapthorn 44 TL 0290
Glapwell 53 SK 4766
Glasbury 30 SO 1739
Glascote 42 SK 2203
Glascwm 30 SO 1553
Glasdrum 96 NN 0046
Glasfryn 49 SH 9150
Glasgow 84 NS 5865
Glasinfryn 48 SH 5868
Glaspwll 39 SN 7397
Glasserton 68 NX 4238
Glassford 84 NS 7247
Glasshouse Hill 32 SO 7020
Glasshouses 65 SE 1764
Glasslaw 105 NJ 8659
Glasslie 92 NO 2305
Glasson (Cumbr.) 70 NY 2560
Glasson (Lancs.) 64 SD 4455
Glassonby 63 NY 5738
Glasterlaw 99 NO 6051
Glaston 44 SK 8900
Glastonbury 17 ST 4938
Glatton 45 TL 1586
Glazebury 58 SJ 6796
Glazeley 41 SO 7088
Gleadless Townend 53 SK 3883
Gleadsmoss 51 SJ 8469
Gleaston 64 SD 2570
Glemsford 36 TL 8247
Glen Auldyn 56 SC 4393
Glen Parva 43 SP 5798
Glen Vine 56 SC 3378
Glenancross 95 NM 6691
Glenbarr 80 NR 6736
Glenbervie 99 NO 7680
Glenboig 84 NS 7268
Glenbreck 77 NT 0521
Glenbuck 76 NS 7429
Glenburn 82 NS 4761
Glencaple 70 NX 9968
Glencarse 92 NO 1922
Glencloy 81 NS 0036
Glencoe 96 NN 1058
Glencraig 92 NT 1795
Glendevon 91 NN 9804
Glendoick 92 NO 2022
Glenduckie 93 NO 2818
Glenegedale 80 NR 3351
Glenelg 101 NG 8119
Glenfarg 92 NO 1310
Glenfield 43 SK 5306
Glenfinart 89 NS 1987
Glenfinnan 95 NM 9080
Glenfoot 92 NO 1715
Glengarnock 82 NS 3252
Glengrasco 100 NG 4444
Glenkindie 104 NJ 4313
Glenlee 69 NX 6080
Glenluce 68 NX 1957
Glenmavis 84 NS 7567
Glenmaye 56 SC 2380
Glenmore (Skye) 100 NG 4340
Glenridding 62 NY 3817
Glenrothes 92 NO 2600
Glensaugh 99 NO 6778
Glensluain 89 NS 0999
Glentham 54 TF 0090
Glentress 85 NT 2839
Glentrool Village 68 NX 3578
Glentworth 54 SK 9488
Glespin 76 NS 8028
Gletness 113 HU 4651
Glewstone 29 SO 5522
Glinton 45 TF 1506
Glooston 44 SP 7596
Glossop 52 SK 0393
Gloster Hill 79 NU 2504
Gloucester 32 SO 8318
Gloup 163 HP 5004
Glusburn 59 SE 0344
Glympton 33 SP 4221
Glyn 49 SH 7457
Glyn Ceiriog 50 SJ 2038
Glyn-Cywarch 48 SH 6034
Glyn-Neath 28 SN 8806
Glynarthen 26 SN 3148
Glyncorrwg 28 SS 8799
Glynde 13 TQ 4509
Glyndebourne 13 TQ 4510
Glyndyfrdwy 50 SJ 1542
Glyntaff 28 ST 0889
Glynteg 26 SN 3637
Gnosall 41 SJ 8220
Gnosall Heath 41 SJ 8419
Goadby 44 SP 7598
Goadby Marwood 44 SK 7826
Goatacre 18 SU 0176
Goathill 9 ST 6717
Goathland 67 NZ 8301
Goathurst 16 ST 2534
Gobowen 50 SJ 3033
Godalming 12 SU 9743
Godmanchester 45 TL 2470
Godmanstone 9 SY 6697
Godmersham 15 TR 0650
Godney 17 ST 4842
Godolphin Cross 2 SW 6031
Godre'r-graig 25 SN 7507
Godshill (Hants.) 10 SU 1714
Godshill (I. of W.) 11 SZ 5281
Godstone 21 TQ 3551
Goetre 29 SO 3205
Goff's Oak 35 TL 3202
Gogar 85 NT 1672
Goginan 39 SN 6981
Golan 48 SH 5242
Golant 4 SX 1254
Golberdon 4 SX 3271
Golborne 51 SJ 6097
Golcar 59 SE 0915
Goldcliff 29 ST 3683
Golden Cross 13 TQ 5312
Golden Green 14 TQ 6348
Golden Grove 26 SN 5919
Golden Pot 12 SU 7143
Golden Valley 32 SO 9022
Goldenhill 51 SJ 8553
Golders Green 21 TQ 2488
Goldhanger 23 TL 9009
Golding 40 SJ 5403
Goldsborough (N Yorks.) 73 NZ 8314
Goldsborough (N Yorks.) 66 SE 3856
Goldsithney 2 SW 5430
Goldthorpe 60 SE 4604
Gollanfield 103 NH 8052
Golspie 108 NH 8399
Golval 111 NC 8962
Gomersal 59 SE 2026
Gomshall 20 TQ 0847
Gonalston 53 SK 6847
Good Easter 22 TL 6212
Gooderstone 46 TF 7602
Goodleigh 6 SS 5934
Goodmanham 60 SE 8842
Goodnestone (Kent) 15 TR 0461
Goodnestone (Kent) 15 TR 2554
Goodrich 29 SO 5719
Goodrington 5 SX 8958
Goodwick 24 SM 9438
Goodworth Clatford 19 SU 3642
Goodyers End 43 SP 3385
Goole 60 SE 7423
Goonbell 2 SW 7249
Goonhavern 2 SW 7953
Gooseham 6 SS 2316
Goosetrey 51 SJ 7769
Goosey 19 SU 3591
Goosnargh 57 SD 5536
Gordon 86 NT 6443
Gordonbush 108 NC 8409
Gordonstown (Grampn.) 104 NJ 5656
Gordonstown (Grampn.) 105 NJ 7138
Gorebridge 85 NT 3461
Gorefield 45 TF 4112
Goring 19 SU 6080
Goring-by-Sea 12 TQ 1102
Gorleston on Sea 47 TG 5203
Gorley 10 SU 1511
Gorrachie 105 NJ 7358
Gorran Haven 4 SX 0141
Gors 27 SN 6277
Gorsedd 50 SJ 1476
Gorseinon 25 SS 5998
Gorslas 25 SN 5713
Gorsley 29 SO 6826
Gorstan 102 NH 3862
Gorsty Common 30 SO 4537
Gorton 58 SJ 8996
Gosbeck 37 TM 1555
Gosberton 55 TF 2331
Gosfield 22 TL 7829
Gosforth (Cumbr.) 62 NY 0603
Gosforth (Tyne and Wear) 72 NZ 2467
Gosmore 35 TL 1927
Gosport 11 SZ 6199
Goswick 87 NU 0545
Gotham 53 SK 5330
Gotherington 32 SO 9629
Goudhurst 14 TQ 7337
Goulceby 55 TF 2579
Gourdas 105 NJ 7741
Gourdon 99 NO 8270
Gourock 82 NS 2477
Govan 84 NS 5464
Gowanhill 105 NK 0363
Gowdall 60 SE 6122
Gowerton 25 SS 5896
Gowkhall 85 NT 0589
Goxhill (Humbs.) 61 TA 1021
Goxhill (Humbs.) 61 TA 1844
Graffham (W Susx.) 12 SU 9216
Grafham (Cambs.) 45 TL 1669
Grafton (Here. and Worc.) 30 SO 4937
Grafton (Here. and Worc.) 31 SO 5761
Grafton (N Yorks.) 66 SE 4163
Grafton (Oxon.) 33 SP 2600
Grafton Flyford 32 SO 9655
Grafton Regis 34 SP 7546
Grafton Underwood 44 SP 9280
Grafty Green 14 TQ 8748
Graianrhyd 50 SJ 2156
Graig (Clwyd) 49 SJ 0872
Graig (Gwyn.) 49 SH 8071
Graig-fechan 50 SJ 1454
Grain 22 TQ 8876
Grainsby 61 TF 2799
Grainthorpe 61 TF 3896
Graizelound 60 SK 7798
Gramisdale 109 NF 8155
Grampound 3 SW 9348
Grampound Road 3 SW 9150
Granborough 34 SP 7625
Granby 54 SK 7536
Grandborough 43 SP 4866
Grandtully 97 NN 9152
Grange (Cumbr.) 62 NY 2517
Grange (Mers.) 50 SJ 2286
Grange (N Yorks.) 66 SE 5796
Grange Hill 21 TQ 4492
Grange Moor 59 SE 2216
Grange Villa 72 NZ 2352
Grange of Lindores 92 NO 2516
Grange-over-Sands 64 SD 4077
Grangemouth 84 NS 9281
Grangepans 85 NT 0282
Grangetown 73 NZ 5420
Granish 103 NH 8914
Gransmoor 67 TA 1259
Grantchester 35 TL 4355
Grantham 54 SK 9135
Grantley 66 SE 2369
Grantlodge 105 NJ 7017
Granton (Dumf. and Galwy.) 77 NT 0709
Granton (Lothian) 85 NT 2277
Grantown-on-Spey 103 NJ 0327
Grantshouse 87 NT 8065
Grappenhall 51 SJ 6385
Grasby 61 TA 0804
Grasmere 62 NY 3307
Grasscroft 59 SD 9704
Grassendale 50 SJ 3985
Grassholme 63 NY 9221
Grassington 65 SE 0064
Grassmoor 53 SK 4067
Grassthorpe 54 SK 7967
Grateley 19 SU 2741
Gratwich 52 SK 0231
Graveley (Cambs.) 35 TL 2564
Graveley (Herts.) 35 TL 2328
Gravelly Hill 42 SP 1090
Graveney 15 TR 0562
Gravesend 22 TQ 6473
Gravir 109 NB 3715
Grayingham 61 SK 9395
Grayrigg 63 SD 5797
Grays 22 TQ 6177
Grayshott 12 SU 8735
Grayswood 12 SU 9234
Grazeley 19 SU 6966
Greasbrough 53 SK 4195
Greasby 50 SJ 2587
Great Abington 35 TL 5348
Great Addington 44 SP 9575
Great Alne 32 SP 1159
Great Altcar 57 SD 3206

Great Amwell 238 Harton (Salop

Great Amwell 35 TL 3712
Great Asby 63 NY 6813
Great Ashfield 36 TM 0068
Great Ayton 73 NZ 5510
Great Baddow 22 TL 7204
Great Badminton 18 ST 8082
Great Bardfield 36 TL 6730
Great Barford 35 TL 1352
Great Barr 42 SP 0495
Great Barrington 33 SP 2013
Great Barrow 50 SJ 4668
Great Barton 36 TL 8967
Great Barugh 67 SE 7478
Great Bavington 79 NY 9880
Great Bedwyn 18 SU 2764
Great Bentley 23 TM 1121
Great Billing 34 SP 8162
Great Bircham 46 TF 7632
Great Blakenham 37 TM 1150
Great Bolas 41 SJ 6421
Great Bookham 21 TQ 1454
Great Bosullow 2 SW 4133
Great Bourton 33 SP 4545
Great Bowden 44 SP 7488
Great Bradley 36 TL 6753
Great Braxted 22 TL 8614
Great Bricett 37 TM 0350
Great Brickhill 34 SP 9030
Great Bridgeford 41 SJ 8827
Great Brington 43 SP 6665
Great Bromley 23 TM 0826
Great Broughton 66 NZ 5406
Great Budworth 51 SJ 6677
Great Burdon 72 NZ 3116
Great Burstead 22 TQ 6892
Great Busby 66 NZ 5105
Great Canfield 22 TL 5917
Great Carlton 55 TF 4185
Great Casterton 45 TF 0009
Great Chart 15 TQ 9842
Great Chatwell 41 SJ 7914
Great Chesterford 35 TL 5042
Great Cheverell 18 ST 9858
Great Chishill 35 TL 4238
Great Clacton 23 TM 1716
Great Coates 61 TA 2310
Great Comberton 32 SO 9542
Great Corby 71 NY 4754
Great Cornard 36 TL 8840
Great Coxwell 18 SU 2693
Great Cransley 44 SP 8376
Great Cressingham 46 TF 8501
Great Crosby 50 SJ 3199
Great Cubley 52 SK 1637
Great Dalby 44 SK 7414
Great Doddington 34 SP 8864
Great Driffield 67 TA 0257
Great Dunham 46 TF 8714
Great Dunmow 22 TL 6221
Great Durnford 10 SU 1338
Great Easton (Essex) 22 TL 6125
Great Easton (Leic.) 44 SP 8493
Great Eccleston 57 SD 4240
Great Edstone 66 SE 7084
Great Ellingham 46 TM 0196
Great Elm 18 ST 7449
Great Eversden 35 TL 3653
Great Finborough 36 TM 0157
Great Fransham 46 TF 8913
Great Gaddesden 35 TL 0211
Great Gidding 45 TL 1183
Great Givendale 61 SE 8153
Great Glemham 37 TM 3361
Great Glen 43 SP 6597
Great Gonerby 54 SK 9038
Great Gransden 35 TL 2756
Great Green (Norf.) 47 TM 2789
Great Green (Suff.) 36 TL 9155
Great Habton 67 SE 7576
Great Hale 55 TF 1443
Great Hallingbury 22 TL 5119
Great Hanwood 40 SJ 4309
Great Harrowden 44 SP 8871
Great Harwood 58 SD 7332
Great Haseley 34 SP 6401
Great Hatfield 61 TA 1842
Great Heck 60 SE 5920
Great Henny 36 TL 8738
Great Hinton 18 ST 9058
Great Hockham 46 TL 9592
Great Holland 23 TM 2119
Great Horkesley 36 TL 9731
Great Hormead 35 TL 4030
Great Horwood 34 SP 7731
Great Houghton (Northants.) 34 SP 7958
Great Houghton (S Yorks.) 59 SE 4206
Great Hucklow 52 SK 1777
Great Kelk 67 TA 1058
Great Kingshill 20 SU 8798
Great Langton 66 SE 2996
Great Leighs 22 TL 7317
Great Limber 61 TA 1308
Great Livermere 36 TL 8871
Great Longstone 53 SK 1971
Great Lumley 72 NZ 2949
Great Lyth 40 SJ 4507
Great Malvern 32 SO 7845
Great Maplestead 36 TL 8034
Great Marton 57 SD 3335
Great Massingham 46 TF 7922
Great Milton 34 SP 6302
Great Missenden 34 SP 8901
Great Mitton 58 SD 7138
Great Mongeham 15 TR 3451
Great Moulton 47 TM 1690
Great Musgrave 63 NY 7613
Great Ness 40 SJ 3918
Great Oakley (Essex) 23 TM 1927
Great Oakley (Northants.) 44 SP 8686
Great Offley 35 TL 1427
Great Ormside 63 NY 7017
Great Orton 70 NY 3254
Great Oxendon 44 SP 7383
Great Palgrave 46 TF 8312
Great Parndon 35 TL 4308
Great Paxton 35 TL 2164
Great Plumstead 47 TG 3010
Great Ponton 54 SK 9230
Great Postland 45 TF 2612
Great Preston 59 SE 4029
Great Raveley 45 TL 2581
Great Rissington 33 SP 1917
Great Rollright 33 SP 3231
Great Ryburgh 46 TF 9527
Great Ryle 79 NU 0212
Great Saling 22 TL 7025
Great Salkeld 63 NY 5536
Great Sampford 36 TL 6435
Great Sankey 51 SJ 5688
Great Saxham 36 TL 7862
Great Shefford 19 SU 3875
Great Shelford 35 TL 4652
Great Smeaton 66 NZ 3404
Great Snoring 46 TF 9434
Great Somerford 18 ST 9682
Great Soudley 41 SJ 7228
Great Stainton 72 NZ 3322
Great Stambridge 23 TQ 9092
Great Staughton 35 TL 1264
Great Steeping 55 TF 4364
Great Stonar 15 TR 3359
Great Strickland 63 NY 5522
Great Stukeley 45 TL 2275
Great Sturton 55 TF 2176
Great Swinburne 78 NY 9375
Great Tew 33 SP 3929
Great Tey 22 TL 8925
Great Torrington 6 SS 4919
Great Tosson 79 NU 0300
Great Totham (Essex) 22 TL 8511
Great Totham (Essex) 22 TL 8613
Great Wakering 23 TQ 9487
Great Waldingfield 36 TL 9143
Great Walsingham 46 TF 9437
Great Waltham 22 TL 6913
Great Warley 21 TQ 5890
Great Washbourne 32 SO 9834
Great Welnetham 36 TL 8759
Great Wenham 37 TM 0738
Great Whittington 79 NZ 0070
Great Wigborough 23 TL 9615
Great Wilbraham 36 TL 5557
Great Wishford 10 SU 0835
Great Witcombe 32 SO 9014
Great Witley 32 SO 7566
Great Wolford 33 SP 2434
Great Wratting 36 TL 6848
Great Wyrley 41 SJ 9907
Great Wytheford 41 SJ 5719
Great Yarmouth 47 TG 5207
Great Yeldham 36 TL 7638
Greatford 45 TF 0811
Greatham (Cleve.) 73 NZ 4927
Greatham (Hants.) 12 SU 7730
Greatham (W Susx) 12 TQ 0415
Greatstone-on-Sea 15 TR 0822
Greatworth 33 SP 5542
Green Hammerton 66 SE 4656
Green Hill (Wilts.) 18 SU 0686
Green Ore 17 ST 5749
Green Street 21 TQ 1998
Green Street Green (Gtr London) 21 TQ 4563
Green, The (Cumbr.) 62 SD 1784
Green, The (Wilts.) 10 ST 8731
Greenburn 84 NS 9360
Greendykes 87 NU 0628
Greenfield (Beds.) 35 TL 0534
Greenfield (Clwyd) 50 SJ 1977
Greenfield (Oxon.) 20 SU 7191
Greenford 21 TQ 1382
Greengairs 84 NS 7870
Greenham 19 SU 4865
Greenhaugh 78 NY 7987
Greenhead (Northum.) 71 NY 6665
Greenhill (Central) 84 NS 8278
Greenhill (Gtr London) 21 TQ 1688
Greenhill (S Yorks.) 53 SK 3481
Greenhithe 21 TQ 5974
Greenholm 84 NS 5637
Greenhow Hill 65 SE 1164
Greenigo 113 HY 4107
Greenland 112 ND 2367
Greenlaw 86 NT 7145
Greenloaning 91 NN 8307
Greenmount 58 SD 7714
Greenock 82 NS 2776
Greenodd 62 SD 3182
Greens Norton 34 SP 6649
Greenside 72 NZ 1362
Greenskairs 105 NJ 7863
Greenstead Green 22 TL 8227
Greensted 22 TL 5302
Greenwich 21 TQ 3877
Greet 32 SP 0230
Greete 41 SO 5770
Greetham (Leic.) 44 SK 9214
Greetham (Lincs.) 55 TF 3070
Greetland 59 SE 0821
Greinton 17 ST 4136
Grendon (Northants.) 34 SP 8760
Grendon (Warw.) 43 SK 2800
Grendon Common 42 SP 2799
Grendon Green 31 SO 5957
Grendon Underwood 34 SP 6720
Grenoside 53 SK 3394
Gresford 50 SJ 3454
Gresham 47 TG 1738
Greshornish 100 NG 3454
Gress 109 NB 4842
Gressenhall 46 TF 9615
Gressenhall Green 46 TF 9616
Gressingham 64 SD 5769
Greta Bridge 72 NZ 0813
Gretna 70 NY 3167
Gretna Green 70 NY 3268
Gretton (Glos.) 32 SP 0030
Gretton (Northants.) 44 SP 9094
Gretton (Salop) 40 SO 5195
Grewelthorpe 66 SE 2276
Greysouthen 62 NY 0729
Greystoke 62 NY 4330
Greystone 99 NO 5343
Greywell 20 SU 7151
Griff 43 SP 3588
Griffithstown 28 ST 2999
Grigghall 63 SD 4691
Grimeford Village 58 SD 6112
Grimethorpe 59 SE 4109
Grimley 32 SO 8360
Grimoldby 55 TF 3988
Grimsargh 57 SD 5834
Grimsby 61 TA 2810
Grimscote 34 SP 6553
Grimscott 6 SS 2606
Grimshader 109 NB 4026
Grimsthorpe 44 TF 0423
Grimston (Leic.) 43 SK 6821
Grimston (Norf.) 46 TF 7221
Grimstone 9 SY 6393
Grindale 67 TA 1371
Grindle 41 SJ 7403
Grindleford 53 SK 2477
Grindleton 58 SD 7545
Grindlow 52 SK 1877
Grindon (Northum.) 87 NT 9144
Grindon (Staffs.) 52 SK 0854
Gringley on the Hill 54 SK 7390
Grinsdale 70 NY 3758
Grinshill 40 SJ 5223
Grinton 65 SE 0498
Gristhorpe 67 TA 0882
Griston 46 TL 9499
Grittenham 18 SU 0382
Grittleton 18 ST 8579
Grizebeck 62 SD 2384
Grizedale 62 SD 3394
Groby 43 SK 5207
Groes (Clwyd) 49 SJ 0064
Groes (W Glam.) 28 SS 7986
Groes-faen 28 ST 0780
Groesffordd Marli 49 SJ 0073
Groeslon 48 SH 4755
Grogport 81 NR 8044
Gronant 49 SJ 0883
Groombridge 13 TQ 5337
Grosebay 109 NG 1592
Grosmont (Gwent) 29 SO 4024
Grosmont (N Yorks.) 67 NZ 8205
Groton 36 TL 9641
Grove (Dorset) 9 SY 6972
Grove (Kent) 15 TR 2362
Grove (Notts.) 54 SK 7379
Grove (Oxon.) 19 SU 4090
Grove Park 21 TQ 4172
Grovesend 25 SN 5900
Gruids 108 NC 5604
Grula 100 NG 3826
Gruline 88 NM 5440
Grundisburgh 37 TM 2251
Gruting 113 HU 2748
Gualachulain 96 NN 1145
Guardbridge 93 NO 4519
Guarlford 32 SO 8145
Guay 98 NO 0049
Guestling Green 14 TQ 8513
Guestwick 47 TG 0627
Guide Post 79 NZ 2585
Guilden Morden 35 TL 2744
Guilden Sutton 50 SJ 4468
Guildford 20 TQ 0049
Guildtown 92 NO 1331
Guilsborough 43 SP 6773
Guilsfield 40 SJ 2111
Guisborough 73 NZ 6115
Guiseley 59 SE 1941
Guist 46 TF 9925
Guiting Power 32 SP 0924
Gullane 86 NT 4882
Gulval 2 SW 4831
Gumfreston 24 SN 1101
Gumley 43 SP 6890
Gunby (Lincs.) 44 SK 9021
Gundleton 11 SU 6133
Gunn 6 SS 6333
Gunnerside 65 SD 9598
Gunnerton 78 NY 9074
Gunness 60 SE 8411
Gunnislake 4 SX 4371
Gunnista 113 HU 5043
Gunthorpe (Norf.) 46 TG 0135
Gunthorpe (Notts.) 53 SK 6744
Gurnard 11 SZ 4795
Gurney Slade 17 ST 6249
Gurnos 28 SN 7709
Gussage All Saints 10 SU 0010
Gussage St. Michael 10 ST 9811
Guston 15 TR 3244
Gutcher 113 HU 5498
Guthrie 99 NO 5650
Guy's Head 45 TF 4825
Guy's Marsh 10 ST 8420
Guyhirn 45 TF 3903
Guyzance 79 NU 2103
Gwaenysgor 49 SJ 0780
Gwalchmai 48 SH 3975
Gwaun-Cae-Gurwen 25 SN 7011
Gwbert-on-Sea 26 SN 1650
Gweek 2 SW 7026
Gwehelog 29 SO 3804
Gwenddwr 27 SO 0643
Gwennap 2 SW 7340
Gwenter 2 SW 7418
Gwernaffield 50 SJ 2064
Gwernesney 29 SO 4101
Gwernogle 26 SN 5234
Gwernymynydd 50 SJ 2162
Gwespyr 50 SJ 1183
Gwinear 2 SW 5937
Gwithian 2 SW 5841
Gwyddelwern 49 SJ 0746
Gwyddgrug 26 SN 4635
Gwytherin 49 SH 8761

H

Habberley (Here. and Worc.) 41 SO 8077
Habberley (Salop) 40 SJ 3903
Habrough 61 TA 1514
Hacconby 45 TF 1025
Haceby 54 TF 0236
Hacheston 37 TM 3059
Hackenthorpe 53 SK 4183
Hacketts 35 TL 3208
Hackford 47 TG 0502
Hackforth 66 SE 2493
Hackleton 34 SP 8055
Hackness (N Yorks.) 67 SE 9690
Hackney 21 TQ 3585
Hackthorn 54 SK 9882
Hackthorpe 63 NY 5423
Hadden 87 NT 7836
Haddenham (Bucks.) 34 SP 7408
Haddenham (Cambs.) 45 TL 4675
Haddington 86 NT 5174
Haddiscoe 47 TM 4497
Haddon 45 TL 1392
Hademore 42 SK 1708
Hadfield 59 SK 0296
Hadham Cross 35 TL 4218
Hadham Ford 35 TL 4321
Hadleigh (Essex) 22 TQ 8087
Hadleigh (Suff.) 36 TM 0242
Hadley 41 SJ 6712
Hadley End 42 SK 1320
Hadlow 14 TQ 6349
Hadlow Down 13 TQ 5324
Hadnall 40 SJ 5120
Hadstock 36 TL 5645
Hadzor 32 SO 9162
Haffenden Quarter 14 TQ 8841
Hafod-Dinbych 49 SH 8953
Haggbeck 71 NY 4774
Hagley (Here. and Worc.) 31 SO 5641
Hagley (Here. and Worc.) 41 SO 9181
Hagworthingham 55 TF 3469
Haigh 58 SD 6108
Haighton Green 57 SD 5634
Hail Weston 35 TL 1662
Haile 62 NY 0308
Hailes 32 SP 0530
Hailey (Herts.) 35 TL 3710
Hailey (Oxon.) 33 SP 3512
Hailsham 13 TQ 5909
Hainault 21 TQ 4691
Hainford 47 TG 2218
Hainton 55 TF 1784
Haisthorpe 67 TA 1264
Halam 53 SK 6754
Halberton 8 ST 0012
Halcro 112 ND 2260
Hale (Ches.) 50 SJ 4682
Hale (Gtr Mches.) 51 SJ 7786
Hale (Hants.) 10 SU 1919
Hale Bank 50 SJ 4784
Hale Street 14 TQ 6749
Halebarns 51 SJ 7985
Hales (Norf.) 47 TM 3897
Hales (Staffs.) 51 SJ 7134
Hales Place 15 TR 1459
Halesowen 41 SO 9683
Halesworth 37 TM 3877
Halewood 50 SJ 4585
Halford (Salop) 40 SO 4383
Halford (Warw.) 33 SP 2545
Halfpenny Green 41 SO 8292
Halfway (Berks.) 16 SU 4068
Halfway (Dyfed) 27 SN 6430
Halfway House 40 SJ 3411
Halfway Houses 23 TQ 9373
Halifax 59 SE 0825
Halistra 100 NG 2459
Halket 82 NS 4252
Halkirk 112 ND 1359
Halkyn 50 SJ 2071
Hall Green 42 SP 1181
Hall's Green 35 TL 2728
Halland 13 TQ 5016
Hallaton 44 SP 7896
Hallatrow 17 ST 6356
Hallbankgate 71 NY 5859
Hallen 29 ST 5479
Hallin 100 NG 2559
Halling 14 TQ 7063
Hallington 79 NY 9875
Halloughton 53 SK 6851
Hallow 32 SO 8258
Hallrule 78 NT 5914
Hallsands 5 SX 8138
Halltoft End 55 TF 3645
Hallworthy 4 SX 1787
Hallyne 85 NT 1940
Halmer End 51 SJ 7949
Halmore 29 SO 6902
Halmyre Mains 85 NT 1749
Halnaker 12 SU 9108
Halsall 57 SD 3710
Halse (Northants.) 33 SP 5640
Halse (Somer.) 16 ST 1327
Halsetown 2 SW 5038
Halsham 61 TA 2627
Halsinger 6 SS 5138
Halstead (Essex) 36 TL 8130
Halstead (Kent) 21 TQ 4961
Halstead (Leic.) 44 SK 7505
Halstock 9 ST 5308
Haltham 55 TF 2463
Halton (Bucks.) 34 SP 8710
Halton (Ches.) 50 SJ 5381
Halton (Clwyd) 50 SJ 3039
Halton (Lancs.) 64 SD 5065
Halton East 65 SE 0454
Halton Gill 65 SD 8876
Halton Holegate 55 TF 4165
Halton Lea Gate 71 NY 6558
Halton West 65 SD 8454
Haltwhistle 71 NY 7064
Halvergate 47 TG 4206
Halwell 5 SX 7753
Halwill 6 SX 4299
Halwill Junction 6 SS 4400
Ham (Glos.) 29 ST 6898
Ham (Gtr London) 21 TQ 1772
Ham (Highld.) 112 ND 2373
Ham (Kent) 15 TR 3354
Ham (Wilts.) 19 SU 3262
Ham Green (Here. and Worc.) 32 SP 0063
Ham Street (Somer.) 17 ST 5534
Hamble 11 SU 4806
Hambleden (Bucks.) 20 SU 7886
Hambledon (Hants.) 11 SU 6414
Hambledon (Surrey) 12 SU 9638
Hambleton (Lancs.) 57 SD 3742
Hambleton (N Yorks.) 60 SE 5430
Hambridge 9 ST 3921
Hambrook (Avon) 29 ST 6378
Hambrook (W Susx.) 12 SU 7806
Hameringham 55 TF 3167
Hamerton 45 TL 1379
Hamilton 84 NS 7255
Hammersmith 21 TQ 2279
Hammerwich 42 SK 0707
Hammoon 10 ST 8114
Hamnavoe (Shetld.) 113 HU 4971
Hamnavoe (West Burra) 113 HU 3635
Hampden 34 SP 8603
Hampden Park 13 TQ 6002
Hampden Row 34 SP 8402
Hampnett 32 SP 0915
Hampole 60 SE 5010
Hampreston 10 SZ 0598
Hampstead 21 TQ 2485
Hampstead Norris 19 SU 5276
Hampsthwaite 66 SE 2558
Hampton (Gtr London) 20 TQ 1369
Hampton (Salop) 41 SO 7486
Hampton Bishop 31 SO 5538
Hampton Heath 50 SJ 4949
Hampton Lovett 32 SO 8865
Hampton Lucy 33 SP 2557
Hampton Poyle 33 SP 5015
Hampton in Arden 42 SP 2081
Hampton on the Hill 33 SP 2564
Hamsey 13 TQ 4112
Hamstall Ridware 42 SK 1019
Hamstead (I. of W.) 11 SZ 4091
Hamstead (W Mids) 42 SP 0593
Hamstead Marshall 19 SU 4165
Hamsterley (Durham) 72 NZ 1131
Hamsterley (Durham) 72 NZ 1156
Hamstreet (Kent) 15 TR 0034
Hamworthy 10 SY 9990
Hanbury (Here and Worc.) 32 SO 9663
Hanbury (Staffs.) 42 SK 1727
Hanchurch 51 SJ 8441
Handbridge 50 SJ 4164
Handcross 13 TQ 2630
Handforth 51 SJ 8883
Handley 50 SJ 4657
Handsacre 42 SK 0916
Handsworth (S Yorks.) 53 SK 4086
Handsworth (W Mids) 42 SP 0490
Hanford 51 SJ 8642
Hanging Langford 10 SU 0237
Hanham 29 ST 6372
Hankelow 51 SJ 6645
Hankerton 18 ST 9690
Hankham 13 TQ 6105
Hanley 51 SJ 8847
Hanley Castle 32 SO 8342
Hanley Swan 32 SO 8143
Hanley William 41 SO 6765
Hanlith 65 SD 9061
Hanmer 50 SJ 4540
Hannington (Hants.) 19 SU 53
Hannington (Northants.) 44 SP 81
Hannington (Wilts.) 18 SU 17
Hannington Wick 18 SU 17
Hanslope 34 SP 80
Hanthorpe 45 TF 08
Hanwell 33 SP 43
Hanworth (Gtr London) 20 TQ 12
Hanworth (Norf.) 47 TG 19
Happendon 84 NS 85
Happisburgh 47 TG 37
Happisburgh Common 47 TG 37
Hapsford 50 SJ 47
Hapton (Lancs.) 58 SD 79
Hapton (Norf.) 47 TM 17
Harberton 5 SX 77
Harbertonford 5 SX 78
Harbledown 15 TR 13
Harborne 42 SP 03
Harborough Magna 43 SP 47
Harbottle 78 NT 93
Harbury 33 SP 37
Harby (Leic.) 54 SK 74
Harby (Notts.) 54 SK 87
Harcombe 8 SY 15
Harden 59 SE 08
Hardenhuish 18 ST 90
Hardgate 99 NJ 78
Hardham 12 TQ 03
Hardingham 46 TG 04
Hardings Wood 51 SJ 80
Hardingstone 34 SP 76
Hardington 18 ST 74
Hardington Mandeville 9 ST 51
Hardington Marsh 9 ST 50
Hardley 11 SU 42
Hardley Street 47 TG 38
Hardmead 34 SP 93
Hardrow 65 SD 86
Hardstoft 53 SK 44
Hardway (Hants.) 11 SU 61
Hardway (Somer.) 17 ST 71
Hardwick (Bucks.) 34 SP 80
Hardwick (Cambs.) 35 TL 37
Hardwick (Norf.) 47 TM 22
Hardwick (Northants.) 44 SP 85
Hardwick (Oxon.) 33 SP 37
Hardwick (Oxon.) 33 SP 57
Hardwicke (Glos.) 32 SO 79
Hardwicke (Glos.) 32 SO 91
Hare Hatch 20 SU 80
Hare Street 35 TL 39
Hareby 55 TF 33
Hareden 64 SD 63
Harefield 20 TQ 05
Harehope 79 NU 09
Harescombe 32 SO 84
Haresfield 32 SO 81
Harewood 59 SE 32
Harford 5 SX 63
Hargrave (Ches.) 50 SJ 48
Hargrave (Northants.) 44 TL 03
Hargrave Green 36 TL 77
Haringey 21 TQ 32
Harker 70 NY 39
Harkstead 37 TM 19
Harlaston 42 SK 21
Harlaxton 54 SK 88
Harle Syke 58 SD 86
Harlech 48 SH 58
Harlesden 21 TQ 23
Harleston (Norf.) 47 TM 24
Harleston (Suff.) 36 TM 01
Harlestone 34 SP 70
Harley 41 SJ 59
Harling Road 46 TL 97
Harlington 35 TL 03
Harlosh 100 NG 28
Harlow 35 TL 47
Harlow Hill 72 NZ 07
Harlthorpe 60 SE 73
Harlton 35 TL 38
Harman's Cross 10 SY 98
Harmby 65 SE 12
Harmer Green 35 TL 25
Harmer Hill 40 SJ 48
Harmston 54 SK 97
Harnhill 32 SP 06
Harold Hill 21 TQ 53
Harold Wood 21 TQ 55
Haroldston West 24 SM 86
Haroldswick 113 HP 64
Harome 66 SE 64
Harpenden 35 TL 13
Harpford 8 SY 08
Harpham 67 TA 09
Harpley (Here. and Worc.) 31 SO 68
Harpley (Norf.) 46 TF 78
Harpole 34 SP 69
Harpsdale 112 ND 12
Harpsden 20 SU 76
Harpswell 54 SK 93
Harpur Hill 52 SK 06
Harpurhey 58 SD 87
Harrapool 101 NG 65
Harrietfield 91 NN 98
Harrietsham 14 TQ 87
Harrington (Cumbr.) 62 NX 99
Harrington (Lincs.) 55 TF 36
Harrington (Northants.) 44 SP 77
Harringworth 44 SP 91
Harriseahead 51 SJ 86
Harrogate 66 SE 30
Harrold 34 SP 94
Harrow 20 TQ 13
Harrow on the Hill 21 TQ 15
Harrowbarrow 4 SX 39
Harrowden 35 TL 06
Harston (Cambs.) 35 TL 42
Harston (Leic.) 54 SK 83
Hart 73 NZ 47
Hartburn 79 NZ 08
Hartest 36 TL 83
Hartfield 13 TQ 47
Hartford (Cambs.) 45 TL 25
Hartford (Ches.) 51 SJ 63
Hartford End 22 TL 68
Hartfordbridge 20 SU 77
Harthill (Ches.) 50 SJ 49
Harthill (Lothian) 84 NS 90
Harthill (S Yorks.) 53 SK 49
Hartington 52 SK 13
Hartland 6 SS 26
Hartlebury 41 SO 84
Hartlepool 73 NZ 50
Hartley (Cumbr.) 65 NY 78
Hartley (Kent) 21 TQ 61
Hartley (Kent) 14 TQ 76
Hartley (Northum.) 79 NZ 34
Hartley Wespall 19 SU 69
Hartley Wintney 20 SU 77
Hartlip 14 TQ 83
Harton (N Yorks.) 66 SE 70
Harton (Salop) 40 SO 48

Harton (Tyne and Wear) 239 Holton (Somer.)

arton (Tyne and Wear) 72 NZ 3864
artpury 32 SO 7924
artshill 43 SP 3293
artshorne 43 SK 3221
artwell 34 SP 7850
artwood 84 NS 8459
arvel 14 TQ 6563
arvington 32 SP 0548
arvington Cross 32 SP 0549
arwell 19 SU 4989
arwich 37 TM 2431
arwood (Durham) 63 NY 8133
arwood (Gtr Mches.) 58 SD 7411
arwood Dale 67 SE 9595
arworth 53 SK 6291
ascombe 12 TQ 0039
aselbech 44 SP 7177
aselbury Plucknett 9 ST 4711
aseley 42 SP 2368
aselor 32 SP 1257
asfield 32 SO 8227
asguard 24 SM 8509
askayne 57 SD 3507
asketon 37 TM 2550
asland 53 SK 3969
aslemere 12 SU 9032
aslingden 58 SD 7823
aslingden Grane 58 SD 7523
aslingfield 35 TL 4052
aslington 51 SJ 7355
assall 51 SJ 7657
assall Green 51 SJ 7758
assell Street 15 TR 0946
assendean 78 NT 5420
assingham 47 TG 3605
assocks 13 TQ 3015
assop 53 SK 2272
astigrow 112 ND 2661
astingleigh 15 TR 0945
astings 14 TQ 8009
astingwood 35 TL 4807
astoe 34 SP 9209
aswell 72 NZ 3743
atch (Beds.) 35 TL 1547
atch (Hants.) 19 SU 6752
atch (Wilts.) 10 ST 9228
atch Beauchamp 8 ST 3020
atch End 20 TQ 1391
atching Green 35 TL 1313
atchmere 50 SJ 5571
atcliffe 61 TA 2100
atfield (Here. and Worc.) 31 SO 5859
atfield (Herts.) 35 TL 2309
atfield (S Yorks.) 60 SE 6609
atfield Broad Oak 22 TL 5516
atfield Heath 22 TL 5215
atfield Peverel 22 TL 7911
atfield Woodhouse 60 SE 6708
atford 19 SU 3394
atherden 19 SU 3450
atherleigh 6 SS 5404
athern 43 SK 5022
atherop 32 SP 1505
athersage 53 SK 2381
atherton (Ches.) 51 SJ 6847
atherton (Staffs.) 41 SJ 9610
atley St. George 35 TL 2851
attingley 11 SU 6437
atton (Ches.) 51 SJ 5982
atton (Derby.) 53 SK 2130
atton (Grampn.) 105 NK 0537
atton (Gtr London) 20 TQ 1075
atton (Lincs.) 55 TF 1776
atton (Salop) 40 SO 4690
atton (Warw.) 42 SP 2367
atton Heath 50 SJ 4561
atton of Fintray 105 NJ 8316
attoncrook 105 NJ 8424
augh Head 79 NU 0026
augh of Urr 69 NX 8066
augham 55 TF 3381
aughley 36 TM 0262
aughley Green 36 TM 0364
aughton (Notts.) 53 SK 6772
aughton (Salop) 40 SJ 3727
aughton (Salop) 40 SJ 5516
aughton (Salop) 41 SO 6795
aughton (Staffs.) 41 SJ 8620
aughton Green 51 SJ 9393
aughton Moss 51 SJ 5756
aunton 42 SK 2411
auxley 79 NU 2703
auxton 35 TL 4352
avant 12 SU 7106
aven 30 SO 4054
avenstreet 11 SZ 5690
averfordwest 24 SM 9515
averhill 36 TL 6745
averigg 62 SD 1578
avering 21 TQ 5587
avering's Grove 22 TQ 6594
avering-atte-Bower 21 TQ 5193
aversham 34 SP 8343
averthwaite 62 SD 3483
awarden 50 SJ 3165
awes 64 SD 8789
awford 32 SO 8460
awick 78 NT 5014
awkchurch 8 ST 3400
awkedon 36 TL 7952
awkeridge 18 ST 8653
awkerland 8 SY 0588
awkes End 43 SP 2983
awkesbury 18 ST 7687
awkesbury Upton 18 ST 7786
awkhill 79 NU 2212
awkhurst 14 TQ 7630
awkinge 15 TR 2139
awkley 12 SU 7429
awkridge 7 SS 8630
awkshead 62 SD 3598
awkswick 65 SD 9570
awksworth (Notts.) 54 SK 7543
awksworth (W Yorks.) 59 SE 1641
awkwell 22 TQ 8691
awley (Hants.) 20 SU 8558
awley (Kent) 21 TQ 5571
awling 32 SP 0623
awnby 66 SE 5389
aworth 59 SE 0337
awsker 67 NZ 9207
awstead 36 TL 8559
awthorn Hill 20 SU 8873
awton 54 SK 7851
axby 66 SE 6057
axey 60 SK 7699
ay-on-Wye 30 SO 2342
aydock 50 SJ 5696
aydon 9 ST 6615
aydon Bridge 71 NY 8464
aydon Wick 18 SU 1388
aye 4 SX 3570
ayes (Gtr London) 20 TQ 0980
ayes (Gtr London) 21 TQ 4165
Hayfield 52 SK 0386
Hayhillock 99 NO 5242
Hayle 2 SW 5537
Hayling Island 12 SU 7201
Haynes 35 TL 0841
Hayscastle Cross 24 SM 9125
Hayton (Cumbr.) 70 NY 1041
Hayton (Cumbr.) 71 NY 5057
Hayton (Humbs.) 60 SE 8145
Hayton (Notts.) 54 SK 7284
Hayton's Bent 40 SO 5280
Haytor Vale 5 SX 7677
Haywards Heath 13 TQ 3324
Haywood Oaks 53 SK 6055
Hazel Grove 51 SJ 9287
Hazelbank 84 NS 8344
Hazelbury Bryan 9 ST 7408
Hazeley 20 SU 7459
Hazelslade 42 SK 0212
Hazelton Walls 93 NO 3321
Hazelwood 53 SK 3245
Hazlemere 20 SU 8895
Hazlerigg 79 NZ 2472
Hazleton 32 SP 0718
Heacham 46 TF 6737
Head of Muir 84 NS 8080
Headbourne Worthy 11 SU 4831
Headcorn 14 TQ 8344
Headington 33 SP 5407
Headlam 72 NZ 1818
Headley (Hants.) 19 SU 5162
Headley (Hants.) 12 SU 8236
Headley (Surrey) 21 TQ 2054
Headon 54 SK 7476
Heads Nook 71 NY 4955
Heage 53 SK 3650
Healaugh (N Yorks.) 65 SE 0198
Healaugh (N Yorks.) 60 SE 4947
Heale 7 SS 6446
Healey (Lancs.) 58 SD 8817
Healey (N Yorks.) 65 SE 1780
Healey (Northum.) 72 NZ 0158
Healeyfield 72 NZ 0648
Healing 61 TA 2110
Heamoor 2 SW 4631
Heanish 94 NM 0343
Heanor 53 SK 4346
Heanton Punchardon 6 SS 5035
Heapham 54 SK 8788
Hearthstane 77 NT 1125
Heast 100 NG 6417
Heath 53 SK 4467
Heath End (Hants.) 19 SU 5762
Heath Hayes 42 SK 0110
Heath Hill 41 SJ 7614
Heath House 17 ST 4146
Heath and Reach 34 SP 9228
Heathcote 52 SK 1460
Heather 43 SK 3910
Heathfield (Devon.) 5 SX 8376
Heathfield (E Susx) 13 TQ 5821
Heathfield (Somer.) 16 ST 1526
Heathrow Airport — London 20 TQ 0775
Heathton 41 SO 8192
Heatley 51 SJ 6988
Heaton (Lancs.) 57 SD 4460
Heaton (Staffs.) 51 SJ 9462
Heaton (Tyne and Wear) 72 NZ 2665
Heaverham 21 TQ 5758
Hebburn 72 NZ 3265
Hebden 65 SE 0263
Hebden Bridge 59 SD 9927
Hebden Green 51 SJ 6365
Hebron 79 NZ 1989
Heckfield 20 SU 7260
Heckfield Green 37 TM 1875
Heckington 55 TF 1444
Heckmondwike 59 SE 2123
Heddington 18 ST 9966
Heddon-on-the-Wall 72 NZ 1366
Hedenham 47 TM 3193
Hedge End 11 SU 4812
Hedgerley 20 SU 9787
Hedging 17 ST 3029
Hedley on the Hill 72 NZ 0759
Hednesford 42 SK 0012
Hedon 61 TA 1828
Hedsor 20 SU 9187
Hegdon Hill 31 SO 5854
Heighington (Durham) 72 NZ 2522
Heighington (Lincs.) 54 TF 0269
Heights of Brae 102 NH 5161
Heilam 110 NC 4560
Heiton 86 NT 7130
Hele (Devon.) 6 SS 5347
Hele (Devon.) 8 SS 9902
Helensburgh 90 NS 2982
Helford 2 SW 7526
Helhoughton 46 TF 8626
Helions Bumpstead 36 TL 6541
Helland 4 SX 0770
Hellesdon 47 TG 2010
Hellidon 33 SP 5158
Hellifield 65 SD 8556
Hellingly 13 TQ 5812
Hellington 47 TG 3103
Helmdon 33 SP 5843
Helmingham 37 TM 1857
Helmsdale 112 ND 0215
Helmshore 58 SD 7821
Helmsley 66 SE 6183
Helperby 66 SE 4369
Helperthorpe 67 SE 9570
Helpringham 55 TF 1340
Helpston 45 TF 1205
Helsby 50 SJ 4875
Helston 2 SW 6527
Helstone 4 SX 0881
Helton 63 NY 5122
Hemblington 47 TG 3411
Hemel Hempstead 35 TL 0506
Hemingbrough 60 SE 6730
Hemingby 55 TF 2374
Hemingford Abbots 45 TL 2870
Hemingford Grey 45 TL 2970
Hemingstone 37 TM 1453
Hemington (Northants.) 45 TL 0985
Hemington (Somer.) 17 ST 7253
Hemley 37 TM 2842
Hempholme 67 TA 0850
Hempnall 47 TM 2494
Hempnall Green 47 TM 2593
Hempriggs 103 NJ 1064
Hempstead (Essex) 36 TL 6338
Hempstead (Norf.) 47 TG 4028
Hempsted (Glos) 32 SO 8117
Hempstead (Norf.) 47 TG 1037
Hempton (Norf.) 46 TF 9129
Hempton (Oxon.) 33 SP 4431
Hemsby 47 TG 4917
Hemswell 54 SK 9290
Hemsworth 59 SE 4213
Hemyock 8 ST 1313
Henbury (Avon) 29 ST 5478
Henbury (Ches.) 51 SJ 8873
Hendon (Gtr London) 21 TQ 2389
Hendon (Tyne and Wear) 72 NZ 4055
Hendy 25 SN 5804
Heneglwys 48 SH 4276
Henfield 13 TQ 2116
Hengoed (Mid Glam.) 28 ST 1495
Hengoed (Powys) 30 SO 2253
Hengoed (Salop) 50 SJ 2833
Hengrave 36 TL 8268
Henham 22 TL 5428
Heniarth 40 SJ 1108
Henley (Salop) 40 SO 5476
Henley (Somer.) 17 ST 4232
Henley (Suff.) 37 TM 1551
Henley (W Susx) 12 SU 8926
Henley Park 20 SU 9352
Henley on Thames 20 SU 7682
Henley-in-Arden 32 SP 1465
Henllan (Clwyd) 49 SJ 0268
Henllan (Dyfed) 26 SN 3540
Henllan Amgoed 24 SN 1820
Henllys 28 ST 2693
Henlow 35 TL 1738
Hennock 5 SX 8380
Henryd 49 SH 7674
Hensall 60 SE 5923
Henshaw 71 NY 7664
Henstead 47 TM 4986
Henstridge 9 ST 7219
Henstridge Marsh 9 ST 7420
Henton (Oxon.) 34 SP 7602
Henton (Somer.) 17 ST 4845
Henwick 32 SO 8354
Henwood 4 SX 2673
Heol Senni 28 SN 9223
Heol-y-Cyw 28 SS 9484
Hepburn 79 NU 0724
Hepple 79 NT 9800
Hepscott 79 NZ 2284
Heptonstall 59 SD 9827
Hepworth (Suff.) 36 TL 9874
Hepworth (W Yorks.) 59 SE 1606
Herbrandston 24 SM 8707
Hereford 31 SO 5040
Hergest 30 SO 2655
Heriot 85 NT 3952
Hermitage (Berks.) 19 SU 5072
Hermitage (Borders) 78 NY 5095
Hermitage (Dorset.) 9 ST 6306
Hermitage (Hants.) 12 SU 7505
Hermon (Dyfed) 26 SN 2032
Hermon (Dyfed) 26 SN 3630
Herne 15 TR 1866
Herne Bay 15 TR 1768
Herner 6 SS 5926
Hernhill 15 TR 0660
Herodsfoot 4 SX 2160
Herongate 22 TQ 6391
Heronsgate 20 TQ 0294
Herriard 19 SU 6645
Herringfleet 47 TM 4797
Herringswell 36 TL 7170
Herrington 72 NZ 3553
Hersden 15 TR 1961
Hersham 20 TQ 1164
Herstmonceux 13 TQ 6312
Herston 113 ND 4291
Hertford 35 TL 3212
Hertford Heath 35 TL 3510
Hertingfordbury 35 TL 3112
Hesket Newmarket 62 NY 3438
Hesketh Bank 57 SD 4323
Hesketh Lane 58 SD 6141
Hesleden 73 NZ 4438
Hesleyside 78 NY 8183
Heslington 66 SE 6250
Hessay 66 SE 5253
Hessenford 4 SX 3057
Hessett 36 TL 9361
Hessle 61 TA 0326
Hest Bank 64 SD 4566
Heston 20 TQ 1277
Heswall 50 SJ 2682
Hethe 33 SP 5929
Hethersett 47 TG 1505
Hethersgill 71 NY 4767
Hethpool 87 NT 8928
Hett 72 NZ 2836
Hetton 65 SD 9658
Hetton-le-Hole 72 NZ 3548
Heugh 79 NZ 0873
Heugh-Head 104 NJ 3711
Heveningham 37 TM 3372
Hever 21 TQ 4744
Heversham 63 SD 4983
Hevingham 47 TG 2021
Hewelsfield 29 SO 5602
Hewish (Avon) 17 ST 4064
Hewish (Somer.) 9 ST 4108
Hexham 71 NY 9364
Hextable 21 TQ 5170
Hexton 35 TL 1030
Hexworthy 5 SX 6572
Heybridge (Essex) 22 TL 8508
Heybridge (Essex) 22 TQ 6498
Heybridge Basin 22 TL 8707
Heybrook Bay 5 SX 4948
Heydon (Cambs.) 35 TL 4340
Heydon (Norf.) 47 TG 1127
Heydour 54 TF 0039
Heylipoll 94 NL 9643
Heylor 113 HU 2881
Heysham 64 SD 4161
Heyshott 12 SU 8918
Heytesbury 18 ST 9242
Heythrop 33 SP 3527
Heywood (Gtr Mches.) 58 SD 8510
Heywood (Wilts.) 18 ST 8753
Hibaldstow 61 SE 9702
Hickleton 60 SE 4805
Hickling (Norf.) 47 TG 4124
Hickling (Notts.) 43 SK 6929
Hickling Green 47 TG 4023
Hickling Heath 47 TG 4022
Hidcote Boyce 32 SP 1742
High Ackworth 59 SE 4317
High Beach 21 TQ 4097
High Bentham 64 SD 6669
High Bickington 6 SS 5920
High Birkwith 65 SD 8076
High Blantyre 84 NS 6756
High Bonnybridge 84 NS 8378
High Buston 79 NU 2308
High Callerton 79 NZ 1670
High Cogges 33 SP 3709
High Coniscliffe 72 NZ 2215
High Cross (Hants.) 12 SU 7126
High Cross (Herts.) 35 TL 3618
High Cross Bank 43 SK 3018
High Easter 22 TL 6214
High Ellington 65 SE 1983
High Ercall 41 SJ 5917
High Etherley 72 NZ 1628
High Garrett 22 TL 7726
High Grange 72 NZ 1731
High Green (Norf.) 47 TG 1305
High Green (S Yorks.) 59 SK 3397
High Halden 14 TQ 9037
High Halstow 22 TQ 7875
High Ham 17 ST 4231
High Hatton 41 SJ 6024
High Hesket 71 NY 4744
High Hoyland 59 SE 2710
High Hunsley 61 SE 9535
High Hurstwood 13 TQ 4926
High Lane 31 SO 6760
High Laver 22 TL 5208
High Legh 51 SJ 6984
High Littleton 17 ST 6458
High Lorton 62 NY 1625
High Melton 60 SE 5001
High Newton 62 SD 4082
High Newton-by-the-Sea 79 NU 2325
High Offley 41 SJ 7826
High Ongar 22 TL 5603
High Onn 41 SJ 8216
High Roding 22 TL 6017
High Salvington 12 TQ 1206
High Shaw 65 SD 8791
High Spen 72 NZ 1359
High Street (Corn.) 3 SW 9753
High Street (Suff.) 37 TM 4355
High Street Green 36 TM 0055
High Toynton 55 TF 2869
High Trewhitt 79 NU 0105
High Wray 62 SD 3799
High Wych 35 TL 4614
High Wycombe 29 SU 8593
Higham (Derby.) 53 SK 3959
Higham (Kent) 14 TQ 7171
Higham (Lancs.) 58 SD 8036
Higham (Suff.) 36 TL 7465
Higham (Suff.) 36 TM 0335
Higham Dykes 79 NZ 1375
Higham Ferrers 44 SP 9669
Higham Gobion 35 TL 1033
Higham on the Hill 43 SP 3895
Highampton 6 SS 4804
Highbridge 17 ST 3147
Highbrook 13 TQ 3630
Highburton 59 SE 1813
Highbury 17 ST 6849
Highclere 19 SU 4360
Highcliffe 11 SZ 2193
Higher Ansty 9 ST 7603
Higher Ballam 57 SD 3630
Higher Penwortham 57 SD 5128
Higher Tale 8 ST 0601
Higher Walreddon 5 SX 4771
Higher Walton (Ches.) 51 SJ 5985
Higher Walton (Lancs.) 57 SD 5727
Higher Wych 50 SJ 4943
Highfield (Strath.) 82 NS 3050
Highfield (Tyne and Wear) 72 NZ 1459
Highfields 35 TL 3559
Highleadon 32 SO 7623
Highleigh 12 SZ 8498
Highley 41 SO 7483
Highmoor Cross 19 SU 7084
Highmoor Hill 29 ST 4689
Highnam 32 SO 7919
Highsted 14 TQ 9161
Hightown (Ches.) 51 SJ 8762
Hightown (Mers.) 57 SD 2903
Highway 18 SU 0474
Highweek 5 SX 8472
Highworth 18 SU 2092
Hilborough (Norf.) 46 TF 8200
Hildenborough 21 TQ 5648
Hildersham 36 TL 5448
Hilderstone 51 SJ 9434
Hilderthorpe 67 TA 1765
Hilgay 46 TL 6298
Hill 29 ST 6495
Hill Brow 12 SU 7926
Hill Dyke 55 TF 3447
Hill End (Durham) 72 NZ 0135
Hill End (Fife.) 92 NT 0495
Hill Head (Hants.) 11 SU 5402
Hill Ridware 42 SK 0718
Hill Row 45 TL 4475
Hill Top (Hants.) 11 SU 4002
Hill Top (W Yorks.) 59 SE 3315
Hill of Fearn 108 NH 8377
Hill, The 62 SD 1783
Hillam 60 SE 5028
Hillbeck 63 NY 7915
Hillberry 56 SC 3879
Hillborough (Kent) 15 TR 2168
Hillbrae (Grampn.) 104 NJ 6047
Hillbrae (Grampn.) 105 NJ 7923
Hillend (Fife.) 85 NT 1483
Hillesden 34 SP 6828
Hillesley 18 ST 7689
Hillfarrance 8 ST 1624
Hillhead (Devon.) 5 SX 9053
Hillhead (Strath.) 75 NS 4219
Hillhead of Auchentumb 105 NJ 9258
Hillhead of Cocklaw 105 NK 0844
Hilliard's Cross 42 SK 1412
Hilliclay 112 ND 1764
Hillingdon 20 TQ 0882
Hillington 46 TF 7225
Hillmorton 43 SP 5374
Hillockhead 104 NJ 3809
Hillside (Grampn.) 99 NO 9298
Hillside (Tays.) 99 NO 7061
Hillswick 113 HU 2877
Hilmarton 18 SU 0175
Hilperton 18 ST 8759
Hilsea 11 SU 6503
Hilton (Cambs.) 45 TL 2966
Hilton (Cleve.) 73 NZ 4611
Hilton (Cumbr.) 63 NY 7320
Hilton (Derby.) 53 SK 2430
Hilton (Dorset) 9 ST 7802
Hilton (Durham) 72 NZ 1621
Hilton (Grampn.) 105 NJ 9434
Hilton (Salop) 41 SO 7795
Hilton of Cadboll 108 NH 8776
Himbleton 32 SO 9458
Himley 41 SO 8891
Hincaster 63 SD 5148
Hinckley 43 SP 4294
Hinderclay 36 TM 0276
Hinderwell 73 NZ 7916
Hindford 50 SJ 3333
Hindhead 12 SU 8736
Hindley 58 SD 6104
Hindley Green 58 SD 6403
Hindlip 32 SO 8758
Hindolveston 46 TG 0329
Hindon 10 ST 9032
Hindringham 46 TF 9836
Hingham 46 TG 0202
Hinstock 41 SJ 6926
Hintlesham 37 TM 0843
Hinton (Avon) 29 ST 7376
Hinton (Hants.) 11 SZ 2095
Hinton (Northants.) 33 SP 5352
Hinton (Salop) 40 SJ 4008
Hinton Ampner 11 SU 5927
Hinton Blewett 17 ST 5956
Hinton Charterhouse 18 ST 7758
Hinton Marsh 11 SU 5827
Hinton Martell 10 SU 0106
Hinton Parva 18 SU 2283
Hinton St. George 9 ST 4212
Hinton St. Mary 10 ST 7816
Hinton Waldrist 19 SU 3799
Hinton on the Green 32 SP 0204
Hinton-in-the-Hedges 33 SP 5537
Hints (Salop) 41 SO 6175
Hints (Staffs.) 42 SK 1503
Hinwick 34 SP 9361
Hinxhill 15 TR 0442
Hinxton 35 TL 4945
Hinxworth 35 TL 2340
Hipperholme 59 SE 1225
Hirnant 39 SJ 0423
Hirst 79 NZ 2787
Hirst Courtney 60 SE 6124
Hirwaun 28 SN 9505
Hiscott 6 SS 5426
Histon 35 TL 4363
Hitcham 36 TL 9851
Hitchin 35 TL 1829
Hither Green 21 TQ 3874
Hittisleigh 7 SX 7395
Hixon 42 SK 0026
Hoaden 15 TR 2759
Hoaldalbert 29 SO 3923
Hoar Cross 42 SK 1223
Hoarwithy 29 SO 5429
Hoath 15 TR 2064
Hobarris 40 SO 3078
Hobkirk 78 NT 5810
Hobson 72 NZ 1755
Hoby 42 SK 6617
Hockering 47 TG 0713
Hockerton 54 SK 7156
Hockley 22 TQ 8293
Hockley Heath 42 SP 1572
Hockliffe 34 SP 9726
Hockwold cum Wilton 46 TL 7288
Hockworthy 8 ST 0319
Hoddesdon 35 TL 3709
Hoddlesdon 58 SD 7122
Hodgeston 24 SS 0399
Hodnet 41 SJ 6128
Hodthorpe 53 SK 5476
Hoe 46 TF 9916
Hoe Gate 11 SU 6213
Hoggeston 34 SP 8025
Hoghton 58 SD 6125
Hognaston 53 SK 2350
Hogsthorpe 55 TF 5372
Holbeach 45 TF 3625
Holbeach Bank 45 TF 3627
Holbeach Drove 45 TF 3212
Holbeach Hurn 45 TF 3927
Holbeach St. Johns 45 TF 3418
Holbeach St. Marks 55 TF 3731
Holbeach St. Matthew 55 TF 4132
Holbeck 53 SK 5473
Holberrow Green 32 SP 0259
Holbeton 5 SX 6150
Holbrook (Derby) 53 SK 3645
Holbrook (Suff.) 37 TM 1636
Holburn 87 NU 0436
Holbury 11 SU 4303
Holcombe (Devon.) 8 SX 9574
Holcombe (Somer.) 17 ST 6649
Holcombe Rogus 8 ST 0519
Holcot 44 SP 7969
Holden 58 SD 7749
Holdenby 43 SP 6967
Holdgate 40 SO 5589
Holdingham 54 TF 0547
Holestane 76 NX 8799
Holford 16 ST 1541
Holker 65 SD 3577
Holkham 46 TF 8944
Hollacombe 6 SS 3702
Holland (Stronsay) 113 HY 6622
Holland-on-Sea 23 TM 2016
Hollandstoun 113 HY 7553
Hollesley 37 TM 3544
Hollingbourne 14 TQ 8455
Hollington (Derby) 53 SK 2239
Hollington (E Susx.) 14 TQ 7911
Hollington (Staffs.) 52 SK 0538
Hollingworth 52 SK 0096
Hollins 58 SD 8108
Hollins Green 51 SJ 6990
Hollinsclough 52 SK 0666
Hollinswood 41 SJ 6909
Hollinwood 50 SJ 5236
Hollocombe 6 SS 6311
Holloway 53 SK 3256
Hollowell 43 SP 6972
Holly End 45 TF 4906
Hollybush (Gwent) 28 SO 1603
Hollybush (Here. and Worc.) 32 SO 7636
Hollybush (Strath.) 75 NS 3914
Hollym 61 TA 3425
Holmbury St. Mary 12 TQ 1144
Holme (Cambs.) 45 TL 1987
Holme (Cumbr.) 63 SD 5278
Holme (Notts.) 54 SK 8059
Holme (W Yorks.) 59 SE 1005
Holme Chapel 58 SD 8728
Holme Hale 46 TF 8807
Holme Lacy 31 SO 5535
Holme Marsh 30 SO 3354
Holme next the Sea 46 TF 7043
Holme on the Wolds 61 SE 9646
Holme upon Spalding Moor 60 SE 8138
Holmer Green 20 SU 9097
Holmes Chapel 51 SJ 7667
Holmesfield 53 SK 3277
Holmeswood 57 SD 4316
Holmewood 53 SK 4365
Holmfirth 59 SE 1408
Holmhead 75 NS 5620
Holmpton 61 TA 3623
Holmrook 62 SD 0799
Holne 5 SX 7069
Holnest 9 ST 6509
Holsworthy 6 SS 3403
Holsworthy Beacon 6 SS 3508
Holt (Clwyd) 50 SJ 4053
Holt (Dorset) 10 SU 0203
Holt (Here. and Worc.) 32 SO 8262
Holt (Norf.) 47 TG 0738
Holt (Wilts.) 18 ST 8661
Holt End 42 SP 0769
Holt Heath 32 SO 8163
Holtby 66 SE 6754
Holton (Oxon.) 33 SP 6006
Holton (Somer.) 17 ST 6826

Holton (Suff.) 240 Kennyhi

Holton (Suff.)	37	TM 4077
Holton Heath	10	SY 9491
Holton St. Mary	37	TM 0537
Holton cum Beckering	55	TF 1181
Holton le Clay	61	TA 2802
Holton le Moor	61	TF 0797
Holwell (Herts.)	35	TL 1633
Holwell (Leic.)	44	SK 7323
Holwell (Oxon)	33	SP 2309
Holwick	63	NY 9026
Holy Cross	41	SO 9279
Holybourne	12	SU 7341
Holyhead	48	SH 2482
Holymoorside	53	SK 3369
Holyport	20	SU 8977
Holystone	78	NT 9502
Holytown	84	NS 7760
Holywell (Cambs.)	45	TL 3370
Holywell (Clwyd)	50	SJ 1875
Holywell (Corn.)	5	SW 7658
Holywell (Dorset)	9	ST 5904
Holywell Green	59	SE 0918
Holywell Lake	8	ST 1020
Holywell Row	36	TL 7077
Holywood	69	NX 9480
Hom Green	29	SO 5822
Homer	41	SJ 6101
Homersfield	47	TM 2885
Homington	10	SU 1226
Honey Hill	15	TR 1161
Honeyborough	24	SM 9506
Honeybourne	32	SP 1144
Honeychurch	6	SS 6202
Honiley	42	SP 2472
Honing	47	TG 3227
Honingham	47	TG 1011
Honington (Lincs.)	54	SK 9443
Honington (Suff.)	36	TL 9174
Honington (Warw.)	33	SP 2642
Honiton	8	ST 1600
Honley	59	SE 1311
Hoo (Kent)	22	TQ 7872
Hoo Green	37	TM 2559
Hooe (Devon.)	5	SX 5052
Hooe (E Susx)	13	TQ 6809
Hook (Dyfed)	24	SM 9811
Hook (Hants.)	20	SU 7254
Hook (Humbs.)	60	SE 7525
Hook (Surrey)	21	TQ 1764
Hook (Wilts.)	18	SU 0784
Hook Norton	33	SP 3533
Hooke (Dorset)	9	ST 5300
Hookgate	51	SJ 7435
Hookway	7	SX 8598
Hookwood	13	TQ 2643
Hoole	50	SJ 4367
Hooton	50	SJ 3679
Hooton Levitt	53	SK 5291
Hooton Pagnell	60	SE 4808
Hooton Roberts	60	SK 4897
Hop Pole	45	TF 1813
Hope (Clwyd)	50	SJ 3058
Hope (Derby.)	52	SK 1783
Hope (Devon.)	5	SX 6740
Hope (Powys)	40	SJ 2507
Hope (Salop)	40	SJ 3401
Hope Bagot	41	SO 5874
Hope Bowdler	40	SO 4792
Hope Mansell	29	SO 6219
Hope under Dinmore	30	SO 5052
Hopeman	104	NJ 1469
Hopesay	40	SO 3883
Hopton (Salop)	41	SJ 5926
Hopton (Staffs.)	41	SJ 9426
Hopton (Suff.)	36	TL 9979
Hopton Cangeford	40	SO 5480
Hopton Castle	40	SO 3678
Hopton Wafers	41	SO 6476
Hopton on Sea (Norf.)	47	TG 5200
Hopwas	42	SK 1705
Hopwood	42	SP 0375
Horam	13	TQ 5717
Horbling	55	TF 1135
Horbury	59	SE 2918
Horden	73	NZ 4441
Horderley	40	SO 4086
Hordle	11	SZ 2795
Hordley	40	SJ 3730
Horeb	26	SN 3942
Horham	37	TM 2172
Horkesley Heath	23	TL 9829
Horkstow	61	SE 9818
Horley (Oxon.)	33	SP 4143
Horley (Surrey)	13	TQ 2843
Horn Hill	20	TQ 0292
Hornblotton Green	17	ST 5833
Hornby (Lancs.)	64	SD 5868
Hornby (N Yorks.)	66	NZ 3605
Horncastle	55	TF 2669
Hornchurch	21	TQ 5487
Horncliffe	87	NT 9249
Horndean	11	SU 7013
Horndon on the Hill	22	TQ 6683
Horne	13	TQ 3344
Horning	47	TG 3417
Horninghold	44	SP 8097
Horninglow	42	SK 2324
Horningsea	35	TL 4962
Horningsham	18	ST 8241
Horningtoft	46	TF 9323
Hornsby	71	NY 5150
Hornsea	61	TA 2047
Hornsey	21	TQ 3089
Hornton	33	SP 3945
Horrabridge	5	SX 5169
Horringer	36	TL 8261
Horsebridge (E Susx)	13	TQ 5711
Horsebridge (Hants.)	11	SU 3430
Horsebrook	41	SJ 8810
Horsehay	41	SJ 6707
Horseheath	36	TL 6147
Horsehouse	65	SE 0481
Horsell	20	SU 9959
Horseman's Green	50	SJ 4441
Horseway	45	TL 4287
Horsey	47	TG 4523
Horsford	47	TG 1916
Horsforth	59	SE 2337
Horsham (Here. and Worc.)	32	SO 7357
Horsham (W Susx)	12	TQ 1730
Horsham St. Faith	47	TG 2114
Horsington (Lincs.)	55	TF 1868
Horsington (Somer.)	9	ST 7023
Horsley (Derby.)	53	SK 3744
Horsley (Glos.)	18	ST 8398
Horsley (Northum.)	78	NY 8496
Horsley (Northum.)	72	NZ 0966
Horsley Cross	23	TM 1227
Horsley Woodhouse	53	SK 3945
Horsleycross Street	23	TM 1228
Horsleyhill	78	NT 5319
Horsmonden	14	TQ 7040
Horspath	33	SP 5704
Horstead	47	TG 2619
Horsted Keynes	13	TQ 3828
Horton (Avon)	29	ST 7684
Horton (Berks.)	20	TQ 0175
Horton (Bucks.)	34	SP 9219
Horton (Dorset)	10	SU 0307
Horton (Northants.)	34	SP 8254
Horton (Northum.)	87	NU 0230
Horton (Staffs.)	51	SJ 9457
Horton (W Glam.)	25	SS 4785
Horton (Wilts.)	18	SU 0463
Horton Green	50	SJ 4549
Horton Heath	11	SU 4916
Horton Kirby	21	TQ 5668
Horton in Ribblesdale	65	SD 8172
Horwich	58	SD 6311
Horwood	6	SS 5027
Hose	44	SK 7329
Hosh	91	NN 8523
Hotham	60	SE 8934
Hothfield	15	TQ 9644
Hoton	43	SK 5722
Hough	51	SJ 7151
Hough Green	50	SJ 4885
Hough-on-the-Hill	54	SK 9246
Hougham	54	SK 8844
Hougharry	109	NF 7071
Houghton (Cambs.)	45	TL 2871
Houghton (Cumbr.)	70	NY 4159
Houghton (Dyfed)	24	SM 9807
Houghton (Hants.)	11	SU 3331
Houghton (W Susx)	12	TQ 0111
Houghton Conquest	35	TL 0441
Houghton Regis	34	TL 0224
Houghton St. Giles	46	TF 9235
Houghton le Spring	72	NZ 3450
Houghton on the Hill	43	SK 6703
Houll	113	HU 3792
Houlsyke	67	NZ 7308
Hound Green	20	SU 7259
Houndslow	86	NT 6347
Houndwood	87	NT 8464
Hounslow	20	TQ 1276
Housetter	113	HU 3784
Houston	82	NS 4067
Houstry	112	ND 1534
Hove	13	TQ 2805
Hoveringham	53	SK 6946
Hoversta	113	HU 4940
Hoveton	47	TG 3018
Hovingham	66	SE 6675
How	71	NY 5056
How Caple	31	SO 6030
Howden	60	SE 7428
Howden-le-Wear	72	NZ 1633
Howe (Cumbr.)	63	SD 4588
Howe (Highld.)	112	ND 3062
Howe (Norf.)	47	TM 2799
Howe Green	22	TL 7403
Howe Street (Essex)	22	TL 6914
Howe Street (Essex)	36	TL 6934
Howe of Teuchar	105	NJ 7947
Howe, The	56	SC 1967
Howell	27	TF 1346
Howey	30	SO 0558
Howgate	85	NT 2457
Howick	79	NU 2517
Howlaws	86	NT 7242
Howle	41	SJ 6823
Howlett End	36	TL 5834
Howmore	109	NF 7636
Hownam	78	NT 7719
Hownam Mains	78	NT 7820
Howsham (Humbs.)	61	TA 0404
Howsham (N Yorks.)	67	SE 7362
Howton	29	SO 4129
Howwood	82	NS 3960
Hoxne	37	TM 1877
Hoylake	50	SJ 2189
Hoyland Nether	59	SE 3600
Hoyland Swaine	59	SE 2604
Hubbert's Bridge	55	TF 2643
Huby	66	SE 5665
Hucclecote	32	SO 8717
Hucking	14	TQ 8358
Hucknall	53	SK 5349
Huddersfield	59	SE 1416
Huddington	32	SO 9457
Hudswell	65	NZ 1400
Huggate	67	SE 8855
Hugh Town	2	SV 9010
Hughenden Valley	20	SU 8695
Hughley	40	SO 5697
Hugmore	50	SJ 3752
Huish (Devon.)	6	SS 5311
Huish (Wilts.)	18	SU 1463
Huish Champflower	16	ST 0429
Huish Episcopi	17	ST 4226
Hulcott	34	SP 8516
Hulland	53	SK 2447
Hullavington	18	ST 8982
Hullbridge	22	TQ 8194
Hulme End	52	SK 1059
Hulme Walfield	51	SJ 8465
Hulver Street	47	TM 4686
Humber Court	31	SO 5356
Humberston	61	TA 3105
Humberstone	43	SK 6206
Humbie	86	NT 4562
Humbleton (Humbs.)	61	TA 2234
Humbleton (Northum.)	87	NT 9728
Hume	86	NT 7041
Humshaugh	78	NY 9171
Huna	112	ND 3573
Huncoat	58	SD 7730
Huncote	43	SP 5197
Hundalee	78	NT 6418
Hunderthwaite	72	NY 9821
Hundleby	55	TF 3966
Hundleton	24	SM 9600
Hundon	36	TL 7348
Hundred Acres	11	SU 5911
Hundred End	57	SD 4122
Hundred, The	31	SO 5264
Hungarton	43	SK 6807
Hungerford (Berks.)	19	SU 3368
Hungerford (Hants.)	10	SU 1612
Hungerford Newtown	19	SU 3571
Hunmanby	67	TA 0977
Hunningham	43	SP 3768
Hunsdon	35	TL 4114
Hunsingore	66	SE 4253
Hunsonby	63	NY 5835
Hunspow	112	ND 2172
Hunstanton	46	TF 6741
Hunstanworth	72	NY 9449
Hunston (Suff.)	36	TL 9768
Hunston (W Susx)	12	SU 8601
Hunstrete	17	ST 6462
Hunt End	32	SP 0364
Hunt's Cross	50	SJ 4385
Huntingdon	45	TL 2371
Huntingfield	37	TM 3374
Huntington (Here. and Worc.)	30	SO 2553
Huntington (Lothian)	86	NT 4875
Huntington (N Yorks.)	66	SE 6156
Huntington (Staffs)	41	SJ 9713
Huntingtower	92	NO 0725
Huntley	32	SO 7219
Huntly	104	NJ 5339
Hunton (Kent)	14	TQ 7149
Hunton (N Yorks.)	65	SE 1892
Huntsham	8	ST 0020
Huntspill	17	ST 3045
Huntworth	17	ST 3134
Hunwick	72	NZ 1832
Hunworth	47	TG 0635
Hurdsfield	51	SJ 9274
Hurley (Berks.)	20	SU 8283
Hurley (Warw.)	42	SP 2495
Hurlford	82	NS 4536
Hurliness	113	ND 2888
Hurn	10	SZ 1296
Hursley	11	SU 4225
Hurst (Berks.)	20	SU 7972
Hurst (Gtr Mches.)	58	SD 9400
Hurst Green (E Susx)	14	TQ 7327
Hurst Green (Lancs.)	58	SD 6838
Hurst Green (Surrey)	21	TQ 3951
Hurstbourne Priors	19	SU 4346
Hurstbourne Tarrant	19	SU 3853
Hurstpierpoint	13	TQ 2816
Hurtiso	113	HY 5001
Hurworth-on-Tees	72	NZ 3010
Hury	72	NY 9619
Husbands Bosworth	43	SP 6484
Husborne Crawley	34	SP 9535
Husinish	109	NA 9812
Husthwaite	66	SE 5175
Huthwaite	53	SK 4659
Huttoft	55	TF 5176
Hutton (Avon)	17	ST 3458
Hutton (Borders)	87	NT 9053
Hutton (Cumbr.)	62	NY 4326
Hutton (Essex)	22	TQ 6394
Hutton (Lancs.)	57	SD 4926
Hutton (N Yorks.)	67	SE 7667
Hutton Bonville	66	NZ 3300
Hutton Buscel	67	SE 9784
Hutton Conyers	66	SE 3273
Hutton Cranswick	67	TA 0252
Hutton End	63	NY 4538
Hutton Henry	72	NZ 4236
Hutton Magna	72	NZ 1212
Hutton Roof (Cumbr.)	62	NY 3734
Hutton Roof (Cumbr.)	63	SD 5777
Hutton Rudby	66	NZ 4606
Hutton Sessay	66	SE 4776
Hutton Wandesley	66	SE 5050
Hutton-le-Hole	66	SE 7090
Huxley	50	SJ 5061
Huyton	50	SJ 4490
Hycemoor	62	SD 0989
Hyde (Glos.)	32	SO 8801
Hyde (Gtr. Mches.)	51	SJ 9294
Hyde Heath	34	SP 9300
Hydestile	12	SU 9740
Hynish	94	NL 9839
Hyssington	40	SO 3194
Hythe (Hants.)	11	SU 4207
Hythe (Kent)	15	TR 1635

I

Ibberton	10	ST 7807
Ible	53	SK 2457
Ibsley	10	SU 1509
Ibstock	43	SK 4010
Ibstone	20	SU 7593
Ibthorpe	19	SU 3753
Ibworth	19	SU 5654
Ickburgh	46	TL 8195
Ickenham	20	TQ 0786
Ickford	34	SP 6407
Ickham	15	TR 2258
Ickleford	35	TL 1831
Icklesham	14	TQ 8816
Ickleton	35	TL 4943
Icklingham	36	TL 7772
Ickwell Green	35	TL 1545
Icomb	33	SP 2122
Idbury	33	SP 2320
Iddesleigh	6	SS 5608
Ide	5	SX 8990
Ide Hill	21	TQ 4851
Ideford	5	SX 8977
Iden	14	TQ 9123
Iden Green	14	TQ 8031
Idlicote	33	SP 2844
Idmiston	11	SU 1937
Idridgehay	53	SK 2849
Idrigil	100	NG 3863
Idstone	18	SU 2584
Ifield (W Susx)	13	TQ 2537
Ifold	12	TQ 0231
Iford	13	TQ 4007
Ifton Heath	50	SJ 3236
Ightfield	51	SJ 5938
Ightham	21	TQ 5956
Iken	37	TM 4155
Ilam	52	SK 1351
Ilchester	9	ST 5222
Ilderton	79	NU 0121
Ilford	21	TQ 4586
Ilfracombe	6	SS 5147
Ilkeston	53	SK 4642
Ilketshall St. Andrew	47	TM 3887
Ilketshall St. Margaret	47	TM 3485
Ilkley	59	SE 1147
Illey	41	SO 9881
Illingworth	59	SE 0728
Illogan	2	SW 6643
Illston on the Hill	44	SP 7099
Ilmer	34	SP 7605
Ilmington	33	SP 2143
Ilminster	8	ST 3614
Ilsington	5	SX 7876
Ilston	25	SS 5590
Ilton (N. Yorks.)	65	SE 1878
Ilton (Somer.)	8	ST 3517
Imachar	81	NR 8640
Immingham	61	TA 1714
Immingham Dock	61	TA 1816
Impington	35	TL 4463
Ince	50	SJ 4476
Ince Blundell	57	SD 3203
Ince-in-Makersfield	58	SD 5903
Inchbare	99	NO 6065
Inchberry	104	NJ 3155
Inchinnan	82	NS 4768
Inchlaggan	96	NH 1801
Inchnacardoch	102	NH 3710
Inchnadamph	110	NC 2522
Inchture	93	NO 2728
Inchyra	92	NO 1820
Indian Queens	3	SW 9158
Ingatestone	22	TQ 6499
Ingbirchworth	59	SE 2205
Ingestre	41	SJ 9724
Ingham (Lincs.)	54	SK 9483
Ingham (Norf.)	47	TG 3825
Ingham (Suff.)	36	TL 8570
Ingleby Arncliffe	66	NZ 4400
Ingleby Greenhow	66	NZ 5806
Inglesbatch	17	ST 7061
Inglesham	18	SU 2098
Ingleton (Durham)	72	NZ 1720
Ingleton (N Yorks.)	64	SD 6972
Inglewhite	57	SD 5439
Ingoe	79	NZ 0374
Ingoldisthorpe	46	TF 6832
Ingoldmells	55	TF 5668
Ingoldsby	44	TF 0030
Ingram	79	NU 0116
Ingrave	22	TQ 6292
Ings	63	SD 4498
Ingst	29	ST 5887
Ingworth	47	TG 1929
Inkberrow	32	SP 0157
Inkhorn	105	NJ 9239
Inkpen	19	SU 3564
Inkstack	112	ND 2570
Inn	96	NM 9956
Innellan	82	NS 1469
Innerleithen	85	NT 3336
Innerleven	93	NO 3700
Innermessan	68	NX 0863
Innerwick (Lothian)	86	NT 7273
Innerwick (Tays.)	97	NN 5947
Insch	104	NJ 6327
Insh	97	NH 8101
Inskip	57	SD 4537
Instow	6	SS 4730
Inver (Grampn.)	98	NO 2393
Inver (Highld.)	108	NH 8682
Inverailort	95	NM 7681
Inveralligin	101	NG 8457
Inverallochy	105	NK 0464
Inveramsay	105	NJ 7424
Inveran	108	NH 5797
Inveraray	89	NN 0908
Inverarish	100	NG 5535
Inverarnan	90	NN 3118
Inverbervie	99	NO 8372
Invercreran	96	NN 0147
Inverdruie	103	NJ 9010
Inverebrie	105	NJ 9233
Inveresk	85	NT 3471
Inverey	98	NO 0889
Inverfarigaig	102	NH 5224
Invergarry	96	NH 3101
Invergeldie	91	NN 7427
Invergordon	103	NH 7168
Invergowrie	93	NO 3430
Inverhadden	97	NN 6757
Inverharroch	104	NJ 3831
Inverie	95	NG 7600
Inverinate	101	NG 9122
Inverkeilor	99	NO 6649
Inverkeithing	85	NT 1383
Inverkeithny	104	NJ 6246
Inverkip	82	NS 2071
Inverkirkaig	110	NC 0819
Inverlael	107	NH 1885
Inverlochlarig	90	NN 4318
Invermoriston	102	NH 4117
Invernaver	111	NC 7060
Inverness	103	NH 6645
Invernoaden	89	NS 1197
Inverquharity	98	NO 4057
Inverquhomery	105	NK 0246
Inverroy	96	NN 2581
Invershin	109	NH 5796
Inverugie	105	NK 0947
Inveruglas	90	NN 3109
Inverurie	105	NJ 7721
Invervar	97	NN 6648
Inwardleigh	6	SX 5599
Inworth	22	TL 8717
Iping	12	SU 8522
Ipplepen	5	SX 8366
Ipsden	19	SU 6385
Ipstones	52	SK 0249
Ipswich	37	TM 1744
Irby	50	SJ 2584
Irby in the Marsh	55	TF 4763
Irby upon Humber	61	TA 1904
Irchester	34	SP 9265
Ireby (Cumbr.)	62	NY 2338
Ireby (Lancs.)	64	SD 6575
Ireleth	64	SD 2277
Ireshopeburn	63	NY 8638
Irlam	51	SJ 7194
Irnham	44	TF 0226
Iron Acton	29	ST 6783
Iron Cross	32	SP 0552
Iron-Bridge	41	SJ 6703
Ironside	105	NJ 8852
Ironville	53	SK 4351
Irstead	47	TG 3620
Irthington	71	NY 4961
Irthlingborough	44	SP 9470
Irton	67	TA 0084
Irvine	82	NS 3239
Isauld	111	NC 9765
Isfield	13	TQ 4417
Isham	44	SP 8873
Isle Abbotts	8	ST 3520
Isle Brewers	8	ST 3621
Isle of Whithorn	69	NX 4736
Isleham	36	TL 6474
Isleornsay	101	NG 6912
Isleworth	21	TQ 1675
Isley Walton	43	SK 4225
Islington	21	TQ 3085
Islip (Northants.)	44	SP 9879
Islip (Oxon.)	33	SP 5214
Islivig	109	NA 9927
Itchen Abbas	11	SU 5332
Itchen Stoke	11	SU 5532
Itchingfield	12	TQ 1328
Itchington	29	ST 6586
Itteringham	47	TG 1430
Itton (Devon.)	7	SX 6898
Itton (Gwent)	29	ST 4896
Ivegill	70	NY 4143
Iver	20	TQ 0381
Iver Heath	20	TQ 0283
Iveston	72	NZ 1350
Ivinghoe	34	SP 9416
Ivinghoe Aston	34	SP 9518
Ivington	30	SO 4756
Ivington Green	30	SO 4656
Ivy Hatch	21	TQ 5854
Ivybridge	5	SX 6356
Ivychurch	15	TR 0227
Iwade	14	TQ 9067
Iwerne Courney or Shroton	10	ST 8512
Iwerne Minster	10	ST 8614
Ixworth	36	TL 9370
Ixworth Thorpe	36	TL 91

J

Jack Hill	65	SE 19
Jackstown	105	NJ 75
Jackton	84	NS 59
Jacobstow (Corn.)	6	SX 19
Jacobstowe (Devon)	6	SS 58
Jameston	24	SS 05
Jamestown (Dumf. and Galwy.)	77	NY 29
Jamestown (Highld.)	102	NH 47
Jamestown (Strath.)	90	NS 39
Janetstown	112	ND 19
Jarrow	72	NZ 32
Jawcraig	84	NS 84
Jaywick	23	TM 15
Jedburgh	78	NT 65
Jeffreyston	24	SN 09
Jemimaville	103	NH 71
Jevington	13	TQ 56
Johnby	62	NY 43
Johnshaven	99	NO 79
Johnston (Dyfed)	24	SM 93
Johnstone (Strath.)	82	NS 42
Johnstonebridge	77	NY 10
Jordans	20	SU 97
Jump	59	SE 37
Juniper Green	85	NT 20
Jurby East	56	SC 38
Jurby West	56	SC 35

K

Kaber	63	NY 79
Kaimes (Lothian)	85	NT 27
Kames (Strath.)	89	NM 82
Kames (Strath.)	81	NR 97
Kames (Strath.)	76	NS 69
Kea	2	SW 80
Keadby	60	SE 83
Keal	55	TF 37
Keal Cotes	55	TF 36
Kearsley	58	SD 75
Kearstwick	63	SD 60
Kearton	65	SD 99
Keasden	65	SD 72
Keddington (Lincs.)	55	TF 33
Kedington (Suff.)	36	TL 70
Kedleston	53	SK 29
Keelby	61	TA 16
Keele	51	SJ 80
Keeley Green	34	TL 00
Keeston	24	SM 90
Keevil	18	ST 91
Kegworth	43	SK 48
Kehelland	2	SW 62
Keig	104	NJ 61
Keigar	113	HY 55
Keighley	59	SE 06
Keilarsbrae	91	NS 89
Keilhill	105	NJ 72
Keillor	93	NO 26
Keillour	91	NN 97
Keils	80	NR 52
Keinton Mandeville	17	ST 54
Keir Mill	76	NX 85
Keisby	44	TF 03
Keiss	112	ND 34
Keith	104	NJ 43
Keithock	99	NO 60
Kelbrook	58	SD 90
Kelby	54	TF 00
Keld (Cumbr.)	63	NY 55
Keld (N Yorks.)	65	NY 89
Kelfield	60	SE 59
Kelham	54	SK 77
Kellan	88	NM 53
Kellas (Grampn.)	104	NJ 16
Kellas (Tays.)	93	NO 45
Kellaton	5	SX 80
Kelleth	63	NY 66
Kelling	47	TG 09
Kellington	60	SE 55
Kelloe	72	NZ 34
Kelly	4	SX 39
Kelly Bray	4	SX 35
Kelmarsh	44	SP 73
Kelmscot	18	SU 24
Kelsale	37	TM 38
Kelsall	50	SJ 52
Kelshall	35	TL 32
Kelso	86	NT 73
Kelstern	55	TF 25
Kelston	29	ST 69
Keltneyburn (Tays.)	97	NN 77
Kelty	92	NT 14
Kelvedon	22	TL 86
Kelvedon Hatch	21	TQ 56
Kelynack	2	SW 37
Kemback	93	NO 41
Kemberton	41	SJ 72
Kemble	18	ST 98
Kemerton	32	SO 94
Kemnay	105	NJ 73
Kemp Town	13	TQ 33
Kempley	29	SO 67
Kempsey	32	SO 85
Kempsford	18	SU 15
Kempston	34	TL 03
Kempston Hardwick	35	TL 02
Kempton	40	SO 35
Kemsing	21	TQ 55
Kenardington	15	TQ 97
Kenchester	30	SO 43
Kencot	33	SP 25
Kendal	63	SD 51
Kenfig	28	SS 80
Kenfig Hill	28	SS 84
Kenilworth	43	SP 28
Kenley (Gtr London)	21	TQ 32
Kenley (Salop)	40	SJ 56
Kenmore (Highld.)	101	NG 75
Kenmore (Tays.)	97	NN 77
Kenn (Avon)	29	ST 41
Kenn (Devon.)	8	SX 92
Kennacraig	81	NR 82
Kennerleigh	7	SS 81
Kennet	91	NS 92
Kennethmont	104	NJ 53
Kennett	36	TL 70
Kennford	8	SX 91
Kenninghall	47	TM 03
Kennington (Kent)	15	TR 02
Kennington (Oxon)	33	SP 52
Kennoway	93	NO 34
Kennyhill	36	TL 66

Kennythorpe 241 Langrick

ennythorpe 67 SE 7865
enovay 94 NL 9946
ensaleyre 100 NG 4251
ensington and Chelsea 21 TQ 2778
ensworth 34 TL 0318
ensworth Common 35 TL 0317
ent's Green 32 SO 7423
ent's Oak 11 SU 3224
entallen 96 NN 0057
entford 36 TL 7066
entisbeare 8 ST 0608
entisbury 6 SS 6144
entmere 63 NY 4504
enton (Devon.) 8 SX 9583
enton (Suff.) 37 TM 1965
entra 95 NM 6568
ents Bank 64 SD 3975
enwick 40 SJ 4230
enwyn 2 SW 8145
enyon 58 SJ 6295
eoldale 110 NC 3866
eppanach 96 NN 0262
eppoch 101 NG 9621
epwick 66 SE 4690
eresley 43 SP 3182
erne Bridge 29 SO 5819
erridge 51 SJ 9376
erris 2 SW 4427
erry 40 SO 1490
erry's Gate 30 SO 3933
errycroy 82 NS 1061
ersall 54 SK 7162
ersey 36 TM 0044
ershader 109 NB 3419
ersoe 32 SO 9939
erswell 8 ST 0806
erswell Green 32 SO 8646
esgrave 37 TM 2245
essingland 47 TM 5286
estle Mill 2 SW 8459
eston 21 TQ 4164
eswick (Cumbr.) 62 NY 2723
eswick (Norf.) 47 TG 2004
eswick (Norf.) 47 TG 3533
ettering 44 SP 8778
etteringham 47 TG 1503
ettins 92 NO 2338
ettlebaston 36 TL 9650
ettlebridge 93 NO 3007
ettlebrook 42 SK 2103
ettleburgh 37 TM 2660
ettleshulme 51 SJ 9879
ettlestone 46 TF 9631
ettlethorpe 54 SK 8475
ettlewell 65 SD 9772
etton 44 SK 9704
ew 21 TQ 1877
ewstoke 17 ST 3363
exbrough 59 SE 3009
exby (Lincs.) 54 SK 8785
exby (N Yorks.) 66 SE 7050
ey Green 51 SJ 8963
eyham 43 SK 6606
eyhaven 11 SZ 3091
eymer 13 TQ 3115
eyningham 61 TA 2425
eynsham 29 ST 6568
eysoe 35 TL 0763
eysoe Row 35 TL 0861
eyston 44 TL 0475
eyworth 53 SK 6130
ibblesworth 72 NZ 2456
ibworth Beauchamp 43 SP 6893
ibworth Harcourt 43 SP 6894
idbrooke 21 TQ 4076
iddemore Green 41 SJ 8509
idderminster 41 SO 8376
iddington 33 SP 4122
idlington 33 SP 4913
idmore End 20 SU 6979
idsgrove 51 SJ 8354
idwelly 25 SN 4106
ielder 78 NY 6293
iells 80 NR 4168
ilbarchan 82 NS 4063
ilbeg 95 NG 6506
ilberry 81 NR 7164
ilbirnie 82 NS 3154
ilbride (S. Uist) 109 NF 7514
ilbride (Skye) 100 NG 5820
ilbride (Strath.) 89 NM 8525
ilburn (Derby.) 53 SK 3845
ilburn (N Yorks.) 66 SE 5179
ilby 43 SP 6295
ilcadzow 84 NS 8848
ilchattan (Bute) 82 NS 1054
ilchattan (Colonsay) 88 NR 3795
lchenzie 74 NR 6725
lchiaran 80 NR 2060
ilchoan 95 NM 4963
ilchoman 80 NR 2163
ilchrenan 89 NN 0322
ilconquhar 93 NO 4802
ilcot 29 SO 6925
ilcoy 102 NH 5751
lcreggan 90 NS 2380
ldale 66 NZ 6009
ldalloig 74 NR 7518
ildonan (Highld.) 111 NC 9121
ildonan (Island of Arran) 74 NS 0321
ildonan Lodge 111 NC 9122
ildrummy 104 NJ 4617
ldwick 59 SE 0145
lfinan 81 NR 9378
lfinnan 96 NN 2795
lgetty 24 SN 1207
ilgwrrwg Common 29 ST 4797
ilham (Humbs.) 67 TA 0564
ilham (Northumb.) 87 NT 8832
ilkhampton 6 SS 2511
illamarsh 53 SK 4680
illay 25 SS 6092
illchianaig 88 NR 6486
illean 81 NR 6944
illearn 90 NS 5286
illerby 72 NZ 1919
illichonan 97 NN 5458
illichronan 95 NM 5441
illiechanate 96 NN 2481
illiecrankie 97 NN 9162
illilan 101 NG 9430
illimster 112 ND 3156
illin 90 NN 5732
illinghall 66 SE 2858
illington 63 SD 6188
illochyett 86 NT 4545
lmacolm 82 NS 3569
lmahumaig 89 NR 7893
lmaluag 100 NG 4374
lmany 93 NO 3821
ilmarie 100 NG 5417
ilmarnock 82 NS 4237
ilmartin 89 NR 8398
ilmaurs 82 NS 4141
Kilmelford 89 NM 8413
Kilmersdon 17 ST 6952
Kilmeston 11 SU 5825
Kilmichael Glassary 89 NR 8593
Kilmington (Devon.) 8 SY 2798
Kilmington (Wilts.) 17 ST 7736
Kilmorack 102 NH 4944
Kilmore (Island of Skye) 95 NG 6507
Kilmory (Highld.) 95 NM 5270
Kilmory (Island of Arran) 74 NR 9621
Kilmory (Strath.) 81 NR 7075
Kilmuir (Highld.) 103 NH 6749
Kilmuir (Highld.) 108 NH 7573
Kilmuir (Island of Skye) 100 NG 2547
Kilmun 89 NS 1781
Kiln Pit Hill 72 NZ 0454
Kilnave 80 NR 2871
Kilndown 13 TQ 7035
Kilninian 94 NM 3945
Kilninver 89 NM 8221
Kilnsea 61 TA 4015
Kilnsey 65 SD 9767
Kilnwick 61 SE 9949
Kiloran 88 NR 3996
Kilpatrick 74 NR 9027
Kilpeck 30 SO 4430
Kilphedir 112 NC 9818
Kilpin 60 SE 7726
Kilrenny 93 NO 5705
Kilsby 43 SP 5671
Kilspindie 92 NO 2225
Kilsyth 84 NS 7178
Kiltarlity 102 NH 5041
Kilton 16 ST 1644
Kilvaxter 100 NG 3869
Kilve 16 ST 1443
Kilvington 54 SK 8042
Kilwinning 82 NS 3043
Kimberley (Norf.) 47 TG 0704
Kimberley (Notts.) 53 SK 4944
Kimble 34 SP 8206
Kimble Wick 34 SP 8007
Kimblesworth 72 NZ 2547
Kimbolton (Cambs.) 45 TL 0967
Kimbolton (Here. and Worc.) 31 SO 5261
Kimcote 43 SP 5888
Kimmeridge 10 SY 9179
Kimmerston 87 NT 9535
Kimpton (Hants.) 19 SU 2746
Kimpton (Herts.) 35 TL 1718
Kinbrace 111 NC 8631
Kinbuck 91 NN 7905
Kincaple 93 NO 4518
Kincardine (Fife.) 84 NS 9387
Kincardine (Highld.) 108 NH 6089
Kincardine O'Neil 99 NO 5999
Kinclaven 92 NO 1538
Kincraig 103 NH 8305
Kincraigie 98 NN 9849
Kindallachan 98 NN 9950
Kineton (Glos.) 32 SP 0926
Kineton (Warw.) 33 SP 3351
Kinfauns 92 NO 1622
King Sterndale 52 SK 0972
King's Bromley 42 SK 1216
King's Cliffe 44 TL 0097
King's Coughton 32 SP 0858
King's Heath 42 SP 0781
King's Lynn 46 TF 6220
King's Norton (Leic.) 44 SK 6800
King's Norton (W Mids) 42 SP 0579
King's Nympton 7 SS 6819
King's Pyon 30 SO 4350
King's Somborne 11 SU 3631
King's Stag 9 ST 7210
King's Stanley 32 SO 8103
King's Sutton 33 SP 5036
King's Walden 35 TL 1623
Kingarth 981 NS 0956
Kingcoed 29 SO 4205
Kingham 33 SP 2523
Kingholm Quay 70 NX 9773
Kinghorn 85 NT 2686
Kinglassie 92 NT 2298
Kingoodie 93 NO 3329
Kings Caple 29 SO 5628
Kings Langley 35 TL 0702
Kings Meaburn 63 NY 6221
Kings Muir (Borders) 85 NT 2539
Kings Ripton 45 TL 2576
Kings Worthy 11 SU 4932
Kingsand 4 SX 4350
Kingsbarns 93 NO 5912
Kingsbridge (Devon.) 5 SX 7344
Kingsbridge (Somer.) 16 SS 9837
Kingsburgh 100 NG 3955
Kingsbury (Gtr London) 21 TQ 1989
Kingsbury (Warw.) 42 SP 2196
Kingsbury Episcopi 9 ST 4320
Kingsclere 19 SU 5258
Kingscote 18 ST 8196
Kingscott 6 SS 5318
Kingscross 74 NS 0428
Kingsdon 17 ST 5126
Kingsdown 15 TR 3748
Kingseat 92 NT 1290
Kingsey 34 SP 7406
Kingsfold 12 TQ 1636
Kingsford 41 SO 8281
Kingshall Street 36 TL 9161
Kingshouse 90 NN 5620
Kingskerswell 5 SX 8767
Kingskettle 93 NO 3008
Kingsland 30 SO 4461
Kingsley (Ches) 50 SJ 5474
Kingsley (Hants.) 12 SU 7838
Kingsley (Staffs.) 52 SK 0047
Kingsley Green 12 SU 8930
Kingsmuir (Fife) 93 NO 5409
Kingsmuir (Tays.) 98 NO 4849
Kingsnorth 15 TR 0039
Kingstanding 42 SP 0794
Kingsteignton 5 SX 8773
Kingsthorne 30 SO 4932
Kingsthorpe 34 SP 7563
Kingston (Cambs.) 35 TL 3455
Kingston (Devon.) 5 SX 6347
Kingston (Dorset) 9 ST 7509
Kingston (Dorset) 10 SY 9579
Kingston (Grampn.) 104 NJ 3365
Kingston (Hants.) 10 SU 1401
Kingston (I. of W.) 11 SZ 4781
Kingston (Kent) 15 TR 1951
Kingston (Lothian) 86 NT 5482
Kingston Bagpuize 19 SU 4098
Kingston Blount 20 SU 7399
Kingston Deverill 10 ST 8436
Kingston Lisle 19 SU 3287
Kingston Russell 9 SY 5891
Kingston Seymour 29 ST 3966
Kingston St. Mary 16 ST 2229
Kingston by Sea 13 TQ 2205
Kingston near Lewes 13 TQ 3908
Kingston on Soar 43 SK 5027
Kingston upon Hull 61 TA 0929
Kingston upon Thames 21 TQ 1869
Kingstone (Here. and Worc.) 30 SO 4235
Kingstone (Somer.) 8 ST 3713
Kingstone (Staffs.) 42 SK 0629
Kingstown 70 NY 3959
Kingswear 5 SX 8851
Kingswells 105 NJ 8606
Kingswinford 41 SO 8888
Kingswood (Avon) 29 ST 6473
Kingswood (Bucks) 34 SP 6819
Kingswood (Glos.) 29 ST 7491
Kingswood (Kent) 14 TQ 8351
Kingswood (Powys) 40 SJ 2402
Kingswood (Surrey) 21 TQ 2455
Kingswood (Warw.) 42 SP 1871
Kington (Here. and Worc.) 30 SO 2956
Kington (Here. and Worc.) 32 SO 9955
Kington Langley 18 ST 9276
Kington Magna 9 ST 7622
Kington St. Michael 18 ST 9077
Kingussie 97 NH 7500
Kingweston 17 ST 5230
Kinharrachie (Grampn.) 105 NJ 9231
Kinkell Bridge 91 NN 9316
Kinlet 41 SO 7280
Kinloch (Highld.) 110 NC 3434
Kinloch (Rhum) 94 NM 4099
Kinloch (Tays.) 98 NO 1444
Kinloch (Tays.) 98 NO 2644
Kinloch Hourn 95 NG 9407
Kinloch Rannoch 97 NN 6658
Kinlochard 90 NN 4502
Kinlochbervie 110 NC 2156
Kinlocheil 96 NM 9779
Kinlochewe 101 NH 0261
Kinlochleven 96 NN 1861
Kinloss 103 NJ 0661
Kinmuck 105 NJ 8119
Kinmundy 105 NJ 8817
Kinnadie 105 NJ 9643
Kinnaird 92 NO 2428
Kinneff 99 NO 8574
Kinnelhead 76 NT 0201
Kinnell 99 NO 6050
Kinnerley 40 SJ 3321
Kinnersley (Here. and Worc.) 30 SO 3449
Kinnersley (Here. and Worc.) 32 SO 8743
Kinnerton (Ches.) 50 SJ 3361
Kinnerton (Powys) 30 SO 2463
Kinnesswood 92 NO 1702
Kinninvie 72 NZ 0521
Kinnordy 98 NO 3654
Kinoulton 53 SK 6730
Kinross 92 NO 1102
Kinrossie 92 NO 1832
Kinsham 30 SO 3664
Kinsley 59 SE 4114
Kintbury 19 SU 3866
Kintessack 103 NJ 0060
Kintillo 92 NO 1317
Kintocher 104 NJ 5709
Kintore 105 NJ 7916
Kinveachy 103 NH 9118
Kinver 41 SO 8433
Kippax 59 SE 4130
Kippen 91 NS 6594
Kippford or Scaur 69 NX 8355
Kirby Bedon 47 TG 2705
Kirby Cane 47 TM 3794
Kirby Cross 23 TM 2120
Kirby Grindalythe 67 SE 9067
Kirby Hill (N Yorks.) 65 NZ 1306
Kirby Hill (N Yorks.) 66 SE 3868
Kirby Knowle 66 SE 4687
Kirby Misperton 67 SE 7779
Kirby Muxloe 43 SK 5104
Kirby Row 47 TM 3792
Kirby Sigston 66 SE 4194
Kirby Underdale 67 SE 8158
Kirby Wiske 66 SE 3784
Kirby le Soken 23 TM 2222
Kirdford 12 TQ 0226
Kirk 112 ND 2859
Kirk Bramwith 60 SE 6111
Kirk Connel (Dumf. and Galwy.) 76 NS 7312
Kirk Deighton 66 SE 3950
Kirk Ella 61 TA 0129
Kirk Hallam 53 SK 4540
Kirk Hammerton 66 SE 4655
Kirk Ireton 53 SK 2650
Kirk Langley 53 SK 2838
Kirk Merrington 72 NZ 2631
Kirk Michael (I. of M.) 56 SC 3190
Kirk Sandall 60 SE 6007
Kirk Smeaton 60 SE 5116
Kirk Yetholm 87 NT 8227
Kirk of Shotts 84 NS 8462
Kirkabister 113 HU 4938
Kirkandrews upon Eden 70 NY 3558
Kirkbampton 70 NY 3056
Kirkbean 70 NX 9859
Kirkbride 70 NY 2356
Kirkbuddo 99 NO 5043
Kirkburn (Humbs.) 67 SE 9855
Kirkburton 59 SE 1912
Kirkby (Lincs.) 54 TF 0692
Kirkby (Mers.) 50 SJ 4098
Kirkby (N Yorks.) 66 NZ 5306
Kirkby Fleetham 66 SE 2984
Kirkby Green 54 TF 0857
Kirkby Lonsdale 63 SD 6178
Kirkby Malham 65 SD 8960
Kirkby Mallory 43 SK 4500
Kirkby Malzeard 66 SE 2374
Kirkby Overblow 59 SE 3249
Kirkby Stephen 65 NY 7708
Kirkby Thore 63 NY 6325
Kirkby Underwood 45 TF 0727
Kirkby in Ashfield 53 SK 5056
Kirkby la Thorpe 54 TF 0946
Kirkby on Bain 55 TF 2362
Kirkbymoorside 66 SE 6986
Kirkcaldy 93 NT 2791
Kirkcambeck 71 NY 5368
Kirkcarswell 69 NX 7549
Kirkcolm 68 NX 0268
Kirkcowan 68 NX 3260
Kirkcudbright 69 NX 6851
Kirkfieldbank 84 NS 8643
Kirkgunzeon 69 NX 8666
Kirkham (Lancs.) 57 SD 4231
Kirkham (N Yorks.) 67 SE 7365
Kirkhamgate 59 SE 2922
Kirkharle 79 NZ 0182
Kirkheaton (Northum.) 79 NZ 0177
Kirkheaton (W Yorks.) 59 SE 1817
Kirkhill (Highld.) 102 NH 5545
Kirkhill (Tays.) 99 NO 6860
Kirkhope (Borders) 77 NT 3823
Kirkhouse 85 NT 3233
Kirkibost (Island of Skye) 100 NG 5417
Kirkinch 98 NO 3144
Kirkinner 68 NX 4251
Kirkintilloch 84 NS 6573
Kirkland (Cumbr.) 62 NY 0718
Kirkland (Cumbr.) 63 NY 6432
Kirkland (Dumf. and Galwy.) 76 NS 7214
Kirkland (Dumf. and Galwy.) 76 NX 8090
Kirkleatham 73 NZ 5921
Kirklevington 66 NZ 4309
Kirkley 47 TM 5491
Kirkleyditch 51 SJ 8778
Kirklington (N Yorks.) 66 SE 3181
Kirklington (Notts.) 53 SK 6757
Kirklinton 70 NY 4366
Kirkliston 85 NT 1274
Kirkmaiden 68 NX 1236
Kirkmichael (Strath.) 75 NS 3408
Kirkmichael (Tays.) 98 NO 0860
Kirkmuirhill 84 NS 7943
Kirknewton (Lothian) 85 NT 1166
Kirknewton (Northum.) 87 NT 9130
Kirkoswald (Cumbr.) 71 NY 5541
Kirkoswald (Strath.) 75 NS 2407
Kirkpatrick Durham 69 NX 7870
Kirkpatrick-Fleming 70 NY 2770
Kirksanton 62 SD 1380
Kirkstall 59 SE 2635
Kirkstile (Dumf. and Galwy.) 77 NY 3690
Kirkton (Borders) 78 NT 5413
Kirkton (Dumf. and Galwy.) 70 NX 9781
Kirkton (Fife.) 93 NO 3625
Kirkton (Grampn.) 104 NJ 6112
Kirkton (Grampn.) 104 NJ 6425
Kirkton (Grampn.) 105 NJ 6950
Kirkton (Grampn.) 105 NJ 8243
Kirkton (Grampn.) 105 NK 1050
Kirkton (Highld.) 101 NG 9141
Kirkton (Highld.) 108 NH 7998
Kirkton (Tays.) 91 NN 9618
Kirkton (Tays.) 98 NO 4246
Kirkton Manor 85 NT 2137
Kirkton of Airlie 98 NO 3151
Kirkton of Auchterhouse 93 NO 3338
Kirkton of Barevan 103 NH 8347
Kirkton of Collace 92 NO 1931
Kirkton of Craig 99 NO 7055
Kirkton of Durris 99 NO 7796
Kirkton of Glenbuchat 104 NJ 3715
Kirkton of Glenisla 98 NO 2160
Kirkton of Kingoldrum 98 NO 3354
Kirkton of Largo 93 NO 4203
Kirkton of Lethendy 98 NO 1241
Kirkton of Logie Buchan 105 NJ 9829
Kirkton of Maryculter 99 NO 8599
Kirkton of Menmuir 99 NO 5364
Kirkton of Monikie 93 NO 5138
Kirkton of Rayne 105 NJ 6930
Kirkton of Skene 105 NJ 8007
Kirkton of Strathmartine 93 NO 3735
Kirkton of Tealing 93 NO 4037
Kirktown 105 NK 0952
Kirktown of Auchterless 105 NJ 7141
Kirktown of Bourtie 105 NJ 8024
Kirktown of Deskford 104 NJ 5061
Kirktown of Fetteresso 99 NO 8585
Kirkwall 113 HY 4410
Kirkwhelpington 79 NY 9984
Kirmington 61 TA 1011
Kirmond le Mire 55 TF 1892
Kirn 82 NS 1878
Kirriemuir 98 NO 3854
Kirstead Green 47 TM 2997
Kirtlebridge 70 NY 2372
Kirtling 36 TL 6857
Kirtling Green 36 TL 6855
Kirtlington 33 SP 4919
Kirtomy 111 NC 7463
Kirton (Highld.) 101 NG 8327
Kirton (Lincs.) 55 TF 3038
Kirton (Notts.) 63 SK 6869
Kirton (Suff.) 37 TM 2739
Kirton End 55 TF 2840
Kirton Holme 55 TF 2642
Kirton in Lindsey 61 SK 9398
Kislingbury 34 SP 6959
Kites Hardwick 43 SP 4668
Kittybrewster 105 NJ 9208
Kitwood 11 SU 6633
Kiveton Park 53 SK 4982
Knaith 54 SK 8284
Knap Corner 10 ST 8023
Knaphill 20 SU 9658
Knapp (Somer.) 17 ST 3025
Knapp (Tays.) 93 NO 2831
Knapton (N Yorks.) 66 SE 5652
Knapton (N Yorks.) 67 SE 8775
Knapton (Norf.) 47 TG 3034
Knapwell 35 TL 3362
Knaresborough 66 SE 3557
Knarsdale 71 NY 6753
Knaven 105 NJ 8943
Knayton 66 SE 4387
Knebworth 35 TL 2520
Kneesall 54 SK 7064
Kneesworth 35 TL 3444
Kneeton 54 SK 7146
Knelston 25 SS 4689
Knightacott 7 SS 6439
Knightcote 33 SP 3954
Knighton (Devon.) 5 SX 5249
Knighton (Leic.) 43 SK 6001
Knighton (Powys) 40 SO 2872
Knighton (Staffs.) 51 SJ 7240
Knighton (Staffs.) 41 SJ 7427
Knightwick 32 SO 7355
Knill 30 SO 2960
Knipton 54 SK 8231
Knitsley 72 NZ 1148
Kniveton 53 SK 2050
Knock (Cumbr.) 63 NY 6826
Knock (Grampn.) 104 NJ 5452
Knock (Island of Mull) 88 NM 5438
Knock (Isle of Lewis) 109 NB 4931
Knockally 112 ND 1428
Knockan 107 NC 2110
Knockando 104 NJ 1941
Knockbain 102 NH 6255
Knockbrex 69 NX 5849
Knockdee 112 ND 1761
Knockdolian 68 NX 1285
Knockenkelly 74 NS 0426
Knockentiber 82 NS 3939
Knockholt 21 TQ 4658
Knockholt Pound 21 TQ 4859
Knockin 40 SJ 3322
Knocknaha 74 NR 6817
Knockrome 80 NR 5571
Knocksharry 56 SC 2785
Knodishall 37 TM 4261
Knolls Green 51 SJ 8079
Knolton 50 SJ 3738
Knook 18 ST 9341
Knossington 44 SK 8008
Knott End-on-Sea 57 SD 3548
Knotting 34 TL 0063
Knottingley 60 SE 5023
Knowbury 41 SO 5774
Knowe 68 NX 3171
Knowehead 76 NX 6090
Knowesgate 79 NY 9885
Knoweside 75 NS 2512
Knowl Hill 20 SU 8279
Knowle (Avon) 29 ST 6170
Knowle (Devon.) 6 SS 4938
Knowle (Devon.) 7 SS.7801
Knowle (W Mids) 42 SP 1876
Knowle Green 58 SD 6337
Knowlton 15 TR 2853
Knowsley 50 SJ 4395
Knowstone 7 SS 8223
Knucklas 40 SO 2574
Knutsford 51 SJ 7578
Knypersley 51 SJ 8856
Kyle of Lochalsh 101 NG 7627
Kyleakin 101 NG 7526
Kylerhea 101 NG 7820
Kylesku 110 NC 2334
Kylestrome 110 NC 2234
Kyloe 87 NU 0540
Kynnersley 41 SJ 6716
Kyre Park 31 SO 6263

L

Laceby 61 TA 2106
Lacey Green 20 SP 8200
Lach Dennis 51 SJ 7071
Lackford 36 TL 7970
Lacock 18 ST 9168
Ladbroke 33 SP 4158
Laddingford 14 TQ 6948
Lade Bank 55 TF 3954
Ladock 3 SW 8950
Ladybank (Fife.) 93 NO 3009
Ladykirk 87 NT 8847
Ladysford 105 NJ 9060
Lagavulin 80 NR 4045
Lagg (Island of Arran) 74 NR 9521
Lagg (Jura) 80 NR 5978
Laggan (Highld.) 97 NN 6194
Lagganulva 95 NM 4541
Laide 106 NG 8992
Laindon 22 TQ 6889
Lair 101 NH 0148
Lairg 108 NC 5806
Lake 10 SU 1239
Lake Side 62 SD 3787
Lakenham 47 TG 2307
Lakenheath 46 TL 7182
Lakesend 45 TL 5196
Laleham 20 TQ 0568
Laleston 28 SS 8779
Lamarsh 36 TL 8935
Lamas 47 TG 2423
Lamberhurst 13 TQ 6735
Lamberton 87 NT 9657
Lambeth 21 TQ 3078
Lambfell Moar 56 SC 2984
Lambley (Northum.) 71 NY 6758
Lambley (Notts.) 53 SK 6245
Lambourn 19 SU 3278
Lambourne End 21 TQ 4894
Lambs Green 13 TQ 2136
Lambston 24 SM 9016
Lamerton 5 SX 4476
Lamesley 72 NZ 2557
Lamington (Highld.) 108 NH 7577
Lamington (Strath.) 85 NS 9730
Lamlash 81 NS 0231
Lamonby 62 NY 4135
Lamorna 2 SW 4524
Lamorran 3 SW 8741
Lampeter 27 SN 5748
Lampeter-Velfrey 24 SN 1514
Lamphey 24 SN 0100
Lamplugh 62 NY 0820
Lamport 44 SP 7574
Lamyatt 17 ST 6535
Lana 6 SX 3496
Lanark 84 NS 8843
Lancaster 64 SD 4761
Lanchester 72 NZ 1647
Landbeach 45 TL 4765
Landcross 6 SS 4524
Landerberry 99 NJ 7404
Landewednack 2 SW 7012
Landford 11 SU 2519
Landimore 25 SS 4693
Landkey 6 SS 5931
Landrake 4 SX 3760
Landscove 5 SX 7766
Landshipping 24 SN 0211
Landulph 4 SX 4261
Landwade 36 TL 6268
Landywood 41 SJ 9806
Lane End 20 SU 8091
Laneast 4 SX 2283
Laneham 54 SK 8076
Laneshaw Bridge 58 SD 9240
Langar 54 SK 7234
Langbank 82 NS 3873
Langbar 65 SE 0951
Langcliffe 65 SD 8264
Langdale End 67 SE 9391
Langdon Hills 22 TQ 6786
Langdyke 93 NO 3304
Langenhoe 23 TM 0018
Langford (Beds.) 35 TL 1841
Langford (Devon.) 8 ST 0203
Langford (Essex) 22 TL 8408
Langford (Notts.) 54 SK 8258
Langford (Oxon.) 33 SP 2402
Langford Budville 8 ST 1122
Langford End 35 TL 1654
Langham (Essex) 36 TM 0233
Langham (Leic.) 44 SK 8411
Langham (Norf.) 46 TG 0041
Langham (Suff.) 36 TL 9769
Langho 58 SD 7034
Langholm 70 NY 3684
Langley (Berks.) 20 TQ 0078
Langley (Ches.) 51 SJ 9471
Langley (Essex) 35 TL 4435
Langley (Hants.) 11 SU 4400
Langley (Herts.) 35 TL 2122
Langley (Kent) 14 TQ 8051
Langley (W Susx) 12 SU 8029
Langley (Warw.) 33 SP 1962
Langley Burrell 18 ST 9275
Langley Marsh 16 ST 0729
Langley Park 72 NZ 2144
Langley Street 47 TG 3601
Langney 13 TQ 6302
Langold 53 SK 5887
Langore 4 SX 3086
Langport 17 ST 4226
Langrick 55 TF 2648

Langridge 242 Llanfair Talhaiarn

Langridge 29 ST 7369
Langrigg 70 NY 1645
Langrish 12 SU 7023
Langsett 59 SE 2100
Langshaw 86 NT 5139
Langskaill 113 HY 4443
Langstone 12 SU 7104
Langthorne 66 SE 2491
Langthorpe 66 SE 3867
Langthwaite 65 NZ 0002
Langtoft (Humbs.) 67 TA 0166
Langtoft (Lincs.) 45 TF 1212
Langton (Durham) 72 NZ 1719
Langton (Lincs.) 55 TF 2368
Langton (Lincs.) 55 TF 3970
Langton (N Yorks.) 67 SE 7967
Langton Green 13 TQ 5439
Langton Herring 9 SY 6182
Langton Matravers 10 SY 9978
Langton by Wragby 55 TF 1476
Langtree 6 SS 4415
Langwathby 63 NY 5733
Langworth 54 TF 0676
Lanivet 4 SX 0364
Lanlivery 4 SX 0759
Lanner 2 SW 7139
Lanreath 4 SX 1756
Lansallos 4 SX 1751
Lanteglos Highway 4 SX 1453
Lanton (Borders) 78 NT 6221
Lanton (Northum.) 87 NT 9231
Lapford 7 SS 7308
Laphroaig 80 NR 3845
Lapley 41 SJ 8713
Lapworth 42 SP 1671
Larbert 84 NS 8582
Largie 104 NJ 6131
Largiemore 89 NR 9486
Largoward 93 NO 4607
Largs 82 NS 2058
Largybeg 74 NS 0423
Largymore 74 NS 0424
Larkfield 82 NS 2376
Larkhall 84 NS 7651
Larkhill 18 SU 1243
Larling 46 TL 9889
Larriston 78 NY 5494
Lartington 72 NZ 0117
Lasham 19 SU 6742
Lassodie 92 NT 1292
Lasswade 85 NT 3066
Lastingham 66 SE 7290
Latchingdon 22 TL 8800
Latchley 4 SX 4173
Lately Common 58 SJ 6797
Lathbury 34 SP 8745
Latheron 112 ND 1933
Lathones 93 NO 4708
Latimer 20 TQ 0099
Latteridge 29 ST 6684
Lattiford 17 ST 6926
Latton 18 SU 0995
Lauder 86 NT 5347
Laugharne 25 SN 3011
Laughterton 54 SK 8375
Laughton (E Susx) 13 TQ 4913
Laughton (Leic.) 53 SP 6589
Laughton (Lincs.) 60 SK 8497
Laughton-en-le-Morthen 53 SK 5188
Launcells 6 SS 2405
Launceston 4 SX 3384
Launton 34 SP 6022
Laurencekirk 99 NO 7171
Laurieston 69 NX 6864
Lavant 12 SU 8608
Lavendon 34 SP 9153
Lavenham 36 TL 9149
Laverhay 77 NY 1498
Laverstock 10 SU 1530
Laverstoke 19 SU 4948
Laverton (Glos.) 32 SP 0735
Laverton (N Yorks) 66 SE 2273
Laverton (Somer.) 18 ST 7753
Law 84 NS 8252
Lawers (Tays.) 91 NN 6739
Lawford 37 TM 0830
Lawhitton 4 SX 3582
Lawkland 65 SD 7766
Lawley 41 SJ 6608
Lawnhead 41 SJ 8224
Lawrenny 24 SN 0107
Lawshall 36 TL 8654
Lawton 30 SO 4459
Laxay 109 NB 3321
Laxdale 109 NB 4234
Laxey 56 SC 4384
Laxfield 37 TM 2972
Laxo 113 HU 4463
Laxton (Humbs.) 60 SE 7825
Laxton (Northants.) 44 SP 9496
Laxton (Notts.) 54 SK 7266
Laycock 59 SE 0340
Layer Breton 23 TL 9417
Layer-de-la-Haye 23 TL 9620
Layham 36 TM 0340
Layland's Green 19 SU 3866
Laysters Pole 31 SO 5563
Laytham 60 SE 7439
Lazenby 73 NZ 5719
Lazonby 63 NY 5439
Lea (Derby.) 53 SK 3357
Lea (Here. and Worc.) 29 SO 6521
Lea (Lincs.) 54 SK 8286
Lea (Salop) 40 SJ 4108
Lea (Salop) 40 SO 3589
Lea (Wilts.) 18 ST 9586
Lea Marston 42 SP 2093
Lea Town 57 SD 4930
Lea yeat 65 SD 7587
Leachkin 103 NH 6344
Leadburn 85 NT 2355
Leaden Roding 22 TL 5913
Leadenham 54 SK 9452
Leadgate (Cumbr.) 71 NY 7043
Leadgate (Durham) 72 NZ 1251
Leadhills 76 NS 8814
Leafield 33 SP 3115
Leake Common Side 55 TF 3952
Leake Hurn's End 55 TF 4248
Lealholm 67 NZ 7607
Lealt (Island of Skye) 100 NG 5060
Leamington Hastings 43 SP 4467
Leargybreck 80 NR 5371
Learmouth 87 NT 8537
Leasgill 63 SD 4984
Leasingham 54 TF 0548
Leask 105 NK 0232
Leatherhead 21 TQ 1656
Leathley 59 SE 2346
Leaton 50 SJ 4618
Leaveland 15 TR 0054
Leavening 67 SE 7863
Leaves Green 21 TQ 4162
Lebberston 67 TA 0882
Lechlade 18 SU 2199
Leckford 11 SU 3737
Leckfurin 111 NC 7059
Leckgruinart 80 NR 2769
Leckhampstead (Berks.) 19 SU 4375
Leckhampstead (Bucks.) 34 SP 7237
Leckhampton 32 SO 9419
Leckmelm 106 NH 1690
Leckwith 28 ST 1574
Leconfield 61 TA 0143
Ledaig 89 NM 9037
Ledburn 34 SP 9022
Ledbury 32 SO 7037
Ledgemoor 30 SO 4150
Ledicot 30 SO 4162
Ledmore Junction 110 NC 2412
Ledsham (Ches.) 50 SJ 3574
Ledsham (W Yorks.) 59 SE 4529
Ledston 59 SE 4328
Ledwell 33 SP 4128
Lee (Devon.) 6 SS 4846
Lee (Hants.) 11 SU 3517
Lee (Lancs.) 64 SD 5655
Lee (Salop) 40 SJ 4032
Lee Brockhurst 40 SJ 5426
Lee Clump 34 SP 9004
Lee Green 51 SJ 6561
Lee Moor 5 SX 5862
Lee, The 34 SP 9004
Lee-on-the-Solent 11 SU 5600
Leebotwood 40 SO 4798
Leece 64 SD 2469
Leeds (Kent) 14 TQ 8253
Leeds (W Yorks.) 59 SE 3034
Leedstown 2 SW 6034
Leek 51 SJ 9856
Leek Wootton 43 SP 2868
Leeming 66 SE 2989
Leeming bar 66 SE 2889
Lees (Derby.) 53 SK 2637
Lees (Gtr Mches) 58 SD 9504
Leeswood 50 SJ 2759
Legbourne 55 TF 3684
Legerwood 86 NT 5843
Legsby 55 TF 1385
Leicester 43 SK 5904
Leigh (Dorset) 9 ST 6108
Leigh (Glos.) 32 SO 8725
Leigh (Gtr Mches) 58 SJ 6699
Leigh (Here. and Worc.) 32 SO 7853
Leigh (Kent) 21 TQ 5546
Leigh (Salop) 40 SJ 3303
Leigh (Surrey) 21 TQ 2246
Leigh (Wilts.) 18 SU 0692
Leigh Beck 22 TQ 8182
Leigh Common 17 ST 7329
Leigh Green 14 TQ 9033
Leigh Sinton 32 SO 7750
Leigh Woods 29 ST 5572
Leigh upon Mendip 17 ST 6847
Leigh-on-Sea 22 TQ 8385
Leighterton 18 ST 8290
Leighton (Powys) 40 SJ 2405
Leighton (Salop) 41 SJ 6105
Leighton (Somer.) 17 ST 7043
Leighton Bromswold 45 TL 1175
Leighton Buzzard 34 SP 9225
Leinthall Earls 40 SO 4467
Leinthall Starkes 40 SO 4369
Leintwardine 40 SO 4074
Leire 43 SP 5290
Leirinmore 110 NC 4267
Leishmore 102 NH 3940
Leiston 37 TM 4462
Leitfie 98 NO 2545
Leith 85 NT 2676
Leitholm 87 NT 7944
Lelant 2 SW 5437
Lelley 61 TA 2032
Lem Hill 41 SO 7274
Lempitlaw 87 NT 7832
Lemreway 109 NB 3711
Lendalfoot 75 NX 1390
Lenham 14 TQ 8952
Lenham Heath 14 TQ 9249
Lenie 102 NH 5127
Lennel 87 NT 8540
Lennoxtown 84 NS 6277
Lenton 54 TF 0230
Lenwade 47 TG 0918
Lenzie 84 NS 6571
Leoch 93 NO 3638
Leochel-Cushnie 104 NJ 5210
Leominster 30 SO 4959
Leonard Stanley 32 SO 8003
Lepe 11 SZ 4498
Lephin 100 NG 1749
Lephinmore 89 NR 9892
Leppington 67 SE 7661
Lepton 59 SE 2015
Lerryn 4 SX 1356
Lerwick (Shetld.) 113 HU 4741
Lesbury 79 NU 2311
Leslie (Fife.) 92 NO 2401
Leslie (Grampn.) 104 NJ 5924
Lesmahagow 84 NS 8139
Lesnewth 4 SX 1390
Lessingham 47 TG 3928
Lessonhall 70 NY 2250
Leswalt 68 NX 0263
Letchmore Heath 21 TQ 1597
Letchworth 35 TL 2132
Letcombe Bassett 19 SU 3785
Letcombe Regis 19 SU 3786
Letham (Fife.) 93 NO 3014
Letham (Tays.) 99 NO 5248
Lethenty 105 NJ 8041
Letheringham 37 TM 2757
Letheringsett 47 TG 0638
Lettaford 5 SX 7084
Letterfearn 101 NG 8823
Letters 106 NH 1687
Letterston 24 SM 9429
Lettoch 103 NJ 0932
Letton (Here. and Worc.) 30 SO 3346
Letton (Here. and Worc.) 30 SO 3770
Letty Green 35 TL 2810
Letwell 53 SK 5587
Leuchars 93 NO 4521
Levedale 41 SJ 8916
Leven (Fife.) 93 NO 3700
Leven (Humbs.) 61 TA 1045
Levens 63 SD 4886
Levenshulme 51 SJ 8794
Leverburgh 109 NG 0186
Leverington 45 TF 4410
Leverton 55 TF 3947
Levington 37 TM 2339
Levisham 67 SE 8390
Lew 33 SP 3206
Lewannick 4 SX 2780
Lewdown 5 SX 4486
Lewes 13 TQ 4110
Leweston 24 SM 9422
Lewisham 21 TQ 3875
Lewiston 102 NH 5029
Lewknor 20 SU 7197
Leworthy 7 SS 6638
Lewtrenchard 5 SX 4586
Ley (Corn.) 4 SX 1766
Leybourne 14 TQ 6858
Leyburn 65 SE 1190
Leycett 51 SJ 7846
Leyland 57 SD 5421
Leylodge 105 NJ 7713
Leys (Grampn.) 105 NK 0052
Leys (Tays.) 93 NO 2537
Leys of Cossans 98 NO 3749
Leysdown-on-Sea 15 TR 0370
Leysmill 99 NO 6047
Leyton 21 TQ 3886
Lezant 4 SX 3378
Lhanbryde 104 NJ 2761
Lhen, The 56 NX 3801
Libberton 85 NS 9943
Liberton 85 NT 2769
Lichfield 42 SK 1209
Lickey 41 SO 0075
Lickey End 41 SO 9772
Lickfold 12 SU 9225
Liddington 18 SU 2081
Lidgate 36 TL 7258
Lidlington 34 SP 9939
Lidstone 33 SP 3524
Liff 93 NO 3332
Lifton 4 SX 3885
Lighthorne 33 SP 3355
Lightwater 20 SU 9262
Lightwood 51 SJ 9041
Lightwood Green 50 SJ 3840
Lilbourne 43 SP 5677
Lilleshall 41 SJ 7315
Lilley 35 TL 1226
Lilliesleaf 78 NT 5325
Lillingstone Dayrell 34 SP 7039
Lillingstone Lovell 34 SP 7140
Lillington 9 ST 6212
Lilstock 16 ST 1644
Limbrick 58 SD 6016
Limefield 58 SD 8012
Limekilnburn 84 NS 7050
Limekilns 85 NT 0783
Limerigg 84 NS 8570
Limington 9 ST 5422
Limpenhoe 47 TG 3903
Limpley Stoke 18 ST 7760
Limpsfield 21 TQ 4152
Linby 53 SK 5350
Linchmere 12 SU 8630
Lincoln 54 SK 9771
Lincomb 41 SO 8268
Lincombe 5 SX 7458
Lindal in Furness 64 SD 2575
Lindale 63 SD 4180
Lindean 86 NT 4931
Lindfield 13 TQ 3425
Lindford 12 SU 8136
Lindores 93 NO 2616
Lindridge 41 SO 6769
Lindsell 22 TL 6427
Lindsey 36 TL 9744
Linford (Essex) 22 TQ 6779
Linford (Hants.) 10 SU 1707
Lingague 56 SC 2172
Lingdale 73 NZ 6716
Lingen 40 SO 3667
Lingfield 13 TQ 3943
Lingwood 47 TG 3609
Linicro 100 NG 3967
Linkenholt 19 SU 3657
Linkinhorne 4 SX 3173
Linktown 93 NT 2790
Linley 40 SO 3593
Linley Green 31 SO 6953
Linlithgow 85 NS 9977
Linsidemore 108 NH 5498
Linslade 34 SP 9125
Linstead Parva 37 TM 3377
Linstock 70 NY 4258
Linthwaite 59 SE 0913
Lintlaw 87 NT 8258
Lintmill 104 NJ 5165
Linton (Borders) 87 NT 7726
Linton (Cambs.) 36 TL 5646
Linton (Derby.) 53 SK 2716
Linton (Here. and Worc.) 29 SO 6625
Linton (Kent) 14 TQ 7550
Linton (N Yorks.) 65 SD 9962
Linton-on-Ouse 66 SE 4960
Linwood (Hants.) 10 SU 1809
Linwood (Lincs.) 55 TF 1186
Linwood (Strath.) 82 NS 4464
Lionel 109 NB 5263
Liphook 12 SU 8431
Liscombe 7 SS 8732
Liskeard 4 SX 2564
Liss 12 SU 7727
Liss Forest 12 SU 7929
Lissett 67 TA 1458
Lissington 55 TF 1083
Lisvane 28 ST 1983
Liswerry 29 ST 3487
Litcham 46 TF 8817
Litchborough 34 SP 6354
Litchfield 19 SU 4553
Litherland 50 SJ 3397
Litlington (Cambs.) 35 TL 3142
Litlington (E Susx) 13 TQ 5201
Little Abington 35 TL 5349
Little Addington 44 SP 9573
Little Alne 32 SP 1361
Little Amwell 35 TL 3511
Little Aston 42 SK 0900
Little Atherfield 11 SZ 4680
Little Ayre 113 ND 3091
Little Ayton 73 NZ 5710
Little Baddow 22 TL 7807
Little Badminton 18 ST 8084
Little Bardfield 36 TL 6530
Little Barford 35 TL 1857
Little Barningham 47 TG 1333
Little Barrington 33 SP 2012
Little Barugh 67 SE 7579
Little Bedwyn 19 SU 2966
Little Bentley 23 TM 1125
Little Berkhamsted 35 TL 2907
Little Billing 34 SP 8061
Little Birch 30 SO 5031
Little Blakenham 37 TM 1048
Little Bowden 44 SP 7487
Little Bradley 36 TL 6852
Little Brampton 40 SO 3681
Little Brechin 99 NO 5862
Little Brickhill 34 SP 9032
Little Brington 34 SP 6663
Little Bromley 23 TM 0928
Little Budworth 51 SJ 5965
Little Burstead 22 TQ 6691
Little Bytham 44 TF 0118
Little Carlton 55 TF 3985
Little Casterton 44 TF 0109
Little Cawthorpe 55 TF 3583
Little Chalfont 20 SU 9997
Little Chart 15 TQ 9445
Little Chesterford 35 TL 5141
Little Cheverell 18 ST 9853
Little Chishill 35 TL 4237
Little Clacton 23 TM 1618
Little Comberton 32 SO 9643
Little Common 14 TQ 7107
Little Compton 33 SP 2530
Little Cowarne 31 SO 6051
Little Coxwell 19 SU 2893
Little Cressingham 46 TF 8600
Little Dalby 44 SK 7714
Little Dens 105 NK 0744
Little Dewchurch 31 SO 5231
Little Dunham 46 TF 8613
Little Dunkeld 98 NO 0242
Little Dunmow 22 TL 6521
Little Easton 22 TL 6023
Little Eaton 53 SK 3641
Little Ellingham 46 TM 0099
Little Eversden 35 TL 3752
Little Fakenham 36 TL 9076
Little Faringdon 33 SP 2201
Little Fenton 60 SE 5135
Little Fransham 46 TF 9011
Little Gaddesden 34 SP 9913
Little Garway 29 SO 4424
Little Gidding 45 TL 1382
Little Glemham 37 TM 3458
Little Gransden 35 TL 2755
Little Gruinard 106 NG 9484
Little Hadham 35 TL 4422
Little Hale 55 TF 1441
Little Hallingbury 22 TL 5017
Little Harrowden 44 SP 8771
Little Haseley 34 SP 6400
Little Hautbois 47 TG 2521
Little Haven 24 SM 8513
Little Hay 42 SK 1202
Little Haywood 42 SK 0021
Little Hereford 40 SO 5568
Little Horkesley 36 TL 9531
Little Horsted 13 TQ 4718
Little Horwood 34 SP 7930
Little Houghton (Northants.) 34 SP 8059
Little Hucklow 52 SK 1678
Little Hulton 58 SD 7103
Little Kingshill 20 SU 8999
Little Langford 10 SU 0436
Little Laver 22 TL 5409
Little Leigh 51 SJ 6175
Little Leighs 22 TL 7116
Little Lever 58 SD 7507
Little London (E Susx) 13 TQ 5719
Little London (Hants.) 19 SU 3749
Little London (Hants.) 19 SU 6259
Little London (Lincs.) 45 TF 2321
Little Longstone 52 SK 1871
Little Malvern 32 SO 7741
Little Maplestead 36 TL 8233
Little Marcle 31 SO 6736
Little Marlow 20 SU 8788
Little Massingham 46 TF 7924
Little Melton 47 TG 1506
Little Mill (Gwent) 29 SO 3102
Little Milton 19 SP 6100
Little Missenden 20 SU 9298
Little Ness (Salop) 40 SJ 4019
Little Newcastle 24 SM 9829
Little Newsham 72 NZ 1217
Little Oakley (Essex) 23 TM 2229
Little Oakley (Northants.) 44 SP 8985
Little Orton 70 NY 3555
Little Paxton 35 TL 1862
Little Petherick 3 SW 9172
Little Plumstead 47 TG 3112
Little Raveley 45 TL 2579
Little Ribston 66 SE 3853
Little Rissington 33 SP 1819
Little Ryburgh 46 TF 9628
Little Ryle 79 NU 0211
Little Salkeld 63 NY 5636
Little Sampford 36 TL 6533
Little Saxham 36 TL 8063
Little Scatwell 102 NH 3756
Little Shelford 35 TL 4551
Little Smeaton 60 SE 5219
Little Snoring 46 TF 9532
Little Somerford 18 ST 9684
Little Stainton 72 NZ 3420
Little Stanney 50 SJ 4173
Little Staughton 35 TL 1062
Little Steeping 55 TF 4362
Little Stonham 37 TM 1160
Little Stretton (Leic.) 43 SK 6600
Little Stretton (Salop) 40 SO 4491
Little Strickland 63 NY 5619
Little Stukeley 45 TL 2075
Little Tew 33 SP 3828
Little Thetford 45 TL 5376
Little Thurrock 22 TQ 6477
Little Torrington 6 SS 4816
Little Totham 22 TL 8812
Little Town (Cumbr.) 62 NY 2319
Little Wakering 23 TQ 9388
Little Walden 36 TL 5441
Little Waldingfield 36 TL 9245
Little Walsingham 46 TF 9336
Little Waltham 22 TL 7012
Little Warley 22 TQ 6090
Little Weighton 61 SE 9833
Little Welnetham 36 TL 8860
Little Wenlock 41 SJ 6406
Little Whittingham Green 37 TM 2877
Little Wilbraham 36 TL 5458
Little Witley 32 SO 7863
Little Wittenham 19 SU 5693
Little Wolford 33 SP 2635
Little Wyrley 42 SK 0105
Little Yeldham 36 TL 7739
Littleborough (Gtr Mches) 58 SD 9316
Littleborough (Notts.) 54 SK 8282
Littlebourne 15 TR 2057
Littlebredy 9 SY 5888
Littlebury 35 TL 5139
Littlebury Green 35 TL 4938
Littledean 29 SO 6713
Littleferry 108 NH 8095
Littleham (Devon.) 6 SS 4323
Littleham (Devon.) 8 SY 0281
Littlehampton 12 TQ 0202
Littlehempston 5 SX 8162
Littlehoughton (Northum.) 79 NU 2316
Littlemill (Highld.) 103 NH 9150
Littlemill (Strath.) 75 NS 4515
Littlemore 33 SP 5302
Littleover 53 SK 3234
Littleport 46 TL 5686
Littlestone-on-Sea 15 TR 0824
Littlethorpe 66 SE 326
Littleton (Ches.) 50 SJ 436
Littleton (Hants) 11 SU 453
Littleton (Somer.) 17 ST 483
Littleton (Surrey) 20 TQ 076
Littleton (Tays.) 93 NO 263
Littleton Drew 18 ST 828
Littleton Pannell 18 ST 995
Littleton-on-Severn 29 ST 599
Littletown (Durham) 72 NZ 334
Littlewick Green 20 SU 837
Littleworth (Here. and Worc.) 32 SO 885
Littleworth (Oxon.) 19 SU 319
Littleworth (Staffs.) 42 SK 011
Litton (Derby) 52 SK 167
Litton (N Yorks.) 65 SD 907
Litton (Somer.) 17 ST 595
Litton Cheney 9 SY 549
Liverpool 50 SJ 359
Liversedge 59 SE 202
Liverton 73 NZ 711
Livingston 85 NT 056
Livingston Village 85 NT 036
Lixwm 50 SJ 167
Lizard 2 SW 691
Llanaber 38 SH 601
Llanaehaearn 48 SH 384
Llanafan 27 SN 687
Llanafan-fechan 27 SN 965
Llanallgo 48 SH 508
Llanarmon 48 SH 423
Llanarmon Dyffryn Ceiriog 50 SJ 153
Llanarmon-yn-Ial 50 SJ 185
Llanarth (Dyfed) 26 SN 425
Llanarth (Gwent.) 29 SO 371
Llanarthney 25 SN 532
Llanasa 50 SJ 108
Llanbabo 48 SH 378
Llanbadarn Fawr 38 SN 608
Llanbadarn Fynydd 27 SO 097
Llanbadarn-y-garreg 30 SO 114
Llanbadrig 48 SH 379
Llanbeder 29 ST 389
Llanbedr (Gwyn.) 38 SH 582
Llanbedr (Powys) 30 SO 134
Llanbedr (Powys) 28 SO 232
Llanbedr-Dyffryn-Clwyd 50 SJ 145
Llanbedr-y-cennin 49 SH 765
Llanbedrgoch 48 SH 518
Llanbedrog 48 SH 323
Llanberis 48 SH 576
Llanbister 40 SO 107
Llanblethian 28 SS 987
Llanboidy 24 SN 212
Llanbradach 28 ST 149
Llanbrynmair 39 SH 900
Llancarfan 28 ST 057
Llancayo 29 SO 360
Llancynfelyn 39 SN 649
Llandanwg 38 SH 572
Llandawke 25 SN 281
Llanddaniel Fab 48 SH 497
Llanddarog 25 SN 501
Llanddeiniol 26 SN 567
Llanddeiniolen 48 SH 546
Llandderfel 49 SH 983
Llanddeusant (Dyfed) 28 SN 772
Llanddeusant (Gwyn.) 48 SH 348
Llanddew 27 SO 053
Llanddewi 25 SS 468
Llanddewi Brefi 27 SN 665
Llanddewi Rhydderch 29 SO 341
Llanddewi Velfrey 24 SN 141
Llanddewi Ystradenni 40 SO 106
Llanddewi'r Cwm 27 SO 034
Llanddoget 49 SH 806
Llanddona 48 SH 577
Llanddowror 25 SN 251
Llanddulas 49 SH 907
Llanddyfnan 48 SH 507
Llandebie 25 SN 621
Llandefaelog 25 SN 411
Llandefaelog Fach 27 SO 033
Llandegai 48 SH 597
Llandegfan 48 SH 567
Llandegla 50 SJ 195
Llandegley 30 SO 136
Llandegveth 29 ST 339
Llandeilo 25 SN 632
Llandeilo Graban 27 SO 094
Llandeilo'r Fan 27 SN 894
Llandeloy 24 SM 852
Llandenny 29 SO 410
Llandevenny 29 ST 418
Llandinabo 29 SO 512
Llandinam 39 SO 028
Llandissilio 24 SN 122
Llandogo 29 SO 520
Llandough (S Glam.) 28 SS 997
Llandough (S Glam.) 28 ST 167
Llandovery 27 SN 763
Llandow 28 SS 947
Llandre (Dyfed) 38 SN 628
Llandrillo 49 SJ 033
Llandrillo-yn-Rhos 49 SH 838
Llandrindod Wells 27 SO 056
Llandrinio 40 SJ 291
Llandudno 49 SH 778
Llandudno Junction 49 SH 797
Llandwrog 48 SH 455
Llandyfan 25 SN 641
Llandyfriog 26 SN 324
Llandyfrydog 48 SH 448
Llandygwydd 26 SN 244
Llandyrnog 50 SJ 106
Llandyssil 40 SO 199
Llandysul 26 SN 414
Llanegryn 38 SH 590
Llanegwad 25 SN 512
Llaneilian 48 SH 469
Llanelian-yn-Rhos 49 SH 837
Llanelidan 50 SJ 105
Llanelieu 30 SO 183
Llanellen 29 SO 301
Llanelli (Dyfed) 25 SN 500
Llanelltyd 39 SH 711
Llanelly (Gwent) 28 SO 231
Llanelwedd 27 SO 045
Llanenddwyn 38 SH 582
Llanengan 38 SH 292
Llanerchymedd 39 SH 413
Llanerfyl 39 SJ 030
Llanfachraeth 48 SH 318
Llanfachreth 39 SH 752
Llanfaelog 48 SH 337
Llanfaes 48 SH 607
Llanfaethlu 48 SH 318
Llanfaglan 48 SH 476
Llanfair 38 SH 572
Llanfair Caereinion 40 SJ 100
Llanfair Clydogau 27 SN 625
Llanfair Dyffryn Clwyd 50 SJ 135
Llanfair P. G. 48 SH 537
Llanfair Talhaiarn 49 SH 926

Llanfair Waterdine 243 Maidstone

Llanfair Waterdine 40 SO 2476
Llanfair-Nant-Gwyn 26 SN 1637
Llanfair-yn-Neubwll 48 SH 3077
Llanfairfechan 49 SH 6874
Llanfairynghornwy 48 SH 3290
Llanfallteg 24 SN 1520
Llanfallteg West 24 SN 1519
Llanfaredd 27 SO 0651
Llanfechain 40 SJ 1820
Llanfechelli 48 SH 3691
Llanfendigaid 38 SH 5605
Llanferres 50 SJ 1860
Llanfflewyn 48 SH 3689
Llanfihangel 39 SJ 0817
Llanfihangel Glyn Myfyr 49 SH 9849
Llanfihangel Nant Bran 27 SN 9434
Llanfihangel Rhydithon 40 SO 1466
Llanfihangel Rogiet 29 ST 4487
Llanfihangel ar-Arth 26 SN 4539
Llanfihangel-Tal-y-llyn 28 SO 1128
Llanfihangel-nant-Melan 30 SO 1758
Llanfihangel-uwch-Gwili 25 SN 4822
Llanfihangel-y-Creuddyn 27 SN 6676
Llanfihangel-y-pennant (Gwyn.) 48 SH 5245
Llanfihangel-y-pennant (Gwyn.) 39 SH 6708
Llanfihangel-y-traethau 48 SH 5935
Llanfilo 30 SO 1133
Llanfoist 29 SO 2813
Llanfor 49 SH 9336
Llanfrechfa 29 ST 3193
Llanfrothen 48 SH 6241
Llanfrynach 28 SO 0726
Llanfwrog (Clwyd) 50 SJ 1157
Llanfwrog (Gwyn.) 48 SH 3083
Llanfyllin 40 SJ 1419
Llanfynydd (Clwyd) 50 SJ 2756
Llanfynydd (Dyfed) 25 SN 5527
Llanfyrnach 26 SN 2231
Llangadfan 39 SJ 0010
Llangadog 25 SN 7028
Llangadwaladr (Clwyd) 40 SJ 1730
Llangadwaladr (Gwyn.) 48 SH 3869
Llangaffo 48 SH 4468
Llangain 25 SN 3815
Llangammarch Wells 27 SN 9347
Llangan 28 SS 9577
Llangarron 29 SO 5221
Llangathen 25 SN 5822
Llangattock 28 SO 2117
Llangattock Lingoed 29 SO 3620
Llangattock-Vibon-Avel 29 SO 4515
Llangedwyn 40 SJ 1824
Llangefni 48 SH 4575
Llangeinor 28 SS 9187
Llangeitho 27 SN 6159
Llangeler 26 SN 3739
Llangelynin 38 SH 5707
Llangendeirne 25 SN 4514
Llangennech 25 SN 5601
Llangennith 25 SS 4291
Llangenny 28 SO 2418
Llangernyw 49 SH 8767
Llangian 38 SH 2928
Llanglydwen 24 SN 1826
Llangoed 48 SH 6079
Llangoedmor 26 SN 2045
Llangollen 50 SJ 2141
Llangolman 24 SN 1127
Llangorse 28 SO 1327
Llangovan 29 SO 4505
Llangower 49 SH 9032
Llangranog 26 SN 3154
Llangristiolus 48 SH 4373
Llangrove 29 SO 5219
Llangua 29 SO 3926
Llangunllo 40 SO 2171
Llangunnor 25 SN 4219
Llangurig 39 SN 9080
Llangwm (Clwyd) 49 SH 9644
Llangwm (Dyfed) 24 SM 9909
Llangwm-isaf 29 SO 4200
Llangwnadl 48 SH 2033
Llangwyfan 50 SJ 1266
Llangwyllog 48 SH 4379
Llangwyryfon 27 SN 5970
Llangybi (Dyfed) 27 SN 6053
Llangybi (Gwent) 29 ST 3796
Llangybi (Gwyn.) 48 SH 4240
Llangyfelach 25 SS 6499
Llangynhafal 50 SJ 1263
Llangynidr 28 SO 1519
Llangynin 25 SN 2519
Llangynog (Dyfed) 25 SN 3316
Llangynog (Powys) 39 SJ 0526
Llanharan 28 ST 0083
Llanharry 28 ST 0080
Llanhennock 29 ST 3592
Llanhilleth 28 SO 2100
Llanidloes 39 SN 9584
Llaniestyn 48 SH 2633
Llanigon 30 SO 2139
Llanilar 27 SN 6275
Llanilid 28 SS 9781
Llanishen (Gwent) 29 SO 4703
Llanishen (S Glam.) 28 ST 1781
Llanllechid 48 SH 6268
Llanlleonfel 27 SN 9350
Llanllowell 29 ST 3998
Llanllugan 39 SJ 0402
Llanllwch 25 SN 3818
Llanllwchaiarn 40 SO 1192
Llanllyfni 48 SH 4651
Llanmadoc 25 SS 4493
Llanmaes 28 SS 9869
Llanmartin 29 ST 3989
Llanmerewig 40 SO 1593
Llanmihangel 28 SS 9771
Llanmorlais 25 SS 5294
Llannefydd 49 SH 9770
Llannon 25 SN 5408
Llannor 48 SH 3537
Llanon 26 SN 5167
Llanpumsaint 25 SN 4129
Llanrhaeadr 49 SJ 0763
Llanrhaeadr-ym-Mochnant 40 SJ 1226
Llanrhidian 25 SS 3992
Llanrhos 49 SH 7880
Llanrhyddlad 48 SH 3389
Llanrhystud 26 SN 5369
Llanrian 24 SM 8131
Llanrothal 29 SO 4618
Llanrug 48 SH 5363
Llanrwst 49 SH 7961
Llansadurnen 25 SN 2810
Llansadwrn (Dyfed) 27 SN 6931
Llansadwrn (Gwyn.) 48 SH 5575
Llansaint 25 SN 3808
Llansannan 49 SH 9365
Llansannor 28 SS 9977
Llansantffraed 28 SO 1223
Llansantffraed-Cwmdeuddwr 27 SN 9667
Llansantffraed-in-Elvel 27 SO 0954
Llansantffraid 26 SN 5167
Llansantffraid Glan Conwy 49 SH 8075
Llansantffraid-ym-Mechain 40 SJ 2220
Llansawel 27 SN 6136
Llansilin 40 SJ 2028
Llansoy 29 SO 4402
Llanstadwell 24 SM 9505
Llanstephan (Dyfed) 25 SN 3511
Llanstephan (Powys) 30 SO 1142
Llanthony 29 SO 2827
Llantilio-Crossenny 29 SO 3914
Llantrisant (Gwent) 29 ST 3996
Llantrisant (Mid Glam.) 28 ST 0483
Llantrithyd 28 ST 0472
Llantwit Fardre 28 ST 0785
Llantwit Major 28 SS 9768
Llantysilio 50 SJ 1943
Llanuwchllyn 49 SH 8730
Llanvaches 29 ST 4391
Llanvair-Discoed 29 ST 4492
Llanvapley 29 SO 3614
Llanvetherine 29 SO 3617
Llanveynoe 30 SO 3031
Llanvihangel Crucorney 29 SO 3220
Llanvihangel Gobion 29 SO 3409
Llanvihangel-Ystern-Llewern 29 SO 4313
Llanwarne 29 SO 5028
Llanwddyn 39 SJ 0219
Llanwenog 26 SN 4945
Llanwern 29 ST 3688
Llanwinio 25 SN 2626
Llanwnda (Dyfed) 24 SM 9339
Llanwnda (Gwyn.) 48 SH 4758
Llanwnen 26 SN 5347
Llanwnog 39 SO 0293
Llanwrda 27 SN 7131
Llanwrin 39 SH 7803
Llanwrthwl 27 SN 9763
Llanwrtyd 27 SN 8647
Llanwrtyd Wells 27 SN 8746
Llanwyddelan 39 SJ 0801
Llanybiodwel 40 SJ 2322
Llanybri 25 SN 3312
Llanybydder 26 SN 5244
Llanycefn 24 SN 0923
Llanychaer Bridge 24 SM 9835
Llanycrwys 27 SN 6445
Llanymawddwy 39 SH 9019
Llanymynech 40 SJ 2620
Llanynghenedl 48 SH 3181
Llanynys 50 SJ 1062
Llanyre 27 SO 0462
Llanystumdwy 48 SH 4738
Llanywern 28 SO 1028
Llawhaden 24 SN 0717
Llawnt 40 SJ 2430
Llawryglyn 39 SN 9291
Llay 50 SJ 3255
Llechcynfarwy 48 SH 3881
Llechfaen 28 SO 0828
Llechryd (Dyfed) 26 SN 2243
Llechryd (Mid Glam.) 28 SO 1009
Llechrydau 50 SJ 2234
Lledrod (Clwyd) 40 SJ 2229
Lledrod (Dyfed) 27 SN 6470
Llidiadnenog 26 SN 5437
Llidiardau 38 SH 1929
Llithfaen 48 SH 3543
Llong 50 SJ 2562
Llowes 30 SO 1941
Llwydcoed 28 SN 9905
Llwyn 40 SO 2880
Llwyncelyn 26 SN 4459
Llwyndafydd 26 SN 3755
Llwynderw 40 SJ 2004
Llwyndyrys 48 SH 3741
Llwyngwril 38 SH 5909
Llwynhendy 25 SS 5599
Llwynmawr 50 SJ 2236
Llwynypia 28 SS 9993
Llynclys 40 SJ 2924
Llynfaes 48 SH 4178
Llys-y-fran 24 SN 0424
Llysfaen 49 SH 8977
Llyswen 30 SO 1337
Llysworney 28 SS 9674
Llywel 27 SN 8630
Loan 84 NS 9575
Loanend 87 NT 9450
Loanhead 85 NT 2765
Loans 82 NS 3431
Lochailort (Highld.) 95 NM 7682
Lochaline (Highld.) 95 NM 6744
Lochans 68 NX 0656
Locharbriggs 70 NX 9980
Lochawe (Strath.) 89 NN 1227
Lochboisdale (S. Uist) 109 NF 7820
Lochbuie (Strath.) 88 NM 6125
Lochcarron (Highld.) 101 NG 9039
Lochdonhead 89 NM 7333
Lochead 81 NR 7778
Lochearnhead 90 NN 5823
Lochee 93 NO 3631
Lochend (Highld.) 102 NH 5937
Locheport (N. Uist) 109 NF 8563
Lochfoot 69 NX 8973
Lochgair 89 NR 9290
Lochgarthside 102 NH 5219
Lochgelly 92 NT 1893
Lochgilphead 89 NR 8687
Lochgoilhead 90 NN 1901
Lochhill 104 NJ 2964
Lochinver 110 NC 0922
Lochlane 91 NN 8320
Lochluichart 102 NH 3262
Lochmaben 70 NY 0882
Lochnaw 68 NW 9962
Lochore 92 NT 1796
Lochranza (Island of Arran) 81 NR 9350
Lochside (Grampn.) 99 NO 7464
Lochside (Highland.) 111 NC 8735
Lochton 99 NO 7592
Lochwinnoch 82 NS 3558
Lochwood (Strath.) 84 NS 6966
Lockengate 4 SX 0361
Lockerbie 70 NY 1381
Lockeridge 18 SU 1467
Lockerley 11 SU 2925
Locking 17 ST 3659
Lockington (Humbs.) 67 SE 9947
Lockington (Leic.) 43 SK 4628
Lockleywood 41 SJ 6828
Lockmaddy 109 NF 9168
Locks Heath 11 SU 5207
Lockton 67 SE 8489
Loddington (Leic.) 44 SK 7802
Loddington (Northants.) 44 SP 8178
Loddiswell 5 SX 7148
Loddon 47 TM 3698
Lode 35 TL 5362
Loders 9 SY 4994
Lodsworth 12 SU 9223
Lofthouse (N Yorks.) 65 SE 1073
Lofthouse (W Yorks.) 59 SE 3325
Loftus 73 NZ 7118
Logan 75 NS 5820
Loggerheads 51 SJ 7336
Logie (Fife) 93 NO 4020
Logie (Grampn.) 105 NK 0356
Logie (Tays.) 99 NO 6963
Logie Coldstone 98 NJ 4304
Logie Hill 108 NH 7776
Logie Newton 105 NJ 6638
Logie Pert 99 NO 6664
Logierait 98 NN 9752
Login 24 SN 1623
Lolworth 35 TL 3664
Lonbain 101 NG 6853
Londesborough 60 SE 8645
London 21 TQ 3281
London Colney 35 TL 1603
Londonderry 66 SE 3087
Londonthorpe 54 SK 9537
Londubh 106 NG 8680
Long Ashton 29 ST 5470
Long Bennington 54 SK 8344
Long Bredy 9 SY 5690
Long Buckby 43 SP 6267
Long Clawson 44 SK 7227
Long Common 11 SU 5014
Long Compton (Staffs.) 41 SJ 8522
Long Compton (Warw.) 33 SP 2832
Long Crendon 34 SP 6908
Long Crichel 10 ST 9710
Long Ditton 21 TQ 1666
Long Drax 60 SE 6528
Long Duckmanton 53 SK 4371
Long Eaton 53 SK 4933
Long Hanborough 33 SP 4114
Long Hermiston 85 NT 1770
Long Itchington 33 SP 4165
Long Lawford 43 SP 4775
Long Load 9 ST 4623
Long Marston (Herts.) 34 SP 8915
Long Marston (N Yorks.) 66 SE 4951
Long Marston (Warw.) 32 SP 1548
Long Marton 63 NY 6624
Long Melford 36 TL 8646
Long Newnton (Glos.) 18 ST 9092
Long Preston 65 SD 8357
Long Riston 67 TA 1242
Long Stratton 47 TM 1992
Long Street 34 SP 7946
Long Sutton (Hants.) 20 SU 7347
Long Sutton (Lincs.) 45 TF 4322
Long Sutton (Somer.) 9 ST 4625
Long Whatton 43 SK 4723
Long Wittenham 19 SU 5493
Longbenton 72 NZ 2668
Longborough 33 SP 1729
Longbridge (W Mids) 42 SP 0178
Longbridge (Warw.) 33 SP 2662
Longbridge Deverill 18 ST 8640
Longburton 9 ST 6412
Longcliffe 53 SK 2255
Longcot 18 SU 2790
Longcroft 84 NS 7979
Longden 40 SJ 4306
Longdon (Here. and Worc.) 32 SO 8336
Longdon (Staffs.) 42 SK 0714
Longdon upon Tern 41 SJ 6215
Longdown 5 SX 8691
Longdowns 2 SW 7434
Longfield 14 TQ 6069
Longford (Derby.) 53 SK 2137
Longford (Glos.) 32 SO 8320
Longford (Gtr London) 20 TQ 0576
Longford (Salop) 51 SJ 6433
Longford (Salop) 41 SJ 7218
Longford (W Mids.) 43 SP 3583
Longforgan 93 NO 3129
Longformacus 86 NT 6957
Longframlington 79 NU 1201
Longham (Dorset) 10 SZ 0697
Longham (Norf.) 46 TF 9415
Longhirst 79 NZ 2289
Longhope 29 SO 6819
Longhorsley 79 NZ 1494
Longhoughton 79 NU 2414
Longley Green 32 SO 7350
Longmanhill 105 NJ 7462
Longmoor Camp 12 SU 7930
Longmorn 104 NJ 2358
Longnewton (Bord) 86 NT 5827
Longnewton (Cleve.) 72 NZ 3816
Longney 32 SO 7612
Longniddry 86 NT 4476
Longnor (Salop) 40 SJ 4800
Longnor (Staffs.) 52 SK 0864
Longparish 19 SU 4344
Longridge (Lancs.) 58 SD 6037
Longridge (Lothian) 84 NS 9462
Longriggend 84 NS 8270
Longsdon 51 SJ 9554
Longside 105 NK 0347
Longslow 51 SJ 6535
Longstanton 45 TL 4066
Longstock 11 SU 3536
Longstowe 35 TL 3054
Longthorpe 45 TL 1698
Longton (Lancs.) 57 SD 4725
Longton (Staffs.) 51 SJ 9043
Longtown (Cumbr.) 70 NY 3768
Longtown (Here. and Worc.) 29 SO 3228
Longville in the Dale 40 SO 5393
Longwick 34 SP 7805
Longwitton 79 NZ 0788
Longwood 41 SJ 6007
Longworth 19 SU 3899
Longyester 86 NT 5465
Lonmore 100 NG 2646
Looe 4 SX 2553
Loose 14 TQ 7552
Loosley Row 34 SP 8100
Lootcherbrae 104 NJ 6054
Lopcombe Corner 11 SU 2435
Lopen 9 ST 4214
Loppington 40 SJ 4629
Lorbottle 79 NU 0306
Lornty 98 NO 1746
Loscoe 53 SK 4247
Lossiemouth 104 NJ 2370
Lossit 80 NR 1856
Lostock Gralam 51 SJ 6874
Lostock Junction 67 SD 6708
Lostwithiel 4 SX 1059
Lothbeg 108 NC 9410
Lothersdale 58 SD 9545
Lothmore 111 NC 9611
Loudwater 20 SU 8990
Loughborough 43 SK 5319
Loughor 25 SS 5898
Loughton (Bucks.) 34 SP 8337
Loughton (Essex) 21 TQ 4296
Loughton (Salop) 41 SO 6183
Lound (Lincs.) 45 TF 0618
Lound (Notts.) 53 SK 6986
Lound (Suff.) 47 TM 5099
Lount 43 SK 3819
Louth 55 TF 3287
Love Clough 58 SD 8126
Lover 11 SU 2120
Loversall 60 SK 5798
Loves Green 22 TL 6404
Loveston 24 SN 0808
Lovington 17 ST 5931
Low Bradfield 53 SK 2691
Low Bradley 59 SE 0048
Low Braithwaite 70 NY 4242
Low Brunton 71 NY 9269
Low Burnham 60 SE 7702
Low Catton 66 SE 7053
Low Crosby 71 NY 4459
Low Dinsdale 72 NZ 3411
Low Eggborough 60 SE 5522
Low Gate 71 NY 9064
Low Ham 17 ST 4329
Low Hesket 71 NY 4646
Low Hesleyhurst 79 NZ 0997
Low Moor 58 SD 7241
Low Redford 72 NZ 0731
Low Row (Cumbr.) 71 NY 5863
Low Row (N Yorks.) 65 SD 9897
Low Santon 61 SE 9312
Low Street 47 TG 3424
Low Torry 85 NT 0086
Low Worsall 66 NZ 3909
Lowca 62 NX 9821
Lowdham 53 SK 6646
Lower Aisholt 16 ST 2035
Lower Assendon 20 SU 7484
Lower Beeding 13 TQ 2227
Lower Benefield 44 SP 9888
Lower Bentham 64 SD 6469
Lower Bentley 32 SO 9865
Lower Boddington 33 SP 4752
Lower Bullingham 30 SO 5038
Lower Cam 32 SO 7401
Lower Chapel 27 SO 0235
Lower Chute 19 SU 3153
Lower Cwmtwrch 28 SN 7710
Lower Darwen 58 SD 6824
Lower Down 40 SO 3384
Lower Dunsforth 66 SE 4464
Lower Farringdon 12 SU 7035
Lower Frankton 50 SJ 3732
Lower Froyle 12 SU 7544
Lower Gledfield 108 NH 5990
Lower Green 46 TF 9837
Lower Greenbank 64 SD 5254
Lower Halstow 14 TQ 8567
Lower Hardres 15 TR 1453
Lower Heyford 33 SP 4824
Lower Higham 22 TQ 7172
Lower Hordley 40 SJ 3929
Lower Killeyan 80 NR 2743
Lower Langford 17 ST 4660
Lower Largo 93 NO 4102
Lower Lemington 33 SP 2134
Lower Lye 40 SO 4067
Lower Maes-coed 30 SO 3431
Lower Mayland 23 TL 9101
Lower Moor 32 SO 9847
Lower Nazeing 35 TL 3906
Lower Penarth 28 ST 1869
Lower Penn 41 SO 8696
Lower Pennington 11 SZ 3193
Lower Peover 51 SJ 7474
Lower Quinton 33 SP 1847
Lower Shelton 34 SP 9942
Lower Shiplake 20 SU 7779
Lower Shuckburgh 33 SP 4862
Lower Slaughter 32 SP 1622
Lower Stanton St. Quintin 18 ST 9180
Lower Sundon 35 TL 0526
Lower Swanwick 11 SU 4909
Lower Swell 32 SP 1725
Lower Thurlton 47 TM 4299
Lower Tysoe 33 SP 3445
Lower Upham 11 SU 5219
Lower Vexford 16 ST 1135
Lower Weare 17 ST 4053
Lower Wield 19 SU 6340
Lower Winchendon 34 SP 7312
Lower Woodend 20 SU 8187
Lower Woodford 10 SU 1235
Lowesby 44 SK 7207
Lowestoft 47 TM 5493
Lowestoft End 47 TM 5394
Loweswater 62 NY 1421
Lowgill (Lancs.) 64 SD 6564
Lowick (Cumbr.) 62 SD 2985
Lowick (Northants.) 44 SP 9781
Lowick (Northum.) 87 NU 0139
Lownie Moor 99 NO 4848
Lowsonford 42 SP 1867
Lowthorpe 67 TA 0860
Lowton 58 SJ 6197
Lowton Common 58 SJ 6397
Loxbeare 8 SS 9116
Loxhill 12 TQ 0037
Loxhore 6 SS 6138
Loxley 33 SP 2553
Loxton 17 ST 3755
Loxwood 12 TQ 0431
Lubenham 44 SP 7087
Luccombe 16 SS 9144
Luccombe Village 11 SZ 5880
Lucker 87 NU 1530
Luckett 4 SX 3873
Luckington 18 ST 8383
Lucklawhill 93 NO 4222
Luckwell Bridge 16 SS 9038
Lucton 30 SO 4364
Ludborough 55 TF 2995
Ludchurch 24 SN 1411
Luddenden 59 SE 0425
Luddesdown 14 TQ 6766
Luddington 60 SE 8216
Ludford (Lincs.) 55 TF 1989
Ludford (Salop) 40 SO 5173
Ludgershall (Bucks.) 34 SP 6617
Ludgershall (Wilts.) 18 SU 2650
Ludgvan 2 SW 5033
Ludham 47 TG 3818
Ludlow 40 SO 5175
Ludwell 10 ST 9122
Ludworth 72 NZ 3641
Luffincott 4 SX 3394
Luffness 86 NT 4780
Lugar 75 NS 5821
Luggiebank 84 NS 7672
Lugton 82 NS 4152
Lugwardine 31 SO 5441
Luib 100 NG 5628
Lulham 30 SO 4041
Lullington (Derby.) 42 SK 2513
Lullington (Somer.) 18 ST 7851
Lulsgate Bottom 29 ST 5065
Lulsley 32 SO 7455
Lumb 59 SE 0221
Lumby 60 SE 4830
Lumloch 84 NS 6369
Lumphanan 104 NJ 5804
Lumphinnans 92 NT 1692
Lumsden 104 NJ 4722
Lunan 99 NO 6851
Lunanhead 99 NO 4752
Luncarty 92 NO 0929
Lund (Humbs.) 61 SE 9648
Lund (N Yorks.) 60 SE 6532
Lundie (Tays.) 93 NO 2836
Lundin Links 93 NO 4002
Lunna 113 HU 4969
Lunning 113 HU 5066
Lunsford's Cross 14 TQ 7210
Lunt 57 SD 3401
Luntley 30 SO 3955
Luppitt 8 ST 1606
Lupton 63 SD 5581
Lurgashall 12 SU 9326
Lurgmore 102 NH 5937
Lusby 55 TF 3367
Luss 90 NS 3592
Lusta 100 NG 2756
Lustleigh 5 SX 7881
Luston 30 SO 4863
Luthermuir 99 NO 6568
Luthrie 93 NO 3219
Luton (Beds.) 35 TL 0821
Luton (Devon) 8 SX 9076
Luton (Kent) 14 TQ 7766
Lutterworth 43 SP 5484
Lutton (Devon.) 5 SX 5959
Lutton (Lincs.) 45 TF 4325
Lutton (Northants.) 45 TL 1187
Luxborough 16 SS 9738
Luxulyan 4 SX 0458
Lybster 112 ND 2435
Lydbury North 40 SO 3486
Lydcott 7 SS 6936
Lydd 15 TR 0421
Lydd-on-Sea 15 TR 0819
Lydden 15 TR 2645
Lyddington 44 SP 8797
Lydeard St. Lawrence 16 ST 1232
Lydford (Devon.) 5 SX 5084
Lydford (Somer.) 17 ST 5731
Lydgate 58 SD 9225
Lydham 40 SO 3391
Lydiard Millicent 18 SU 0986
Lydiate 57 SD 3604
Lydlinch 9 ST 7413
Lydney 29 SO 6203
Lydstep 24 SS 0898
Lye 41 SO 9284
Lye Green 34 SP 9703
Lyford 19 SU 3994
Lymbridge Green 15 TR 1243
Lyme Regis 8 SY 3492
Lyminge 15 TR 1641
Lymington 11 SZ 3295
Lyminster 12 TQ 0204
Lymm 51 SJ 6786
Lymore 11 SZ 2992
Lympne 15 TR 1235
Lympsham 17 ST 3454
Lympstone 8 SX 9984
Lynchat 97 NH 7801
Lyndhurst 11 SU 2907
Lyndon 44 SK 9004
Lyne 20 TQ 0166
Lyne of Gorthleck 102 NH 5420
Lyne of Skene 105 NJ 7610
Lyneal 50 SJ 4433
Lynegar 112 ND 2357
Lyneham (Oxon.) 33 SP 2720
Lyneham (Wilts.) 18 SU 0179
Lynemouth 79 NZ 2991
Lyness 113 ND 3094
Lyng (Norf.) 47 TG 0617
Lyng (Somer.) 17 ST 3328
Lynmouth 7 SS 7249
Lynsted 15 TQ 9461
Lynton 7 SS 7149
Lyon's Gate 9 ST 6605
Lyonshall 30 SO 3356
Lytchett Matravers 10 SY 9495
Lytchett Minster 10 SY 9593
Lyth 112 ND 2763
Lytham 57 SD 3727
Lytham St. Anne's 57 SD 3427
Lythe 73 NZ 8413

M

Mabe Burnthouse 2 SW 7634
Mabie 69 NX 9570
Mablethorpe 55 TF 5085
Macclesfield 51 SJ 9173
Macduff 105 NJ 7064
Macharioch 74 NR 7309
Machen 28 ST 2189
Machrihanish 74 NR 6220
Machynlleth 39 SH 7401
Mackworth 53 SK 3137
Macmerry 86 NT 4372
Madderty 91 NN 9522
Maddiston 84 NS 9476
Madehurst 12 SU 9810
Madeley (Salop) 41 SJ 6904
Madeley (Staffs.) 51 SJ 7744
Madingley 35 TL 3960
Madley 30 SO 4138
Madresfield 32 SO 8047
Madron 2 SW 4532
Maenclochog 24 SN 0827
Maendy 28 ST 0176
Maentwrog 49 SH 6640
Maer 51 SJ 7938
Maerdy (Clwyd) 49 SJ 0144
Maerdy (Mid Glam.) 28 SS 9798
Maes-glas 29 ST 2985
Maes-y-cwmmer 28 ST 1794
Maesbrook 40 SJ 3121
Maesbury Marsh 40 SJ 3125
Maesgwynne 24 SN 2024
Maeshafn 50 SJ 2061
Maesllyn 26 SN 3644
Maesmynis 27 SO 0148
Maesteg 28 SS 8591
Maesybont 25 SN 5616
Magdalen Laver 22 TL 5108
Maggieknockater 104 NJ 3145
Magham Down 13 TQ 6111
Maghull 57 SD 3702
Magor 29 ST 4287
Maiden Bradley 17 ST 8038
Maiden Law 72 NZ 1749
Maiden Newton 9 SY 5997
Maidencombe 8 SX 9268
Maidenhead 20 SU 8881
Maidens 75 NS 2107
Maidford 34 SP 6052
Maids' Moreton 34 SP 7035
Maidstone 14 TQ 7656

Monkleigh 245 Newton Toney

Monkleigh 6 SS 4520
Monknash 28 SS 9270
Monkokehampton 6 SS 5805
Monks Eleigh 36 TL 9647
Monks Kirby 43 SP 4683
Monks' Heath 51 SJ 8873
Monkshill 105 NJ 7941
Monksilver 16 ST 0737
Monkswood 29 SO 3403
Monkton (Devon.) 8 ST 1803
Monkton (Kent) 15 TR 2865
Monkton (Strath.) 75 NS 3527
Monkton (Tyne and Wear) 72 NZ 3463
Monkton Combe 18 ST 7761
Monkton Deverill 10 ST 8537
Monkton Farleigh 18 ST 8065
Monkton Heathfield 16 ST 2526
Monkton Up Wimborne 10 SU 0113
Monkwood 11 SU 6730
Monmouth 29 SO 5113
Monnington on Wye 30 SO 3743
Monreith 68 NX 3641
Monreith Mains 68 NX 3643
Montacute 9 ST 4916
Montford 40 SJ 4114
Montgarrie 104 NJ 5717
Montgomery 40 SO 2296
Montgreenan 82 NS 3343
Montrave 93 NO 3706
Montrose 99 NO 7157
Monxton 19 SU 3144
Monyash 52 SK 1566
Monymusk 105 NJ 6815
Monzie 91 NN 8725
Moonzie 93 NO 3317
Moor Crichel 10 ST 9908
Moor Monkton 66 SE 5056
Moor Nook 58 SD 6537
Moor, The 14 TQ 7529
Moorby 55 TF 2964
Moorcot 30 SO 3555
Moordown 10 SZ 0994
Moore 51 SJ 5584
Moorends 60 SE 6915
Moorhall 53 SK 3175
Moorhampton 30 SO 3846
Moorhouse (Cumbr.) 70 NY 3356
Moorhouse (Notts.) 54 SK 7566
Moorland or Northmoor Green 17 ST 3332
Moorlinch 17 ST 3936
Moorsholm 73 NZ 6814
Moorside 58 SD 9507
Moortown (I. of W.) 11 SZ 4283
Moortown (Lincs.) 61 TF 0699
Morborne 45 TL 1391
Morchard Bishop 7 SS 7607
Morcombelake 8 SY 4093
Morcott 44 SK 9200
Morda 40 SJ 2827
Morden (Dorset) 10 SY 9195
Morden (Gtr London) 21 TQ 2567
Mordiford 31 SO 5637
Mordon 72 NZ 3326
More 40 SO 3491
Morebath 8 SS 9525
Morebattle 78 NT 7724
Morecambe 64 SD 4364
Morefield 106 NH 1195
Moreleigh 5 SX 7652
Morenish 90 NN 6035
Moresby 62 NX 9821
Morestead 11 SU 5125
Moreton (Dorset) 10 SY 8089
Moreton (Essex) 22 TL 5307
Moreton (Mers.) 50 SJ 2689
Moreton (Oxon.) 34 SP 6904
Moreton Corbet 40 SJ 5523
Moreton Jeffries 31 SO 6048
Moreton Morrell 43 SP 3155
Moreton Pinkney 33 SP 5749
Moreton Say 51 SJ 6234
Moreton Valence 32 SO 7809
Moreton on Lugg 30 SO 5045
Moreton-in-Marsh 33 SP 2032
Moretonhampstead 5 SX 7586
Morfa Bychan 48 SH 5437
Morfa Glas 28 SN 8606
Morfa Nefyn 48 SH 2840
Morgan's Vale 11 SU 1921
Morland 63 NY 6022
Morley (Derby.) 53 SK 3941
Morley (Durham) 72 NZ 1227
Morley (W Yorks.) 59 SE 2627
Morley Green 51 SJ 8282
Morley St. Botolph 47 TM 0799
Morningside 85 NT 2471
Morningthorpe 47 TM 2192
Morpeth 79 NZ 2085
Morphie 99 NO 7164
Morrey 42 SK 1218
Morriston 25 SS 6698
Morston 46 TG 0043
Mortehoe 6 SS 4545
Mortimer 19 SU 6564
Mortimer West End 19 SU 6363
Mortimer's Cross 30 SO 4263
Mortlake 21 TQ 2075
Morton (Avon) 29 ST 6491
Morton (Derby.) 53 SK 4060
Morton (Lincs.) 54 SK 8091
Morton (Lincs.) 45 TF 0924
Morton (Norf.) 47 TG 1217
Morton (Salop) 40 SJ 2824
Morton Bagot 32 SP 1164
Morton-on-Swale 66 SE 3292
Morvah 2 SW 4035
Morval 4 SX 2556
Morvich 101 NG 9621
Morville 41 SO 6694
Morwenstow 6 SS 2015
Mosborough 53 SK 4281
Moscow 82 NS 4840
Mosedale 62 NY 3532
Moseley (Here. and Worc.) 32 SO 8159
Moseley (W Mids) 42 SP 0883
Moss (Clwyd) 50 SJ 3052
Moss (S Yorks.) 60 SE 5914
Moss (Tiree) 94 NL 9644
Moss Bank 50 SJ 5198
Moss Nook 51 SJ 8385
Moss Side 57 SD 3830
Moss of Barmuckity 104 NJ 2461
Mossat 104 NJ 4719
Mossbank (Shetld.) 113 HU 4475
Mossburnford 78 NT 6616
Mossdale 69 NX 6571
Mossend 84 NS 7460
Mosside 98 NO 4252
Mossley 58 SD 9702
Mosston 99 NO 5444
Mosterton 9 ST 4505
Mostyn 50 SJ 1680
Motcombe 10 ST 8425
Motherwell 84 NS 7557
Mottingham 21 TQ 4272
Mottisfont 11 SU 3226
Mottistone 11 SZ 4083
Mottram in Longendale 59 SJ 9995
Mouldsworth 50 SJ 5171
Moulin 97 NN 9459
Moulsecoomb 13 TQ 3307
Moulsford 19 SU 5984
Moulsoe 34 SP 9041
Moulton (Ches.) 51 SJ 6569
Moulton (Lincs.) 45 TF 3023
Moulton (N Yorks.) 66 NZ 2303
Moulton (Northants.) 44 SP 7866
Moulton (Suff.) 36 TL 6964
Moulton Chapel 45 TF 2918
Moulton Seas End 45 TF 3227
Mount (Corn.) 2 SW 7856
Mount (Corn.) 4 SX 1467
Mount Bures 36 TL 9032
Mount Hawke 2 SW 7147
Mount Pleasant 37 TM 5077
Mountain Ash 28 ST 0498
Mountain Cross 85 NT 1446
Mountain Water 24 SM 9224
Mountbenger 77 NT 3125
Mountfield 14 TQ 7320
Mountgerald 102 NH 5661
Mountjoy 3 SW 8760
Mountnessing 22 TQ 6297
Mounton 29 ST 5193
Mountsorrel 43 SK 5814
Mousehole 2 SW 4626
Mouswald 70 NY 0672
Mow Cop 51 SJ 8557
Mowhaugh 78 NT 8120
Mowsley 43 SP 6489
Mowtie 99 NO 8388
Moy (Highld.) 96 NN 4282
Moylgrove 26 SN 1244
Muasdale 81 NR 6840
Much Birch 30 SO 5030
Much Cowarne 31 SO 6147
Much Dewchurch 30 SO 4831
Much Hadham 35 TL 4319
Much Hoole 57 SD 4723
Much Marcle 31 SO 6533
Much Wenlock 41 SO 6199
Muchalls 99 NO 9091
Muchelney 9 ST 4224
Muchlarnick 4 SX 2156
Mucking 22 TQ 6881
Mucklestone 51 SJ 7237
Muckleton 41 SJ 5821
Muckletown 104 NJ 5621
Muckton 55 TF 3781
Muddiford 6 SS 5638
Mudeford 10 SZ 1892
Mudford 9 ST 5719
Mudgley 17 ST 4445
Mugdock 84 NS 5576
Mugeary 100 NG 4438
Mugginton 53 SK 2843
Muggleswick 72 NZ 0450
Muie 108 NC 6704
Muir of Fowlis 104 NJ 5612
Muir of Ord 102 NH 5250
Muirdrum 93 NO 5637
Muirhead (Fife.) 93 NO 2805
Muirhead (Strath.) 84 NS 6869
Muirhead (Tays.) 93 NO 3434
Muirhouses 85 NT 0180
Muirkirk 76 NS 6927
Muirshearlich 96 NN 1380
Muirskie 99 NO 8295
Muirtack (Grampn.) 105 NJ 8146
Muirtack (Grampn.) 105 NJ 9937
Muirton 103 NH 7463
Muirton of Ardblair 98 NO 1743
Muirton of Ballochy 99 NO 6462
Muirtown 91 NN 9211
Muiryfold 105 NJ 7651
Muker 65 SD 9198
Mulbarton 47 TG 1901
Mulben 104 NJ 3450
Mullion 2 SW 6719
Mumbles, The 25 SS 6287
Mumby 55 TF 5174
Munderfield Row 31 SO 6451
Munderfield Stocks 31 SO 6550
Munderno 105 NJ 9614
Mundesley 47 TG 3136
Mundford 46 TL 8093
Mundham (Norf.) 47 TM 3298
Mundon Hill 22 TL 8702
Mundorno 105 NJ 9413
Munerigie 96 NH 2602
Mungrisdale 62 NY 3630
Munlochy 103 NH 6453
Munsley 31 SO 6640
Munslow 40 SO 5187
Munslow Aston 40 SO 5086
Murcott 33 SP 5815
Murkle 112 ND 1668
Murlaggan (Highld.) 96 NN 3181
Murrow 45 TF 3707
Mursley 34 SP 8128
Murthill 98 NO 4657
Murthly 92 NO 0938
Murton (Cumbr.) 63 NY 7221
Murton (Durham) 72 NZ 3947
Murton (N Yorks.) 66 SE 6452
Murton (Northum.) 87 NT 9748
Musbury 8 SY 2794
Muscoates 66 SE 6880
Musselburgh 85 NT 3472
Muston (Leic.) 54 SK 8237
Muston (N Yorks.) 67 TA 0979
Mustow Green 41 SO 8774
Mutford 47 TM 4888
Muthill 91 NN 8616
Mutterton 8 ST 0304
Mybster 112 ND 1652
Myddfai 28 SN 7730
Myddle 40 SJ 4623
Mydroilyn 26 SN 4555
Mylor Bridge 2 SW 8036
Mynachlog-ddu 26 SN 1430
Myndtown 40 SO 3889
Mynytho 48 SH 3031
Myrebird 99 NO 7498
Mytchett 20 SU 8855
Mytholm 58 SD 9827
Mytholmroyd 59 SE 0125
Myton-on-Swale 66 SE 4366

N

Naburn 60 SE 5945
Nackington 15 TR 1554
Nacton 37 TM 2240
Nafferton 67 TA 0559
Nailsea 29 ST 4670
Nailstone 43 SK 4107
Nailsworth 18 ST 8499
Nairn 103 NH 8756
Nancegollan 2 SW 6632
Nanhoron 48 SH 2831
Nannau 39 SH 7420
Nannerch 50 SJ 1669
Nanpantan 43 SK 5017
Nanpean 3 SW 9556
Nant-ddu 28 SO 0015
Nant-glas 27 SN 9965
Nant-y-derry 29 SO 3306
Nant-y-moel 28 SS 9393
Nanternis 26 SN 3756
Nantgaredig 25 SN 4921
Nantgarw 28 ST 1285
Nantglyn 49 SJ 0061
Nantlle 48 SH 5053
Nantmawr 40 SJ 2424
Nantmel 27 SO 0366
Nantwich 51 SJ 6552
Nantyffyllon 28 SS 8492
Nantyglo 28 SO 1910
Naphill 20 SU 8496
Napton on the Hill 33 SP 4661
Narberth 24 SN 1114
Narborough (Leic.) 43 SP 5497
Narborough (Norf.) 46 TF 7413
Nasareth 48 SH 4749
Naseby 43 SP 6878
Nash (Bucks.) 34 SP 7734
Nash (Gwent) 29 ST 3483
Nash (Here. and Worc.) 30 SO 3062
Nash (Salop) 41 SO 6071
Nash Lee 34 SP 8408
Nassington 45 TL 0696
Nasty 35 TL 3624
Nateby (Cumbr.) 65 NY 7706
Nateby (Lancs.) 57 SD 4644
Natland 63 SD 5289
Naughton 36 TM 0249
Naunton (Glos.) 32 SP 1123
Naunton (Here. and Worc.) 32 SO 8739
Naunton Beauchamp 32 SO 9652
Naust 106 NG 8283
Navenby 54 SK 9857
Navestock 21 TQ 5397
Navestock Side 21 TQ 5697
Nawton 66 SE 6584
Nayland 36 TL 9734
Nazeing 35 TL 4106
Neacroft 10 SZ 1897
Neal's Green 43 SP 3384
Neap 113 HU 5060
Near Cotton 52 SK 0646
Neasham 72 NZ 3210
Neath 28 SS 7597
Neatishead 47 TG 3421
Nebo (Dyfed) 26 SN 5465
Nebo (Gwyn.) 48 SH 4750
Nebo (Gwyn.) 49 SH 8356
Necton 46 TF 8709
Nedd 110 NC 1332
Nedging Tye 36 TM 0149
Needham 47 TM 2281
Needham Market 37 TM 0855
Needingworth 45 TL 3472
Neen Savage 41 SO 6777
Neen Sollars 41 SO 6572
Neenton 41 SO 6487
Nefyn 48 SH 3040
Neilston 82 NS 4657
Nelson (Lancs.) 58 SD 8737
Nelson (Mid Glam.) 28 ST 1195
Nelson Village 79 NZ 2577
Nemphlar 84 NS 8544
Nempnett Thrubwell 17 ST 5360
Nenthead 71 NY 7743
Nenthorn 86 NT 6837
Nercwys 50 SJ 2260
Nereabolls 80 NR 2255
Nerston 84 NS 6457
Nesbit 87 NT 9833
Ness (Ches.) 50 SJ 3075
Ness (N Yorks.) 66 SE 6878
Ness (Shapinsay) (Ork.) 113 HY 5423
Ness (Westray) (Ork.) 113 HY 5039
Nesscliffe 40 SJ 3819
Neston (Ches.) 50 SJ 2877
Neston (Wilts.) 18 ST 8667
Nether Alderley 51 SJ 8476
Nether Blainslie 86 NT 5443
Nether Broughton 44 SK 6925
Nether Burrow 64 SD 6174
Nether Cerne 9 SY 6698
Nether Compton 9 ST 5917
Nether Crimond 105 NJ 8222
Nether Exe 8 SS 9300
Nether Handwick 98 NO 3641
Nether Haugh 59 SK 4196
Nether Heyford 34 SP 6658
Nether Howecleuch 76 NT 0312
Nether Kellet 64 SD 5067
Nether Kinmundy 105 NK 0444
Nether Kirkton 82 NS 4757
Nether Langwith 53 SK 5371
Nether Padley 53 SK 2478
Nether Poppleton 66 SE 5654
Nether Silton 66 SE 4592
Nether Stowey 16 ST 1939
Nether Wallop 11 SU 3036
Nether Wasdale 62 NY 1204
Nether Whitacre 42 SP 2393
Nether Worton 33 SP 4230
Netheravon 18 SU 1448
Netherbrae 105 NJ 7959
Netherburn 84 NS 7947
Netherbury 9 SY 4799
Netherby 70 NY 3971
Netherend 29 SO 5900
Netherfield 14 TQ 7018
Netherhampton 10 SU 1029
Netherlaw 69 NX 7445
Netherley 99 NO 8593
Nethermill 70 NY 0487
Nethermuir 105 NJ 9143
Netherplace 82 NS 5155
Netherseal 43 SK 2813
Netherstreet 18 ST 9764
Netherthird 75 NS 5818
Netherthong 59 SE 1309
Netherton (Devon.) 5 SX 8971
Netherton (Here. and Worc.) 32 SO 9941
Netherton (Northum.) 79 NT 9907
Netherton (Tays.) 98 NO 1452
Netherton (Tays.) 99 NO 5457
Netherton (W Yorks.) 59 SE 2716
Nethertown (Cumbr.) 62 NX 9807
Nethertown (Highld.) 112 ND 3578
Netherwitton 79 NZ 1090
Nethy Bridge 103 NJ 0020
Netley 11 SU 4508
Netley Marsh 11 SU 3312
Nettlebed 19 SU 7086
Nettlebridge 17 ST 6448
Nettlecombe 9 SY 5195
Nettleden 34 TL 0210
Nettlestead 14 TQ 6852
Nettlestead Green 14 TQ 6850
Nettlestone 11 SZ 6290
Nettleton 54 TF 0075
Nettleton (Lincs.) 61 TA 1000
Nettleton (Wilts.) 18 ST 8178
Neuk, The 99 NO 7397
Nevendon 22 TQ 7390
Nevern 24 SN 0840
New Abbey 70 NX 9665
New Aberdour 105 NJ 8863
New Addington 21 TQ 3863
New Alresford 11 SU 5832
New Alyth 98 NO 2447
New Annesley 53 SK 5153
New Ash Green 14 TQ 6065
New Bewick 79 NU 0620
New Bolingbroke 55 TF 3058
New Brighton 50 SJ 3093
New Brinsley 53 SK 4550
New Buckenham 47 TM 0890
New Byth 105 NJ 8254
New Clipstone 53 SK 5863
New Costessey 47 TG 1710
New Cross 27 SN 6376
New Cumnock 76 NS 6113
New Deer 105 NJ 8846
New Duston 34 SP 7162
New Earswick 66 SE 6155
New Edlington 60 SK 5399
New Ellerby 61 TA 1639
New Eltham 21 TQ 4573
New End 32 SP 0560
New Farnley 59 SE 2431
New Ferry 50 SJ 3385
New Fryston 60 SE 4526
New Galloway 69 NX 6377
New Gilston 93 NO 4207
New Hartley 79 NZ 3076
New Hedges 24 SN 1302
New Holland 61 TA 0724
New Houghton (Derby.) 53 SK 5065
New Houghton (Norf.) 46 TF 7827
New Houses 65 SD 8073
New Hutton 63 SD 5691
New Hythe 14 TQ 7159
New Inn (Gwent) 29 SO 4800
New Inn (Gwent) 29 ST 3099
New Inn (N Yorks.) 65 SD 8072
New Invention 40 SO 2976
New Kelso 101 NG 9442
New Lanark 84 NS 8742
New Lane 57 SD 4212
New Leake 55 TF 4057
New Leeds 105 NJ 9954
New Longton 57 SD 5125
New Luce 68 NX 1764
New Mains of Ury 99 NO 8787
New Marton 50 SJ 3334
New Mill (Corn.) 3 SW 4534
New Mill (Herts.) 34 SP 9212
New Mill (W Yorks.) 59 SE 1608
New Mills (Corn.) 2 SW 8952
New Mills (Derby.) 52 SK 0085
New Mills (Powys) 39 SJ 0901
New Milton 11 SZ 2495
New Moat 24 SN 0625
New Pitsligo 105 NJ 8855
New Polzeath 3 SW 9379
New Prestwick 75 NS 3424
New Quay (Dyfed) 26 SN 3859
New Rackheath 47 TG 2812
New Radnor 30 SO 2161
New Rent 63 NY 4536
New Romney 15 TR 0624
New Rossington 60 SK 6198
New Sauchie 91 NS 8993
New Scone 92 NO 1325
New Silksworth 72 NZ 3853
New Stevenston 84 NS 7659
New Tolsta 109 NB 5349
New Town (Lothian) 86 NT 4470
New Tredegar 28 SO 1403
New Tupton 53 SK 3966
New Ulva 88 NR 7080
New Walsoken 45 TF 4709
New Waltham 61 TA 2804
New Wimpole 35 TL 3450
New Winton 86 NT 4271
New Yatt 33 SP 3713
New York (Lincs.) 55 TF 2455
New York (Tyne and Wear) 72 NZ 3270
Newark (Cambs.) 45 TF 2100
Newark (Ork.) 113 HY 7242
Newark-on-Trent 54 SK 7953
Newarthill 84 NS 7859
Newbald 60 SE 9136
Newbiggin (Cumbr.) 71 NY 5649
Newbiggin (Cumbr.) 63 NY 6228
Newbiggin (Cumbr.) 64 SD 2669
Newbiggin (Durham) 65 NY 9127
Newbiggin (N Yorks.) 65 SD 9591
Newbiggin (N Yorks.) 65 SD 9985
Newbiggin-by-the-Sea 79 NZ 3187
Newbiggin-on-Lune 65 NY 7005
Newbigging (Strath.) 85 NT 0145
Newbigging (Tays.) 98 NO 2841
Newbigging (Tays.) 93 NO 4237
Newbigging (Tays.) 93 NO 4936
Newbold (Derby) 53 SK 3773
Newbold (Leic.) 43 SK 4018
Newbold Pacey 33 SP 2957
Newbold Verdon 43 SK 4403
Newbold on Avon 43 SP 4877
Newbold on Stour 33 SP 2446
Newborough (Cambs.) 45 TF 2006
Newborough (Gwyn.) 48 SH 4265
Newborough (Staffs.) 42 SK 1325
Newbottle 33 SP 5236
Newbourn 37 TM 2743
Newbridge (Clwyd) 50 SJ 2841
Newbridge (Corn.) 2 SW 4231
Newbridge (Gwent) 28 ST 2197
Newbridge (Hants.) 11 SU 2915
Newbridge (I. of W.) 11 SZ 4187
Newbridge (Lothian) 85 NT 1272
Newbridge on Wye 27 SO 0158
Newbridge-on-Usk 29 ST 3894
Newbrough 71 NY 8767
Newburgh (Fife) 92 NO 2318
Newburgh (Grampn.) 105 NJ 9925
Newburgh (Lancs.) 57 SD 4810
Newburn 72 NZ 1765
Newbury 19 SU 4666
Newby (Cumbr.) 63 NY 5921
Newby (N Yorks.) 73 NZ 5012
Newby (N Yorks.) 65 SD 7269
Newby Bridge 62 SD 3686
Newby East 71 NY 4758
Newby West 70 NY 3653
Newby Wiske 66 SE 3687
Newcastle (Gwent) 29 SO 4417
Newcastle (Salop) 40 SO 2482
Newcastle Emlyn 26 SN 3040
Newcastle upon Tyne 72 NZ 2464
Newcastle-under-Lyme 51 SJ 8445
Newcastleton 71 NY 4887
Newchapel (Dyfed) 26 SN 2239
Newchapel (Staffs.) 51 SJ 8654
Newchapel (Surrey) 13 TQ 3642
Newchurch (Dyfed) 27 SN 3724
Newchurch (Gwent) 29 ST 4597
Newchurch (I. of W.) 11 SZ 5585
Newchurch (Kent) 15 TR 0531
Newchurch (Powys) 30 SO 2150
Newchurch in Pendle 58 SD 8239
Newcott 8 ST 2309
Newdigate 12 TQ 2042
Newell Green 20 SU 8771
Newenden 14 TQ 8327
Newent 32 SO 7226
Newfield (Durham) 72 NZ 2033
Newfield (Highld.) 108 NH 7877
Newgale 24 SM 8422
Newgate 47 TG 0443
Newgate Street 35 TL 3005
Newhall (Ches.) 51 SJ 6045
Newhall (Derby.) 43 SK 2821
Newham (Gtr London) 21 TQ 4082
Newham (Northum.) 87 NU 1728
Newham Hall 87 NU 1729
Newhaven 13 TQ 4401
Newholm 73 NZ 8610
Newhouse 84 NS 7961
Newick 13 TQ 4121
Newington (Kent) 14 TQ 8665
Newington (Kent) 15 TR 1737
Newington (Oxon.) 19 SU 6196
Newland (Glos.) 29 SO 5509
Newland (Here. and Worc.) 32 SO 7948
Newland (N Yorks.) 60 SE 6824
Newlandrig 85 NT 3662
Newlands (Grampn.) 104 NJ 3051
Newlands (Northum.) 72 NZ 0955
Newlands of Geise 112 ND 0865
Newlyn 2 SW 4628
Newlyn East 2 SW 8256
Newmachar 105 NJ 8819
Newmains 84 NS 8256
Newmarket (Isle of Lewis) 109 NB 4235
Newmarket (Suff.) 36 TL 6463
Newmill (Borders) 77 NT 4510
Newmill (Grampn.) 104 NJ 4352
Newmill of Inshewan 98 NO 4260
Newmills (Lothian) 85 NT 1667
Newmiln 92 NO 1230
Newmilns 84 NS 5337
Newnham (Glos.) 29 SO 6911
Newnham (Hants) 20 SU 7054
Newnham (Herts.) 35 TL 2437
Newnham (Kent) 15 TQ 9557
Newnham (Northants.) 33 SP 5859
Newnham Bridge 41 SO 6469
Newport (Devon) 6 SS 5631
Newport (Dyfed) 24 SN 0639
Newport (Essex) 35 TL 5234
Newport (Glos.) 29 ST 7097
Newport (Gwent) 29 ST 3187
Newport (Highld.) 112 ND 1224
Newport (Humbs) 60 SE 8530
Newport (I. of W.) 11 SZ 4989
Newport (Norf.) 47 TG 5017
Newport (Salop) 41 SJ 7419
Newport Pagnell 34 SP 8743
Newport-on-Tay 93 NO 4228
Newpound Common 12 TQ 0627
Newquay (Corn.) 2 SW 8161
Newseat (Grampn.) 105 NJ 7033
Newsham (N Yorks.) 65 NZ 1010
Newsham (Northum.) 79 NZ 3079
Newsholme (Humbs.) 60 SE 7229
Newsholme (Lancs.) 65 SD 8451
Newstead (Borders) 86 NT 5634
Newstead (Northum.) 87 NU 1526
Newstead (Notts.) 53 SK 5252
Newthorpe 60 SE 4632
Newtimber Place 13 TQ 2613
Newton (Borders) 78 NT 6020
Newton (Cambs.) 45 TF 4314
Newton (Cambs.) 35 TL 4349
Newton (Ches.) 50 SJ 5059
Newton (Ches.) 60 SJ 5274
Newton (Cumbr.) 64 SD 2371
Newton (Dumf. and Galwy.) 77 NY 1194
Newton (Grampn.) 104 NJ 1663
Newton (Here. and Worc.) 30 SO 3433
Newton (Here. and Worc.) 30 SO 5054
Newton (Highld.) 110 NC 2331
Newton (Highld.) 112 ND 3449
Newton (Highld.) 103 NH 7448
Newton (Highld.) 103 NH 7866
Newton (Lancs.) 64 SD 5974
Newton (Lancs.) 58 SD 6950
Newton (Lincs.) 54 TF 0436
Newton (Lothian) 85 NT 0877
Newton (Mid Glam.) 28 SS 8377
Newton (N. Uist.) 109 NF 8877
Newton (Norf.) 46 TF 8315
Newton (Northants.) 44 SP 8883
Newton (Northum.) 72 NZ 0364
Newton (Notts.) 53 SK 6841
Newton (Staffs.) 42 SK 0325
Newton (Strath.) 84 NS 6560
Newton (Strath.) 84 NS 9331
Newton (Suff.) 36 TL 9140
Newton (W Glam.) 25 SS 6088
Newton (W Yorks.) 59 SE 4427
Newton (Warw.) 43 SP 5378
Newton Abbot 5 SX 8671
Newton Arlosh 70 NY 1955
Newton Aycliffe 72 NZ 2824
Newton Bewley 73 NZ 4626
Newton Blossomville 34 SP 9251
Newton Bromswold 44 SP 9966
Newton Burgoland 43 SK 3609
Newton Ferrers 5 SX 5447
Newton Flotman 47 TM 2198
Newton Harcourt 43 SP 6397
Newton Kyme 60 SE 4644
Newton Longville 34 SP 8431
Newton Mearns 84 NS 5456
Newton Mountain 24 SM 9807
Newton Poppleford 8 SY 0889
Newton Purcell 34 SP 6230
Newton Regis 43 SK 2707
Newton Reigny 63 NY 4731
Newton Solney 43 SK 2825
Newton St. Cyres 7 SX 8797
Newton St. Faith 47 TG 2117
Newton St. Loe 17 ST 7064
Newton St. Petrock 6 SS 4112
Newton Stacey 19 SU 4040
Newton Stewart 68 NX 4165
Newton Toney 18 SU 2140

O

P

Prescott (Salop) 248 Rottingdean

Prescott (Salop) 40 SJ 4221
Pressen 87 NT 8335
Prestatyn 49 SJ 0682
Prestbury (Ches.) 51 SJ 8976
Presteigne 30 SO 3164
Presthope 41 SO 5897
Prestleigh 17 ST 6340
Preston (Borders) 87 NT 7957
Preston (Devon.) 5 SX 8574
Preston (Dorset) 9 SY 7082
Preston (E Susx) 13 TQ 3107
Preston (Glos.) 31 SO 6734
Preston (Glos.) 32 SP 0400
Preston (Herts.) 35 TL 1724
Preston (Humbs.) 61 TA 1830
Preston (Kent) 15 TR 0260
Preston (Kent) 15 TR 2561
Preston (Lancs.) 57 SD 5329
Preston (Leic.) 44 SK 8602
Preston (Lothian) 86 NT 5977
Preston (Suff.) 36 TL 9450
Preston (Wilts.) 18 SU 0377
Preston Bagot 33 SP 1766
Preston Bissett 34 SP 6530
Preston Brockhurst 40 SJ 5324
Preston Brook 51 SJ 5680
Preston Candover 19 SU 6041
Preston Capes 33 SP 5754
Preston Gubbals 40 SJ 4819
Preston Wynne 31 SO 5646
Preston on Stour 33 SP 2049
Preston on Wye 30 SO 3842
Preston upon the Weald Moors 41 SJ 6815
Preston-under-Scar 65 SE 0791
Prestonpans 85 NT 3874
Prestwich 58 SD 8103
Prestwick (Northum.) 79 NZ 1872
Prestwick (Strath.) 75 NS 3525
Prestwood 20 SP 8700
Price Town 28 SS 9392
Prickwillow 46 TL 5982
Priddy 17 ST 5250
Priest Hutton 64 SD 5273
Priestweston 40 SO 2997
Primethorpe 43 SP 5293
Primrose Green 47 TG 0616
Primrose Hill (Cambs.) 45 TL 3889
Primrose Hill (Herts.) 35 TL 0803
Princes Risborough 34 SP 8003
Princethorpe 43 SP 4070
Princetown 5 SX 5873
Prior Muir 93 NO 5213
Priors Hardwick 33 SP 4756
Priors Marston 33 SP 4857
Priory Wood 30 SO 2545
Priston 17 ST 6960
Prittlewell 22 TQ 8787
Privett 11 SU 6726
Probus 3 SW 8947
Prudhoe 72 NZ 0962
Puckeridge 35 TL 3823
Puckington 8 ST 3718
Pucklechurch 29 ST 6976
Puddington (Ches.) 50 SJ 3273
Puddington (Devon) 7 SS 8310
Puddledock 47 TM 0592
Puddletown 9 SY 7594
Pudleston 31 SO 5659
Pudsey 59 SE 2232
Pulborough 12 TQ 0418
Puleston 41 SJ 7322
Pulford 50 SJ 3758
Pulham 9 ST 7008
Pulham Market 47 TM 1986
Pulham St. Mary 47 TM 2185
Pulloxhill 35 TL 0634
Pumpherston 85 NT 0669
Pumsaint 27 SN 6540
Puncheston 24 SN 0029
Puncknowle 9 SY 5388
Punnett's Town 13 TQ 6220
Purbrook 11 SU 6707
Purfleet 21 TQ 5578
Puriton 17 ST 3241
Purleigh 22 TL 8301
Purley (Berks.) 19 SU 6676
Purley (Gtr Lon.) 21 TQ 3161
Purlogue 40 SO 2877
Purls Bridge 45 TL 4787
Purse Caundle 9 ST 6917
Purslow 40 SO 3680
Purston Jaglin 59 SE 4319
Purton (Glos.) 29 SO 6605
Purton (Glos.) 29 SO 6904
Purton (Wilts.) 18 SU 0887
Purton Stoke 18 SU 0890
Pury End 34 SP 7045
Pusey 19 SU 3596
Putley 31 SO 6437
Putney 21 TQ 2274
Puttenham (Herts.) 34 SP 8814
Puttenham (Surrey) 20 SU 9347
Puxton 17 ST 4063
Pwll 25 SN 4801
Pwll-y-glaw 28 SS 7993
Pwllcrochan 24 SM 9202
Pwlldefaid 38 SH 1526
Pwllheli 48 SH 3735
Pwllmeyric 29 ST 5192
Pye Corner 29 ST 3485
Pye Green 41 SJ 9814
Pyecombe 13 TQ 2912
Pyle (I. of W.) 11 SZ 4879
Pyle (Mid Glam.) 28 SS 8282
Pylle 17 ST 6038
Pymore 45 TL 4986
Pyrford 20 TQ 0458
Pyrton 19 SU 6895
Pytchley 44 SP 8574
Pyworthy 6 SS 3102

Q

Quabbs 40 SO 2080
Quadring 55 TF 2233
Quainton 34 SP 7420
Quarff 113 HU 4235
Quarley 18 SU 2743
Quarndon 53 SK 3340
Quarrier's Homes 82 NS 3666
Quarrington 54 TF 0544
Quarrington Hill 72 NZ 3337
Quarry Bank (W Mids.) 41 SO 9386
Quarrybank (Ches.) 50 SJ 5465
Quarrywood 104 NJ 1864
Quarter 84 NS 7251
Quatford 41 SO 7390
Quatt 41 SO 7588
Quebec 72 NZ 1743
Quedgeley 32 SO 8114
Queen Adelaide 46 TL 5681
Queen Camel 9 ST 5924
Queen Charlton 29 ST 6366
Queenborough 23 TQ 9172
Queensbury 59 SE 1030
Queensferry (Clwyd) 50 SJ 3168
Queensferry (Lothian) 85 NT 1278
Queenzieburn 84 NS 6977
Quendale 113 HU 3713
Quendon 35 TL 5130
Queniborough 43 SK 6412
Quenington 32 SP 1404
Quernmore 64 SD 5160
Quethiock 4 SX 3164
Quidenham 46 TM 0287
Quidhampton (Hants) 19 SU 5150
Quidhampton (Wilts.) 10 SU 1030
Quilquox 105 NJ 9038
Quine's Hill 56 SC 3473
Quinton 34 SP 7754
Quoditch 6 SX 4097
Quoig 91 NN 8222
Quorndon 43 SK 5616
Quothquan 85 NS 9939

R

Raby 50 SJ 3179
Rachub 48 SH 6268
Rackenford 7 SS 8418
Rackham 12 TQ 0514
Rackheath 47 TG 2814
Racks 70 NY 0374
Rackwick (Hoy) 113 ND 1999
Radcliffe (Gtr Mches) 58 SD 7806
Radcliffe (Northum.) 79 NU 2602
Radcliffe on Trent 53 SK 6439
Radclive 34 SP 6734
Radcot 19 SU 2899
Radernie 93 NO 4609
Radford Semele 33 SP 3464
Radlett 20 TL 1600
Radley 19 SU 5398
Radnage 20 SU 7897
Radstock 17 ST 6854
Radstone 33 SP 5840
Radway 33 SP 3648
Radway Green 51 SJ 7754
Radwell 35 TL 2335
Radwinter 36 TL 6037
Radyr 28 ST 1380
Rafford 103 NJ 0656
Ragdale 43 SK 6619
Raglan 29 SO 4107
Ragnall 54 SK 8073
Rahane 90 NS 2386
Rainford 57 SD 4700
Rainham (Gtr London) 21 TQ 5282
Rainham (Kent) 14 TQ 8165
Rainhill 50 SJ 4990
Rainhill Stoops 50 SJ 5090
Rainow 51 SJ 9575
Rainton 66 SE 3775
Rainworth 53 SK 5958
Raisbeck 63 NY 6407
Rait 92 NO 2226
Raithby (Lincs.) 55 TF 3084
Raithby (Lincs.) 55 TF 3767
Rake 12 SU 8027
Ram Lane 15 TQ 9646
Ramasaig 100 NG 1644
Rame (Corn.) 2 SW 7233
Rame (Corn.) 4 SX 4249
Rampisham 9 ST 5502
Rampside 64 SD 2366
Rampton (Cambs.) 45 TL 4268
Rampton (Notts.) 54 SK 7978
Ramsbottom 58 SD 7916
Ramsbury 18 SU 2771
Ramscraigs 112 ND 1427
Ramsdean 12 SU 7021
Ramsdell 19 SU 5957
Ramsden 33 SP 3515
Ramsden Bellhouse 22 TQ 7194
Ramsden Heath 22 TQ 7195
Ramsey (Cambs.) 45 TL 2885
Ramsey (Essex) 37 TM 2130
Ramsey (I. of M.) 56 SC 4594
Ramsey Forty Foot 45 TL 3187
Ramsey Mereside 45 TL 2889
Ramsey St. Mary's 45 TL 2588
Ramsgate 15 TR 3865
Ramsgill 65 SE 1170
Ramshorn 52 SK 0845
Ranby 53 SK 6480
Rand 55 TF 1078
Randwick 32 SO 8206
Ranfurly 82 NS 3865
Rangemore 42 SK 1822
Rangeworthy 29 ST 6886
Rankinston 75 NS 4514
Ranskill 53 SK 6587
Ranton 41 SJ 8524
Ranworth 47 TG 3514
Rascarrel 69 NX 7948
Raskelf 66 SE 4971
Rassau 28 SO 1411
Rastrick 59 SE 1321
Ratagan 101 NG 9220
Ratby 43 SK 5105
Ratcliffe Culey 43 SP 3299
Ratcliffe on the Wreake 43 SK 6314
Rathen 105 NK 0060
Rathillet 93 NO 3620
Rathmell 65 SD 8059
Ratho 85 NT 1370
Rathven 104 NJ 4465
Ratley 33 SP 3847
Ratlinghope 40 SO 4096
Rattar 112 ND 2672
Ratten Row 57 SD 4241
Rattery 5 SX 7361
Rattlesden 36 TL 9758
Rattray 98 NO 1745
Rauceby 54 TF 0146
Raughton Head 70 NY 3745
Raunds 44 SP 9972
Ravenfield 53 SK 4895
Ravenglass 62 SD 0896
Raveningham 47 TM 3996
Ravenscar 67 NZ 9801
Ravensdale 56 SC 3592
Ravensden 35 TL 0754
Ravenshead 53 SK 5654
Ravensmoor 51 SJ 6250
Ravensthorpe (Northants.) 43 SP 6670
Ravensthorpe (W Yorks.) 59 SE 2220
Ravenstone (Bucks.) 34 SP 8450
Ravenstone (Leic.) 43 SK 4013
Ravenstonedale 65 NY 7203
Ravenstruther 84 NS 9245
Ravensworth 65 NZ 1407
Raw 67 NZ 9305
Rawcliffe (Humbs.) 60 SE 6822
Rawcliffe (N Yorks.) 66 SE 5855
Rawcliffe Bridge 60 SE 6921
Rawdon 59 SE 2139
Rawmarsh 59 SK 4396
Rawreth 22 TQ 7793
Rawridge 8 ST 2006
Rawtenstall 58 SD 8122
Raydon 37 TM 0438
Raylees 78 NY 9291
Rayleigh 22 TQ 8090
Rayne 22 TL 7222
Reach 36 TL 5666
Read 58 SD 7634
Reading 20 SU 7272
Reading Street 14 TQ 9230
Reagill 63 NY 6017
Rearquhar 108 NH 7492
Rearsby 43 SK 6514
Rease Heath 51 SJ 6454
Reaster 112 ND 2565
Reawick 113 HU 3244
Reay 111 NC 9664
Reculver 15 TR 2269
Red Dial 70 NY 2545
Red Roses 24 SN 2012
Red Row 79 NZ 2599
Red Street 51 SJ 8251
Red Wharf Bay (Gwyn.) 48 SH 5281
Redberth 24 SN 0804
Redbourn 35 TL 1012
Redbourne 54 SK 9699
Redbridge 21 TQ 4389
Redbrook 29 SO 5310
Redbrook Street 15 TQ 9336
Redburn (Highld.) 102 NH 5767
Redburn (Highld.) 103 NH 9447
Redcar 73 NZ 6024
Redcastle (Highld.) 102 NH 5849
Redcastle (Tays.) 99 NO 6850
Redcliff Bay 29 ST 4475
Redding 84 NS 9178
Reddingmuirhead 84 NS 9177
Reddish 51 SJ 8993
Redditch 42 SP 0468
Rede 36 TL 8055
Redenhall 47 TM 2684
Redford 99 NO 5644
Redgrave 37 TM 0478
Redheugh 98 NO 4463
Redhill (Avon) 17 ST 4962
Redhill (Grampn.) 105 NJ 6837
Redhill (Grampn.) 99 NJ 7704
Redhill (Surrey) 21 TQ 2850
Redisham 47 TM 4084
Redland (Avon) 29 ST 5875
Redland (Orkney) 113 HY 3724
Redlingfield 37 TM 1871
Redlynch (Somer.) 17 ST 6933
Redlynch (Wilts.) 10 SU 2020
Redmarley D'Abitot 32 SO 7531
Redmarshall 72 NZ 3821
Redmile 54 SK 7935
Redmire 65 SE 0491
Redmoor 4 SX 0761
Rednal 40 SJ 3628
Redpath 86 NT 5835
Redpoint (Highld.) 101 NG 7368
Redruth 2 SW 6941
Redwick (Avon) 29 ST 5485
Redwick (Gwent) 29 ST 4184
Redworth 72 NZ 2423
Reed 35 TL 3636
Reedham 47 TG 4201
Reedness 60 SE 7922
Reepham (Lincs.) 54 TF 0373
Reepham (Norf.) 47 TG 1023
Reeth 65 SE 0499
Regaby 56 SC 4397
Reiff 110 NB 9614
Reigate 21 TQ 2550
Reighton 67 TA 1275
Reiss 112 ND 3354
Rejerrah 2 SW 8055
Relubbus 2 SW 5632
Relugas 103 NH 9948
Remenham 20 SU 7784
Remenham Hill 20 SU 7883
Rempstone 43 SK 5724
Rendcomb 32 SP 0109
Rendham 37 TM 3564
Renfrew 82 NS 4967
Renhold 35 TL 0953
Renishaw 53 SK 4477
Rennington 79 NU 2118
Renton 82 NS 3878
Renwick 71 NY 5943
Repps 47 TG 4116
Repton 43 SK 3026
Resipole 95 NM 7264
Resolis 103 NH 6765
Resolven 28 SN 8202
Reston 87 NT 8861
Reswallie 99 NO 5051
Retew 3 SW 9256
Retford 54 SK 7080
Rettendon 22 TQ 7698
Revesby 55 TF 2961
Rewe 8 SX 9499
Reydon 37 TM 4977
Reymerston 46 TG 0206
Reynalton 24 SN 0909
Reynoldston 25 SS 4890
Rhandirmwyn 27 SN 7843
Rhayader 27 SN 9668
Rhedyn 48 SH 3032
Rheindown 102 NH 5147
Rhemore 95 NM 5750
Rhes-y-cae 50 SJ 1870
Rhewl (Clwyd) 50 SJ 1060
Rhewl (Clwyd) 50 SJ 1744
Rhiconich 110 NC 2552
Rhicullen 108 NH 6971
Rhifail 111 NC 7349
Rhigos 28 SN 9205
Rhilochan 108 NC 7407
Rhiwbryfdir 49 SH 6946
Rhiwderyn 28 ST 2587
Rhiwlas (Clwyd) 50 SJ 1931
Rhiwlas (Gwyn.) 48 SH 5765
Rhiwlas (Gwyn.) 49 SH 9237
Rhodes Minnis 15 TR 1542
Rhodesia 53 SK 5680
Rhodiad 24 SM 7627
Rhonehouse or Kelton Hill 69 NX 7459
Rhoose 28 ST 0666
Rhos (Dyfed) 26 SN 3835
Rhos (W Glam.) 25 SN 7303
Rhos-fawr 48 SH 3838
Rhos-on-Sea 50 SH 8480
Rhos-y-gwaliau 49 SH 9434
Rhos-y-llan 48 SH 2337
Rhoscolyn 48 SH 2675
Rhoscrowther 24 SM 9002
Rhosesmor 50 SJ 2168
Rhosgadfan 48 SH 5057
Rhosgoch (Gwyn.) 48 SH 4189
Rhoslan 48 SH 4841
Rhoslefain 38 SH 5705
Rhosllanerchrugog 50 SJ 2946
Rhosmeirch 48 SH 4677
Rhosneigr 48 SH 3172
Rhosnesni 50 SJ 3451
Rhossili 25 SS 4188
Rhosson 24 SM 7225
Rhostryfan 48 SH 4958
Rhostyllen 50 SJ 3148
Rhosybol 43 SH 4288
Rhu (Strath.) 90 NS 2783
Rhualit 49 SJ 0774
Rhuddlan 49 SJ 0277
Rhulen 30 SO 1349
Rhunahaorine 81 NR 7048
Rhyd (Gwyn.) 48 SH 6341
Rhyd-Ddu 48 SH 5652
Rhyd-lydan 49 SH 8950
Rhyd-y-clafdy 48 SH 3235
Rhyd-y-meirch 29 SO 3107
Rhyd-yr-onnen 38 SH 6102
Rhydargaeau 25 SN 4326
Rhydcymerau 25 SN 5738
Rhydd 32 SO 8345
Rhydding 25 SS 7498
Rhydlewis 26 SN 3447
Rhydlios 48 SH 1830
Rhydowen 26 SN 4445
Rhydrosser 26 SN 5667
Rhydtalog 50 SJ 2354
Rhydycroesau 50 SJ 2330
Rhydyfelin (Dyfed) 26 SN 5979
Rhydyfro 25 SN 7105
Rhydymain 39 SH 7922
Rhydymwyn 50 SJ 2066
Rhyl 49 SJ 0181
Rhymney 28 SO 1107
Rhynd 92 NO 1520
Rhynie (Grampn.) 104 NJ 4927
Rhynie (Highld.) 108 NH 8578
Ribbesford 41 SO 7874
Ribbleton 57 SD 5630
Ribchester 58 SD 6435
Ribigill 111 NC 5854
Riby 61 TA 1807
Riccall 60 SE 6237
Riccarton 82 NS 4235
Richards Castle 40 SO 4969
Richmond 65 NZ 1701
Richmond upon Thames 21 TQ 1874
Rickarton 99 NO 8188
Rickinghall Inferior 37 TM 0475
Rickinghall Superior 37 TM 0475
Rickling 35 TL 4931
Rickmansworth 20 TQ 0594
Riddell 78 NT 5124
Riddlecombe 6 SS 6013
Riddlesden 59 SE 0742
Ridge (Dorset) 10 SY 9386
Ridge (Herts.) 21 TL 2100
Ridge (Wilts.) 10 ST 9531
Ridge Lane 43 SP 2994
Ridgehill (Avon) 17 ST 5362
Ridgemont 34 SP 9736
Ridgeway Cross 32 SO 7147
Ridgewell 36 TL 7340
Ridgewood 13 TQ 4719
Riding Mill 72 NZ 0161
Ridlington (Leic.) 44 SK 8402
Ridlington (Norf.) 47 TG 3430
Ridsdale 78 NY 9084
Rienachachait 110 NC 0530
Rievaulx 66 SE 5785
Rigg 70 NY 2966
Riggend 84 NS 7670
Righoul 103 NH 8851
Rigside 84 NS 8734
Rileyhill 42 SK 1115
Rilla Mill 4 SX 2973
Rillington 67 SE 8574
Rimington 58 SD 8045
Rimpton 9 ST 6021
Rimswell 61 TA 3128
Rinaston 24 SM 9825
Ring's End 45 TF 3902
Ringford 69 NX 6857
Ringland 47 TG 1313
Ringmer 13 TQ 4412
Ringmore 5 SX 6545
Ringorm 104 NJ 2644
Ringsfield 47 TM 4088
Ringsfield Corner 47 TM 4187
Ringshall (Bucks.) 34 SP 9814
Ringshall (Suff.) 37 TM 0452
Ringshall Stocks 37 TM 0551
Ringstead (Norf.) 46 TF 7040
Ringstead (Northants.) 44 SP 9875
Ringwood 10 SU 1405
Ringwould 15 TR 3648
Rinsey 2 SW 5927
Ripe 13 TQ 5010
Ripley (Derby.) 53 SK 3950
Ripley (Hants.) 10 SZ 1698
Ripley (N Yorks.) 66 SE 2860
Ripley (Surrey) 20 TQ 0556
Riplingham 61 SE 9631
Ripon 66 SE 3171
Rippingale 45 TF 0927
Ripple (Here. and Worc.) 32 SO 8737
Ripple (Kent) 15 TR 3550
Ripponden 59 SE 0319
Risabus 80 NR 3143
Risbury 31 SO 5455
Risby (Suff.) 36 TL 7966
Risca 28 ST 2391
Rise 61 TA 1541
Risegate 45 TF 2029
Riseley (Beds.) 35 TL 0463
Riseley (Berks.) 20 SU 7263
Rishangles 37 TM 1568
Rishton 58 SD 7229
Rishworth 59 SE 0317
Risley 53 SK 4635
Risplith 66 SE 2467
Rispond 110 NC 4565
Rivar 19 SU 3161
Rivenhall End 22 TL 8316
Riverhead 21 TQ 5156
Rivington 58 SD 6214
Roa Island 64 SD 2364
Roade 34 SP 7551
Roadmeetings 84 NS 8649
Roadside 112 ND 1560
Roadside of Kinneff 99 NO 8476
Roadwater 16 ST 0238
Roag 100 NG 2744
Roath 28 ST 1978
Roberton (Borders) 77 NT 4314
Roberton (Strath.) 76 NS 9428
Robertsbridge 14 TQ 7323
Roberttown 59 SE 1922
Robeston Cross 24 SM 8809
Robeston Wathen 24 SN 0815
Robin Hood's Bay 67 NZ 9505
Roborough 6 SS 5717
Roby 50 SJ 4291
Roby Mill 57 SD 5106
Rocester 52 SK 1039
Roch 24 SM 8821
Rochdale 58 SD 8913
Roche 3 SW 9860
Rochester (Kent) 14 TQ 7467
Rochester (Northum.) 78 NY 8397
Rochford (Essex) 22 TQ 8790
Rochford (Here. and Worc.) 41 SO 6268
Rock (Corn.) 3 SW 9475
Rock (Here. and Worc.) 41 SO 7371
Rock (Northum.) 79 NU 2020
Rock Ferry 50 SJ 3386
Rockbeare 8 SY 0195
Rockbourne 10 SU 1118
Rockcliffe (Cumbr.) 70 NY 3561
Rockcliffe (Dumf. and Galwy.) 69 NX 8553
Rockfield (Gwent) 29 SO 4814
Rockfield (Highld.) 108 NH 9282
Rockhampton 29 ST 6593
Rockingham 44 SP 8691
Rockland All Saints 46 TL 9896
Rockland St. Mary 47 TG 3104
Rockland St. Peter 46 TL 9897
Rockley 18 SU 1571
Rockwell End 20 SU 7988
Rodbourne 18 ST 9383
Rodd 30 SO 3162
Roddam 79 NU 0220
Rodden 9 SY 6184
Rode 18 ST 8053
Rode Heath (Ches.) 51 SJ 8056
Rodeheath (Ches.) 51 SJ 8766
Rodel 113 NG 0483
Roden 41 SJ 5716
Rodhuish 16 ST 0139
Rodington 41 SJ 5814
Rodley 32 SO 7411
Rodmarton 18 ST 9397
Rodmell 13 TQ 4106
Rodmersham 14 TQ 9261
Rodney Stoke 17 ST 4849
Rodsley 53 SK 2040
Roecliffe 66 SE 3765
Roehampton 21 TQ 2373
Roewen 49 SH 7571
Roffey 12 TQ 1931
Rogart 108 NC 7303
Rogate 12 SU 8023
Rogerstone 28 ST 2688
Rogerton 84 NS 6256
Rogiet 29 ST 4587
Roker 72 NZ 4059
Rollesby 47 TG 4415
Rolleston (Leic.) 44 SK 7300
Rolleston (Notts.) 54 SK 7452
Rolleston (Staffs.) 42 SK 2337
Rolston 61 TA 2145
Rolvenden 14 TQ 8431
Rolvenden Layne 14 TQ 8530
Romaldkirk 72 NY 9921
Romanby 66 SE 3693
Romannobridge 85 NT 1547
Romansleigh 7 SS 7220
Romford 21 TQ 5188
Romiley 51 SJ 9390
Romsey 11 SU 3521
Romsley (Here. and Worc.) 41 SO 9679
Romsley (Salop) 41 SO 7883
Ronague 56 SC 2472
Rookhope 71 NY 9342
Rookley 11 SZ 5084
Rooks Bridge 17 ST 3752
Roos 61 TA 2830
Rootpark 84 NS 9554
Ropley 11 SU 6431
Ropley Dean 11 SU 6331
Ropsley 54 SK 9834
Rora 105 NK 0650
Rorrington 40 SJ 3000
Rose 2 SW 7754
Rose Ash 7 SS 7821
Roseacre 57 SD 4336
Rosebank 84 NS 8049
Rosebrough 79 NU 1326
Rosedale Abbey 66 SE 7296
Roseden 79 NU 0321
Rosehearty 105 NJ 9367
Rosehill 41 SJ 6630
Roseisle 104 NJ 1367
Rosemarket 24 SM 9508
Rosemarkie 103 NH 7357
Rosemary Lane 8 ST 1514
Rosemount (Strath.) 75 NS 3729
Rosemount (Tays) 98 NO 2043
Rosewell 85 NT 2862
Roseworthy 2 SW 6139
Rosgill 63 NY 5316
Roshven 95 NM 7078
Roskhill 100 NG 2745
Rosley 70 NY 3245
Roslin 85 NT 2663
Rosliston 42 SK 2416
Rosneath 82 NS 2583
Ross (Dumf. and Galwy.) 69 NX 6444
Ross (Northum.) 87 NU 1336
Ross (Tays.) 91 NN 7621
Ross-on-Wye 29 SO 6024
Rossett 50 SJ 3657
Rossington 60 SK 6298
Rosskeen 103 NH 6869
Roster 112 ND 2639
Rostherne 51 SJ 7483
Rosthwaite 62 NY 2514
Roston 52 SK 1241
Rosyth 85 NT 1183
Rothbury 79 NU 0601
Rotherby 43 SK 6716
Rotherfield 13 TQ 5529
Rotherfield Greys 20 SU 7282
Rotherfield Peppard 20 SU 7081
Rotherham 53 SK 4492
Rothersthorpe 34 SP 7156
Rotherwick 20 SU 7156
Rothes 104 NJ 2749
Rothesay 81 NS 0864
Rothiebrisbane 105 NJ 7437
Rothienorman 105 NJ 7235
Rothiesholm 113 HY 6123
Rothley 43 SK 5812
Rothmaise 105 NJ 6832
Rothwell (Lincs.) 61 TF 1599
Rothwell (Northants.) 44 SP 8181
Rothwell (W Yorks.) 59 SE 3428
Rotsea 67 TA 0651
Rottal 98 NO 3769
Rottingdean 13 TQ 3602

Rottington 249 Shirburn

ottington 62 NX 9613
oud 11 SZ 5280
ough Close 51 SJ 9239
ougham 46 TF 8320
ougham Green 36 TL 9061
oughburn 96 NN 3781
oughlee 58 SD 8440
oughley 42 SP 1399
oughsike 71 NY 5275
oughton (Lincs.) 55 TF 2364
oughton (Norf.) 47 TG 2136
oughton (Salop) 41 SO 7594
oundhay 59 SE 3235
oundstreet Common 12 TQ 0528
oundway 18 SU 0163
ounton 66 NZ 4103
ous Lench 32 SP 0153
ousdon 8 SY 2990
outenburn 82 NS 1961
outh 61 TA 0842
ow (Corn.) 4 SX 0976
ow (Cumbr.) 63 SD 4589
owanburn 70 NY 4177
owde 18 ST 9762
owfoot 71 NY 6860
owhedge 23 TM 0221
owhook 12 TQ 1234
owington 42 SP 2069
owland 53 SK 2072
owland's Castle 12 SU 7310
owland's Gill 72 NZ 1658
owledge 12 SU 8243
owley (Humbs.) 61 SE 9732
owley (Salop) 40 SJ 3006
owley Regis 41 SO 9787
owlstone 29 SO 3727
owly 12 TQ 0441
owney Green 42 SP 0471
ownhams 11 SU 3816
owsham 34 SP 8518
owsley 53 SK 2566
owston 54 TF 0856
owton (Ches.) 50 SJ 4464
owton (Salop) 41 SJ 6119
oxburgh 86 NT 6930
oxby (Humbs.) 60 SE 9217
oxby (N Yorks) 73 NZ 7616
oxton 35 TL 1554
oxwell 22 TL 6408
oy Bridge 96 NN 2781
oyal Lemington Spa 43 SP 3166
oyal Tunbridge Wells 13 TQ 5839
oydon (Essex) 35 TL 4009
oydon (Norf.) 46 TF 7022
oydon (Norf.) 37 TM 0980
oyston (Herts.) 35 TL 3541
oyston (S Yorks.) 59 SE 3611
oyton 58 SD 9207
uabon 50 SJ 3043
uaig 94 NM 0647
uan Lanihorne 3 SW 8942
uan Minor 2 SW 7115
uardean 29 SO 6117
uardean Woodside 29 SO 6216
ubery 41 SO 9777
uckcroft 71 NY 5344
uckinge 15 TR 0233
uckland 55 TF 3378
uckley 40 SJ 5300
uddington 53 SK 5733
udge 18 ST 8252
udgeway 29 ST 6286
udgwick 12 TQ 0934
udhall 29 SO 6225
udry 28 ST 1986
udston 67 TA 0967
udyard 51 SJ 9557
ufford 57 SD 4515
ufforth 66 SE 5251
ugby 43 SP 5075
ugeley 42 SK 0418
uilick 102 NH 5046
uishton 8 ST 2624
uislip 20 TQ 0987
umbling Bridge 92 NT 0199
umburgh 47 TM 3581
umford 3 SW 8970
umney 28 ST 2179
uncorn 50 SJ 5182
uncton 12 SU 8802
uncton Holme 46 TF 6109
unfold 20 SU 8747
unhall 47 TG 0507
unham 47 TG 4610
unnington 8 ST 1121
unswick 73 NZ 8016
untaleave 98 NO 2867
unwell 22 TQ 7494
ush Green 21 TQ 5187
ushall (Here. and Worc.) 31 SO 6434
ushall (Norf.) 47 TM 1982
ushall (W Mids.) 42 SK 0201
ushall (Wilts.) 18 SU 1255
ushbrooke 36 TL 8961
ushbury 40 SO 5191
ushden (Herts.) 35 TL 3031
ushden (Northants.) 44 SP 9566
ushford 46 TL 9281
ushlake Green 13 TQ 6218
ushmere 47 TM 4987
ushmere St. Andrew 37 TM 2046
ushmoor 12 SU 8740
ushock 41 SO 8871
usholme 58 SJ 8494
ushton (Ches.) 51 SJ 5863
ushton (Northants) 44 SP 8483
ushton (Salop) 41 SJ 6008
ushton Spencer 51 SJ 9363
ushwick 32 SO 8353
ushyford 72 NZ 2828
uskie 90 NN 6200
uskington 54 TF 0850
usland 62 SD 3488
usper 13 TQ 2037
uspidge 29 SO 6512
ussell's Water 20 SU 7089
ustington 12 TQ 0502
uston Parva 67 TA 0661
uswarp 67 NZ 8809
utherford 86 NT 6530
utherglen 84 NS 6161
uthernbridge 4 SX 0166
uthin 50 SJ 1257
uthrieston 99 NJ 9204
uthven (Grampn.) 104 NJ 5046
uthven (Tays.) 98 NO 2848
uthvoes 3 SW 9360
uthwell 70 NY 1067
uyton-XI-Towns 40 SJ 3922
yal 79 NZ 0174
yal Fold 58 SD 6621
yall 9 SY 4094
yarsh 14 TQ 6659
ydal 62 NY 3606
Ryde 11 SZ 5992
Rye 14 TQ 9220
Rye Foreign 14 TQ 8822
Rye Harbour 15 TQ 9419
Ryhall 44 TF 0311
Ryhill 59 SE 3814
Ryhope 72 NZ 4152
Rylstone 65 SD 9758
Ryme Intrinseca 9 ST 5810
Ryther 60 SE 5539
Ryton (Glos.) 32 SO 7232
Ryton (N Yorks.) 67 SE 7975
Ryton (Salop) 41 SJ 7502
Ryton (Tyne and wear) 72 NZ 1564
Ryton-on-Dunsmore 43 SP 3874

S

Sabden 58 SD 7737
Sacombe 35 TL 3419
Sacriston 72 NZ 2447
Sadberge 72 NZ 3416
Saddell 81 NR 7832
Saddington 43 SP 6591
Saddle Bow 46 TF 6015
Saffron Walden 35 TL 5438
Saham Toney 46 TF 9002
Saighton 50 SJ 4462
Saint Hill 13 TQ 3835
Saintbury 32 SP 1139
Salcombe 5 SX 7338
Salcombe Regis 8 SY 1488
Salcott 23 TL 9413
Sale 51 SJ 7990
Sale Green 32 SO 9358
Saleby 55 TF 4578
Salehurst 14 TQ 7424
Salem (Dyfed) 25 SN 6226
Salem (Dyfed) 39 SN 6684
Salem (Gwyn.) 48 SH 5456
Salen (Highld.) 95 NM 6864
Salen (Island of Mull) 95 NM 5743
Salesbury 58 SD 6732
Salford (Beds.) 34 SP 9339
Salford (Gtr Mches.) 58 SJ 7796
Salford (Oxon.) 33 SP 2828
Salford Priors 32 SP 0751
Salfords 21 TQ 2846
Salhouse 47 TG 3114
Saline 92 NT 0292
Salisbury 10 SU 1429
Sall 47 TG 1024
Sallachy (Highld.) 101 NG 9130
Salmonby 55 TF 3273
Salmond's Muir 93 NO 5837
Salperton 32 SP 0720
Salph End 35 TL 0752
Salsburgh 84 NS 8262
Salt 41 SJ 0994
Saltash 4 SX 4258
Saltburn 103 NH 7269
Saltburn-by-the-Sea 73 NZ 6621
Saltby 44 SK 8426
Saltcoats 82 NS 2441
Saltdean 13 TQ 3802
Salter 64 SD 6063
Salterforth 58 SD 8845
Salterswall 51 SJ 6267
Saltfleet 55 TF 4593
Saltfleetby All Saints 55 TF 4590
Saltfleetby St. Clements 55 TF 4591
Saltfleetby St. Peter 55 TF 4389
Saltford 29 ST 6867
Salthouse 47 TG 0743
Saltmarshe 60 SE 7824
Saltness 113 ND 2790
Saltney 50 SJ 3864
Salton 66 SE 7180
Saltwick 79 NZ 1780
Saltwood 15 TR 1536
Salwarpe 32 SO 8762
Salwayash 9 SY 4596
Sambourne 32 SP 0561
Sambrook 41 SJ 7124
Samlesbury 57 SD 5829
Samlesbury Bottoms 58 SD 6229
Sampford Arundel 8 ST 1018
Sampford Brett 16 ST 0940
Sampford Courtnay 6 SS 6301
Sampford Peverell 8 ST 0214
Sampford Spiney 5 SX 5372
Samuelston 86 NT 4870
Sanaigmore 80 NR 2370
Sancreed 2 SW 4029
Sancton 60 SE 8939
Sand 113 HU 3447
Sand Hutton (N Yorks.) 66 SE 6958
Sand Side 62 SD 2282
Sandbach 51 SJ 7560
Sandbank 82 NS 1580
Sandbanks 10 SZ 0487
Sandend 104 NJ 5566
Sanderstead 21 TQ 3461
Sandford (Avon) 17 ST 4159
Sandford (Cumbr.) 63 NY 7216
Sandford (Devon) 7 SS 8202
Sandford (Dorset) 10 SY 9289
Sandford (Strath.) 84 NS 7143
Sandford Orcas 9 ST 6220
Sandford St. Martin 33 SP 4226
Sandford-on-Thames 33 SP 5301
Sandfordhill 105 NK 1141
Sandgarth 113 HY 5215
Sandgate 15 TR 2035
Sandgreen 69 NX 5752
Sandhaven 105 NJ 9667
Sandhead 68 NX 0949
Sandhoe 72 NY 9766
Sandholme (Humbs.) 60 SE 8230
Sandholme (Lincs.) 55 TF 3337
Sandhurst (Berks.) 20 SU 8361
Sandhurst (Glos.) 32 SO 8223
Sandhurst (Kent) 14 TQ 8028
Sandhutton (N Yorks.) 66 SE 3881
Sandiacre 53 SK 4736
Sandilands 55 TF 5280
Sandiway 51 SJ 6070
Sandleheath 10 SU 1214
Sandleigh 33 SP 4501
Sandling 14 TQ 7558
Sandness 113 HU 1956
Sandon (Essex) 22 TL 7404
Sandon (Herts) 35 TL 3234
Sandon (Staffs.) 41 SJ 9429
Sandown 11 SZ 5984
Sandplace 4 SX 2457
Sandridge (Herts.) 35 TL 1710
Sandridge (Wilts.) 18 ST 9465
Sandringham 46 TF 6928
Sandsend 73 NZ 8512
Sandtoft 60 SE 7408
Sandvoe 113 HU 3692
Sandwich 15 TR 3358
Sandwick (Shetld) 113 HU 4323
Sandy 35 TL 1649
Sandy Lane 18 ST 9668
Sandycroft 50 SJ 3366
Sandygate 56 SC 3797
Sangobeg 110 NC 4266
Sanna 95 NM 4569
Sanquhar 76 NS 7809
Santon Bridge 62 NY 1001
Santon Downham 46 TL 8187
Sapcote 43 SP 4893
Sapey Common 32 SO 7064
Sapiston 36 TL 9175
Sapperton (Glos.) 32 SO 9403
Sapperton (Lincs.) 54 TF 0133
Saracen's Head 45 TF 3427
Sarclet 112 ND 3443
Sarisbury 11 SU 5008
Sarn (Mid Glam.) 28 SS 9083
Sarn (Powys) 40 SO 2090
Sarn Meyllteyrn 48 SH 2432
Sarn-bach 38 SH 3026
Sarnau (Dyfed) 25 SN 3151
Sarnau (Dyfed) 26 SN 3318
Sarnau (Gwyn.) 49 SH 9739
Sarnau (Powys) 40 SJ 2315
Sarnesfield 30 SO 3750
Saron (Dyfed) 26 SN 3738
Saron (Dyfed) 25 SN 6012
Sarratt 20 TQ 0499
Sarre 15 TR 2565
Sarsden 33 SP 2822
Satley 72 NZ 1143
Satterleigh 7 SS 6622
Satterthwaite 62 SD 3392
Sauchchrie 75 NS 3014
Sauchen 105 NJ 7010
Saucher 92 NO 1933
Sauchieburn 99 NO 6669
Saughall 50 SJ 3669
Saughtree 78 NY 5696
Saul 32 SO 7409
Saundby 54 SK 7888
Saundersfoot 24 SN 1304
Saunderton 34 SP 7901
Saunton 6 SS 4537
Sausthorpe 55 TF 3869
Savalmore 108 NC 5908
Sawbridgeworth 35 TL 4814
Sawdon 67 SE 9485
Sawley (Lancs.) 58 SD 7746
Sawley (N Yorks.) 66 SE 2467
Sawrey (Near) 62 SD 3694
Sawston 35 TL 4849
Sawtry 45 TL 1683
Saxby (Leic.) 44 SK 8220
Saxby (Lincs.) 54 TF 0086
Saxby All Saints 61 SE 9816
Saxelbye 44 SK 7021
Saxilby 54 SK 8875
Saxlingham 46 TG 0239
Saxlingham Nethergate 47 TM 2397
Saxmundham 37 TM 3863
Saxon Street 36 TL 6859
Saxondale 53 SK 6839
Saxtead 37 TM 2665
Saxtead Green 37 TM 2564
Saxthorpe 47 TG 1130
Saxton 60 SE 4736
Sayers Common 13 TQ 2618
Scackleton 66 SE 6472
Scaftworth 53 SK 6691
Scagglethorpe 67 SE 8372
Scalasaig 88 NR 3894
Scalby 67 TA 0090
Scaldwell 44 SP 7672
Scale Houses 71 NY 5845
Scaleby 71 NY 4563
Scalebyhill 70 NY 4363
Scales (Cumbr.) 64 SD 2772
Scalford 44 SK 7624
Scalloway 113 HU 4039
Scamblesby 55 TF 2778
Scampston 67 SE 8575
Scampton 54 SK 9479
Scar 113 HY 6745
Scarborough 67 TA 0388
Scarcliffe 53 SK 4968
Scarcroft 59 SE 3540
Scardroy 102 NH 2151
Scarfskerry 112 ND 2673
Scargill 72 NZ 0510
Scarinish 94 NM 0444
Scarisbrick 57 SD 3713
Scarning 46 TF 9512
Scarrington 54 SK 7341
Scarth Hill 57 SD 4206
Scartho 61 TA 2606
Scarwell 113 HY 2421
Scaur or Kippford 69 NX 8355
Scawby 61 SE 9605
Scawton 66 SE 5483
Scayne's Hill 13 TQ 3723
Scethrog 28 SO 1025
Scholes (W Yorks.) 59 SE 1507
Scholes (W Yorks.) 59 SE 3736
Sciberscross 108 NC 7810
Scleddau 24 SM 9434
Sco Ruston 47 TG 2821
Scole 37 TM 1579
Scolton 24 SM 9922
Sconser 100 NG 5232
Scopwick 54 TF 0658
Scorborough 61 TA 0145
Scorrier 2 SW 7244
Scorton (Lancs.) 57 SD 5048
Scorton (N Yorks.) 66 NZ 2400
Scotby 71 NY 4454
Scotforth 64 SD 4759
Scothern 54 TF 0377
Scotland Gate 79 NZ 2584
Scotlandwell 92 NO 1801
Scots' Gap 79 NZ 0486
Scotsburn 108 NH 7275
Scotscraig 93 NO 4428
Scotstown 95 NM 8263
Scotter 60 SE 8800
Scotterthorpe 60 SE 8701
Scotton (Lincs.) 60 SK 8899
Scotton (N Yorks.) 65 SE 1895
Scotton (N Yorks.) 66 SE 3259
Scottow 47 TG 2623
Scoughall 86 NT 6183
Scoulton 46 TF 9800
Scourie 110 NC 1544
Scousburgh 113 HU 3717
Scrabster 112 ND 0970
Scrainwood 79 NT 9909
Scrane End 55 TF 3841
Scraptoft 43 SK 6405
Scratby 47 TG 5115
Scrayingham 66 SE 7360
Scredington 55 TF 0940
Scremby 55 TF 4467
Scremerston 87 NU 0049
Screveton 54 SK 7343
Scriven 66 SE 3458
Scrooby 53 SK 6590
Scropton 52 SK 1930
Scrub Hill 55 TF 2355
Scruton 66 SE 2992
Sculthorpe 46 TF 8931
Scunthorpe 60 SE 8910
Sea Palling 47 TG 4327
Seaborough 9 ST 4205
Seacombe 50 SJ 3190
Seacroft 55 TF 5660
Seafield 85 NT 0066
Seaford 13 TV 4899
Seaforth 50 SJ 3297
Seagrave 43 SK 6117
Seaham 72 NZ 4149
Seahouses 87 NU 2132
Seal 21 TQ 5556
Sealand 50 SJ 3268
Seamer (N Yorks.) 73 NZ 4910
Seamer (N Yorks.) 67 TA 0183
Seamill 82 NS 2047
Searby 61 TA 0605
Seasalter 15 TR 0864
Seascale 62 NY 0301
Seathwaite (Cumbr.) 62 SD 2296
Seaton (Corn.) 4 SX 3054
Seaton (Cumbr.) 62 NY 0130
Seaton (Devon.) 8 SY 2490
Seaton (Durham) 72 NZ 4049
Seaton (Humbs.) 61 TA 1646
Seaton (Leic.) 44 SP 9098
Seaton (Northum.) 79 NZ 3276
Seaton Carew 73 NZ 5229
Seaton Delaval 79 NZ 3075
Seaton Ross 60 SE 7741
Seaton Sluice 79 NZ 3376
Seave Green 66 NZ 5600
Seaview Seavington St. Mary 9 ST 3914
Seavington St. Michael 9 ST 4015
Sebergham 70 NY 3541
Seckington 42 SK 2607
Sedbergh 63 SD 6592
Sedbusk 65 SD 8891
Sedgeberrow 32 SP 0238
Sedgebrook 54 SK 8537
Sedgefield 72 NZ 3528
Sedgeford 46 TF 7136
Sedgehill 10 ST 8627
Sedgley 41 SO 9193
Sedgwick 63 SD 5186
Sedlescombe 14 TQ 7818
Seend 18 ST 9460
Seend Cleeve 18 ST 9260
Seer Green 20 SU 9691
Seething 47 TM 3197
Sefton 57 SD 3500
Seghill 79 NZ 2874
Seighford 41 SJ 8725
Seisdon 41 SO 8394
Selattyn 50 SJ 2633
Selborne 12 SU 7433
Selby 60 SE 6132
Selham 12 SU 9320
Selkirk 77 NT 4728
Sellack 29 SO 5627
Sellindge 15 TR 0938
Selling 15 TR 0358
Sells Green 18 ST 9462
Selly Oak 42 SP 0482
Selmeston 13 TQ 5007
Selsden 21 TQ 3562
Selsey 12 SZ 8593
Selsfield Common 13 TQ 3434
Selston 53 SK 4553
Selworthy 16 SS 9146
Semer 36 TM 0046
Semington 18 ST 8960
Semley 10 ST 8926
Send 20 TQ 0155
Senghenydd 28 ST 1191
Sennen 2 SW 3525
Sennen Cove 2 SW 3425
Sennybridge 28 SN 9228
Sessay 66 SE 4575
Setchey 46 TF 6313
Setley 11 SU 3000
Setter 113 HU 4683
Settle 65 SD 8263
Settrington 67 SE 8370
Seven Kings 21 TQ 4586
Seven Sisters 28 SN 8108
Sevenhampton (Glos.) 32 SP 0321
Sevenhampton (Wilts.) 18 SU 2090
Sevenoaks 21 TQ 5355
Sevenoaks Weald 21 TQ 5351
Severn Beach 29 ST 5384
Severn Stoke 32 SO 8544
Sevington 15 TR 0340
Sewards End 36 TL 5738
Sewerby 67 TA 2068
Seworgan 2 SW 7030
Sewstern 44 SK 8821
Sezincote 33 SP 1731
Shabbington 34 SP 6606
Shackerstone 43 SK 3706
Shackleford 20 SU 9345
Shadforth 72 NZ 3441
Shadingfield 47 TM 4383
Shadoxhurst 15 TQ 9737
Shaftesbury 10 ST 8622
Shafton 59 SE 3810
Shalbourne 19 SU 3163
Shalcombe 11 SZ 3985
Shalden 20 SU 6941
Shaldon 8 SX 9272
Shalfleet 11 SZ 4189
Shalford (Essex) 22 TL 7229
Shalford (Surrey) 20 TQ 0047
Shalford Green 22 TL 7127
Shallowford 7 SS 7144
Shalstone 34 SP 6436
Shamley Green 12 TQ 0344
Shandon 90 NS 2586
Shangton 44 SP 7196
Shanklin 11 SZ 5881
Shap 63 NY 5615
Shapwick (Somer.) 17 ST 4137
Shardlow 53 SK 4330
Shareshill 41 SJ 9406
Sharlston 59 SE 3818
Sharnbrook 34 SP 9959
Sharnford 43 SP 4891
Sharoe Green 57 SD 5332
Sharow 66 SE 3271
Sharpenhoe 35 TL 0630
Sharperton 79 NT 9503
Sharpness 29 SO 6702
Sharpthorne 13 TQ 3732
Sharrington 47 TG 0337
Shatterford 41 SO 7980
Shaugh Prior 5 SX 5463
Shaughlaige-e-Caine 56 SC 3187
Shavington 51 SJ 6951
Shaw (Gtr Mches.) 58 SD 9308
Shaw (Wilts.) 18 ST 8865
Shaw Mills 66 SE 2562
Shawbost 109 NB 2646
Shawbury 40 SJ 5521
Shawell 43 SP 5480
Shawford 11 SU 4624
Shawforth 58 SD 8920
Shawhead 69 NX 8675
Shawwood 75 NS 5325
Shear Cross 18 ST 8642
Shearsby 43 SP 6291
Shebbear 6 SS 4309
Shebdon 41 SJ 7525
Shebster 112 ND 0164
Shedfield 11 SU 5512
Sheen 52 SK 1161
Sheepscombe 32 SO 8910
Sheepstor 5 SX 5567
Sheepwash 6 SS 4806
Sheepy Magna 43 SK 3201
Sheepy Parva 43 SK 3301
Sheering 22 TL 5013
Sheerness 23 TQ 9274
Sheet 12 SU 7524
Sheffield 53 SK 3587
Sheffield Bottom 19 SU 6469
Shefford 35 TL 1439
Sheigra 110 NC 1861
Sheinton 41 SJ 6104
Shelderton 40 SO 4077
Sheldon (Derby.) 52 SK 1768
Sheldon (Devon.) 8 ST 1208
Sheldon (W Mids.) 42 SP 1584
Sheldwich 15 TR 0156
Shelf 59 SE 1228
Shelfanger 47 TM 1083
Shelfield 42 SK 0302
Shelford 53 SK 6642
Shelley 59 SE 2011
Shellingford 19 SU 3193
Shellow Bowells 22 TL 6108
Shelsley Beauchamp 32 SO 7362
Shelsley Walsh 32 SO 7263
Shelton (Beds.) 34 TL 0368
Shelton (Norf.) 47 TM 2191
Shelton (Notts.) 54 SK 7744
Shelton Green 47 TM 2390
Shelve 40 SO 3399
Shelwick 31 SO 5243
Shenfield 22 TQ 6094
Shenington 33 SP 3642
Shenley 35 TL 1900
Shenley Brook End 34 SP 8335
Shenley Church End 34 SP 8336
Shenleybury 35 TL 1802
Shenmore 30 SO 3938
Shenstone (Here. and Worc.) 41 SO 8673
Shenstone (Staffs.) 42 SK 1004
Shenton 43 SK 3800
Shenval 104 NJ 2129
Shepherd's Green 20 SU 7183
Shepherdswell or Sibertswold 15 TR 2548
Shepley 59 SE 1909
Shepperdine 29 ST 6195
Shepperton 20 TQ 0867
Shepreth 35 TL 3947
Shepshed 43 SK 4719
Shepton Beauchamp 9 ST 4016
Shepton Mallet 17 ST 6143
Shepton Montague 17 ST 6731
Shepway 14 TQ 7753
Sheraton 73 NZ 4334
Sherborne (Dorset) 9 ST 6316
Sherborne (Glos.) 33 SP 1714
Sherborne St. John 19 SU 6155
Sherbourne 33 SP 2661
Sherburn (Durham) 72 NZ 3142
Sherburn (N Yorks.) 67 SE 9577
Sherburn in Elmet 60 SE 4933
Shere 20 TQ 0747
Shereford 46 TF 8829
Sherfield English 11 SU 2922
Sherfield on Loddon 19 SU 6757
Sherford 5 SX 7744
Sheriff Hutton 66 SE 6566
Sheriffhales 41 SJ 7512
Sheringham 47 TG 1543
Sherington 34 SP 8846
Shernborne 46 TF 7132
Sherrington 10 ST 9638
Sherston 18 ST 8585
Sherwood Green 6 SS 5520
Shettleston 84 NS 6464
Shevington 57 SD 5408
Shevington Moor 57 SD 5410
Sheviock 4 SX 3655
Shiel Bridge 101 NG 9318
Shieldaig 101 NG 8154
Shieldhill (Central) 84 NS 8976
Shielfoot 95 NM 6669
Shifnal 41 SJ 7407
Shilbottle 79 NU 1908
Shildon 72 NZ 2226
Shillingford (Devon.) 8 SS 9723
Shillingford (Oxon.) 19 SU 5992
Shillingford St. George 8 SX 9087
Shillingstone 10 ST 8211
Shillington 35 TL 1234
Shillmoor (Northum.) 78 NT 8807
Shilton (Oxon.) 33 SP 2608
Shilton (Warw.) 43 SP 4084
Shimpling (Norf.) 47 TM 1583
Shimpling (Suff.) 36 TL 8551
Shimpling Street 36 TL 8652
Shiney Row 72 NZ 3252
Shinfield 20 SU 7368
Shinness 111 NC 5314
Shipbourne 21 TQ 5952
Shipdham 46 TF 9607
Shipham 17 ST 4457
Shiphay 5 SX 8965
Shiplake 20 SU 7678
Shipley (Salop) 41 SO 8095
Shipley (W Susx.) 12 TQ 1422
Shipley (W Yorks.) 59 SE 1337
Shipmeadow 47 TM 3789
Shippon 19 SU 4898
Shipston on Stour 33 SP 2540
Shipton (Glos.) 32 SP 0318
Shipton (N Yorks) 66 SE 5558
Shipton (Salop) 40 SO 5591
Shipton Bellinger 18 SU 2345
Shipton Gorge 9 SY 4991
Shipton Green 12 SU 8000
Shipton Moyne 18 ST 8889
Shipton-on-Cherwell 33 SP 4716
Shipton-under-Wychwood 33 SP 2717
Shiptonthorpe 60 SE 8543
Shirburn 20 SU 6995

St Stephens (Corn.) 251 Swithland

St. Stephens (Corn.) 4 SX 4158
St. Teath 4 SX 0680
St. Twynnells 24 SR 9597
St. Vigeans 99 NO 6443
St. Wenn 3 SW 9664
St. Weonards 29 SO 4924
Stackhouse 65 SD 8165
Stacksteads 58 SD 8421
Staddiscombe 5 SX 5151
Staddlethorpe 60 SE 8428
Stadhampton 19 SU 6098
Staffield 71 NY 5442
Staffin 100 NG 4967
Stafford 41 SJ 9223
Stagsden 34 SP 9849
Stainburn 59 SE 2448
Stainby 44 SK 9022
Staincross 59 SE 3210
Staindrop 72 NZ 1220
Staines 20 TQ 0471
Stainfield (Lincs.) 45 TF 0724
Stainfield (Lincs.) 55 TF 1173
Stainforth (N Yorks.) 65 SD 8267
Stainforth (S Yorks.) 60 SE 6411
Staining 57 SD 3435
Stainland 59 SE 0719
Stainsacre 67 NZ 9108
Stainton (Cleve.) 73 NZ 4714
Stainton (Cumbr.) 63 NY 4827
Stainton (Cumbr.) 63 SD 5285
Stainton (Durham) 72 NZ 0718
Stainton (N Yorks.) 65 SE 1096
Stainton (S Yorks.) 53 SK 5593
Stainton by Langworth 54 TF 0577
Stainton le Vale 55 TF 1794
Stainton with Adgarley 64 SD 2472
Staintondale 67 SE 9898
Stair (Cumbr.) 62 NY 2321
Stair (Strath.) 75 NS 4323
Staithes 73 NZ 7818
Stake Pool 57 SD 4148
Stalbridge 9 ST 7317
Stalbridge Weston 9 ST 7216
Stalham 47 TG 3725
Stalham Green 47 TG 3824
Stalisfield Green 15 TQ 9652
Stalling Busk 65 SD 9185
Stallingborough 61 TA 2011
Stalmine 57 SD 3745
Stalybridge 58 SJ 9698
Stambourne 36 TL 7238
Stamford 44 TF 0207
Stamford Bridge 66 SE 7155
Stamfordham 79 NZ 0772
Stanborough 35 TL 2210
Stanbridge (Beds.) 34 SP 9623
Stanbridge (Dorset) 10 SU 0003
Stand 84 NS 7668
Standburn 84 NS 9274
Standeford 41 SJ 9107
Standen 14 TQ 8540
Standford 12 SU 8134
Standish 57 SD 5609
Standlake 33 SP 3902
Standon (Hants.) 11 SU 4227
Standon (Herts.) 35 TL 3922
Standon (Staffs.) 51 SJ 8134
Stane 84 NS 8859
Stanfield 46 TF 9320
Stanford (Beds.) 15 TL 1641
Stanford (Kent) 15 TR 1238
Stanford Bishop 31 SO 6851
Stanford Bridge 32 SO 7165
Stanford Dingley 19 SU 5771
Stanford Rivers 22 TL 5301
Stanford in the Vale 19 SU 3493
Stanford le Hope 22 TQ 6882
Stanford on Avon 43 SP 5878
Stanford on Soar 43 SK 5422
Stanford on Teme 37 SO 7065
Stanghow 73 NZ 6715
Stanhoe 46 TF 8036
Stanhope 72 NY 9939
Stanhope 85 NT 1230
Stanion 44 SP 9187
Stanley (Derby.) 53 SK 4140
Stanley (Durham) 72 NZ 1953
Stanley (Staffs.) 51 SJ 9252
Stanley (Tays.) 92 NO 1033
Stanley (W Yorks.) 59 SE 3422
Stanmer 13 TQ 3309
Stanmore (Berks.) 19 SU 4778
Stanmore (Gtr London) 21 TQ 1692
Stannington (Northum.) 79 NZ 2179
Stannington (S Yorks.) 53 SK 2988
Stansbatch 30 SO 3461
Stansfield 36 TL 7852
Stanstead 36 TL 8449
Stanstead Abbots 35 TL 3811
Stansted 14 TQ 6062
Stansted Mountfitchet 22 TL 5124
Stanton (Glos.) 32 SP 0634
Stanton (Northum.) 79 NZ 1390
Stanton (Staffs.) 52 SK 1246
Stanton (Suff.) 36 TL 9673
Stanton Drew 17 ST 5963
Stanton Fitzwarren 18 SU 1790
Stanton Harcourt 33 SP 4105
Stanton Hill 53 SK 4860
Stanton Lacy 40 SO 4978
Stanton Long 41 SO 5690
Stanton Prior 17 ST 6762
Stanton St. Bernard 18 SU 0962
Stanton St. John 33 SP 5709
Stanton St. Quintin 18 ST 9079
Stanton Street 36 TL 9566
Stanton Wick 17 ST 6162
Stanton by Bridge 43 SK 3627
Stanton by Dale 53 SK 4637
Stanton in Peak 53 SK 2464
Stanton on the Wolds 53 SK 6330
Stanton under Bardon 43 SK 4610
Stanton upon Hine Heath 40 SJ 5624
Stanwardine in the Fields 40 SJ 4124
Stanway (Essex) 23 TL 9324
Stanway (Glos.) 32 SP 0532
Stanwell 20 TQ 0574
Stanwell Moor 20 TQ 0474
Stanwick 44 SP 9871
Stape 67 SE 7993
Stapehill 10 SU 0500
Stapeley 51 SJ 6749
Staple 15 TR 2756
Staple Cross 14 TQ 7822
Staple Fitzpaine 8 ST 2618
Staplefield 13 TQ 2728
Stapleford (Cambs.) 35 TL 4751
Stapleford (Herts.) 35 TL 3117
Stapleford (Leic.) 44 SK 8118
Stapleford (Lincs.) 54 SK 8757
Stapleford (Notts.) 53 SK 4837
Stapleford (Wilts.) 10 SU 0637
Stapleford Abbotts 21 TQ 5096
Stapleford Tawney 21 TQ 5098
Staplegrove 16 ST 2126
Staplehurst 14 TQ 7843
Staplers 11 SZ 5189
Stapleton (Avon) 29 ST 6175
Stapleton (Cumbr.) 71 NY 5071
Stapleton (Here. and Worc.) 30 SO 3265
Stapleton (Leic.) 43 SP 4398
Stapleton (N Yorks.) 72 NZ 2612
Stapleton (Salop) 40 SJ 4604
Stapleton (Somer.) 9 ST 4621
Stapley 8 ST 1813
Staploe 35 TL 1460
Star (Dyfed) 26 SN 2435
Star (Fife.) 93 NO 3103
Star (Somer.) 17 ST 4358
Starbotton 65 SD 9574
Starcross 8 SX 9781
Starston 47 TM 2384
Startforth 72 NZ 0416
Startley 18 ST 9482
Stathe 17 ST 3728
Stathern 54 SK 7731
Station Town 72 NZ 4036
Staughton Highway 35 TL 1364
Staunton (Glos.) 29 SO 5412
Staunton (Glos.) 32 SO 7929
Staunton on Arrow 30 SO 3660
Staunton on Wye 30 SO 3645
Staveley (Cumbr.) 62 SD 3786
Staveley (Cumbr.) 63 SD 4698
Staveley (Derby.) 53 SK 4374
Staveley (N Yorks.) 66 SE 3662
Staverton (Devon.) 5 SX 7964
Staverton (Glos.) 32 SO 9823
Staverton (Northants.) 33 SP 5461
Staverton (Wilts.) 18 ST 8560
Stawell 17 ST 3638
Staxigoe 112 ND 3852
Staxton 67 TA 0179
Staylittle 39 SN 8892
Staythorpe 54 SK 7554
Stean 65 SE 0873
Stearsby 66 SE 6171
Steart 17 ST 2745
Stebbing 22 TL 6624
Stedham 12 SU 8622
Steele Road 78 NY 5292
Steen's Bridge 31 SO 5457
Steep 12 SU 7525
Steeple (Dorset) 10 SY 9080
Steeple (Essex) 23 TL 9303
Steeple Ashton 18 ST 9056
Steeple Aston 33 SP 4725
Steeple Barton 33 SP 4424
Steeple Bumpstead 36 TL 6741
Steeple Claydon 34 SP 7027
Steeple Gidding 45 TL 1381
Steeple Langford 10 SU 0337
Steeple Morden 35 TL 2842
Steeton 59 SE 0344
Steinmanhill 105 NJ 7642
Stelling Minnis 15 TR 1446
Stenalees 4 SX 0157
Stenhousemuir 84 NS 8682
Stenness 113 HU 2176
Stenton 86 NT 6274
Steppingley 34 TL 0135
Stepps 84 NS 6668
Sternfield 37 TM 3861
Stert 18 SU 0259
Stetchworth 36 TL 6458
Stevenage 35 TL 2325
Stevenston 82 NS 2642
Steventon (Hants.) 19 SU 5547
Steventon (Oxon.) 19 SU 4691
Stevington 34 SP 9853
Stewartby 35 TL 0242
Stewarton 82 NS 4246
Stewton 55 TF 3687
Steyning 12 TQ 1711
Steynton 24 SM 9108
Stibb 6 SS 2210
Stibb Cross 6 SS 4314
Stibb Green 18 SU 2262
Stibbard 46 TF 9828
Stibbington 45 TL 0898
Stichill 86 NT 7138
Sticker 3 SW 9750
Stickford 55 TF 3560
Sticklepath 5 SX 6394
Stickney 55 TF 3456
Stiffkey 46 TF 9743
Stifford's Bridge 32 SO 7348
Stilligarry 109 NF 7638
Stillingfleet 60 SE 5940
Stillington (Cleve.) 72 NZ 3723
Stillington (N Yorks.) 66 SE 5867
Stilton 45 TL 1689
Stinchcombe 29 ST 7298
Stinsford 9 SY 7191
Stirchley 41 SJ 6906
Stirling 91 NS 7993
Stisted 22 TL 8024
Stithians 2 SW 7336
Stivichall 43 SP 3376
Stixwould 55 TF 1765
Stoak 50 SJ 4273
Stobo 85 NT 1837
Stoborough 10 SY 9286
Stoborough Green 10 SY 9184
Stock 22 TQ 6998
Stock Green 32 SO 9859
Stock Wood 32 SP 0058
Stockbridge 11 SU 3535
Stockbriggs 84 NS 7936
Stockbury 14 TQ 8461
Stockcross 19 SU 4368
Stockdalewath 70 NY 3845
Stockerston 44 SP 8397
Stocking Pelham 35 TL 4529
Stockingford 43 SP 3391
Stockland 8 ST 2404
Stockland Bristol 16 ST 2443
Stockleigh English 7 SS 8406
Stockleigh Pomeroy 7 SS 8703
Stockley 18 SU 0067
Stockport 51 SJ 8989
Stocksbridge 59 SK 2798
Stocksfield 72 NZ 0561
Stockton (Here. and Worc.) 30 SO 5161
Stockton (Norf.) 47 TM 3894
Stockton (Salop) 41 SO 7299
Stockton (Warw.) 33 SP 4363
Stockton (Wilts.) 10 ST 9738
Stockton Heath 51 SJ 6185
Stockton on Teme 41 SO 7167
Stockton on the Forest 66 SE 6556
Stockton-on-Tees 72 NZ 4419
Stockwith 54 SK 7994
Stodmarsh 15 TR 2160
Stody 41 TG 0535
Stoer 110 NC 0428
Stoford (Somer.) 9 ST 5613
Stoford (Wilts.) 10 SU 0835
Stogumber 16 ST 0937
Stogursey 16 ST 2042
Stoke (Devon.) 6 SS 2324
Stoke (Hants.) 19 SU 4051
Stoke (Hants.) 12 SU 7202
Stoke (Kent) 22 TQ 8275
Stoke Abbott 9 ST 4500
Stoke Albany 44 SP 8088
Stoke Ash 37 TM 1170
Stoke Bardolph 53 SK 6441
Stoke Bliss 31 SO 6562
Stoke Bruerne 34 SP 7450
Stoke Canon 8 SX 9397
Stoke Charity 11 SU 4839
Stoke Climsland 4 SX 3574
Stoke D'Abernon 20 TQ 1259
Stoke Doyle 44 TL 0286
Stoke Dry 44 SP 8597
Stoke Ferry 46 TF 7000
Stoke Fleming 5 SX 8648
Stoke Gabriel 5 SX 8457
Stoke Gifford 29 ST 6280
Stoke Golding 43 SP 3997
Stoke Goldington 34 SP 8348
Stoke Hammond 34 SP 8829
Stoke Holy Cross 47 TG 2301
Stoke Lacy 31 SO 6149
Stoke Lyne 33 SP 5628
Stoke Mandeville 34 SP 8310
Stoke Newington 21 TQ 3286
Stoke Orchard 32 SO 9128
Stoke Poges 20 SU 9884
Stoke Prior (Here. and Worc.) 30 SO 5256
Stoke Prior (Here. and Worc.) 41 SO 9467
Stoke Rivers 6 SS 6335
Stoke Rochford 44 SK 9127
Stoke Row 19 SU 6883
Stoke St. Gregory 17 ST 3426
Stoke St. Mary 8 ST 2622
Stoke St. Michael 17 ST 6646
Stoke St. Milborough 40 SO 5682
Stoke Talmage 19 SU 6799
Stoke Trister 17 ST 7328
Stoke by Clare 36 TL 7443
Stoke sub Hamdon 9 ST 4717
Stoke upon Tern 41 SJ 6327
Stoke-by-Nayland 36 TL 9836
Stoke-on-Trent 51 SJ 8745
Stokeford 10 SY 8787
Stokeham 54 SK 7876
Stokeinteignhead 8 SX 9170
Stokenchurch 20 SU 7596
Stokenham 5 SX 8042
Stokesay 40 SO 4381
Stokesby 47 TG 4310
Stokesley 66 NZ 5208
Stolford 16 ST 2245
Ston Easton 17 ST 6253
Stondon Massey 22 TL 5800
Stone (Bucks.) 34 SP 7812
Stone (Glos.) 29 ST 6895
Stone (Here. and Worc.) 41 SO 8675
Stone (Kent) 21 TQ 5774
Stone (Kent) 15 TQ 9427
Stone (Staffs.) 51 SJ 9034
Stone Allerton 17 ST 3950
Stone Cross 13 TQ 6104
Stone House (Cumbr.) 65 SD 7785
Stonebroom 53 SK 4159
Stonegate 13 TQ 6628
Stonegate Crofts 105 NK 0339
Stonegrave 66 SE 6577
Stonehaugh 78 NY 7976
Stonehaven 99 NO 8685
Stonehouse (Glos.) 32 SO 8005
Stonehouse (Northum.) 71 NY 6958
Stonehouse (Strath.) 76 NS 7546
Stoneleigh 43 SP 3272
Stonely 45 TL 1067
Stones Green 23 TM 1626
Stonesby 44 SK 8224
Stonesfield 33 SP 3917
Stoney Cross 11 SU 2511
Stoney Middleton 53 SK 2275
Stoney Stanton 43 SP 4894
Stoney Stratton 17 ST 6539
Stoney Stretton 40 SJ 3809
Stoneybridge 109 NF 7433
Stoneyburn 85 NS 9762
Stoneygate 43 SK 6102
Stoneyhills 23 TQ 9497
Stoneykirk 68 NX 0853
Stoneywood 105 NJ 8910
Stonham Aspal 37 TM 1359
Stonnall 42 SK 0603
Stonor 20 SU 7388
Stonton Wyville 44 SP 7395
Stony Stratford 34 SP 7840
Stoodleigh 8 SS 9218
Stopham 12 TQ 0219
Stopsley 35 TL 1023
Storeton 50 SJ 3084
Stornoway 109 NB 4333
Storridge 32 SO 7448
Storrington 12 TQ 0814
Storth 63 SD 4780
Stotfold 35 TL 2136
Stottesdon 41 SO 6782
Stoughton (Leic.) 43 SK 6402
Stoughton (Surrey) 20 SU 9851
Stoughton (W Susx) 12 SU 8011
Stoulton 32 SO 9049
Stour Provost 10 ST 7921
Stour Row 10 ST 8220
Stourbridge 41 SO 8984
Stourpaine 10 ST 8509
Stourport-on-Severn 41 SO 8171
Stourton (Here. and Worc.) 41 SO 8585
Stourton (Warw.) 33 SP 2936
Stourton (Wilts.) 17 ST 7733
Stourton Caundle 9 ST 7114
Stoven 47 TM 4481
Stow (Borders) 86 NT 4644
Stow (Lincs.) 54 SK 8781
Stow Bardolph 46 TF 6205
Stow Bedon 46 TL 9596
Stow Longa 45 TL 1171
Stow Maries 22 TQ 8399
Stow cum Quy 35 TL 5260
Stow-on-the-Wold 33 SP 1925
Stowbridge 46 TF 6007
Stowe (Salop) 40 SO 3173
Stowe (Staffs.) 42 SK 0027
Stowell 9 ST 6822
Stowford 4 SX 4386
Stowlangtoft 36 TL 9568
Stowmarket 37 TM 0458
Stowting 15 TR 1241
Stowupland 37 TM 0659
Straad 81 NS 0462
Strachan 99 NO 6792
Strachur 89 NN 0901
Stradbroke 37 TM 2373
Stradishall 36 TL 7452
Stradsett 46 TF 6605
Stragglethorpe 54 SK 9152
Straiton (Lothian) 85 NT 2766
Straiton (Strath.) 75 NS 3804
Straloch (Grampn.) 105 NJ 8621
Straloch (Tays.) 98 NO 0463
Stramshall 52 SK 0735
Stranraer 68 NX 0660
Strata Florida 27 SN 7465
Stratfield Mortimer 19 SU 6764
Stratfield Saye 19 SU 6961
Stratfield Turgis 19 SU 6959
Stratford St. Andrew 37 TM 3560
Stratford St. Mary 37 TM 0434
Stratford Tony 10 SU 0926
Stratford-upon-Avon 33 SP 2055
Strath 112 ND 2753
Strath Gairloch 106 NG 7977
Strathan (Highld.) 110 NC 0821
Strathaven 84 NS 7044
Strathblane (Central) 84 NS 5679
Strathcarron (Highld.) 101 NG 9442
Strathdon 104 NJ 3513
Strathkanaird (Highld.) 106 NC 1501
Strathkinness 93 NO 4516
Strathmiglo 92 NO 2109
Strathmore Lodge 113 ND 1048
Strathpeffer 102 NH 4858
Strathwhillan 81 NS 0235
Strathy 111 NC 8465
Strathyre 90 NN 5617
Stratton (Corn.) 6 SS 2306
Stratton (Dorset) 9 SY 6593
Stratton (Glos.) 32 SP 0103
Stratton Audley 34 SP 6026
Stratton St. Margaret 18 SU 1787
Stratton St. Michael 47 TM 2093
Stratton Strawless 47 TG 2220
Stratton-on-the-Fosse 17 ST 6550
Stravithie 93 NO 5311
Streat 13 TQ 3515
Streatham 21 TQ 2972
Streatley (Beds.) 35 TL 0728
Streatley (Berks.) 19 SU 5980
Street (Lancs.) 64 SD 5252
Street (Somer.) 17 ST 4836
Street End 12 SZ 8599
Streethay 42 SK 1410
Streetly 42 SP 0898
Strefford 40 SO 4485
Strensall 66 SE 6360
Strensham 32 SO 9040
Stretcholt 17 ST 2943
Strete 5 SX 8447
Stretford 51 SJ 7894
Stretford Court 30 SO 4455
Strethall 35 TL 4840
Stretham 45 TL 5174
Strettington 12 SU 8807
Stretton (Ches.) 50 SJ 4452
Stretton (Ches.) 51 SJ 6182
Stretton (Derby.) 53 SK 3961
Stretton (Leic.) 44 SK 9415
Stretton (Staffs.) 41 SJ 8811
Stretton (Staffs.) 42 SK 2526
Stretton Grandison 31 SO 6344
Stretton Heath 40 SJ 3610
Stretton Westwood 41 SO 5998
Stretton en le Field 43 SK 3012
Stretton on Fosse 33 SP 2238
Stretton under Fosse 43 SP 4581
Stretton-on-Dunsmore 43 SP 4072
Strichen 105 NJ 9455
Stringston 16 ST 1742
Strixton 34 SP 9061
Stroat 29 ST 5798
Stromeferry 101 NG 8634
Stromness (Orkney) 113 HY 2509
Stronachlachar 90 NN 4010
Strone (Highld.) 96 NN 1582
Strone (Strath.) 96 NS 1880
Stronenaba 96 NN 2084
Strònmilchan 89 NN 1528
Strontian 95 NM 8161
Strood 14 TQ 7369
Stroud (Glos.) 32 SO 8504
Stroud (Hants.) 12 SU 7223
Struan (Highld.) 100 NG 3438
Strubby 55 TF 4582
Strumpshaw 47 TG 3507
Strutherhill 84 NS 7650
Struy 102 NH 4039
Stuartfield 105 NJ 9745
Stubbington 11 SU 5503
Stubbins 58 SD 7918
Stubhampton 10 ST 9113
Stubton 54 SK 8748
Stuckton 10 SU 1613
Studham 34 TL 0215
Studland 10 SZ 0382
Studley (Oxon.) 34 SP 6012
Studley (Warw.) 32 SP 0763
Studley (Wilts.) 18 ST 9671
Studley Roger 66 SE 2970
Stump Cross 35 TL 5044
Stuntney 36 TL 5578
Sturbridge 51 SJ 8330
Sturmer 36 TL 6944
Sturminster Common 10 ST 7812
Sturminster Marshall 10 SY 9499
Sturminster Newton 10 ST 7813
Sturry 15 TR 1760
Sturton by Stow 54 SK 8980
Sturton le Steeple 54 SK 7884
Stuston 37 TM 1378
Stutton (N Yorks.) 60 SE 4741
Stutton (Suff.) 37 TM 1434
Stwekley 34 SP 8525
Styal 51 SJ 8383
Suckley 32 SO 7151
Sudborough 44 SP 9682
Sudbourne 37 TM 4153
Sudbrook 29 ST 5087
Sudbrooke 54 TF 0276
Sudbury (Derby.) 52 SK 1631
Sudbury (Suff.) 36 TL 8741
Suddie 103 NH 6654
Sudgrove 32 SO 9307
Suffield 47 TG 2332
Sugnall 41 SJ 7930
Sulby 56 SC 3994
Sulgrave 33 SP 5545
Sulham 19 SU 6474
Sulhamstead 19 SU 6368
Sullington 12 TQ 0913
Sullom 113 HU 3573
Sully 28 ST 1568
Summerbridge 65 SE 1962
Summercourt 3 SW 8856
Summerleaze 29 ST 4284
Summerseat 58 SD 7914
Summit 58 SD 9418
Sunadale 81 NR 8145
Sunbury 20 TQ 1069
Sunderland (Cumbr.) 62 NY 1735
Sunderland (Tyne and Wear) 72 NZ 3957
Sunderland Bridge 72 NZ 2637
Sundhope 77 NT 3324
Sundon Park 35 TL 0525
Sundridge 21 TQ 4854
Sunk Island 61 TA 2619
Sunningdale 20 SU 9567
Sunninghill 20 SU 9367
Sunningwell 33 SP 4900
Sunniside (Durham) 72 NZ 1438
Sunniside (Tyne and Wear) 72 NZ 2159
Sunny Bank 62 SD 2992
Sunnylaw 91 NS 7998
Sunnyside 13 TQ 3937
Surbiton 21 TQ 1867
Surfleet 45 TF 2528
Surfleet Seas End 45 TF 2628
Surlingham 47 TG 3106
Surrigarth 113 HY 4945
Sustead 47 TG 1837
Susworth 60 SE 8302
Sutcombe 6 SS 3411
Sutterton 55 TF 2835
Sutton (Beds.) 35 TL 2247
Sutton (Cambs.) 45 TL 4479
Sutton (Gtr London) 21 TQ 2463
Sutton (Kent) 15 TR 3349
Sutton (Norf.) 47 TG 3823
Sutton (Notts.) 53 SK 6784
Sutton (Notts.) 54 SK 7637
Sutton (Oxon.) 33 SP 4106
Sutton (Salop) 51 SJ 6631
Sutton (Salop) 40 SO 5082
Sutton (Salop) 41 SO 7286
Sutton (Staffs.) 41 SJ 7622
Sutton (Suff.) 37 TM 3046
Sutton (Surrey) 20 TQ 1046
Sutton (W Susx) 12 SU 9715
Sutton Bassett 44 SP 7790
Sutton Benger 18 ST 9478
Sutton Bonington 43 SK 5025
Sutton Bridge 45 TF 4821
Sutton Cheney 43 SK 4100
Sutton Coldfield 42 SP 1296
Sutton Courtenay 19 SU 5093
Sutton Crosses 45 TF 4321
Sutton Grange 66 SE 2874
Sutton Howgrave 66 SE 3179
Sutton Lane Ends 51 SJ 9270
Sutton Maddock 41 SJ 7201
Sutton Mallet 17 ST 3736
Sutton Mandeville 10 ST 9828
Sutton Montis 9 ST 6224
Sutton Scotney 11 SU 4539
Sutton St. Edmund 45 TF 3613
Sutton St. James 45 TF 3918
Sutton St. Nicholas 31 SO 5345
Sutton Valence 14 TQ 8148
Sutton Veny 18 ST 9041
Sutton Waldron 10 ST 8615
Sutton Weaver 50 SJ 5479
Sutton at Hone 21 TQ 5570
Sutton in Ashfield 53 SK 5058
Sutton on Sea 55 TF 5282
Sutton on Trent 54 SK 7965
Sutton on the Hill 53 SK 2333
Sutton upon Derwent 60 SE 7046
Sutton-in-Craven 59 SE 0044
Sutton-on-Hull 61 TA 1132
Sutton-on-the-Forest 66 SE 5864
Sutton-under-Brailes 33 SP 2937
Sutton-under-Whitestonecliffe 66 SE 4882
Swaby 55 TF 3877
Swadlincote 43 SK 3019
Swaffham 46 TF 8109
Swaffham Bulbeck 36 TL 5562
Swaffham Prior 36 TL 5764
Swafield 47 TG 2832
Swainby 66 NZ 4701
Swainsthorpe 47 TG 2101
Swainswick 29 ST 7568
Swalcliffe 33 SP 3738
Swalecliffe 15 TR 1367
Swallow 61 TA 1703
Swallowcliffe 10 ST 9626
Swallowfield 20 SU 7264
Swanage 10 SZ 0278
Swanbourne 34 SP 8027
Swanland 61 SE 9927
Swanley 21 TQ 5168
Swanmore 11 SU 5815
Swannington (Leic.) 43 SK 4116
Swannington (Norf.) 47 TG 1319
Swanscombe 21 TQ 6074
Swansea 25 SS 6593
Swanton Abbot 47 TG 2625
Swanton Morley 46 TG 0117
Swanton Novers 46 TG 0132
Swanwick (Derby.) 53 SK 4053
Swanwick (Hants.) 11 SU 5109
Swarby 54 TF 0440
Swardeston 47 TG 2002
Swarkestone 43 SK 3728
Swarland 79 NU 1601
Swarland Estate 79 NU 1603
Swaton 55 TF 1337
Swavesey 45 TL 3668
Sway 11 SZ 2798
Swayfield 44 SK 9822
Swaythling 11 SU 4315
Swefling 37 TM 3463
Swepstone 43 SK 3610
Swerford 33 SP 3731
Swettenham 51 SJ 8067
Swilland 37 TM 1853
Swillington 59 SE 3830
Swimbridge 6 SS 6230
Swinbrook 33 SP 2812
Swinderby 54 SK 8662
Swindon (Glos.) 32 SO 9325
Swindon (Staffs.) 41 SO 8690
Swindon (Wilts.) 18 SU 1484
Swine 61 TA 1335
Swinefleet 60 SE 7621
Swineshead (Beds.) 45 TL 0565
Swineshead Bridge 55 TF 2142
Swiney 112 ND 2335
Swinford (Leic.) 43 SP 5679
Swinford (Oxon.) 33 SP 4408
Swingfield Minnis 15 TR 2142
Swinhill 84 NS 7748
Swinhoe 87 NU 2028
Swinhope 55 TF 2196
Swinithwaite 65 SE 0489
Swinscoe 52 SK 1347
Swinstead 44 TF 0122
Swinton (Borders) 87 NT 8447
Swinton (Gtr Mches.) 58 SD 7701
Swinton (N Yorks.) 65 SE 2179
Swinton (N Yorks.) 67 SE 7573
Swinton (S Yorks.) 60 SK 4499
Swintonmill 87 NT 8145
Swithland 43 SK 5413

Swordale 252 Towto

Place	Page	Grid ref.
Swordale	102	NH 5765
Swordly	111	NC 7363
Sworton Heath	51	SJ 6884
Swyddffynnon	27	SN 6966
Swynnerton	51	SJ 8435
Swyre	9	SY 5288
Syde	32	SO 9411
Sydenham (Gtr London)	21	TQ 3571
Sydenham (Oxon.)	34	SP 7301
Sydenham Damerel	4	SX 4075
Syderstone	46	TF 8332
Sydling St. Nicholas	9	SY 6399
Sydmonton	19	SU 4857
Syerston	54	SK 7447
Syke	58	SD 8915
Sykehouse	60	SE 6216
Sylen	25	SN 5107
Symbister	113	HU 5362
Symington (Strath.)	82	NS 3831
Symington (Strath.)	85	NS 9935
Symonds Yat	29	SO 5516
Symondsbury	9	SY 4493
Synod Inn	26	SN 4054
Syre	111	NC 6843
Syreford	32	SP 0320
Syresham	34	SP 6241
Syston (Leic.)	43	SK 6211
Syston (Lincs.)	54	SK 9240
Sytchampton	32	SO 8466
Sywell	44	SP 8267

T

Place	Page	Grid ref.
Tackley	33	SP 4720
Tacolneston	47	TM 1395
Tadcaster	60	SE 4843
Tadden	10	ST 9801
Taddington (Derby)	52	SK 1471
Taddington (Glos.)	32	SP 0831
Tadley	19	SU 6060
Tadlow	35	TL 2847
Tadmarton	33	SP 3937
Tadworth	21	TQ 2356
Tafarn-y-Gelyn	50	SJ 1861
Tafarnaubach	28	SO 1110
Taff's Well	28	ST 1283
Tafolwern	39	SH 8902
Tai'n-lon	48	SH 4450
Tai'r Bull	28	SN 9926
Tai-bach (Clwyd)	40	SJ 1528
Taibach (W Glam.)	28	SS 7789
Tain (Highld.)	112	ND 2266
Tain (Highld.)	108	NH 7782
Takeley	22	TL 5521
Tal-y-Bont (Gwyn.)	49	SH 7668
Tal-y-bont (Gwyn.)	38	SH 5921
Tal-y-cafn	49	SH 7971
Tal-y-llyn (Gwyn.)	39	SH 7109
Talachddu	27	SO 0733
Talacre	50	SJ 1284
Talaton	8	SY 0699
Talbenny	24	SM 8412
Talerddig	39	SH 9300
Talgarreg	26	SN 4251
Talgarth	30	SO 1534
Taliesin	39	SN 6591
Talisker	100	NG 3230
Talke	51	SJ 8253
Talkin	71	NY 5557
Talladale	106	NG 9270
Tallentire	62	NY 1035
Talley	27	SN 6332
Tallington	45	TF 0908
Talmine	111	NC 5862
Talog	25	SN 3325
Talsarn	26	SN 5456
Talsarnau	48	SH 6135
Talskiddy	3	SW 9165
Talwrn	48	SH 4876
Talybont (Dyfed)	39	SN 6589
Talybont (Powys)	28	SO 1122
Talysarn	48	SH 4852
Talywern	39	SH 8200
Tamerton Foliot	5	SX 4761
Tamworth	42	SK 2004
Tan-y-fron	49	SH 9564
Tan-y-groes	26	SN 2849
Tandridge	21	TQ 3750
Tanfield	72	NZ 1855
Tangley	19	SU 3352
Tangmere	12	SU 9006
Tankersley	59	SK 3499
Tannach	112	ND 3247
Tannadice	99	NO 4758
Tannington	37	TM 2467
Tansley	53	SK 3259
Tansor	45	TL 0590
Tantobie	72	NZ 1754
Tanton	73	NZ 5210
Tanworth in Arden	42	SP 1170
Tanygrisiau	49	SH 6845
Taplow	20	SU 9182
Tarbert (Harris)	109	NB 1500
Tarbert (Jura)	88	NR 6082
Tarbert (Strath.)	81	NR 8668
Tarbet (Highld.)	110	NC 1648
Tarbet (Highld.)	95	NM 7992
Tarbet (Strath.)	90	NN 3104
Tarbock Green	50	SJ 4687
Tarbolton	75	NS 4327
Tarbrax	85	NT 0255
Tardebigge	41	SO 9969
Tarfside	99	NO 4979
Tarland	99	NJ 4804
Tarleton	57	SD 4420
Tarlscough	57	SD 4313
Tarlton	18	ST 9599
Tarnbrook	64	SD 5855
Tarporley	50	SJ 5562
Tarr	16	ST 1030
Tarrant Crawford	10	ST 9203
Tarrant Gunville	10	ST 9212
Tarrant Hinton	10	ST 9310
Tarrant Keyneston	10	ST 9204
Tarrant Launceston	10	ST 9409
Tarrant Monkton	10	ST 9408
Tarrant Rawston	10	ST 9306
Tarrant Rushton	10	ST 9305
Tarring Neville	13	TQ 4404
Tarrington	31	SO 6140
Tarsappie	92	NO 1220
Tarskavaig	100	NG 5810
Tarves	105	NJ 8631
Tarvin	50	SJ 4867
Tasburgh	47	TM 2096
Tasley	41	SO 6994
Taston	33	SP 3521
Tatenhill	42	SK 2022
Tathwell	55	TF 3282
Tatsfield	21	TQ 4156
Tattenhall	50	SJ 4858
Tatterford	46	TF 8628
Tattersett	46	TF 8429
Tattershall	55	TF 2157
Tattershall Bridge	55	TF 1956
Tattershall Thorpe	55	TF 2159
Tattingstone	37	TM 1337
Taunton	8	ST 2324
Taverham	47	TG 1513
Tavernspite	24	SN 1812
Tavistock	5	SX 4774
Taw green	7	SX 6497
Tawstock	6	SS 5529
Taxal	52	SK 0079
Tayinloan	81	NR 6945
Taynton (Glos.)	32	SO 7221
Taynton (Oxon.)	32	SP 2313
Taynuilt	89	NN 0031
Tayport	93	NO 4528
Tayvallich	89	NR 7386
Tealby	55	TF 1590
Teangue	101	NG 6609
Tebay	63	NY 6104
Tebworth	34	SP 9926
Tedburn St. Mary	5	SX 8194
Teddington (Glos.)	32	SO 9632
Teddington (Gtr London)	21	TQ 1671
Tedstone Delamere	31	SO 6958
Tedstone Wafre	31	SO 6759
Teeton	43	SP 6970
Teffont Evias	10	ST 9831
Teffont Magna	10	ST 9832
Tegryn	26	SN 2233
Teigh	44	SK 8616
Teigngrace	5	SX 8474
Teignmouth	5	SX 9473
Telford	41	SJ 6909
Tellisford	18	ST 8055
Telscombe	13	TQ 4003
Templand	70	NY 0886
Temple (Corn.)	4	SX 1473
Temple (Lothian)	85	NT 3158
Temple (Strath.)	84	NS 5469
Temple Bar	26	SN 5354
Temple Cloud	17	ST 6157
Temple Ewell	15	TR 2844
Temple Grafton	32	SP 1254
Temple Guiting	32	SP 0928
Temple Hirst	60	SE 6025
Temple Normanton	53	SK 4167
Temple Sowerby	63	NY 6127
Templecombe	9	ST 7022
Templeton (Devon.)	7	SS 8813
Templeton (Dyfed)	24	SN 1111
Tempsford	35	TL 1653
Ten Mile Bank	46	TL 6097
Tenbury Wells	41	SO 5968
Tenby	24	SN 1300
Tendring	23	TM 1424
Tenterden	14	TQ 8833
Terling	22	TL 7715
Ternhill	51	SJ 6332
Terrington	66	SE 6670
Terrington St. Clement	45	TF 5520
Terrington St. John	45	TF 5416
Teston	14	TQ 7053
Testwood	11	SU 3514
Tetbury	18	ST 8993
Tetbury Upton	18	ST 8795
Tetchill	50	SJ 3832
Tetcott	6	SX 3396
Tetford	55	TF 3374
Tetney	61	TA 3101
Tetney Lock	61	TA 3402
Tetsworth	34	SP 6802
Teversal	53	SK 4861
Teversham	35	TL 4958
Teviothead	77	NT 4005
Tewin	35	TL 2714
Tewkesbury	32	SO 8933
Teynham	15	TQ 9663
Thakeham	12	TQ 1017
Thame	34	SP 7006
Thames Ditton	21	TQ 1567
Thames Haven	22	TQ 7581
Thamesmead	21	TQ 4779
Thaneston	99	NO 6375
Thanington	15	TR 1356
Thankerton	85	NS 9737
Tharston	47	TM 1894
Thatcham	19	SU 5167
Thatto Heath	50	SJ 5093
Thaxted	36	TL 6131
The City	20	SU 7896
Theakston	66	SE 3085
Thealby	60	SE 8917
Theale (Berks.)	19	SU 6371
Theale (Somer.)	17	ST 4646
Thearne	61	TA 0736
Theberton	37	TM 4365
Theddingworth	43	SP 6685
Theddlethorpe All Saints	55	TF 4688
Theddlethorpe St. Helen	55	TF 4788
Thelbridge Barton	7	SS 7812
Thelnetham	36	TM 0178
Thelwall	51	SJ 6587
Themelthorpe	47	TG 0524
Thenford	33	SP 5141
Therfield	35	TL 3337
Thetford	46	TL 8783
Theydon Bois	21	TQ 4598
Thickwood	18	ST 8272
Thimbleby (Linc.)	55	TF 2369
Thimbleby (N Yorks.)	66	SE 4495
Thirkleby	66	SE 4778
Thirlby	66	SE 4884
Thirlestane	86	NT 5647
Thirn	65	SE 2185
Thirsk	66	SE 4282
Thistleton	44	SK 9118
Thistley Green	36	TL 6776
Thixendale	67	SE 8461
Thockrington	78	NY 9579
Tholomas Drove	45	TF 4006
Tholthorpe	66	SE 4766
Thomas Chapel	24	SN 1008
Thomastown	104	NJ 5737
Thompson	46	TL 9296
Thomshill	104	NJ 2157
Thong	14	TQ 6770
Thoralby	65	SE 0086
Thoresby	53	SK 6371
Thoresway	61	TF 1696
Thorganby (Lincs.)	61	TF 2097
Thorganby (N Yorks.)	60	SE 6841
Thorgill	66	SE 7096
Thorington	37	TM 4274
Thorington Street	36	TM 0135
Thorlby	65	SD 9652
Thorley	35	TL 4719
Thormanby	66	SE 4974
Thornaby-on-Tees	73	NZ 4518
Thornage	47	TG 0436
Thornborough (Bucks.)	34	SP 7433
Thornborough (N Yorks.)	66	SE 2979
Thornbury (Avon)	29	ST 6390
Thornbury (Devon.)	6	SS 4008
Thornbury (Here and Worc.)	31	SO 6159
Thornby	43	SP 6675
Thorncliff	52	SK 0158
Thorncombe	8	ST 3703
Thorncombe Street	12	TQ 0042
Thorndon	37	TM 1469
Thorne	60	SE 6813
Thorne St. Margaret	8	ST 0920
Thorner	59	SE 3740
Thorney (Cambs.)	45	TF 2804
Thorney (Notts.)	54	SK 8572
Thorney Hill	11	SZ 2099
Thorney Island	12	SU 7503
Thornfalcon	8	ST 2723
Thornford	9	ST 6013
Thorngumbald	61	TA 2026
Thornham	46	TF 7343
Thornham Magna	37	TM 1071
Thornham Parva	37	TM 1072
Thornhaugh	45	TF 0600
Thornhill (Central)	91	NS 6699
Thornhill (Derby.)	52	SK 1983
Thornhill (Dump. and Galwy.)	76	NX 8795
Thornhill (Hants.)	11	SU 4612
Thornhill (Mid Glam.)	28	ST 1584
Thornhill (W Yorks.)	59	SE 2418
Thornicombe	10	ST 8703
Thornley (Durham)	72	NZ 1137
Thornley (Durham)	72	NZ 3639
Thornliebank	84	NS 5459
Thorns	36	TL 7455
Thornthwaite (Cumbr.)	62	NY 2225
Thornthwaite (N Yorks.)	65	SE 1858
Thornton (Bucks.)	34	SP 7535
Thornton (Fife.)	93	NT 2897
Thornton (Humbs.)	60	SE 7545
Thornton (Lancs.)	57	SD 3342
Thornton (Leic.)	43	SK 4607
Thornton (Lincs.)	55	TF 2467
Thornton (Mers.)	57	SD 3300
Thornton (Northum.)	87	NT 9547
Thornton (Tays.)	98	NO 3946
Thornton (W Yorks.)	59	SE 1032
Thornton Curtis	61	TA 0817
Thornton Dale	67	SE 8383
Thornton Hough	50	SJ 3080
Thornton Rust	65	SD 9788
Thornton Steward	65	SE 1787
Thornton Watlass	66	SE 2385
Thornton le Moor (Lincs.)	61	TF 0496
Thornton-in-Craven	58	SD 9048
Thornton-le-Beans	66	SE 3990
Thornton-le-Clay	66	SE 6875
Thornton-le-Moor (N Yorks.)	66	SE 3988
Thornton-le-Moors	50	SJ 4474
Thorntonhall	84	NS 5955
Thorntonloch	86	NT 7574
Thorntonpark	87	NT 9448
Thornwood Common	35	TL 4705
Thoroton	54	SK 7642
Thorp Arch	59	SE 4346
Thorpe (Derby.)	52	SK 1550
Thorpe (Lincs.)	55	TF 4982
Thorpe (N Yorks.)	65	SE 0161
Thorpe (Norf)	47	TM 4398
Thorpe (Notts.)	54	SK 7649
Thorpe (Surrey)	20	TQ 0268
Thorpe Abbotts	37	TM 1979
Thorpe Acre	43	SK 5120
Thorpe Arnold	44	SK 7620
Thorpe Audlin	60	SE 4715
Thorpe Bassett	67	SE 8573
Thorpe Bay	23	TQ 9284
Thorpe Constantine	42	SK 2608
Thorpe End Garden Village	47	TG 2811
Thorpe Green	36	TL 9354
Thorpe Hesley	59	SK 3796
Thorpe Langton	44	SP 7492
Thorpe Larches	72	NZ 3862
Thorpe Malsor	44	SP 8379
Thorpe Mandeville	33	SP 5345
Thorpe Market	47	TG 2436
Thorpe Morieux	36	TL 9453
Thorpe Salvin	53	SK 5281
Thorpe Satchville	44	SK 7311
Thorpe St. Andrew	47	TG 2609
Thorpe St. Peter	55	TF 4861
Thorpe Thewless	72	NZ 4023
Thorpe Waterville	44	TL 0281
Thorpe Willoughby	60	SE 5731
Thorpe by Water	44	SP 8996
Thorpe in Balne	60	SE 5910
Thorpe in the Fallows	54	SK 9180
Thorpe on the Hill	54	SK 9065
Thorpe-le-Soken	23	TM 1822
Thorpeness	37	TM 4759
Thorrington	23	TM 0920
Thorverton	8	SS 9202
Thrandeston	37	TM 1176
Thrapston	44	SP 9978
Threapwood	50	SJ 4345
Three Bridges	13	TQ 2837
Three Cocks	30	SO 1737
Three Crosses	25	SS 5794
Three Holes	45	TF 5000
Three Legged Cross (Dorset)	10	SU 0806
Three Mile Cross	20	SU 7168
Threekingham	54	TF 0836
Threlkeld	62	NY 3225
Threshfield	65	SD 9963
Thrigby	47	TG 4512
Thringarth	63	NY 9323
Thringstone	43	SK 4217
Thrintoft	66	SE 3293
Thriplow	35	TL 4446
Throcking	35	TL 3330
Throckley	72	NZ 1567
Throckmorton	32	SO 9749
Throphill	79	NZ 1385
Thropton	79	NU 0202
Throwleigh	5	SX 6690
Throwley	15	TQ 9955
Thrumpton	53	SK 5131
Thrumster	112	ND 3345
Thrunton	79	NU 0810
Thrupp (Glos.)	32	SO 8603
Thrupp (Oxon.)	33	SP 4715
Thrushelton	5	SX 4487
Thrushgill	64	SD 6462
Thrussington	43	SK 6416
Thruxton (Hants.)	19	SU 2845
Thruxton (Here. and Worc.)	31	SO 4334
Thrybergh	53	SK 4694
Thundersley	23	TQ 7788
Thurcaston	43	SK 5610
Thurcroft	53	SK 4988
Thurgarton (Norf.)	47	TG 1835
Thurgarton (Notts.)	53	SK 6949
Thurgoland	59	SE 2801
Thurlaston (Leic.)	43	SP 5099
Thurlaston (Warw.)	43	SP 4671
Thurlby (Lincs.)	54	SK 9061
Thurlby (Lincs.)	45	TF 1017
Thurleigh	35	TL 0558
Thurlestone	5	SX 6742
Thurlow	36	TL 6750
Thurloxton	17	ST 2730
Thurlstone	59	SE 2303
Thurlton	47	TM 4198
Thurmaston	43	SK 6109
Thurnby	43	SK 6404
Thurne	47	TG 4015
Thurnham (Kent)	14	TQ 8057
Thurnham (Lancs.)	64	SD 4554
Thurning (Norf.)	47	TG 0729
Thurning (Northants.)	45	TL 0883
Thurnscoe	60	SE 4605
Thursby	70	NY 3250
Thursford	46	TF 9833
Thursley	12	SU 9039
Thurso	12	ND 1168
Thurstaston	50	SJ 2483
Thurston	36	TL 9365
Thurstonfield	70	NY 3156
Thurstonland	59	SE 1610
Thurton	47	TG 3200
Thurvaston	53	SK 2437
Thuxton	47	TG 0307
Thwaite (N Yorks.)	65	SD 8998
Thwaite (Suff.)	37	TM 1168
Thwaite St. Mary	47	TM 3395
Thwing	67	TA 0570
Tibbermore	92	NO 0523
Tibberton (Glos.)	32	SO 7521
Tibberton (Here. and Worc.)	32	SO 9054
Tibberton (Salop)	41	SJ 6720
Tibbie Shiels Inn	77	NT 2320
Tibenham	47	TM 1389
Tibshelf	53	SK 4360
Tibthorpe	67	SE 9555
Ticehurst	13	TQ 6930
Tichborne	11	SU 5630
Tickencote	44	SK 9809
Tickenham	29	ST 4571
Tickhill	53	SK 5993
Ticklerton	40	SO 4890
Ticknall	43	SK 3524
Tickton	61	TA 0641
Tidcombe	19	SU 2858
Tiddington (Oxon.)	34	SP 6404
Tiddington (Warw.)	33	SP 2256
Tidebrook	13	TQ 6130
Tideford	4	SX 3459
Tidenham	29	ST 5596
Tideswell	52	SK 1575
Tidmarsh	19	SU 6374
Tidmington	33	SP 2538
Tidpit	10	SU 0718
Tiers Cross	24	SM 9010
Tiffield	34	SP 6951
Tifty	105	NJ 7740
Tigerton	99	NO 5364
Tigharry	109	NF 7171
Tighnabruaich	81	NR 9772
Tighnafiline	106	NG 8789
Tigley	5	SX 7560
Tilbrook	45	TL 0769
Tilbury	22	TQ 6376
Tile Cross	42	SP 1687
Tile Hill	43	SP 2777
Tilehurst	19	SU 6673
Tilford	12	SU 8743
Tillathrowie	104	NJ 4634
Tillicoultry	91	NS 9197
Tillingham	23	TL 9903
Tillington (Here. and Worc.)	30	SO 4645
Tillington (W Susx.)	12	SU 9621
Tillington Common	30	SO 4546
Tillyarblet	99	NO 5267
Tillycorthie	105	NJ 9123
Tillyfourie	104	NJ 6412
Tillygarmond	99	NO 6393
Tillygreig	105	NJ 8823
Tilmanstone	15	TR 3051
Tilney All Saints	46	TF 5618
Tilney High End	46	TF 5617
Tilney St. Lawrence	46	TF 5414
Tilshead	18	SU 0347
Tilstock	50	SJ 5337
Tilston	50	SJ 4551
Tilstone Fearnall	51	SJ 5660
Tilsworth	34	SP 9724
Tilton on the Hill	44	SK 7405
Timberland	55	TF 1158
Timbersbrook	51	SJ 8962
Timberscombe	16	SS 9542
Timble	65	SE 1752
Timperley	51	SJ 7988
Timsbury (Avon)	17	ST 6658
Timsbury (Hants.)	11	SU 3424
Timworth Green	36	TL 8669
Tincleton	10	SY 7691
Tindale	71	NY 6159
Tingewick	34	SP 6533
Tingley	59	SE 2826
Tingrith	34	TL 0032
Tinhay	4	SX 4085
Tinshill	59	SE 2540
Tinsley	53	SK 3990
Tintagel	4	SX 0588
Tintern Parva	29	SO 5200
Tintinhull	9	ST 5019
Tintwistle	59	SK 0297
Tinwald	70	NY 0081
Tinwell	44	TF 0006
Tipperty	105	NJ 9627
Tipton	41	SO 9592
Tipton St. John	8	SY 0991
Tiptree	23	TL 8916
Tirabad	27	SN 8741
Tirley	32	SO 8328
Tirphil	28	SO 1303
Tirril	63	NY 5026
Tisbury	10	ST 9429
Tissington	52	SK 1752
Titchberry	6	SS 2427
Titchfield	11	SU 5305
Titchmarsh	44	TL 0279
Titchwell	46	TF 7543
Tithby	54	SK 6936
Titley	30	SO 3260
Titlington	79	NU 1015
Tittensor	51	SJ 8738
Tittleshall	46	TF 8920
Tiverton (Ches.)	50	SJ 5560
Tiverton (Devon.)	8	SS 9512
Tivetshall St. Margaret	47	TM 1787
Tivetshall St. Mary	47	TM 1686
Tixall	41	SJ 9722
Tixover	44	SK 9700
Toab	113	HU 3811
Tobermory	95	NM 5055
Toberonochy	89	NM 7408
Tocher	105	NJ 6932
Tockenham	18	SU 0379
Tockenham Wick	18	SU 0381
Tockholes	58	SD 662
Tockington	29	ST 618
Tockwith	66	SE 465
Todber	10	ST 792
Toddington (Beds.)	34	TL 012
Toddington (Glos.)	32	SP 043
Todenham	33	SP 243
Todhills	70	NY 366
Todmorden	58	SD 932
Todwick	53	SK 498
Toft (Cambs.)	35	TL 365
Toft (Ches.)	51	SJ 767
Toft (Lincs.)	45	TF 061
Toft Monks	47	TM 429
Toft next Newton	54	TF 048
Toftrees	46	TF 892
Tofts	112	ND 376
Toftwood	46	TF 981
Togston	79	NU 240
Tokavaig	100	NG 601
Tokers Green	20	SU 707
Toll of Birness	105	NK 003
Tolland	16	ST 103
Tollard Royal	10	ST 941
Toller Fratrum	9	SY 579
Toller Porcorum	9	SY 569
Tollerton (N Yorks.)	66	SE 516
Tollerton (Notts.)	53	SK 613
Tollesbury	23	TL 951
Tolleshunt D'Arcy	23	TL 931
Tolleshunt Major	23	TL 901
Tolpuddle	10	SY 799
Tolstachaolais	109	NB 193
Tolworth	21	TQ 196
Tomatin	103	NH 802
Tombreck	103	NH 693
Tomich (Highld.)	102	NH 534
Tomich (Highld.)	108	NH 707
Tomintoul (Grampn.)	104	NJ 161
Tomintoul (Grampn.)	98	NO 149
Tomnavoulin	104	NJ 202
Ton	29	SO 330
Tonbridge	14	TQ 584
Tondu	28	SS 898
Tong (Isle of Lewis)	109	NB 443
Tong (Salop)	41	SJ 790
Tonge	43	SK 412
Tongham	20	SU 884
Tongland	69	NX 695
Tongue	111	NC 595
Tongwynlais	28	ST 158
Tonna	28	SS 779
Tonwell	35	TL 331
Tonypandy	28	SS 999
Tonyrefail	28	ST 018
Toot Baldon	33	SP 560
Toot Hill (Essex)	22	TL 510
Toot Hill (Hants.)	11	SU 371
Topcliffe	66	SE 397
Topcroft	47	TM 269
Topcroft Street	47	TM 269
Toppesfield	36	TL 733
Toppings	58	SD 721
Topsham	8	SX 978
Torbay	5	SX 896
Torbeg	74	NR 892
Torbryan	5	SX 826
Torcastle	96	NN 137
Torcross	5	SX 824
Tore	107	NH 605
Torksey	54	SK 837
Torlundy	96	NN 147
Tormarton	18	ST 767
Tormitchell	75	NX 239
Tormore	81	NR 893
Tornagrain	108	NH 764
Tornahaish	104	NJ 290
Tornaveen	104	NJ 610
Torness	102	NH 572
Torpenhow	62	NY 203
Torphichen	84	NS 967
Torphins	99	NJ 620
Torpoint	4	SX 435
Torquay	8	SX 916
Torquhan	86	NT 444
Torran (Strath.)	89	NM 870
Torrance	84	NS 617
Torridon	101	NG 905
Torrin	100	NG 572
Torrisdale	111	NC 676
Torrish	111	NC 971
Torrisholme	64	SD 446
Torroble	108	NC 590
Torry (Grampn.)	104	NJ 433
Torry (Grampn.)	105	NJ 940
Torryburn	85	NT 028
Torrylin	74	NR 962
Torterston	105	NK 074
Torthorwald	70	NY 037
Tortington	12	TQ 000
Tortworth	29	ST 699
Torvaig	100	NG 494
Torver	62	SD 289
Torwood	84	NS 848
Torworth	53	SK 658
Toscaig	101	NG 713
Toseland	35	TL 236
Tosside	65	SD 765
Tostock	36	TL 956
Totaig	100	NG 205
Tote	100	NG 414
Totegan	111	NC 826
Totland	11	SZ 328
Totley	53	SK 317
Totnes	5	SX 806
Toton	53	SK 503
Tottenham	21	TQ 349
Tottenhill	46	TF 631
Totteridge	21	TQ 249
Totternhoe	34	SP 992
Tottington	58	SD 771
Totton	11	SU 351
Tournaig	106	NG 878
Toux (Grampn.)	104	NJ 545
Toux (Grampn.)	105	NJ 985
Tovil	14	TQ 755
Tow Law	72	NZ 113
Toward	82	NS 136
Towcester	34	SP 694
Towednack	2	SW 483
Tower Hamlets	21	TQ 358
Towersey	34	SP 730
Towie	104	NJ 441
Towiemore	104	NJ 394
Town End (Cambs.)	45	TL 419
Town End (Cumbr.)	63	SD 448
Town Street	46	TL 778
Town Yetholm	87	NT 822
Townhead	69	NX 694
Townhead of Greenlaw	69	NX 746
Townhill	85	NT 108
Townshend	2	SW 593
Towthorpe	66	SE 625
Towton	60	SE 483

Wanswell 254 Whiteston

Wanswell 29 SO 6801
Wantage 19 SU 4087
Wapley 29 ST 7179
Wappenbury 43 SP 3769
Wappenham 34 SP 6245
Warbleton 13 TQ 6018
Warborough 19 SU 5993
Warboys 45 TL 3080
Warbstow 4 SX 2090
Warburton 51 SJ 7089
Warcop 63 NY 7415
Ward Green 37 TM 0564
Warden 15 TR 0271
Wardington 33 SP 4946
Wardle (Ches.) 51 SJ 6057
Wardle (Gtr Mches.) 58 SD 9116
Wardley 44 SK 8300
Wardlow 52 SK 1874
Wardy Hill 45 TL 4782
Ware 35 TL 3614
Wareham 10 SY 9287
Warehorne 15 TQ 9832
Waren Mill 87 NU 1534
Warenford 87 NU 1328
Warenton 87 NU 1030
Wareside 35 TL 3915
Waresley 35 TL 2454
Warfield 20 SU 8872
Wargrave 20 SU 7878
Warham All Saints 46 TF 9441
Warham St. Mary 46 TF 9441
Wark (Northum.) 87 NT 8238
Wark (Northum.) 78 NY 8576
Warkleigh 7 SS 6422
Warkton 44 SP 8980
Warkworth 79 NU 2406
Warlaby 66 SE 3591
Warland 58 SD 9419
Warleggan 4 SX 1569
Warley 42 SP 0086
Warlingham 21 TQ 3658
Warmfield 59 SE 3720
Warmingham 51 SJ 7161
Warmington (Northants.) 45 TL 0791
Warmington (Warw.) 33 SP 4147
Warminster 18 ST 8644
Warmsworth 60 SE 5400
Warmwell 9 SY 7585
Warndon 32 SO 8856
Warnford 11 SU 6223
Warnham 12 TQ 1633
Warninglid 13 TQ 2526
Warren (Ches.) 51 SJ 8870
Warren (Dyfed) 24 SR 9397
Warren Row 20 SU 8180
Warren Street 14 TQ 9253
Warrington (Bucks.) 34 SP 8954
Warrington (Ches.) 51 SJ 6088
Warsash 11 SU 4905
Warslow 52 SK 0858
Warsop 53 SK 5667
Warter 67 SE 8750
Warthill 66 SE 6755
Wartling 13 TQ 6509
Wartnaby 34 SK 7123
Warton (Lancs) 57 SD 4028
Warton (Lancs.) 64 SD 4972
Warton (Northum) 79 NU 0002
Warton (Warw) 42 SK 2803
Warwick (Cumbr.) 71 NY 4656
Warwick (Warw.) 33 SP 2865
Warwick Bridge 71 NY 4756
Washaway 4 SX 0369
Washbourne 5 SX 7954
Washfield 8 SS 9315
Washfold 65 NZ 0502
Washford 16 ST 0441
Washford Pyne 7 SS 8111
Washingborough 54 TF 0170
Washington (Tyne and Wear) 72 NZ 3356
Washington (W Susx) 12 TQ 1212
Wasing 19 SU 5764
Waskerley 72 NZ 0545
Wasperton 33 SP 2659
Wass 66 SE 5579
Watchet 16 ST 0743
Watchfield (Oxon.) 18 SU 2490
Watchfield (Somer.) 17 ST 3446
Watchgate 63 SD 5399
Water 58 SD 8425
Water End (Herts.) 35 TL 0310
Water End (Herts.) 35 TL 2304
Water Meetings 76 NS 9513
Water Newton 45 TL 1097
Water Orton 42 SP 1791
Water Stratford 34 SP 6534
Water Yeat 62 SD 2889
Waterbeach 45 TL 4965
Waterbeck 70 NY 2477
Waterden 46 TF 8835
Waterfall 52 SK 0851
Waterfoot (Lancs.) 58 SD 8321
Waterfoot (Strath.) 84 NS 5654
Waterford 35 TL 3114
Waterheads 85 NT 2451
Waterhouses (Durham) 72 NZ 1841
Waterhouses (Staffs.) 52 SK 0850
Wateringbury 14 TQ 6853
Wateringhouse 113 ND 3090
Waterloo (Dorset) 10 SZ 0194
Waterloo (Mers.) 50 SJ 3297
Waterloo (Norf.) 47 TG 2219
Waterloo (Strath.) 84 NS 8153
Waterloo (Tays.) 92 NO 0636
Waterlooville 11 SU 6809
Waterperry 34 SP 6206
Waterrow 16 ST 0525
Waters Upton 41 SJ 6319
Watersfield 12 TQ 0115
Waterside (Strath.) 75 NS 4308
Waterside (Strath.) 82 NS 4843
Waterside (Strath.) 82 NS 5160
Waterside (Strath.) 84 NS 6773
Waterstock 34 SP 6305
Waterston 24 SM 9306
Watford (Herts.) 20 TQ 1196
Watford (Northants.) 43 SP 6069
Wath (N Yorks.) 66 SE 3277
Wath (N. Yorks.) 65 SE 1467
Wath Upon Dearne 59 SE 4300
Watlington (Norf.) 46 TF 6211
Watlington (Oxon.) 19 SU 6994
Watnall Chaworth 53 SK 5046
Watten 112 ND 2454
Wattisfield 36 TM 0174
Wattisham 36 TM 0151
Watton (Humbs.) 67 TA 0150
Watton (Norf.) 46 TF 9100
Watton-at-Stone 35 TL 3019
Wattston 84 NS 7770
Wattstown 28 ST 0194
Waunarlwydd 25 SS 6095
Waunfawr 48 SH 5259
Wavendon 34 SP 9137
Waverton (Ches.) 50 SJ 4663
Waverton (Cumbr.) 70 NY 2247
Wawne 61 TA 0836
Waxham 47 TG 4326
Waxholme 61 TA 3229
Way Village 7 SS 8810
Wayford 9 ST 4006
Wealdstone 21 TQ 1689
Weare 17 ST 4152
Weare Giffard 6 SS 4721
Weasenham All Saints 46 TF 8421
Weasenham St. Peter 46 TF 8522
Weaverham 51 SJ 6173
Weaverthorpe 67 SE 9670
Webheath 42 SP 0266
Weddington 43 SP 3693
Wedhampton 18 SU 0557
Wedmore 17 ST 4347
Wednesbury 42 SP 0095
Wednesfield 41 SJ 9400
Weedon 34 SP 8118
Weedon Bec 34 SP 6259
Weedon Lois 33 SP 6047
Weeford 42 SK 1404
Week 7 SS 7316
Week St. Mary 6 SX 2397
Weekley 44 SP 8880
Weeley 23 TM 1422
Weeley Heath 23 TM 1520
Weem 97 NN 8449
Weeping Cross 41 SJ 9421
Weeting 46 TL 7788
Weeton (Lancs.) 57 SD 3834
Weeton (W Yorks.) 59 SE 2846
Weir 58 SD 8724
Welbeck Colliery Village 53 SK 5869
Welborne 47 TG 0610
Welbourn 54 SK 9654
Welburn 66 SE 7168
Welbury 66 NZ 3902
Welby 54 SK 9738
Welches Dam 45 TL 4786
Welcombe 6 SS 2218
Weldon 44 SP 9289
Welford (Berks.) 19 SU 4073
Welford (Northants.) 43 SP 6480
Welford-on-Avon 32 SP 1552
Welham 44 SP 7692
Welham Green 35 TL 2305
Well (Hants.) 20 SU 7646
Well (Lincs.) 55 TF 4473
Well (N Yorks.) 66 SE 2682
Well Hill (Kent) 21 TQ 4963
Welland 32 SO 7940
Wellesbourne 33 SP 2755
Wellhill (Highld.) 108 NH 9962
Welling 21 TQ 4575
Wellingborough 44 SP 8968
Wellingham 46 TF 8722
Wellingore 54 SK 9856
Wellington (Here. and Worc.) 30 SO 4948
Wellington (Salop) 41 SJ 6411
Wellington (Somer.) 8 ST 1320
Wellington Heath 32 SO 7140
Wellow (Avon) 18 ST 7358
Wellow (I. of W.) 11 SZ 3887
Wellow (Notts.) 53 SK 6666
Wells 17 ST 5445
Wells of Ythan 104 NJ 6338
Wells-Next-The-Sea 46 TF 9143
Wellsborough 43 SK 3602
Wellwood 85 NT 0888
Welney 45 TL 5294
Welsh End 50 SJ 5035
Welsh Frankton 50 SJ 3633
Welsh Hook 24 SM 9327
Welsh Newton 29 SO 4918
Welsh St. Donats 28 ST 0276
Welshampton 50 SJ 4334
Welshpool (Trallwng) 40 SJ 2207
Welton (Cumbr.) 70 NY 3544
Welton (Humbs.) 61 SE 9527
Welton (Lincs.) 54 TF 0079
Welton (Northants.) 33 SP 5865
Welton le Marsh 55 TF 4768
Welton le Wold 55 TF 2787
Welwick 61 TA 3421
Welwyn 35 TL 2316
Welwyn Garden City 35 TL 2412
Wem 40 SJ 5129
Wembdon 17 ST 2837
Wembley 21 TQ 1985
Wembury 5 SX 5148
Wembworthy 7 SS 6609
Wemyss Bay 82 NS 1869
Wenallt 49 SH 9842
Wendens Ambo 35 TL 5036
Wendlebury 34 SP 5519
Wendling 46 TF 9213
Wendover 34 SP 8708
Wendron 2 SW 6731
Wendy 35 TL 3247
Wenhaston 37 TM 4275
Wennington (Cambs.) 45 TL 2379
Wennington (Essex) 21 TQ 5381
Wennington (Lancs.) 64 SD 6169
Wensley (Derby) 53 SK 2661
Wensley (N Yorks) 65 SE 0989
Wentbridge 60 SE 4817
Wentnor 40 SO 3892
Wentworth (Cambs.) 45 TL 4878
Wentworth (S Yorks.) 53 SK 3898
Wenvoe 28 ST 1272
Weobley 30 SO 4051
Weobley Marsh 30 SO 4151
Wereham 46 TF 6801
Wergs 41 SJ 8601
Wernrheolydd 29 SO 3913
Werrington (Devon.) 4 SX 3287
Werrington (Staffs.) 51 SJ 9647
Wervin 50 SJ 4171
Wesham 57 SD 4132
Wessington 53 SK 3757
West Acre 46 TF 7715
West Allerdean 87 NT 9646
West Alvington 5 SX 7243
West Anstey 7 SS 8527
West Ashby 55 TF 2672
West Ashling 12 SU 8007
West Ashton 18 ST 8755
West Auckland 72 NZ 1826
West Bagborough 16 ST 1633
West Barkwith 55 TF 1580
West Barns 86 NT 6578
West Barsham 46 TF 9033
West Bay 9 SY 4690
West Beckham 47 TG 1339
West Bergholt 36 TL 9527
West Bexington 9 SY 5386
West Bilney 46 TF 7115
West Blatchington 13 TQ 2706
West Bradenham 46 TF 9208
West Bradford 58 SD 7444
West Bradley 17 ST 5536
West Bretton 59 SE 2813
West Bridgford 53 SK 5837
West Bromwich 42 SP 0091
West Buckland (Somer.) 8 ST 1720
West Burton (N Yorks) 65 SE 0186
West Burton (W Susx) 12 TQ 0014
West Caister 47 TG 5011
West Calder 85 NT 0163
West Camel 9 ST 5724
West Challow 19 SU 3688
West Charleton 5 SX 7542
West Chelborough 9 ST 5405
West Chevington 79 NZ 2297
West Chiltington 12 TQ 0918
West Clandon 20 TQ 0452
West Cliffe 15 TR 3445
West Clyne 108 NC 8906
West Clyth 112 ND 2736
West Coker 9 ST 5113
West Compton (Dorset) 9 SY 5694
West Compton (Somer.) 17 ST 5942
West Cross 25 SS 6189
West Curry 4 SX 2893
West Curthwaite 70 NY 3248
West Dean (W Susx) 12 SU 8512
West Dean (Wilts.) 11 SU 2526
West Deeping 45 TF 1009
West Derby 50 SJ 3993
West Dereham 46 TF 6500
West Ditchburn 79 NU 1320
West Down (Devon) 6 SS 5142
West Drayton (Gtr London) 20 TQ 0679
West Drayton (Notts.) 54 SK 7074
West Dunnet 112 ND 2273
West End (Avon) 29 ST 4469
West End (Beds.) 34 SP 9853
West End (Hants) 11 SU 4614
West End (Herts.) 35 TL 3306
West End (Norf.) 47 TG 4911
West End (Oxon.) 33 SP 4204
West End (Surrey) 20 SU 9461
West End Green 19 SU 6661
West Farleigh 14 TQ 7152
West Felton 40 SJ 3425
West Firle 12 TQ 4707
West Geirnish 109 NF 7741
West Ginge 19 SU 4386
West Grafton 18 SU 2460
West Green 20 SU 7456
West Grimstead 11 SU 2026
West Grinstead 12 TQ 1721
West Haddlesey 60 SE 5526
West Haddon 43 SP 6371
West Hagbourne 19 SU 5187
West Hallam 53 SK 4341
West Halton 60 SE 9020
West Ham (Gtr London) 21 TQ 4083
West Handley 53 SK 3977
West Hanney 19 SU 4092
West Hanningfield 22 TQ 7399
West Harnham 10 SU 1229
West Harptree 17 ST 5556
West Hatch 8 ST 2820
West Helmsdale 112 ND 0114
West Hendred 19 SU 4488
West Heslerton 67 SE 9175
West Hill 8 SY 0694
West Hoathly 13 TQ 3632
West Holme 10 SY 8885
West Horndon 22 TQ 6288
West Horrington 17 ST 5747
West Horsley 20 TQ 0753
West Hougham 15 TR 2640
West Humble 21 TQ 1652
West Hyde 20 TQ 0391
West Ilsley 19 SU 4682
West Itchenor 12 SU 7900
West Kennet 18 SU 1167
West Kilbride 82 NS 2048
West Kingsdown 21 TQ 5762
West Kington 18 ST 8077
West Kirby 50 SJ 2186
West Knighton 9 SY 7387
West Knoyle 10 ST 8532
West Langdon 15 TR 3247
West Langwell 108 NC 6909
West Lavington (W Susx.) 12 SU 8920
West Lavington (Wilts.) 18 SU 0052
West Layton 72 NZ 1409
West Leake 43 SK 5226
West Lexham 46 TF 8417
West Lilling 66 SE 6465
West Linton (Borders) 85 NT 1551
West Littleton 29 ST 7575
West Looe 4 SX 2553
West Lulworth 10 SY 8280
West Lutton 67 SE 9269
West Lynn 46 TF 6120
West Mains 84 NS 9550
West Malling 14 TQ 6857
West Malvern 32 SO 7646
West Marden 12 SU 7613
West Markham 54 SK 7272
West Marton 65 SD 8850
West Meon 11 SU 6424
West Mersea 23 TM 0112
West Milton 9 SY 5096
West Monkton 16 ST 2528
West Moors 10 SU 0802
West Muir (Tays.) 99 NO 5661
West Newton (Humbs.) 61 TA 2038
West Newton (Norf.) 46 TF 6927
West Norwood 21 TQ 3171
West Ogwell 5 SX 8170
West Overton 18 SU 1367
West Parley 10 SZ 0997
West Peckham 14 TQ 6452
West Pennard 17 ST 5438
West Pentire 2 SW 7760
West Putford 6 SS 3515
West Quantoxhead 16 ST 1141
West Rainton 72 NZ 3246
West Rasen 54 TF 0589
West Raynham 46 TF 8725
West Row 36 TL 6775
West Rudham 46 TF 8127
West Runton 47 TG 1842
West Saltoun 86 NT 4667
West Sandwick 113 HU 4488
West Scrafton 65 SE 0783
West Stafford 9 SY 7289
West Stoke 12 SU 8208
West Stonesdale 65 NY 8802
West Stoughton 17 ST 4149
West Stour 10 ST 7822
West Stourmouth 15 TR 2562
West Stow 36 TL 8170
West Stowell 18 SU 1362
West Street 14 TQ 9054
West Tanfield 66 SE 2778
West Tarbert 81 NR 8467
West Thorney 12 SU 7602
West Thurrock 21 TQ 5877
West Tilbury 22 TQ 6677
West Tisted 11 SU 6429
West Tofts 92 NO 1134
West Torrington 55 TF 1381
West Town 29 ST 4767
West Tytherley 11 SU 2730
West Tytherton 18 ST 9474
West Walton 45 TF 4713
West Walton Highway 45 TF 4912
West Wellow 11 SU 2818
West Wemyss 93 NT 3294
West Wick (Avon) 17 ST 3661
West Wickham (Cambs.) 36 TL 6149
West Wickham (Gtr. London) 21 TQ 3866
West Winch 46 TF 6316
West Wittering 12 SZ 7898
West Witton 65 SE 0688
West Woodburn 78 NY 8986
West Woodhay 19 SU 3962
West Worldham 12 SU 7436
West Wratting 36 TL 6052
West Wycombe 20 SU 8394
Westbere 15 TR 1961
Westbourne (Dorset) 10 SZ 0690
Westbourne (W Susx.) 12 SU 7507
Westbury 57 SD 3731
Westbury (Salop) 50 SJ 3509
Westbury (Wilts.) 18 ST 8751
Westbury Leigh 18 ST 8649
Westbury-on-Severn 32 SO 7114
Westbury-sub-Mendip 17 ST 5049
Westcliff-on-Sea 22 TQ 8685
Westcombe 17 ST 6739
Westcote 33 SP 2120
Westcott (Bucks.) 34 SP 7117
Westcott (Devon) 8 ST 0104
Westcott (Surrey) 20 TQ 1348
Westcott Barton 33 SP 4224
Westdean (E Susx) 13 TV 5299
Wester Culbeuchly Crofts 104 NJ 6562
Wester Denoon 98 NO 3543
Wester Fintray 105 NJ 8116
Wester Gruinards 108 NH 5292
Wester Lonvine 108 NH 7172
Westerdale (Highld.) 112 ND 1251
Westerdale (N Yorks.) 66 NZ 6605
Westerfield (Suff.) 37 TM 1747
Westergate 12 SU 9305
Westerham 21 TQ 4454
Westerleigh 29 ST 6979
Westerloch 112 ND 3358
Westerton 99 NO 6654
Westfield (Caithness) 112 ND 0564
Westfield (E Susx.) 14 TQ 8115
Westfield (Lothian) 84 NS 9372
Westfield (Norf.) 46 TF 9909
Westgate (Durham) 63 NY 9038
Westgate (Humbs.) 60 SE 7707
Westgate (Norf.) 46 TF 9740
Westgate on Sea 15 TR 3270
Westhall (Cumbr.) 71 NY 5667
Westhall (Suff.) 47 TM 4280
Westham (E Susx.) 13 TQ 6404
Westham (Somer.) 17 ST 4046
Westhampnett 12 SU 8706
Westhay 17 ST 4342
Westhead 57 SD 4407
Westhide 31 SO 5844
Westhope (Here. and Worc.) 30 SO 4651
Westhope (Salop) 40 SO 4786
Westhorpe (Lincs.) 55 TF 2131
Westhorpe (Suff.) 37 TM 0469
Westhoughton 58 SD 6505
Westhouse 64 SD 6673
Westhouses 53 SK 4257
Westing 113 HP 5705
Westlake 5 SX 6253
Westleigh (Devon) 6 SS 4628
Westleigh (Devon) 8 ST 0517
Westleton 37 TM 4469
Westley (Salop) 40 SJ 3507
Westley (Suff.) 36 TL 8264
Westley Waterless 36 TL 6256
Westlington 34 SP 7610
Westlinton (Cumbr.) 70 NY 3964
Westmarsh 15 TR 2761
Westmeston 13 TQ 3313
Westmill 35 TL 3627
Westmuir (Tays.) 98 NO 3652
Westnewton (Cumbr.) 70 NY 1344
Weston (Avon) 29 ST 7266
Weston (Berks.) 19 SU 3973
Weston (Ches.) 50 SJ 5080
Weston (Ches.) 51 SJ 7252
Weston (Dorset) 9 SY 6870
Weston (Hants.) 12 SU 7221
Weston (Herts.) 35 TL 2630
Weston (Lincs.) 45 TF 2925
Weston (Northants.) 33 SP 5847
Weston (Notts.) 54 SK 7767
Weston (Salop) 41 SJ 5628
Weston (Salop) 41 SO 5993
Weston (Staffs.) 41 SJ 9727
Weston (W Yorks.) 59 SE 1747
Weston Beggard 31 SO 5841
Weston Colville 36 TL 6153
Weston Corbett 19 SU 6846
Weston Favel 34 SP 7862
Weston Green 36 TL 6252
Weston Heath 41 SJ 7813
Weston Hills 45 TF 2821
Weston Jones 41 SJ 7524
Weston Longville 47 TG 1116
Weston Lullingfields 40 SJ 4224
Weston Patrick 19 SU 6946
Weston Rhyn 50 SJ 2835
Weston Subedge 32 SP 1240
Weston Turville 34 SP 8511
Weston Underwood (Bucks.) 34 SP 8650
Weston Underwood (Derby) 53 SK 2942
Weston by Welland 44 SP 7791
Weston under Penyard 29 SO 6323
Weston under Wetherley 43 SP 3569
Weston-in-Gordano 29 ST 4474
Weston-on-Trent 43 SK 4027
Weston-on-the-Green 33 SP 5318
Weston-super-Mare 17 ST 3261
Weston-under-Lizard 41 SJ 8010
Westoning 35 TL 0332
Westonzoyland 17 ST 3534
Westow 67 SE 7565
Westport 9 ST 3819
Westrigg 84 NS 9067
Westruther 86 NT 6349
Westry 45 TL 3998
Westward 70 NY 2744
Westward Ho! 6 SS 4329
Westwell (Kent) 15 TQ 9947
Westwell (Oxon) 33 SP 2210
Westwell Leacon 15 TQ 9647
Westwick (Cambs.) 45 TL 4265
Westwick (Norf.) 47 TG 2727
Westwood (Devon.) 8 SY 0199
Westwood (Wilts.) 18 ST 8059
Westwoodside 60 SK 7499
Wetheral 71 NY 465
Wetherby 59 SE 404
Wetherden 36 TM 006
Wetheringsett 29 TM 126
Wethersfield 36 TL 713
Wetherup Street 37 TM 146
Wetley Rocks 51 SJ 964
Wettenhall 51 SJ 626
Wetton 52 SK 105
Wetwang 67 SE 935
Wetwood 51 SJ 773
Wexcombe 19 SU 275
Weybourne 47 TG 114
Weybread 37 TM 248
Weybridge 20 TQ 076
Weydale 112 ND 146
Weyhill 19 SU 314
Weymouth 9 SY 677
Whaddon (Bucks.) 34 SP 803
Whaddon (Cambs.) 35 TL 354
Whaddon (Glos.) 32 SO 831
Whaddon (Wilts.) 10 SU 192
Whale 63 NY 522
Whaley 53 SK 517
Whaley Bridge 52 SK 018
Whaligoe 112 ND 324
Whalley 58 SD 733
Whalton 79 NZ 128
Wham 65 SD 776
Whaplode 45 TF 322
Whaplode Drove 45 TF 311
Wharfe 65 SD 786
Wharles 57 SD 443
Wharncliffe Side 59 SK 299
Wharram le Street 67 SE 866
Wharton (Ches.) 51 SJ 666
Wharton (Here. and Worc.) 30 SO 505
Whaston 65 NZ 140
Whatcombe 10 ST 830
Whatcote 33 SP 294
Whatfield 36 TM 024
Whatley 19 ST 734
Whatlington 14 TQ 761
Whatstandwell 53 SK 335
Whatton 54 SK 743
Whauphill 68 NX 404
Whaw 65 NY 980
Wheatacre 47 TM 459
Wheathampstead 35 TL 171
Wheatley (Hants.) 12 SU 784
Wheatley (Notts) 54 SK 768
Wheatley (Oxon) 33 SP 590
Wheatley Hill 72 NZ 383
Wheatley Lane 58 SD 833
Wheaton Aston 41 SJ 841
Wheddon Cross 16 SS 923
Wheedlemont 104 NJ 472
Wheelerstreet 12 SU 944
Wheelock 51 SJ 745
Wheelton 58 SD 602
Wheldrake 60 SE 674
Whelford 18 SU 169
Whelpley Hill 34 TL 000
Whenby 66 SE 636
Whepstead 36 TL 835
Wherstead 37 TM 154
Wherwell 19 SU 384
Wheston 52 SK 137
Whetsted 14 TQ 654
Whicham 62 SD 138
Whichford 33 SP 313
Whickham 72 NZ 206
Whiddon Down 5 SX 699
Whigstreet 99 NO 484
Whilton 34 SP 636
Whim 85 NT 215
Whimple 8 SY 049
Whimpwell Green 47 TG 382
Whinburgh 46 TG 000
Whinnyfold 105 NK 073
Whippingham 11 SZ 519
Whipsnade 34 TL 011
Whipton 8 SX 949
Whissendine 44 SK 821
Whissonsett 46 TF 912
Whistley Green 20 SU 797
Whiston (Mers.) 50 SJ 479
Whiston (Northants.) 34 SP 856
Whiston (S Yorks.) 53 SK 448
Whiston (Staffs.) 41 SJ 891
Whiston (Staffs.) 52 SK 034
Whitbeck 62 SD 118
Whitbourne 32 SO 715
Whitburn (Lothian) 34 NS 946
Whitburn (Tyne and Wear) 72 NZ 406
Whitby (Ches.) 50 SJ 407
Whitby (N Yorks.) 73 NZ 891
Whitchurch (Avon) 29 ST 616
Whitchurch (Bucks.) 34 SP 802
Whitchurch (Devon) 5 SX 497
Whitchurch (Dyfed) 24 SM 802
Whitchurch (Hants.) 19 SU 464
Whitchurch (Here. and Worc.) 29 SO 541
Whitchurch (Oxon) 19 SU 637
Whitchurch (S Glam) 28 ST 168
Whitchurch (Salop) 50 SJ 544
Whitchurch Canonicorum 9 SY 399
Whitcott Keysett 40 SO 278
White Chapel 57 SD 554
White Coppice 58 SD 611
White Court 22 TL 742
White Lackington 9 SY 719
White Ladies Aston 32 SO 925
White Notley 22 TL 781
White Roding 22 TL 561
White Waltham 20 SU 857
Whitecairns 105 NJ 921
Whitechurch 26 SN 143
Whitecraig (Lothian) 85 NT 357
Whitecroft 29 SO 610
Whitecross 85 NS 967
Whiteface 108 NH 718
Whitefield (Gtr Mches.) 58 SD 800
Whitefield (Tays) 92 NO 173
Whiteford 105 NJ 712
Whitehall 113 HY 652
Whitehaven 62 NX 971
Whitehill (Hants.) 12 SU 793
Whitehills 104 NJ 656
Whitehouse (Grampn.) 104 NJ 621
Whitehouse (Strath) 81 NR 816
Whitekirk 86 NT 598
Whiteley Village 20 TQ 096
Whitemans Green 13 TQ 302
Whitemire 103 NH 985
Whitemoor 3 SW 975
Whiteparish 11 SU 242
Whiterashes 105 NJ 852
Whiterow 112 ND 354
Whiteshill 32 SO 830
Whiteside (Lothian) 85 NS 966
Whitesmith 13 TQ 521
Whitestaunton 8 ST 281
Whitestone 5 SX 869

Whiteway 255 Yaxley (Cambs.)

Whiteway	32	SO 9110
Whitewell	58	SD 6546
Whitewreath	104	NJ 2356
Whitfield (Avon)	29	ST 6791
Whitfield (Kent)	15	TR 3146
Whitfield (Northants)	34	SP 6039
Whitfield (Northum)	71	NY 7758
Whitford	50	SJ 1477
Whitgift	60	SE 8022
Whitgreave	41	SJ 8928
Whithorn	69	NX 4440
Whiting Bay (Island of Arran)	74	NS 0425
Whitington	46	TL 7199
Whitland	24	SN 1916
Whitletts	75	NS 3622
Whitley (Berks)	20	SU 7170
Whitley (Ches.)	51	SJ 6178
Whitley (N Yorks)	60	SE 5521
Whitley Bay	79	NZ 3577
Whitley Chapel	71	NY 9257
Whitley Row	21	TQ 5052
Whitlock's End	42	SP 1076
Whitminster	32	SO 7708
Whitmore	51	SJ 8041
Whitnage	8	ST 0215
Whitnash	33	SP 3263
Whitney	30	SO 2647
Whitrigg (Cumbr.)	62	NY 2038
Whitrigg (Cumbr.)	70	NY 2257
Whitsbury	10	SU 1218
Whitsome	87	NT 8650
Whitson	29	ST 3783
Whitstable	15	TR 1166
Whitstone	6	SX 2698
Whittingham	79	NU 0611
Whittingslow	40	SO 4288
Whittington (Derby)	53	SK 3975
Whittington (Glos.)	32	SP 0120
Whittington (Here. and Worc.)	41	SO 8582
Whittington (Here. and Worc.)	32	SO 8752
Whittington (Lancs.)	64	SD 5976
Whittington (Salop)	50	SJ 3230
Whittington (Staffs.)	42	SK 1508
Whittle-le-Woods	57	SD 5822
Whittlebury	34	SP 6943
Whittlesey	45	TL 2797
Whittlesford	35	TL 4748
Whitton (Clev.)	72	NZ 3822
Whitton (Humbs.)	60	SE 9034
Whitton (Northum.)	79	NU 0501
Whitton (Powys)	40	SO 2667
Whitton (Salop)	41	SO 5772
Whitton (Suff.)	37	TM 1447
Whittonditch	19	SU 2872
Whittonstall	72	NZ 0757
Whitwell (Derby.)	53	SK 5276
Whitwell (Herts.)	35	TL 1821
Whitwell (I of W.)	11	SZ 5277
Whitwell (Leic.)	44	SK 9208
Whitwell (N Yorks.)	66	SE 2899
Whitwell-on-the-Hill	66	SE 7265
Whitwick	43	SK 4316
Whitwood	59	SE 4124
Whitworth	58	SD 8818
Whixall	50	SJ 5034
Whixley	66	SE 4457
Whorlton (Durham)	72	NZ 1014
Whorlton (N Yorks.)	66	NZ 4802
Whygate	78	NY 7675
Whyle	31	SO 5560
Whyteleafe	21	TQ 3358
Wibdon	29	ST 5797
Wibtoft	43	SP 4787
Wichenford	32	SO 7860
Wichling	14	TQ 9256
Wick (Avon)	29	ST 7072
Wick (Dorset)	10	SZ 1591
Wick (Here. and Worc.)	32	SO 9645
Wick (Highld.)	112	ND 3650
Wick (S Glam.)	28	SS 9272
Wick (W Susx)	12	TQ 0203
Wick (Wilts.)	18	SU 1621
Wick Rissington	33	SP 1821
Wick St. Lawrence	29	ST 3665
Wicken (Cambs.)	36	TL 5770
Wicken (Northants.)	34	SP 7439
Wicken Bonhunt	35	TL 5033
Wickenby	54	TF 0882
Wickersley	53	SK 4891
Wickford	22	TQ 7593
Wickham (Berks.)	19	SU 3971
Wickham (Hants.)	11	SU 5711
Wickham Bishops	22	TL 8412
Wickham Market	37	TM 3056
Wickham Skeith	37	TM 0969
Wickham St. Paul	36	TL 8336
Wickham Street (Suff.)	36	TL 7554
Wickham Street (Suff.)	37	TM 0869
Wickhambreaux	15	TR 2158
Wickhambrook	36	TL 7454
Wickhamford	32	SP 0642
Wickhampton	47	TG 4205
Wickmere	47	TG 1733
Wickwar	29	ST 7288
Widdington	35	TL 5331
Widdrington	79	NZ 2595
Wide Open	79	NZ 2472
Widecombe in the Moor	5	SX 7176
Widford (Essex)	22	TL 6905
Widford (Herts.)	35	TL 4115
Widmerpool	43	SK 6327
Widnes	50	SJ 5185
Wigan	57	SD 5805
Wiggaton	8	SY 1093
Wiggenhall St. Germans	46	TF 5914
Wiggenhall St. Mary Magdalen	46	TF 5911
Wiggenhall St. Mary the Virgin	46	TF 5814
Wigginton (Herts.)	34	SP 9410
Wigginton (N Yorks.)	66	SE 5958
Wigginton (Oxon.)	33	SP 3833
Wigginton (Staffs.)	42	SK 2106
Wigglesworth	65	SD 8056
Wiggonby	70	NY 2953
Wiggonholt	12	TQ 0616
Wighill	60	SE 4746
Wighton	46	TF 9339
Wigmore (Here. and Worc.)	40	SO 4169
Wigmore (Kent)	14	TQ 8063
Wigsley	54	SK 8570
Wigsthorpe	44	TL 0482
Wigston	43	SP 6099
Wigtoft	55	TF 2636
Wigton	70	NY 2548
Wigtown	68	NX 4355
Wigtwizzle	53	SK 2495
Wilbarston	44	SP 8188
Wilberfoss	66	SE 7350
Wilburton	45	TL 4875
Wilby (Norf.)	46	TM 0389
Wilby (Northants.)	44	SP 8666
Wilby (Suff.)	37	TM 2472
Wilcot	18	SU 1461
Wildboarclough	51	SJ 9868
Wilden	35	TL 0955
Wildhern	19	SU 3550
Wildsworth	60	SK 8097
Wilford	53	SK 5637
Wilkesley	51	SJ 6241
Wilkhaven	108	NH 9486
Wilkieston	85	NT 1168
Willand	8	ST 0310
Willaston (Ches.)	50	SJ 3277
Willaston (Ches.)	51	SJ 6752
Willenhall (W Mids.)	41	SO 9698
Willenhall (W Mids.)	43	SP 3676
Willerby (Humbs.)	61	TA 0230
Willerby (N Yorks.)	67	TA 0079
Willersey	32	SP 1039
Willersley	30	SO 3147
Willesborough	15	TR 0441
Willesden	21	TQ 2284
Willett	16	ST 1033
Willey (Salop)	41	SO 6799
Willey (Warw.)	43	SP 4984
Williamscot	33	SP 4745
Willian	35	TL 2230
Willimontswick	71	NY 7763
Willingale	22	TL 5907
Willingdon	13	TQ 5902
Willingham (Cambs)	45	TL 4070
Willingham by Stow	54	SK 8784
Willington (Beds.)	35	TL 1150
Willington (Derby.)	43	SK 2928
Willington (Durham)	72	NZ 1935
Willington (Tyne and Wear)	72	NZ 3167
Willington (Warw.)	33	SP 2638
Willington Corner	50	SJ 5367
Willitoft	60	SE 7434
Williton	16	ST 0740
Willoughby (Lincs.)	55	TF 4772
Willoughby (Warw.)	43	SP 5167
Willoughby Waterleys	43	SP 5792
Willoughby-on-the-Wolds	43	SK 6325
Willoughton	54	SK 9293
Wilmcote	32	SP 1658
Wilmington (Devon.)	8	SY 2199
Wilmington (E Susx)	13	TQ 5404
Wilmington (Kent)	21	TQ 5372
Wilmslow	51	SJ 8480
Wilnecote	42	SK 2201
Wilpshire	58	SD 6832
Wilsden	59	SE 0935
Wilsford (Lincs.)	54	TF 0043
Wilsford (Wilts.)	18	SU 1057
Wilsford (Wilts.)	18	SU 1339
Wilshamstead	35	TL 0643
Wilsill	65	SE 1864
Wilson	43	SK 4024
Wilsthorpe	45	TF 0913
Wilstone	34	SP 9014
Wilton (Cleve.)	73	NZ 5819
Wilton (N Yorks.)	67	SE 8582
Wilton (Wilts.)	10	SU 0931
Wilton (Wilts.)	19	SU 2661
Wilton Dean (Borders)	77	NT 4914
Wimbish	36	TL 5936
Wimbish Green	36	TL 6035
Wimbledon	21	TQ 2470
Wimblington	45	TL 4192
Wimborne Minster	10	SZ 0199
Wimborne St. Giles	10	SU 0212
Wimbotsham	46	TF 6205
Wimpstone	33	SP 2148
Wincanton	17	ST 7128
Wincham	51	SJ 6675
Winchburgh	85	NT 0874
Winchcombe	32	SP 0228
Winchelsea	14	TQ 9017
Winchelsea Beach	14	TQ 9115
Winchester	11	SU 4829
Winchfield	20	SU 7654
Winchmore Hill (Bucks.)	20	SU 9394
Winchmore Hill (Gtr London)	21	TQ 3195
Wincle	51	SJ 9565
Windermere (Cumbr.)	62	SD 4198
Winderton	33	SP 3240
Windlesham	20	SU 9363
Windley	53	SK 3045
Windmill Hill (E Susx)	13	TQ 6412
Windmill Hill (Somer.)	8	ST 3116
Windrush	33	SP 1913
Windsor	20	SU 9676
Windygates	93	NO 3400
Wineham	13	TQ 2320
Winestead	61	TA 2924
Winfarthing	47	TM 1085
Winford	29	ST 5364
Winforton	30	SO 2947
Winfrith Newburgh	10	SY 8084
Wing (Bucks.)	34	SP 8822
Wing (Leic.)	44	SK 8903
Wingate (Durham)	72	NZ 4036
Wingates (Gtr Mches.)	58	SD 6507
Wingates (Northum.)	79	NZ 0995
Wingerworth	53	SK 3867
Wingfield (Beds.)	34	SP 9926
Wingfield (Suff.)	37	TM 2276
Wingfield (Wilts.)	18	ST 8256
Wingham	15	TR 2457
Wingrave	34	SP 8719
Winkburn	54	SK 7158
Winkfield	20	SU 9072
Winkfield Row	20	SU 9071
Winkhill	52	SK 0651
Winkleigh	6	SS 6308
Winksley	66	SE 2471
Winless	112	ND 3054
Winmarleigh	57	SD 4748
Winnersh	20	SU 7870
Winscales	62	NY 0226
Winscombe	17	ST 4157
Winsford (Ches.)	51	SJ 6566
Winsford (Somer.)	16	SS 9034
Winsham	8	ST 3706
Winshill	42	SK 2623
Winskill	63	NY 5835
Winslade	19	SU 6547
Winsley	18	ST 7960
Winslow	34	SP 7627
Winson	32	SP 0908
Winster (Cumbr.)	62	SD 4193
Winster (Derby.)	53	SK 2460
Winston (Durham)	72	NZ 1416
Winston (Suff.)	37	TM 1861
Winstone	32	SO 9609
Winswell	6	SS 4913
Winterborne Clenston	10	ST 8302
Winterborne Herringston	9	SY 6887
Winterborne Houghton	10	ST 8104
Winterborne Kingston	10	SY 8697
Winterborne Monkton (Dorset)	9	SY 6787
Winterborne Stickland	10	ST 8304
Winterborne Whitechurch	10	SY 8399
Winterborne Zelston	10	SY 8997
Winterbourne (Avon)	29	ST 6480
Winterbourne Abbas	9	SY 6190
Winterbourne Bassett	18	SU 1074
Winterbourne Dauntsey	10	SU 1734
Winterbourne Earls	10	SU 1633
Winterbourne Gunner	10	SU 1735
Winterbourne Monkton (Wilts.)	18	SU 0972
Winterbourne Steepleton	9	SY 6289
Winterbourne Stoke	18	SU 0740
Winterburn	65	SD 9358
Winteringham	61	SE 9222
Winterley	51	SJ 7457
Wintersett	59	SE 3815
Winterslow	11	SU 2232
Winterton	61	SE 9218
Winterton-on-Sea	47	TG 4919
Winthorpe (Lincs.)	55	TF 5665
Winthorpe (Notts.)	54	SK 8156
Winton (Cumbr.)	63	NY 7810
Winton (Dorset)	10	SZ 0894
Wintringham	67	SE 8873
Winwick (Cambs.)	45	TL 1080
Winwick (Ches.)	51	SJ 6092
Winwick (Northants.)	43	SP 6273
Wirksworth	53	SK 2854
Wirswall	50	SJ 5444
Wisbech	45	TF 4609
Wisbech St. Mary	45	TF 4208
Wisborough Green	12	TQ 0526
Wiseton	54	SK 7189
Wishaw (Strath.)	84	NS 7954
Wishaw (Warw.)	42	SP 1794
Wispington	55	TF 2071
Wissett	37	TM 3679
Wistanstow	40	SO 4385
Wistanswick	41	SJ 6629
Wistaston	51	SJ 6853
Wiston (Dyfed)	24	SN 0218
Wiston (Strath.)	84	NS 9531
Wiston (W Susx)	12	TQ 1512
Wistow (Cambs.)	45	TL 2781
Wistow (N Yorks.)	60	SE 5835
Wiswell	58	SD 7437
Witcham	45	TL 4680
Witchampton	10	ST 9806
Witchford	45	TL 5078
Witham	22	TL 8114
Witham Friary	18	ST 7440
Witham on the Hill	45	TF 0516
Witherenden Hill	13	TQ 6426
Witheridge	7	SS 8014
Witherley	43	SP 3297
Withern	55	TF 4382
Withernsea	61	TA 3328
Withernwick	61	TA 1940
Withersdale Street	47	TM 2781
Withersfield	36	TL 6547
Witherslack	63	SD 4384
Withiel	3	SW 9965
Withiel Florey	16	SS 9832
Withington (Ches.)	51	SJ 8170
Withington (Glos.)	32	SP 0315
Withington (Gtr Mches.)	51	SJ 8392
Withington (Here. and Worc.)	31	SO 5643
Withington (Salop)	40	SJ 5713
Withington Green	51	SJ 8071
Withleigh	8	SS 9012
Withnell	58	SD 6322
Withybrook	43	SP 4384
Withycombe	16	ST 0141
Withyham	13	TQ 4935
Withypool	7	SS 8435
Witley	12	SU 9439
Witnesham	37	TM 1850
Witney	33	SP 3509
Wittering	45	TF 0502
Wittersham	14	TQ 8927
Wittingslow	40	SO 4388
Witton	47	TG 3331
Witton Gilbert	72	NZ 2345
Witton Park	72	NZ 1730
Witton le Wear	72	NZ 1431
Wiveliscombe	16	ST 0827
Wivelsfield	13	TQ 3420
Wivelsfield Green	13	TQ 3519
Wivenhoe	23	TM 0321
Wivenhoe Cross	23	TM 0423
Wiveton	46	TG 0343
Wix	23	TM 1628
Wixford	32	SP 0854
Wixoe	36	TL 7142
Woburn	34	SP 9433
Woburn Sands	34	SP 9235
Wokefield Park	19	SU 6765
Woking	20	TQ 0058
Wokingham	20	SU 8068
Wold Newton (Humbs.)	61	TA 0473
Wold Newton (Humbs.)	55	TF 2496
Woldingham	21	TQ 3755
Wolf's Castle	24	SM 9627
Wolferlow	31	SO 6661
Wolferton	46	TF 6528
Wolfhill	92	NO 1533
Wolfsdale	24	SM 9321
Wollaston (Northants.)	34	SP 9062
Wollaston (Salop)	40	SJ 3212
Wollerton	41	SJ 6229
Wolsingham	72	NZ 0737
Wolston	43	SP 4175
Wolvercote	33	SP 4809
Wolverhampton	41	SO 9198
Wolverley (Here. and Worc.)	41	SO 8279
Wolverley (Salop)	40	SJ 4631
Wolverton (Bucks.)	34	SP 8141
Wolverton (Hants.)	19	SU 5557
Wolverton (Warw.)	33	SP 2062
Wolvey	43	SP 4387
Wolviston	73	NZ 4525
Wombleton	66	SE 6683
Wombourne	41	SO 8793
Wombwell	59	SE 3902
Womenswold	15	TR 2250
Womersley	60	SE 5319
Wonastow	29	SO 4811
Wonersh	20	TQ 0145
Wonston	11	SU 4739
Wooburn	20	SU 9187
Wooburn Green	20	SU 9188
Wood Dalling	47	TG 0927
Wood End (Herts.)	35	TL 3225
Wood End (Warw.)	42	SP 1071
Wood End (Warw.)	42	SP 2498
Wood Enderby	55	TF 2764
Wood Green (Gtr London)	21	TQ 3191
Wood Hayes	41	SJ 9501
Wood Norton	46	TG 0128
Wood Street	20	SU 9551
Wood Walton	45	TL 2180
Woodale	65	SE 0279
Woodbastwick	47	TG 3315
Woodbeck	54	SK 7777
Woodborough (Notts.)	53	SK 6347
Woodborough (Wilts.)	18	SU 1059
Woodbridge	37	TM 2749
Woodbury	8	SY 0087
Woodbury Salterton	8	SY 0189
Woodchester	32	SO 8302
Woodchurch	15	TQ 9434
Woodcote (Oxon.)	19	SU 6481
Woodcote (Salop)	41	SJ 7715
Woodcroft	29	ST 5495
Woodditton	36	TL 6559
Woodeaton	33	SP 5311
Woodend (Northants.)	34	SP 6149
Woodend (W Susx)	12	SU 8108
Woodfalls	10	SU 1920
Woodford (Corn.)	6	SS 2113
Woodford (Gtr Mches.)	51	SJ 8982
Woodford (Northants.)	44	SP 9676
Woodford Bridge	21	TQ 4291
Woodford Green	21	TQ 4192
Woodford Halse	33	SP 5452
Woodgate (Here. and Worc.)	41	SO 9666
Woodgate (Norf.)	46	TG 0215
Woodgate (W Mids.)	41	SO 9982
Woodgate (W Susx)	12	SU 9304
Woodgreen (Hants.)	10	SU 1717
Woodhall	65	SD 9790
Woodhall Spa	55	TF 1963
Woodham	20	TQ 0462
Woodham Ferrers	22	TQ 7999
Woodham Mortimer	22	TL 8205
Woodham Walter	22	TL 8006
Woodhaven	93	NO 4127
Woodhead (Grampn.)	105	NJ 7938
Woodhill	41	SO 7384
Woodhorn	79	NZ 2988
Woodhouse (Leic.)	43	SK 5315
Woodhouse (S Yorks.)	53	SK 4184
Woodhouse Eaves	43	SK 5214
Woodhouselee	85	NT 2364
Woodhurst	45	TL 3176
Woodingdean	13	TQ 3605
Woodland (Devon)	5	SX 7968
Woodland (Durham)	72	NZ 0726
Woodlands (Dorset)	10	SU 0508
Woodlands (Grampn.)	99	NO 7895
Woodlands (Hants.)	11	SU 3111
Woodlands Park	20	SU 8578
Woodleigh	5	SX 7348
Woodlesford	59	SE 3629
Woodley	20	SU 7773
Woodmancote (Glos.)	32	SP 0008
Woodmancote (W Susx)	12	SU 7707
Woodmancott	19	SU 5642
Woodmansey	61	TA 0537
Woodmansterne	21	TQ 2760
Woodminton	10	SU 0122
Woodnesborough	15	TR 3156
Woodnewton	44	TL 0394
Woodplumpton	57	SD 4934
Woodrising	46	TF 9803
Woodseaves (Salop)	41	SJ 6830
Woodseaves (Staffs.)	41	SJ 7925
Woodsend	18	SU 2275
Woodsetts	53	SK 5483
Woodsford	9	SY 7690
Woodside (Berks.)	20	SU 9371
Woodside (Herts.)	35	TL 2506
Woodside (Tays.)	92	NO 2037
Woodstock	33	SP 4416
Woodthorpe (Derby.)	53	SK 4574
Woodthorpe (Leic.)	43	SK 5417
Woodton	47	TM 2894
Woodtown	6	SS 4926
Woodville	43	SK 3119
Woodyates	10	SU 0219
Woofferton	40	SO 5168
Wookey	17	ST 5145
Wookey Hole	17	ST 5347
Wool	10	SY 8486
Woolacombe	6	SS 4543
Woolage Green	15	TR 2449
Woolaston	29	ST 5999
Woolavington	17	ST 3441
Woolbeding	12	SU 8722
Wooler	87	NT 9928
Woolfardisworthy (Devon)	6	SS 3321
Woolfardisworthy (Devon)	7	SS 8208
Woolhampton	19	SU 5766
Woolhope	31	SO 6135
Woolland	10	ST 7706
Woolley (Cambs.)	45	TL 1474
Woolley (W Yorks.)	59	SE 3113
Woolmer Green	35	TL 2518
Woolpit	36	TL 9762
Woolscott	43	SP 4968
Woolstaston	40	SO 4498
Woolsthorpe (Lincs.)	54	SK 8334
Woolston (Ches.)	51	SJ 6589
Woolston (Hants.)	11	SU 4410
Woolston (Salop)	40	SJ 3224
Woolston (Salop)	40	SO 4287
Woolstone (Oxon.)	19	SU 2987
Woolton	50	SJ 4286
Woolton Hill	19	SU 4261
Woolverstone	37	TM 1838
Woolverton	18	ST 7853
Woolwich	21	TQ 4478
Wooperton	79	NU 0420
Woore	51	SJ 7242
Wootton (Beds.)	34	TL 0045
Wootton (Hants.)	11	SZ 2498
Wootton (Humbs.)	61	TA 0815
Wootton (Kent)	15	TR 2246
Wootton (Northants.)	34	SP 7656
Wootton (Oxon.)	33	SP 4319
Wootton (Oxon.)	33	SP 4701
Wootton (Staffs.)	41	SJ 8227
Wootton (Staffs.)	52	SK 1045
Wootton Bassett	18	SU 0682
Wootton Bridge	11	SZ 5491
Wootton Common	11	SZ 5390
Wootton Courtenay	16	SS 9343
Wootton Fitzpaine	8	SY 3695
Wootton Rivers	18	SU 1962
Wootton St. Lawrence	19	SU 5953
Wootton Wawen	32	SP 1563
Worcester	32	SO 8555
Worcester Park	21	TQ 2266
Wordsley	41	SO 8887
Worfield	41	SO 7595
Workington	62	NX 9928
Worksop	53	SK 5879
Worlaby	61	TA 0113
World's End (Berks.)	19	SU 4876
Worle	17	ST 3562
Worleston	51	SJ 6856
Worlingham	47	TM 4489
Worlington (Devon.)	7	SS 7713
Worlington (Suff.)	36	TL 6973
Worlingworth	37	TM 2368
Wormbridge	30	SO 4230
Wormegay	46	TF 6611
Wormhill	52	SK 1274
Wormiehills	93	NO 6239
Wormingford	36	TL 9332
Worminghall	34	SP 6408
Wormington	32	SP 0336
Worminster	17	ST 5742
Wormit	93	NO 3925
Wormleighton	33	SP 4453
Wormley	35	TL 3605
Wormshill	14	TQ 8857
Wormsley	30	SO 4248
Worplesdon	20	SU 9753
Worrall	53	SK 3092
Worsbrough	59	SE 3503
Worsley	58	SD 7400
Worstead	47	TG 3026
Worsthorne	58	SD 8732
Worston	58	SD 7642
Worth (Kent)	15	TR 3356
Worth Matravers	10	SY 9777
Wortham	37	TM 0777
Worthen	40	SJ 3204
Worthenbury	50	SJ 4146
Worthing (Norf.)	46	TF 9919
Worthing (W Susx)	12	TQ 1402
Worthington	43	SK 4020
Wortley	59	SK 3099
Worton	18	ST 9757
Wortwell	47	TM 2784
Wotherton	40	SJ 2800
Wotton	20	TQ 1247
Wotton Under Edge	29	ST 7593
Wotton Underwood	34	SP 6815
Wouldham	14	TQ 7164
Wrabness	37	TM 1731
Wragby	55	TF 1378
Wramplingham	47	TG 1106
Wrangham	104	NJ 6331
Wrangle	55	TF 4250
Wrangway	8	ST 1217
Wrantage	8	ST 3022
Wrawby	61	TA 0108
Wraxall (Avon)	29	ST 4872
Wraxall (Somer.)	17	ST 5936
Wray	64	SD 6067
Wraysbury	20	TQ 0173
Wrea Green	57	SD 3931
Wreay (Cumbr.)	71	NY 4349
Wreay (Cumbr.)	63	NY 4423
Wrekenton	72	NZ 2758
	67	SE 7686
Wrenbury	51	SJ 5947
Wreningham	47	TM 1699
Wrentham	47	TM 4982
Wressle	60	SE 7031
Wrestlingworth	35	TL 2547
Wretton	46	TF 6800
Wrexham	50	SJ 3349
Wribbenhall	41	SO 7975
Wrightington Bar	57	SD 5313
Wrinehill	51	SJ 7546
Wrington	17	ST 4662
Writtle	22	TL 6606
Wrockwardine	41	SJ 6212
Wroot	60	SE 7102
Wrotham	14	TQ 6159
Wrotham Heath	14	TQ 6258
Wroughton	18	SU 1480
Wroxall (I. of W.)	11	SZ 5579
Wroxall (Warw.)	42	SP 2271
Wroxeter	40	SJ 5608
Wroxham	47	TG 3017
Wroxton	33	SP 4141
Wyaston	52	SK 1842
Wyberton	55	TF 3240
Wyboston	35	TL 1656
Wybunbury	51	SJ 6949
Wych Cross	13	TQ 4231
Wychbold	32	SO 9166
Wyche	32	SO 7643
Wyck	12	SU 7539
Wycombe Marsh	20	SU 8992
Wyddial	35	TL 3731
Wye	15	TR 0546
Wyke (Dorset)	17	ST 7926
Wyke (Salop)	41	SJ 6402
Wyke (W Yorks.)	59	SE 1526
Wyke Regis	9	SY 6677
Wyke, The (Salop)	41	SJ 7306
Wykeham (N Yorks.)	67	SE 9683
Wykey	40	SJ 3925
Wylam	72	NZ 1164
Wylde Green	42	SP 1293
Wylye	10	SU 0037
Wymering	11	SU 6405
Wymeswold	43	SK 6023
Wymington	34	SP 9564
Wymondham (Leic.)	44	SK 8518
Wymondham (Norf.)	47	TG 1101
Wymondley	35	TL 2128
Wyndham	28	SS 9391
Wynford Eagle	9	SY 5895
Wyre Piddle	32	SO 9647
Wysall	43	SK 6027
Wythall	42	SP 0775
Wytham	33	SP 4708
Wyverstone	37	TM 0468
Wyverstone Street	36	TM 0367

Y

Y Fan	39	SN 9487
Y Rhiw	38	SH 2228
Yaddlethorpe	60	SE 8806
Yafford	11	SZ 4581
Yafforth	66	SE 3494
Yalding	14	TQ 7050
Yanworth	32	SP 0713
Yapham	67	SE 7851
Yapton	12	SU 9703
Yarburgh	55	TF 3493
Yarcombe	8	ST 2408
Yardley	42	SP 1385
Yardley Gobion	34	SP 7644
Yardley Hastings	34	SP 8656
Yardro	30	SO 2258
Yarkhill	31	SO 6042
Yarlet	41	SJ 9129
Yarlington	17	ST 6529
Yarm	72	NZ 4111
Yarmouth	11	SZ 3589
Yarnfield	51	SJ 8632
Yarnscombe	6	SS 5523
Yarnton	33	SP 4711
Yarpole	30	SO 4665
Yarrow	77	NT 3527
Yarrow Feus	77	NT 3325
Yarwell	45	TL 0697
Yate	29	ST 7082
Yateley	20	SU 8160
Yatesbury	18	SU 0671
Yattendon	19	SU 5474
Yatton (Avon)	29	ST 4265
Yatton (Here. and Worc.)	40	SO 4367
Yatton (Here. and Worc.)	31	SO 6330
Yatton Keynell	18	ST 8676
Yaverland	11	SZ 6185
Yaxham	46	TG 0010
Yaxley (Cambs.)	45	TL 1892

Z